PAINTING IN
NINETEENTH CENTURY
HUNGARY

Júlia Szabó

PAINTING IN NINETEENTH CENTURY HUNGARY

Corvina

Title of the original: *A XIX. század festészete Magyarországon*
Corvina Kiadó, 1985
Translated by Ilona Patay
Translation revised by Elizabeth West
Designed by Vera Köböl
© Júlia Szabó, 1985

On the cover: János Rombauer: *Youth in a Landscape,* 1804
(Detail, Plate 14)
On the back cover: Mihály Zichy: *The Triumph of the Genius of Destruction,* 1878
(Detail, Plate 277)

ISBN 963 13 2193 2

With special thanks to Judith E. Sollosy, the English editor of this volume.

Printed in Hungary, 1988
Kner Printing House, Békéscsaba
CO 2559–h–8892

Contents

Nineteenth Century Painting in Hungary

Between the two world wars, Elek Petrovics, the foremost authority and Director of the Museums of Fine Arts, wrote an illustrated book on the history of Hungarian painting. In selecting masterpieces from the 15th century up to the 20th, he found that most of them belonged to the 19th century. In his introduction he wrote: "It is becoming increasingly obvious that in the history of Hungarian art, the 19th century occupies a unique place, having been so far the most important epoch of all. It was at this time that art became an organic part of the intellectual life of the nation... The task of the first fifty years was to awaken an interest in the arts... The task of the second half of the century was to free Hungarian art from its confines of provincialism and to raise the standard to that of European art in general."

This is still true today, though we should add that developments at the turn of the century and during the first decades of the 20th century can now be seen more clearly. Until the Second World War there were two views of 19th century art: on the one hand, a highly critical attitude, on the other, an acceptance of its tradition. Yet the development in art of the early 20th century in Hungary and in East-Central Europe would not have been possible but for the endeavours of our predecessors. Neither could an artistic movement of such universal significance have taken place. Artists in the 19th century prepared the way for a cultural revival. A more profound understanding of the lives and works of those artists helps us to understand even our own age better. It also enables us to perceive the link between the different periods in the history of art throughout the centuries.

The peaceful, even prosperous centuries, so well suited to the development of art and favourable to the patronage of art, ended with the Turkish conquest of Hungary (1526) and the division of the country into three parts (1541).

Architects, sculptors and painters remained active in all three areas, but in a variety of circumstances, at different levels and in difficult social and political conditions. The western part of the country came under the Austrian and Italian influence in the 16th and 17th centuries; later, the influence of the French Enlightenment made itself felt. The central part of Hungary was under Turkish domination, and maintained the old traditions; but in the more or less self-governed, independent cities, there was an attempt to maintain contact with the principality of Transylvania, where far more spiritual freedom was allowed than in the territory under Turkish rule. In Transylvania, where members of different religions (Protestants, Catholics and the Orthodox Churches) and different nationalities (Hungarians, Székelys, Saxons, and later Rumanians) lived side by side by mutual consent in relative political harmony, there was more opportunity for dynamic and distinguished artistic activity. The Protestant rulers of Transylvania sought contact with the Netherlands, Switzerland and England; also, partly as a matter of expediency and partly under the pressure of necessity they attempted to keep on good terms with Turkey, Austria, and the Kingdom of Poland. In the principality of Transylvania artistic life at many levels reflected a fusion of Eastern and Western culture. But in a country ravaged by war, its boundaries changing with each conflict, it is astonishing that any architect was able to build a palace, church or town house, and equally surprising that masterpieces of fine art from Europe were brought in to enrich the local heritage. As a general rule we can say that the local art of both Hungary and Transylvania, lively and varied as it was, clearly reflects the characteristic traits of Central and East-European art. This local or "provincial" art based on late Renaissance patterns and influenced by the artistic trends of the Netherlands, of Poland and the Protestant principalities of Germany, enjoyed widespread popularity, and was much preferred to the classical and High Baroque style encouraged by the House of Habsburg, as Austria sought means of unifying the face of the Empire. Austrian works of art were regarded as imported goods in Hungary even towards the end of the 18th century, by which time, following the defeat of Prince Ferenc Rákóczi II's War of Independence (1703–1711) the whole of Hungary had been incorporated into the Habsburg Empire.

By the end of the 18th century the philosophy of the Enlightenment exerted a marked influence upon the evolution of art. This intellectual movement helped to shape a striving for a Hungary with an improved administration and a developed economy and a superior cultural life. It must be conceded, however, that not all the social and political groups followed the movement towards the Enlightenment with the same enthusiasm. During the reign of Emperor Joseph II and in the decades that followed the Emperor and his successors together with the aristocracy planned the cultural revival in Hungary. Quite different was the aim of the middle classes (the lesser nobility) and the bourgeoisie from whose ranks a new group arose, the intelligentsia. Their aim was to achieve partial, if not total, political autonomy by means of various reforms. Their greatest concern was for the revival of the mother tongue, and a desire to see national poetry flourish once again. Hand in hand with this striving came the desire to enrich the fine arts—all its branches and genres—with new forms of artistic expression.

The Enlightenment found its supporters among both rich and poor. It had its heroes and servants, people who shaped its great intellectual ideas and others who helped to unify them. Their aims were related to political ideas, and they had the difficult task of struggling to gain general support in a period of constant conflict. The Hungarian high nobility were hostile to the centralization planned by the absolutists and were encouraged when, shortly before his death, Emperor Joseph II reaffirmed his statutes, excepting only the two decrees concerning religious tolerance and serfdom. But it was much less acceptable to them when, following a plot led by freemason Ignác (Ignatius) Martinovics, their enlightened monarch inaugurated a period of political terror and tried to prevent the dissemination of French revolutionary ideas. At the dawn of the 19th century when the most eminent members of the Hungarian intelligentsia were already in prison, some aristocrats favoured the Restoration of the monarchy and it seemed that the lesser nobility and the bourgeoisie were abandoning any hope of political reform. Nevertheless, some years later, attempts were made to resume the revival of the 1790s, which first became apparent in the field of language and literature.

Plate 1

The most eminent of those who were encouraging patronage of the arts and the development of literature in Hungary during this period was the poet, writer and critic, Ferenc Kazinczy. In 1800 he was among those held in the prison fortress of Munkács for his part in the Martinovics plot. Yet for thirty years after his release (1801) he devoted himself unsparingly to the task of achieving the general recognition that painting and sculpture were part of the cultural life of Hungary. He expressed this idea in letters and essays, describing the different regions of Hungary, each with its particular monuments and cultural life. It was by no means his desire to create an isolated national art; on the contrary, he longed to see his native country as one of the great artistic centres of Europe. In 1791, he wrote, "There are no art galleries as yet in my country, nor is there any active academy of art at the moment; but we will achieve all of this just as Vienna did and eventually will have our own institutions like those of Dresden, Paris and London."

Many contemporary painters shared Kazinczy's desire. During the first decades of the 19th century, several young painters who had studied at the Academy of Vienna tried to establish an academy of painting and drew up theories on the teaching of art in order to form institution. In 1820, for example, Mihály János Hesz presented to the Palatine Joseph plans for an academy of fine arts to be established in Pest. Hesz was a professor at the Institutium Geometricum, the Imperial Academy of Engineering in Vienna, and Archduke Habsburg Joseph, the Palatine, was a great patron of the arts. As Hesz's project did not materialize, another was put forward in 1841 by Joó János, a painter in Debrecen, this time circulated in the form of an illustrated book. In this he published the plans for an Athenaeum, a building that could be used for instruction and exhibitions as well as for research.

Around 1810 there was a drawing school in practically every important city and town in Hungary. In these schools, however, no theories of painting were taught, no traditional approaches to the pictorial representation of nature, nor methods of conveying ideas in works of art. The teachers concentrated chiefly on the drawing of ornaments for the decoration of craft objects, crested letters and simple sketches to facilitate the making of an object. We learn from the curriculum of some of these schools that by 1810 basic theories of landscape painting were being taught and that there was a cautious attempt to introduce figure, flower and animal painting. In the teaching of drawing, monastic grammar schools (above all the Piarists) played a role "which must not be underestimated". By 1820, the journal entitled *Hazai és Külföldi Tudósítások* (Reports on Events at Home and Abroad) was commenting that even Pest University offered an increasing number of "drawing courses, in addition to scientific studies". This innovation was stimulated by the need to meet a growing demand for portraiture and the representation of the historical and natural sights of the surrounding countryside, even though the pictorial means to do so were as yet rather primitive.

In 1828 Kazinczy wrote to András Fáy: "We may draw the conclusion that if we are glad to have portraits of our friends and relatives who are no longer with us, then our friends and children will, in their turn, be glad to have our portraits."

In the first decades of the 19th century the most favoured form of painting was portraiture. The higher and lesser nobility and other members of the middle classes, writers and politicians, religious and secular leaders, merchants and industrialists all felt it necessary to have themselves portrayed at least once in their lives. They wanted to leave to their heirs a likeness by which they would be remembered; usually the artist would add some object to indicate their way of life. Their dress, a sword or another attribute would indicate their social status. It was even more important to represent a significant action or to indicate learning and wisdom. Objects related to intellectual activities, above all books, were often depicted in portraits during the age of Enlightenment. A likeness of a nobleman involved in politics was inconceivable without a volume of the *Corpus Iuris Hungariae,* of Horatio, Cicero or Seneca. In other portraits a book by Montesquieu or Jean-Jacques Rousseau can be seen, while ladies were sometimes portrayed reading a novel by Sir Walter Scott.

In the early 19th century in Hungary and Transylvania alike, every town of importance had its established portrait painters. There were also itinerant artists, some more skilled than others. The value of portraits painted by artists trained in Vienna and other European Academies was, of course, much greater than that of portraits painted by minor artists from provincial towns. Artists inspired by Heinrich Füger who followed the classical tradition, **Plates 3, 8, 11** Johann Jakob Stunder and János Donát, for instance, were very skilled in the creation of mythological references or elegant backgrounds indicating social status. The minor artists, however, such as József Czauczik, Carl Wieland, **Plates 7, 16, 18, 42, 43,** Ignác Klimkovics, János Ehrlinger, Johann Nepomuk Höfel and, towards the **44, 46, 49, 50** end of this era, Alajos Stech, were very willing but less able to make these additions. The greatest of all Hungarian portrait painters at the beginning of the century was undoubtedly the Lőcse-born János Rombauer. In his portraits, inspired by literary sources, we find beautiful English garden backgrounds which add conviction to the representation of character, beliefs and **Plate 14** achievements.

Artists were especially fond of creating portraits of connoisseurs. Their aim was to convey the model's strength of character and the historical significance of his or her life.

Kazinczy and his friends dreamed about a national picture gallery where portraits of the famous would be exhibited, including portraits of themselves, their scholar-friends and historical persons, all idealists fighting for a great cause; there would also be a place in the future gallery for historical landscapes and paintings of dramatic historical events. Kazinczy regarded historical landscape painting as a means of recording picturesque valleys and ruined fortresses, "places which remain sacred to the nation for ever". Thus he conceived the idea of creating a series of paintings comprising views of Visegrád, Vajdahunyad and other historic sites, as well as landscapes of the famous Tokaj mountains and the majestic range of the High Tatras. He hoped that these works would be produced by a new generation of artists in Hungary who, painting in the classical style of Claude Lorraine, would have the necessary skill and reverence for their task to create a worthy series of paintings.

By propagating these ideas Kazinczy and his contemporaries were responsible for the survival of historical landscape painting in Hungary until as late as the 1870s, and intermittently even beyond this date, when it was already out of date in the rest of Europe. Yet, in Hungary, this form persisted, producing works that were sometimes remarkable, sometimes much less so. Travellers with a taste for the Romantic, such as Alajos Mednyánszky, shared Kazinczy's hopes. In 1825 Mednyánszky undertook a "picturesque journey" along the River Vág, meticulously noting all geographical, historical or ethnographical details of interest in each particular region. These he later published in a book illustrated by Joseph Fischer's lithographed drawings of Hungarian fortresses. Early 19th century poetry and literature formed the conceptual background to the topics chosen by topographical writers and landscapists. There were elegies and epigrams by Ferenc Kazinczy, the two Kisfaludys (Sándor and Károly), Ferenc Kölcsey and Mihály Vörösmarty about the old, medieval fortresses and historical sites. All this poetry expressed a deep respect for historical landscapes and provided topics for an increasing number of painters and graphic artists—especially from the 1830s onwards.

In Hungary the first landscapists were often engineers, land-surveyors or cartographers, whose training included a thorough observation of landscapes. The general and engineer András Petrich, for example, gave vivid expression in his paintings and drawings to everyday scenes. Sometimes these draughtsmen elaborated their drawings, creating artistic compositions for their own amusement or to give to their friends. Contemporary provincial artists also felt it a duty to record their own regions in paintings or drawings. This was particularly obvious in the towns of Upper Hungary where German Romanticism exerted a particularly strong influence. This early interest in Romantic painting is best illustrated by János Jakab Müller's series in gouache, an example of average quality. A notable work of this style is János Rombauer's *View of Eperjes*.

Besides topographical landscape painting there developed also in the 1820s a more dramatic conception of the representation of nature. This is evident in the works of Károly Kisfaludy, painter and poet, whose art was influenced by some earlier foreign examples. Historical themes in heroic landscape settings were now conceived from literary sources. A theme was seized upon, elaborated, then carried out in drawings and finally in oils.

In all these drawings and paintings, the subject remained closely linked to contemporary literary works. Sándor Kisfaludy's poems about Hungarian castles, the historical elegies of Károly Kisfaludy and Mihály Vörösmarty, as well as their engraved and later lithographed illustrations, provided a real challenge for contemporary painters anxious to create large oil paintings of those landscapes or the historic events with which they were associated. The illustrations were published sometimes in books, sometimes in Károly Kisfaludy's "Aurora", a literary yearbook of great importance in the history of the fine arts in Hungary (1822–1832). In the years when Kazinczy was describing a series of places of historical importance in his letters or journals as he travelled through Hungary and Transylvania (1789, 1824, 1831) this form of landscape depiction was not yet practised in Hungary. Those paintings which did depict narrative or dramatic episodes were used to illustrate Biblical stories and the lives of the saints, and were mostly altar-pieces of outstanding quality. Kazinczy generally praised those religious compositions created in the manner of Raphael, Guido Reni, Anton Raphael Mengs, Heinrich Füger and Angelica Kaufmann. Or again those executed by such highly accomplished academically trained artists as Hubert Maurer (the St. Stephen's altar-piece of the parish church in Pápa) or by a Romantic painter like Adam Friedrich Oeser (altar-piece of the Evangelical Church in Pozsony). Religious painting was looked upon by the Academy as a more solemn form of historical painting. Kazinczy also thought of it in such terms and valued its significance in the hierarchy of academic genres. Other patrons who were more closely related to the Nazarenes' Catholicism, like Ferenc Széchényi, or learned prelates like János László Pyrker, Archbishop of Eger, wanted to support the newly built churches and the revival of Christian faith, and so paid even more attention to it. **Plate 6** **Plate 5**

The rising prosperity of the middle classes introduced a more secular note into the contemporary views of art. There was more concern now to promote a general improvement of standards. Altar-pieces became a consecrated form of genre-painting in which figures and incidents were depicted against a beautiful landscape. The most successful of these paintings are those in which the Baroque tradition of representing the lives of Hungarian saints and holy kings is maintained; thus they too are historical paintings. **Plates 19, 20, 21**

When Kazinczy visited Pest in 1829 he found that battle-scenes enjoyed the greatest popularity with the general public. When these were on view in private collections or shown by art dealers, they were greeted with enthusiasm: "Noblemen and noblewomen, law students and common soldiers indulged in heated discussions about the time and place of the events described." This remark of Kazinczy's shows the contemporary basis for evaluation; a precise representation of a story which the viewer could recognize and describe. The public was less interested in the media (oil or etching). Most of these so-called battle-pieces were mainly circulated as aquatints or engravings made, first of all, from Horace Vernet's works. The only large painting on view in the building of the Royal University was the huge oil by Peter Krafft, the Elder (a Viennese), entitled *Zrínyi's Charge on the Turks from the Fortress of Sziget*. This large canvas was made for the projected national art gallery, the theme having been specified by the Hungarian counties that commissioned it. In Vienna, Krafft, the Elder was to paint first a suitable companion piece to this painting (The coronation of the Hungarian King Emperor Francis I) which, however, never became popular in Hungary. Zrínyi, the defender of a fortress against the Turks, had been celebrated as a hero in a majestic epic poem by one of his descendants (named Miklós after him), written in the 17th century, and he was honoured as a national hero even in the 19th century. Allegorical paintings on national history now lost some of their previous appeal as Krafft created a precedent for other 19th century historical painters who wished to depict such dramatic actions based on antecedent pictorial sources or else making an original visualization of a historical event. Equally popular were the mythological paintings in which artists fused past and present, also paintings of theatrical performances and *tableaux-vivants* in which the figures were posed in pleasing **Plate 58** **Plate 59**

Plate 9 costumes and were often masked. The most typical of this group of paintings is possibly Pál Balkay's allegorical work completed, as the title indicates, to commemorate the arts and sciences. It shows Minerva and Apollo, the Olympian patrons of the arts and sciences, on Mount Parnassus with the nine Muses, while Mars, the God of War, is seen taking off his armour. Immediately beside them can be seen the medieval Hungarian coat of arms with the double cross. The painter donated his work to the National Museum. In spite of all its technical shortcomings it became almost as popular as Krafft's painting; indeed, in a period marked by great enthusiasm for the theatre, similar compositions were often copied on the stage curtains of some theatres, for instance the Hungarian Theatre in Székesfehérvár.

An allegorical representation of major historical events was considered to be one of the main tasks of Hungarian artists in the 19th century. Other forms of art like portraits, landscapes and still–lifes, were considered less valuable, even though they far outnumbered the historical pieces. In the 1830s and 1840s every painter attempted at least one historical piece or allegorical composition. In several engravings and paintings the figure of Pannonia was depicted with the attributes of Minerva, Tyche or other Greek and Roman goddesses. Pannonia symbolized the "mother goddess" of Hungary, the protectress of her arts and culture. It was therefore only natural that her likeness should be seen in numerous places, for example, at the inner main entrance of the Széchényi Library in the National Museum. The Széchényi collections, which Ferenc Széchényi donated to the nation in 1802, formed the foundation of the National Library and Museum. It was further enlarged and declared a museum in 1807. In 1847 it received its own Neo-Classical building worthy of such a noble institution and in the 1870s it was further decorated by statues and wall paintings. This institution and its contribution to the arts and sciences undoubtedly played a major part in promoting cultural development in Hungary.

Plate 6 A portrait of the dignified figure of Ferenc Széchényi, the founder, was painted posthumously in 1823 by Johann Ender. Ferenc Széchényi was one of the most important patrons of art and literature in the history of Hungary, a much respected figure. Széchényi's son, István, carried on his father's work and when in 1826 he saw the portrait, he recorded his appreciation as did Kazinczy in 1829. The Széchényi family gave commissions to a number of Austrian painters, the most important being Johann Ender, Anton Einsle, Josef Kriehuber, Friedrich von Amerling, Moritz Daffinger and Franz Schrotzberg. Like other members of the nobility, for example, the Festetich, Pálffy, Orczy and Batthyány families, Széchényi patronized Austrian painters and in doing so established a precedent followed for many years in Hungary. Sometime in the 1830s István Széchenyi followed his father's example by commissioning Johann Ender, a master at the Academy of Vienna, to complete another painting of the same significance and size as of his father's portrait in the Széchényi Library. He intended this painting to be an emblem or allegory for the newly

Plate 63 formed Learned Society (the Academy of Sciences). Like the National Museum, the Society had no building of its own. István Széchenyi commissioned this portrait, therefore, as a gesture of faith in the new institution. In addition to this generous present, a portrait of himself by Friedrich von Amerling, was given to the Academy of Sciences by his family, thus laying **Plate 65** the foundations for a future picture gallery. A custom was thus established that portraits were to be commissioned not only of the founding members, but of other members too; later, paintings of general interest were added to the collection. Thus the presidents and members of the Academy of Sciences shared with the directors of the National Museum a similar aim—the realization of a national portrait gallery. However, treasures of the museum, a public institution, were more accessible; and it was further expanded and enriched by donations from generous patrons in all walks of life.

In the 1830s Pest-Buda became a very important town, a true capital, and the first among the intellectual and political centres of Hungary. Exhibitions were held there with increasing frequency and these were visited by everyone interested in art. The most important artistic centre had until then been Pozsony, situated near Vienna, and until 1848 the seat of the Hungarian Parliament. Other cities of importance where a parallel cultural evolution took place were Kassa and Eperjes in the north of the country, and Kolozsvár in Transylvania, which had a strong Hungarian cultural tradition. There were several well-trained painters or dynasties of painters in these towns; and from these towns came many of the great scholars and critics of the 1830s and 1840s.

From the 1830s onwards the ideological background to all artistic activities was provided by critical reflections presented in the form of publications or lectures emanating from the capital and principal towns. It was as a result of Ferenc Pulszky's lecture at the Academy of Sciences and Emmerich Henszlmann's lecture at a Meeting of Doctors and Natural Scientists, in the Church of St. Elisabeth in Kassa that the history of art in Hungary became a subject for serious and academic study. The nature of art, its significance, its development, had, however, been discussed earlier, and artistic questions had been considered by scholars, articles and letters had been published in newspapers and art had been the concern of novelists and poets.

The study of art, art criticism and the patronage of art inspired by the ideas of the Age of Enlightenment, in Hungary as in Western Europe, was of lasting value, esteemed by the most learned men of the time. Yet the demand for a specifically Hungarian art, emerging in a more and more conscious form, was becoming increasingly evident. In 1832, in one of his last works, the poet and prose writer Dániel Berzsenyi warned that "the object of your judgement —that is the artistic work—results from a fusion of interior and exterior tendencies, so you must base your criticism upon opinions on works from home and abroad". For him, each criticism necessitated a historical judgement, an examination of whether the work of art in question accorded with the aims of the nation and of mankind, as well as the philosophy of the whole civilization. Emmerich Henszlmann, a most eminent art critic and art historian of his time, held similar views. He was a doctor born in Kassa, who became more and more interested in architectural theories and historical questions. In 1841 he published an essay entitled "Parallelism Between Artistic Views and Educational Theories of Olden Times and the Present, with Special Reference to the

Development of the Arts in Hungary". In this work he also discussed contemporary art in the light of historical precedents and its aesthetic value. His own view was that art should depict individuals and their relationships with each other in "a life-like, characteristic and essentially national" manner. These claims differ from both the "symbolic" style of the oldest (ancient and medieval) art and from the "idealized" style attributed to classical Greek and Roman artists and representatives of several "Neo-Classicisms". As a third to these two approaches, he proposed a "realistic" description of nature. Henszlmann's theory conflicted with the Neo-Classical Academic methods of the early 19th century. This "realistic" method is further differentiated in his treatise when he distinguishes between the Christian (i.e. the Romantic) approach and the materialistic approach (i.e. the manner of the Realists).

Incidentally, in his essay, Henszlmann considers that this third approach has not yet fully materialized. He rightly attributes this fact to the lack of appropriate artistic training and the conservatism of public taste in Hungary. He does not acknowledge as a work of art any painting that does not merge the individual, the national and the natural together in perfect harmony. Furthermore, he declares that art "deserves to be called such only when it displays its essential relationship with the artist's personality, his country and the imagined subject."

A most important factor in Henszlmann's artistic programme is his rejection of Academic patterns. Instead of slavish application of learned compositional rules he suggests a direct confrontation with the subject itself. At the same time, he insists on the importance of artistic training and the necessity for reform. Strangely, he does not refuse Academic art as such, but demands a "realistic Academy". These ideas came to fruition much later in Hungary, in the artistic training and practice of art adopted afterwards, in the 1860s. In his lifetime Henszlmann was often criticized: he was attacked for his opposition to classical idealization or simply because the critics wanted to defend some purely decorative or pragmatic point of view which was absolutely alien to him. All the same, from 1830 onwards—and this was before Henszlmann published his essay—at various exhibitions and also in the "Pesti Műegylet" (Association for the Promotion of Arts and Exhibitions), which had its first exhibition in 1841, some of the exhibits could indeed be described as examples of a life-like, characteristic and national art. In most of the works however there was a simplistic attempt to portray individuality, the "life-like" and "national" aspects being displayed only in the external form.

In the 1830s and 1840s Henszlmann's ideas were embraced by painters living in Hungary who were active in contemporary political and cultural movements. Artists who achieved fame abroad were not yet concerned with the creation of an independent style different from that of their adopted countries, and they seldom chose Hungarian themes for their paintings. Their fame abroad, however, served to increase the reputation of Hungarian art, while at home they were held up as examples of success to their colleagues.

The effect of Henszlmann's theories is best demonstrated in the work of Károly Markó, the Elder and Charles Brocky. Markó had studied in Vienna **Plate 41** and Italy before he painted his first famous historical landscape, the view of

Visegrád (representing a medieval royal castle and fortress and its setting). Afterwards he settled in Italy because he feared poverty at home. In 1840, however, he was elected a member of the Hungarian Academy of Sciences. Art collectors, both foreign and Hungarian, thought very highly of his work, which was truly an excellent 19th century Academic landscape painting in the classical tradition. Art experts and art students from Hungary, Austria and other countries visited his studio in Pisa, and later near Florence. The young Hungarian painters held him in high esteem and admired the subtle style of his mythological, Biblical and Italian genre-scenes, which he introduced into his landscapes. Yet, apart from his own children, he had no direct followers at home. His influence extended only to certain painters of landscapes in the 1850s who adopted some elements of his painting. The Hungarian public, and especially the critics, wanted him to compose paintings on Hungarian history, a wish he sometimes attempted to satisfy. He composed one meticulous historical painting on a medieval subject. He also created a visual interpretation of a poem which had been written by the Archbishop János László Pyrker and was translated into Hungarian from the German by Ferenc Kazinczy ("Die Perle der heiligen Vorzeit"—The Pearls of the Biblical Past). Finally, Markó occasionally chose to paint Hungarian landscapes; more than twenty years after his famous *Visegrád,* in the 1850s, he completed a representation of the Great Plain in two versions. But he was not able to develop closer contact with the artistic life of his own country, which, from around 1830 onwards, and in contrast to his Neo-Classical style, was overwhelmed by a number of more up-to-date artistic theories and trends.

It was during this period that Charles Brocky, having first embarked upon a career as an itinerant painter, proceeded to Vienna where he studied at the Academy in conditions of great poverty. It was not until 1837 that he tried to make contact again with his own country. In the meantime he moved to London where he became a successful portraitist, even portraying members of the royal family. His achievements were acknowledged at home and Miklós Barabás visited him while travelling in England. Brocky's art came closer to the criterion of "naturalness" than that of Markó. This ideal had indeed preoccupied even the painters in Vienna (where Brocky had studied) long before it became a major criterion in Hungary. In Austria, by the end of the 1840s, the very idea of a "nation" being middle class in character was also linked to the notion of "naturalness".

In his portraits of his fellow countrymen, his altar-piece in Eperjes and the sketches for a historical painting—the latter was unfortunately lost, Brocky's attempts to represent his subjects with life-like Naturalism, were combined with well-done accurate characterization and local colour. His interest in the European and Hungarian political movements of the 1840s and 1850s served to nourish this particular aspect of his art.

The contemporary Hungarian press nevertheless praised other painters more highly than they did Brocky and Markó. The "heroes" of artistic circles in Hungary were those painters, whether originally Hungarian or not, who came from abroad to settle in Hungary. The most publicized artists in those days were, primarily, Miklós Barabás (from 1830), Henrik Weber, József

Plates 29, 30, 76, 77, 78

Plate 77

Plate 152

Plates 94, 95, 96, 138

Borsos, Friedrich Lieder, and from 1850 Jakab (Giacomo) Marastoni. Their popularity was, in most instances, justly deserved and was most often due to their ability to adapt themselves and their work to given requirements of fashion, and to their support for the various art institutions. It was for these reasons that Giacomo Marastoni, for example, was so popular.

Painters with a talent for combining art and acting also enjoyed great popularity. In 1848 in the "Honderű" (a literary, artistic and fashion magazine) there was an account of a performance by Imre Róth, an Academic painter "whose pictures on a misty screen have been shown with great success for two successive nights in the National Theatre". Theatre and fine arts were no longer considered to share the same muse. Their relation can be seen in various illustrations of actions or life-like representations. Such were the above-mentioned "misty" pictures, presumably projected onto an illuminated screen of tulle or steam. Bearing this in mind, it is understandable that when photography was finally discovered in 1839, it quickly gained followers in Hungary, many of whom were painters or graphic artists.

At that time, theoreticians did not reject techniques used to achieve more accurate representations of reality. Some artists accepted the scientific approach, but for the majority the chief concern was to "express inherent spiritual and artistic values". At first portraiture was the form of art considered most appropriate for this purpose. Later genre-painting, a development from a narrative type of group portrait, became as important as portrait painting. Life-genre painting also evolved out of landscapes, topographical drawings, sketches of people, towns and villages. To a greater or lesser extent all these forms represented truth to nature and the principles of rational and conscious artistic composition. Scenes taken from village or town life flourished alongside those literary trends which rejected strict Neo-Classicism and sought to achieve the simplicity, verisimilitude and naturalness found in the world of folk poetry.

Perhaps no peasant-genre painter shared poet Sándor Petőfi's radical understanding of people of lower social rank, whom he declared were destined to assume a leading role both in literary and political life. Yet painters now chose their subjects from everyday life rather than Greek and Roman mythology; this was also partly due to the fact that their patrons were no longer confined exclusively to members of the highly educated upper classes and the nobility. Miklós Barabás, a Transylvanian painter who had studied in Nagyszeben, Vienna and Italy, produced as his first exhibit in the Pest Casino (1834) a work based on a mythological theme, *The Rape of Europa,* modelled on a picture by Paolo Veronese which he had copied in water colours. However, after returning home to settle in Pest, he painted no more large oils from water-colours made during his travels. Compared with earlier painters he executed relatively few religious compositions (only two or three are known). While abroad he had particularly enjoyed painting water-colour landscapes but oddly enough he did not use them as models for oil paintings. Instead he produced some very beautiful water-colours of the countryside near Pest and Buda, and in the same medium some lively scenes of everyday life in the town and along the shores of the Danube. His finest work is a water-colour dating from 1838 depicting

Plates 81–83

Plate 85

the *Puszta,* anticipating in the choice of subject matter the great poems by Petőfi as well as paintings by Markó. Yet, from the 1840s onwards landscape became merely incidental, a background in his portraits and large genre-scenes painted in oils.

The drawings, often executed in series, and the oil paintings, few in number, which date from the early years of the 19th century show that during this time in Hungary genre-painting was either practised for ethnographical or topographical purposes, or to illustrate literary works, and followed no strict stylistic rules. By the 1840s all earlier forms of life-genre painting became synthesized into one form and were looked upon as recording contemporary history, literary motifs or, more seldom, contemporary morals. This form is most clearly seen in genre-paintings depicting everyday life or traditional festivities from past history, and on these, the normative requirements are even more apparent.

Barabás produced drawings and lithographs depicting actual events, while his large works are elaborations of these events following more closely the requirements of the accurate representation of an episode and a story according to the rules of Academic composition. In his trade-sign for the *Zöldfa* **Plate 84** Drapery Shop, he depicts an incident from real life: a traveller sits waiting in the shade of a huge tree as a wagon approaches. In contrast, Barabás's finest work, *Vlachs from the Mountains off to the Fair* (now known as *Rumanian* **Plate 109** *Family off to the Fair),* has been carefully composed in every detail. Barabás's first teacher was a Saxon, Franz Neuhauser, jr., living in Transylvania, who **Plate 38** painted and produced lithographs of folk-scenes and landscapes. He often chose to paint fairs because of the great variety of social and national types to be found there. Barabás's painting retains the quality of his earlier graphic works. Yet his aim was not to represent a multitude of people hurrying to the fair, but to catch one group in a composition reminiscent of the Neo-Classicists. The narrative character of the painting and the beauty of the landscape were much praised by Barabás's contemporaries. The large painting of the *Vlachs from the Mountains* was bought by the Civil Rifle Club of Pest for the Picture Gallery of the National Museum. Barabás was even asked to complete five replicas of the same painting, though Henszlmann criticized the stiffness of the composition and the affected style. It cannot be denied that compared to the genre scenes of bourgeois life in Austria by Ferdinand Waldmüller (an artist Barabás admired) **Plate 107** the *Rumanian Family* is somewhat conservative and comes closer to the idealized style of the Viennese painters of around 1810–1830 such as Johann Ender. Waldmüller's *Peasant Wedding in Lower Austria* dates from the same **Plate 110** year as Barabás's *Rumanian Family.* This Austrian painter deliberately drew his composition with loose, casually formed groups of people. Barabás did not endeavour to paint a Hungarian equivalent until the mid-1850s, when he completed *Arrival of the Bride.* **Plate 111**

Contemporary with Barabás were numerous artists producing works in a similar free, quick style to that of his drawings and water-colours of everyday life. The most important themes of the period all represented the period itself: the flourishing towns, the great flood of the Danube in Pest (1838), the suffering of the victims, the reconstruction it necessitated, social gatherings,

Plates 100–106 balls and theatrical events. The heroes of this era were the poets, politicians and scholars; and in poetry and painting alike, the *citoyen* types of the nobility and the middle-classes. The ladies and the bourgeois housewives were portrayed in single portraits or in family group portraits, sometimes wearing elaborate jewellery, sometimes simply dressed with only a fine silk or velvet ribbon at the throat, and always with a flower in their hair or in their hands. They sometimes sit in front of a mirror completing their toilet, or they pose fully dressed, usually in fine white fabrics, sometimes in velvet or heavy silk. The ideal woman of the period, however, was not exclusively this noble mother-figure, or a gentle wife. She could be a celebrated actress, rich, highly educated and active in the social and political life of the day. In those days an actress could be a living legend, her portrait the dream of the painter come true. In portraying **Plates 115, 116** her, an artist would introduce more flowers than usual. In her lifetime, the celebrated actress Fanny Ellsler was sculpted in the finest porcelain. There were also numerous painted or engraved portraits of actors wearing splendid costumes depicted against a stage set or posed for a single portrait. Famous actors wearing appropriate costumes were also portrayed as historical figures **Plate 91** or even introduced into trade-signs as in Barabás's painting of Miklós Zrínyi, which could be seen both in the theatre tailor's workshop and the café named after him.

Trade-signs were in those days fashionable pieces of painting. They were executed even by academically trained painters such as Ferdinand Waldmüller in Vienna, Johann Nepomuk Höfel, Ferdinand Lütgendorff, Miklós Barabás and others in Pozsony and Pest. In shops and other public places it was customary to paint scenes of everyday life. The bourgeois inhabitants of the towns tended to see everything from their own point of view. It was therefore that artists portrayed the enlightened reformers of the day as worthy citizens. This was the image of Széchenyi with his newspaper **Plate 71** portrayed by Ágost Schoefft; and there were similar representations of the Palatine Joseph of Hungary, the aristocratic patrons of the Academy; also poets and writers of all social levels. The countryside itself was now seen as a pleasant bourgeois environment, as evidenced by the painting of the High **Plate 88** Tátra by Károly Tibély, an Upper Hungarian. Talented painters concerned themselves with the different forms of painting from the middle-class point of view. The only distinction that can be made is that in addition to portraiture, landscape and genre-scenes, they also began to introduce historical subjects into their genre-paintings. The most popular of these historical genre-paintings was an excessively sentimental composition portraying a Protestant minister in prison during the time of the Counter-Reformation, saying good-**Plate 112** bye to his daughter; it was painted by Bálint Kiss, curator of the National Museum, in 1846.

Bálint Kiss's life could be considered typical of the painters of the middle of the century. He entered the Protestant College in Debrecen in 1819, and in 1827 proceeded to Vienna where he studied at the Faculty of Historical Painting at the Academy. He returned to Hungary in 1830, but not finding enough work in Szentes, his native town, he lived from 1832 to 1834 in Italy and Switzerland. He then stayed for three years in Debrecen before moving on to Pest.

After a year in Pest, he produced several portraits and historical paintings. One of these, *The Death of János Hunyadi,* depicted a subject that was popular with many artists, so that although the painting by Kiss was lost, József Schmidt's version of the same subject shows how it was handled at that time. The dying Hunyadi, who led his army against the Turks in the 15th century, is depicted taking leave of his sons and soldiers, is a typical sentimental frame subject of 19th century European art, though the handling is typically Hungarian. Hunyadi is not depicted as an Oriental despot, like Delacroix's Sardanapalus dying together with his harem, nor is he shown as an ancient hero like Germanicus in Heinrich Füger's painting, *The Death of Germanicus.* Hunyadi is represented not so much as a leader of high rank but rather as an ordinary soldier faithfully serving his country, setting an example to posterity, expressing noble thoughts as he gives up his life which were popularized by lyrical descriptions of his death. The success of this painting prompted Bálint Kiss to plan a complete series of drawings and paintings depicting the history of Hungary, an enterprise he was not able, however, to carry out until 1858. After the defeat of the War of Independence in which he took an active part as a National Guard, he was removed from his post as curator of the National Museum. But in due course he was allowed to resume his work in the Museum. Once again he commissioned the preservation of paintings, had them copied, and provided tuition for younger artists in the composition of historical painting.

Similarities can be seen in the life of Henrik Weber, another remarkable painter of the period. After studying drawing in Pest, Henrik Weber went to the Academy of Vienna in 1835, two years later than Bálint Kiss. There was at the time another student named Weber who, however, was subsequently forgotten. Gyula Fleischer, in his book about Hungarians at the Academy of Vienna, says that both Webers took drawing lessons from Leopold Kupelwieser, a gifted teacher of drawing, who also painted many altar-pieces for Hungary. From Kupelwieser the Webers went to the classes of Carl Gsellhofer and Johann Nepomuk Ender in the Department of Historical Painting. In 1840, the better known of the two Webers went to Munich. He spent two years there at the Academy where the school of drawing had a better reputation than that in Vienna. From Munich he went to Italy, and did not settle in Hungary until 1847. The fact that he spent twelve years studying different techniques indicates just how conscientious and serious he was, an artist who developed his own system of values. In his portraits and genre-paintings the *citoyen* ideal of his age appears in its best form, exemplified by some figures of the group portrait of his family. Nevertheless, it is not the work of this much travelled man which can be compared with that of Barabás, but the work of the other Weber, who probably worked in Pest or Vienna. This Weber often exhibited at the "Pesti Műegylet" (Association for the Promotion of Arts and Exhibitions in the capital). His somewhat bland, historical genre-paintings and allegories met with more success in Hungary. Over the years, however, the work of these two painters became so similar that it was difficult to make attributions, and they became registered as one and the same person.

The finest and most celebrated painter of portraits in Pest, Buda and Vienna in the 1840s was József Borsos. At the Viennese Academy, he studied for only a short time under Leopold Kupelwieser, and then went to study at the school of Ferdinand Waldmüller. He exhibited at the "Műegylet" and at the Viennese *Kunstverein* from 1844 onwards. Already in 1837 he was painting historical works based on earlier compositions and he was copying Baroque works. But the form in which he was to excel was not historical painting, but portraiture, genre-pieces, water-colour drawings and lithographs representing genre scenes.

His drawing technique was excellent and he possessed an acute sense of the pictorial. He made use of his time in Vienna not only by studying assiduously under his masters but also by copying classical works in the art galleries. The influence of some of the Dutch masters was decisive in his works. Of his contemporaries he preferred the elegant portraits and life-like compositions of Friedrich von Amerling rather than the more accurate works of Ferdinand Waldmüller. As a painter, his talent for characterization merits special attention. He achieved a note of individuality by using finely detailed clothing, rich interiors and beautiful scenery to enhance the subject's features, bearing, and social standing. In a series of excellent drawings and paintings Borsos recorded the revolution of 1848 in Pest, in Vienna and the 1848–49 Hungarian War of Independence. Travelling to Pest and Buda from Vienna, he was able to observe the course of events and their influence on the arts in both cities. His masterpiece, a painting of a National Guardsman from 1848, especially if we consider the attitude of the figure, is rendered in a Realistic-Romantic style and must be ranked with the finest of European paintings of the period.

In 1848–1849, there occurred the most heroic and tragic political events of the century in Europe. These have been expressed in many works of art, though initially they were only perceptible in a few graphic representations of the battle-fields and in portraits of revolutionary figures. In Hungary these were either published in political journals such as the "Képesújság", an illustrated paper published in Kassa, or were circulated in the form of lithographs and water-colour series. These drawings are an invaluable part of the national heritage of Hungary.

1848 was a turning point in the history of Europe with some consequence also for the history of art. Being much influenced by French politics, the bourgeoisie increased their power and status in Central and Western Europe. This development, accompanied by political unrest, was leading inevitably towards the events of 1848. In France, successive revolutions (1830, 1848) ensured victory and power to the high bourgeoisie, while the more radical failed to achieve their aims.

The revolutions in Central and Eastern Europe only indirectly assisted the development of a capitalistic society. This was most obvious in the German provinces. However, the Austrian Empire experienced its first significant crisis in 1848, when the various nations living uneasily within the bonds of the Empire, all striving for independence, often turned against each other. The radical elements in the Vienna Revolution of 1848, for example, were weakened by lack of support from Hungary's revolutionary leaders and army. In spite of the defeat of the Viennese Revolution, an Austrian bourgeois Parlia-

21

ment was called into being and a new era began in Austria with a definite trend towards bourgeois development, though within the feudal framework of the Empire. The Revolution of 1848 in Prague failed to achieve its immediate goals, but the evolution towards a middle-class society was ensured through its close relationship with Austria. The 1848–1849 Revolution and the ensuing War of Independence in Hungary lasted longer than anywhere in Europe and despite its defeat, gained general acknowledgement and respect for the country and nation. It was defeated with the help of Tsarist Russia and a difficult period under a new oppression was to come. The War of Independence was looked upon as a noble endeavour by thoughtful Europeans: Hungary was mentioned together with Poland as a nation with the moral courage to resist oppression and fight for freedom and independence. It was respected by Europe's great thinkers and poets and the educated middle classes. When they came to analyse the significance of 1848, Karl Marx, Michael Bakunin, Heinrich Heine and Friedrich Nietzsche all praised Hungary. The activities of respected Hungarian politicians and soldiers living in exile were followed with interest by artists and men of letters who, like these refugees, were not able to accept the fact of defeat, but were able to express their views only in art and literature (political essays).

Although at first it seemed that everything had been lost and nothing gained, there were developments in the fine arts and in culture generally in Hungary after 1848–1849. Overtly political art at first was destroyed, statues and graphic leaflets were burned, thinkers and artists had to emigrate or were imprisoned. Emmerich Henszlmann and Ferenc Pulszky, two of the first historians and theoreticians of art, like the leaders of the War of Independence, Lajos Kossuth and György Klapka among them, were obliged to emigrate. Artists like Mihály Kovács, the young Antal Ligeti, Mór Than, Soma Orlai Petrich and others went into hiding, using false names, or left the country for a while. Curiously, it was in Vienna that they were most secure from harassment, always provided that they confined their activities to the pursuit of art. Among these was József Borsos. Naturally, they were asked to adjust to the   **Plate 131** new political situation if they wished to retain their aristocratic and bourgeois patrons. Unlike the poets, artists living in Hungary did not remain silent for as long as it has previously been presumed by certain art historians. Even in 1851 literary and art magazines were being published and exhibitions were organized once again. Censorship was not strict, even when articles were published in which writers openly analysed the events of the War of Independence. Painters were given commissions for portraits, genre-paintings and religious compositions. Soon, presumably for financial gain, many Hungarian artists were producing elegant portraits of the Austrian Emperor Franz Joseph I, intended for various public institutions. Numbers of these portraits are now stored in museums.

Genre-painting and portraiture continued also in Vienna, taking on even more enriched forms, and with a concentration on skill and technical solutions. In the 1850s Austrian painters were mainly concerned to develop a new "true to life" Academic style influenced by Biedermeier Naturalism. The same task was undertaken by the Hungarian artists living in Vienna: József Borsos,   **Plates 145, 146, 148**

Plate 162	Adalbert Schäffer, Alajos Györgyi Giergl (as yet a student) and many others.
Plate 111	In Pest in the 1850s, Barabás was working on the continuation of genre paint-

Plate 162
Plate 111 Adalbert Schäffer, Alajos Györgyi Giergl (as yet a student) and many others.
In Pest in the 1850s, Barabás was working on the continuation of genre painting in Waldmüller's style. He continued as before to portray public figures, politicians, writers, actors and actresses, and wealthy members of the nobility and the bourgeoisie. In his treatment of background, setting and clothing, and in his skilled portrayal of character, Barabás maintained the tradition of the 1840s even into the late 1880s, and at a very high artistic level.

In the Viennese institutions of art in the 1850s, old and new trends existed side by side. However, innovation came not from the Academy of Arts but from private schools. At the Academy traditional religious painting in the style of the Nazarenes was taught under the professorship of Leopold Kupelwieser and Joseph Führich. Kupelwieser had close contacts with several Hungarian

Plate 159 patrons of religious art for whom, during the 1850s, he executed several altarpieces. Both masters taught their pupils the art of harmonious composition marked by a mature use of line and colour, free of political implication and concerned only with "absolute values". They created rather nostalgic Biblical scenes for which they devised new interpretations. Several of their pupils followed this path, having been similarly inspired by the Nazarene tradition encountered during their travels in Italy. In order to make the Biblical scenes more life-like and authentic, the painters studied Oriental landscapes and costumes. Their study-trips to the Holy Land were subsidized by prelates and aristocratic patrons so that by the late 1850s many of them were exhibiting paintings of high quality. This same stylistic approach and choice of subject (incorporating the earlier religious Italian influence by way of Vienna), was

Plates 157, 158, 161, 207 represented in Hungary by Mihály Kovács, József Molnár, Antal Haan and Ferenc Szoldatics (a late exponent of the movement). Similar features could

Plate 208 still be seen in the 1850s in the early works of Bertalan Székely, who started his career by undertaking religious subjects of this kind, while studying in Vienna under Führich and Kupelwieser. The Academy of Munich presumably encouraged its pupils to follow the same path, particularly in the field of landscape painting. From the beginning of the century many painters set out from Munich to visit first the classical remains in Greece, then to go on to the Holy Land to study the places mentioned in the Bible.

Plates 155, 156 In Hungary, it was Antal Ligeti whose paintings and drawings represented this nostalgic Neo-Classical-Romantic trend. His artistic talent developed in the 1850s after spending a short time in Vienna and Munich, and was chiefly inspired by his travels in Italy and the Near East. He was active until 1890, all his work being of high quality. Equally notable was the work of Károly Lajos

Plates 154, 214, 215 Libay, Károly Telepy and Sándor Brodszky. Like Ligeti, they travelled widely, used similar methods and all their paintings showed great craftsmanship.

Throughout the 1850s Vienna continued to be a centre of interest to artists, while Munich became increasingly important for the development of art in Hungary.

In Vienna Waldmüller's free school, in which students could study naturalist genre-painting and portraiture, was no longer the only rival of the Academy.

In 1850 Carl Rahl opened a school which was to exert a major influence on the Hungarian painting of the 1850s and 1860s. Rahl had been trained in Munich and Stuttgart before, in 1836, he went to live in Rome from where he returned to the Austrian capital.

Art historians have described Rahl's painting as typical of Academic Historicism and Eclecticism. Though he had studied at the Academy in Munich, Rahl did not adopt the formal type of drawing taught in the Academy but modelled his work on that of the Classical painters. In his historical paintings, genre-scenes and portraits he tried to imitate the opulent style and rich compositions of the great masters of High Renaissance and Baroque art. Rahl was consciously trying to give his paintings an appearance of remoteness from his own age; his aim was to achieve in his work a timeless absolute value, unlike his contemporary, Friedrich von Amerling, who was more responsive to a middle-class concern for the present. Rahl probably did not realize—or did not want to realize—that in his descriptive and decorative paintings for new buildings he was supporting the current political situation. To understand this more fully, one must realize that Rahl, who was not really accepted by the Emperor's court, upheld values that were essentially democratic. In his school, he laid the foundations for the careers of many painters who became celebrated artists acknowledged by the Monarchy, and of others who laboured to propagate democratic ideals and national traditions by means of their portraits and historical genre-paintings.

Several young Hungarian artists profited by their studies under Carl Rahl. Two of his most successful pupils, Mór Than and Károly Lotz, assisted him in the execution of his monumental paintings in Vienna and in the University of Athens, where he had so many commissions that he could not complete them without assistance.

These superb historical paintings from the early 1850s helped the talented Hungarian painter Mór Than to revive the tradition of the Baroque battle-scenes of the previous century characterized by dramatic action and elaborate figure painting. As a colourist, Than united instinct and acquired knowledge to create his harmonious, often powerful effects. His sole aim was to remind visitors to his exhibitions, whether Hungarian or foreign, of the heroic struggles of the Hungarian people. For this purpose he created his large canvas depicting the last stage of *The Battle of Mohács,* painted in Paris in 1856. This painting commemorates the heroes who refused to surrender: the king is depicted fleeing with his escort. The principal figures represent László Szalkai, Archbishop of Esztergom, Pál Tomori, the wounded commander of the tragic battle, and János Drágfi, the standard bearer holding the white flag with the figure of the Holy Virgin and the Infant Jesus. (The same flag was also used during the War of Independence.) Meanwhile, all around the battle rages, Hungarians clashing with Turkish soldiers, commoners and noblemen alike. Mór Than was probably influenced by Rahl's sketch for a mural entitled *The Battle at the Lajta,* depicting an ancient Germanic tribe's fight, but his own, painted in Paris, is far more colourful and vigorous than his model. It is clearly conceived within the manners of French historical painting of the 19th century.

The interpretation of historic events in the light of contemporary political situations became common in French painting from the end of the 18th century, in the period of Napoleon's first consulship. The device continued, though with different symbolism, during the Empire, the Restoration and the revolutions. After 1848, historical themes became purely academic tasks for artists who liked to uphold the tradition. French critics as early as 1830 rejected the pure archaeological approach to historical events. During the 1840s and 1850s, the belief grew that the artist's most important task was to concern himself with the Romanticism of the present, with "the heroism of modern life" (Baudelaire) and to express "the morality of the present time" (Courbet). Historical painting, however, did not disappear from the salons. Some painters who subscribed to the new ideals raised contemporary events or those of the immediate past onto the pedestal previously reserved for ancient and medieval historic incidents. Even the most advanced critics acknowledged the unques-

Plates 175, 176   tionable value of works painted by Delacroix and Daumier, with their representation of the "history" of the present, objecting only to the idle repetitions of dramatic, moving or tragic scenes of the past without introducing some link with contemporary life. Historical paintings exhibited in the salons were for the most part sentimental or awe-inspiring representations of events of timeless significance. Their subjects included prison scenes, murders and executions of the innocent, watched by mourners, the idle and the curious. These works were intended to point out a moral, to exemplify the cruelty of life. As early as 1831, Heine and later Baudelaire strongly criticised these scenes of horror and urged artists to pay more attention to their own time; he even indicated one suitable subject—the Polish revolt of 1830.

It is probable that neither Heine, Baudelaire, nor other critics were aware that in 1833 a painting was exhibited in Pest showing a Polish hero with a broken sword. It represented a participant in the 1830 uprising and was painted by Ede Heinrich after Leon Cogniet, a French Academic painter. Heinrich's painting is unfortunately lost.

This approach to contemporary history in the academic style attracted Hungarian painters to Paris even after the passage of twenty or twenty-five years, where they studied under the famous masters of the 1830s, such as Leon Cogniet, Horace Vernet and Paul Delaroche, all teaching by then in their own schools of painting.

In the 1850s the Academic style of Munich also began to reveal a more materialistic approach to history. Carl von Piloty, a German painter who lived for a time in Belgium and who was later influenced by Paul Delaroche and Louis Gallait, was acclaimed for a historical work executed in 1855. The paint-

Plate 198   ing described, without too much regard for the facts, the murder of Wallenstein during the Thirty Years War. There are stylistic similarities with

Plate 183   Delaroche's *The Death of the Duc de Guise* and *Jeanne d'Arc in Prison,* painted some twenty-five years earlier. The following year Piloty was appointed to teach at the Academy and so he could freely develop his style, which exerted an influence mainly in Central and Eastern Europe.

It was indeed the same pictorial approach which attracted Hungarian painters to Munich and Paris. Driven by ambition and a desire to uphold the Hungarian tradition, they were not content to follow the Nazarene, Neo-Renaissance or Neo-Baroque style of Vienna, but even the by now exaggerated, sweet sophistication of the *Biedermeierstil,* intended to satisfy bourgeois taste, was equally unacceptable to them. It was stylized and affected in contrast to the Academic naturalism or natural Academism, which they found in the Salons, private studios and schools of Paris. The influence of the French schools reached Munich in 1856 when one class at the Academy began to follow the French example. In the 1850s, the number of Hungarian pupils in Munich rapidly increased. All those who, for obvious reasons, had no liking for Vienna, chose either Paris or Munich. However since Vienna was nearer and cheaper it often became only the first "port of call" for artists intending to continue their training in Munich or Paris and they frequently returned to Vienna after one or two years of study further afield.

Historical themes continued to dominate Hungarian painting in the 1850s. Tragic themes abounded in the history of Hungary and could be illustrated by events since 1848–1849 as well as those of the distant past. Artists had to create only the setting for heroic episodes in which men could be seen facing a brutal death with honour. These scenes were painted in compositions of the utmost sentimentality. A variety of *clichés* were employed to depict human **Plate 141** tragedies: sometimes the victor was shown forgiving the enemy and paying homage to the defeated.

The water-colour by the Austrian painter August von Pettenkofen is a faithful representation of an Austrian soldier burying the dead enemy. József **Plate 140** Borsos also completed a painting showing the grieving widow of an Austrian officer, a work that is far more realistic than his coldly beautiful *Girls after the Ball.* **Plate 146**

Pictures of honorable women from Hungarian history mourning their heroes were respected almost to the point of veneration at this time, in both paintings and graphic works. They held a symbolic significance like Antigone of the Greeks. This cult was due to the fact that the greatest of all contemporary Hungarian poets, Sándor Petőfi, disappeared on the battlefield in 1849, and his body was never found. Thus artists sought from historical and literary sources stories of widows mourning by the grave and gave their subject a more general actual meaning.

One of these paintings reached the Exhibition in Pest in 1851 too late to be hung in an appropriate place, nor was it approved by the critics; yet it became very popular. This painting was executed by Soma Orlai Petrich that same **Plate 142** year. Orlai received an education and lived in a style typical of his age and his art was typical of the period in that it reflects his commitment to the national cause. He was a friend of Petőfi, of whom he made several realistic portraits. He worked seriously and conscientiously, his interests being divided between literature, poetry and history. In 1846 he decided to become an artist and went to Marastoni's school in Pest. He also attended Waldmüller's school in Vienna for a while. In 1848 he composed his painting, *The Recall of St. Stephen, the First King of Hungary,* which was widely praised in the press. He fought in the War of Independence as a *honvéd* officer, a defender of the motherland. After the defeat he escaped to Munich where he attended Wilhelm Kaulbach's classes. He only stayed in Munich for two years and it was then that he sent the painting mentioned above to Pest. It represented the discovery of the body of the Hungarian king Louis II in 1526 and marked a new development in the pictorial representation of the Battle of Mohács, although it was in fact based on a 17th century German engraving on a similar theme. Orlai places the king's body at the centre of the composition, making it seem much larger than in the engraving. The mourners paying their last respects to the dead king are arranged in groups and are posed in a similar way to the mourners of the dead Christ in Pietà compositions. The kneeling woman dressed in blue is presumably Dorottya Kanizsai or Queen Mary, the widow of the king, with her are two other female mourners. Orlai's composition was considered to be completely successful, in spite of his heavy-handed figure-drawing and the lack of colour harmony. Not only did it move the public, but it also impressed young artists, despite its more calculated Academic formality, learned in Kaulbach's school. In the Turkish-Hungarian Battle of Mohács it was not only the king who lost his life; the sacrifice was made by countless followers, the humble together with the great. This line of thought led inevitably to another theme for artists—the defeat of the War of Independence. Years later both Orlai and **Plates 143, 144**   Mihály Kovács painted another incident at Mohács, when the wife of Imre Perényi searched for her husband's body on the battlefield, and commanded that he should be buried together with the rest of the unidentified dead. Both paintings represent dramatic scenes of mourning by night, with Perényi's wife as the central figure. In Kovács's painting she lifts her right hand as she orders the burial, in Orlai's she is seen with both arms raised to heaven in an imploring gesture. The act of national mourning is further emphasized by the groups of knights, grave-diggers, monks and grieving women.

Mihály Kovács had come home to Hungary from Italy on learning of the uprising in 1848 and his Hungarian historical works reveal much empathy. He intended to complete a series of historical paintings under the guidance of his friend Béla Tárkányi, who was a priest. He was unfortunately never able to complete the series. After his studies in Vienna he chose as the theme for his next work the origins of Hungary and depicted the scene in which Árpád is lifted to the shield. It was only in sketches that he depicted the more recent past, but one of these, an oil sketch which the artist described as an "allegorical **Plate 177**   sketch", deserves special attention. It is a composition with many figures, entitled *The Oppression of Hungary in 1849*. The principal figure is a woman, barefooted and dressed in ragged red and white garments. This figure had of course appeared in earlier historical paintings and was to be represented in the future. There comes to mind Delacroix's allegory representing the subjuga- **Plate 175**   tion of Greece, the lively figure of the heroine in his *Liberty Leading the People* and Daumier's allegorical representation of France as a very simply dressed **Plate 176**   proletarian mother.

The poor woman in Kovács's painting represents the young independent Hungarian state, called into being by the 1849 Declaration of Independence and the Kossuth Government. The great powers (the Austrian Empire and Tsarist Russia) and the minorities living near and in Hungary, are represented by figures attacking the poor woman. The Habsburg policy of "divide and conquer" practised for over a hundred years, and a lack of understanding on the part of Hungary itself, caused other nationalities to forsake the cause of Hungarian freedom and independence and to fight against the new independent state.

Kovács could not paint his subject in the large size he had wished because it referred too openly to the contemporary political situation and its tragic consequences. By 1861–1862, when the sketch was made, the War of Independence was already past history, but the memory of it was still alive in the minds of the people, and its main conflicts remained unsolved.

Many historical paintings and drawings, typical of and acceptable to the contemporary public, in no way reflected the dramatic conflicts that had sometimes divided the people. Some of the pictorial arts were more naive and biased in their descriptions, and also in their interpretation of history, than were literary works or essays by contemporary historians. The remorse and note of apology present in Hungarian literature, expressed by 16th century preachers, by later philosophers and by Kölcsey in his National Anthem, did not manifest itself in the arts. It was replaced by a resentment of injustice and a sense of undeserved suffering. Painters conceived their history as a story of a blameless and heroic nation attacked by enemies who were the agents of Fate. The historical paintings of this period were conceived as elaborate symbols and allegories, the central motif being always the death of a hero or heroine who had fought to the death (Dobozi and His Spouse, for example), **Plates 200, 201, 202** or a victim unjustly executed (László Hunyadi, Péter Zrínyi and Ferenc Frangepán). **Plates 184, 185, 187**

Strikingly enough, similar tragic themes can be found in Hungarian folklore; but here tragedy is often based on chance. The same is represented in folk-genre-paintings, as, for example, when a peasant lad is drowned in the river or a coach overturned into a ditch. Other folk-genres, however, retained their idyllic style until 1870, when a new social conception of genre-painting emerged. Humour helped the people to endure their state of subjection and to cope with their difficulties, and their own courage in a difficult situation strengthened their self-esteem. Thus, both the pathetic historical portraits and the anecdotic genre-paintings (or those interpreting literary works) serve to heighten the nation's awareness of its identity. Contemporary artists could experiment with both approaches or chose the approach best suited to their talents.

Nearly all painters trained in Vienna experimented with both forms, while those from Munich were more apt to choose one or the other. Important literary sources for folk scenes were to be found in Hungarian poems by Csokonai, Petőfi and János Arany; also in the folk-songs which were just beginning to be collected at this time.

From the 1850s onwards, a more Academic approach was represented by Mór Than, Károly Lotz and Soma Orlai Petrich, while the more instinctive approach to genre-painting was practised by Mihály Szemlér and János Jankó, who also enlivened their paintings with an element of caricature. They particularly liked to represent people dancing and singing, especially peasants and **Plates 169, 170** shepherds. Dancing figures demonstrating old Hungarian dances were also the chief subject chosen by Hungary's greatest 19th century sculptor, Miklós Izsó. In fact, paintings with dancing figures all show some affinity with Izsó's small figurines. Their aim was to represent this branch of Hungarian folk-art. Whereas in the paintings of the 1830s and 1840s we find scenes from everyday life, such themes were not chosen in the later representations of the life of middle-classes in the towns. Paintings executed for the newly-rich patrons of the 1850s and 1860s tended to feature both false glamour and sentimentalism. Everyday life is best represented by traditional scenes of weddings, burials, fêtes, or work. Another popular subject was life in the *Puszta;* shepherds, swine-herds or horse trainers were depicted enjoying the beauty of nature, removed from all political strife. Mór Than tried to experience and reproduce

Plates 169, 170, 171, 249

this way of life in accordance with Rahl's methods of narration. Szemlér and János Jankó painted either caricatures or idealized representations of life in the *Puszta,* while Orlai and Antal Ligeti aimed at dispassionate objectivity.

The most significant painter of these landscape folk scenes was the young Károly Lotz. These were the scenes he chose to paint in most of the works he sent from Vienna to Hungary. At the beginning of his career, he composed historical paintings only occasionally, as he was less skilled in this field (cf. his Dobozi sketch). But he depicted the life of the *Puszta* in a complete series and it is certainly significant that his first painting to be accepted by the National

Plate 166

Museum was *Stud in a Thunderstorm.*

Mihály Szemlér, a fashionable genre-painter and caricaturist, was born into a family of craftsmen, fought in the War of Independence, and afterwards

Plate 249

studied under both Rahl and Waldmüller in Vienna. His first ambition was to become a historical painter, but eventually he found his individual style in painting and drawing folk scenes.

Plate 163

Gusztáv Kelety, another painter and a remarkable art critic, spent only a short time in Rahl's school and then returned to Hungary to become the private tutor of József Eötvös's children. He made a conscious choice to paint land-scapes, in which he sometimes introduced elements of portraiture, a style much favoured in the first half of the 19th century. He also wrote art criticism, concentrating mainly on serious artists whose work was free from all extrava-gance. He wrote serious studies of the landscapes of Markó, Ligeti, Telepy and their friends, noting especially those artists whose drawings showed their lack of affectation and their closeness to nature.

Antal Ligeti began his career as a portrait-painter, though he also completed a historical painting in collaboration with Henrik Weber. Later on he aban-doned literary connotations. Although the small figures or architectural details

Plates 156, 167, 168

introduced into his landscapes are well observed, he did not arrange these details to create a narrative composition. Accordingly, he was one of the most remarkable painters of views of historically significant places, both sacred and exotic.

Plates 162, 164

Alajos Györgyi Giergl painted portraits, genre-scenes and religious composi-tions without showing a preference for one of the other. He cultivated a ver-satile talent and developed an elegant style in which he composed truly great and noble paintings. József Borsos was another painter of wide-ranging inter-ests who used his brush with great skill. Yet he totally abandoned painting in

29

the 1860s, first taking up photography, and then becoming the owner of an inn in Buda. Antal Haan and Ferenc Szoldatics settled in Italy, and after a period in Hungary, Károly Telepy and Mór Than also returned to that country.

Mihály Zichy, whose career was the most exciting of the 19th century Hungarian painters, also studied first in Giacomo Marastoni's school of painting in Pest before moving on to study under Ferdinand Waldmüller in Vienna. During the 1840s he painted some of the most impressive of the bourgeois genre-paintings. In 1847 he left Vienna for St. Petersburg where after working for a time as an independent artist he was appointed court-painter to the Tsar. Except for a few short periods he lived in St. Petersburg until 1874, when he moved to Paris. At that time he already knew Théophile Gautier who had visited him in St. Petersburg on several occasions and had written a laudatory analysis of his work, praising it as truly Romantic. Although Zichy stayed for any length of time in Hungary only once, in 1880, he followed with interest the literary and political developments in his native country. These he also illustrated in his paintings and drawings with eagerness, enthusiasm, and sometimes with despair, always seeing the fate of Hungary within the wider context of European history.

Mihály Kovács, Soma Orlai Petrich, Mór Than and Mihály Zichy attempted to practise every form of art in the Academic hierarchy; they continued to do so throughout their lives, achieving success in each form. Viktor Madarász, however, who was born in 1830 and began to paint in 1853, decided to be a true historical painter. He painted excellent portraits but here too his aim was to commemorate his subjects as historical characters. After 1858, Madarász conceived a series of works reflecting an international trend in historical painting; and during the fourteen years of his stay in Paris his style underwent an even more radical change than that of Mór Than who stayed there for a shorter period of time.

Madarász deliberately broke with the Waldmüller-like genre painting and sought new pictorial examples; this was already obvious in *The Fugitive's Dream* painted in Vienna.

Plate 179

In the view of experts in the iconology of the 19th century, the greatest novelty in French Academic painting of the time was the change in the process of composition. The very first step of the process, (that is, capturing the essence of the picture in one sweeping movement in a colour sketch), came to be considered the most important phase in painting. This was certainly due to the influence of Romanticism. The colour sketch was then shown to the professors at the Academies, who based their critical judgements on the emotional power of the subject and the spontaneity of the pictorial style.

Madarász soon became aware of the importance of condensing both thematic and pictorial elements in his sketches and to remain as concise as possible in the final version too.

Earlier Hungarian historical painting with its detailed and anecdotic narrative was created quite differently. Madarász was thus confronted with the problem of finding his way between two opposite systems of requirements. In his picture entitled *Felicián Zách,* painted in Paris in 1859, he followed dramatic

Plate 181

interpretation by placing the two very strongly and clearly characterized figures of the story side by side. The subject of 14th century nobleman Felicián Zách and his daughter (who had been seduced by a relative of the Queen), convey the artist's image of an unhappy girl and her elderly but passionate father, wild with grief and impatient for revenge. Even Parisian visitors to the exhibition must surely have felt some of the implication of this family drama. The "exotic" costumes from what was to the French a far distant country only enhanced for them the curious quality of the work.

One year later, Madarász, determined to break into the wider world of European art, experimented with an even more impressive composition. His subject was the lying in state of László Hunyadi, a young Hungarian nobleman, the son of the famous János Hunyadi, who had been executed by Ladislas V in the 15th century on charges of high treason. Madarász depicted the body of Hunyadi, shrouded and lying on his bier, in the light of two candles in a Gothic chapel; his mother and his bride are seen weeping over his corpse. This tragic episode was known to all Hungarians as was its contemporary relevance and later interpretations. Albert Berzeviczy wrote that the painting *The Mourning of László Hunyadi,* does not merely relate an historic event, but also makes us feel the tribulations of the human being and the tragic fate of a nation. This Hungarian Pietà symbolizes the tragic fate of Hungary. (The interpretations furnish proof that several social strata under several historical circumstances identified themselves with the young victim of a bad sovereign's unjust sentence.) The message expressed by Madarász was also understood in Paris, and famous critics of the time, such as Théophile Gautier, analysed his works. At that time, this painting was thought to symbolize the defeated War of Independence rather than depict a historic episode of the 15th century. It was rightly felt that apart from the universal nature of such an issue as national independence, the Hungarian nation was finding its place in European world of art and that by means of the tragic condition of the people, this nation was sending a special message to Paris and to the rest of Europe.

Madarász was duly awarded the Gold Medal of the Salon of 1859 in the year when Hungarian emigrants tried to get help from Napoleon III for a new war of independence. Apart from its political significance, his painting still remains more powerful than any work previously executed on a similar theme. Madarász was never again able to produce an equally powerful work. His portrait head of Péter Zrínyi from 1858 seemed to promise a similar or perhaps even greater dramatic tension and a development towards a style comparable to that of Courbet's self-portraits of the 1840s, and his painting *The Wounded Youth,* preserved in Vienna. Yet the heroic figures in Madarász's historical paintings dating from the 1860s reveal little of the artistic insight which enabled him to create the portrait head of Zrínyi or the colour sketches for the László Hunyadi composition.

Madarász's most successful work in his homeland was *Péter Zrínyi and Ferenc Frangepán in the Wiener-Neustadt Prison,* representing another subject to which it was easy to give contemporary significance. The same subject can be seen in a 17th century engraving, which was used to illustrate an account of Wesselényi's conspiracy against the Habsburgs; and in a play by Petőfi there is reference to certain fairground farceurs who, because they played the story of Zrínyi's and Frangepán's 1671 execution as criminals, were themselves physically attacked by a crowd of Hungarians. The memory of the Hungarian aristocrats of the 17th century who conspired against the Habsburgs was alive in Hungary before and after the War of Independence of 1848. Madarász movingly portrays the two noblemen taking leave of each other as they go to the scaffold; Péter Zrínyi calm and resolute, Ferenc Frangepán young and tearful. Madarász visited Wiener Neustadt to see the town where they were executed and the fortress for himself. In one version of his painting the two-headed eagle of Austria can be seen in the background on a window. This version, however, could not be exhibited at that time in Hungary. Consequently, a new version was made; but even without the two-headed eagle, visitors to the exhibition had no doubt about the anti-Habsburg meaning of the picture. Madarász was intensely aware of contemporary issues, he felt deeply about them and could always choose a subject from history to actualize and create a dramatic situation. His passionate nature caused him to intensify primary pictorial values, contrasting dark and light by using broad, powerful strokes of his brush. He was capable of evoking both sympathy and aversion for the persons he depicted. His portrayal of the death of László Hunyadi was the work most frequently discussed by historians, and it was also one of the most popular of his works. In 1875 he again chose to paint the death of a hero, this time a contemporary hero, Petőfi. Engravings were made and all over the country **Plate 190** prints were to be seen in the homes of rich and poor alike, in village hostelries and other public places where people gathered to discuss politics.

These works preserved the politically heated atmosphere of the 1860s, when Hungary stood at a cross-roads in its history. For the country had to choose between the exiled Kossuth's plan to join neighbouring nations of the projected Danube Alliance in a renewed struggle for independence, or to reach a compromise with Austria as advocated by Ferenc Deák and his party at home. István Széchenyi, who lived in a private asylum in Döbling (Austria), became very anti-Austrian during the 1850s. He even published in London under a pseudonym a biting satire of the political system of Alexander Bach, governor of the Hungarian territories whose absolutism followed General Haynau's reign of terror after 1849. Széchenyi sent his pamphlet to Napoleon III, the British Prime Minister and representatives of the other great nations in the hope of gaining some support for the Hungarian people. All he gained was a period of harassment for himself by the Austrian police. In April 1860, Széchenyi finally committed suicide. In the following year it was Count László **Plate 189** Teleki who succumbed to political harassment and put an end to his life. In spite of using a pseudonym, when he was on a private visit to Dresden he was arrested by the Saxon police and deported under police escort to Austria. Later he gained the Emperor's pardon and was freed, but when he was again a candidate for the Hungarian Parliament and joined the more radical wing in the preparatory stages of the Austro-Hungarian Compromise, his life was threatened once more. Just before he was to appear in an important political debate, he committed suicide, or was possibly murdered the previous night. The death of Széchenyi and Teleki deeply moved the whole nation. Memorial

Plate 188 leaflets were produced, showing the allegorical figure of Hungary in tears, with allegorical and life-like representations of their deaths and funerals. These leaflets were preserved by the people with a zeal reflecting the strength of political feeling.

Madarász retained his radical views throughout his life. He did not waver in the years following the 1867 Compromise with Austria, when Hungarian artists began to occupy themselves with historical representation of the newly established Austro-Hungarian Monarchy. His painting of the dying Petőfi reflects, perhaps even more dramatically, the message of the Teleki and Széchenyi memorial leaflets: Petőfi is seen in the gloom of twilight, his eyes

Plate 190 turned to heaven, and in the dusty earth he has traced the word "Hazám", (My Homeland). The painting, especially as cheaply reproduced, was similar in tone to the crude sentimental works such as Delaroche's *The Execution of Lady Jane Grey* and other European historical horror pictures. In the final decades of the century Madarász's painting was acclaimed as much in Hungary as Bálint

Plate 112 Kiss's picture of János Pethes Jablonczay, the 17th century Protestant preacher, taking leave of his daughter. The great success of both paintings is an indication of the development of political and artistic awareness throughout the lowest strata of society.

Madarász returned to Hungary in 1870, at the height of his career. But officially his work was not well received and after some harsh criticism by the professional critics of the period, he gave up painting about ten years later. His failure was also the consequence of the popularity of the more refined requirements of a German-type Academicism with its rejection of exaggerated and emotional display of Paris "manners" and "tasteless" manifestation of the cult of heroes. In Hungary in the 1860s the respected Academic painters were not impressed by Paris or Vienna, but by the Academy of Munich which had already been praised in the highest terms by Emmerich Henszlmann. In Madarász's *László Hunyadi* the treatment of the body is much more straightforward and direct, despite the shroud, than anything to be seen in the work of his Hungarian forerunners or contemporaries who were influenced by a more rigid type of Academism.

Bertalan Székely, the great Academic painter whose career was more soundly based than that of Madarász, at first studied in Vienna under Führich and Kupelwieser, then in the schools of Carl Rahl and Waldmüller, which laid special emphasis on the works of Carl von Blaas. Later Székely went to Munich to study under Karl von Piloty. This training deeply influenced his work, although later he tried to purge his style of all influences reminiscent of Paul Delaroche and Horace Vernet, acquired during his Paris visits and in Piloty's school in Munich. His ambition was to return to the Neo-Classical Academism represented by Wilhelm von Kaulbach. He also revered other German painters whom he considered to be the greatest artists of the century. He thoroughly analysed Moritz von Schwind's lyrical paintings which were equally inspired by the description of nature and literary source. His drawings, on the other hand, are occasionally reminiscent of drawings by Alfred Rethel, the early naturalist of this period. Rethel was a master of detail, and in his drawing was as precise in his representation of the beauty of nature as in his figure drawing; nor did he neglect the detail in the characterization of his minor figures.

Székely zealously studied his contemporaries' interpretation of nature and the classics of the Renaissance but was also guided by his own system of values. By sheer diligence he achieved a standard higher than that of some of his teachers. His *Self-portrait* from 1860 already indicates that Székely's main characteristics are an objective rationalism and a high degree of artistic sensibility. His working methods betray his early beginnings as an engineer accustomed to the keen and objective examination of objects. These qualities enabled him to become an excellent portraitist, though his meticulously composed historical paintings, based on hundreds of previous sketches, were more successful in his lifetime than his portraits.

When Székely first began to paint, every significant historic event had already been depicted at least once in Hungary by some other artist. His task was consequently to rearrange the *déjà vu* in the most perfect composition possible, eliminating all the naive elements, improper and unnecessary details of his predecessors' works. The fact that he had studied in Munich was of great help to him for it was probably there that he first learned to develop a sketch in faultless linear form before going on to find the balance through patches of colour in brush and colour sketches; in the third stage of his development, he merged the two approaches, using his brush to achieve plastic representation. Thus in his treatment of best known themes he achieved an effect of timelessness and verisimilitude.

Székely always respected the strict rules of proportion and measurement. Only in more intimate forms, (genre-painting or less official portraiture) did he create a freer atmosphere, and in some rare landscape sketches he conveyed a certain longing for infinity.

He noted in his diaries in Vienna and Munich that he could only work seriously on subjects which stirred his imagination. He did make experimental sketches on themes from a wider historical context, but his real aim was to put his art to the service of his country. For this reason, his note and sketch books and later his oil paintings preserve enthralling episodes of Hungarian history. He chose as the theme for one of his first great endeavours *The Discovery of the Body of King Louis II* after the battle of Mohács in 1526. He was obviously acquainted with Orlai's previous composition, and had recognized Orlai's impressive arrangement of figures as well as the faults of the work itself. He was also acquainted with motifs of mourning present in contemporary Austrian and German painting. He may well have known the young Anton Romako's sketch, made in 1855, *The Decisive Battle of Dürnkrut* (Austria), a battle which brought Rudolf Habsburg the Austrian throne following the death of Prince Ottokar Přemysl on the battlefield. It is an excellent sketch dominated by the brownish grey tones of the evening sky over the battlefield; Rudolph Habsburg, obviously moved, is seen with his escort, standing over his dead enemy. The sketch is a good example of a reserved, more moderate Academic style. Similar in conception, but emotionally more effective is Carl von Piloty's previously mentioned painting from 1855. The work was extremely popular at the time. It is an indoor scene, showing the body of General Wallenstein and the grieving friend, an astrologer, who had prophesied his death and now stands in front of the body in deep sorrow. The restrained grief of the friend is a motif largely retained by Székely in his work. Although he was far too inventive an artist to simply borrow motifs from any of his contemporaries, he undoubtedly observed and adapted the solutions he judged most appropriate to express a dramatic situation: his *Discovery of the Body of King Louis II* not only linked him with Hungarian pictorial tradition, it represented a solution to the problem of representing death in a historical setting. It had been a frame-subject among 19th century painters, who attempted to solve the representation of this subject in various settings. Jan Białostocki, who thoroughly analysed this question in his study on "framework" subjects, saw in the stories of the famous deaths the representation of the ill-fate of the individual, and beyond it, that of the community, and instances of the lessons to be learnt from political defeat. Székely's painting is certainly closely related to similar works of which there are numerous variations produced to meet national requirements. In the literature, Székely's *Louis II* is usually associated with two works by Alfred Rethel (who died in 1859), which depict the discovery of the bodies of Gustavus Adolphus and Frederick Barbarossa. There are also affinities with Benjamin West's *Death of General Wolfe* and numerous other Romantic and Academic works on the subject of death. Székely's painting deserves a special place in European as well as in Hungarian art, for it represents an attempt to answer the challenge formerly posed by Ferenc Kazinczy, Dániel Berzsenyi and Emmerich Henszlmann to the Hungarian painters—that is, to solve a pictorial problem on a high level, and express a typical national-historical feeling.

Székely's historical works, his sketches as well as his oil paintings, provide us with a list of subjects which could be related to contemporary issues in Hungary and throughout the world. One such theme is depicted in *Dobozi and His Spouse,* a painting which he began to plan in the late 1850s and finally completed in 1861. In Székely's view the dramatic flight-motif is not the high-point of the tragedy, as it was in minor works of the early 19th century, and also in one of Madarász's paintings. Székely's painting is a character study of this tragic couple. A similar interest in human character determined his pictorial solution for *The Women of Eger,* another piece on which he toiled for more than a decade. Here, in his depiction of the desperate defence of a fortress besieged by the Turks, Székely emphasizes the choice of self-sacrifice, which, however, he does not idealize. The incident which inspired this work was the fearless resistance of the women of Eger in the 16th century, who fought beside their husbands to defend the fortress against the Turks. Similar actions can be found in sources everywhere and have been represented in numerous of historical and allegorical paintings of courageous women, for example in the *Girl of Saragossa* by Sir David Wilkie (who died in 1841), or Delacroix's monumental painting in which the figure of a *citoyenne* with one bare breast becomes the famous symbol of Liberty. Székely purposely avoided allegorical interpretations in his monumental paintings, the actual historical settings of the events being significant enough for him. Nevertheless, both a universal meaning and abstract ideals are evident in his painting. That this was fully understood by the

Hungarian public is best shown by the fact that *Dobozi and His Spouse* and *Women of Eger* were very soon in the collection of the National Museum, the pantheon of Hungarian heroes. The cost of these paintings, as well as Krafft's painting at the beginning of the 19th century, was born by public donation. Until 1867, Székely's career ran parallel to other politically minded artists committed to the cause of liberty and freedom. Later, although he occasionally expressed his interest in politics and never once denied his past, he adopted a rather different attitude to history which is very obviously reflected in his *King Ladislas V and Ulrik Cillei* of around 1870. This picture depicts the young 15th century king as a careless youth unaware of the tragic conditions of his own time, allowing his courtiers to divert his attention from social unrest by means of games, love affairs and other indulgences of the wealthy. Traditionally, Székely should have painted a second picture to show that the king's behaviour would surely be punished by death. Instead the artist adopted a new device, indicating that by weakly allowing himself to be influenced by his courtiers, the king's foolishness deteriorated into self indulgence.

After 1867 Romantic interpretations of historical subjects were less frequently used and artists began to introduce into them new attitudes and meanings. Before the turning point of 1867, the ideological and historical conditions responsible for the growth of the Romantic revolution and the later rebellious gestures remained constant and even influenced artists living abroad in their choice of subject matter.

Sándor Liezen-Mayer was born in Győr and studied in Vienna until 1856. Later he studied in Munich where he presented a painting on a Hungarian historical subject when applying for admission to Karl von Piloty's class. The subject of his painting was the first phase of the decline of Hungary, the period when, after the death of the Hungarian king Louis Anjou the Great (died in 1383), the country was torn between two factions. The followers of the former king, his wife and daughter, can only bitterly lament beside the king's tomb, bewailing their own fate and the declining fortunes of their countrymen, while through the chapel doorway, the coronation of the new king (in their eyes a usurper) can be seen in all its splendour. The elegance of the painting and the masterly gradations of tone and application of colour values were intended to gain the approval of the senior teachers at the Academy, Piloty in particular. By choosing the theme of national mourning, Liezen-Mayer hoped to secure the favourable opinion of the judges who, in competitions for historical paintings, always concentrated on the subject matter. In the choice of subject and its execution, the artist's intentions were clearly sincere. The same straightforward honesty is evident in Alexander Wagner's paintings from Hungarian history. Wagner was another distinguished historical painter, later a professor at the Academy of Munich. In the work which he sent from Munich to Pest for the historical paintings competition of 1859, he paid a tribute to the memory of Titusz Dugovics, who died a heroic death in 1456 in the Battle of Nándorfehérvár when he prevented a Turk from climbing the wall of the fortress, by throwing himself from the ramparts, thus falling to his death together with the Turk. In the painting he is shown just as he is about to

Plate 211

Plate 217

leap. Wagner's other remarkable work dates from the early 1860s. Both the colour sketch and the final version are of a quality comparable to that of Székely's grandiose national paintings. Wagner's picture shows Queen Isabella, widow of King János Zápolyai, taking leave of the country on a day in autumn. (When Buda fell to the Turks in 1541, she was allowed to keep only Transylvania for herself and her infant son. However, due to the politics of Ferdinand I and the intrigues of her own court, she was even forced to abdicate Transylvania in the name of her son, and to go into exile.) Isabella is depicted grieving as like the queen in the picture of Louis Anjou the Great; she looks into the distance, sad but dignified, mourning a lost cause.

In time, however, artists abandoned this manner, in which famous women personified Hungary, their individual misfortune indicating the declining fortune of the country. In Hungary, just before 1867, painters began to introduce a new, less pessimistic symbolism. Initially it seemed the natural consequence of an easing of the political situation and the possibility of inaugurating a new era. In fact, even in the late 1850s, in spite of many difficulties, there were signs of renewed vigour in the arts and sciences. In the autumn of 1858, the Academy of Sciences was allowed to hold a general assembly—though this was conditional upon certain modifications of the statutes proposed by the Emperor. Scientific reviews, historical sources and literary reminiscences were published. The poet János Arany, the historian László Szalay, and the writer, politician and historian József Eötvös, played an important part in the revival of the Academy. At the same time, the Academy also embodied the ideals of the conservative aristocracy, and their resistance to the development of a widely based culture. This was an attitude expressed by Emil Dessewffy, who was elected as president and József Eötvös as vice-president in 1855. However, conditions were still too repressive to permit free development in any subject except the natural sciences. In the realm of literature, too, the tradition of freedom and liberty was preserved. Painters and sculptors who decorated buildings on the other hand, were still dependent in some respects on their patrons. They had to suppress their revolutionary views, choosing only the themes and styles favoured by those who were in a position to give them commissions for monuments and decorative painting.

The aristocracy was the first social group to accept the Compromise with the House of Habsburg, but the discontent of the lower classes continued. Internally and internationally, conditions were unfavourable to the movement for freedom. The lesser nobility, who were inclined to accept the Compromise, and the bourgeoisie who, like the nobility, realized its historical necessity, declared that the recovery of Hungary should take place within the existing framework of the Habsburg Empire. It was nevertheless the defeat suffered by Austria in 1866 in the war against Italy and Prussia, which finally hastened the Compromise. This agreement did not serve to strengthen the national struggle for independence in Hungary, rather, it made the minorities and neighbouring countries resent her for her privileges.

Kossuth wrote from exile in 1867, when the agreement was signed: "The Compromise isolates us from the rest of the world—and the only honour that is left for us is to be the fire which scorches the Austrian eagle."

Little heed was paid to these words in 1867. Indeed Austria seemed to be gaining power, both economic and military. The Austrian army continued to occupy Hungary until 1867, and the Emperor nominated Gyula Andrássy as Prime Minister of Hungary; furthermore, in the spring of that year, Parliament passed a bill introducing common ministries for financial, military and foreign affairs. In June 1867, Franz Joseph I was crowned King of Hungary in a most magnificent ceremony.

Hungarian artists and their patrons either took an active part in this historic process, or watched, passive and bewildered. This was the reaction of Bertalan Székely who even represented in his drawings and paintings some of the events at the time of the coronation. It was a turning point for Hungary. Artists had to choose one of three alternatives: they could endeavour to maintain their artistic integrity within the new historical context, they could use their talents to serve the new conception of "nation state", or they could withdraw from all political movements and devote themselves to the pursuit of art, especially the questions of "decorum", or the proper approach to Nature.

There were no precise lines of demarcation between these three approaches. Some artists and patrons of art tried all of them—understandably enough when we consider the general mood of the age of compromises.

Before 1867, few institutions were well housed and such public buildings as existed were rarely decorated with works of art. From 1859 on, the erection and decoration of one public building occupied artists and critics alike. It was the Redoute (Municipal Concert Hall) in Pest intended for balls, concerts and exhibitions. Sándor Wagner, then in Munich, provided two historical paintings, while Mór Than and Károly Lotz completed wall-paintings and other compositions in consultation with the architect to whom they had been recommended by Carl Rahl himself, who believed that their work would be a worthy expression of "the cultural standard of the nation".

The theme for the series of wall paintings in the Redoute, known in Pest as the Vigadó, was conceived by the historian Arnold Ipolyi. In 1855 he published *Magyar Mithológia* (Hungarian Mythology), in which he considered the relationship between old folk tales and of their possible connection with Asian and European culture in general, especially with Greek and Roman mythology. The paintings of the Redoute and the preliminary sketches, were approved by Emmerich Henszlmann and Gusztáv Kelety. Henszlmann wrote about the project in a Leipzig magazine; Kelety was working in Pest planning classes in the theory and practice of art at the Academy.

The Redoute was commissioned by the Council of the City of Pest. Their choice of a theme for the wall-paintings—in the words of Gusztáv Kelety,—was "diplomatically taken from the realm of folk tales". This "diplomacy" consisted in ensuring that historical paintings should show no reference to contemporary politics. The wall-paintings in the Redoute represent an attempt to introduce a new type of subject matter. The story of Prince Argyrus and his love for the Fairy Ilona had been familiar in Hungary from the early 16th century. It runs through both literature and folklore. Lotz and Than were influenced by Moritz von Schwind's series, *The Beautiful Melusina,* when they

Plates 220, 221, 222

created a new pictorial form devoid of national symbolism and intended only as a means for the representation of mythological themes.

The scenes painted by Lotz, situated so high that they could not be enjoyed, became known to the German and Hungarian public chiefly in the form of illustrations in magazines, while Mór Than's huge painting of Fairy Ilona's meeting with Prince Argyrus was a magnificent work to be appreciated at first hand. The original idea of the decoration is probably better expressed in Than's *The Feast of Attila,* painted in the dining hall of the Redoute. In this composition the painter made use of a description of Attila's court by Priskos Rhetor, the Greek historian. The dignified figure of Attila, the proud Hun sovereign, is seen with his courtiers feasting and listening to songs about the military exploits and victories of his courageous people. In Kelety's view, "Mór Than has carried out his task with due respect". Indeed, this respect for his subject is conspicuous in Than's historical composition. In the Redoute, however, the decoration of which was being continued until 1873, no more such compositions seemed to be necessary. Additional smaller paintings were consequently entrusted to Lotz, whose livelier brushwork, dancing cherubs and mythological scenes in the classical style were much appreciated. In the new era when there was a growing demand for decorative painting, it was definitely to his advantage to have studied under Rahl, in Vienna.

While completing their work in the Redoute, Than and Lotz were commissioned by the Chancellery on the 8th January, 1867 to create wall-paintings for the main staircase and ceiling of the entrance hall of the National Museum. They obtained this commission through the good offices of Eitelberger von Edelberg, court counsellor of the museums of Vienna, and although the Compromise had not yet been signed, the political climate of the moment influenced even this commission. The sketches provided by Than and Lotz were approved by the commissioners and were held to satisfy the prevailing national requirements as well. For the ceiling Lotz devised a composition to include a multitude of allegorical figures representing the arts and sciences. Above the entrance on the first floor, Mór Than depicted Hungaria (or Pannonia), no longer in a mourning pose, but crowned and dignified, the patroness of the arts and sciences represented by two naked immature youths. The history of Hungary can be followed in a frieze which runs round the staircase wall at first floor level, which includes scenes from the history of Hungary: the Asian Huns, the Magyars accepting Christianity, medieval scenes, and events in the reign of Maria-Theresa. It was Lotz's task to illustrate the legendary events of the Hungarian past, while the more politically minded Than painted scenes from later history and also contemporary scenes, for instance Palatine Joseph Habsburg shown as a patron of the arts. The figures of István Széchenyi and Ferenc Deák, which close the series, indicate cultural achievements during the Age of Reform.

The wall-paintings in the National Museum are rather dull and uninteresting, typical examples of work resulting from an attempt to synthesize several approaches to history. These paintings were based on a conception of historical pieces and a scholarly representation of mythological subjects which reflected the anachronistic political system of the dual monarchy and the belief that art

39

should serve politics. The style is reminiscent of the wall-paintings in Viennese palaces and the University of Athens executed by Rahl with the assistance of his pupils. **Plate 223**

In the period after 1867, a divergence could be observed in Hungarian culture, sculpture and graphic art in theme, style and form. From 1861 onwards, painting was for the first time taught in a state academy called the "Mintarajzis-kola" (High School of Decorative Drawing and Arts), and from 1880 onwards in master's schools comparable to the European Academies, though the notion of art in Europe was by this time no longer limited to the forms and patterns taught there.

The most fashionable painter of the period was indisputably Károly Lotz. He no longer painted only landscapes and genre-scenes; instead he used his skill to decorate public institutions and private homes. Lotz made no attempt to give a new interpretation to mythology, nor did he specify the hidden meanings of his allegories. He liked to paint, without allusions, purely decorative scenes and figures. Mostly he painted beautiful women, scantily clad, symbolizing **Plates 226, 227** the senses, the muses or forms of art. In an allegorical composition made in 1877 for the former Műcsarnok (Art Gallery), he painted a figure to represent Reality. In contrast to his other models, Lotz chose to depict in this work an old naked woman who sees in her mirror the reality of her condition, and through it, the inevitable progress of time. Yet in most of his works, Lotz was **Plate 228** not concerned with reality except when painting some portraits or illustrating certain books. It was for Petőfi's poems published after 1859 that Lotz made his most successful illustrations, for example, those made for "Childe John" (János Vitéz) and "The Shepherd on his Donkey" (Megy a juhász a szamáron). About twenty years earlier, Gustave Courbet had abandoned the representation of mythological figures and winged angels for the idea of Reality. Lotz continued to please his patrons in his great public commissions and it might well be thought that some other artist of this type was responsible for the portraits, so clearly intended to please and so aptly described by the term "society painting", or *l'art pompier*. He frequently portrayed his step-daughter **Plate 282** whom he depicted as an elegant and respectable upper middle-class lady, emancipated to a degree, but essentially feminine, like all his models. Lotz's **Plate 283** female nudes, on the other hand, have the same quality of naive eroticism seen in the painting of his first master, Giacomo Marastoni, although with a higher degree of pictorial virtuosity. Lotz worked industriously until the turn of the 19th–20th centuries, skilfully adapting his art to the changing requirements of the time. He avoided the great pitfalls that faced the talented painters when art flourished and declined in the second half of the 19th century, an age dangerous for its cultural prosperity; on the other hand, his art always merely skimmed the surface of the question raised by the epoch in which he worked. In some of the paintings he comes close to Impressionism, but he did not deliberately choose this way. He painted beautiful allegorical scenes with little concern for meaning, and was a successful painter of landscapes with no wish to specialize in them. In short, he always chose the easy way out and adhered to convention.

In Hungary, even during the second half of the century, landscape painting was not held in great esteem, despite the fact that it required more contemplation of a high order and possibly gave more lasting satisfaction to the painter. Gusztáv Kelety was one of those who fully appreciated the art of landscape painting. As a critic he also demanded from the artists a keen observation and a sensitive reproduction of nature. He opposed hasty innovations and the rejection of tradition. But he was not only an art critic, he was also an excellent landscapist. He produced a grandiose painting of the Tátra, based on numerous drawings in ink and water-colour. In this work Kelety realized the ideal of landscape painting conceived by one of his predecessors, the poet and critic Kazinczy. In some of Kelety's landscapes the Romantic conception of dramatic scenery exists together with the classical form, and his choice of Visegrád as a subject was certainly not accidental. In his large oil paintings he wished to enrich tradition by the detailed description of natural phenomena in a realistic, almost photographic, style.

Antal Ligeti showed even greater persistence than Kelety by continuing to paint landscapes in his mature style of the 1850s. While travelling in Italy and the Holy Land he carefully noted ancient ruins, Biblical landscapes and natural settings, observing with great accuracy and care the flora of various regions, the climate and sometimes the inhabitants wearing exotic dress. His compositions are not of enclosed scenes as if for a stage setting, but range over a wider view. Although he sometimes used engravings as pictorial sources for his views of cities or landscapes, his chief aim was to compose a standard view that was brought animated by personal experience. Ligeti returned from his travels in the late 1850s and from then onwards till his death in 1890, he completed oil paintings based on water-colours and pencil drawings made abroad. His subjects included the Greek amphitheatre in Taormina, the cedar-groves of the Lebanon, the views of Jerusalem, Bethlehem, Nazareth and other famous places. His paintings sold well as did the wood-cuts and lithographs made after them; their authenticity made them a reliable source for illustrations of travel books and articles, and they were also suitable for representing the holy places of the Christian religion places. Certain critics, however, occasionally show a greater appreciation for Ligeti's Hungarian landscapes. One of his views of Visegrád was published as a wood-cut by the "Képzőművészeti Társulat" (Association for the Fine Arts) in 1863, and in the year of his death, a coloured wood-cut was made of his water-colour entitled *Baalbek,* painted when he was in the Near East.

Károly Telepy completed many more Hungarian landscapes and townscapes than Ligeti. He was also active until the turn of the century. (He died in 1906.) He studied for some time in Munich, and for a longer period in Italy. In some of his early landscapes painted in Italy he juxtaposed realistic and symbolic landscape elements. Like Mihály Kovács in an earlier period, Telepy delighted in painting picturesque Italian national costumes. He attempted very few landscapes with figures, preferring to point accurate but deeply felt skyscapes, both brilliant and subdued. His aim was to discover a balance between the ephemeral and lasting characteristics of a landscape, and he recorded the variations occurring according to the time of day, the weather and the season of the year. This balance he achieved in some of his most distinguished works.

41

Academic landscape painting in the style of Munich was also represented by the work of Sándor Brodszky and József Molnár. The latter painted other genres as well. Both painters worked in an academic style which by 1870 was quite outdated.

By now Munich was no longer a mere temple of Neo-Classical Academism, but had become instead a meeting place for the old and the new; even in the late Academic painting which might be described as a remodelling of the ideals of High Renaissance, Baroque and Rococo art, some degree of Naturalism was present. Teachers and students alike were trying out new artistic methods in order to develop a more naturalistic style in landscape, portraiture and the portrayal of contemporary social life. Mythological scenes were depicted in a more intimate and sensuous style; in historical paintings artists had to recognize the lower classes, and their compositions now included members of the middle classes, peasants and tradesmen.

In the Munich of the 1860s Realism was neither disapproved of nor dismissed as scandalous, as it had been in the Paris of the 1840s. Academic artists themselves admired the harmonious colour effects and the warm tones, and encouraged their less creative pupils to copy the techniques used by French artists. Realism and Naturalism made its début in Munich in 1869 at an exhibition which came straight from Paris and where works by Corot, Courbet, Millet, Théodore Rousseau and Manet were shown. This was, of course, the most extreme manifestation. As a direct consequence, many Munich artists felt as if nature had been revealed to them anew and they felt an urge to paint in a different manner in the future. However a thread of tradition was firmly woven into their experiments, so that their work was exceedingly eclectic.

This many-folded character of art is exemplified in the work of Gyula Benczúr and Pál Szinyei Merse. These two very talented Hungarian artists of the 19th century became friends, and the course of their lives ran parallel at times before diverging in their later years. Benczúr acknowledged tradition, which for him was the sole authority, a choice which was typical for the most of the artists of the Eastern part of Europe divided up by the French-Prussian-Austrian conflicts and wars. The career and achievements of his best friend, Szinyei Merse, represent an exception. Szinyei Merse found his way to fresh insights and clever innovations; he was influenced and inspired by exhibitions, the wider world of modern art and some of its great representatives. Yet in the 1870s in Munich this alternative was not so strongly established that it could provide Szinyei with theoretical arguments to explain and defend his discoveries. After a few successes and some unfavourable criticism, Szinyei did not go further west than Munich; he returned eastward to Vienna and Hungary where he hoped to find a more positive reception, but found neither sympathy nor a theoretical basis for his painting.

As for Gyula Benczúr, by the end of the 1860s, his historical sketches proved him to be Piloty's most faithful pupil. During the 1870s he too felt the influence of the French Realists and Naturalists and of the German Realism of Lenbach and Leibl. Yet he remained faithful to the hierarchy of genres taught at the Academy and continued to paint portraits of public figures and to create large and theatrical historical compositions. His work is more aggressive, more sensuous than anything found in the Hungarian Academic paintings of earlier years. At times it seems as if Benczúr's paintings from this period were overcome by some mad desire to exaggerate the ceremonial until it turns into the grotesque, to create new myths in the name of unconventionality and to merge and devalue even those newly created values that were born of Naturalism and Realism on the soil of bourgeois democratic ideals.

Benczúr and Szinyei were endowed with a very similar creative talent. Benczúr had first studied drawing at the drawing school of Kassa under Béla Klimkovics and his early attempts consisted mainly of portraits and some historical drawings. Szinyei studied in Várad under Lajos Mezey, a stimulating painter and photographer who taught drawing as a discipline in precision. In Munich both Benczúr and Szinyei enrolled in Piloty's class, where the striking difference between the two young artists soon became obvious: while Benczúr could adapt himself with ease to the manners of the old masters such as Caravaggio, Rubens and Van Dyck, Szinyei produced only awkward historical sketches. He lacked the skill to paint as tradition required and he was less interested in history than in conveying human feelings through portraiture. **Plates 232, 233, 234** He made a few experiments in the vein of Anselm Feuerbach and Arnold Böcklin. These works bear witness to his fine sense of the pictorial; yet he still remained basically unfamiliar with the use of symbols to synthesize old and new meanings.

Szinyei made his decisive choice of *plein-air* painting before the 1869 French exhibition in Munich. This is one of the most surprising elements in his career. For Szinyei did not develop his new style solely in Munich. He was able to work in his homeland at Jernye in the North of Hungary where, being of noble birth, he had inherited a castle and estate. There he lived undisturbed, **Plates 229, 230** observing and painting nature and portraying members of his family in the unaffected, natural poses he preferred.

In 1869, in Munich, Szinyei made some lively, fresh oil sketches in the concise style required by the renewed Academy. His paintings were no longer romantic representations of historical events, nor did he attempt to moralize through art; he simply depicted, out of doors, some episode from everyday life. *Hanging out the Wash, The Swing* and *Mother and Child* **Plates 235, 238, 239** all reveal simultaneously various levels of observation and composition. Though he used different colouring and brushwork, in the conception of these paintings Szinyei is linked with Courbet of the 1840s or the *plein-air* genre scenes by Edouard Manet and **Plates 240, 241** Claude Monet painted in the 1860s. The essence of these paintings lies in the free movement of the figures and the cheerful "dialogue" between the patches of colour, as well as the representation of the play of light and shade outdoors, for Szinyei was more concerned with the vivid synthesis of his new experiences than with the analysis of pictorial problems. He conceived painting as a more independent means of expression than did the French *plein-air* painters, and he had no wish to limit the painter's role to that of mere visual perception. He wanted to reproduce what he saw with more intensified colours.

In the course of 1869, Szinyei became popular in Munich, and most of his new **Plate 235** works were acquired by dealers and collectors in Western Europe and

America. These connoisseurs must have sensed Szinyei's special, totally personal contribution to European Naturalism. Yet Szinyei did not take advantage of his success, but returned to Hungary where he lived for the next two years. It seems that he derived special inspiration from being in his own home environment; certainly his art benefited greatly from this atmosphere, which even inspired the landscapes and genre scenes from the 1840s. Yet in 1872, Szinyei returned to Munich. He did not do so at the request of the Academy, but because of an appeal from such as Gabriel Max and Arnold Böcklin, young artists who were working in a similar style and who recognized his great talent. Gabriel Max wrote to him, urging him to return to Munich for, as he said, the time had arrived to turn Szinyei's oil-sketches into paintings. Arnold Böcklin, on his part, no longer wanted him to paint mythological compositions, but rather scenes from everyday life. He now taught Szinyei compositional technique, such as the use of white underpaint and superimposed layers of glazed paint in order to achieve a translucent quality. Karl von Piloty also spoke highly of Szinyei's efforts and told him to go and paint out-of-doors, in the manner of the younger generation.

Curiously enough, Szinyei's most beautiful painting, *Picnic in May,* was not **Plate 243** completed out-of-doors. He painted it in the winter of 1872–1873 from colour sketches which themselves had been made from memory; his aim was to evoke and intensify the glowing tones and the play of light and shade. He uses an everyday theme, an outing on a beautiful spring day. Though the excursion actually took place Szinyei's concern is not topographical accuracy. He had used the same hillside as a motif in a painting executed three years earlier, in which a mother and child are seated on the hillside, now the site of the picnic. **Plate 235** Every detail of *Picnic* has been considered in relation to balance: the figures of the men and women, the picnic basket, the food laid out on a cloth on the grass, the rugs. The figures do not face the viewer; they turn towards each other, they talk, they live; one of them even lies on the ground with his back to us. This arrangement is obviously a deliberate protest against ceremonious theatrical, Academic compositions. In 1863, Edouard Manet had gone so far **Plate 240** in his famous painting entitled *Breakfast Outdoors* as to include a nude model among his picnickers. In 1873, Szinyei, did not wish to scandalize visitors to the exhibition in Vienna or Munich, where he intended to show his painting before sending it to the National Museum in Budapest.

The effectiveness of Szinyei's painting derives not from spectacular experiment but from utter simplicity and genuine naturalness; the composition is strikingly accurate, but there is a total lack of pedantry in the generosity of the palette. From the turn of the century onwards, this work has been judged to be not only the finest Hungarian painting of the 19th century, but also one of the best in Europe.

Here, the landscape is not just a background, nor is it a means to introduce historical relics; it is nature itself, caught in its totality within a fleeting moment, clearly arranged and tangible. The figures serve only to show the joy that can be derived from nature, its beauty, its changing moods. Every detail serves this purpose: clothing, facial features, the gesturing figures, the picnic spread out on the ground and so appetizingly evoked by means of shapes and colours.

Szinyei was a bold and excellent colourist, the harmony and simplicity of his work is unparalleled in contemporary Hungarian art. His masterpiece nevertheless received little praise at first except from one unknown critic at the 1873 World Exhibition. There it was removed from a group of Hungarian paintings and was placed among the exhibits from the Munich Academy before being removed by Szinyei himself. He offered to give it to the Hungarian National Museum, but the offer was refused. When the painting was exhibited again in Vienna in the 1880s, it was not understood at all, nor were the painter's other works. The universal actuality and true aesthetic values of his art were not recognized until 1896.

After his lack of success with *Picnic in May,* Szinyei painted some unfinished colour sketches and landscape-portraits. His most famous picture of this period is his *Lady in Violet,* a portrait of the painter's wife. It is a dignified portrait in rich tones, related to the portraits of women in landscape settings executed by Gustave Courbet, Ludwig Feuerbach and others. Nevertheless it is not comparable with *Picnic in May,* being a more controlled and traditional work in many respects. During the early 1880s, Szinyei tried and failed on a number of occasions to achieve the perfection of his most important painting, but these later works are not comparable to Courbet and Manet. They reflect a kind of rejuvenated Academism, with or without mythological motifs, with nothing but an almost photographic representation of reality.

In the twenty odd years from around 1870 to the 1890s, many talented Hungarian artists reached the pinnacle of their achievement, after which they seemed to falter and lose their way. Nevertheless, the last decade of the century saw, parallel with their decline, the arrival of a new generation of artists who brought new life to Hungarian art.

Among Szinyei's contemporaries of the same rank, though working in a totally different conception, who produced work comparable to his own were Mihály Munkácsy, László Paál and Géza Dósa. Paál died in the 1870s and Géza Dósa's career was also cut short by his early death. All that has survived of Dósa's work are some mediocre historical paintings, a number of colour sketches in which he experimented with *plein-air* and some fine portraits and group portraits in a style similar to those made by Szinyei in the 1870s. He was a very talented artist who studied in Vienna and Munich before committing suicide in 1871, at the age of 25. From contemporary records we learn that he was able to perceive and fully understand the new aesthetic ideals expressed at the 1869 French exhibition in Munich. He also tried to paint in the style of Courbet, Corot and their associates, when this style was still dismissed by many as humble and much too commonplace. In the few paintings he completed, however, he introduced a highly individual realistic style.

Mihály Munkácsy was only one year older than Dósa when he was awarded the golden medal at the Paris Salon for his *The Condemned Cell.*

He was of humble birth, his success being entirely due to outstanding talent and great strength of will. He lost his parents at an early age and his relatives gave little attention to his education. So the sickly and rather nervous child started his training as an apprentice carpenter, but his gift for drawing and painting became increasingly important to him. His first master was Elek

Szamossy, an itinerant painter. He taught the young Munkácsy the technique
of portraiture in a provincial Realistic style fashionable in Hungary around
1860. In 1863 Munkácsy went to Pest to undertake more advanced training.
Not finding an appropriate school, he had to be content with copying the
paintings in the National Museum and making illustrations for newspapers.
His drawing technique was influenced by that of Mihály Szemlér and János
Jankó, and he had by now completed some bold genre-scenes. Antal Ligeti,
Mór Than, and the "Képzőművészeti Társulat" (Association for Art), helped
Munkácsy to go to Vienna. There, for a short time he was able to study under
Carl Rahl and to learn compositional technique as applied to genre-painting
before the great master died six months after Munkácsy's arrival in Vienna.
He returned to Pest and was again sponsored by patrons who enabled him to
go to Munich.

Munkácsy's stay in Munich coincided with that of Szinyei, yet they seemed to
represent two different worlds. They both knew Leibl. It was from his strong
peasant faces and depictions of labourers that Munkácsy, who spoke scarcely
any German, learned that his childhood memories, as well as the genre-scenes
that illustrated the Pest newspapers, could equally provide subject matter for
large canvases.

In 1867 Munkácsy visited Paris for two weeks, thanks to the help of Károly
Telepy, one of the founders of the Association for Art. There he saw Gustave
Courbet's paintings at the World Exhibition, an experience which had a lasting effect on his art. Two years later, Szinyei and Dósa were greatly impressed
by Courbet's rugged Naturalism, independent compositional technique, fresh
colouring, and his unconventional approach. Munkácsy however was most
affected by the social message of Courbet's painting, and so Courbet's understanding and sympathy for the lower classes.

At that time, Munkácsy did not stay longer in Paris. In order to become an
independent artist he felt it necessary to continue his training. The Academy of
Munich however did not appeal to him after the experience of Paris, nor was
he qualified to gain admission on account of his incomplete training in
draughtsmanship. He found that he would be allowed to attend only Sándor
(Alexander) Wagner's preparatory class. Consequently, he soon left for Düsseldorf. At the Düsseldorf Academy there were classes in naturalistic landscape and genre-painting. Another attraction of that city was the presence of
Ludwig Knaus, a German painter of genre scenes whose works Munkácsy   **Plate 254**
had seen in Vienna in cuts and engravings. It is interesting to realize that
though Ludwig Knaus had a much surer drawing technique than Munkácsy
and he executed his folk genre-paintings with more care, he was far less
talented than Munkácsy. Knaus's best work hardly surpassed the thoughtfully
composed, yet caricature-like genre-paintings by Mihály Szemlér, even if they   **Plate 249**
were stylistically more harmonious. Certainly, Munkácsy's first paintings
completed in Düsseldorf, such as the *Yawning Apprentice,* are reminiscent of
Knaus's slightly caricatured genre-scenes. Simultaneously, and perhaps under
the influence of earlier and more dramatic Austrian and Hungarian manners
(seen in the work of Carl Rahl and Mór Than) Munkácsy concerned himself
with a type of genre-painting which represented human tragedies with some

psychological insight, though an element of Romanticism was usually present. This attitude was developed by the young Munkácsy on his own, with no assistance from Ludwig Knaus or his other genre-painter colleague in Düsseldorf, Benjamin Vautier. If we look for an antecedent to *The Condemned Cell* (1869–1870), we inevitably find it in Munkácsy's first really significant work painted in 1865, his portrayal of a *Lovesick Lad*, later known as the *Grieving Betyár*. It shows an outlaw in an inn, his elbows on the table, stubbornly trying to enjoy the gypsy band, though he has little hope of not being discovered by the country police and the Austrian soldiers who seek him because he has not conformed to the social and moral standards of the age. (Outlaws were legendary figures in 19th century Hungary, usually poor peasants or shepherds who went into hiding rather than serve in the Austrian army. They would rob the rich at fairs or on the roads and, according to many a folksong, they would share their gain with the poor. Some of them united in groups to fight in the War of Independence, as regular, though separate units. They were always ready to join later risings against the tyrannical absolutist rule of the years after 1848 and for this reason they were outlawed.) Although it was not possible for artists to publish sympathetic illustrations of outlaws for newspapers, a certain admiration for their bravery mingled with compassion for their miserable lot, was always present in their drawings. Towards the end of the 1860s the young Munkácsy used this theme to convey his own deep sympathy for the outlawed and his real understanding of the tragedy. *The Condemned Cell* depicts the outlaw together with his weeping wife and child, his indifferent gaoler, sympathetic friends and the excited village people.

The painting is not comparable with any of Courbet's genre-paintings, for the subject is treated in a theatrical manner. Yet it is much superior to Knaus's genre painting which always lacks genuine dramatic tension, for which he substitutes mere lively description. As earlier models, from before 1848, one could cite the Romantic historical scenes painted by Mór Than and Viktor Madarász, such as *The Mourning of László Hunyadi* or *Recruiting,* or perhaps some of Leibl's folk scenes in which there is more psychological interest.

Munkácsy was ambitious and therefore experimented by using distinguished pictorial manners. Like the Munich genre painters, he too dressed his models in appropriate costumes, chose the pose, photographed them or had them photographed by someone else. He also made pencil and oil sketches of them and then, assembling these preliminary efforts, arranged the final composition. He composed in parallel, vertical and converging horizontal planes. Verticals were used for the solitary figures, isolated by their own grief, indifference or bitterness. Diagonals were used for the figures turned towards the condemned prisoner and expressing compassion, curiosity or scorn. The prisoner shows no interest in his visitors—yet his outstretched arm involuntarily seeks contact with them. This composition succeeds in conveying a human tragedy. Those who saw it were by no means indifferent to the message. The picture also impressed the jury at the Salon of Paris in 1870, who were receptive to tragic themes past and present, and accepted also its effect of chiaroscuro, and it was a great success in America where connoisseurs described the figures as exotic. Munkácsy's style moved all those critics and viewers who demanded true Realism. In spite of his stylistic remoteness from the forms and drawings of the Munich school and the sentimental colourists of Vienna, he could count on a warm reception both at home and abroad on account of the tone, theme and dramaturgy of his painting.

Yet his success in Paris surprised him, for he himself was painfully aware of his own lack of education and the weakness of his drawing. Of all Hungarian artists, Munkácsy was perhaps the most tormented, torn by dilemmas whenever he was not able to remain true to himself in his choices. By the late 1870s, the great success of *The Condemned Cell* had determined the style he was to follow and had set him on the path to becoming a master of realistic folk genre paintings.

Munkácsy's folk genre-paintings are in the tradition of Hungarian historical painting, though his emphasis on the sociological and dramatic aspects of his chosen theme is quite new. These are noticeable for yet another decade after the success of *The Condemned Cell*. It is especially obvious in the *Lint-Makers*   **Plate 257** (1871) which depicts a typical event from 1848–49. Instead of battles, commanders and politicians, this painting shows an anonymous soldier together with women workers in a military hospital making lint to dress the wounds of the injured soldiers. The wounded soldier on the left is shown telling his story, with suitable gestures, to the village women, young and old, whose illuminated faces are discernible in what is a rather dark scene.

Munkácsy drew some of his inspiration from the psychological figure-paintings of both contemporary artists and the old masters. From his sketches and diaries we learn that he was a great admirer of Rembrandt. He was also indebted to Courbet and his associates, though when Munkácsy moved to Paris in 1872, Courbet was already living in exile. As Munkácsy was neither a born colourist nor yet a painter of the effects of light; his zealous efforts were to paint in the style of his chosen predecessors. Ernst Kállai, the 20th century art critic and theoretician, observed that Munkácsy, like Madarász before him, tended to exaggerate the variations of tone in order to intensify the dramatic effect and conceal his lack of technical ability and academic training. Before 1874, Munkácsy's chiaroscuro was dominated by greyish-white and brownish tones, and it was not until he had several times visited Barbizon that he learned to enrich his colour scheme by the use of lusty reds and yellows and luxuriant greens. The milestones of his burgeoning colour scheme are marked by his smaller genre-paintings, in which there are only one or two figures, painted in the 1870s.

By then, Munkácsy excelled in realistic landscape-painting too; in *Dusty*   **Plate 261** *Country Road* he tried to evoke the very motion of the dust in the air; and in his portraits he paid great attention to detail. Literature was still, however, his main source of inspiration. He developed the theme of *The Condemned Cell* in his representations of tragic episodes in the lives of poor villagers and destitute townsfolk, for example, *The Pawnbroker's Shop, The Debauched Husband,* and *Prowlers of Night*. Later he adopted subjects containing elements of drama calculated to draw tears from the eyes of both the European and American public, and to stir the emotions of others who were mainly interested in the subject and who liked to feel capable of sharing the feelings of the participants in the drama. Towards the end of the 1870s, Munkácsy revived a theme earlier used by Orlai and taken from the life of Milton: the great poet as he continues, in spite of his blindness, to work on "Paradise Lost", dictating it to one of his daughters.

After the warm reception given to his painting of Milton, Munkácsy chose for his next painting a scene from the New Testament which proved to be even more popular and successful. *The Blind Milton Dictating "Paradise Lost"* was acquired by a public library in New York, while the best version of *Christ before Pilate* was acquired for the chapel of a department store, thus becoming part of the Wanemaker Collection in Philadelphia. A smaller replica of *Christ before Pilate,* painted in 1880, was exhibited in Budapest and in Paris and was received in both cities to public and critics alike with similar astonishment. This painting is by no means the usual or traditional religious composition. Munkácsy revives a dramatic moment in the life of Jesus Christ, depicted before his earthly judge, Pilate, in a scene of such vigorous Naturalism and actualization that one critic called out in amazement, demanding to know who this person was—could he be a Nihilist brought before the Tsar?

Even when Munkácsy's sole aim was to compose a picture in a most superb way, his talent for creating true to life situations of conflicts was always in evidence. This overwhelming Realism in Munkácsy has been described by Géza Perneczky as "superproduction".

Like Károly Markó, Sr., at the beginning of the century, Munkácsy spent most of his life abroad. He lived in Paris, but not in that part of the city which was the centre of the artistic revival of 1860–1890. In his most important paintings he complied with the demands of the latest currents in Paris in the 1850s. At the same time his works are typically Hungarian in their arrangement and feeling, and, though more elegant in style, are similar to those painted by artists living in Hungary in the 1850s and 1860s. The Hungarian public preferred his works produced in this style. Of the paintings he hoped to sell in Hungary, the well-known literary or Biblical scenes were received most warmly; his *Magyar Conquest of Hungary* also known as *Árpád, Chief of the Magyars,* one of his last works commissioned for Parliament, was widely praised. Munkácsy was also respected as a landscapist and painter of genre-scenes. But hardly anyone—apart from a few of his followers, appreciated his excellent bourgeois interiors known as "salon-paintings" or "l'art pompier".

Munkácsy never became an Academic painter, yet he cannot be classed as a really modern one. He preferred the Realism of the 1840s and 1850s and watched the development of Impressionism with a certain reserve—his letters and comments were rather fiercely against it—though in a few of his landscapes there are elements of this tendency. His life was that of an exile, an artist in search of a goal, strangely tossed between the real and the sham.

Less turbulent but much shorter was the career of László Paál, who started painting at the same time as Munkácsy, but who met with an untimely death. For some time he studied landscape-painting in Vienna, later in Düsseldorf. From there he moved with Munkácsy to Paris and lived and worked at Barbizon. His last works, which we know only from contemporary descriptions, could perhaps be described as Impressionist. When he died, these so-called

Plate 275

Plate 291

Plate 262

"white" paintings were all destroyed by Munkácsy, who was anxious to save his friend's reputation.

László Paál was a highly skilled landscapist, influenced by the schools of Düsseldorf and Barbizon; and, though he was an introvert, he was also influenced by Munkácsy's dramatic compositions. Paál used the same vernacular as Munkácsy in his genre-paintings. He too built up his pictures by ensuring a contrast between dark and light masses, and, within this, the use of a rich choice of tones. He painted dark forests with contrasting white paths, arid fields lit by the setting sun, or pale rocks against the rich brown of the freshly ploughed soil. Lyrical and pantheistic, László Paál's representation of nature reflects the influence of the Barbizon school, blended with the traditional mood of Hungarian folk ballads. The same sombre Hungarian tones appeared in the paintings of László Mednyánszky, an artist similarly influenced by Barbizon, at the turn of the century.

Plates 267, 268, 270

Mihály Zichy, the outstanding Romantic-Realist painter, lived in Paris from 1874–1878, at the same time as Munkácsy and Paál. He was their elder by many years, a mature, widely travelled artist familiar with the work of others in Vienna, St. Petersburg, Paris and elsewhere.

As we have already seen, Zichy never lost contact with his native country. He was the subject of articles in Hungarian newspapers, his pictures were bought in Hungary and he himself was active in the creation of the "Magyar Egylet" (Hungarian Association) in Paris. He also illustrated some of the most important books published in Hungary during his lifetime. In the 1880s and 1890s his chief sources of inspiration were Petőfi's poems, János Arany's ballads and Imre Madách's drama, "The Tragedy of Man".

Zichy's talent was not restricted to the domain of painting; he was also an intellectual with his own political views. He took a cosmopolitan approach to contemporary history, and was keenly aware of international politics, the devastating effect of war and excessive nationalism, the inner tension of any given social structure, and he knew how members of one institution were liable to manipulate those of another. He did not believe in the unimpeachable conduct of any particular Church, and hoped for the arrival of a new Christianity.

By the end of the 19th century, he gradually came to see his own time as an era in which Evil and Satan held sway. Thus he chose to represent the demon, already described by Byron, Lermontov and Madách, as the hero of one of his most monumental paintings. He gives us a panoramic vision of total destruction in his painting entitled *The Demon's Weapon or the Triumph of the Genius of Destruction*. The painting testifies to Zichy's profound insight into prevailing conditions towards the end of the 19th century, when the glorious ideals of Liberty, Equality and Fraternity had been forgotten, and all hope of reviving them had vanished. The demon is represented as a naked youth, winged, hovering over the Earth, ready to conquer it; beside him is the figure of a beautiful female demon. Destruction, cruelty and death follow in their wake; they lead the righteous astray. Clear references to the Crimean War (1853–56), the Franco-Prussian War (1870–71) and the failure of the Republic and Commune of Paris are to be seen in the painting. The two monarchs—the German

Plate 277

Emperor and the Russian Tsar are depicted as murderers encouraging others to follow their example. Heads of state and Church dignitaries are seen as equally responsible for this scene of carnage, and for the death and suffering of the poor.

The painting remained in the 1878 World Exhibition in Paris for only a few days after which it was removed following the protests made by diplomats of several states. When it was shown in Budapest later the same year, critics for the most part restricted their comments to discussion of Zichy's pictorial weaknesses and "artificial philosophizing". Yet this painting deserves more attention: it is a monumental allegory painted by an independent thinker of aristocratic birth and it is a more dramatic and merciless condemnation of injustice and war than Alfred Rethel's death-dances or Arnold Böcklin's allegories.

In 1880–1881, Jenő Gyárfás, a portraitist and genre-painter trained in Munich, made a series of sketches from which he composed one single work with the same grotesque and dramatic quality as we find in Zichy's painting. However, it must be conceded that Gyárfás's pictorial interpretation of the dramatic **Plates 287, 288** János Arany ballad, "The Ordeal of the Bier," has none of the intellectual vigour of Zichy's historical interpretation.

The ageing János Arany had written the love-ballad some years before, in 1877. Jenő Gyárfás laboured over the theme for more than eighteen months, making numerous large colour sketches and studies. The tragical story of the ballad presumably appealed to the painter. It relates the story of a youth who died under mysterious circumstances. In the belief that when the murderer comes to the bed, the wound will start to bleed, his father summons everyone to his son's death-bed where the body is lying in state. The greatest problem for Gyárfás was the choice of the episode from the ballad that he should depict. One of his first sketches represented the moment when the young man's body was discovered in the forest; later he decided to base his picture on the last scene of the poem. The circumstances of the hero's death were now known: the girl whose love he sought had responded, perhaps driven by some vague inner sadism, by offering him a dagger so that he could prove how great his love really was. Realizing that she had caused his death, she goes mad.

Jenő Gyárfás's painting exemplifies many of the characteristics of the late Munich Academic style. The distraught girl, centrally placed in the composition, is shown dancing wildly, eyes dilated and unseeing. She wears a white bridal gown and attracts the attention of the stunned villagers. The narrative element is clear, the characterization precise, yet Gyárfás was presumably aware that he had failed to achieve what he set out to do. His inability to express his own vision of the story is shown by the fact that he resorted to the device of inscribing lines from the poem on the broad frame of the painting. However, his pictorial solution was by no means unusual in the 19th century. Some decades earlier the English Pre-Raphaelite painters had also represented literary heroes in much the same fashion. This painting, however, is even more closely linked to the Academic paintings on literary subjects that were produced in Germany throughout the century, and were widely known in Hungary as well. János Arany himself thought that the painter's task was to illustrate dramatic episodes in a lively way. Another of his horror-poems, "The Farceurs", describes a fair in Debrecen, where *farceurs* tell and show in pictures stories similar to "The Ordeal of the Bier".

In the last decades of the 19th century, many Hungarians, among whom one must count some of the most distinguished citizens—still demanded a faithful likeness in portraits, and in pictures based on literary subjects they required accurate narrative detail. They were not concerned with the primary formal values of paintings and left the study of drawing, light, colour and shape to the initiated: teachers, painters and critics might discuss these subjects, but only among themselves. It was enough for the public to be able to recognize what the painting represented and to judge whether the representation was accurate. There were occasions when the meeting between art and literature led to the creation of masterpieces, as for example Zichy's illustrations of János Arany's ballads, or Madách's "The Tragedy of Man", and the rather curious paintings by Gyárfás. However, the marriage of painting and literature could not conceive the renewal of painting as a plastic art. Clearly, Hungarian painting had to free itself from the stranglehold of literature, and in the late 19th century this proved to be no easy task. Literary themes appealed to painters and graphic artists, who drew inspiration from Hungarian epics and ballads and sometimes also from translations of foreign works. They could pluck from literature some interesting theme to be expressed anew in pictorial form, but instead created works that were merely illustrations. Hungarian painters never supported the contemporary French Symbolists who proclaimed the equality of painting and literature in both value and rank.

Plate 276

From the late 1880s onwards many artists became convinced that only through objective representation of nature could they bring about the revival they sought, and so escape the visions of destruction and decay of European culture manifested in many works of art. Pál Szinyei Merse made the decisive step soon after 1870. Like so many other painters from Delacroix to Millais, he had already, as a young man, portrayed tragic figures such as Ophelia, the literary predecessor of the heroine of *The Ordeal of the Bier*. By the end of the 1880s an increasing number of painters in Central and Eastern Europe turned away from these dramatic subjects and followed the example of Naturalism and Impressionism. Yet Szinyei's work remained unknown for many years. More tentative experiments in the representation of nature were more widely known; in Hungary for instance, there was considerable interest in the landscapes and genre paintings of the artists working at Szolnok.

The style of the Szolnok School had been evolving ever since the early 1850s. The Austrian artists August von Pettenkofen and Johann Guilbert Raffalt, and, twenty years later, Hungarian artists coming home for the summer from Paris and Munich, among them Lajos Deák Ébner, Pál Böhm and Sándor Bihari, were concentrating single-mindedly on the unbiased observation of nature, and the representation of peasant life. Their first paintings were relatively small, but as they gained experience, they began on larger canvases.

Plates 293, 294

Plate 296

The first two generations of the Szolnok Colony were primarily indebted to the Academies of Vienna and Munich. Géza Mészöly, who came from and worked in Transdanubia, was similarly dependent on the style

Plates 271, 272

of these Academies when he created his simple, unsophisticated landscapes, devoid of narrative allusions. Of all those taught by Albert Zimmermann and Eduard Schleich, he was the only one content to spend hours quietly drawing every detail of the scene he was about to paint; he would note the branches and crowns of tall trees, the sparkling light on the surface of the water, the fine mist rising from it, and the changing colours of the sky. He made a detailed description of each component and then introduced into the landscape the figures of fishermen, shepherds or washerwomen by the river bank. He completed his oil paintings in winter, in his studio, making use of preliminary pencil and water-colour sketches. All this preliminary work enabled him to create paintings that seem to have been executed out of doors.

Mészöly and the Szolnok painters might be compared with László Paál, though the former did not work with the same dramatic intensity as Paál did. They depict the slow, seasonal changes in nature whereas he saw nature as a fearful force. Mészöly was not lacking in determination and he undoubtedly learned much from his stay in Barbizon. During the years remaining before his early death, he continued to paint elaborate landscapes and genre-scenes in a style his contemporaries sometimes compared with that of Camille Corot.

Plates 295, 296 Lajos Deák Ébner, somewhat younger than Mészöly, was active from 1875 to 1887 in Paris and Szolnok. He was also a landscapist of great sensitivity whose rendering of atmosphere and setting were both realistic and detailed; he was especially interested in trying to express traditional pictorial values. In his genre-paintings, however, the figures are dramatically enlarged or overemphasized, as if he were trying to revive the narrative trend of Hungarian painting.

Deák Ébner was appointed director of the Budapest School of Painting for Women in 1887. This gesture was typical of a society where naturalistic landscape and life-scheme painting was considered a "feminine" form. Deák often chose more "masculine" subjects for his own work, for instance, he painted allegorical pictures for the Royal Castle in Buda. At the same time, his style was becoming more eclectic; by the *fin de siècle*, when he returned to Szolnok, he produced a number of artificial genre-paintings.

Naturalistic genre-paintings of peasants or townfolk were arranged with a more modest dramaturgy than compositions on heroic themes. All the same, they had their stereotyped props, and with these, sham *plein-air* paintings which originated in the artist's studio enjoyed their hayday. Károly Lyka has described one such scene in Pál Böhm's studio in Munich: "In the courtyard a battered cart… coming perhaps from a small farm by the River Tisza, … beside it [stands] a fishing boat from Szolnok. The fishing net taken from it is inside the large studio. All these are valuable objects which the artist collected, in the valleys of the Tisza and Zagyva where he often went to refresh his memories of the Hungarian landscape." This kind of stereotyped landscape and genre-painting became fairly fashionable throughout Europe and America, and was even more popular than paintings on historical or literary themes since it was possible to understand them without a knowledge of the classics. In Hungary, painters could always sell such works based on peasant and bourgeois subjects because they introduced into them well-known characters, typical scenes and gestures, and the serene atmosphere which was essential for the approval of the critics.

In addition to Deák Ébner and Pál Böhm, there was a third master of genre-painting, who worked much in the same style, Sándor Bihari. Bihari had studied in Munich and Paris where he went after a lengthy training under a photographer in Hungary. His closely observed scenes of everyday life in and out of doors were very popular. Emperor and King Francis Joseph I, who favoured plain, unsophisticated paintings of his people, preferably without reference to social problems, was an enthusiastic collector of Bihari's work. At the beginning of his career, Bihari had other ambitions; he wanted to create a great picture in the style of the French Impressionists, a large *plein-air* composition with huge figures. But he also wanted to represent contemporary social conditions with open honesty. He had the talent and technical knowledge to achieve his ambition; but unfortunately he lacked the ability to concentrate on a pictorial idiom through which he could solve the problems inherent in a subject. Neither was he able to make an objective assessment of his own capabilities and his own role as an artist. These shortcomings were shared by all the artists working in Szolnok, with the exception of László Mednyán-szky and, a later arrival, Adolf Fényes. Bihari's weaknesses can be seen in many other successful turn-of-the-century artists whose drawing technique was often excellent and who conscientiously studied the views they chose to paint, yet they produced stereotyped, often sentimental landscapes. During the last fifteen years of the century a new generation of painters began to remedy this state of affairs. They, too, studied abroad, in Munich and Paris; but they broke with their predecessors and worked together in groups, or they chose to paint in solitude.

In about 1878 Simon Hollósy, the son of an Armenian living in Máramaros-sziget, arrived in Munich after several years of study under Bertalan Székely at the Academy of Budapest. He showed few signs of achieving any greater distinction as an artist than Pál Böhm or Sándor Bihari, and seemed likely to become a genre painter in the same style. He was associated with a circle including Jenő Gyárfás, who painted a very beautiful study of his head. Influenced by Gyárfás, Hollósy began to share that artist's interest in literary themes.

At the same time, Hollósy's biographers record that he brought the world of the snow-capped Transylvanian mountains with him to Munich. He also brought a deep concern for the poor, the ideals of 1848 propagated by the lesser nobility and the bourgeoisie, and the views of an emerging intelligentsia. The creative foundations for this new intellectual force were the works of Émile Zola and Fyodor Dostoyevsky. Hollósy's progress towards an art in which he could express this new ideal was long and laborious, for his earliest works dating from the 1880s consisted of folk genre scenes similar in inspiration to the fashionable peasant plays of the epoch. Yet these early genre-paintings bore the undeniable presence of his gift for depicting the variation of tones and the effect of light. Also, in these years, though Hollósy painted traditional themes, he gave them a totally fresh interpretation. On the well-used subject of Zrínyi's charge on the Turks from the fortress of Szigetvár, he composed a small colour-sketch, presumably with the intention of using it for a large oil painting. But the political climate was unfavourable for such a project. Hollósy's first teacher, Bertalan Székely himself, was not able to obtain a commission for a large-size painting on this theme. After the Austro–Hungarian Compromise, Zrínyi was no longer honoured as a hero of the struggle against the Turks; a more appropriate subject for large paintings was the reconquest of Buda (1686) and the heroism of Charles de Lorraine and Eugen de Savoy. This **Plate 292** was demonstrated by Gyula Benczúr's huge painting of 1885–1896.

In the early 19th century, historical painters had to show loyalty to both the government and the nation. Later, however, they were divided into two camps and each of them had to make a choice in many cases. Towards the end of the century this division was once again apparent; some artists had commissions for historical paintings in which they could show support for the government and the Empire, others like Simon Hollósy remained faithful to the ideals of the anti-Habsburgian opposition. Eminent art historian Lajos Németh has written that Hollósy's *Zrínyi,* though small in size, is one of the great achievements of Hungarian historical painting, "marking a significant step in the history of painting since the confrontation of the principles of *plein-air* and materiality". This small picture achieves all the goals of the Romantic painters. It embodies all their passionate attempts—from Horace Vernet to Delacroix—to depict both ideals and events. In Hungary these ambitions were embraced in the earlier decades by Peter Krafft, Sr., Mór Than, Bertalan Székely, Mihály Kovács and many other artists, some more talented than others.

Zrínyi was not Hollósy's only historical painting. He made numerous **Plate 304** sketches of the *Rákóczi March,* and these too were not developed as large oil paintings. His sketches portray the endless ranks of the poor and the unknown, the nameless heroes of the Hungarian resistance, who seem to be marching towards the viewer shrouded in the whirling dust of country lanes, called to life by the means of *plein-air* painting. When admiring one of these sketches of *The Rákóczi March,* some critics were reminded of the "Marseillaise".

One of the most pressing *fin de siècle* social issues was the unrest discernible among the poor, who were beginning to unite in revolutionary activities, organized or spontaneous. Members of the intelligentsia who wanted to improve their living conditions, were also joining forces with the lower classes. Hollósy attempted to express this issue in his historical paintings. At the end of the century the condition of the poor was represented in genre scenes, some of them by artists working in Munkácsy's studio in Paris. The plight of the poor also stirred the imagination of Hungarian artists studying in Munich and Paris (Ottó Baditz, Pál Vágó, Tivadar Zemplényi, Imre Révész, László Pataky). One great and solitary figure of the late 19th century, László **Plate 273** Mednyánszky, shared the concern of this group of artists, but his own paintings reflected a deeper insight that went far beyond a wish for social reform. Mednyánszky started his career as a landscapist. He was of aristocratic birth and received his first lessons at the family seat in the valley of the River Vág, from an Austrian landscapist, Thomas Ender. In Paris he studied under Isidore

Pils at the École des Beaux-Arts. He visited Barbizon and Szolnok, and created a number of magnificent landscapes. By the 1880s the influence of Impressionism was also perceptible in his work. Yet his representation of the transitory effects of light on colour never overwhelmed the dramatic quality of his realistic landscapes in which there was even a hint of the Netherlandish tradition. Be that as it may, his landscapes exhibited in 1897 in Paris drew little comment. All attention was focused on his paintings depicting vagabonds of the big European cities, the night-time meetings of revolutionaries, and brawls amongst humble people at night—realistic representations of the outcasts of society. In his journal, Mednyánszky wrote, "Fate condemned me to become well acquainted with the darker side of our society, for I was closely involved with some poor creature whom I learned to love." He himself lived the life of a vagabond in Paris and Vienna, and later even in Budapest. It was as a vagabond that he roamed the Carpathian Mountains and Galicia. His wealth enabled him to help his impecunious friends while with his pencil and brush he **Plates 306, 307** recorded them for posterity. Mednyánszky's expressive, realistic style and mystical trend of thought (he was an admirer of Tolstoy and Dostoyevsky) provided a link between 19th and 20th century art. For him the real problems of his time were not to be found in "artistic orientation" but in the personal quest for truth.

Social problems are very often represented in Hungarian painting with nostalgia, and accompanied by historical allusions, as in István Réti's painting of 1899, *Burial of a Honvéd,* showing a group of old and ragged veterans, **Plate 303** expressing the artist's tribute to those who fought in the War of Independence. They are depicted at the gate of the graveyard in the fading evening light, holding aloft the tattered banner of 1848. Réti, who had studied in Munich and Paris, continued the wake of Courbet's *Funeral of Ornans* with his simple recording of events. His splintered tones, however, lent his work a more poignant sadness than that found in Courbet's painting. His less energetic use of light and colour can be explained not only by Réti's sentiments towards the recent past, but also by his technique and style.

The master par excellence, followed by Hungarian artists who were experimenting with new *plein-air* solutions, was Jules Bastien-Lepage, a French **Plate 308** Naturalist painter much admired by Émile Zola and very popular in Munich. His delicate drawing and restrained characterization, the hazy atmosphere and subdued tones of his paintings, appealed to those young painters who were trying to free themselves from the strident eclecticism of the Munich Academy. This style of "refined Naturalism" appeared in some Hungarian genre-paintings, based on folklore and bourgeois life and historical events.

The young János Thorma was also inspired by events taken from the lives of the bourgeoisie and from history. He went from Nagybánya to Munich and from there to Paris. In 1894 he exhibited his large genre-painting entitled *Suffer-* **Plate 300** *ing* at the Salon aux Champs-Elysées. It depicts a man and his wife coming out of the cemetery of Nagybánya after the burial of their child, and meeting a beggar woman with a healthy child by her side. The atmosphere of the work, similar to that of the novels of Zola, was much appreciated, but later Thorma turned to other themes.

The subject that haunted his imagination all his life was not middle-class genre painting but the heroism and tragedy of the 1848–1849 War of Independence. In the huge painting entitled *The Martyrs of Arad,* the *plein-air* motif is still present but the painter paid more attention to his representation of the execution of the thirteen generals by the Austrians following the defeat of the War of Independence. In another large canvas entitled *Rise Hungarians! plein-air* motifs are no longer discernible; the sole aim of the painting is to commemorate the events of March 15th, 1848, the first day of the revolution, which was, in fact, a rainy day in the Hungarian capital as recorded on Thorma's painting.

Thorma's career clearly illustrates the need felt by the turn of the century for a break with traditional historical themes. Subjects which could be represented without pathos offered a much better opportunity to experiment with new styles and techniques. István Csók, who won a prize in Paris for his *"This do in Remembrance of Me" (Holy Communion)* chose a style in which there was no place for sentimentality. He depicted a whitewashed Calvinist church in which young girls in national costume stand in a semi-circle before the Lord's Table, receiving the bread and wine blessed by the minister. It is a traditional religious ceremony depicted as it was actually practiced by a segment of the population with puritan means. At the beginning of the century, Bálint Kiss had felt obliged to represent the same scene within the framework of a historical subject, namely, the imprisonment of a Protestant minister. When Csók exhibited his painting, the time had not yet come when it could be appreciated in Hungary; he had to wait some years to see its historical significance acknowledged.

The painters at the turn of the century, who were willing to teach the theories of Naturalism and Impressionism within the shelter of foreign academies, were loath to put these theories into practice in their own works. For example, at his private school in Munich, from 1886 Simon Hollósy emphasized the importance of studying nature and the need for colour analysis. His painting could never adequately illustrate his theories, tied as it was to the century-long tradition that Hungarian painting should espouse some national cause. Only those artists who felt that the new Naturalism could compensate them for the loss of the past academism felt free to experiment as they wished. What they accepted was the possibility of representing pictorially that which was fleeting and the new synthesis that went beyond naturalistic representation and aspired rather to the expression of mood and atmosphere.

For decades after Szinyei painted his *Picnic in May* (1873), no other Hungarian painter was able to share the joy of Szinyei and the excitement he felt when he added the red patch of the cloak to the green of the grass and disregard the rules he had learned, and so he set off on the path of true pictorial values. In Hollósy's small genre-paintings, there may be a ray of light stealing in from behind a pink curtain, the shimmering of red fabric or an effect of incandescence in his greyish-white tones. This delight must also have been experienced by Csók when he painted his *Haymakers* and showed how the green of the grass fused into the greenish-brown patches of colour in the background.

However, in paintings by Hollósy and Csók nature has not yet been transformed into the bold, modern harmony of colours we find in the 1890s in the work of Károly Ferenczy. Ferenczy made a more daring break with the Hungarian Academic tradition. It was in Munich and Paris that he reached the period of his maturity as an artist, having previously studied in Naples. His *Boys Throwing Pebbles into the River* of 1890 still shows Jules Bastien Lepage's influence; however, his composition and use of colours verging on grey tones suggest an even greater talent than the French painter's.   **Plate 312**

His *Self-portrait,* painted in 1893 in Munich, is both a self-manifestation and a statement about his relationship to nature. He depicts himself as a man of the same consciousness as Bertalan Székely, but with an additional touch of genuine fresh wonder which transforms his rationalism. It is a portrait representing only the head and shoulders; the artist faces the viewer and wears everyday conventional clothes. Though the face arrests our attention, the background is equally interesting, a forest scene with light filtering through the foliage, to some extent even diminishing the plasticity of the face. The pale face showing no emotion, suggests an inward awe, an intensified concentration on the sights and sounds in nature. Thus we can say that this is a portrait not only of the painter but also of the subject closest to his heart.   **Plate 311**

This love of nature changes to sensuous delight in Ferenczy's *Bird-song* (1893). A young woman in a red dress stands looking upwards to a high tree, her hand on the trunk, listening in wonder to the song of unseen birds in the green foliage. Her face blurs as if into one shape in which we see only the glint of blue eyes, while the play of lights shows her hands more on the tree trunk. The most striking aspect of the painting is the contrast between the red of her dress and the green of the foliage. This is a work of art which links Ferenczy with Szinyei although he had not yet seen the latter's *Picnic in May*.   **Plate 313**

In the 1890s, Ferenczy met those Hungarian painters in Munich who were attempting to create a new relationship with nature. The result of their common effort was the "Secession", the retreat from the world of Academic painting centred in Munich, and the establishment of a *plein-air* school in Hungary. Some vast historical works were still being painted, as well as genre-scenes with a pseudo-folk atmosphere and landscapes after preconceived patterns. And yet at the same time, in 1896, Simon Hollósy took the decisive step of transplanting his private school from Munich to Eastern Hungary and, together with Réti and János Thorma, established what became known as the Nagybánya School. By the summer of 1896 Károly Ferenczy also joined the colony. This new institution was essentially different from the previous Hungarian and Transylvanian drawing schools by its intent and character, and was often referred to as the "Hungarian Barbizon". This name nevertheless does not wholly suit it. The Nagybánya School continued in line with the Naturalist and Impressionist trends. It also embodied, to some extent, the ideas of pantheism. This was not explicit but it is manifest in the art emerging from Nagybánya. The painters worked in the open air and tried consciously to avoid sophisticated composition. They painted landscapes and a new type of naturalistic genre-painting and religious compositions with symbolic meaning and portraits within a landscape, a form which had undergone many changes since the beginning of the 19th century. Thus, the new aspects of their art did not lie in the choice of subject, but in a new pictorial approach and vernacular.

The foundation of the Nagybánya School ended one period of Hungarian art and opened a new one. But it was not only Nagybánya which represented the new ideas which dominated the years around 1900. Several Hungarian painters were trying once to deal systematically with the pictorial problems brought to their attention by Impressionism, while in Paris, a young Hungarian artist, József Rippl Rónai, joined the Post-Impressionists. Rippl Rónai, whose talent and interest embraced drawing, painting and the decorative arts, had studied at the Academy of Munich in the 1880s where, however, he remained an outsider, nor did he associate with other Hungarian artists. When he arrived in Paris he first worked in Munkácsy's studio, by which time several young Hungarian painters were helping the ageing master to complete his many commissions. By the late 1880s, however, Rippl Rónai left his much respected master. He abandoned the bland style of "salon" genre-painting to work on a series of pictures which linked him to the circle who included the Scotsman, James Pittcairn Knowles, and the sculptor Aristide Maillol, and to the Nabis painters, especially Pierre Bonnard, Jean Edouard Vuillard and Maurice Denis. Rippl Rónai was also inspired by the style of James MacNeill Whistler and Henri de Toulouse-Lautrec, while his philosophy of life showed Paul Gauguin's influence in some extent. In Rippl Rónai's paintings and sketches from the period around 1890, most of all linear drawing is important, the curved line being an independent element in itself. What the eye perceives is transformed into a system of decorative forms in dark tones of barely coloured paintings. His style derives from the theories and style of the Nabis painters, to which Rippl Rónai now belonged, though he did not accept the mystical philosophies of the group. In 1894 at the Salon of the Champs de Mars his painting *The Artist's Grandmother* was particularly well received. In addition to the Nabis, both Toulouse-Lautrec and Gauguin were loud in its praise, and this warm reception is more than an acknowledgement of a new painter. As a contemporary critic remarked: "It was a happy surprise and a great delight to discover the picture of this pale-faced little old peasant woman with her bright eyes." How much the painter's colleagues and the Parisian public understood the painting is questionable, for they thought of the model of the painting as if she were a simple peasant woman instead of the educated middle-class lady she really was. The painter had not drawn attention to her background by introducing books or any other attribute of an educated mind. He had found it enough to pose her seated in an elegantly curved armchair, knowing that he could create the impression he desired by indicating the way she held herself and by giving her a lively expression.

The Artist's Grandmother was the first of a series of portraits. The skilful drawing which Rippl Rónai had learnt in Paris enabled him to create portraits of all his relatives in turn—his parents holding hands on their 40th wedding anniversary, uncle Rippl sitting below Lajos Kossuth's portrait, and several citizens of Kaposvár, his native town. In these portraits Rippl Rónai was not only following recent trends, but was also continuing a long-established tradition of portrait-painting in Hungary. His faith in this tradition is further confirmed by his efforts to return to Hungary and to seek commissions there. During the ten years he spent in Paris, he made several short visits to Hungary, where he rep-

59

resented very early the decorative, stylistic approach of the Nabis and Art Nouveau.

In 1897, Rippl Rónai, after exhibiting 130 paintings in the Gallery Art Nouveau, left Paris for several months to stay with his friend Aristide Maillol at Banyuls-sur-Mer, near the French–Spanish border. It was here that he encountered the glowing fields of the South, an experience which enlarged his palette with rich, sensitive colours. There he painted the *Portrait of Aristide Maillol,* which is one of the masterpieces of Post-Impressionism. With its plasticity, its system of colours inherited from Impressionism, its simple, yet monumental character, it is reminiscent of Cézanne's portraits, and represents a milestone in the history of Hungarian art. Through this portrait, Hungarian painting was swept into the currents of contemporary European art.

Rippl Rónai had achieved something which perhaps he did not even realize himself, for he was a modest man who assumed no special role and had no manifested programme. He had achieved the goal of every ambitious painter of the 19th century. By studying at the schools and academies both at home and abroad, by choosing his themes with care, and by learning from the art exhibited in museums, he found himself in the mainstream of European art. Towards the end of the century this was every artist's ambition. To achieve it, painters studied natural history, botany, lived close to nature, sought the very essence of natural forms and the more exceptional of these artists sought the very essence of the universe, that the invisible might reveal itself through the visible.

Painting for most artists in Hungary was a question of mission, message, or vocation. At the beginning and in the middle of the 19th century, *Mater Hungaria* was the patron and inspiration for Hungarian artists. In the last third of the century there were some artists who gained this sense of vocation through the devotion to *Mater Natura.*

It was therefore not altogether surprising when the painter Tivadar Csontváry Kosztka announced that in his youth he had had a vision and heard a heavenly voice directing him to the study of art and assuring him of his great talent. He was yet apprenticed to a pharmacist when he entered into correspondence with professor Gusztáv Kelety about the problems of landscape painting. One day, pausing in his work to draw a haycart, he heard the following words spoken in celestial tones: "Thou shall be the greatest painter to follow the path of the Sun…" The "path of the Sun", as Csontváry realized after many years, was *plein-air.*

Csontváry reacted to this experience in a most practical way. He worked on as a pharmacist and began to save money to pay for lessons. It was many years before he could pay the fees to study in foreign Academies but at last he could devote all his time to art. He visited the museums and in a continual quest for contact with the divine energy of art, travelled widely, visiting places famous for their beauty (Italy, Greece, the Holy Land, the Mount of Lebanon, the Carpathians). He spent much of the 1890s in Munich and in Karlsruhe. He felt that in Munich, in the private school of his fellow countryman Hollósy, and at Professor Kallmorgen in Karlsruhe, he might acquire the techniques necessary for him to fulfil the celestial prophecy and create majestic landscapes and com-

Plate 318

positions. When, during his travels, he encountered a view which he felt to be extremely suitable for a large painting, he was filled with the joy of achievement, having found the place where the glowing colours made vibrant by the Sun can be seen in all their intensity and magnificence. After he had completed the first painting of this kind, he sent a telegram to Hollósy saying, *"Plein-air erfunden"*. He had found the secret of capturing atmosphere and "the way of the Sun".

Plate 321 As the 19th century came to a close, Csontváry was still painting lyrical portraits and well lighted interiors after life. His aims were as yet no different from those of other 19th century painters. He himself declared that while working on his landscapes, figurative compositions and great panoramic views, he "always bore in mind the future of his motherland". He wrote in one letter: "As long as we can serve our country and nation, assist its further development with our spiritual and creative strength, … I think it is our holy duty to do so." In these words Csontváry was expressing the beliefs of the great Hungarian thinkers and reformers of the early 19th century, sharing their wish to contribute to the cultural development and independence of Hungary.

In the 19th century Hungary saw the beginning of a new epoch of spiritual revival in which there was to be a solid ground for a great cultural development. Within Hungary there was no tradition of painting that artists might wish to maintain. Innovations were initially introduced by the simple imitation of foreign models. Another method was to represent nature in a very simple manner, an imitative form many practised in a pleasant naive style at the beginning and in the middle of the century, and in a more elaborate one as it came to an end.

If we try to apply Goethe's aesthetic categories to the evaluation of 19th century painting in Hungary, we might easily conclude that apart from simple imitation or the development of existing mannerism, few paintings revealed either a personal or even a general style. Plurality of styles, which was a more or less defined characteristic of all European art in the 19th century, became a coherent urge in Hungary because of the need to develop a national art. In Central and Eastern Europe all theoretical and creative efforts of any consequence converged in an attempt to raise a national style above simple naive imitation and Academic mannerism. It is for this reason that Hungarian art historians have always concentrated on the relationship between universal values and national significance. In fact, the search for a national style was mainly declined to superficialities. Even works of considerable merit tended to be no more than local variations of international trends. And even when an artist was able to develop a coherent system, he had great difficulty in applying it over a long period of time, much less hand it on to the next generation. Nevertheless, the masterpieces of 19th century art in Hungary did have certain common features. For example, the carefully chosen themes which appealed to a large public and the classical forms based on complex symmetry. But perhaps the most notable characteristic was the more dynamic use of emotion-charged Romantic and later Naturalist. The more complex the political, social message, the greater was the attempt of theatrical gestures, and the more heterogeneous the character.

The 19th century, however, can be subdivided according to one or two of the more dominant styles even in Hungary. The years between 1800 and 1830 were dominated by classicizing Late Baroque; occasionally Rococo or Empire elegance was fused with Romantic ideals. In the 1830s, Neo-Classicism mingled with Romanticism and dominated the different forms of painting, often combined in one work. During the 1840s another trend gained favour; it was called Biedermeierstil in Austria and combined bourgeois sentimentality with a closer relationship to nature without losing a calm Neo-Classicism and the Romantic sensibility. The influence of this style was to be felt in Hungary until the mid-fifties. Around this time, Academic Historicism revived the Neo-Renaissance, Neo-Baroque and then Neo-Rococo styles. These pseudo-styles gave a chance for painters to imitate the tradition of European *grand art*. In fact these works often tended to be extremely out of date, although the intention was to depict nature and society more informally. In the middle of the 19th century painting in Hungary was not a pure visual art form, but visualized history, literary illustration, and a sort of advertisements for political ideas. A great many pictures were created in this way; they should be acknowledged, for they responded to the challenge of history, and to the highest Hungarian poetry and prose of that period.

From the late 1860's onwards, and more specifically from the last decade of the century, painters concerned themselves with the autonomous problems of art and with new ways of capturing nature on the canvas. The strong traditions of long respected Academies continued, however, unaffected by the diverse forms of Naturalism until the last decade of the century. Though some artists involved in the problems of society introduced an element of realism into their genre-paintings, pictorial Realism and an Impressionistic perception of nature were generally not followed in Hungary until the turn of the century. Those artists who were not acknowledged by the public had the choice between withdrawal and emigration. Until 1896–1898, it was not possible to exhibit works of art outside the accepted norms of society.

Nonetheless, painting in Hungary became a very significant branch of art. From 1830 onwards more and more exhibitions were organized, and more and more paintings were bought for public buildings and private homes, and also acquired for the newly established museums. It therefore came about that painters were asked to decorate buildings rather than to analyze a visual problem, and to convey their feelings about a given subject rather than to express deep philosophical concepts. It was even less of a requirement that painting should represent Realistic images of things seen.

In the course of the 19th century, painting had acquired a social status in Hungary. Throughout the century, each generation had produced outstanding artists whose aim was to develop a personal style that would imply national characteristics; and this was often an enormously difficult task. Around and after 1850 this struggle for development gave to Hungarian painting a special significance and brought it into the ranks of European art. Therefore in this survey including the humblest efforts as well as the greatest achievements of the most gifted artists—we have to acknowledge that Hungarian efforts have a place in the history of European painting in the 19th century.

Plate 319

Plates and Plate Descriptions

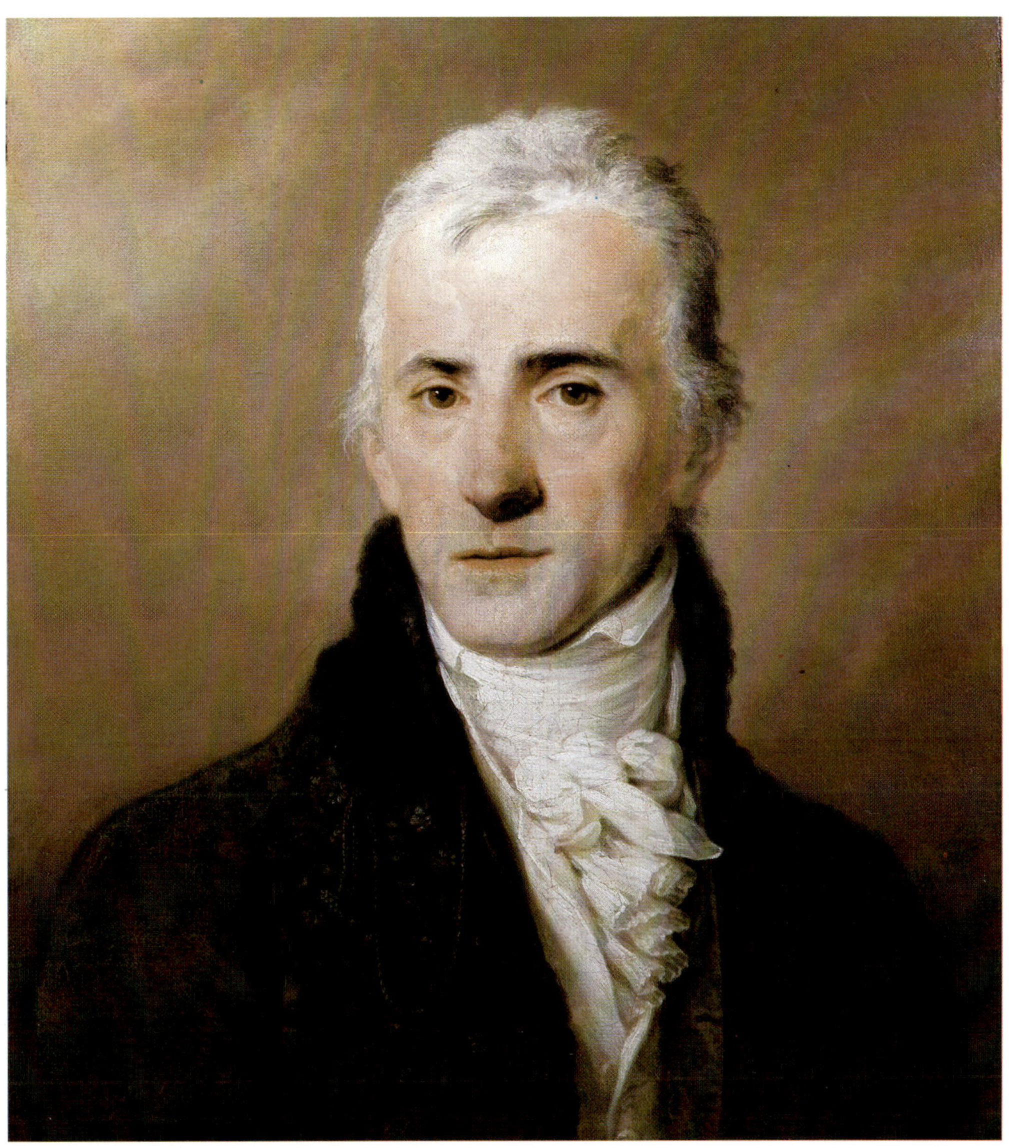

1. JOSEPH KREUTZINGER
Portrait of Ferenc Kazinczy, 1808

Oil on canvas, 51.4 × 45 cm
*Inscription on reverse side: "François de
Kazinczy hongrois, peint par Joseph
Kreutzinger à Vienne, 1808."*
Budapest, Hungarian Academy of Sciences

About twenty six portraits of Ferenc Kazinczy were painted during his lifetime by such important artists as Johann Jakob Stunder, János Rombauer, János Donát, Ferenc Simó and Johann Ender. Many of them—including those in Kazinczy's own collection—have been lost or damaged. According to his friends and biographers, Joseph Kreutzinger's oil painting is the best portrait of Kazinczy. He is portrayed with greying, receding hair, but still vigorous and young-looking, his steady gaze making us aware of the nobility of his character. The high forehead, firm yet sensitive mouth and rosy cheeks all indicate a man with a high degree of intelligence, good powers of judgement and a creative power. The background,

a pink-grey, overcast sky, serves to emphasize the elegance of the sitter.

The French influence, prevalent at the turn of the 18th-19th centuries, is evident in the style of Kazinczy's clothing and the French inscription on the reverse; also in the sensitive colours so typical of late 18th century French portraiture. Completed in 1808, the portrait embodies the gradual change from Rococo to Romanticism.

Art historians refer to Kreutzinger as a Court painter, a title indicating not only social status but also a particular style of painting. In the late 18th and early 19th centuries courtiers required portraits showing themselves elegantly dressed and refined but with marked individuality. These requirements were all met in Kreutzinger's portrayal of a notable Hungarian intellectual.

It was during this period that the presence of Napoleon and the French in and around the city of Vienna clearly contributed to the emergence of a new spirit in many fields of life and art.

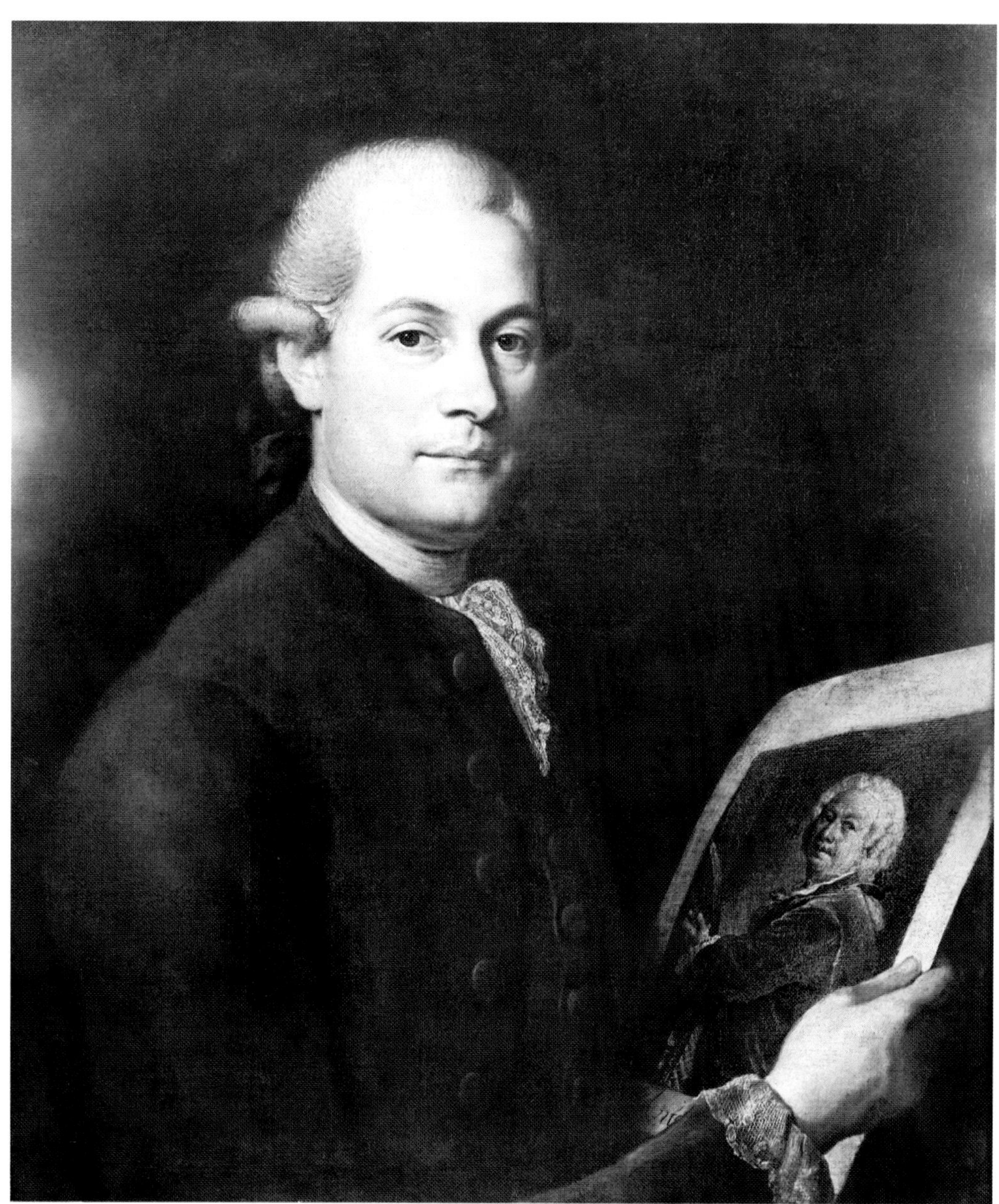

2. JOSEPH KREUTZINGER
Portrait of Carlo Artaria, 1780s
Oil on canvas, 70 × 58 cm
Vienna, Museum der Stadt Wien
Inv. No.: 58.316

The traditional role of art patrons continued into the 19th century, but now there emerged a more dominant figure, the art dealer. The subject of this portrait by Joseph Kreutzinger was a member of a Viennese firm engaged in book publishing, who also bought and sold engravings and pictures. Here the sitter has adopted the pose and dress of a nobleman. As an art dealer, he was in fact able to extend the range of his activities into Hungary because of the interest in his work shown by art patrons such as Kazinczy and his friends.

3. JÁNOS DONÁT
Portrait of József Ürményi, 1804
Oil on canvas, 129 × 93.5 cm
Budapest, Hungarian National Gallery
Inv. No.: L. 5.109

During 64 years as an artist, János Donát portrayed almost every one of the more distinguished inhabitants of Hungary and Transylvania. "His taste in painting was excellent, and he had a gift for reproducing facial likeness," was one comment in an obituary published after his death in 1830, at the age of 86.

The subject of this portrait, József Ürményi, high notability of the counties of Bihar and Nyitra, was appointed Treasurer of Galicia, and later, Head of the Judiciary. His most important achievements were in the field of the advancement of public education. He assisted in the establishment of the *Ratio Educationis* (Education Act). This full-length portrait indicates his achievements by showing a lot of books in the background, as well as the honour with which he was rewarded by the Emperor—the cross of the Order of St. Stephen, established by Empress Maria Theresa in 1664, as a sign of the Empire's recognition of his achievements.

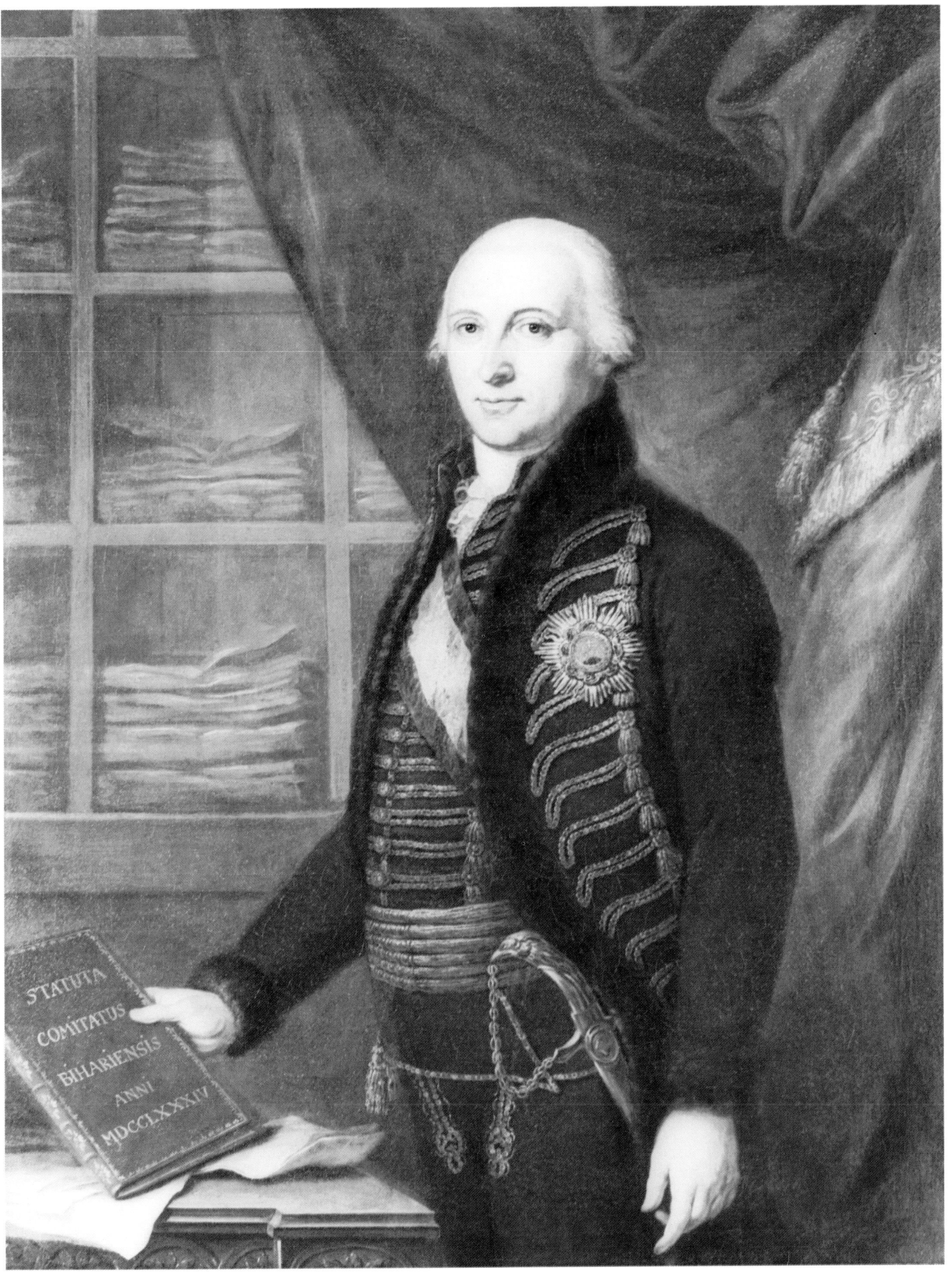

STATUTA
COMITATUS
BIHARIENSIS
ANNI
MDCCLXXXIV

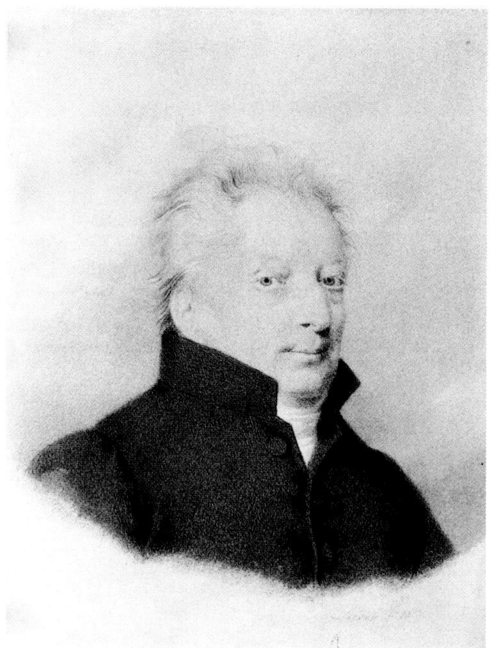

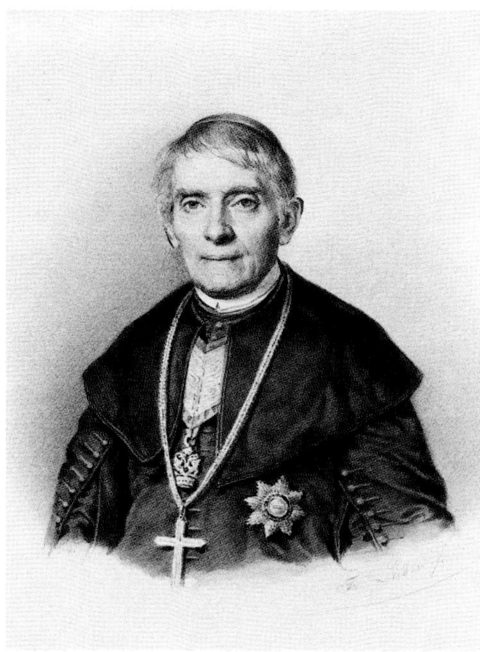

4. FRIEDRICH LIEDER
Portrait of Mihály Hédervári Viczay, 1827
Pencil, water-colour, 195×145 mm
Signed bottom right: "Lieder F. 1827"
Mosonmagyaróvár, Hanság Museum
Inv. No.: 63.3

Friedrich Lieder, a Saxon painter born in Potsdam, worked for some time at the Paris Academy as a pupil of Jacques Louis David. During the French occupation of Vienna, he emerged as a master of water-colours and oil-portraits painted in the French style. In 1824 he was elected a member of the Vienna Academy and from 1830 onwards was active in Pozsony and Nagyszombat where he produced mainly portraits of Hungarian noblemen. In his portrait of Mihály Hédervári Viczay (1756–1831), a friend of the Széchenyis, he immortalized one of the most enthusiastic of the aristocratic patrons and collectors of art. It is a small portrait and was produced in two versions, probably so that one of them could be used for a lithograph. The other version, made in 1826 and housed in the Budapest Museum of Fine Arts, differs from the one in Mosonmagyaróvár only in the style of dress and in the colour of the eyes.

5. FRIEDRICH LIEDER
Portrait of János László Pyrker, Archbishop of Eger, late 1830s
Ink on paper, 263×187 mm
Signed bottom right: "Fr. Lieder fecit."
Budapest, Museum of Fine Arts
Inv. No.: 1912–114

In his detailed study of artistic regions of Hungary in the first half of the 19th century, art historian Károly Lyka describes the entourage of János László Pyrker, Archbishop of Eger (1772–1847), as a colony consisting almost exclusively of foreign artists. According to Lyka those most worthy of mention are Malatesti, Schiavoni, Grigoletti, Danhauser and, of the sculptors, primarily Marco Casagrande. The Archbishop of Eger, ordained in 1827, owned a considerable collection of pictures, consisting of 190 works, which he donated to the National Museum in 1836. There are portraits of him by a number of important artists, for instance Josef Danhauser and later Miklós Barabás.

Lieder's drawing in ink is most likely a preliminary study for a lithograph. The archbishop, who died in 1847, is here characterized with the utmost care as a man in his middle age. The painting emphasizes his studious nature and his gentleness. A large cross is the only ornament on his plain cassock, but he also wears the star of the Order of St. Stephen, an imperial distinction frequently bestowed in the early years of the 19th century on enlightened aristocrats and prelates.

6. JOHANN ENDER
Portrait of Ferenc Széchényi, 1823
Oil on canvas, 318×220 cm
Signed bottom left: "Johann Ender pinx 1823"
Budapest, Hungarian National Museum
(on loan from the Széchényi Library)

Ferenc Széchényi was the most notable Hungarian patron of the arts in the late 18th and early 19th centuries. He gave generously to many who were in need and it was with his help that the greatest but poorest Hungarian poet of the time, Mihály Csokonai Vitéz, was able to publish his work. He also financed the publication of Hungarian journals in Vienna and in Pest-Buda. In 1802 he founded the National Library, which was named after him and which houses not only books but also collections of medals, engravings, maps and antiquities.

After his father's death, István Széchenyi commissioned the Austrian Johann Ender to paint Ferenc Széchényi's full-life portrait based on one he had painted some years earlier. The picture was intended for the Library. It shows Széchényi in his studio, standing, his costume bearing the insignia of the Knights of the Golden Fleece (an honour held also by the Emperor of Austria and King of Hungary). He is portrayed standing in a Neo-Classical colonnaded hall admiring the Castle of Buda which was not even completed in 1823. Four sphinxes, symbolizing wisdom (as we learn from Ender's correspondence with István Széchenyi) support the table. His right hand rests on a book containing the text of the Act of Foundation passed during the 24th Session of Parliament in 1807 which entrusted Parliament with Széchényi's donation. On the table, beside a bronze bust of the Emperor and King Francis I, a small statue of Pallas Athene, Greek pottery vessels, antique rings, medals and plaques, we see the scroll inscribed with the deed of foundation dating from 1802. A folder of engravings and a scroll in front of the table, a globe, an antique vase, a brush and a palette serve to indicate the range of the Széchényi Collection. In the background the wall is decorated with a frieze which shows the family coat of arms surrounded by the seven Muses.

"The conception is bold; the picture is executed in the most beautiful manner, a perfect representation of a great and noble figure, the eternal pride of our nation," wrote Kazinczy in 1829. István Széchenyi's commentary on the picture—and indirectly on his father's legacy—runs as follows: "In the course of my duties I visited the museum where my heart leapt with pride when I saw my father's portrait. Oh, what a joy it is to be honoured by our fellow countrymen."

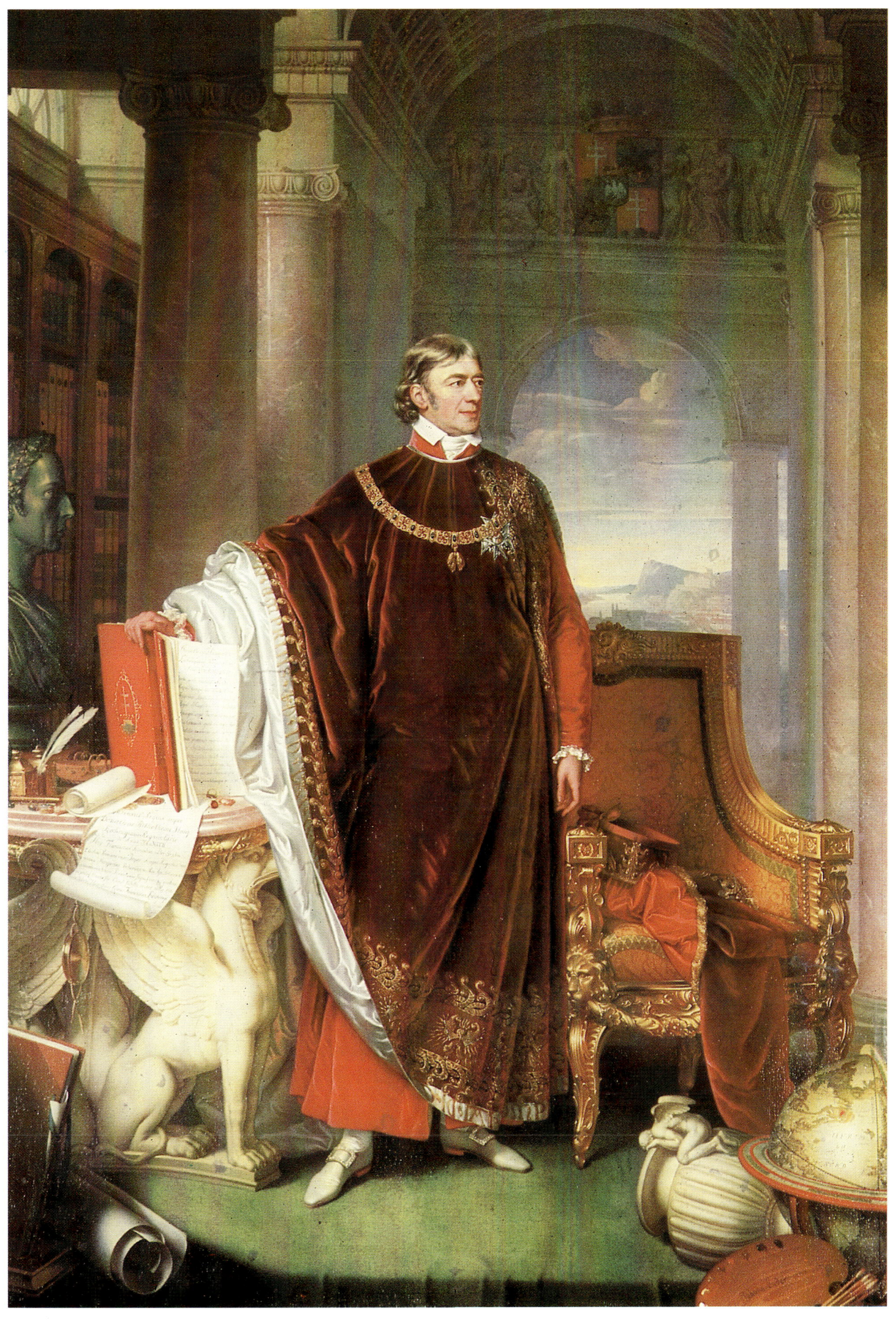

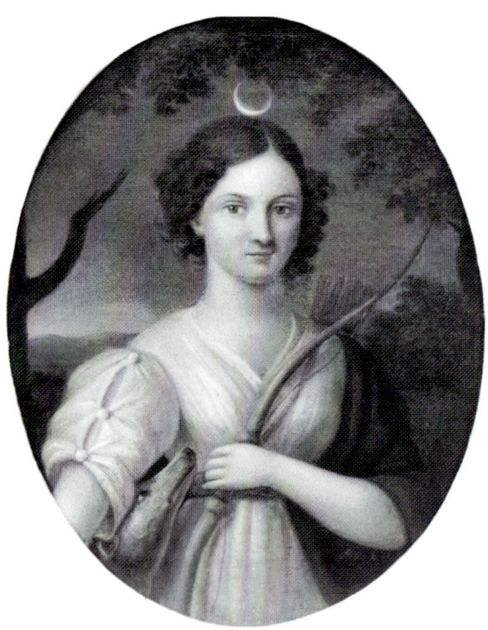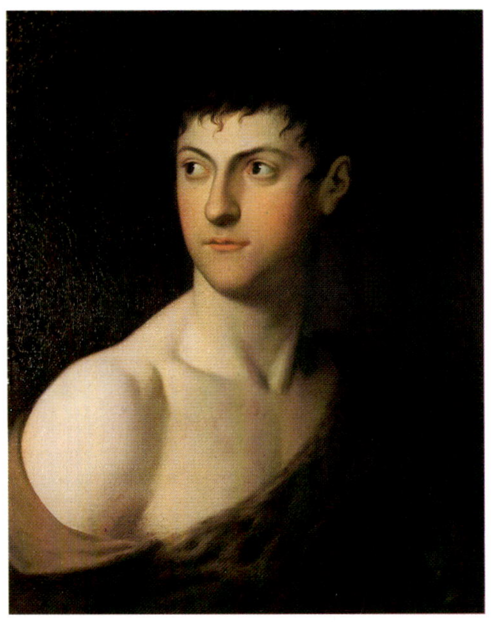

7. JÓZSEF CZAUCZIK
Eugénia Édeskuty as Diana, 1820s
Oil on canvas, 18×15 cm
Levoča, Museum of Szepes County
(A replica of this painting dates from 1838)

During the first decades of the 19th century it was a fashion among the nobility and the middle classes to have themselves portrayed in mythological costumes to celebrate family or social occasions by theatrical performances.

Hungarian painters of the period liked to portray aristocratic ladies in the splendid garments of goddesses or muses and young gentlemen as Greek gods. Later the nobility were portrayed not as isolated figures but as participants in mythological or allegorical scenes.

József Czauczik (Czausig, Zausig) was born in Lőcse and was trained in Vienna. In the small painting here beneath a crescent moon a young girl is portrayed as the goddess Diana. Holding a bow in her left hand and with a quiver over her shoulder, she lovingly enfolds her hound beneath her right arm.

8. JOHANN JAKOB STUNDER
Count László Festetich as Hercules, 1805
Oil on canvas, 51×62 cm
Signed bottom left: "J. Stunder 1805 Juni"
Keszthely, Helicon Library

The young man in the painting is László Festetich, whose father, György Festetich, was one of Hungary's wealthiest landowners and founder of the first important school of agriculture, the Georgicon in Keszthely. During the early years of the 19th century he organized the Helicon Festivals at which students from the Georgicon would demonstrate what they had learned, famous writers and poets (e.g. Sándor Kisfaludy and Dániel Berzsenyi) would read from their works, and pastoral dances would be performed in the "Greek and Roman" style. On one occasion a chestnut tree was planted, the spade used being decked with a wreath. The festivals were originally held to celebrate some family event, when members of the family may possibly have participated, dressed in suitable costumes. This portrait is presumably connected with a precursor of one of these Helicon Festivals, held regularly twice a year from 1817 onwards. Stunder was primarily concerned to represent the face and upper torso in perfect accordance with Academic requirements.

9. PÁL BALKAY
Allegory Commemorating Science and the Arts. The Blessings of Peace, 1820
Oil on canvas, 203.5×145 cm
Signed bottom left: "Balkay Pál 1820"
Budapest, Hungarian National Gallery
Inv. No.: 3104

Pál Balkay, born in Tiszaörs, was a painter very highly regarded by Kazinczy. He studied from 1803 at the Academy of Vienna under Hubert Maurer and Heinrich Füger. Apart from his portraits and altar-pieces, Balkay considered this historical allegory to be his masterpiece. The background consists of a conventional academic representation of Mount Parnassus and Helicon, the Castalian Spring and Pegasus. The two main figures are Minerva and Apollo, patrons of the Sciences and the Arts. The nine Muses are all present in the lower half of the picture; Saturn (or winged Cronus, the god of Time) is seen leading his charges, the Muses of Music and Dance; and on the right of the painting Thalia, the Muse of Comedy, is seated with her attributes as the protector of the fine arts, such as the palette and brush in her hand. In the centre of the composition we see Mars at a feast, while Genius holds aloft the torch of learning. The Hungarian coat of arms protrudes from the earth, making the allegory explicit: it is Hungary to whom Peace presents her blessings, namely a flourishing of the sciences and the arts.

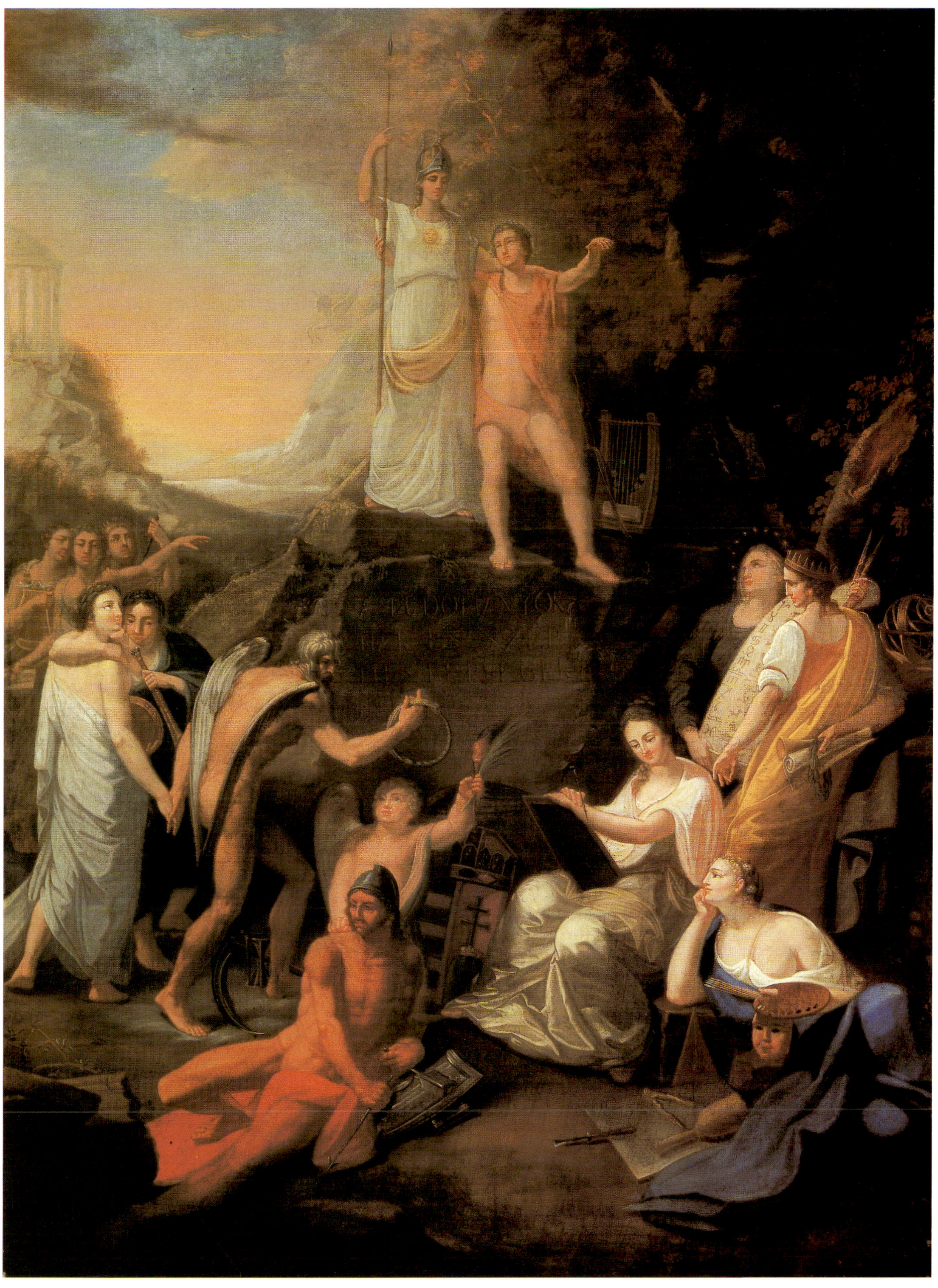

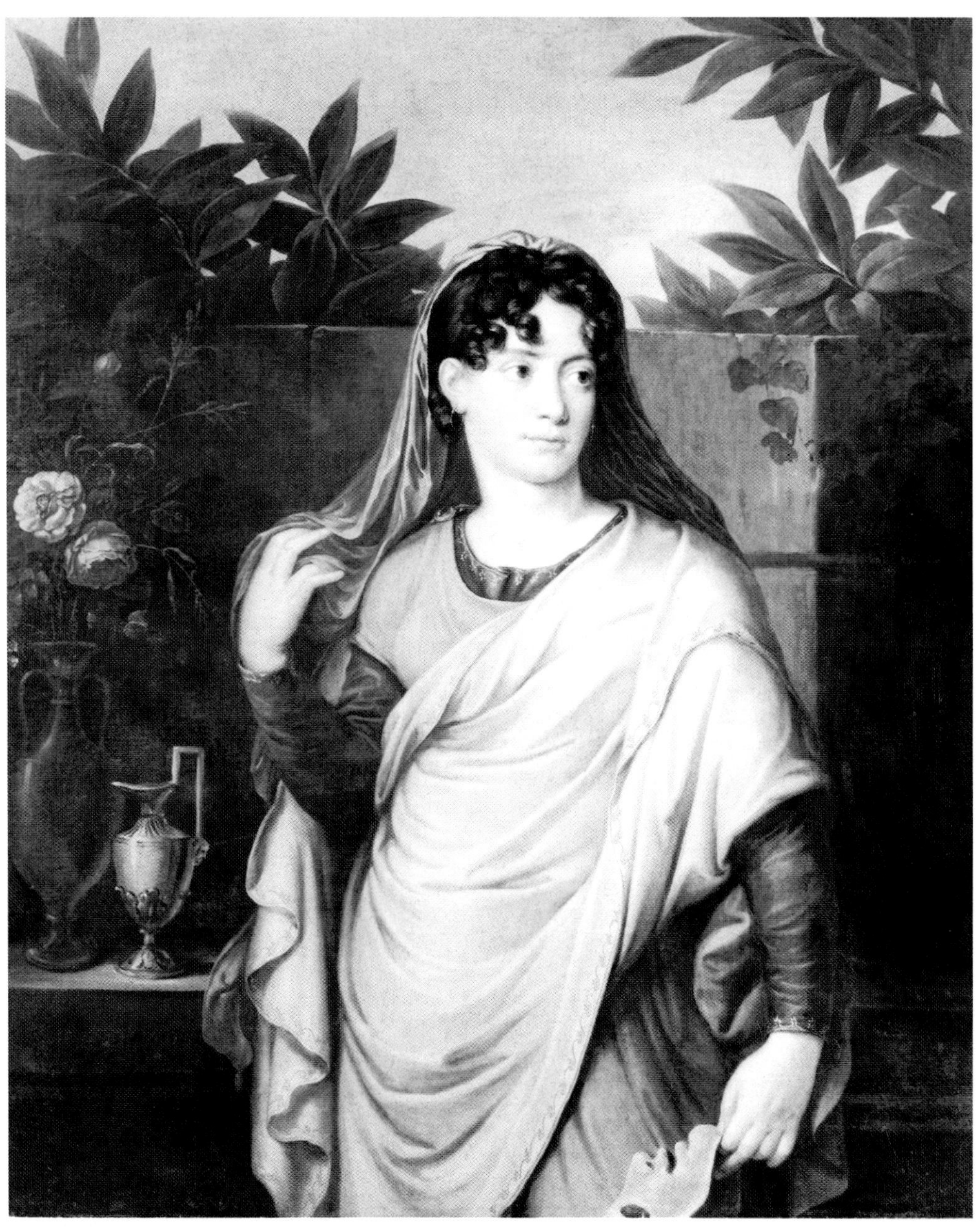

10. JOSEF ABEL
Portrait of Theresia Hudelist, Patron of the Theatre, 1811
Oil on canvas, 122 × 97 cm
Signed bottom left: "Jos Abel fecit 1811"
Vienna, Museum der Stadt Wien
Inv. No.: 46.300

Josef Abel, a Viennese painter and engraver who favoured historical subjects, travelled widely in Eastern Europe. In 1795 he was in Poland and may later have stayed for a while in Hungary too, for he is recorded as having been commissioned to paint individual portraits and group compositions. He executed Heinrich Füger's designs for the Vienna Burg Theatre. He also painted the stage curtains for the German Theatre in the City of Pest. Little remains of either sets of curtains but some of his portraits of theatre-goers have survived. They are sometimes depicted in costume, sometimes in the contemporary fashion, as in this painting preserved in Vienna, but in any case, serve an evocation in the theatre at that time.

The portrait shows an attractive young woman who, judging from the mask she holds in her hand, must personify Thalia, the Muse of Comedy. She stands suitably costumed, in front of a garden wall beside a stone table. The flowers in an ornate vase and the jug in an elaborate wrought stand may well refer to a successful role in a *tableau vivant,* a very fashionable type of theatrical amusement of the period.

11. JÁNOS DONÁT
Portrait of Josef Parkfrieder (Bargfrieder), 1815
Oil on canvas, 226 × 128 cm
Signed: "Donat. p. 1815"
Budapest, Hungarian National Gallery
Inv. No.: 5216

According to art historian Károly Lyka, this portrait represents the owner of a great house in Pest who was a famous collector. Professor Anna Zádor, comparing this with another portrait, has identified the subject as an eccentric court-purveyor who had expressed his great respect for Austrian General Radetzky by having a mausoleum built for him in Heldenberg, in Lower Austria. After Radetzky's death, Parkfrieder was himself buried in the same mausoleum in medieval armour. This unusual middle-class figure, who loved the arts and as we have seen, cherished the hero-cult, is portrayed here dressed in a silk tunic in antique style, leaning against a rock, gesturing with his right arm. We are still unclear as to the significance of the ruins and mountains in the background and the hovering eagle. Possibly they refer to a specific role in a *tableau vivant,* an idea dear to his heart.

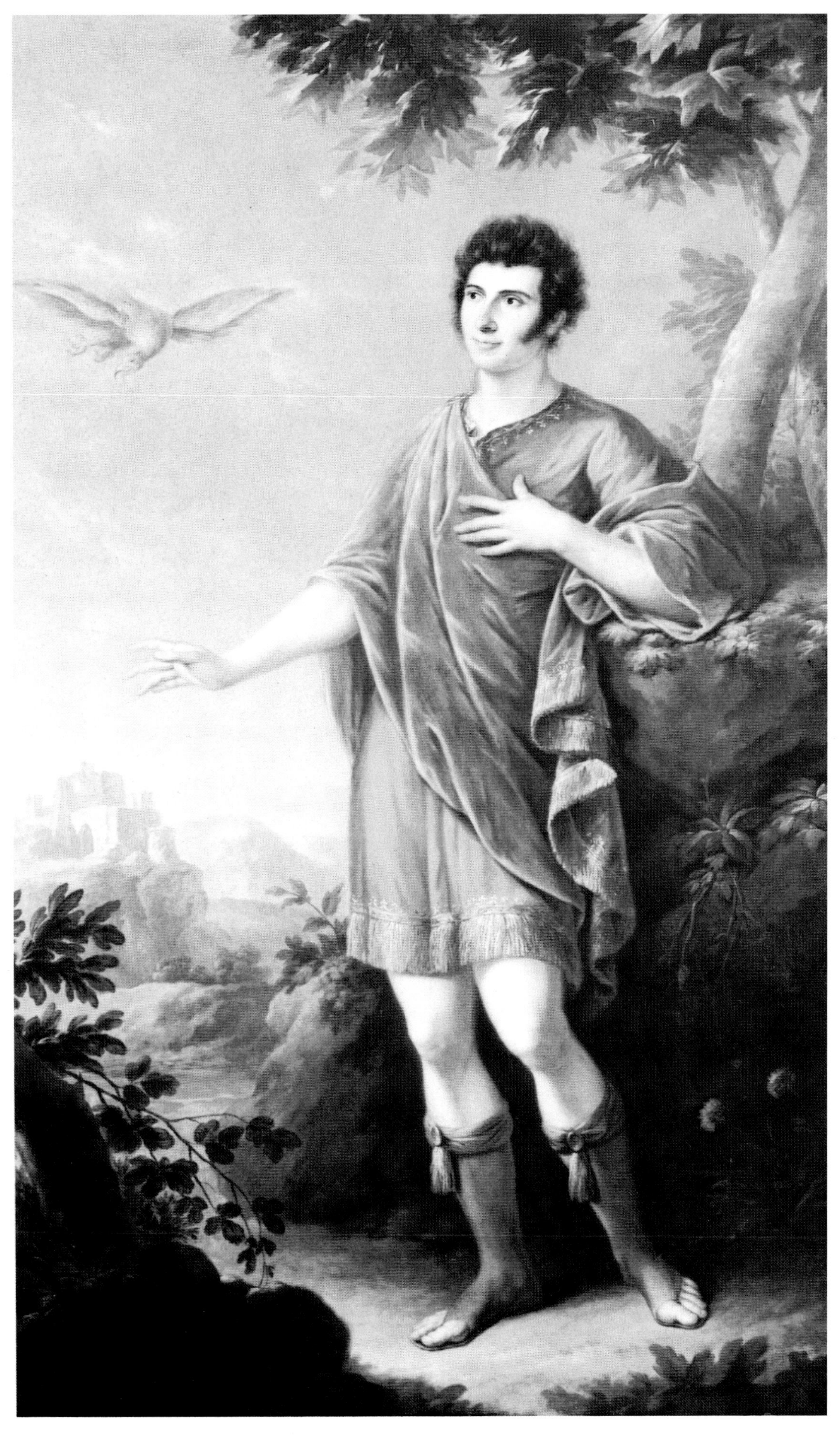

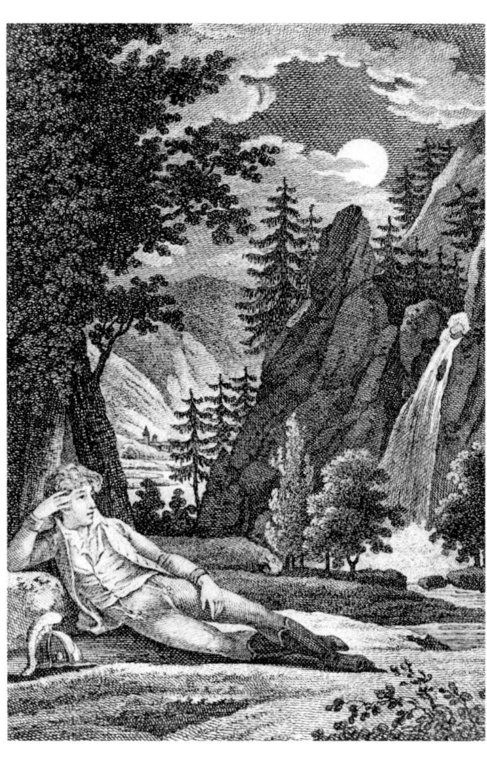

12. VINCENZ GEORG KININGER — JÁNOS BLASCHKE
Love's Lament, 1801

Copper plate engraving, 127 × 78 mm
Inscription: "Az ifjúság kellemeit / Itt hullattya termetem ; / Az életnek Örömeit / E nagy Sírba temetem." (From youthful pleasures / My body takes leave; / All joys of life / I bury in this grave.)
Signed right: "V. Kininger del. J. Blaschke sc."

This copper engraving of 1801 was published in Buda, as the frontispiece to Volume I of Sándor Kisfaludy's "Himfy szerelmei: A kesergő szerelem" (Himfy's Loves: Love's Lament).

Sándor Kisfaludy was chiefly noted for his lyric poetry. While serving in the army as a young man, he lived in Pozsony, where there was a particularly strong interest in music and theatre. Later, he was a Hungarian guard for Maria Theresia in Vienna. During the Napoleonic wars, he visited not only Austria and Italy, but also Provence and the great cultural centres of Germany. In 1800 he returned to Hungary and married his beloved Rosa Szegedi. It was then that Kisfaludy published, first under the pseudonym of Himfy, later in his own name, "Himfy's Loves", a collection of love poems and lyrics, in which he tells the story of his love and marriage. The two volumes and a later edition of epic tales about ruined Hungarian castles were illustrated by engravings.

Kisfaludy's influence is obvious even in Csokonai's poems, known as the "Lilla Songs", another series of lyrical masterpieces of Hungarian poetry. Both poets contributed to a new, sentimental Rousseau-esque style of drawing and painting, in which landscape is no longer a separate, stage-set-like aspect of painting, but an internal part of genre-scenes and portraits.

The copper engravings for "Himfy's Loves" encouraged the creation of a new pictorial vernacular. Commissioned and supervised by Kisfaludy, they were executed by Vincenz Kininger, a Viennese graphic artist.

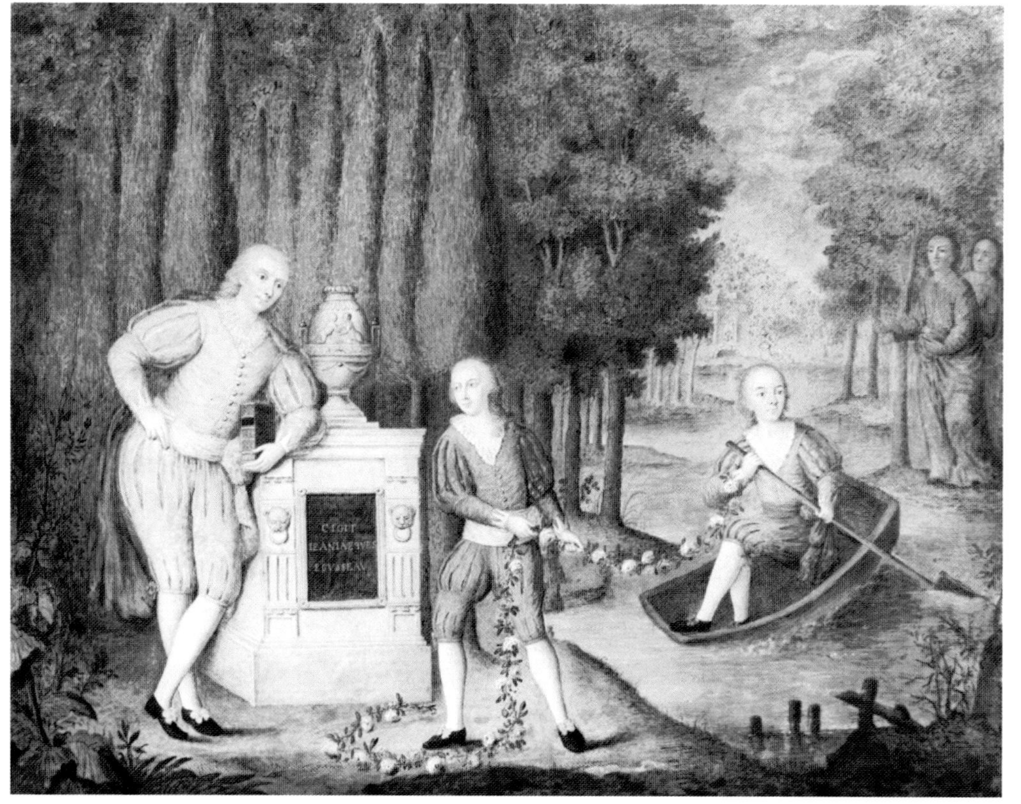

13. UNKNOWN GERMAN PAINTER
Recollections at Rousseau's Grave, c. 1780

Gouache on parchment, 33.5 × 42.5 cm
Budapest, Hungarian National Gallery
Inv. No.: 78.14 M.

This painting represents a type of landscape, which records show to have been appreciated in the years from 1780–1830 in many a Hungarian home, whether castle or town house, by men of letters and by those less erudite. Jean Jacques Rousseau's books were widely read at the time, and his ideas much publicized by admirers who often made the pilgrimage to his grave. Csokonai, the poet, expressed a wish to retire from the world and live in Tihany, by Lake Balaton and become "like Rousseau in Ermenonville" both "a respectable man and citizen".

Although this small painting, probably the work of a German artist, does not bear comparison with Csokonai's poems, it nevertheless expresses a similar emotion and philosophical attitude to life.

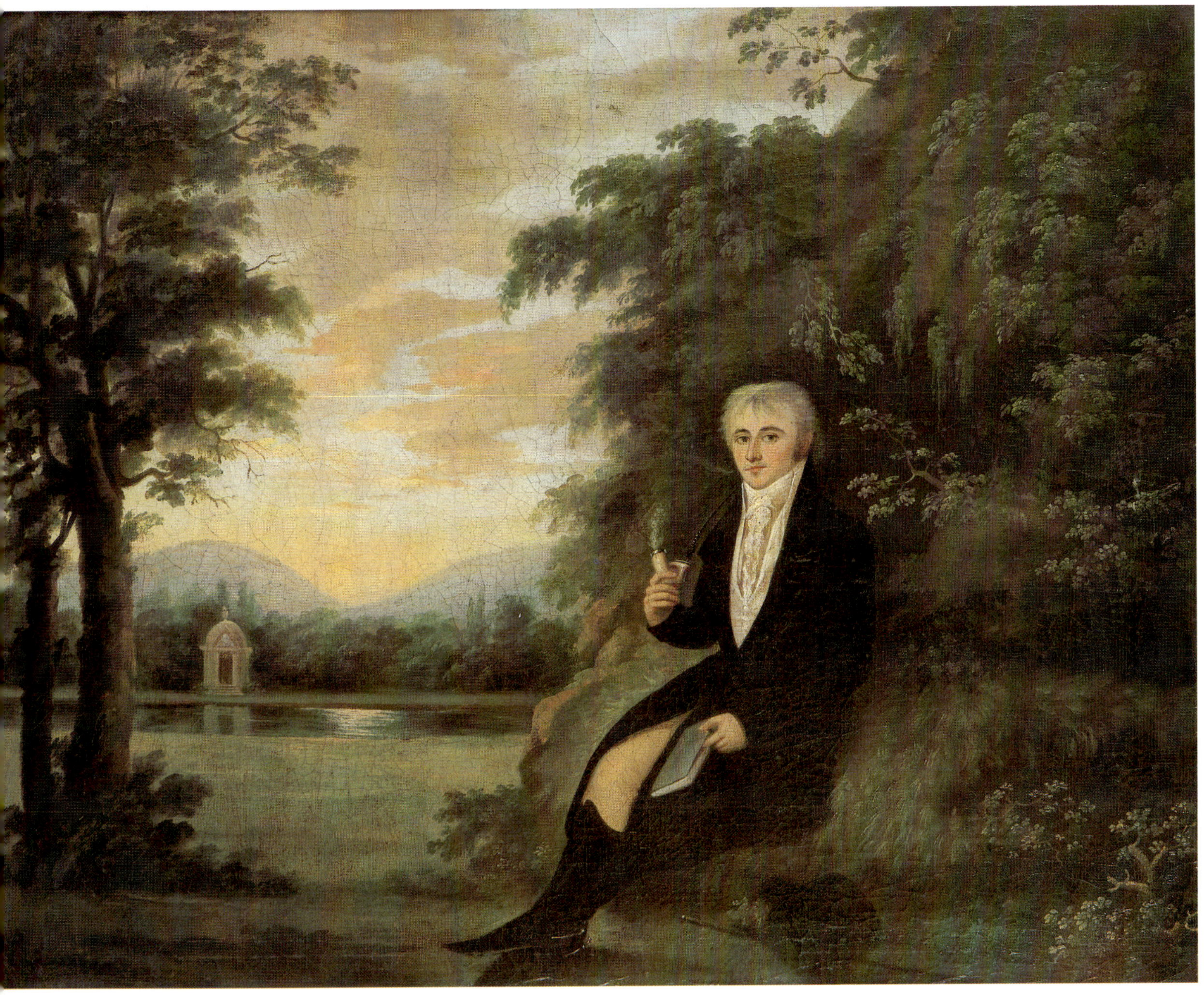

14. JÁNOS ROMBAUER
Youth in a Landscape, 1804
Oil on canvas, 60 × 73.5 cm
Signed bottom right: "Rombauer pinxit 1804"
Košice, Východoslovenská Galéria

Although Johann Jakob Stunder died prematurely in 1811, he left in János Rombauer a remarkable pupil, who gained recognition and fame at home and abroad. An excellent portrait and landscape painter, he was active at Eperjes as a young man when he created one of the most beautiful paintings that has come down to us from the first decade of the 19th century: the portrait of a youth, seated with his pipe and book in the secluded corner of a Romantic English garden. It was clearly commissioned by someone who shared the painter's interest in Rousseau's philosophy and the Romantic attitude to landscapes. Rombauer also painted the county houses of the aristocracy, for example Hotkóc, the property of the Count Csáky family, but this oil painting though retaining a conventional type of composition, reveals an unusual degree of freedom in the representation of both the figure and the landscape.

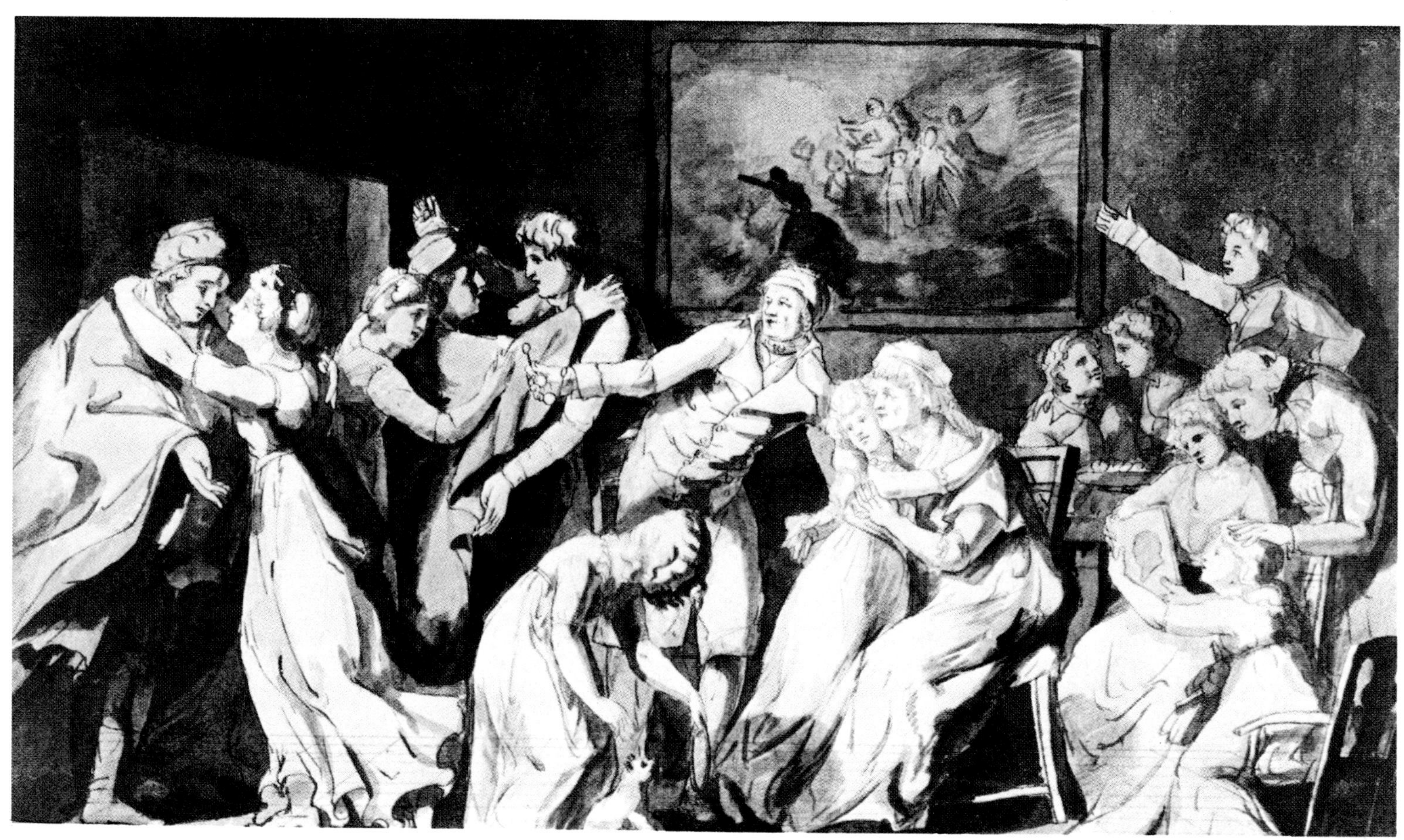

15. PHILIPP OTTO RUNGE
The Sons Come Home, 1800
Pen, Indian ink, brush, 240×405 mm
Berlin, Nationalgalerie
Inv. No.: 23 F III. 2200

In Germany, at the beginning of the 19th
century, the middle class ideal of family life
was embodied at the highest artistic level in
the work of Philipp Otto Runge. Family
portraits and allegorical compositions of the
same kind were being painted in Hungary,
quite apart from those created under the influence of Runge's genre-paintings; however, there is evidence that woodcuts of his
work found their way into the country and
were included in, for instance, the collection
of the Festetich family in Keszthely.
There was in Hungary a development of the
large family group-portrait into a more
dramatized scene, a transformation doubt-
less based on a knowledge of works such as
this lively ink drawing by Runge, which depicts the return of the painter and his brother
Daniel to their father's house.

16. IGNÁC KLIMKOVICS
The Artist as Bridegroom, 1824
Indian ink, water-colour and tempera
on paper, 170×195 mm
Inscription: "Festé Klimkovics Ignác mint
võlegény" (Painted by Ignac Klimkovics as
a bridegroom)
Košice, Východoslovenské Museum

Ignác Klimkovics was one of a family of
painters and sculptors working in Kassa.
Two members of the family, both artists,
were called Ignác. Written sources in the archives of the Hungarian National Gallery
and the style of dress worn by the subject indicate that this small picture is most likely
the work of the Ignác Klimkovics whose
wedding date is recorded as 1824. His descendants still live in Kassa, and the picture
was in their possession until some years ago,
when they sold it to a town museum. It is
a small group-portrait, executed in water-
colour, Indian ink and tempera and, as the
inscription reveals, it represents the artist as
a bridegroom. The figures are crowded together within a confined space. The elegantly dressed young painter looks adoringly at
his fiancée who wears a coronet of flowers.
Her bridesmaids, also elegantly dressed, arrange her curls in preparation for the wedding.

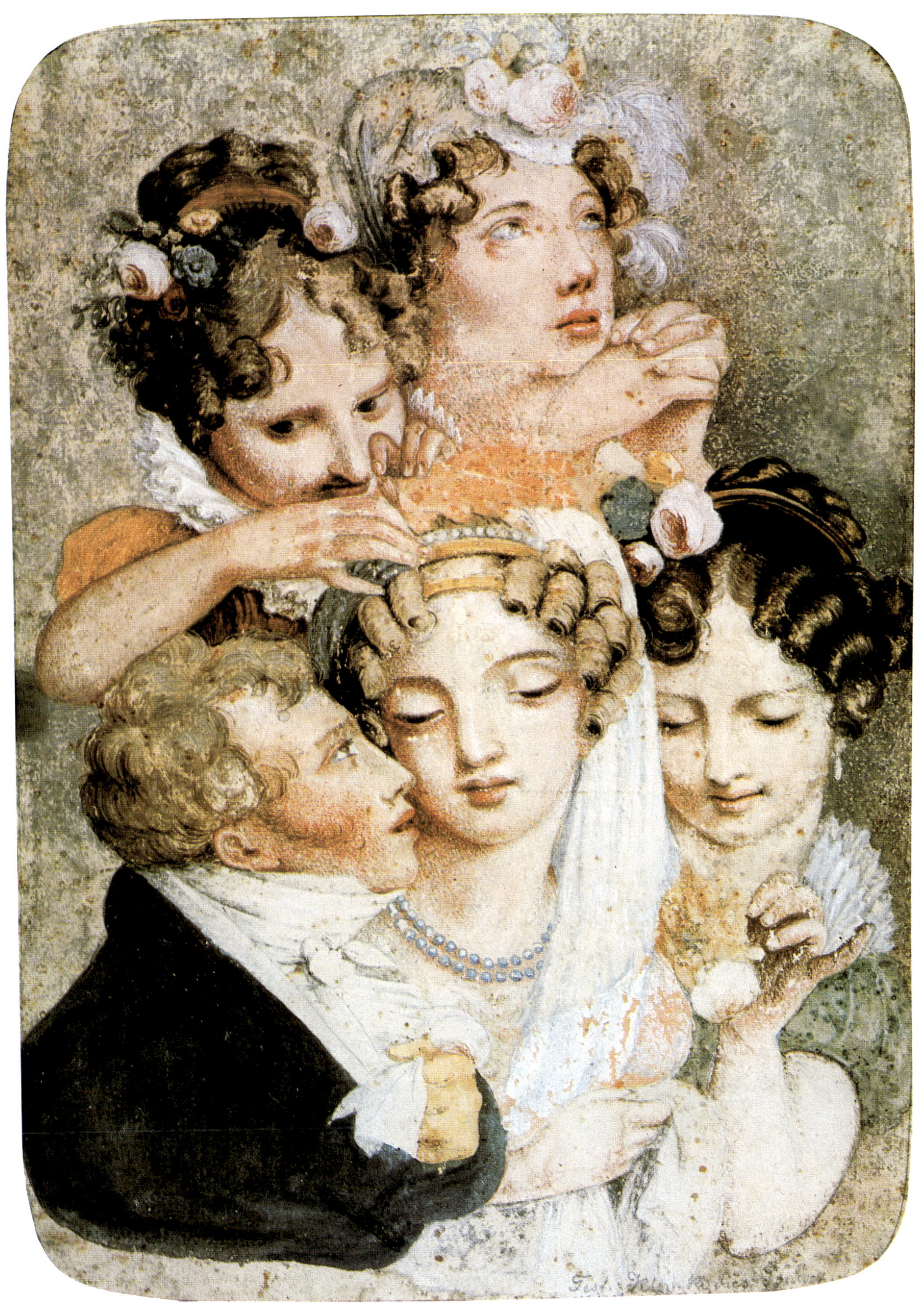

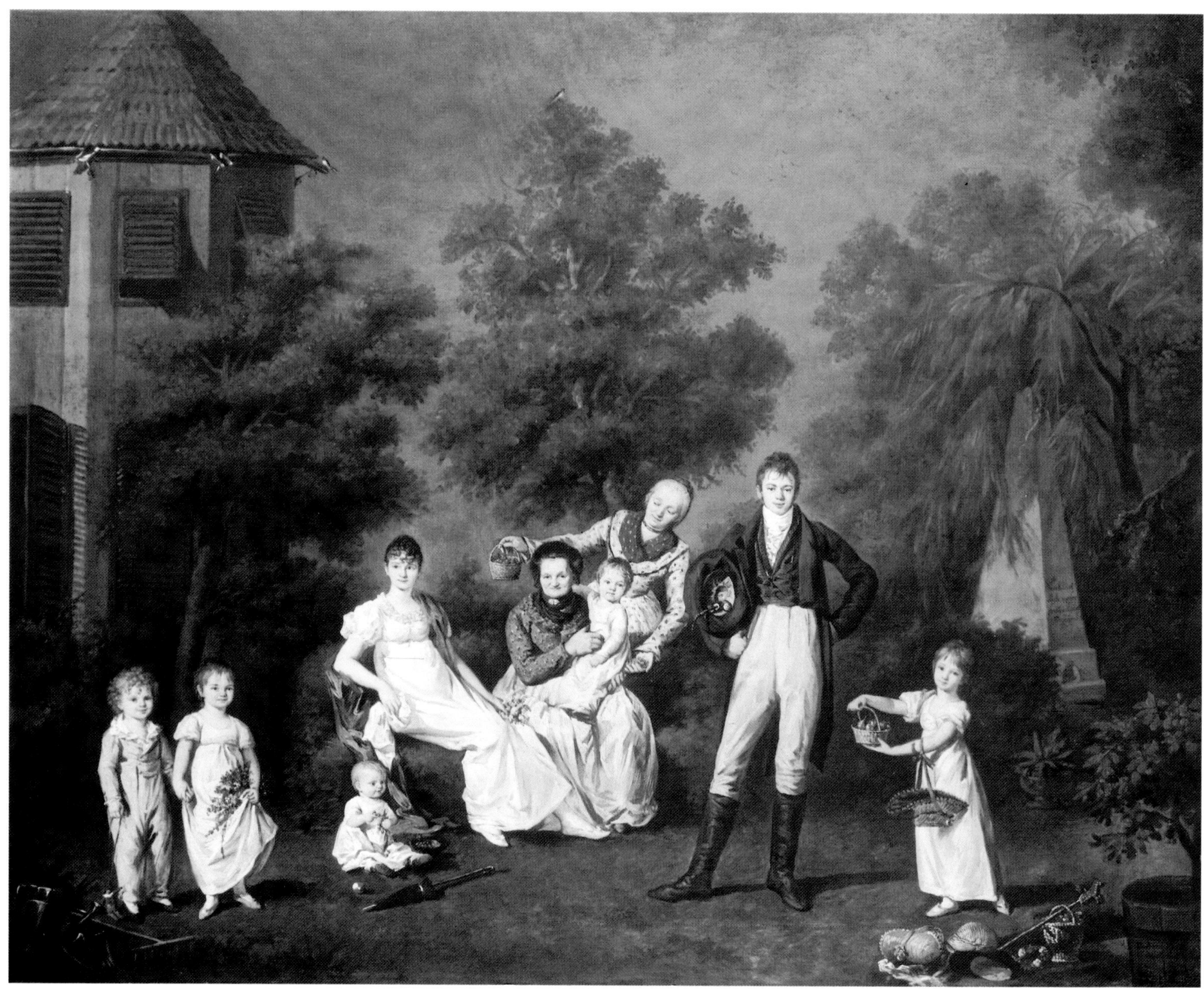

17. BARBARA KRAFFT
Portrait of the Wallner Family, 1809

Oil on canvas, 79 × 65 cm
Inscription on the right, on the tombstone:
"Verklärt dich unser freundliches Daseyn"
Signed bottom right: "Barbara Krafft nata
Steiner pinxit Ano 1809."
Vienna, Österreichische Galerie
Inv. No.: 3682

Bourgeois Romanticism filtered into
Austrian art after the French Revolution, the
Napoleonic and other wars in which the
Austrians were involved and, of course,
through the country's later connection with
France. As a result of this period of war there
were many social changes which fostered
the hope of a new and better world. The
middle classes cherished the idea of the soldier returning from war to rejoin his family
and become a free and prosperous citizen
content to live the simple life in country surroundings; everlasting friendship would
even bind him to the dead.

This painting must have been completed
after Napoleon's first important victory over
the Austrians in 1809; there is confirmation
for this in the fact that as a result of the ensuing peace-treaty the Emperor was to marry
into the Habsburg Family.

Barbara Krafft, born in Moravia, lived in
Vienna, Salzburg and later, Bamberg. She
was not a relative of Peter Krafft, the Elder.
The most successful of her altar-pieces, portraits and genre-paintings were her scenes of
family life.

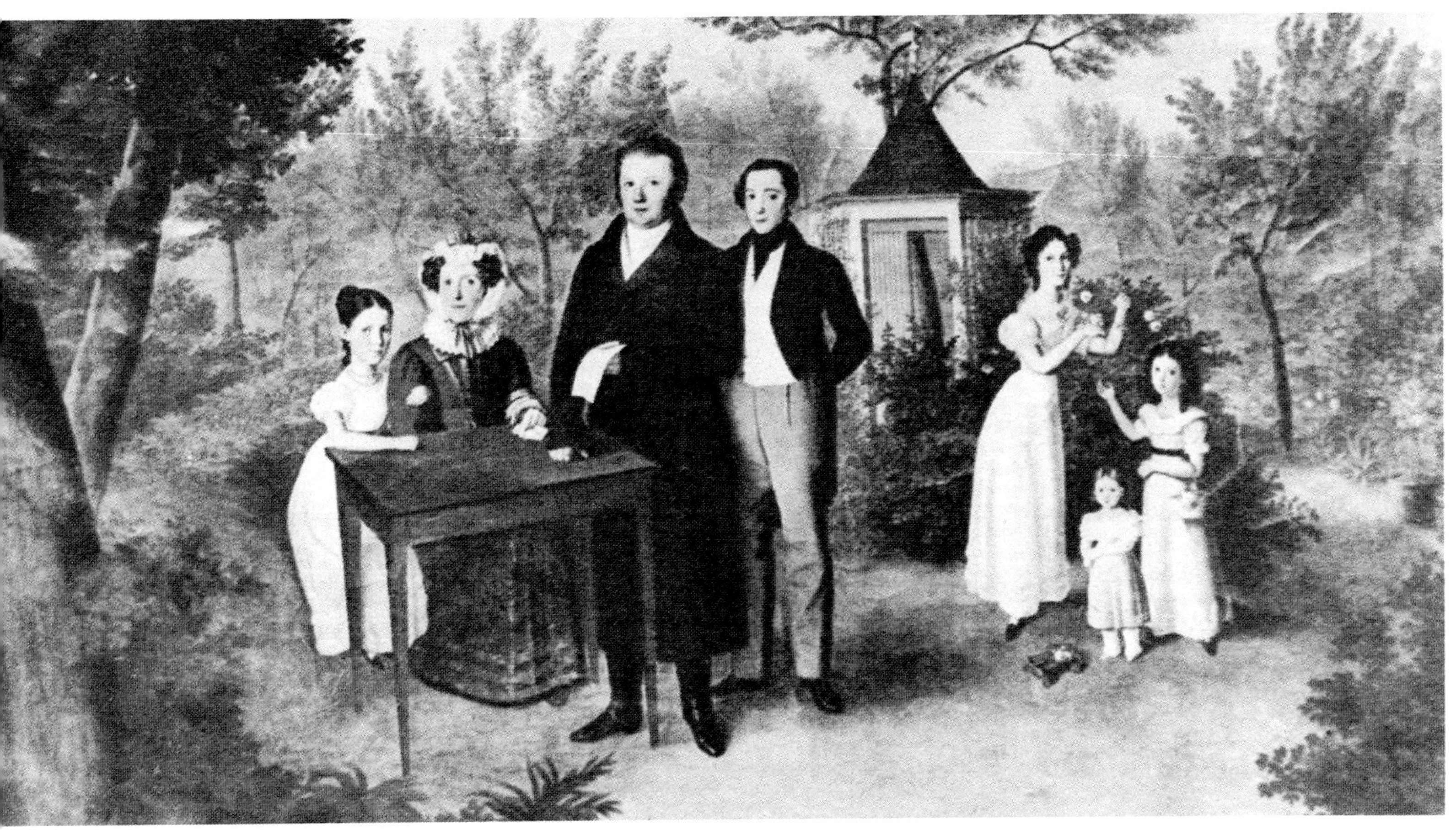

18. JÓZSEF CZAUCZIK
János Dániel Prihradny with his Family, 1820s

Oil on canvas, 120×165 cm
Destroyed during World War II. Formerly in Budapest, in a private collection

By the beginning of the 19th century Hungarians from a variety of social backgrounds felt the urge to own a group-portrait of the whole family. Near the schools of drawing and painting in Lőcse, Eperjes and Kassa, all specializing in landscape painting, portraits in a landscape setting were just as fashionable as individual portraits. Although this picture is much clumsier than Barbara Krafft's painting, there is a similarity of conception. The members of this family from Northern Hungary are seen amidst the bloom of a summer garden. With an excellent feeling for character and a touch of humour, Czauczik depicts the sturdy father with his son, whose elegance indicates the prosperity of the second generation, while the mother, in a simple gown and a lace head-dress, sits with one of the daughters behind a rather clumsily drawn table. The disposition of the figures on the right represents a rather timid attempt to introduce a moving element into the rather formal group portrait: a small child stands in front of two girls of whom the eldest plucks a rose while the younger one holds out her hand to take it. The trees, shrubs and the summer-house in the background all suggest the well-tended garden of a prosperous family.

This painting is dated in the literature as from 1830, but the style of dress and a study of Czauczik's other portraits which he himself dated lead us to believe that it was completed much earlier.

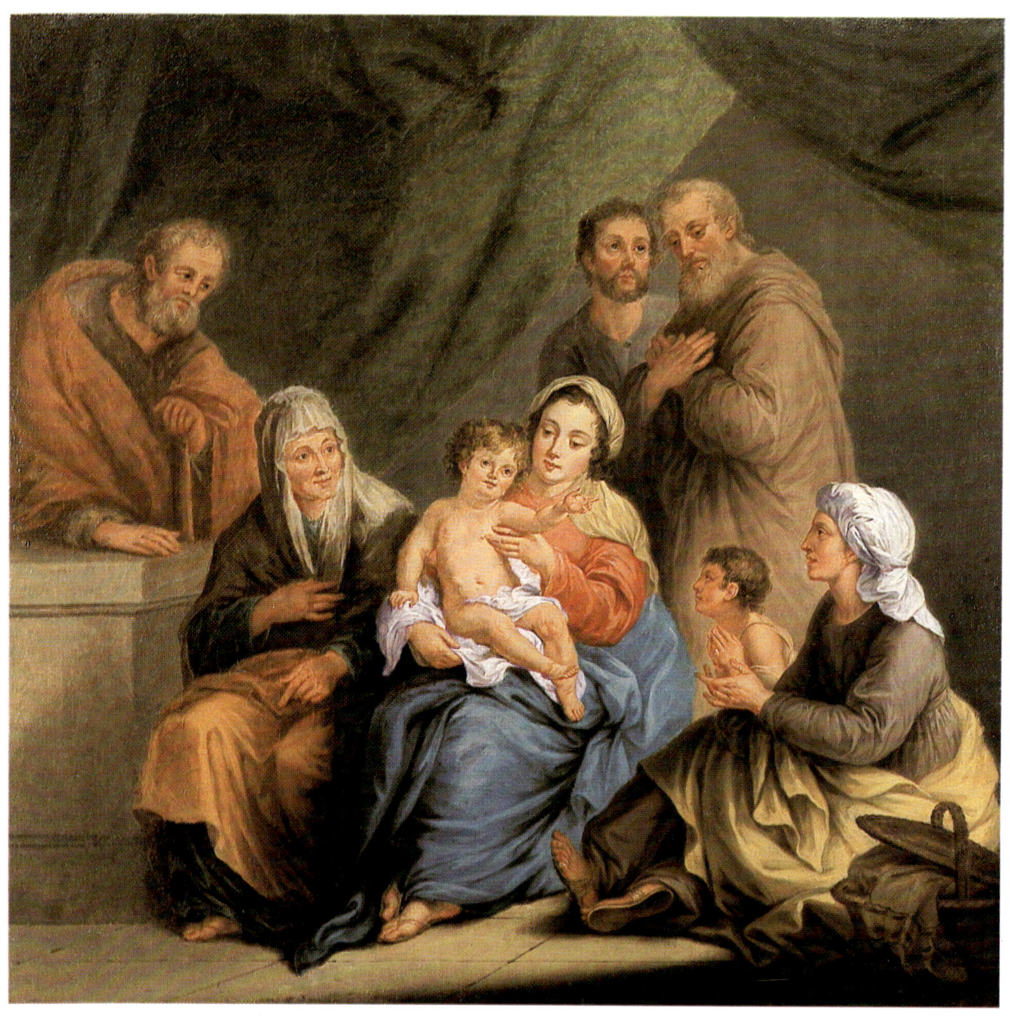

19. JÁNOS DONÁT
The Holy Family, 1808
Oil on canvas, 86 × 86 cm
Signed bottom right: "Donat pinx Vienna 1808"
Bratislava, Mestská Galéria
Inv. No.: A 3043

János Donát painted a great number of altar-pieces for which he créated preliminary cabinet paintings of religious scenes such as this. It is of medium size, a representation of the Holy Family, and an example of the outstanding pictorial quality of his work. It reflects the family ideal of the period. Traditional influence includes that of Murillo, especially his insistence on verisimilitude and a tendency to sentimentality. The great masters of 17th century Dutch painting and even their followers provided inspiration for the handling of religious subjects in a simple everyday manner, while in colouring Donát followed the example of the much imitated Anton Raphael Mengs, Pompeo Batoni, and Angelica Kaufmann.

20. JÁNOS MIHÁLY HESZ
The Holy Family with Saints, 1813
Oil on canvas, 61 × 48 cm
Signed bottom right: "Mih. Hesz. A pinx. Vienna 1813"
Budapest, Hungarian National Gallery
Inv. No.: FK 7088

János Mihály Hesz was the son of a sculptor from Eger. For some years beginning with 1791, he studied under Hubert Maurer in the Department of Historical Painting at the Academy in Vienna. Then he became a professor of free drawing at the highly regarded Viennese "Institutum Geometricum" (Imperial Academy of Engineering).
His ambition was to introduce into Hungary an academic approach to the study of art by creating an institution devoted to the study of art. He aspired to the same idea in his own paintings; his altar-pieces and mythological compositions are characterized by austere Neo-Classicism. The work shown here is a religious cabinet picture. In the figures of the Virgin Mary and St. Elizabeth, there are motifs taken from Raphael's famous painting. The artist's biographer considered the picture to be the most representative example of Academic Classicism in the style of Füger, who sought his models in the works of Raphael and Nicolaus Poussin.

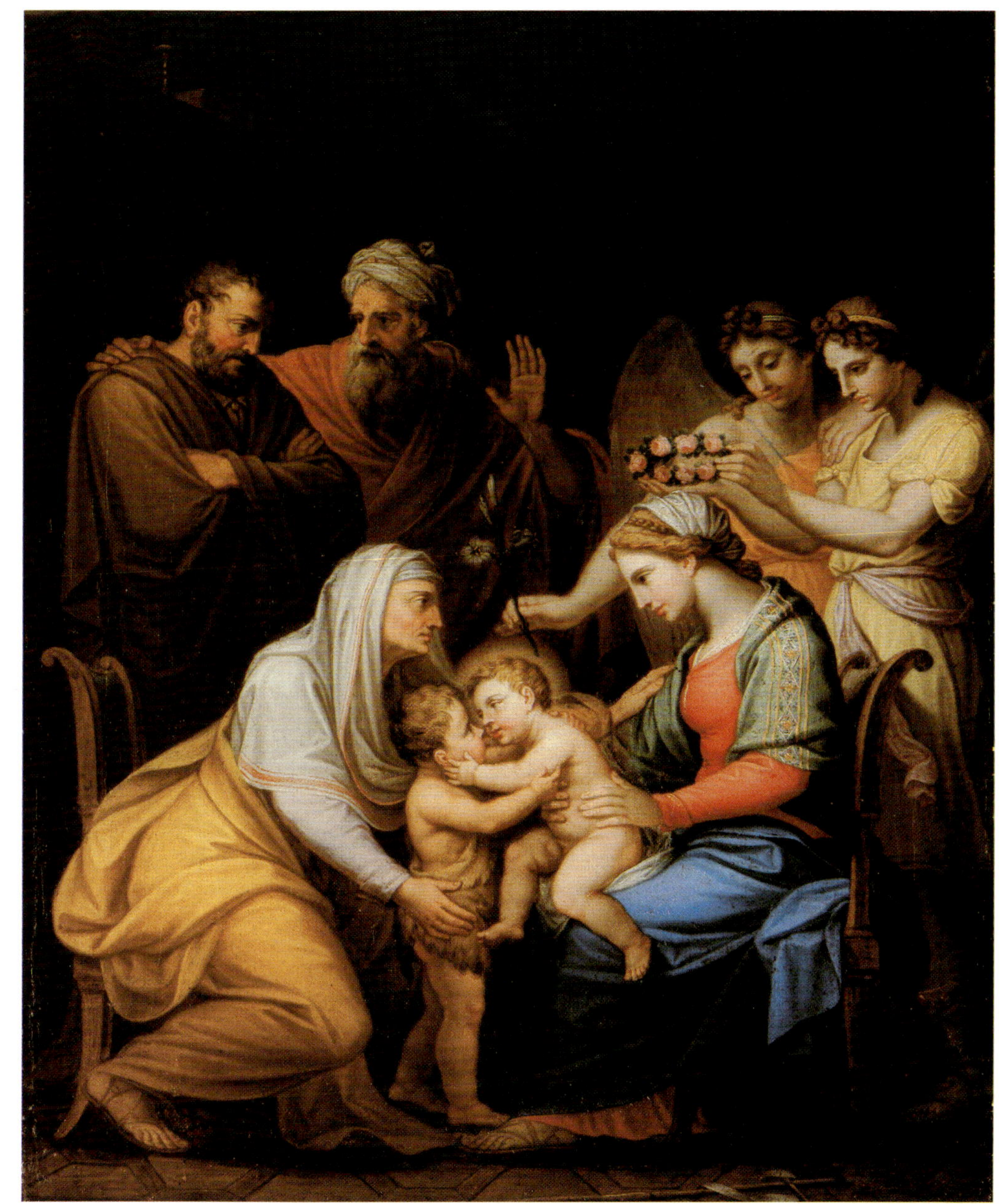

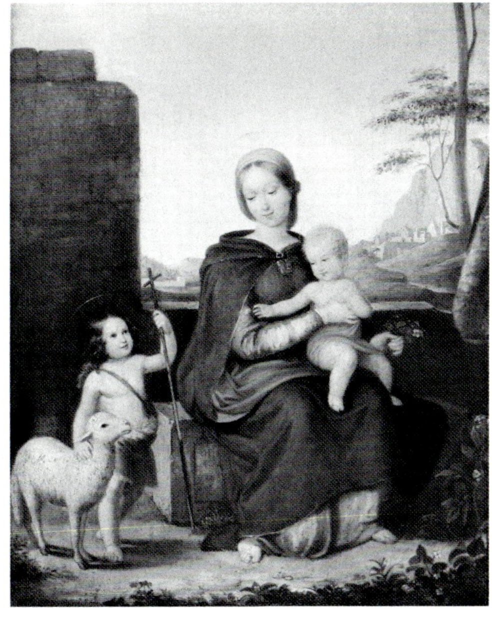

21. GÁBOR MELEGH
The Virgin Mary with the Infant Jesus and St. John the Baptist, 1820
Oil on wood, 36.8 × 18.6 cm
Unsigned
Budapest, Hungarian National Gallery
Inv. No.: FK 4875

The painter and engraver Gábor Melegh left Temesvár in 1817 to study at the Academy of Art in Vienna, where he studied until 1823. He was awarded the Gundel Prize as early as 1819 and in 1823 he won not only the Lampi Prize, but also the Royal Silver Medal, all three in Vienna. The extent to which he applied the principles of Viennese Academic painting is most clearly shown in his altar-piece sketches. This small painting on wood is an almost exact copy of a work by Raphael. It reveals great technical skill, is meticulously executed, and bears witness to the deep respect shown for the Renaissance master by 19th century Viennese and Hungarian Neo-Classical artists.

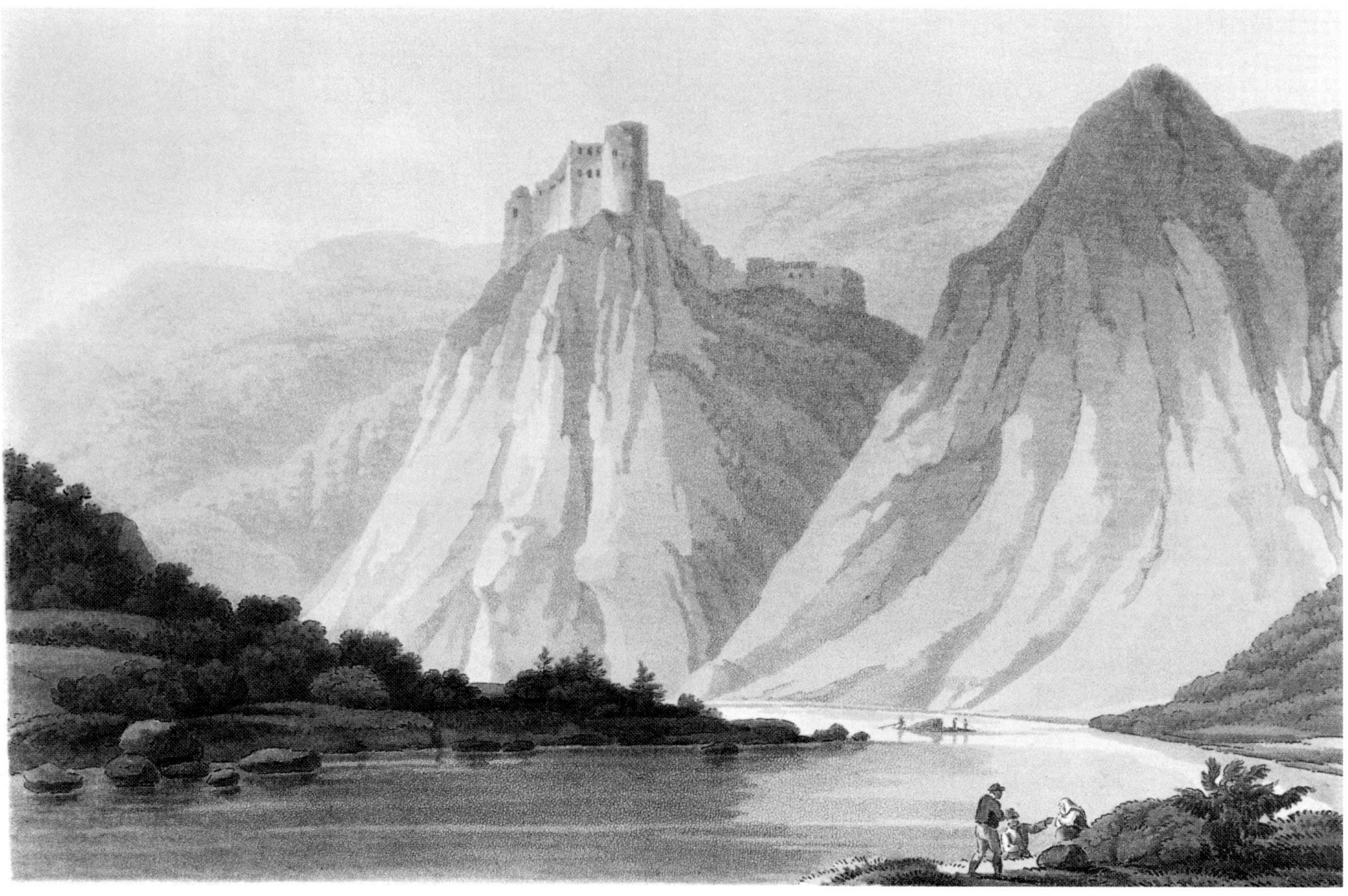

22. JOSEPH FISCHER–
W. F. SCHLOTTERBECK
Óvár, 1817

Aquatint on paper, 175 × 231 mm
Unsigned
Budapest, Museum of Fine Arts

Publications: József Fischer: *Rajzolatokban előadott utazás Magyarországon a Vág vize mentében* [Malerische Reise auf dem Waagflusse in Ungarn]. Pest, 1818. Mednyánszky Alajos: *Malerische Reise auf dem Waagflusse in Ungarn.* Pest, 1826. 2nd edition, Pest, 1844.
—as a lithograph.
Modern edition: Mednyánszky Alajos: *Festői utazás a Vág folyón Magyarországon* (Pictorial Record of a Journey Along the River Vág in Hungary). Bratislava, 1981

Joseph Fischer, a graphic artist connected in many different ways with Hungary, was curator of the Esterházy Collection from 1811 onwards, which was housed first near the Austrian capital, then in Vienna. He painted several landscapes in Hungary. About 1817 he made a series of drawings depicting views along the River Vág. These he published as aquatint reproductions together with a short text. After his death the same works served as illustrations for another more comprehensive book written by Baron Alajos Mednyánszky.

It is essentially in this form that the Hungarian public came to appreciate Fischer's work. His academic training is revealed in the care applied to every detail in order to express the individual character of a landscape. He presumably coloured the original drawings with water-colour, producing the "delicate play of shades, enchanting haze and subtle ethereal effects" praised by Kazinczy. The coloured drawings were then reproduced by Friedrich Wilhelm, a landscapist himself, using aquatint technique. This book was largely instrumental in awakening interest in and appreciation of Hungarian landscape.

23. JÁNOS JAKAB MÜLLER
Bridge over the River, 1815
Gouache on paper, 340 × 475 mm
Signed bottom left: "Joh. Müller pinx. 1815."
Košice, Východoslovenská Galeria

24. JÁNOS JAKAB MÜLLER
Summer Landscape, 1810s
Gouache on paper, 343 × 473 mm
Signed bottom left: "Joh. Müller pinx."
Košice, Východoslovenská Galeria

János Jakab Müller worked in Lőcse, between 1806 and 1827 as a teacher in the Municipal School of Drawing. József Czauczik and Károly Markó, the Elder, were among those who studied under him. He painted a series of landscapes in gouache technique and some water-colours. Of his monumental paintings there exists the altarpiece from Kassa's Lutheranian Church, in which Müller executed the landscape and Czauczik the figures. The medium-sized landscapes reproduced here presumably served as models for the School of Drawing. The technique and treatment of the subject were applied with the aim of demonstrating to pupils a method of reproducing nature directly in pencil sketches.

Müller delighted in depicting the minutest details, whether of changing light or natural movement, as well as the characteristics of townspeople and other local types. Szepes Fortress remained a favourite theme for 19th century painters. The bridges in and around Lőcse and Eperjes, the attractive streams and rivers, figures seen bathing or fishing are themes depicted in Müller's work with unaffected simplicity.

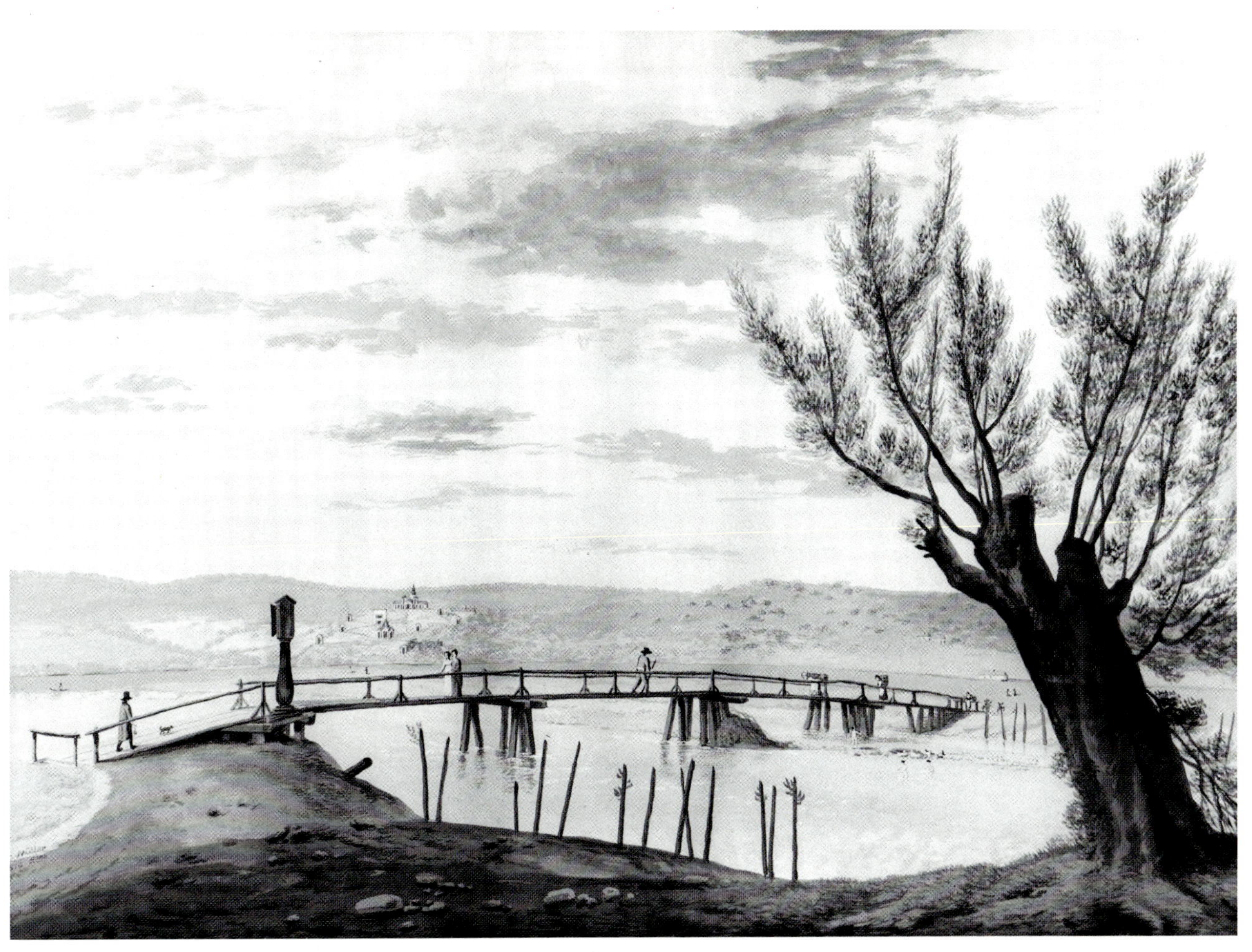

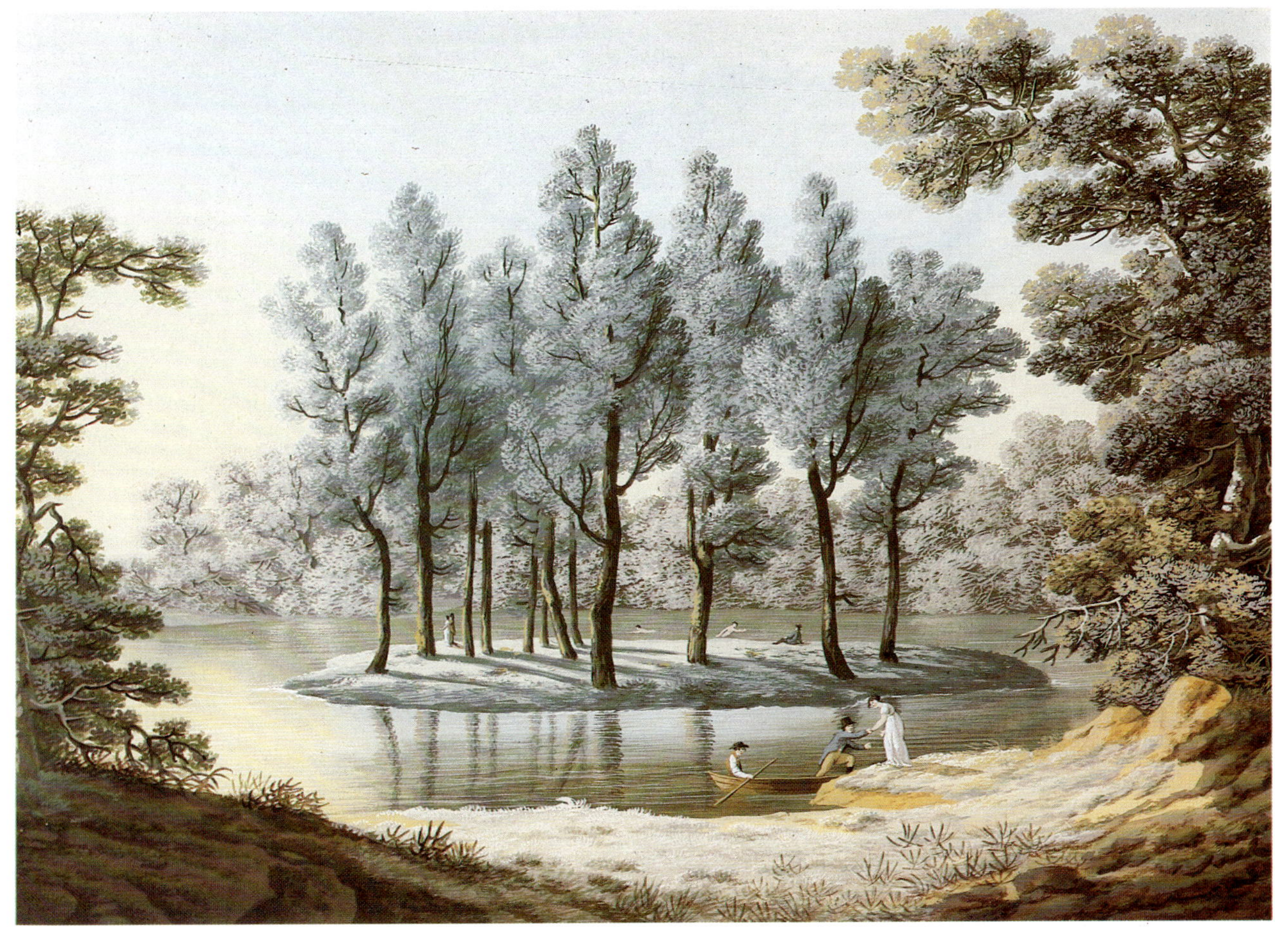

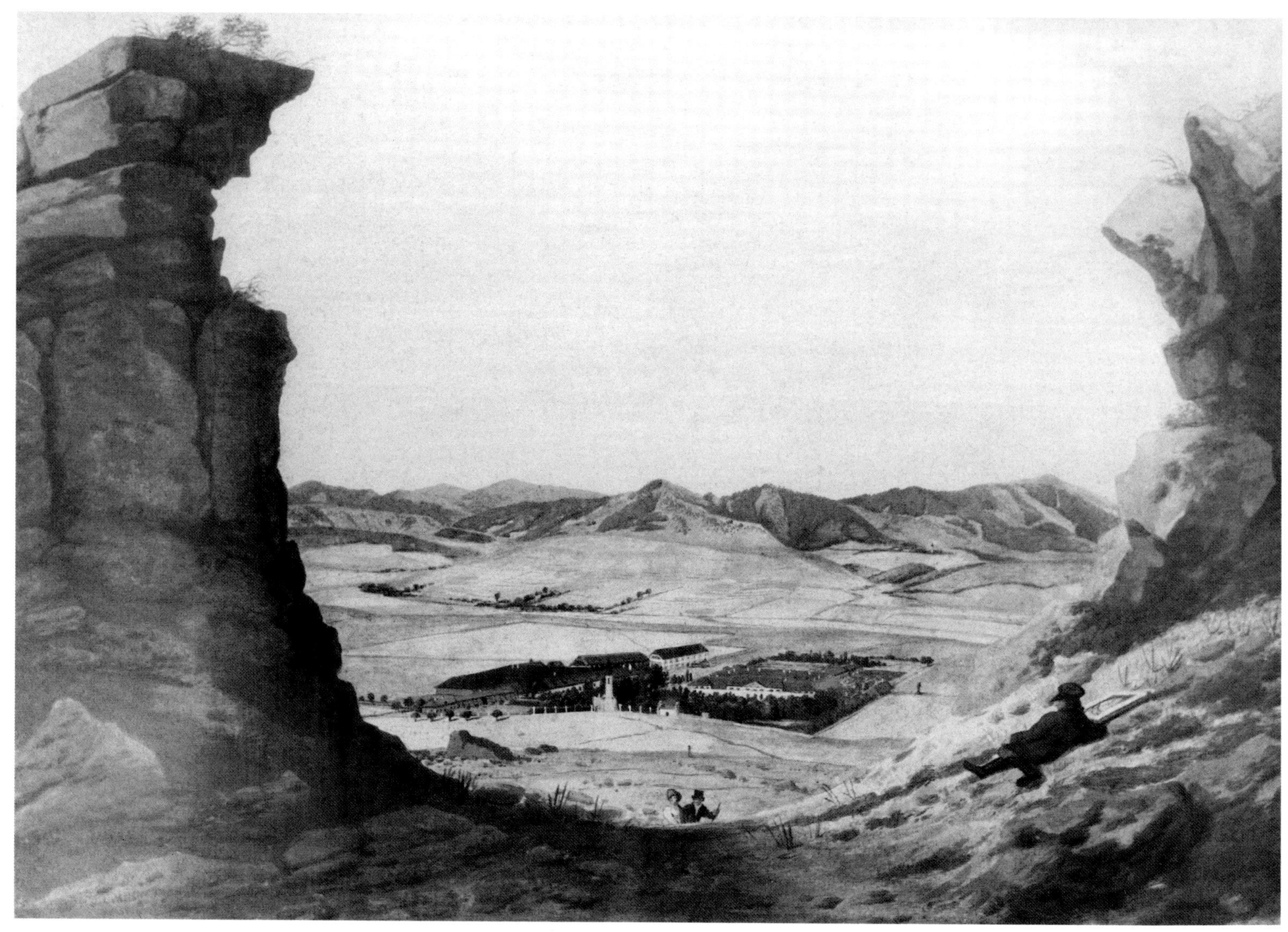

25. JÁNOS JAKAB MÜLLER
View of the Castle of Hotkóc from the Drevenyik, 1819

Gouache on paper, 340×475 mm
Signed bottom left: "John Müller pinx. 1819"
Košice, Východoslovenská Galeria

From 1810–1820 Jakab János Müller wandered about the countryside with his easel and paints, expressing his vision of the landscape, using gouache and showing a preference for large paintings.

This painting is an excellent example of his manner. In the foreground we see the painter with his sketching board as he studies the view. An elegantly dressed couple —perhaps his companions or those who commissioned the work—wave cheerfully as they climb the slope.

Down in the valley one of the famous buildings of the area can be seen—the Castle of Hotkóc, owned by the Csáky family, and its French and English gardens; the annexes and a small chapel are also visible. The castle was built in the early 18th century, but around 1810 a Neo-Classical façade was added. The Csáky family were well-known art patrons; their gardens were filled with statues, a small pavilion and exotic plants, while their castle housed some very fine paintings.

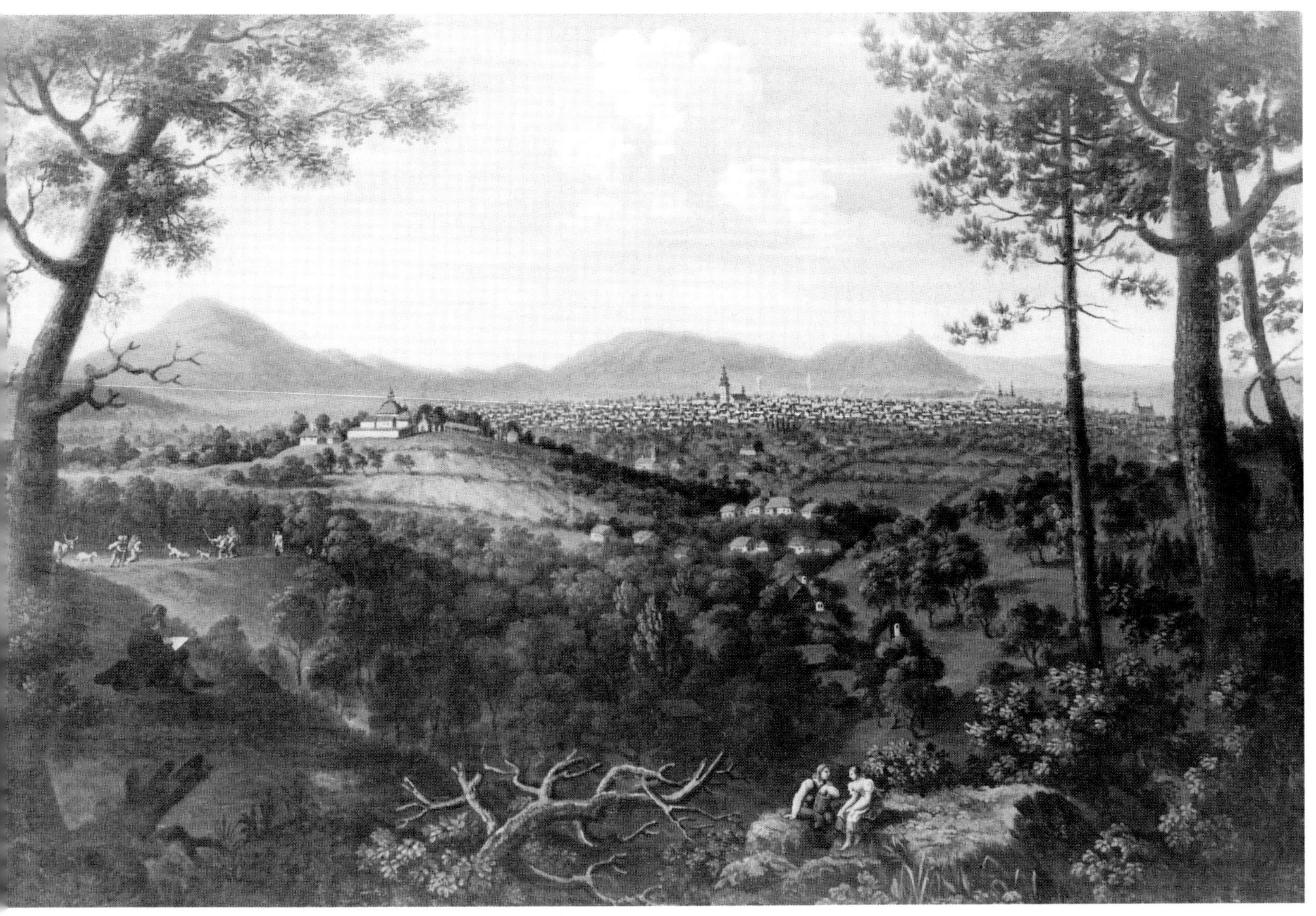

26. JÁNOS ROMBAUER
View of Eperjes, c. 1830
Oil on canvas, 75×112 cm
Unsigned
Prešov, Town Museum
Inv. No.: O-123

About 1806 at Bártfafürdő, János Rombauer met a Russian count who invited him to St. Petersburg. He subsequently lived there for nearly twenty years, completing several notable portraits commissioned by members of the Tzar's Court and by private citizens. However, Rombauer returned to Eperjes in 1824 where he continued to paint portraits and mythological compositions but he also executed landscape painting, a genre he had been deeply interested in even as a young man.

This large panoramic view of Eperjes and its environs was painted around 1830. The foreground is enriched by figures characteristic of genre-painting. Dressed in a black suit and wearing a black top hat, at work on a pencil-sketch for the painting, the painter himself can be seen sitting beneath a tree on the left. Rombauer's use of narrative detail and his accurate rendering of nature give the painting a pictorial quality that takes it beyond the range of topographic depiction as represented in some engravings and drawings of the age.

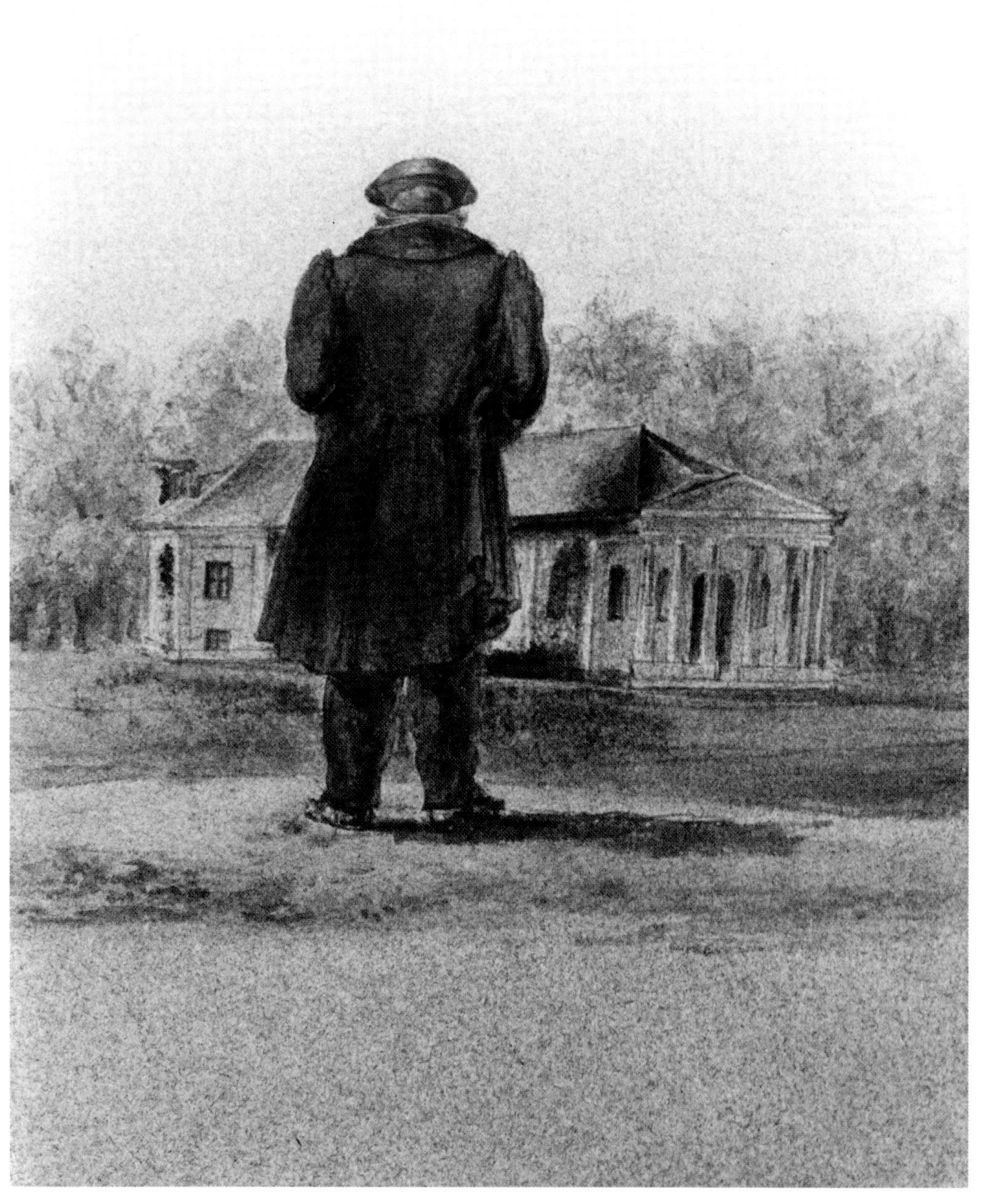

27. ANDRÁS PETRICH
In Front of Kisfaludy's House, 1831

Water-colour on blue paper, 170×111 mm
Inscription on reverse: „Kisfaludy"
Budapest, Hungarian Academy of Sciences,
The Library: Manuscript Archives
Inv. No.: K 380/83

András Petrich, an engineer and general in the Austrian army, worked around Orsova and Belgrade, then near Lake Balaton, and finally at Vác and in Buda. In his leisure time he liked to paint not only accurate landscapes, but also the people typical of each region: peasants, townspeople and noblemen alike, acquaintances and strangers —whoever happened to appear.

On this painting, "Kisfaludy's House" refers to the theatre at Balatonfüred founded by a number of benefactors including Sándor Kisfaludy who donated money for the project. Lost in admiration, a citizen—more German than Hungarian, judging by his clothes—stands in front of the new theatre.

28. ANDRÁS PETRICH
Landscape with Chamois, 1809

Gouache on paper, 630×482 mm
Signed bottom left: "Petrich, 1809"
Budapest, Hungarian National Gallery
Inv. No.: 1898/929

András Petrich was an engineer and Austrian army general who, around 1808 was engaged in a land survey near Salzburg. It was probably there that he made the sketch for his large coloured drawing, though it may have been in the Tyrol, well known for its chamois since the Middle Ages.

Craggy peaks, a snow-covered valley with chamois, a hunter lurking behind a boulder, the most minute details of the landscape are included to create an awe-inspiring composition.

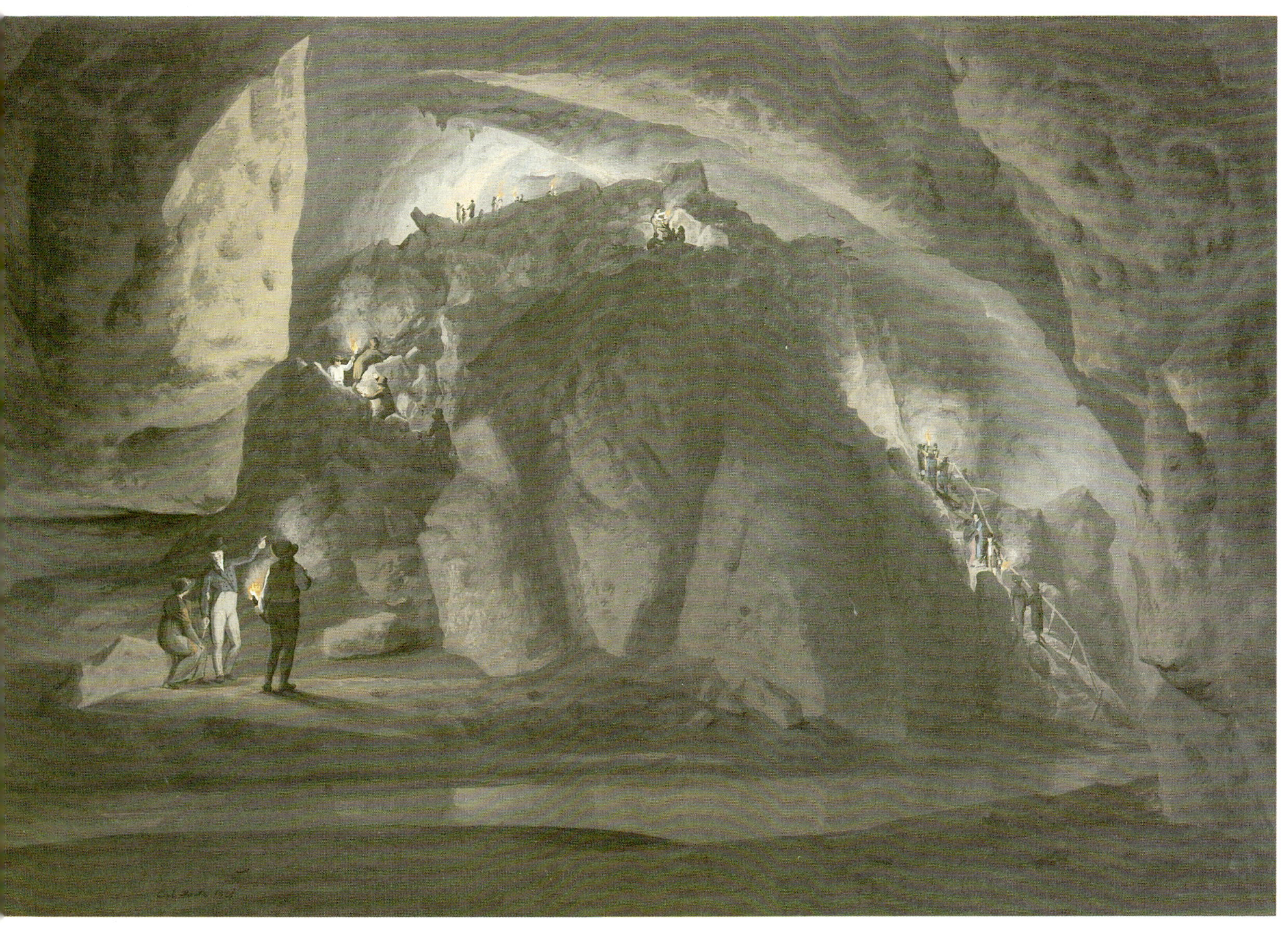

30. KÁROLY MARKÓ, the Elder
The Stalactite Caves of Aggtelek, 1820s

Gouache on paper, 462 × 650 mm
Unsigned
Inscription: "Berg Morea"
Budapest, Hungarian National Gallery
Inv. No.: 1914-34

After finishing his studies in engineering at Kolozsvár and Pest in 1818, Károly Markó worked at Lubló and Rozsnyó as a civic engineer, when he decided to become a painter. As an engineer he had worked on the episcopal estate at Rozsnyó when he was in the habit of visiting the recently discovered Stalactite Caves of Aggtelek. In 1821 he completed a series of six fairly large gouache paintings of the most remarkable phenomena in the caves. This painting is one of a series of six which the painter presumably intended to publish as a guide to this gorgeous site, a project in the tradition of Alajos Mednyánszky's "picturesque journey".

The various chambers of the caves are depicted with meticulous care, the names being given in German. We can also see groups of visitors with their guides as they admire the caves by torchlight. The series was bought by Baron József Brudern who, however, was less interested in publishing these works than in supporting the artist. With the help of his patron, Markó subsequently continued his studies at the Academy of Vienna. The complete series can now be seen in the Hungarian National Gallery.

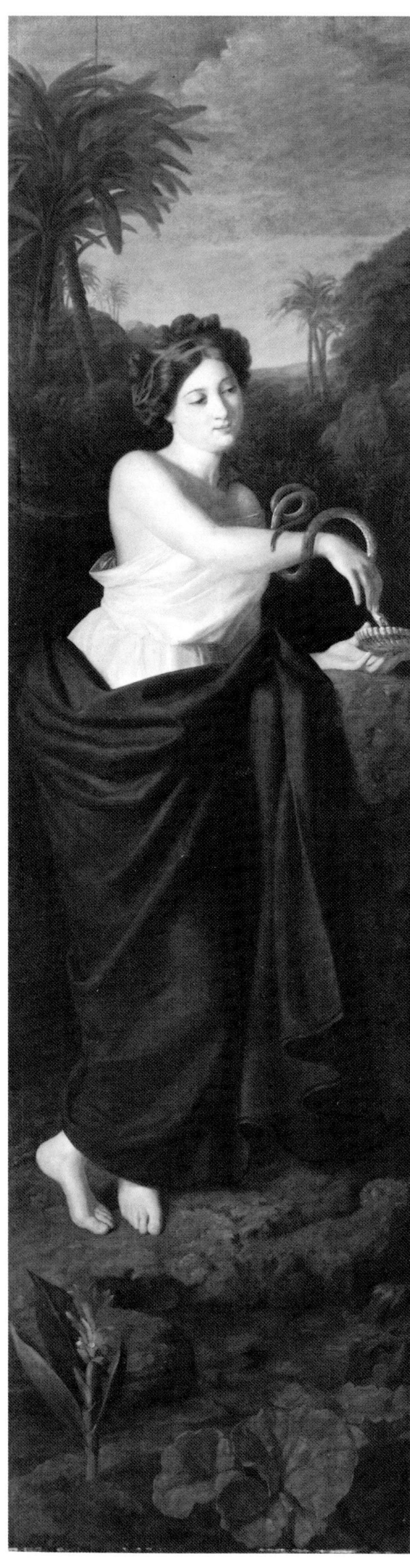

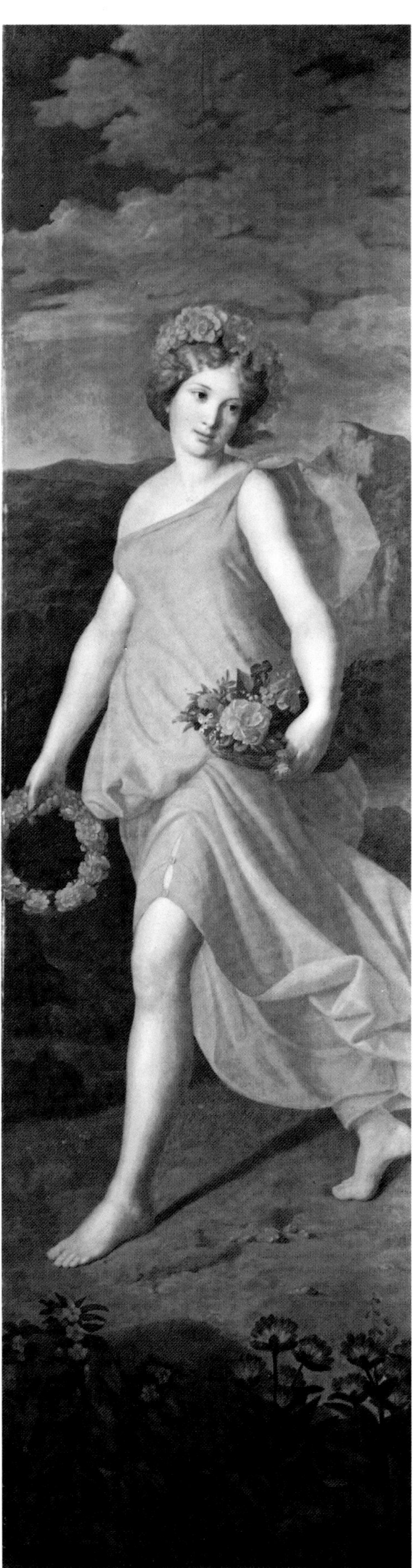

31. FERDINAND GEORG WALDMÜLLER
Two Trade-signs: Hygieia and Flora, 1820s

Oil on wood, both 250×68 cm
Vienna, Österreichische Galerie
Inv. No.: 5624

One of these trade-signs, painted by Waldmüller as a youth, represents Hygieia, goddess of health. She was a daughter of the Night or of Zeus and Themis, who lived in the wonderful garden of the Hesperides. According to another Greek source, she is the daughter of Aesculape and the granddaughter of Apollo.

The serpent twisted round her wrist, who inhabited the garden, had the power to utter many different sounds.

The other trade-sign depicts Gaea or Flora, goddess of flowers and vegetation, who with her magic herbs could make barren lands fertile.

Both paintings served to decorate an elegant pharmacy in Vienna, where there were also other pictures advertising the wonders of medicine and the healing power of herbs and plants.

The trade-signs in Vienna such as these were more exquisite in taste, reflected mythology more accurately, and displayed more pictorial sensibility than those painted in Hungary.

32. JAKAB WARSÁGH
Juno: Trade-sign of a perfume shop in Buda, 1830s

Oil on wood, 173×108 cm
Signed bottom right: "Warságh"
Budapest Historical Museum, the Kiscelli Museum
Inv. No.: 15.520

Jakab Warságh, born in Buda, was a portraitist and decorative painter. His studies under Hermann Neefe, who worked for the theatre in Buda, may have helped him to achieve the expressive power and vivid colouring characteristic of his signboards and altar-pieces.

According to art historian Károly Lyka, "Warságh's signboards were greeted by unpretentious contemporary reporters as cultural events."

Trade-signs sometimes depicted historical figures or landscapes. From Baroque emblem painting onwards it had been fashionable to depict a mythological figure offering the owner's wares. On this trade-sign of a Buda perfumery, Juno, Queen of the Gods and wife of Jupiter, seated in her golden chariot drawn by two peacocks, becomes the symbol of the ideal beauty the goods of the shop will help its patrons achieve.

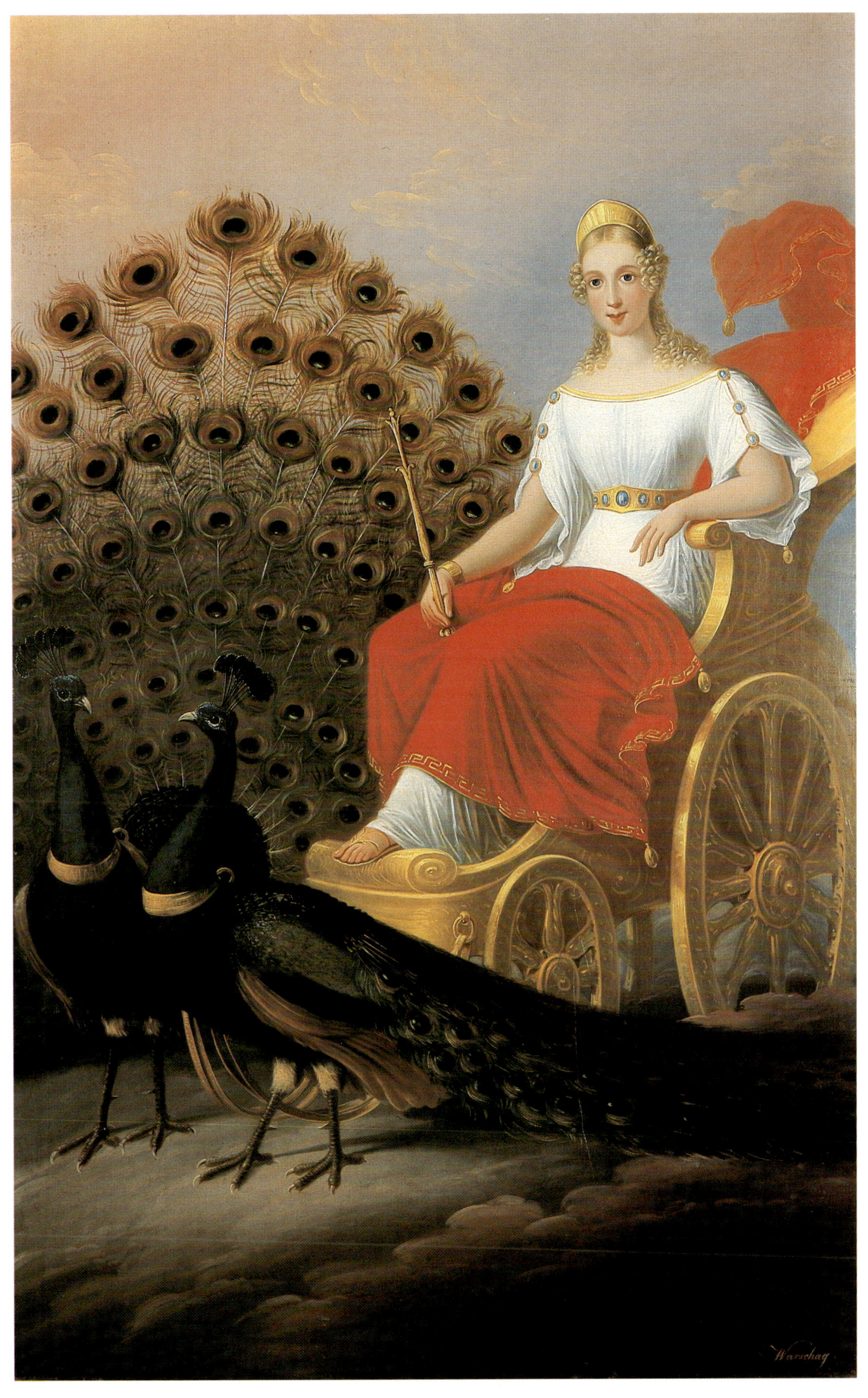

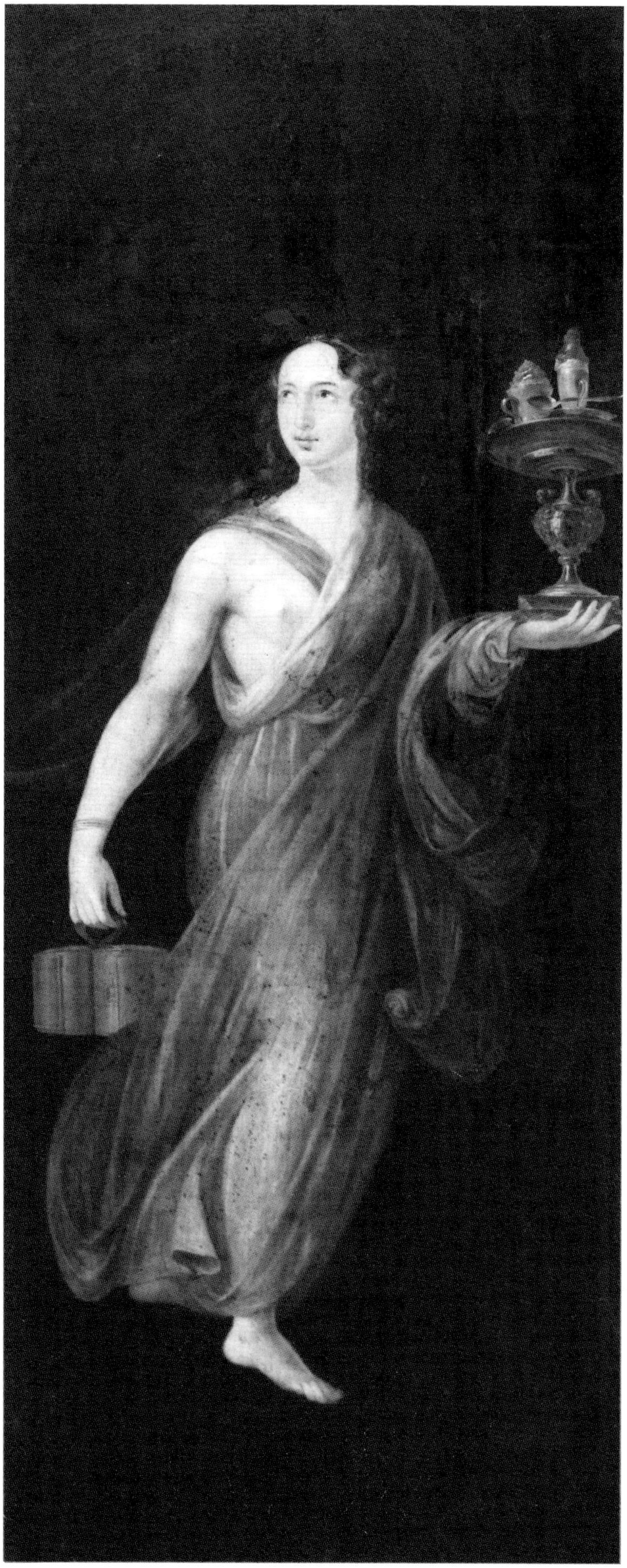

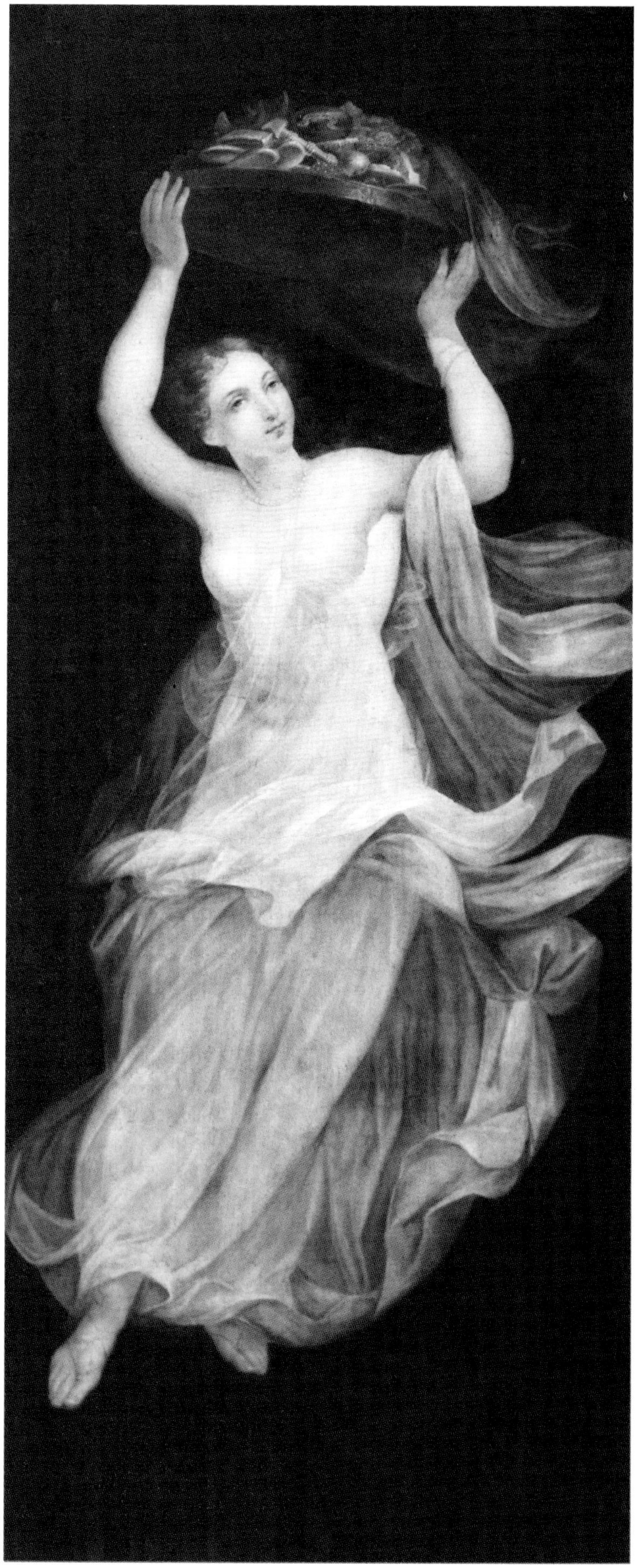

33. FERDINAND LÜTGENDORFF
Two Trade-signs with allegorical figures, painted for the Kőszeghy Confectioner's in Pozsony, 1830s
Oil on wood, both 238 × 94 cm
Bratislava, Mestská Galeria
Inv. No.: A 2065 — 2066

Baron Ferdinand Lütgendorff, a graphic artist and painter who was born in Würzburg and for years worked in Pozsony, did not find it beneath his dignity to paint trade-signs as well as portraits and altar-pieces. For a confectionery in his home town, he depicted Flora and Ceres, the goddesses of Spring and Summer. Compared with Jakab Warságh's technically assured Juno, Lütgendorff's lightly draped female figures have a clumsiness which reveals the painter's lack of experience, but they served their purpose, and probably appealed to the public taste of the times.

34. JÁNOS ROMBAUER
Spring (Flora, May), 1825–1835
Oil on canvas, 46 × 36 cm
Unsigned
Prešov, Mestská Galeria
Inv. No.: O 91

This portrait of a young girl in mythological costume was once believed to be that of the artist's daughter, who died at an early age. However, it is more likely a sketch for a commissioned series of paintings personifying the Four Seasons. The lack of individuality in the features, the stiff bearing of the figure and the over-elaborate arrangement of garlands seem to support the second view of the work's inception.

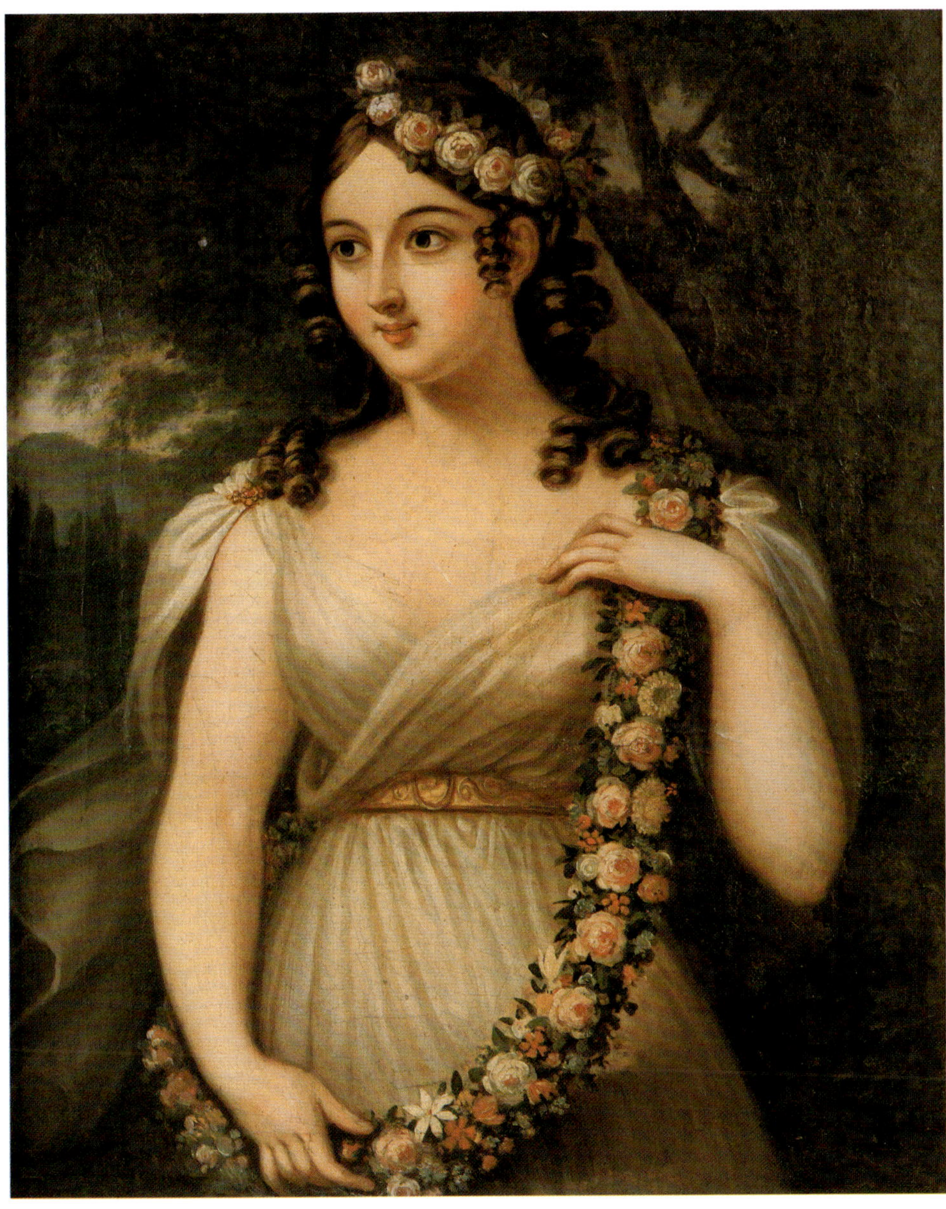

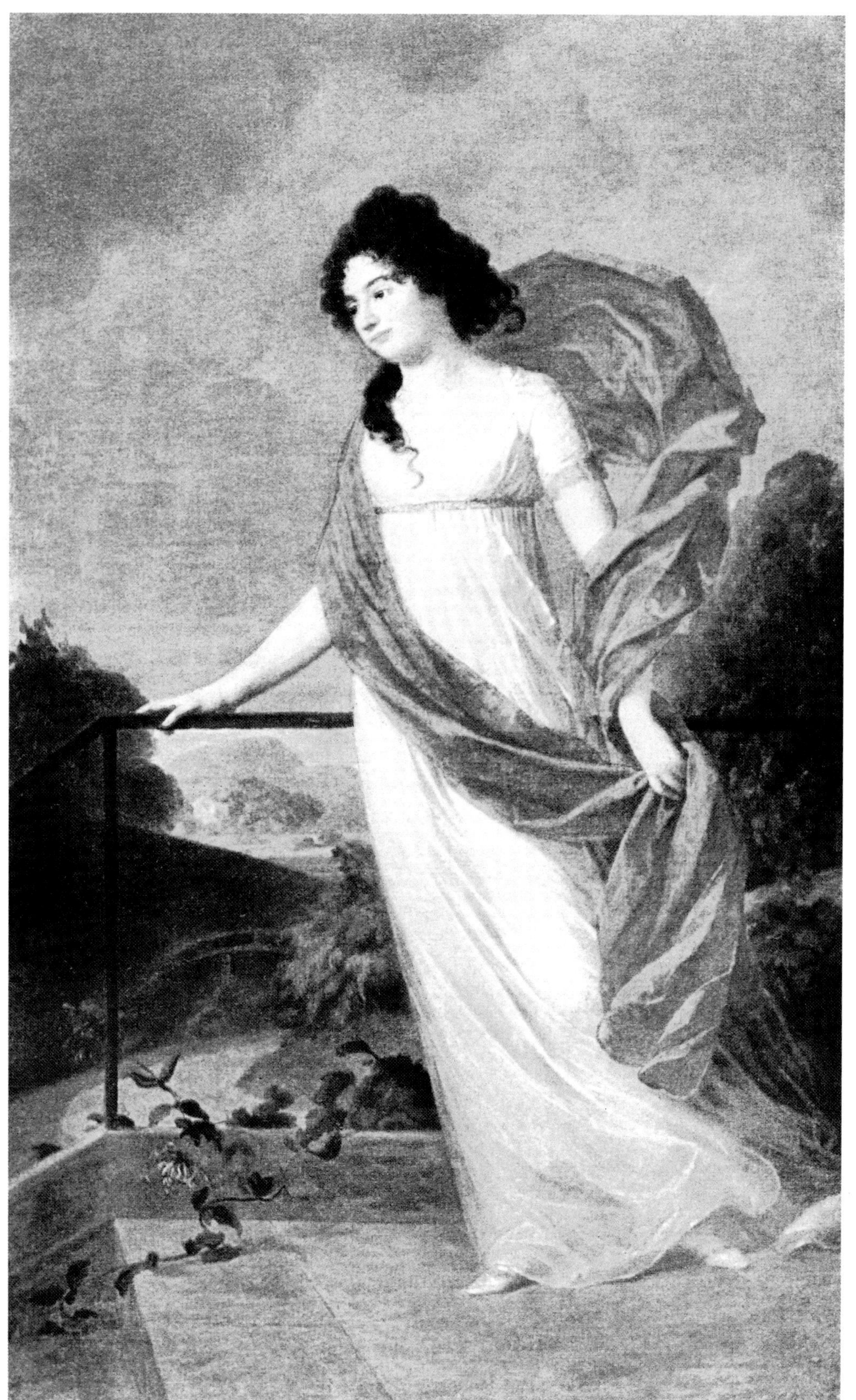

35. JOHANN FRIEDRICH AUGUST TISCHBEIN
Portrait of Countess Theresie Fries, 1801

Oil on canvas, 218 × 128 cm
Signed bottom left: "Tischbein p. 1801"
Hamburg, Kunsthalle
Inv. No.: 604

Johann Friedrich August Tischbein was one of a celebrated line of landscape and portrait painters who around the turn of the 18th–19th centuries adapted French and English artistic conventions. Tischbein himself studied and was active in a number of European cities, including Paris, St. Petersburg, Rome, Berlin and Dresden. In 1800, after the death of Adam Friedrich Oeser, he became a teacher at Leipzig's School of Drawing. A series of portraits shows his preference for painting elegantly dressed aristocrats strolling in leafy surroundings. Several paintings depicting members of the Fries family have now been catalogued.
This type of portrait was later undertaken by Tischbein's pupils.

36. JÓZSEF CZAUCZIK
Girl Fishing, 1818

Oil on canvas, 22 × 18 cm
Signed bottom right: "Joseph Czauczik 1818"
Spišská Nová Ves, Museum and Gallery; on exhibit at Markušovce, The Castle

It is not certain whether József Czauczik conceived the idea for this small picture himself, or whether it is the copy of another painter's work. While Johann Friedrich August Tischbein's influence can be traced from antecedents, the vivid colours unmistakably suggest Czauczik's personal contribution. The heroine could well be the leading lady in a late comedy by Károly Kisfaludy: an attractive young girl of noble birth sits on a river bank, fishing. The red scarf flapping round her shoulders is a vivid and arresting motif. The girl is being watched by young men, half-hidden behind a hill.
Despite its awkwardness, Czauczik's excursion into genre-painting has a special charm of its own.

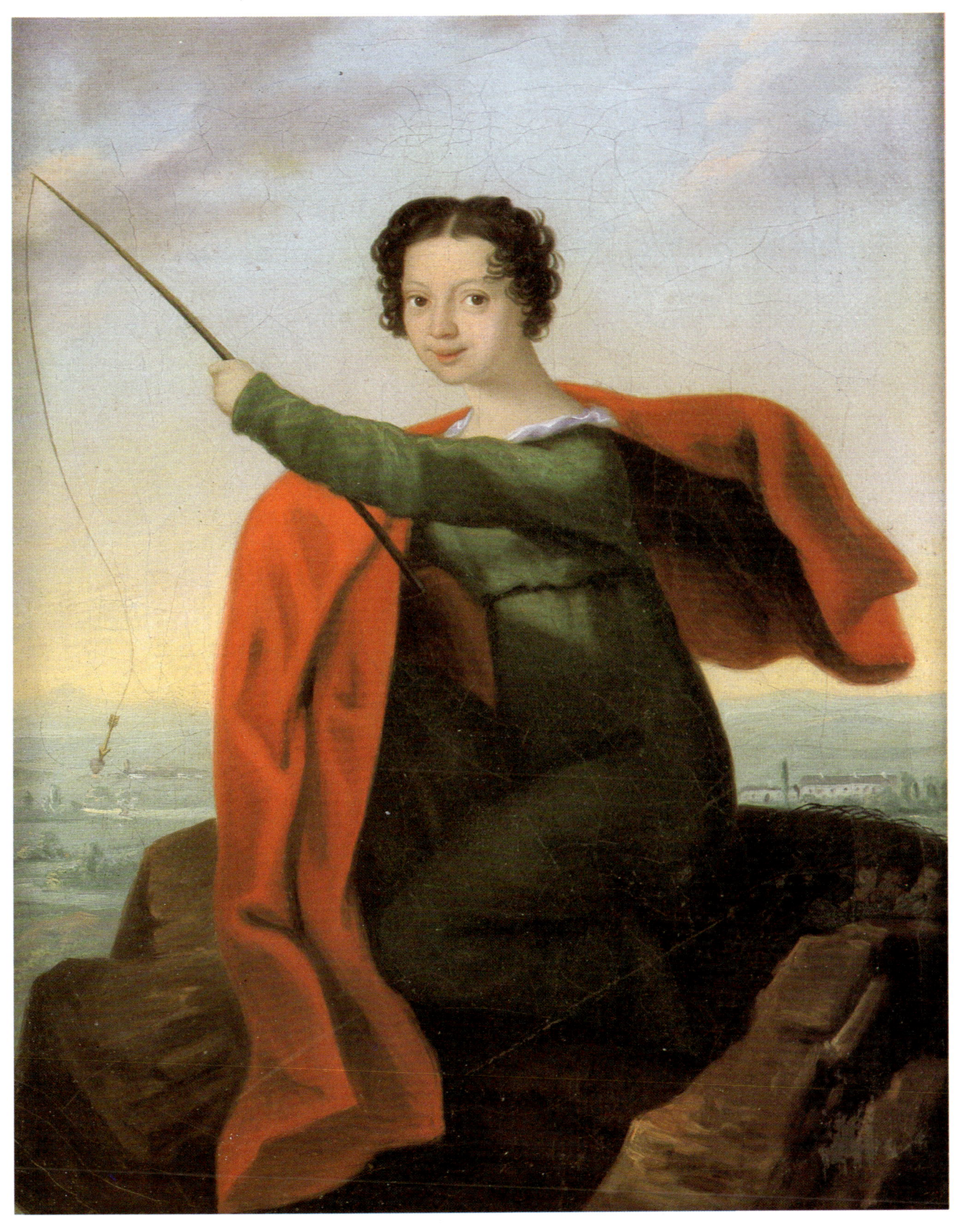

37. DANIEL HAUER
Drawing for a Cartographical Analysis, 1804

Indian ink, water-colour on paper,
620 × 945 mm
Signed bottom right: "Hauer Daniel 1804"
Budapest, Hungarian Academy of Sciences,
Manuscript Archives
Inv. No.: Portfolio I of Miscellaneous
Drawings

At the beginning of the 19th century the first aim of the Imperial Academy of Engineering in Vienna was to produce engineers who were primarily land-surveyors or "geometers", as they were then so appropriately called. Their job was to survey and make charts of the whole of Austria and Hungary. Basic courses for training engineers for this vast enterprise were also offered in provincial towns. The drawing reproduced here is part of a series from Buda or Győr. The aim was to demonstrate how to transpose the measures of a landscape into graphic proportion.

38. FERENC NEUHAUSER, Jr.
Forest Road near Nagyszeben, 1822

Lithograph on paper,
553 × 678 mm
Inscribed bottom left: "Fr. Neuhauser del. ad Natura 1822"
Budapest, the Rudolf Bedő Collection

The artist's father, Franz Adam (1734–1785), was himself a master-draughtsman in Nagyszeben. His four sons were all draughtsmen and graphic artists. One of them was called Ferenc (Franz), which has often led to identification problems for art historians.

Ferenc Neuhauser, Jr. studied in Vienna and in 1783 opened his own school of drawing. Between 1785 and 1836 he supervised several institutions in Nagyszeben, the most important being the Normal High School, and a school of drawing for apprentices.

Several of Neuhauser's life-genre drawings and landscapes were reproduced at the Institute of Lithography in Nagyszeben, founded in 1821, and without doubt this is the origin of this lithograph too. In the inscription the artist declares that his work was drawn from nature: the forest road, the covered wagon, the man walking in front of it, the elderly couple resting with their animals under a tree. Géza Galavics, a Hungarian expert who recently carried out research on works by the Neuhauser family, has pointed out that the composition of the drawing places it within the tradition of early Dutch landscape painting. On the other hand, the work indicates that Neuhauser's intention was to apply to Hungarian landscapes and genre-painting the techniques of composition he had learned at the various Academies and in the Bruckenthal Museum of Nagyszeben.

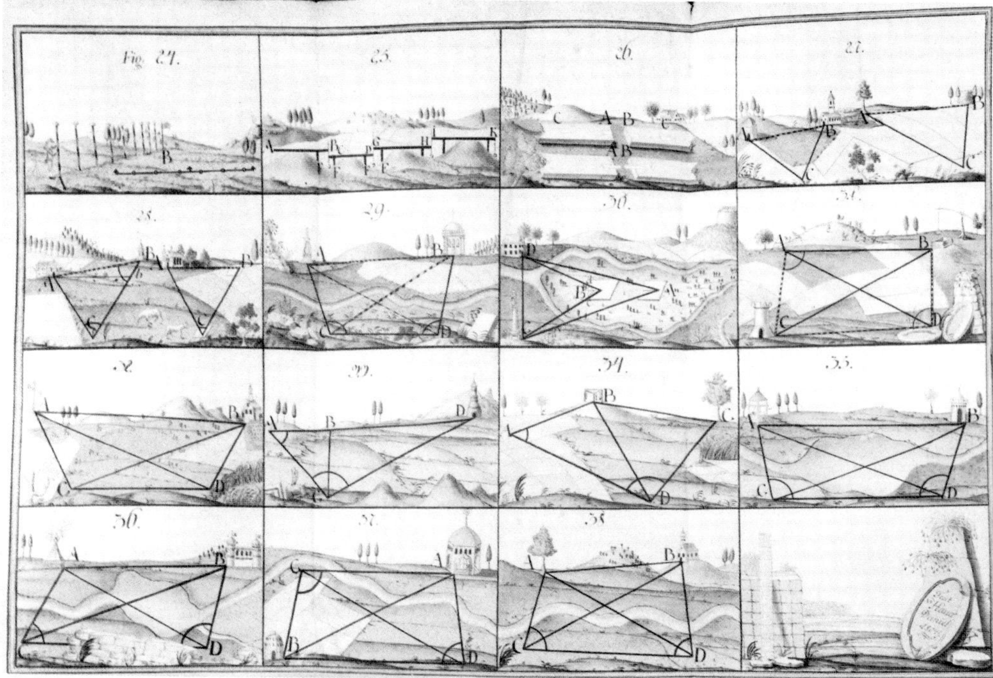

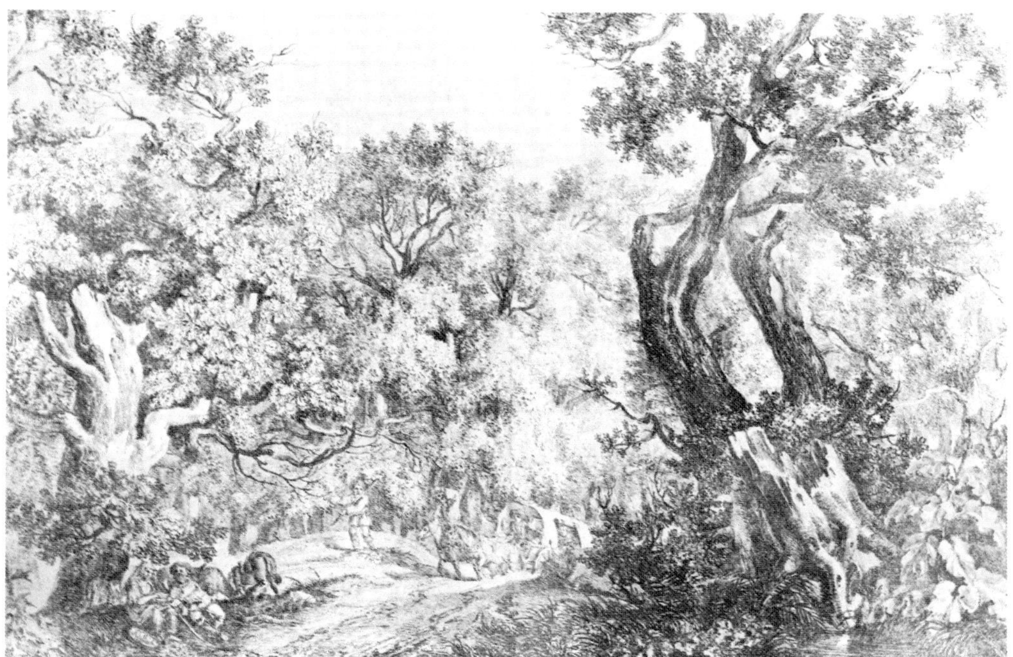

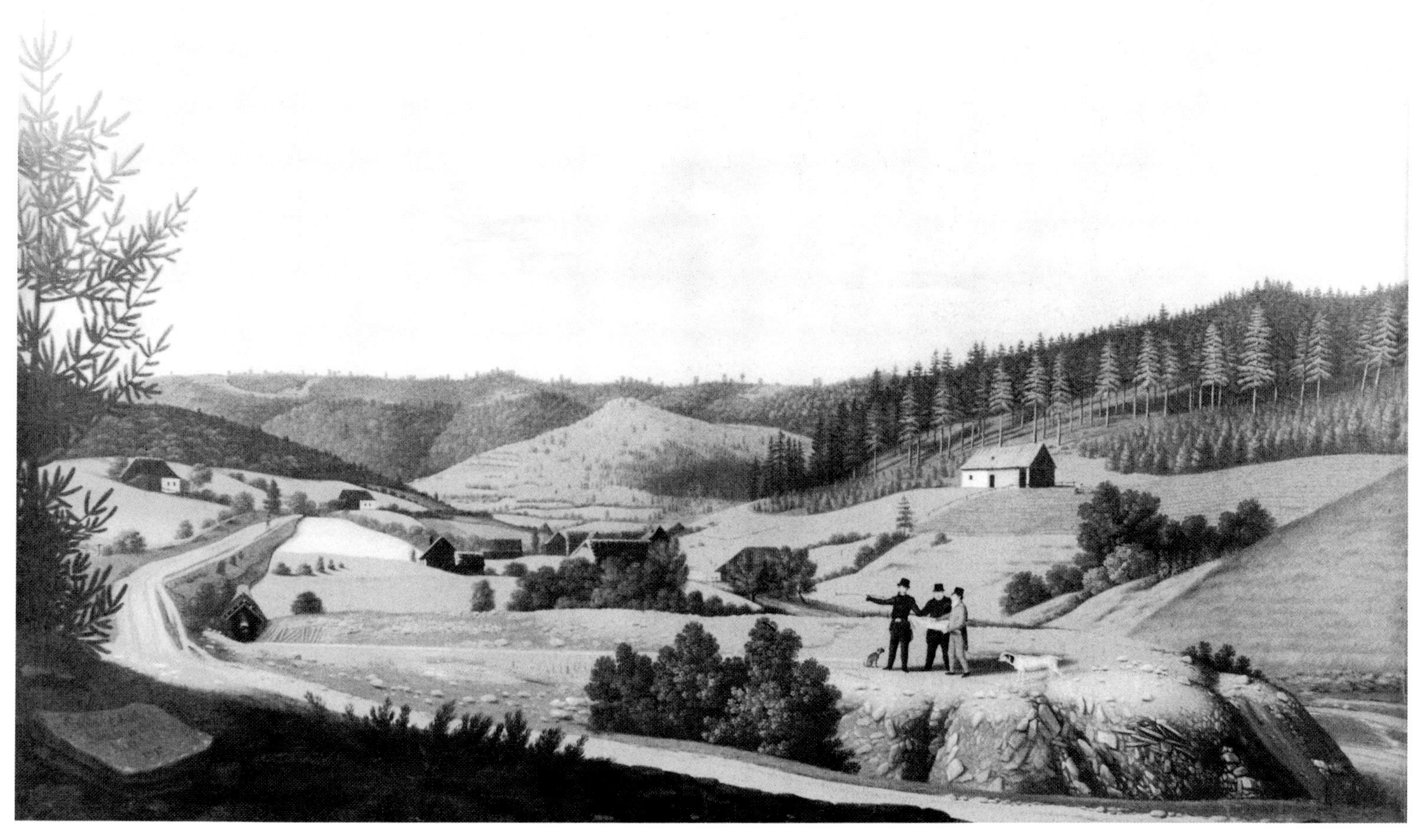

39. JÓZSEF CZAUCZIK
View of Rudnabánya, 1815
Oil on canvas, 87×123 cm
Inscription: "Rochus Erbstrollers Ansicht in der
Rotterbach. 1815"
Košice, Technické Museum

This landscape is a typical example of the work of those artists whose main aim was to represent nature as faithfully as possible. From a viewpoint above the valley, Czauczik has placed in his composition every single bush and hillside exactly as he sees them; from the vantage point a geometer occupies. The three figures holding out a plan are surveying the area with a view to opening up a new pit of the Rudnabánya mine.

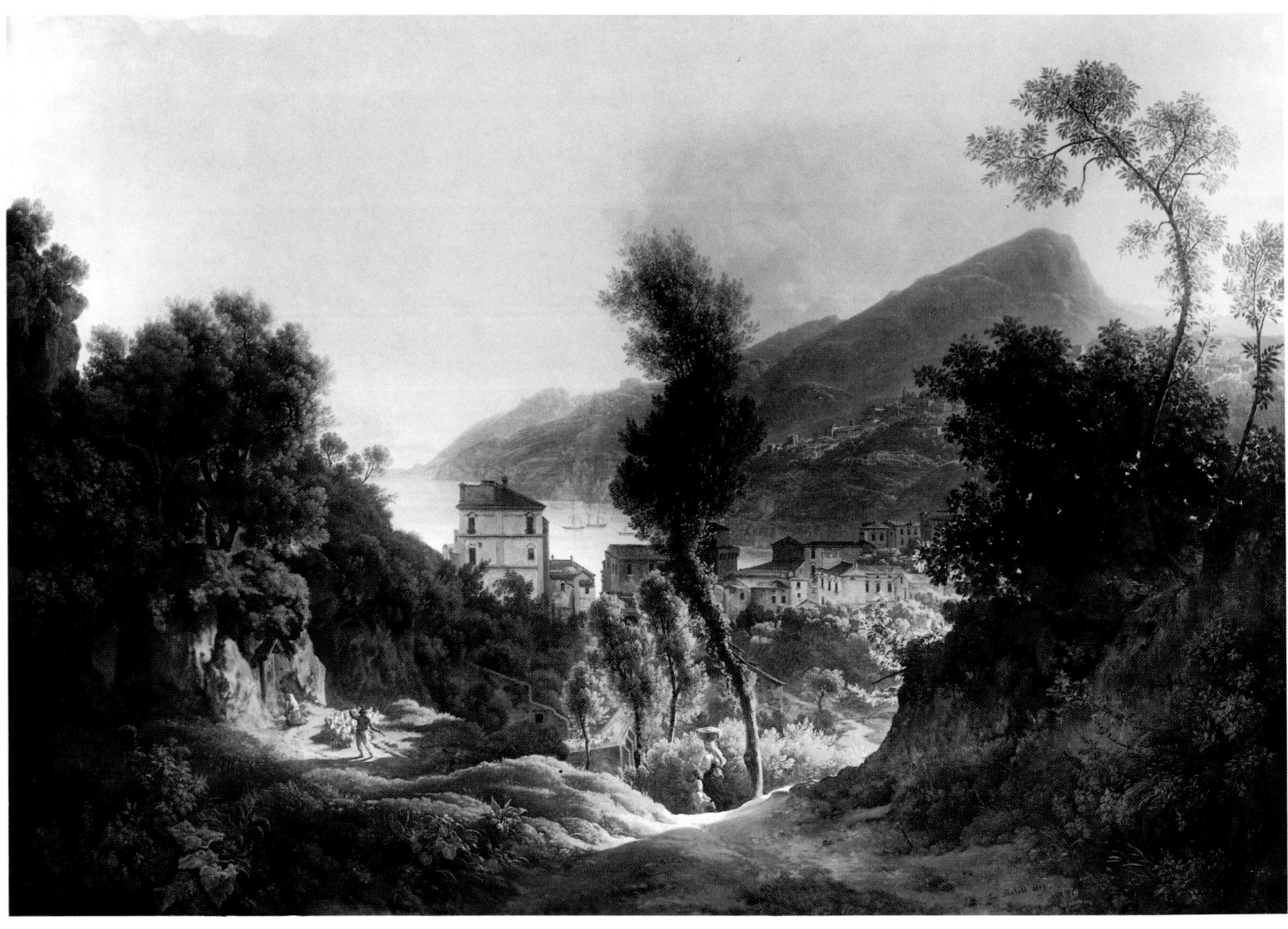

40. JOSEPH REBELL
View of Vietri, 1819

Oil on canvas, 90×130 cm
Signed bottom right: "Jos. Rebell 1819"
Vienna, Österreichische Galerie
Inv. No.: 2369

In the early 19th century, landscape painting was still associated with the meticulously observed and detailed plans used by land surveyors, but at the same time there was an attempt to transpose reality in the process of creating higher Academic art. Although representatives of classical landscape painting —for instance the much respected Joseph Rebell who in 1824 was appointed Director of the Belvedere Collection in Vienna—thought it essential to study every detail of a landscape, they nevertheless transposed the various elements in order to create composition with an artistic significance that went beyond mere topographical representation. Typical elements of such compositions were a dark foreground, a middleground with delicate effects of light and shade, and a townscape or mountain landscape extending into a panoramic background. In all these paintings a winding path on which figures can be seen leads from the foreground towards the central area.

Rebell's paintings became the standard models for art schools. A contemporary copy of this painting may be seen in the Hungarian Academy of Sciences.

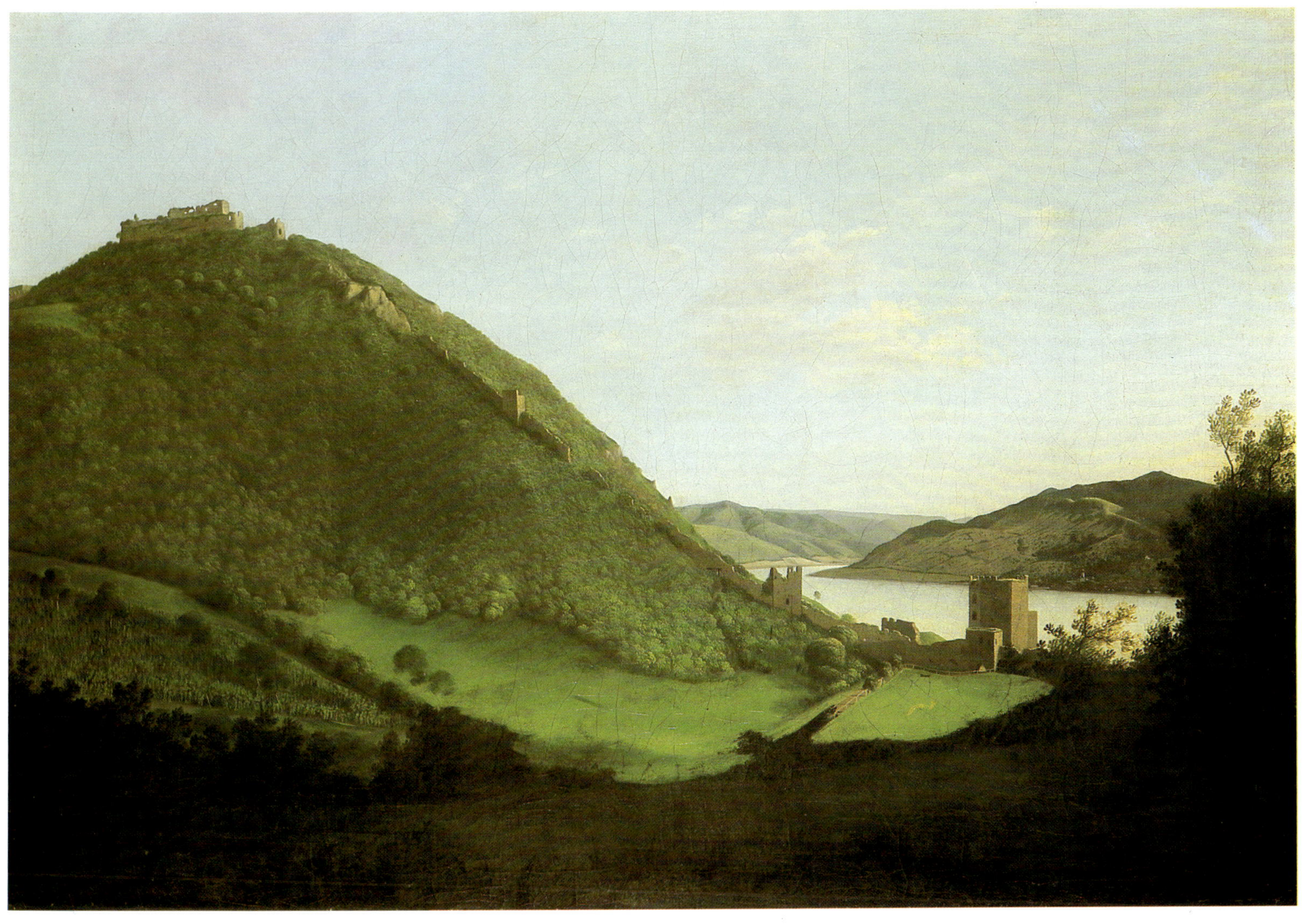

41. KÁROLY MARKÓ, the Elder
Visegrád, 1828–1830
Oil on canvas, 58.5 × 83 cm
Unsigned
Budapest, Hungarian National Gallery
Inv. No.: FK 3097

Károly Markó, the Elder went beyond the
style which art historian Károly Lyka described—perhaps too severely—as "the
mediocre and petty approach to nature typical of Szepes County". This he achieved not
only because of his natural talent, but also
because he had studied and worked so
laboriously during his years in Vienna. He
had a clear understanding of the artistic execution of landscape painting as well as
a knowledge of the historical associations of
the locality. He was aware of the current appeal of historical landscape painting in Hungary when he painted his *Visegrád,* a work
which came to be known as one of the first
purely Hungarian landscapes. It is classified
as a topographical landscape, for it provides
us with a view, in clear daylights of the steep
hill, the Tower of King Solomon, the Upper

Fortress and the medieval stone wall, without the addition of further motifs.

Károly Markó, the Elder did not resort to
Romanticism when he painted the hills and
the medieval ruins; yet we can feel his concern for historical landscape. In this respect
his approach is more closely related to
Kazinczy's Neo-Classical, precise, matter-
of-fact description than to Kisfaludy's
elegiac work entitled *Visegrád;* yet later, this
painting was seen to reflect the approach of
both poets to the subject.

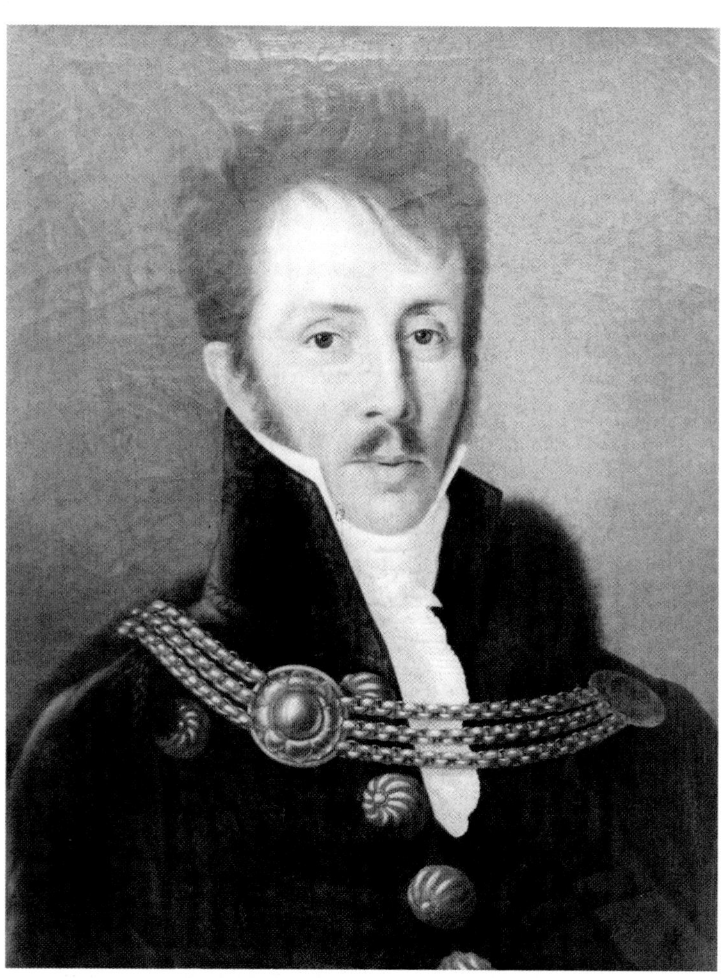

42. JÓZSEF CZAUCZIK
Portrait of Count Emmanuel Csáky, c. 1825

Oil on canvas, 65 × 49 cm
Inscription on reverse: "Count Emmanuel Csáky"
Spišská Nová Ves, Museum and Gallery, Castle Markušovce

The inscription on the reverse side of the painting identifies the sitter as Count Emmanuel Csáky, a famous patron and collector of art. The picture, formerly housed at Hotkóc Castle, later at Márkusfalva Castle, was acquired by the Museum of Igló together with other items from the Csáky Collection and family portrait gallery.

Artists commissioned by the Csáky family included Friedrich von Amerling, Anton Einsle, János Donát, Johann Jakob Stunder, János Rombauer and József Czauczik. Emmanuel Csáky lived in great style in Kassa. His collection of paintings, open to the public, was much praised by the writer Gergely Berzeviczy as early as 1810.

When Czauczik, who had studied at the Vienna Academy, painted the portrait of Emmanuel Csáky, he was already a mature artist. He portrays the Count as a Romantic, his hair short but tousled, his moustache clipped above a sensuous mouth, his handsome features set off by his high white collar.

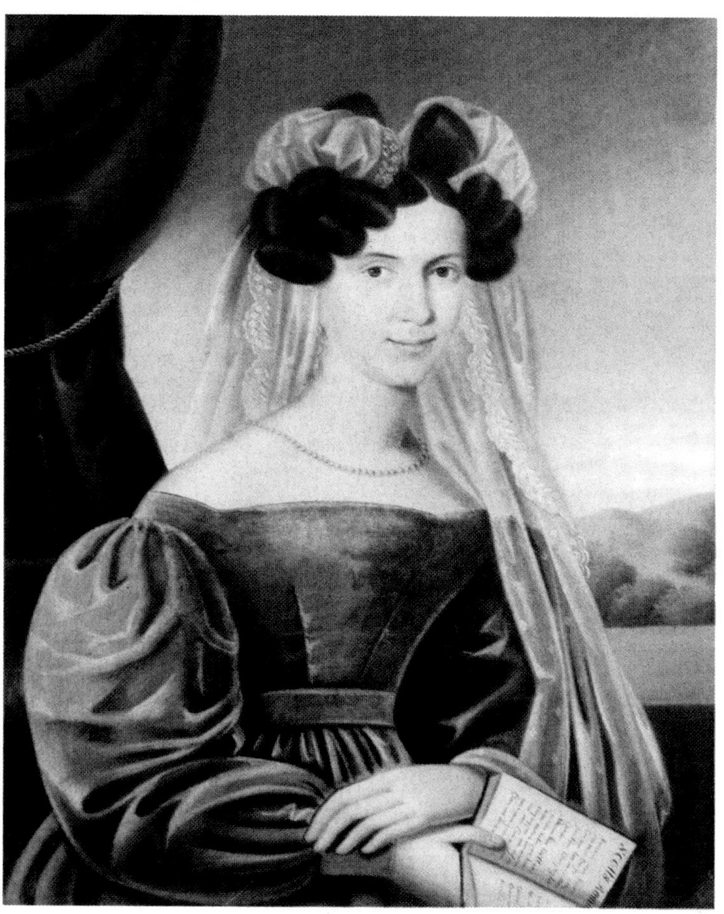

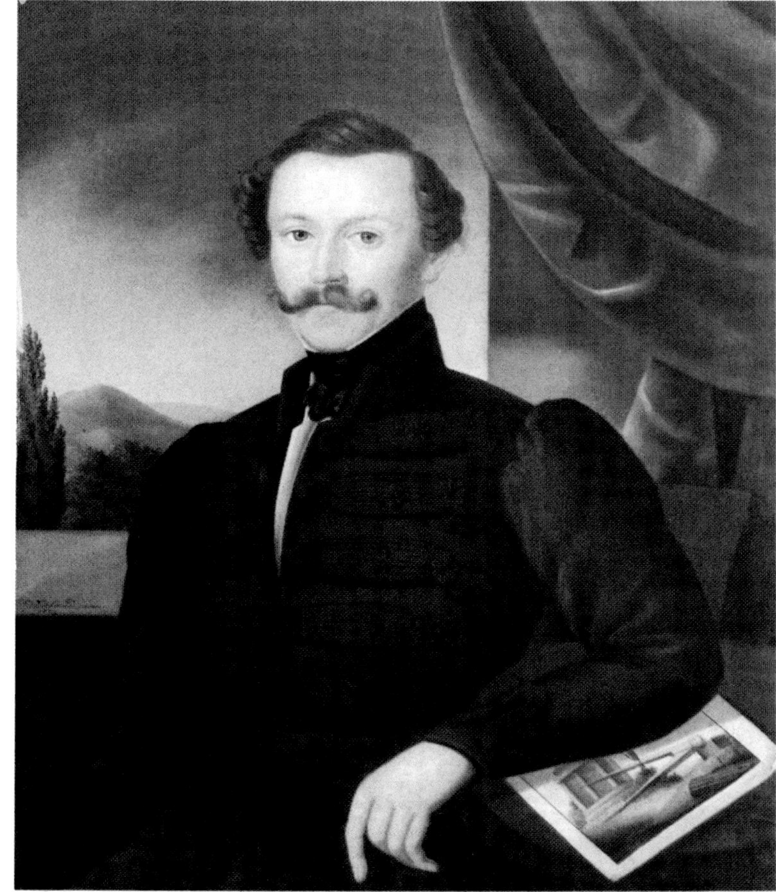

45. JÁNOS ROMBAUER
Portrait of Sámuel Steinhübl,
Merchant of Eperjes, 1804
Oil on canvas, 76 × 61 cm
Signed bottom left: "Rombauer pinxit 1804"
Bratislava, National Gallery
Inv. No.: 0 2512

According to art historian Kornél Divald,
the young János Rombauer worked as an apprentice in the shop of the merchant represented on this portrait. The painter seems
to have kept in contact with Steinbühl even
after he took up painting and the picture
might well have been a trade-sign for display
in the shop. The ship in the background,
laden with Oriental goods, symbolizes the
merchant's trading interests in far off countries.

43. CARL WIELAND
Portrait of a Lady, 1832
Pastel on paper, 67 × 55.8 cm
Košice, Východoslovenská Galéria
Inv. No.: K 579

44. CARL WIELAND
Portrait of a Nobleman, 1832
Pastel on paper, 67 × 55.5 cm
Signed left: "C. Wieland pinx 1832"
Košice, Východoslovenská Galéria
Inv. No.: K 560

At the beginning of the 19th century Carl
Wieland was active in Pest–Buda and in the
small towns of Northern Hungary. We do
not know the details of his career, but it
seems that he may have worked in Pest from
1820 to 1830 and in Késmárk between 1833
and 1840. These two portraits in pastel, representing respectively a nobleman with an
interest in architecture and his wife reading
a novel by Sir Walter Scott, reflect the contemporary interest in culture and are therefore of documentary value.

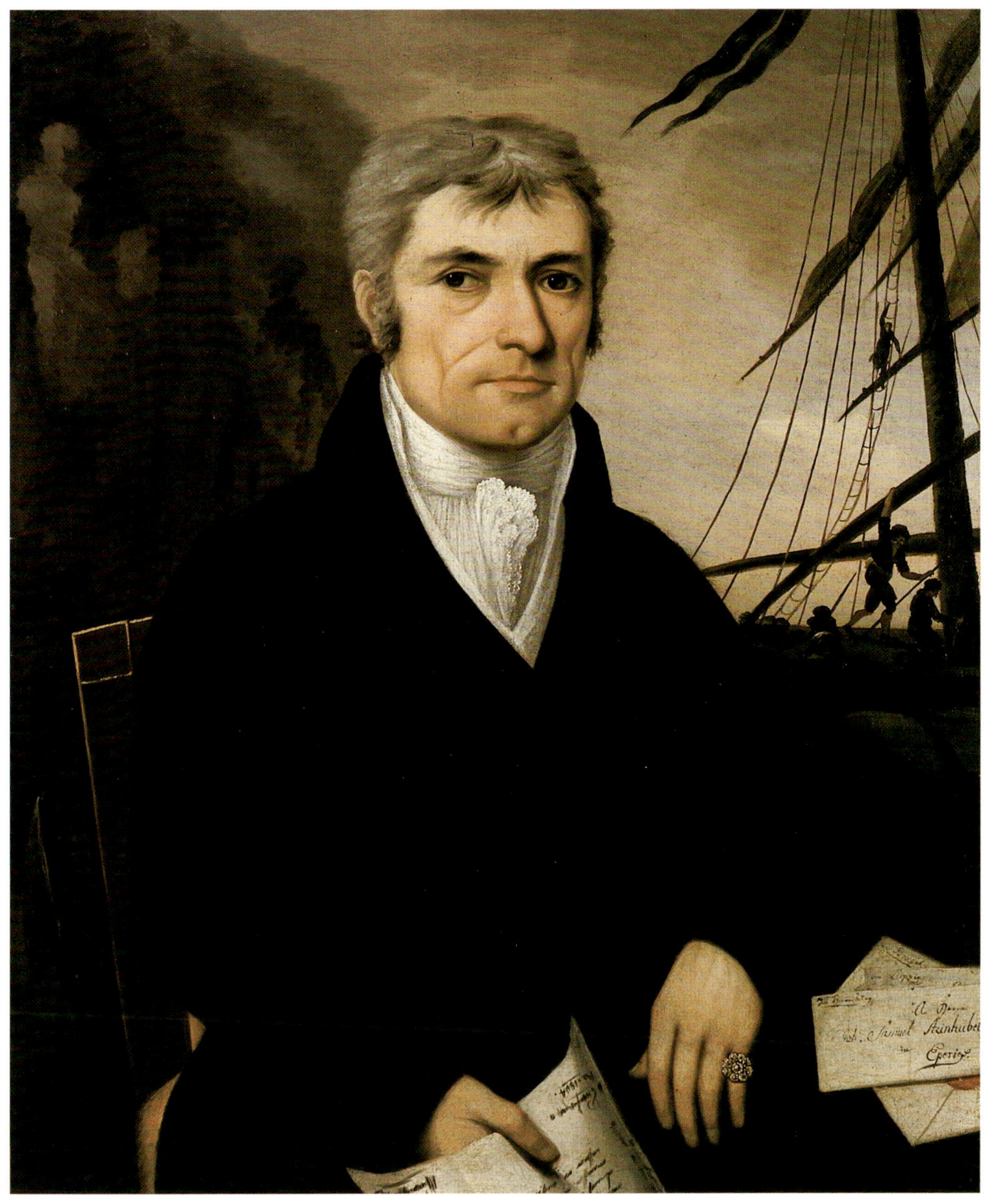

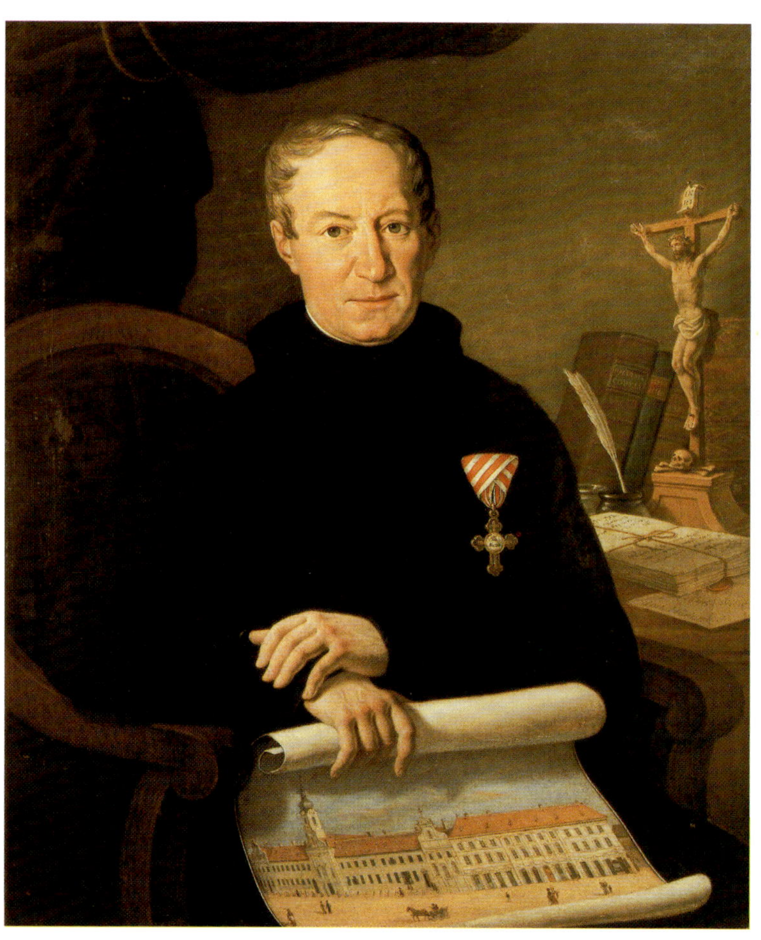

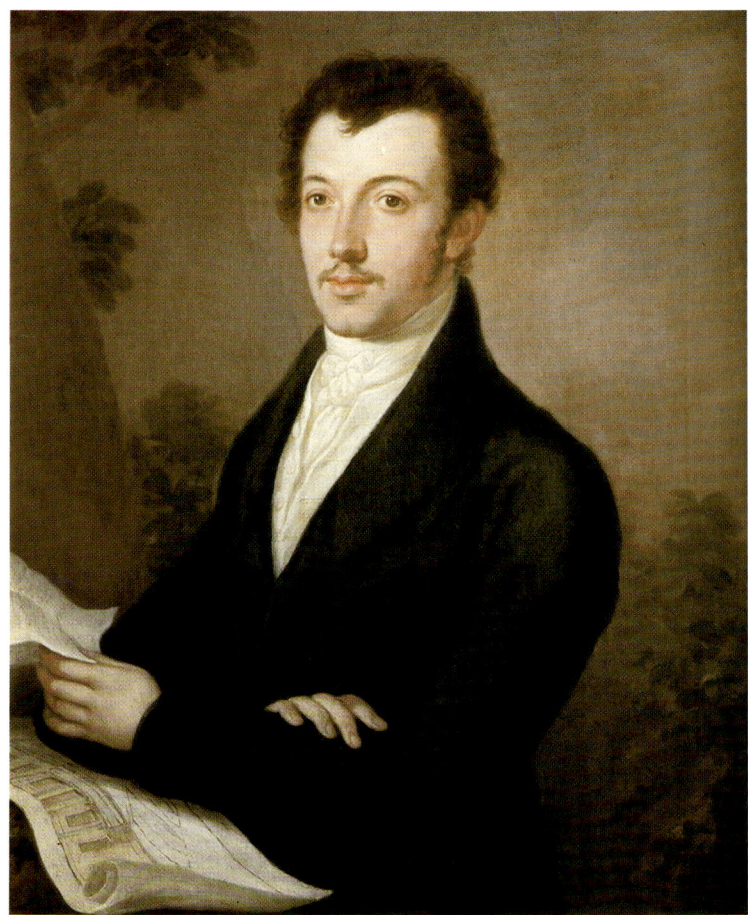

46. JOHANN NEPOMUK HÖFEL
Portrait of Father Sidonius Szakonits,
1846
Oil on canvas, 91.5 × 73.5 cm
Signed bottom right: "1846 Joh. Höfel"
Bratislava, Mestská Galeria
Inv. No.: A 841

Höfel, born in Pest, studied at the Vienna
Academy between 1804 and 1814, where he
was awarded several Academic prizes—the
Silver Medal in 1811 and the Sonnenfeld
Prize in 1812. Later he returned to his native
city, but also accepted commissions in Pozsony and other towns. He was a distinguished Academic painter; his style is therefore somewhat too formal and outdated,
a mélange of the Baroque and the Neo-Classical elements. In this particular painting it
was certainly the sitter's express wish that
the artist should carry out the work in accordance with conservative conventions.
Father Sidonius Szakonits, who commissioned the building of the Piarist Church and
Hospital in Pozsony, is depicted holding
a scroll showing not the plan but the completed building with promenaders and
coaches in front of it. The Crucifix indicates
his ecclesiastical status, while the medical
and pharmaceutical books reflect his concern
of providing medical facilities for the people.

47. JÁNOS DONÁT
Portrait of a Man Holding a Plan,
1823
Oil on canvas, 78 × 62 cm
Signed bottom right: "Donat academicus
Viennensis pinxit 1823"
Miskolc, Herman Ottó Museum
Inv. No.: HOMP 77.80

The sitter has not yet been identified. He
must have been an architect or builder; at
any rate, he was in a position to give commissions since the inscription emphasizes
that the painter had studied at the Vienna
Academy. It is one of the finest of the artist's
late works, an excellent example of his
figurative painting, with a suggestion of
a landscape background of ethereal clouds
and a tree just bursting into leaf. The plan of
the building seen in the sitter's hand and
under his arm could perhaps give some clues
to the sitter's identity.

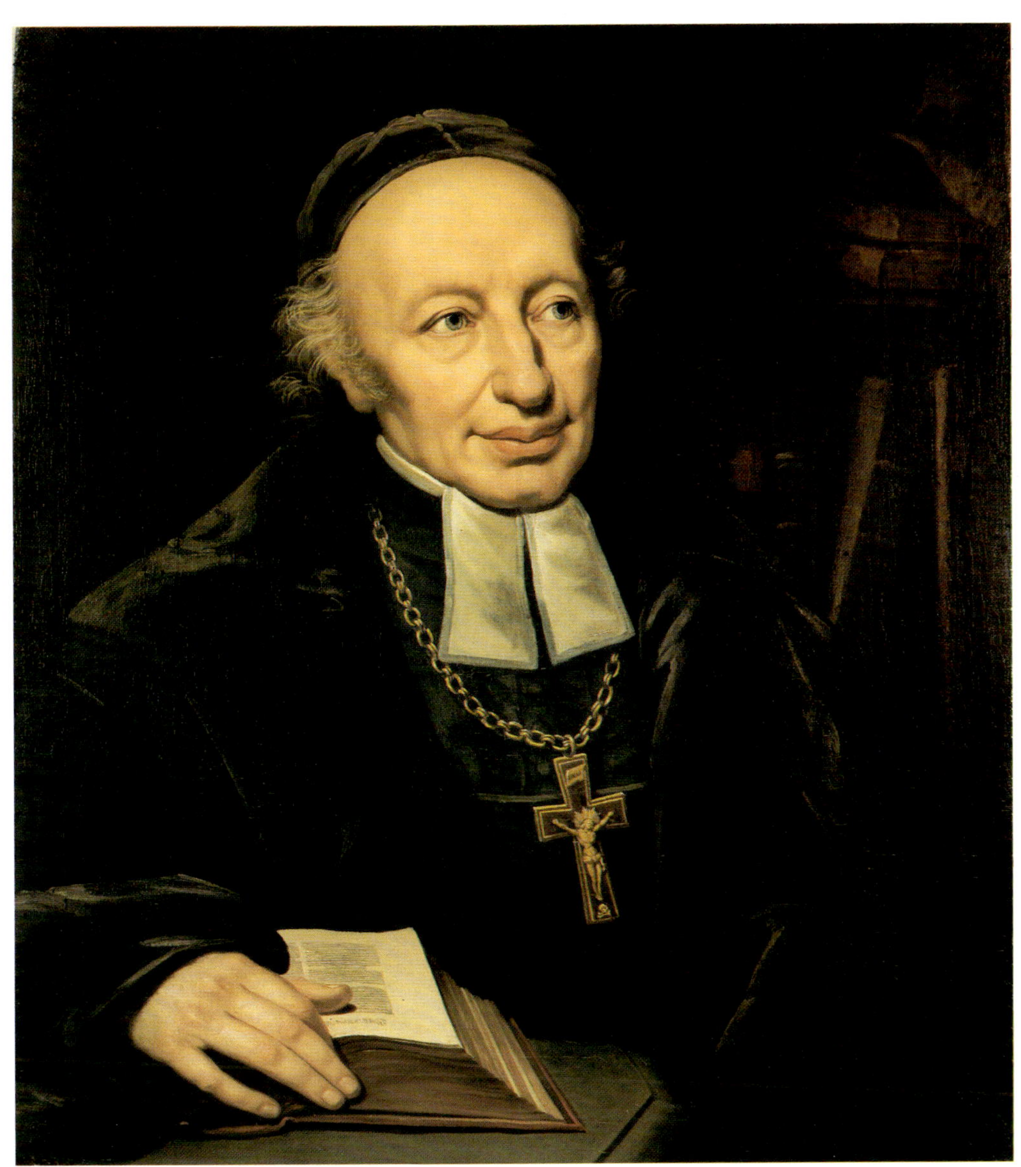

48. JÁNOS ROMBAUER
Portrait of Ignatius Aurelius Fessler,
Historian and Superintendent of the
St. Petersburg Lutheran Church, 1821
Oil on canvas, 80 × 66 cm
Signed: "John. Rombauer pinxit St.
Petersbourgh 1821"
Budapest, Hungarian Academy of Sciences

Rombauer painted this portrait during his
stay in St. Petersburg, and later, in 1840, presented it to the Hungarian Academy of
Sciences.
Though known for his graceful, idealized
pastel portraits and paintings characterized
by French elegance, Rombauer also executed formal, realistic portraits such as this,
where his aim was to give an objective
rendering of the sitter's personality and a feel
for this way of life. This portrait of the historian and superintendent of the German
Lutheran community of St. Petersburg,
a free-mason and respected philosopher, in
which there are indications of all his interests
and activities, is one of the finest in the
Academy of Sciences.

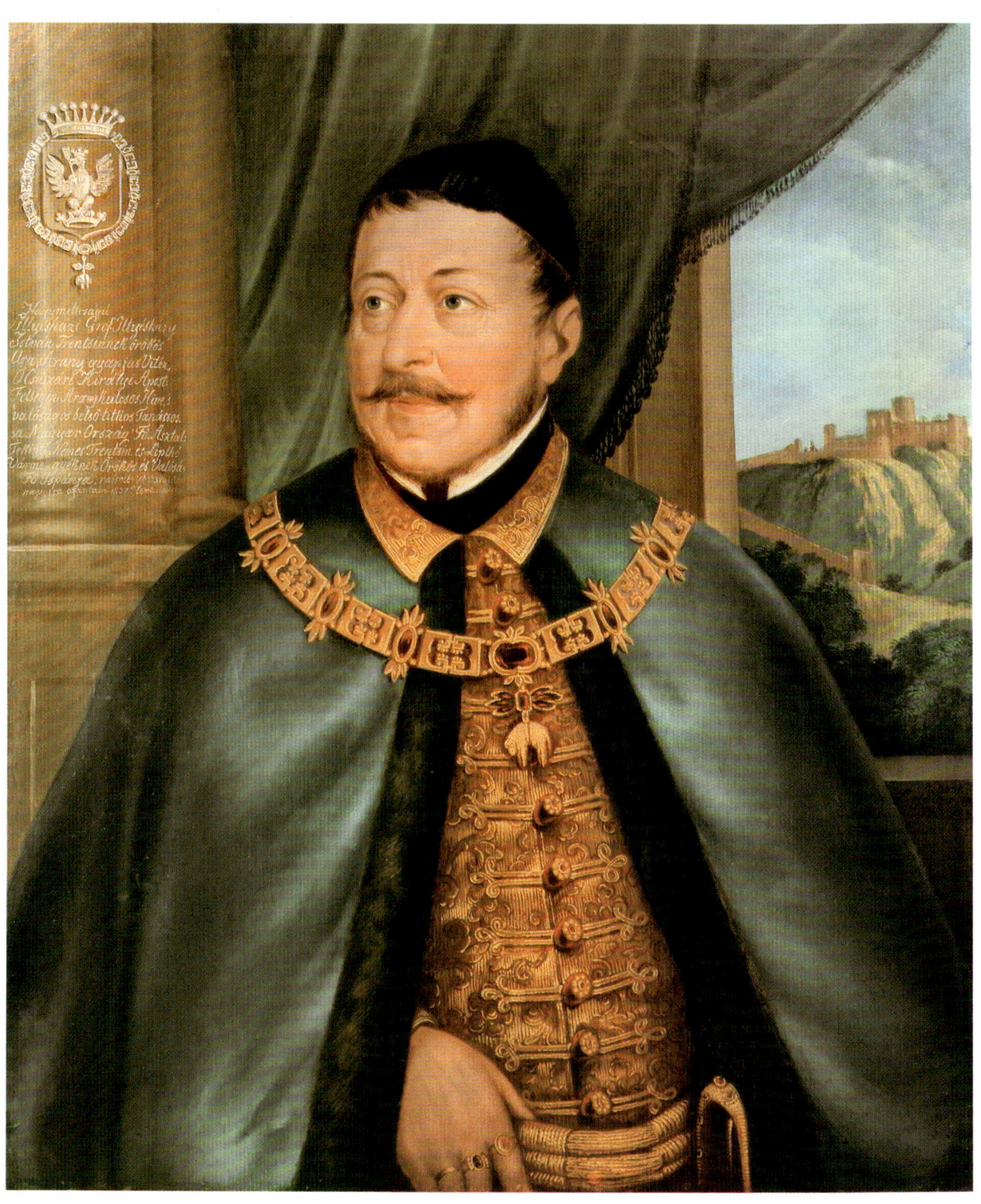

49. JÁNOS EHRLINGER
Portrait of István Illyésházi, 1837

Oil on canvas, 83.5 × 72 cm
Signed: "Erlinger inv. et pinx 1837"
*Inscription: "Nagyméltóságú Illyésházy gróf
Illyésházy István Trentsinnek örökös ura,
aranygyapjas vitéz, Ő császári királyi apost.
felsége Aranykulcsos lovagja, Híres valóságos
belső titkos tanácsos s a magyarországi Fő
Asztal, tekint. nemes Trentsin és Lipthó
Vármegyének örökös és valóságos ispánja."
(His Excellency Count Illyésházy, István
Illyésházy, lord perpetual of Trentsin, knight
of the Golden Fleece, knight of the Golden
Key of the emperor and king, his apostol.
highness, Famous actual Privy Councillor and
actual perpetual bailiff of the Main Table, of
the noble and honourable Counties of Trentsin
and Lipthó.)*
Bratislava, Mestská Galeria
Inv. No.: A 675

Ehrlinger, a modest painter of altar-pieces
and portraits from Pozsony, continued to
portray his subjects as late as the 1840s in the
manner and style of the early years of the
century. The style of dress, the insignia of
office, the indication of the castle of which he
was the owner (seen behind his left shoulder)
as well as a lengthy inscription, illustrate the
main features of the newly popular "social"
portraits of this type. The pictorial treatment
shows that the artist was more an honest
craftsman than a genius.

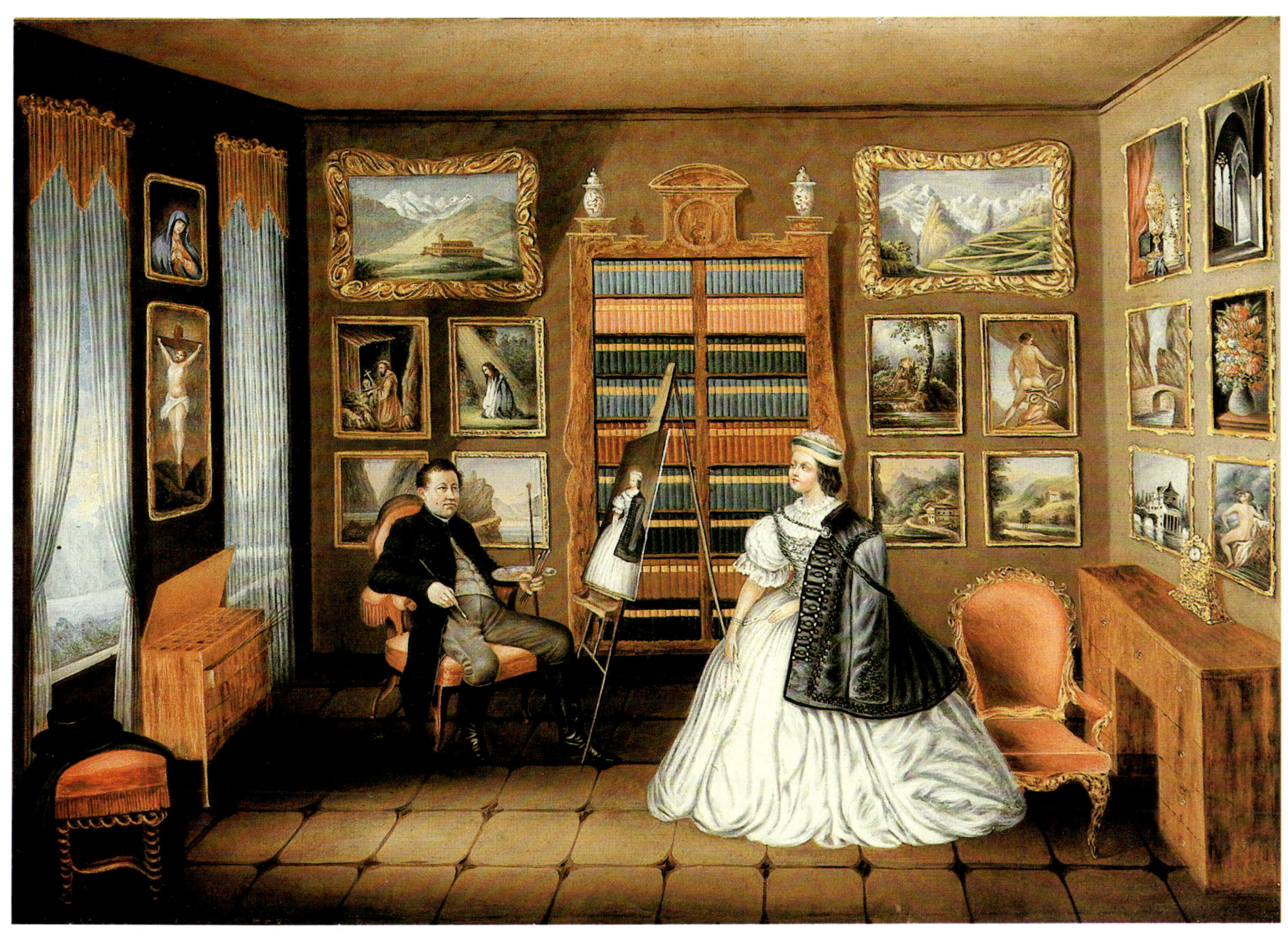

50. ALAJOS STECH
The Artist's Studio, late 1840s
Oil on canvas, 48 × 66 cm
Unsigned
Tata, Kuny Domokos Museum
Inv. No.: 55.66

The picture shows a studio in which we can
see examples of the various styles attempted
by the lesser painters of the period, although
the preference was for portraiture. Alajos
Stech, a Piarist monk and grammar-school
teacher, displays on the walls of his studio
examples of his work, from religious themes
to landscapes, from still-lifes to mythological scenes, thus creating a kind of one-man
show. There is a humorous note in his clear
indication that the noble lady posing for him
is only interested in having her figure and
fine dress immortalized, a task which, it
would seem, the painter found by no means
unacceptable.

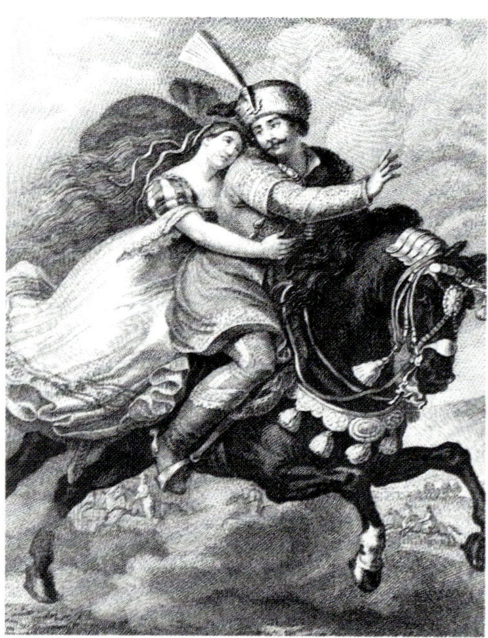

51. KÁROLY KISFALUDY–
MARTIN SCHÄRMER–
JOSEPH AXMANN–
JÁNOS BLASCHKE
Dobozy, 1822

Copperplate engraving, 128 × 82 mm
Inscription: "Schaermer Mar. rajza
— Axmann József bészivatta — Blaschke
János metsz."
Legend: "Dobozy"
Published in: "Aurora" (ed. Károly
Kisfaludy), 1822, as an illustration to the
poem entitled "A Tale of the Olden Days in
Hungary", written by Sándor Kisfaludy,
Károly's brother

Károly Kisfaludy, poet and painter, spent his
youth in the army, after which he travelled
for some time before publishing his drama
"The Tartars in Hungary", which was an
immediate success. He later wrote a series of
dramas in which he incorporated various
historical incidents. In 1822 he launched
"Aurora", a literary almanac described in
contemporary records as comprising "topics
conceived in the Hungarian spirit, also pictures, though engravings still have to be
made abroad." Kisfaludy commissioned illustrations, based on his own ideas. In this
publication, the story of Dobozy and his
wife, in a version written by Kisfaludy's
brother, was illustrated with this engraving,
the first use of the theme in the history of
Hungarian fine arts. (Later it became a popular subject for paintings and engravings.)
According to the story, Mihály Dobozy,
fleeing with his wife from the Turks, killed
her so she would not suffer indignities at
their hands, then killed himself, too.

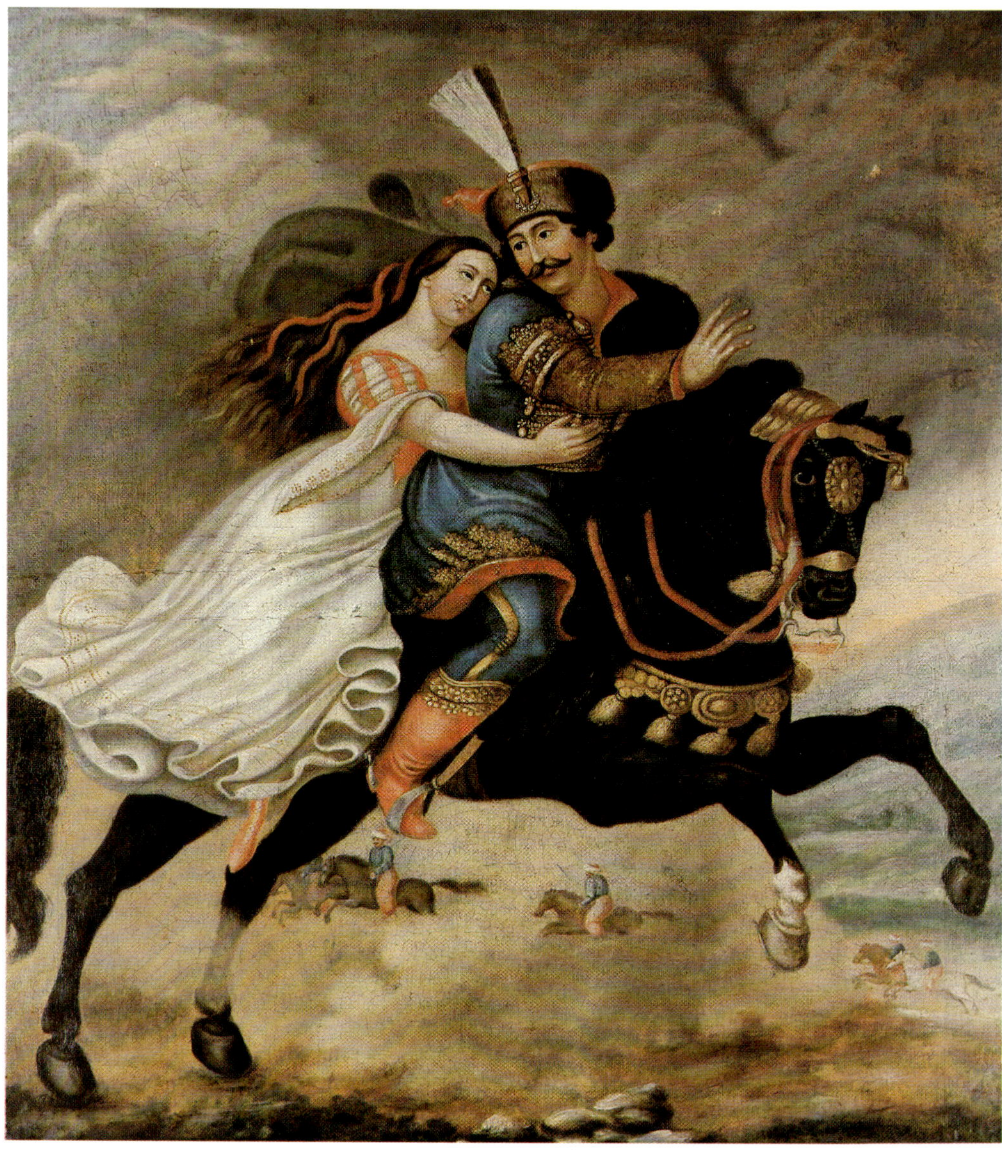

52. UNKNOWN MASTER
after the Dobozy engraving in
"Aurora"
Dobozy and his Wife, after 1822

Oil on canvas, 108 × 95 cm
Unsigned
Budapest, Hungarian Academy of Sciences

The "Aurora" engravings were copied,
coloured and enlarged by Hungarian artists
of greater or lesser significance. Mihály
Dobozy and his wife are sometimes depicted
fleeing from the Turks on a splendidly har-
nessed horse. Dobozy's style of dress in this
version is that seen in portraits of noblemen;
his coat is embroidered with gold thread and
studded with jewels. Dust rises from the
horse's hooves; Dobozy's wife wears
a white silk dress, also embroidered in gold,
which streams in the wind; the Turks, grim-
faced, are hot in pursuit and the drama is
enacted beneath a leaden sky. This naive
composition represents one of the first
fashionable themes of 19th century painting
in Hungary.

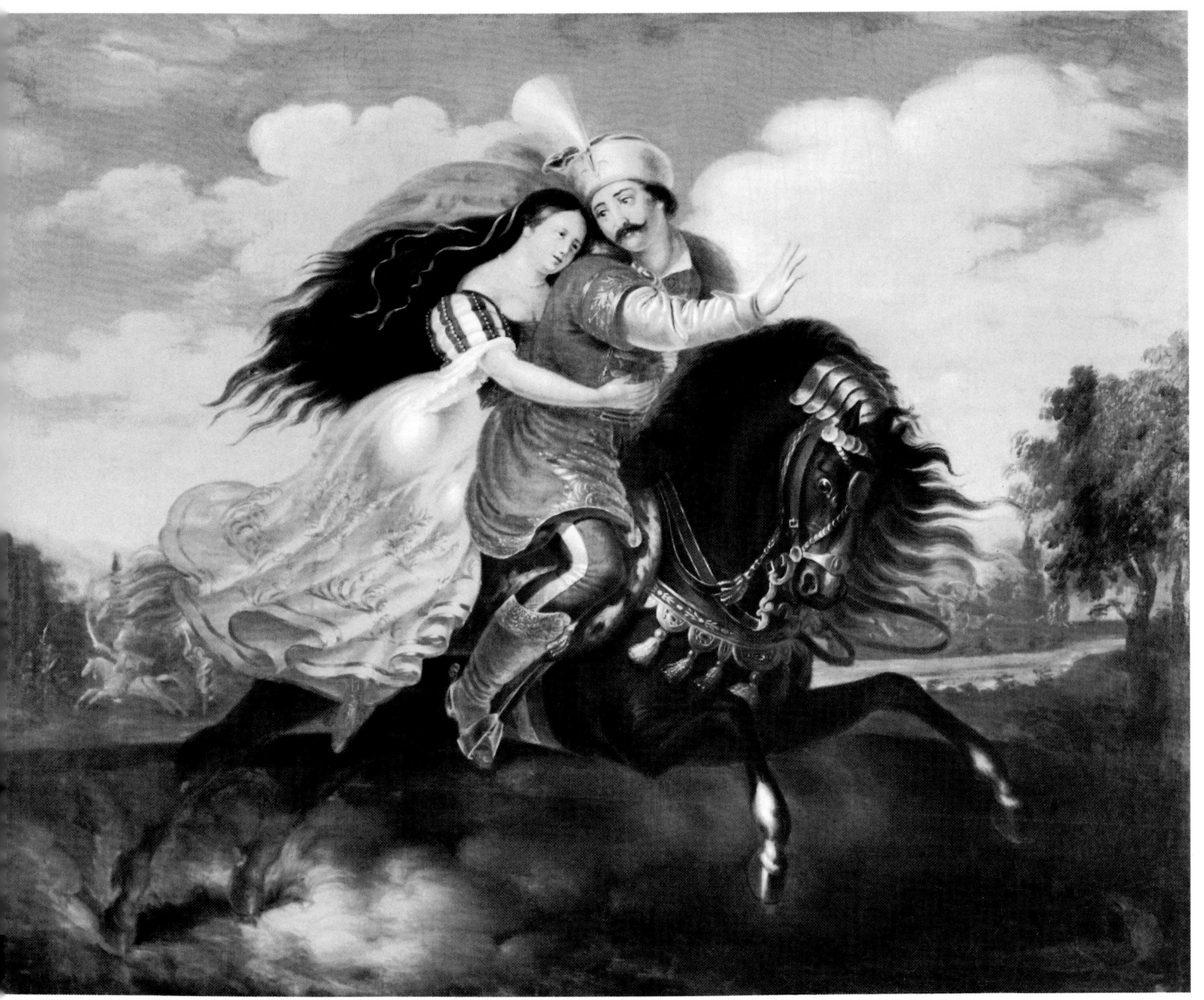

53. DEMETER LACCATARIS (DIAMANTI LACCATÁRI)
Mihály Dobozy and his Wife Fleeing from the Turks, 1830s
Oil on canvas, 61×76 cm
Signed bottom right: "D. Laccataris pinxit"
Budapest, Hungarian National Gallery
Inv. No.: 3109

During the 1830s and 1840s Demeter Laccataris, a man of Greek origin, was making his name as a trade-sign painter. He had studied in Vienna under Josef Danhauser and, like other artists, employed his talent as fashion demanded. He was receptive to the visual potential inherent in the "Aurora" engravings for trade-signs, namely, scenes taken from history which lend themselves to romantic representation. As in other copies of the Dobozy engraving, his picture scarcely deviates from the original except for the overall lay-out, which he changed in order to introduce a more detailed landscape background. The only other noticeable difference is a further exaggeration of the hair and dress of the female figure, Dobozy's wife, and of the horse's mane, streaming in the wind.

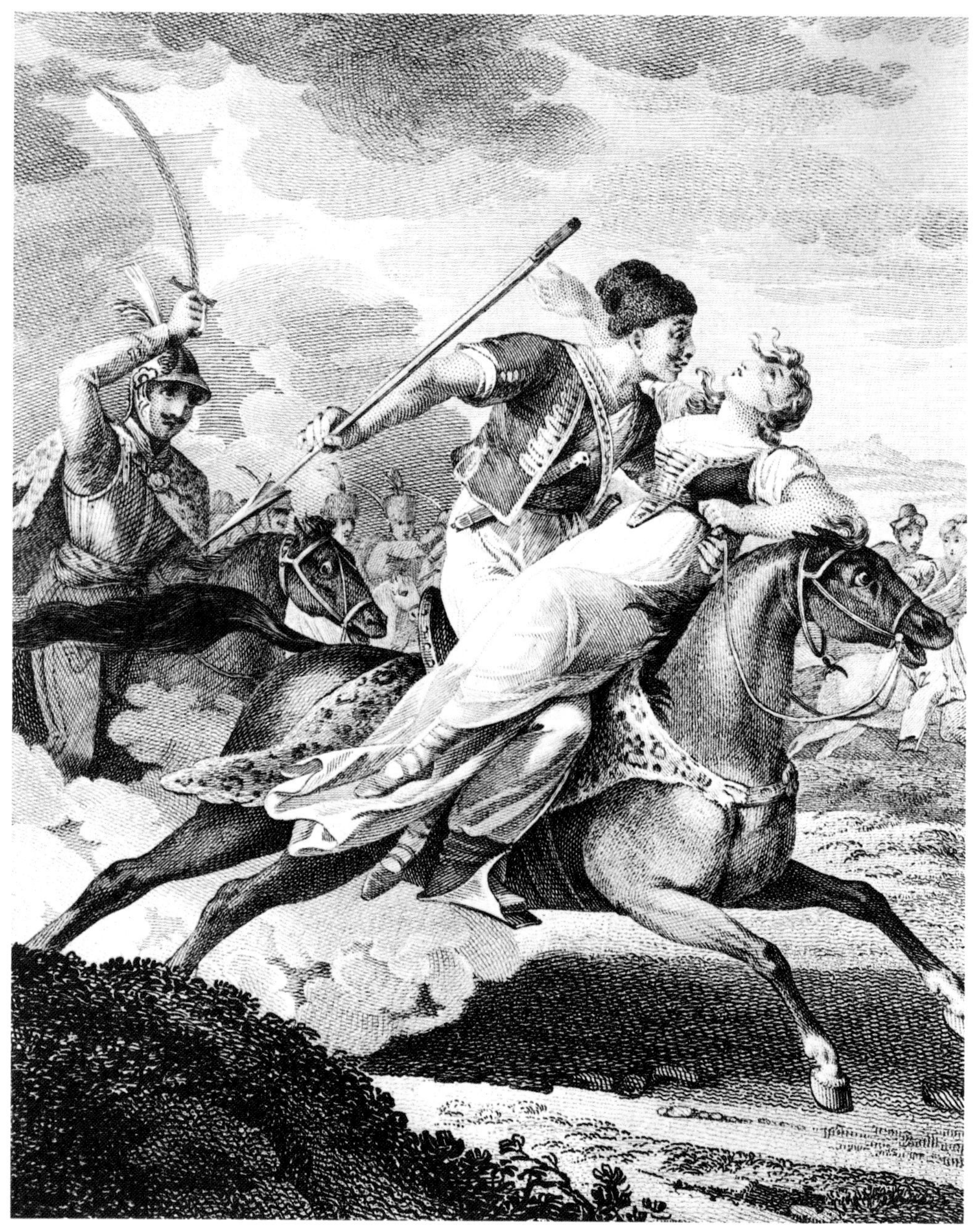

54. KÁROLY KISFALUDY–MICHAEL HOFMANN
King Ladislas at Cserhalom, 1826
Copper engraving, 116 × 82 mm
Inscription: "László Cserhalmon" (King St. Ladislas at Cserhalom)
Published in "Aurora" Vol. I, 1826

Mihály Vörösmarty's poem, "Cserhalom", was first published in 1826 in the literary magazine, "Aurora". Michael Hofmann, a Viennese copper engraver, closely follows the Dobozy painting in his illustration to this poem. Presumably based on Kisfaludy's description and sketch, some minor details are, however, changed: in this picture the fleeing figure is a Cumanian, dressed in Turkish–Tartar fashion, bearing a fainting woman across his saddle while at the head of their pursuers we see King Ladislas himself, clad in armour. According to the medieval legend, King Ladislas was a great warrior and protector of the poor and downtrodden. His story is related to that of Dobozy and his wife, though its happy ending—Ladislas killing the Cumanian and saving the girl—could not vie in popularity with the Gothic horror of the Dobozys' fate.

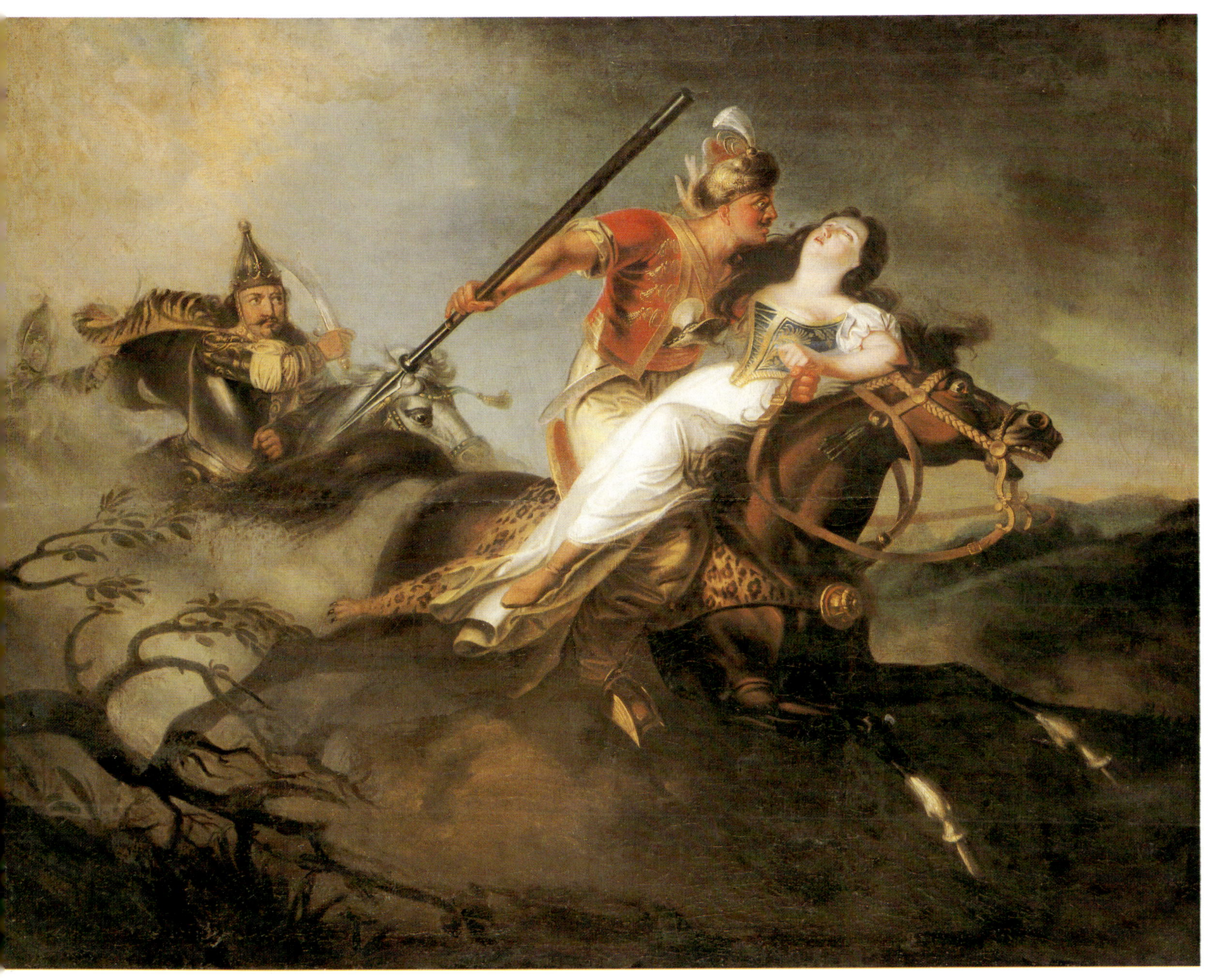

55. UNKNOWN ARTIST
King Ladislas at the Battle
of Cserhalom. Painted after the
"Aurora" engraving, c. 1830
Oil on canvas, 129 × 167 cm
Unsigned
Budapest, Hungarian National Gallery
Inv. No.: 58.276 T.

This painting, based on the "Aurora" engraving of 1826 and attributed by certain art
historians to Károly Kisfaludy, could, however, on the evidence of the format and landscape details, be a work by D. Laccataris.
Yet the subdued colouring and transparent
glaze as well as the elegant technique do not
support this supposition. The painter seems
to have had an academic training and was
certainly deeply involved in this novel subject.

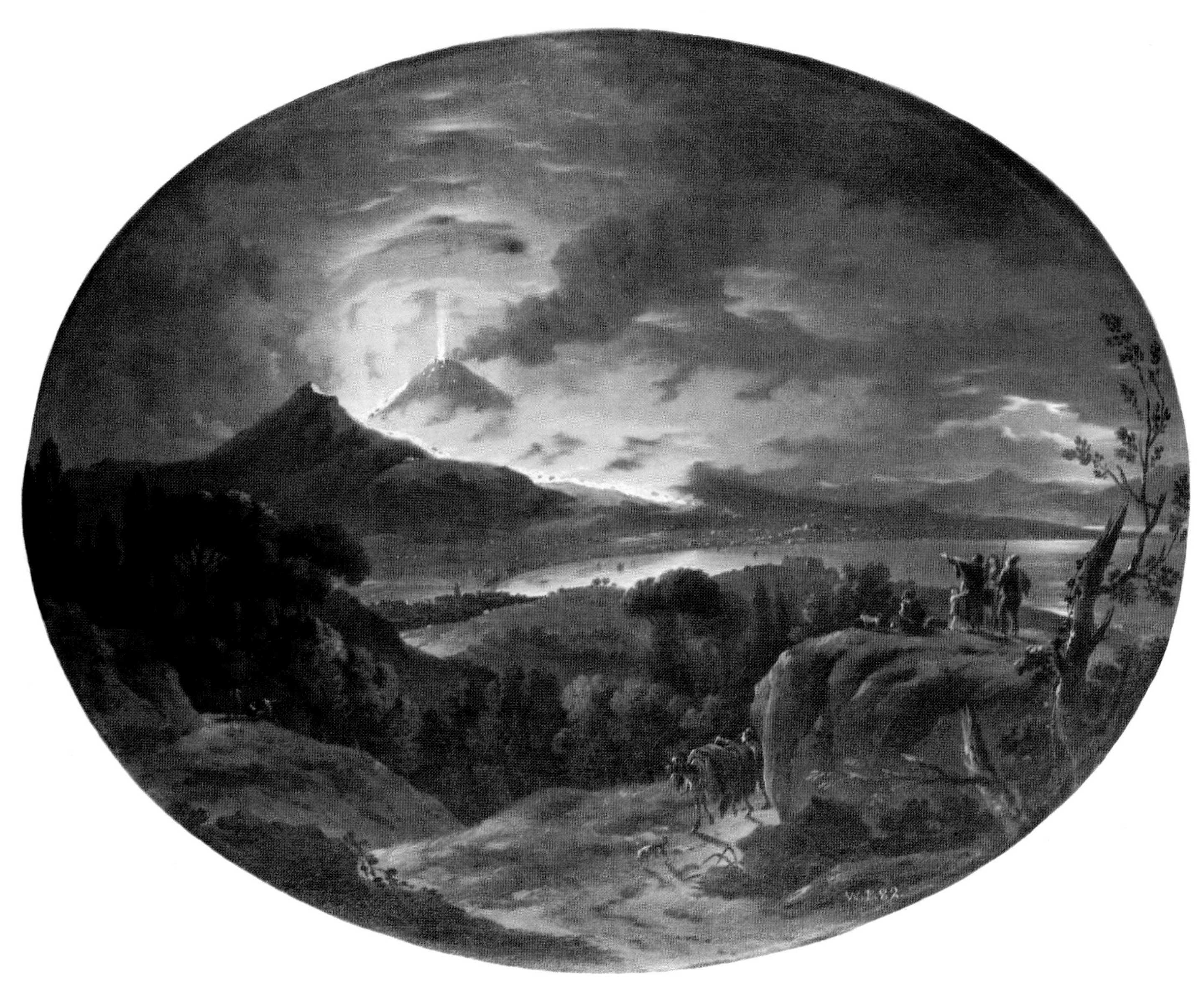

56. MICHAEL WUTKY
Eruption of Vesuvius at Night, 1820s
Oil on canvas, 45 × 55 cm
Marked lower right: "W. E. 82"
Vienna, Österreichische Galerie
Inv. No.: 5584

One of Károly Kisfaludy's chief aims as an artist was to introduce Romantic landscape painting into Hungary. This he tried to achieve by painstakingly copying the sea-scapes and landscapes painted in the Baroque tradition by Joseph Vernet, Michael Wutky and others. Wutky's painting, now in the Österreichische Galerie, serves to emphasize the greater skill of those painters whom Kisfaludy emulated on his own canvases of catastrophies at sea. In their paintings we also find representations of thunderstorms, volcanic eruptions and other violent natural phenomena, watched by small, awestruck figures.

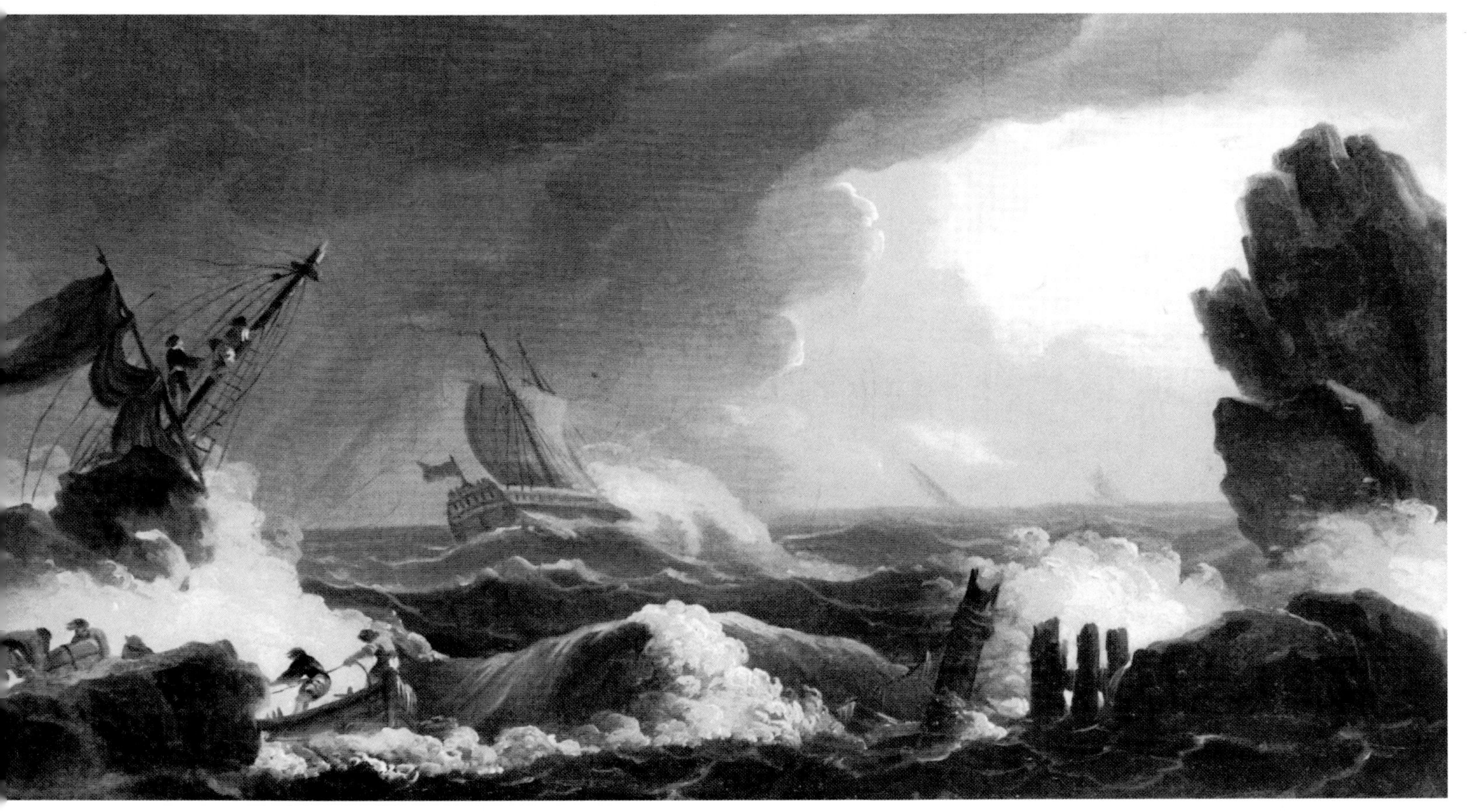

57. KÁROLY KISFALUDY
Catastrophe at Sea (Tempest I), 1820s
Oil on canvas, 22.4 × 39.4 cm
Inscription on reverse: "Tengeri vész, festé
Kisfaludy Károly, ajándékozá Zádor György
1854 Október 5-én" (Catastrophe at sea,
painted by Károly Kisfaludy, given by
György Zádor, the 5th October, 1854).
Formerly owned by the Kisfaludy Society,
now in Budapest, Hungarian Academy of
Sciences, on loan from the Kisfaludy Society

Storms at sea were one of Kisfaludy's favourite themes, which he depicted in numerous variations. In his last years he began work on nearly ten pictures depicting the sea, and according to the aesthetician Ferenc Toldy, he was not always satisfied with the final result. This painting, each motif of which was lifted from other paintings, conveys a perfect understanding of turbulent air, changing light effects, storm-tossed boats, and the rescuers' strenuous efforts in the foreground.

An early death after a life of vicissitudes prevented Kisfaludy from developing his artistic talent to the full. Even so, his paintings demonstrate not only a discerning sense for visual motifs in contemporary prose and poetry, but also a marked skill in depicting them on canvas.

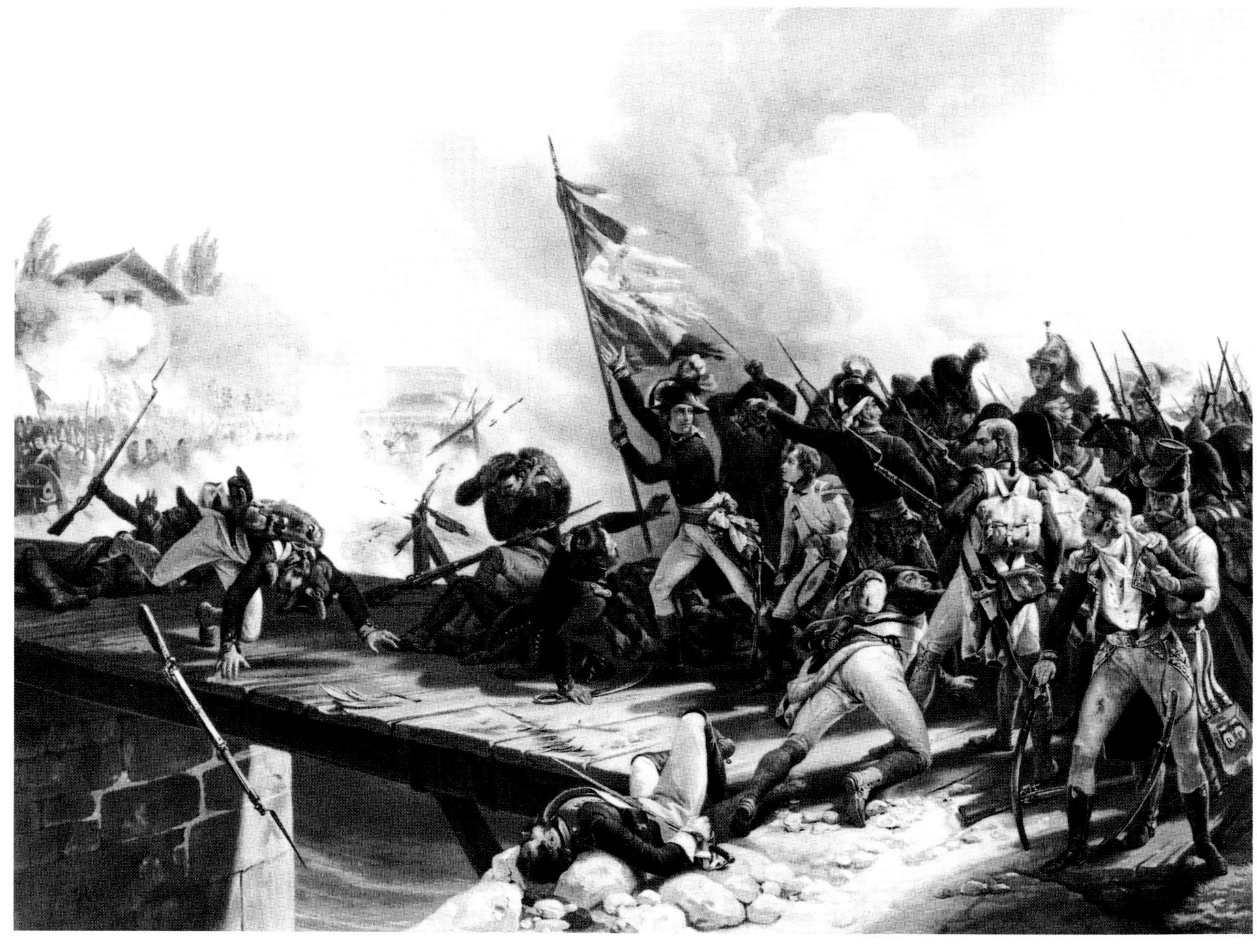

58. HORACE VERNET–JEANNE-PIERRE MARIE JAZET
The Crossing of the Bridge at Arcole, after 1826

Aquatint and copper engraving on paper, after an oil painting, 558 × 730 mm
Inscribed bottom left: "H. Vernet 1826";
underneath: "Peint par Horace Vernet"; in middle: "Arcole"; inscribed bottom right: "gravé par Jazet", underneath: "A Paris a Jazet chez Rue de Lancrey 7, chez AUMONT M'd d'Estampes Rue J. J. Rousseau No. 10. Deposé a la Direction."
Budapest, Museum of Fine Arts
Inv. No.: 64.516
(Formerly in the National Picture Gallery, now incorporated in the Museum of Fine Arts)

When Ferenc Kazinczy saw this aquatint in an art dealer's gallery, either Lichtl's or Tomala's, he noted that it was "the most beautiful historical painting he had ever seen whether painted or engraved".
Horace Vernet was one of the most distin-

guished battle-scene painters in Europe in the early 19th century. During the Napoleonic wars he painted scenes of battle from personal experience. This composition represents an incident in the 1796 Italian campaign, one which inspired several painters and graphic artists: Napoleon Bonaparte, the young general, on foot and wielding a banner, is about to charge the bridge. Napoleon is not portrayed as an isolated hero, but rather as the military leader who ensures before a decisive battle that his soldiers will follow him, while in front of him the way is strewn with the dead and dying.
In Kazinczy's description, there is no mention of the hero's identity. Yet the painting clearly goes beyond a mere description of a battle in which French infantry are led by a fearless youth to whom the drummer boy and all the other soldiers remain faithful to the end.
This print was acquired by the former National Picture Gallery, possibly as a result of Kazinczy's enthusiasm.

59. PETER KRAFFT, the Elder
Zrínyi's Charge on the Turks from the Fortress of Sziget, 1825

Oil on canvas, 455 × 645 cm
Signed bottom right: "Krafft Wien 1825"
Budapest, Museum of Fine Arts
Inv. No.: 137

This large painting was commissioned in 1825 for the National Museum. It represents the last stage of the Siege of Sziget in 1566, when the Hungarian commander of the fortress, Count Miklós Zrínyi, and his followers, broke out of their burning fortress to confront the Turkish Army. As Ferenc Kazinczy wrote, "Zrínyi is not portrayed as a hero knowingly going to meet his inevitable death, but a man going forth to kill the foe." Indeed, this dramatic element is the outstanding feature of the work, which despite its borrowing from compositions seen on Rubens' engravings and its theatrically lit background, ranks among the best of its kind.

Peter Krafft, the Elder studied under David, in Paris, and his work has to some extent been influenced by the Neo-Classical manner in which French artists painted scenes of battle.

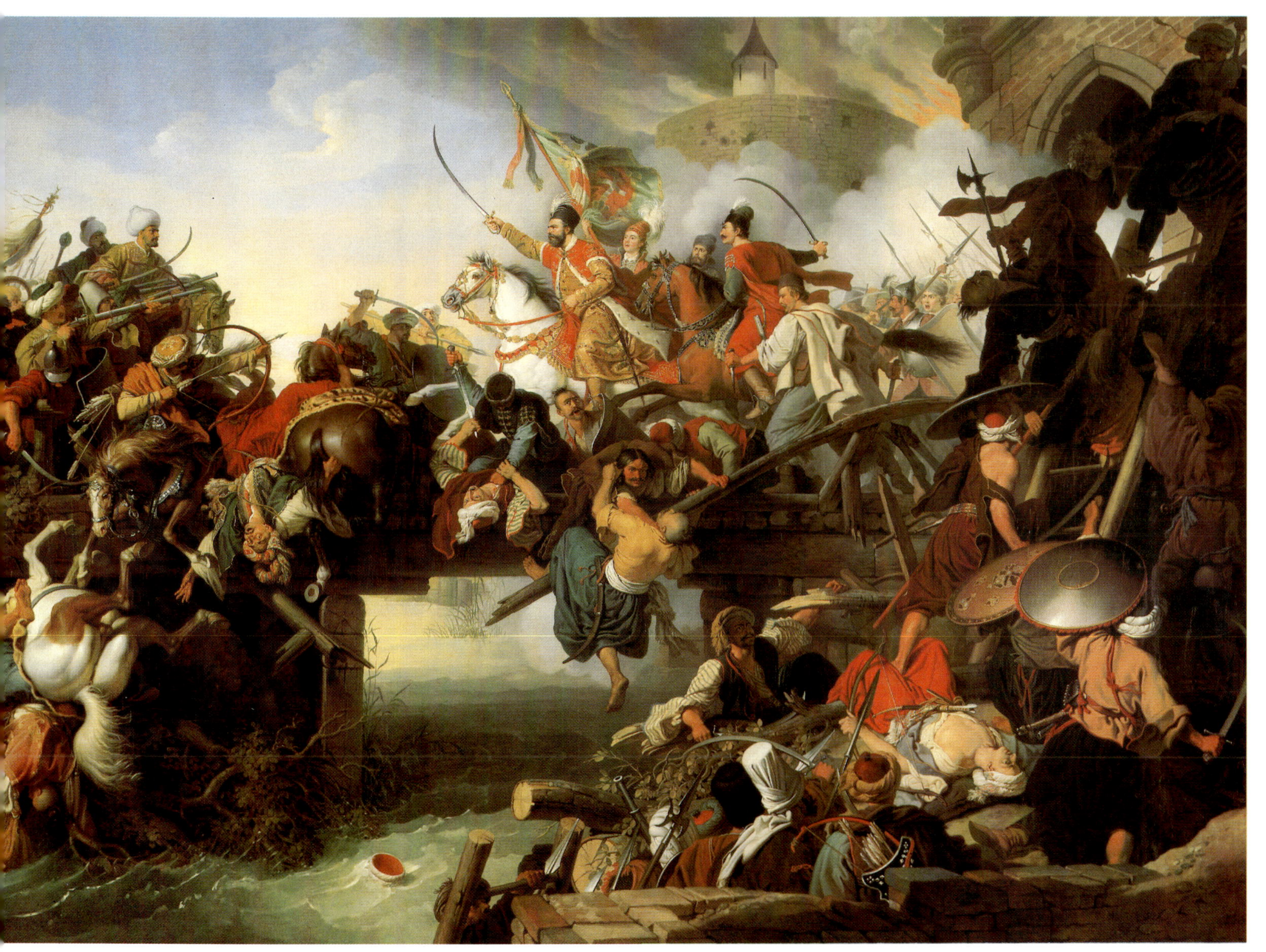

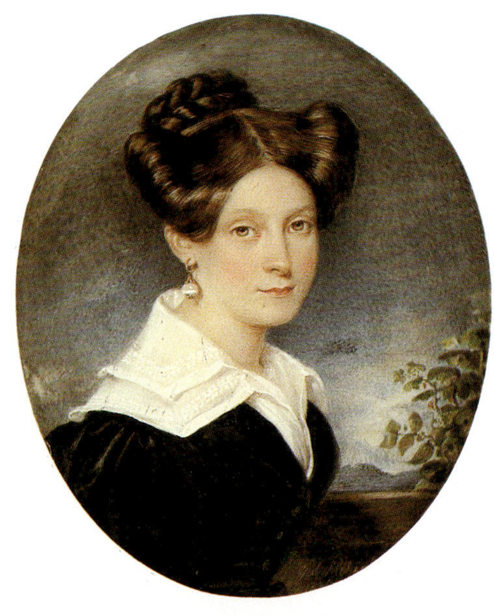

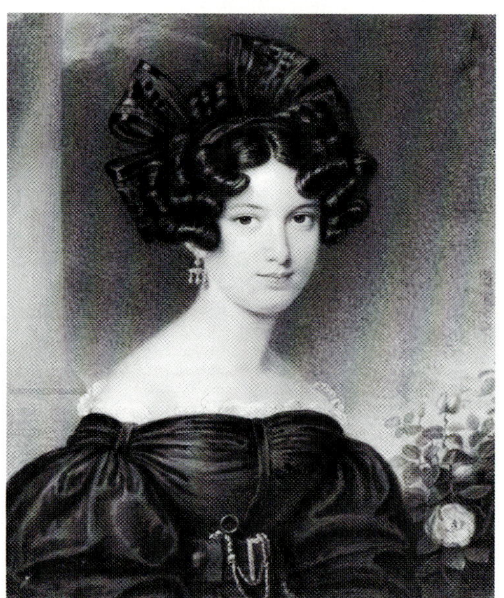

60. GÁBOR MELEGH
Portrait of a Young Lady, 1830
Miniature on ivory plate, 91 × 44 mm
Signed bottom right: "Gab. Melegh 1830"
Budapest, Hungarian National Gallery
Inv. No.: 1955–5293

61. GÁBOR MELEGH
Portrait of a Lady, 1830
Miniature on ivory plate, 89 × 75 mm
Signed bottom right: "Melegh 1830"
Budapest, Hungarian National Gallery
Inv. No.: 1940–3532

In the 1830s Gábor Melegh was one of the most technically accomplished painters in Hungary. He made engravings of historical literary subjects to illustrate works published in "Aurora" as well as genre-scenes. He was active in both Vienna and Hungary, and made a notable contribution to Hungarian art.

These two paintings are exquisite examples of miniature portraiture on ivory plate, a much favoured medium of the period. The faces and figures of the young ladies are executed with the finest brush strokes, their ruffed dresses most delicately delineated, and the details of the coiffure and jewellery portrayed with the utmost care.

62. MIKLÓS BARABÁS
Portrait of a Lady, 1831
Oil on canvas, 80 × 62 cm
Signed top right: "Barabás 1831"
Zalaegerszeg, Göcsej Museum
Inv. No.: 76.1.35

Miklós Barabás was one of the most popular Hungarian 19th century painters. He began his career as an itinerant artist, and after an intensive period of study at the Academy of Vienna from March to November 1831, he set out via Transylvania for Bucharest, where portrait commissions awaited him. He probably painted this portrait of a noble woman somewhere on the way. It rivals in delicacy the miniature portraits of the period, at the same time achieving a bolder pictorial quality. The woman is portrayed as she sits in an armchair, wearing a soft white dress. The beautifully wrought jewellery on her forehead and breast, her earrings, bracelets, and belt all indicate an aristocratic background. The velvet curtain behind her partially conceals a view of the landscape beyond the window—a traditional motif of Viennese portraiture.

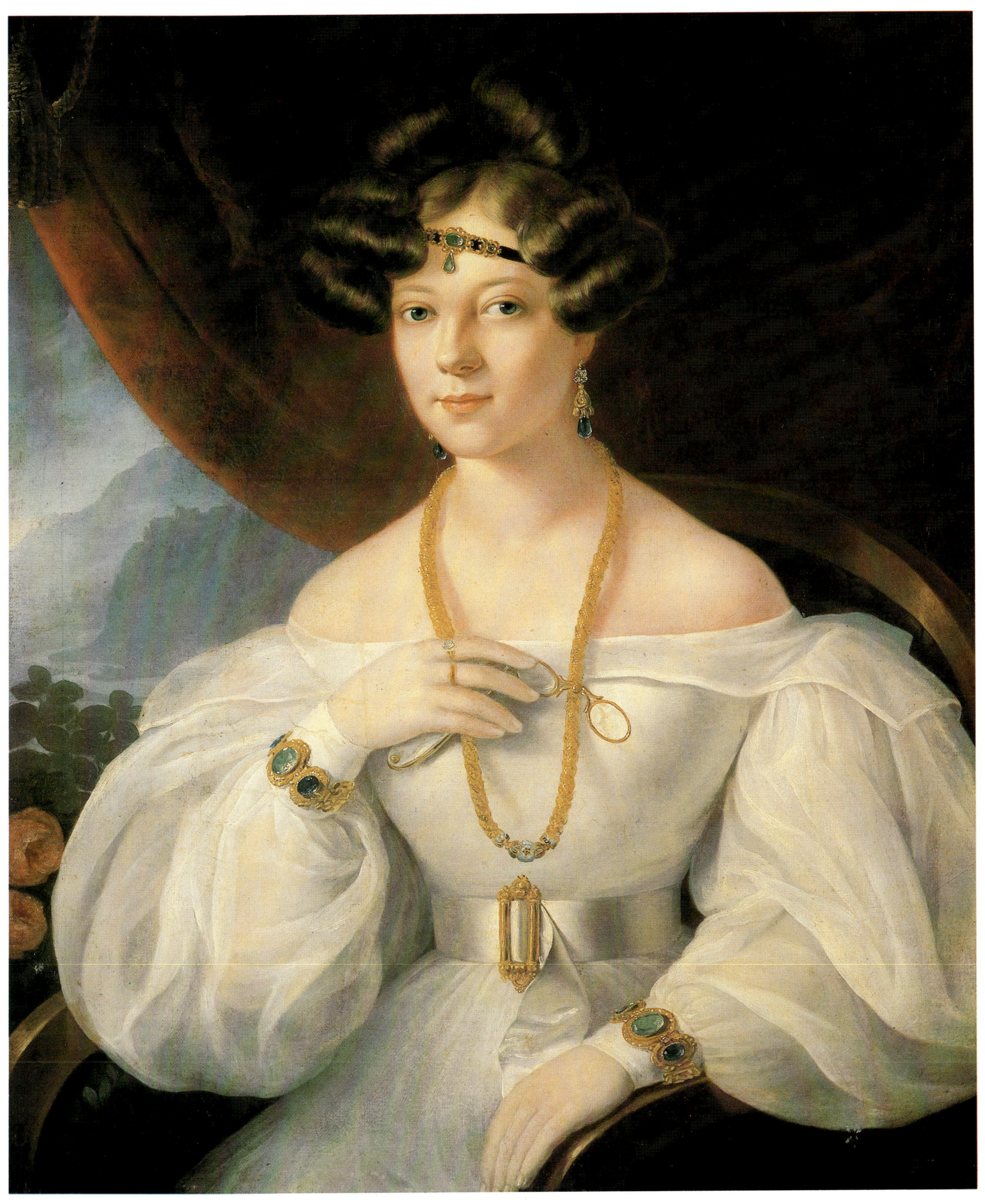

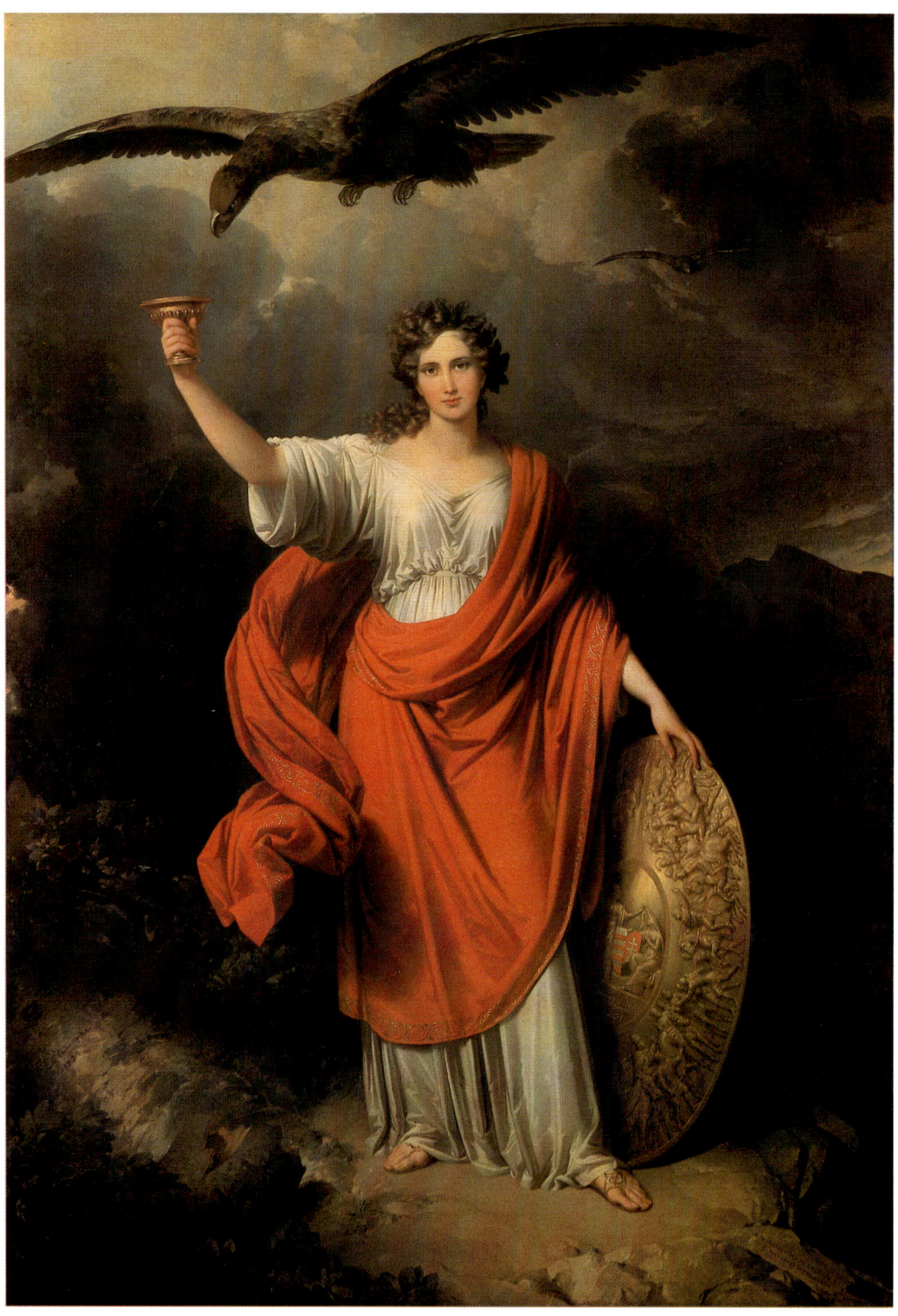

63. JOHANN ENDER
"From Darkness, the Light". Allegory of the Hungarian Academy of Sciences, 1831
Oil on canvas, 273 × 190 cm
Signed bottom left "Johann Ender pinx. 1834"
Legend on the shield: "Borúra derű, 1831"
[From Darkness, the Light]
Legend bottom right: "A. M. Academiának emlékül gr. Széchenyi István 1834" (For the Hungarian Academy from Count István Széchenyi as a keepsake 1834)
Budapest, Hungarian Academy of Sciences

This personification of the Academy of Sciences as a young maid has as its precedents in the seal of the Academy, and the steel-engraving made from the seal. On this large-scale painting, commissioned by Count István Széchenyi, the girl is Hebe, goddess of youth, who nourishes the Hungarian nation symbolized by the eagle swooping down to drink from her potion of science and art. Whereas in the earlier representations Hebe reminds us of Athene, goddess of wisdom, the only similarity between them now is the shield. Athene herself can be discovered in the innermost part of the shield, removing the veil of ignorance from the head of Hungary, seen standing before her. The device on the shield, showing Attila's meeting with Pope Leo, symbolizes the historic encounter between the Eastern Huns and Western European culture.

The focus of interest in the picture is the young woman with a gentle face, wearing classical garments, standing erect beneath a sky with receding storm clouds. In the background, there are topographical details of the Iron Gate region, a romantic but dangerous gorge on the Danube, whose transformation into a safe and navigable waterway was one of the chief tasks of Széchenyi's reform programme. The idealized features of the woman remind us of Crescence Seilern, Széchenyi's future wife. In his journal Széchenyi refers to her as Amphitrite and, confident of his own powers, identifies himself with the eagle.

Though the painting may be interpreted on several symbolic levels, it has one supreme message: praise for Hungarian culture, and for the foundation of the Academy, which ushered in a new era in the history of the Hungarian people.

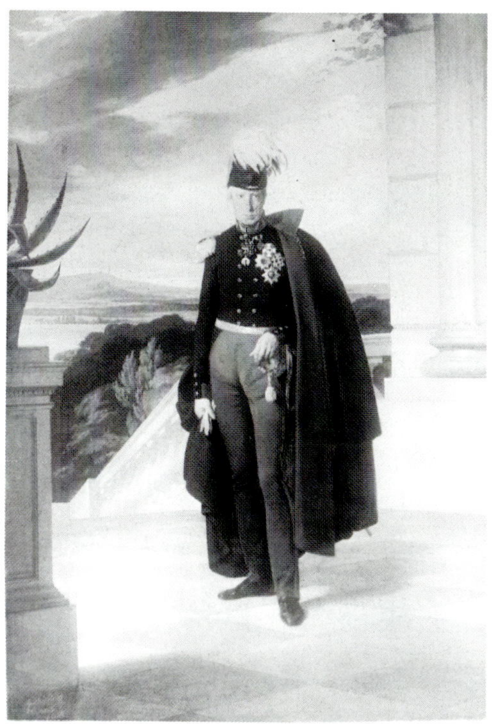

64. FRIEDRICH VON AMERLING
Francz I, Emperor of Austria, Dressed as a General in the Prussian Army, 1834

Oil on canvas, 272 × 182 cm
Vienna, Österreichische Galerie
Inv. No.: 4932

There are a number of sketches extant which show that when Széchenyi was choosing an artist to paint the Allegory of the Academy of Sciences, he seriously considered the Viennese painter, Amerling, who at that time, was already more celebrated than Enders. Amerling began his career as a cartographer and from 1816 to 1824, studied intensively at the Vienna Academy. Later he went first to London to study the portraits of Thomas Lawrence and then to Paris, where his intention was to get in touch with Horace Vernet. He subsequently moved on to Rome and Venice, and was awarded prizes by the Academies of both cities. In 1831, he was distinguished by a commission to paint a full length portrait of Franz I, Emperor of Austria. The Emperor is depicted in the uniform of a Prussian general, standing in an open gallery in the pose characteristic of royal portraits.

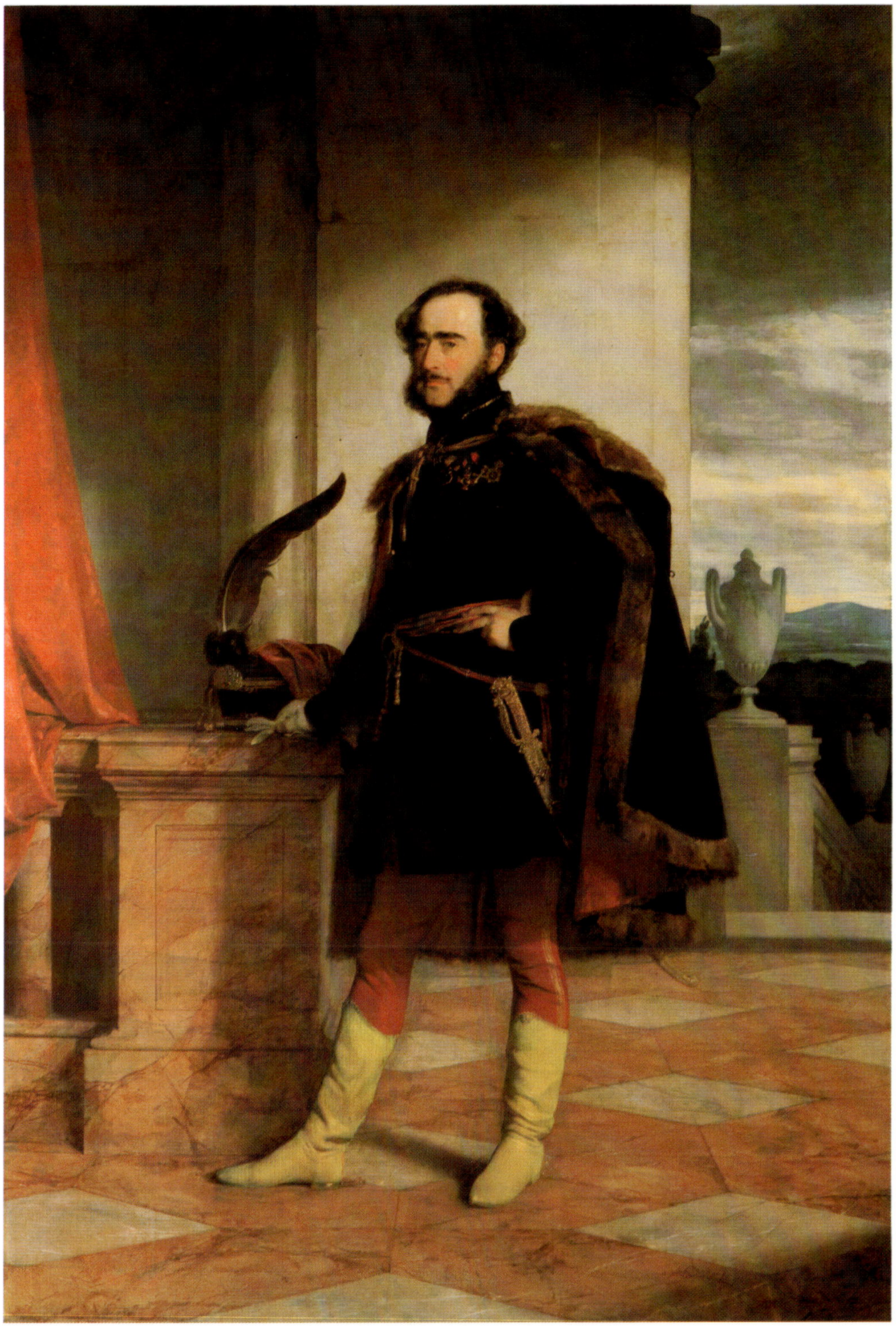

65. FRIEDRICH VON AMERLING
Portrait of Count István Széchenyi, 1836

Oil on canvas, 250 × 165 cm
Signed left: "Fr. Amerling 1836"
Budapest, Hungarian Academy of Sciences

Friedrich von Amerling's portrait of István Széchenyi is not mentioned by Austrian and German art historians whose concern is with more important royalty and noblemen. It was painted soon after the completion of the portrait of Francis I and the background is very similar to that of the royal portrait. It has been classified by art historian Lajos Vayer as one of the best likenesses of István Széchenyi. Vayer described the painting as follows: "Széchenyi is depicted standing on an impressive terrace, wearing the magnificent Hungarian national costume." A flight of steps leads the eye from the castle towards a background of romantic scenery. The artist's concern was not so much to characterize a specific person, as to express, through artistic means, the grandeur of a Hungarian magnate who was ready to make sacrifices in order to enrich the national culture. The picture was presented to the Academy and it is clear from the deed of gift that the donors were aware of the artist's intention: "in hope that our descendants be moved in their hearts to the noblest feelings when they look upon this likeness and be thus urged to work towards the common weal of their people."

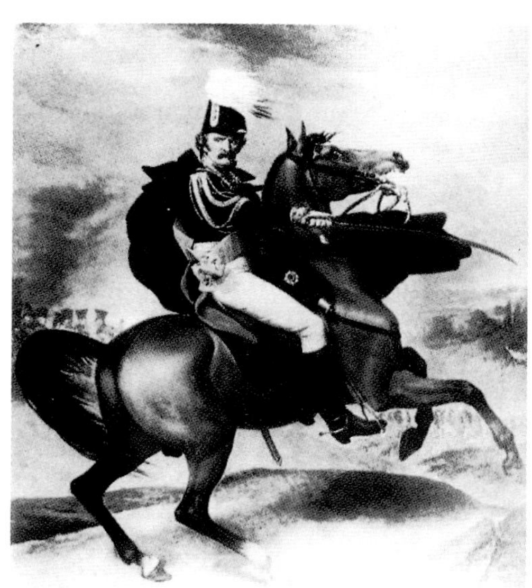

66. SIMON MEISTER
Field-marshal Blücher on Horseback, 1823

Oil on canvas, 293 × 249 cm
Potsdam, Neues Palais

Simon Meister, born in Koblenz, painted portraits, battle-scenes and studies of animals. He was active in Paris from 1821 to 1825 as a pupil of Horace Vernet, and later collaborated with his brother in painting panoramic compositions. Meister's works were sent to Berlin, Vienna and possibly Buda and Pest, thus extending Vernet's influence to these towns. In this portrait of Field-marshal Blücher sitting on his rearing horse, the painter follows a long tradition of military portraits, usually smaller than this and less complex in form. Here the pictorial solution derives from Jacques Louis David's monumental *Bonaparte Crossing the Alps at the St. Bernard Pass,* painted in 1800.

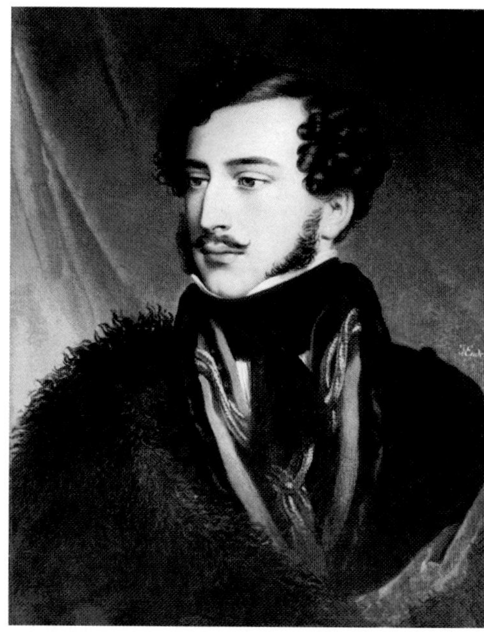

67. JOHANN ENDER
Portrait of Count György Károlyi (One of a series representing the founders of the Hungarian Academy of Sciences), 1830s

Oil on wood, 26 × 20 cm
Signed right: "Ender"
Budapest, Hungarian Academy of Sciences

From the 1830s onwards, the Academy regularly commissioned portraits of its founding members. Several of these portraits were painted by Johann Ender. Here the features of György Károlyi are preserved for posterity in a painting notable for its draughtsmanship and sensitive characterization.

68. TIVADAR ALCONIERE
Allegorical Portrait of Count István Széchenyi at the Iron Gate, 1831 or 1837

Oil on canvas, 51.5 × 59 cm
Signed bottom left: "Alconiere pinx. 1831 (1837)"
Budapest, Hungarian National Gallery
Inv. No.: FK 3097

This painting, identified by Elemér Czakó as an allegorical likeness of Széchenyi, still puzzles art historians. There is a letter from Kazinczy in which he mentions Alconiere as an artist who in 1829 was working for the Pozsony Royal Court of Justice of the Hungarian Kingdom. He was a Jew, born Hermann Kohn in Nagymárton, and studied at the Academy of Vienna from 1812 to 1820. He was also a friend of Amerling and Danhauser. He completed several equestrian portraits, including one of Napoleon which he exhibited in 1840 at the "Műegylet" (Association for Art) in Pest.

The subject of the painting was taken from an engraving depicting a view of the Lower Danube, a place which Széchenyi often visited. Following the course of the river, which cuts a way between sombre and majestic cliffs, an eagle leads the rider of a rearing horse. In the distance a steamboat can be seen on the river, a symbol of the Hungarian Danube Steamship Company. Founded in 1830 and still not functional in 1831, the company began to operate in 1834, and in 1837 it became possible to navigate the river all the way to Constantinople. Edouard Thouvenet, French Minister for Foreign Affairs, greeted Széchenyi's project as a continuation of schemes projected by Julius Caesar, Charlemagne and Napoleon to connect Europe and Asia.

In a paper written on Széchenyi likenesses, Lajos Vayer concluded that the rider's face did not represent that of Széchenyi. The horseman is depicted in Hungarian gala dress, sitting on a horse who trampling under-foot the star of the cross of the Order of St. Stephen founded by Maria Theresa. A little further on lies the emblem of government office with its knot and eagle; and at a little distance from it, an upturned crown. Above, on a small hill on the shore, the Hungarian coat of arms can be seen, wreathed with oak and laurel leaves. The rider's face is more reminiscent of György Károlyi than Széchenyi, but it also bears a resemblance to youthful portraits of "the greatest Hungarian", as Lajos Kossuth called Széchenyi. Count Károlyi in fact never went to the Iron Gate on the Lower Danube. Moreover, whether Széchenyi knew of the painting or not, no one else could have been portrayed at that time in such a Napoleonic pose and with such allusions to great achievements as the great politician and reformer himself.

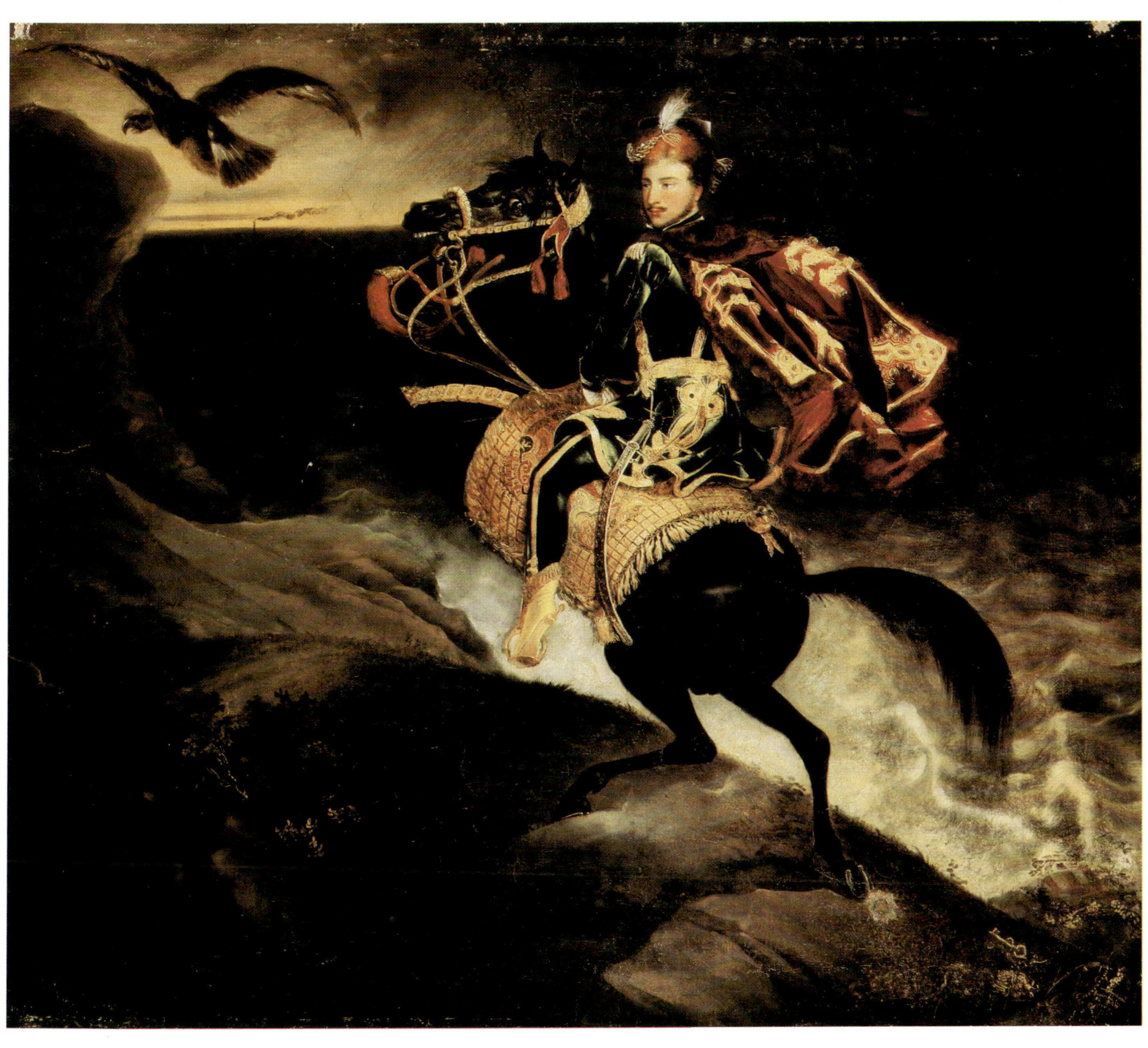

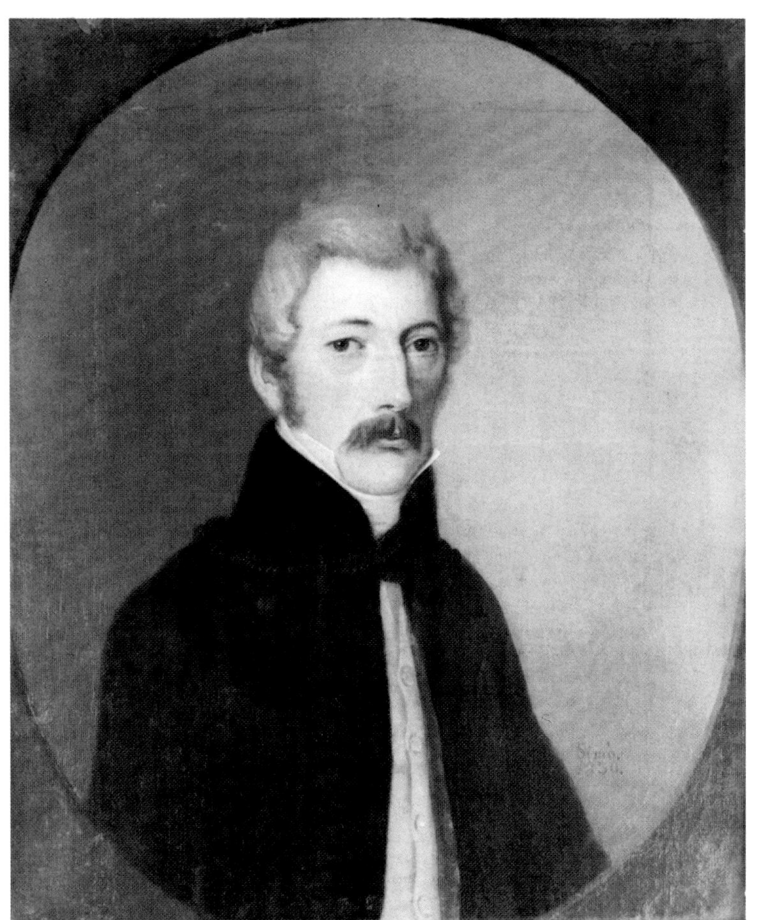 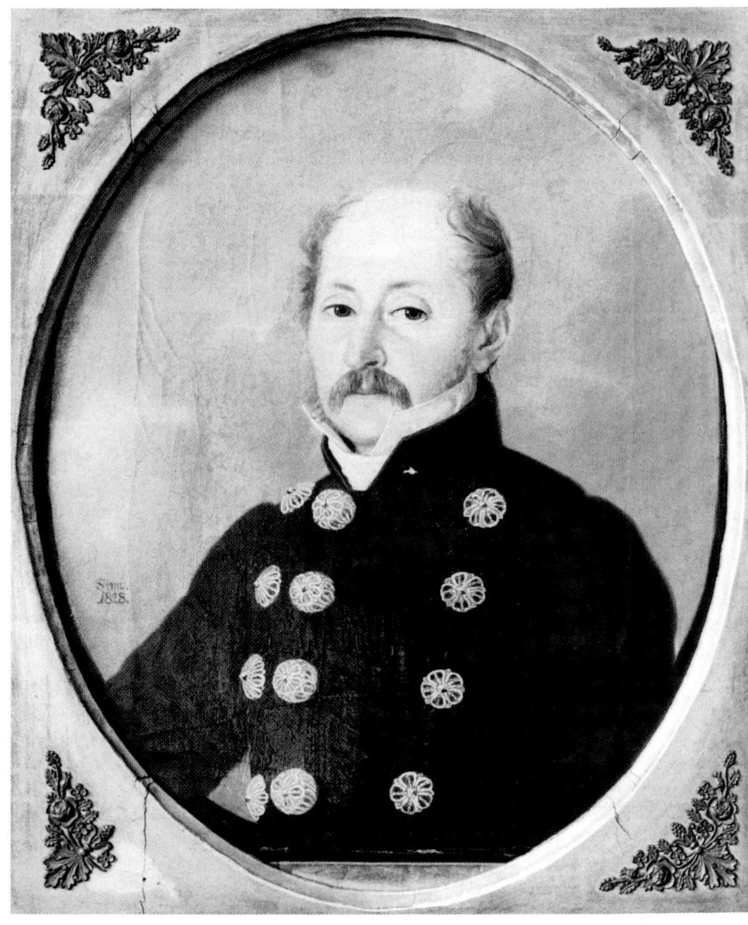

69. FERENC SIMÓ
Portrait of Alajos Mednyánszky, 1830
Oil on canvas, 32 × 26 cm
Signed bottom right: "Simó 1830"
Budapest, Hungarian Academy of Sciences

Ferenc Simó, a Transylvanian artist, settled in Kolozsvár in 1836, where he taught at the School of Drawing. Earlier, however, he had studied for seven years at the Academy of Vienna, then settled in Pest in 1827. There, he devoted himself enthusiastically to the art of portraiture, and painted the likeness of numerous public figures, writers and poets. His talent was first widely acclaimed when he painted a distinguished member of the Academy, Gábor Döbrentei. (At that time, Simó was still in Vienna.) Döbrentei then commissioned Simó to paint portraits of literary figures such as Dániel Berzsenyi, Benedek Virág, Sándor Kisfaludy and Ferenc Kazinczy, for the portrait gallery of the Academy of Sciences.

Two of his small portraits can be seen today in the Academy, mounted in matching oval frames; a third portrait, a likeness of Dániel Berzsenyi, is in the Hungarian National Gallery. The sober expression of the face as well as the sitter's sober dress are features that characterize all the portraits in the series.

70. FERENC SIMÓ
Portrait of Sándor Kisfaludy, 1828
Oil on canvas, 32 × 26 cm
Signed bottom left: "Simo 1828"
Budapest, Hungarian Academy of Sciences

Simó depicted the ageing poet rather freely, taking care, however, to give him a jovial expression. The pink clouds in the background obviously stress the same mood— though it is also possible that they represent an attribute of poets, for they are to be found again in the portrait of Berzsenyi.

71. JÓZSEF SCHOEFFT after AUGUST SCHOEFFT
István Széchenyi at the Iron Gate of the Danube, 1836
Oil on canvas, 150 × 113 cm
Signed bottom right: "Jos. Schoefft"
Veszprém, Bakony Museum
Inv. No.: 53.7.28

Despite considerable experience in studio work, the compositions of the Schoefft family, who lived in Pest, cannot be compared with those of the Viennese masters. Széchenyi nevertheless agreed to sit for the young August Schoefft in a uniform-like gala dress wearing his sword and decorations. In the background, the mountains of the Iron Gate region of the Danube are painted from an engraving in a realistic manner. Realistic detail extends even to the insertion of a copy of Széchenyi's paper "Jelenkor" (Modern Times) from the year 1836.

This portrait was composed with the intention of gaining publicity and support for Széchenyi's grand project to extend the navigable reaches of the Danube and facilitate trade with neighbouring countries, a cause for which he had been pressing the Austrian Chancellor Klemens Metternich and the Hungarian Parliament. This would account for the fact that there are two versions, also several copies by József Schoefft, the painter's father.

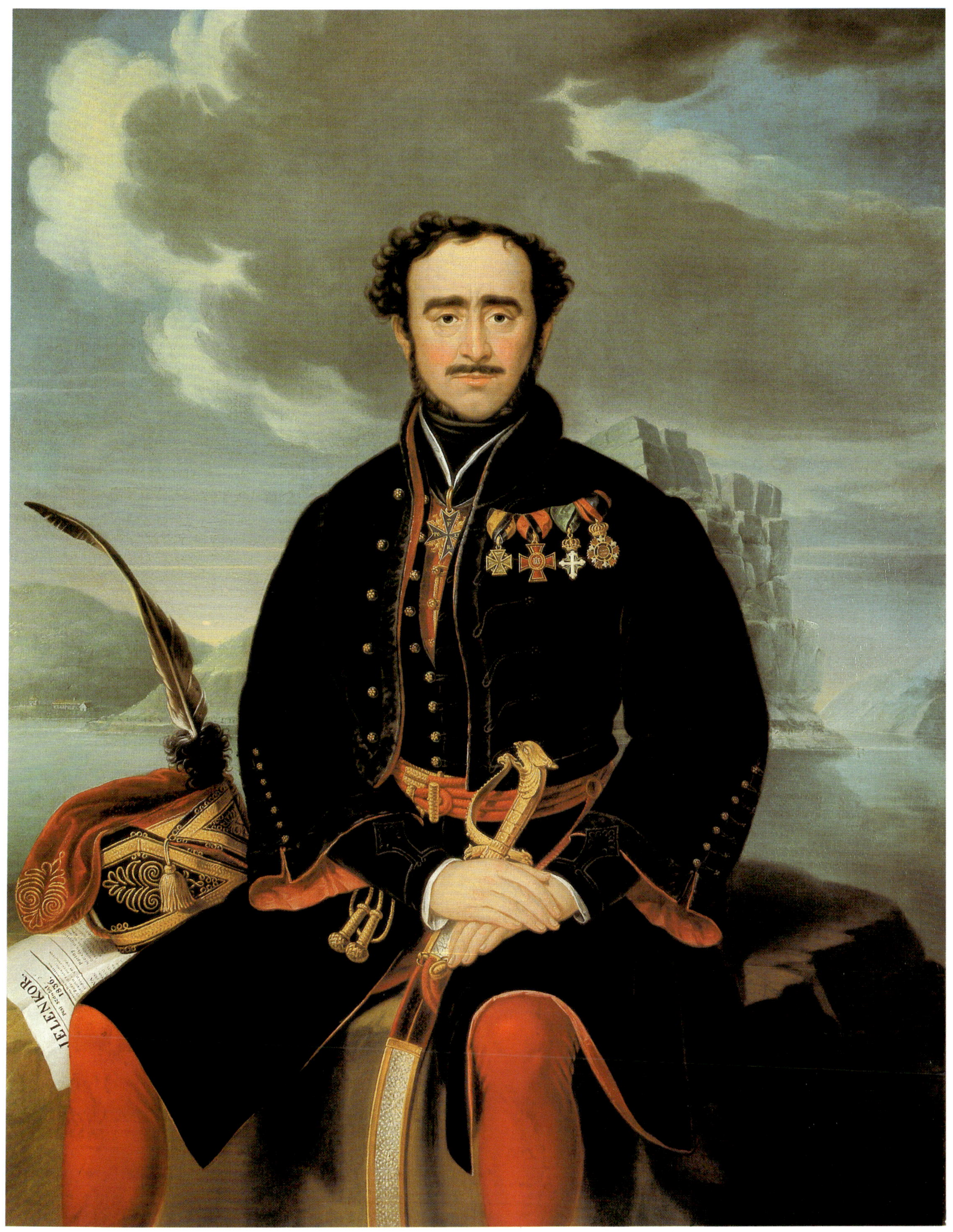
JELENKOR.
Pest Szombat 1836.

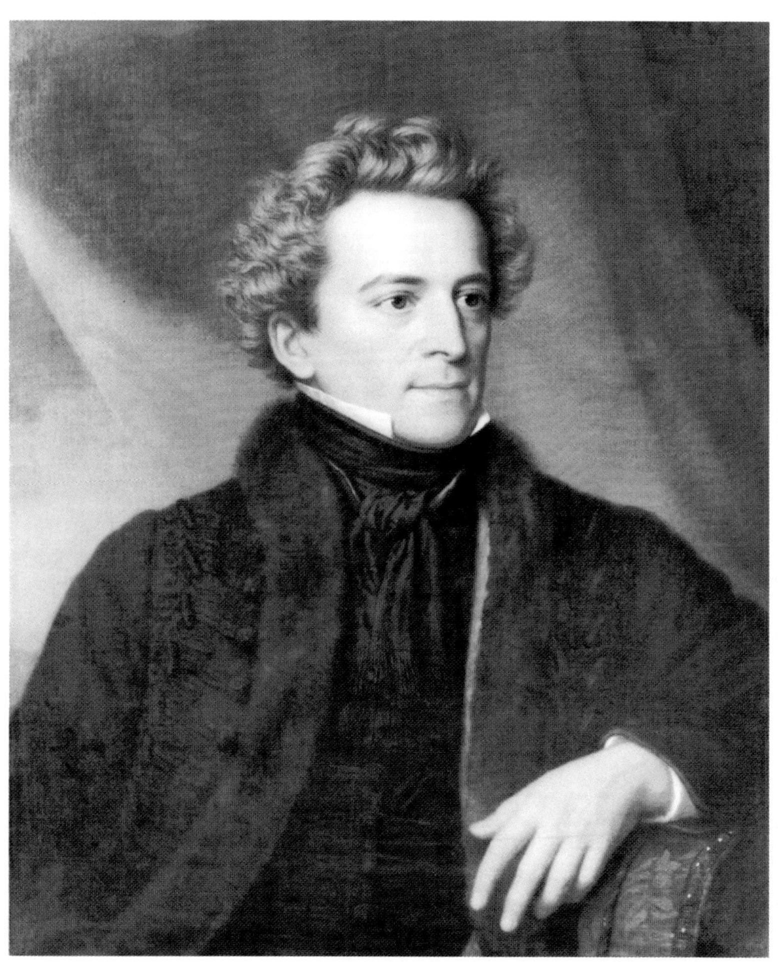

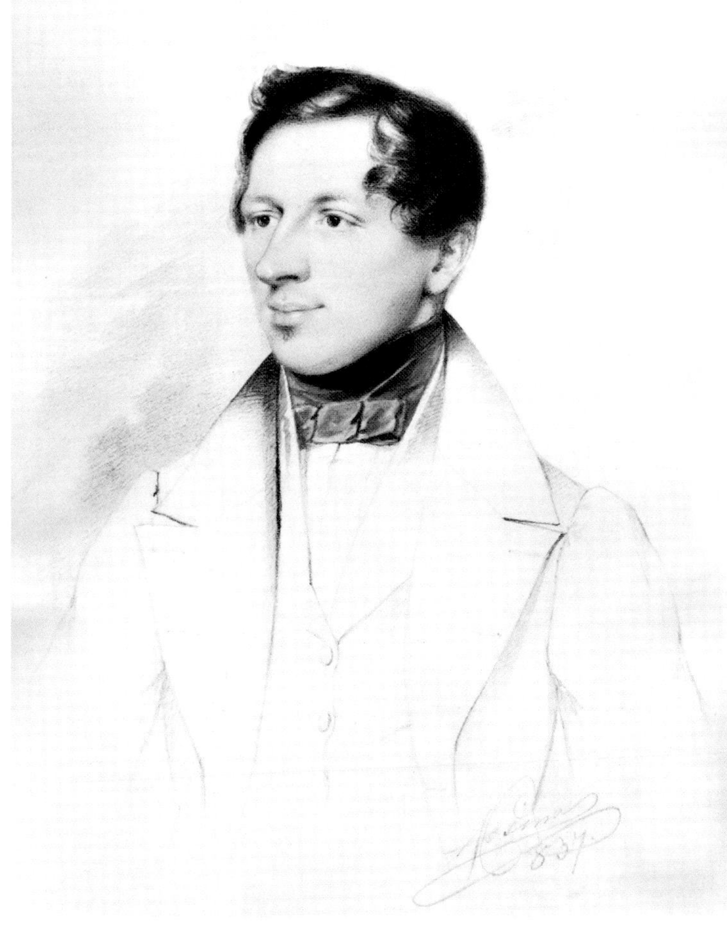

72. JOHANN ENDER
Portrait of Count József Dessewffy, 1830
Oil on canvas, 80×64 cm
Unsigned
Budapest, Hungarian Academy of Sciences

Johann Ender painted two portraits of Count József Dessewffy, also one of the founding members of the Academy of Sciences. The young aristocrat is depicted wearing discreet and elegant clothes, his features being markedly idealized. His intellectual appearance has not been emphasized as a mere gesture of respect to the institution for which the portrait was intended; it genuinely reflects the qualities of the sitter whose political views are of great interest to historians. His view of Széchenyi's famous "Credit" was at one time considered to be too conservative; however, on agrarian questions, Dessewffy took a more radical stand than Széchenyi. For example, he advocated the abolition of serfdom and representation in Parliament for the peasants. Dessewffy's correspondence in which he gives his views on the writing of art history and literary criticism in general, as well as other manuscript writings, has not yet been published.

73. SÁNDOR KOZINA
Portrait of Ferenc Pulszky, 1837
Pencil and water-colour on paper,
226×185 mm
Signed bottom right: "Kozina 837"
Budapest, Hungarian National Gallery
Inv. No.: 1951–4435

This portrait of Ferenc Pulszky, who in the early years of the Romantic movement was a well-known scholar in the field of art history, is one of a series of drawings by Sándor Kozina, who became acquainted with the young scholar in the early 1830s when they were both studying classical remains in Italy. Kozina gives a detailed rendering of the face, the rest of the figure being only delicately sketched so as to facilitate later a possible portrait in oil.

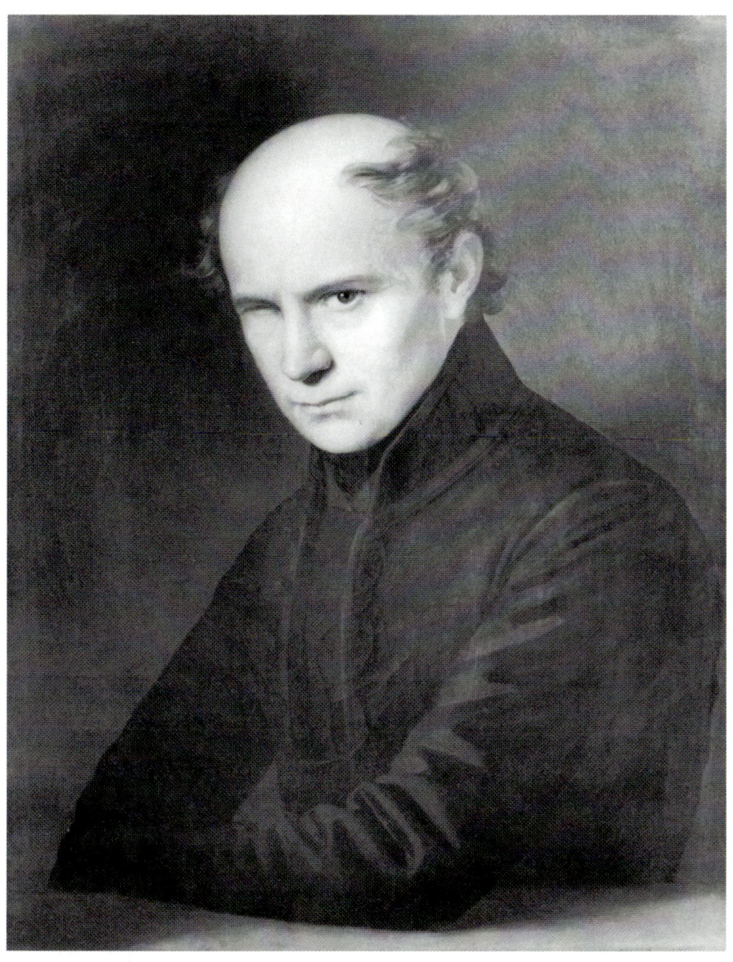

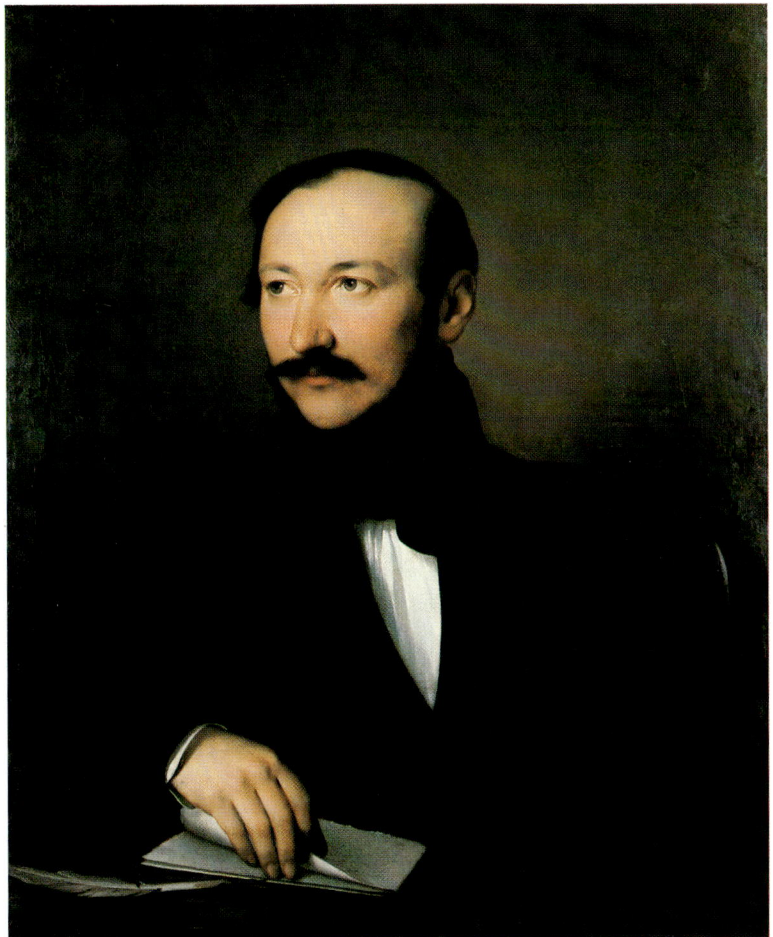

74. ANTON EINSLE
Portrait of Ferenc Kölcsey, 1835
Oil on canvas, 66 × 52.5 cm
Signed bottom right: "Einsle 835"
Budapest, Hungarian Academy of Sciences

In about 1832, Anton Einsle left Vienna for Pest where he was fortunate enough to secure the patronage of Joseph, Palatine of Hungary. This portrait of the distinguished poet and writer, Ferenc Kölcsey, was commissioned by the Academy and is modelled after previous portraits in oil and watercolour. Kölcsey was the author of the "National Anthem", and an epigrammatic poem entitled "Huszt", as well as other memorable Hungarian poems which reflect a romantic sentiment towards the past and the present. These works and his contributions as a Member of Parliament from 1832 onwards, gained him the respect of the nation as well as that of members of the Academy of Sciences.

75. MIKLÓS BARABÁS
Portrait of Mihály Vörösmarty, 1836
Oil on canvas, 76 × 61 cm
Unsigned
Budapest, Hungarian Academy of Sciences

Miklós Barabás was the first Hungarian painter elected to the Academy of Sciences, which was founded to promote equally the arts and sciences. Sensible of the honour accorded him by the Academy in offering him the commission to paint the poet and playwright Mihály Vörösmarty, the great literary figure of Hungarian Romanticism, he posed his subject in a way that shows his respect. The pose is similar to that adopted by Kölcsey in the portrait by Anton Einsle, the high domed forehead being singled out for emphasis. In his right hand Vörösmarty holds the page of a manuscript, a movement which accounts for the tilt of the head; it also reinforces the narrative character of the painting by drawing our attention to the pen, the poet's tool, lying on the table.

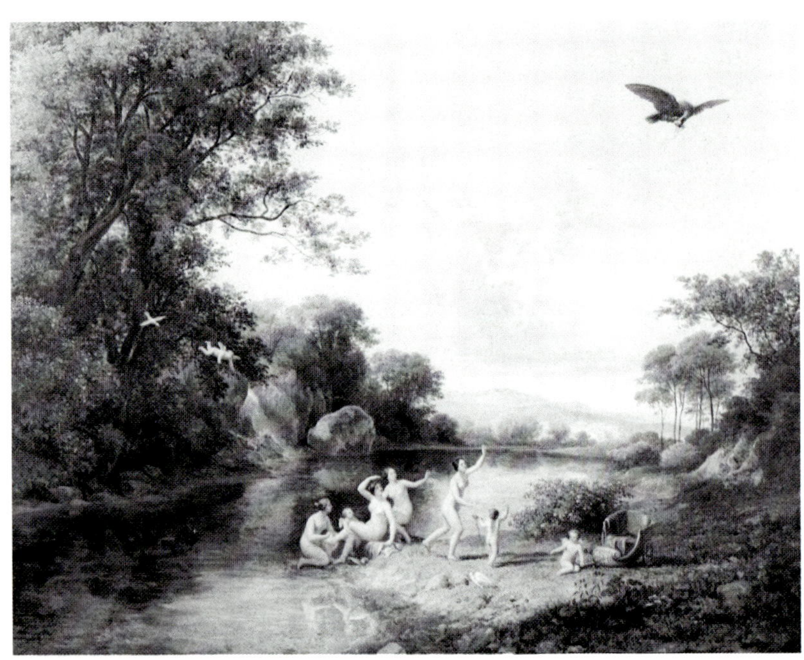

76. KÁROLY MARKÓ, the Elder
Rhodopis's Shoe, 1835
Oil on wood, 37.5 × 48 cm
Signed bottom left: "C. Markó 1835"
Budapest, private collection

In this type of painting, perfected in Italy, Károly Markó achieved a balance between the representation of a group of mythological figures and the strictly Classical landscape. In most of his paintings Markó follows his model, Claude Lorrain, in representing mythological and genre motifs partially concealed within the landscape.

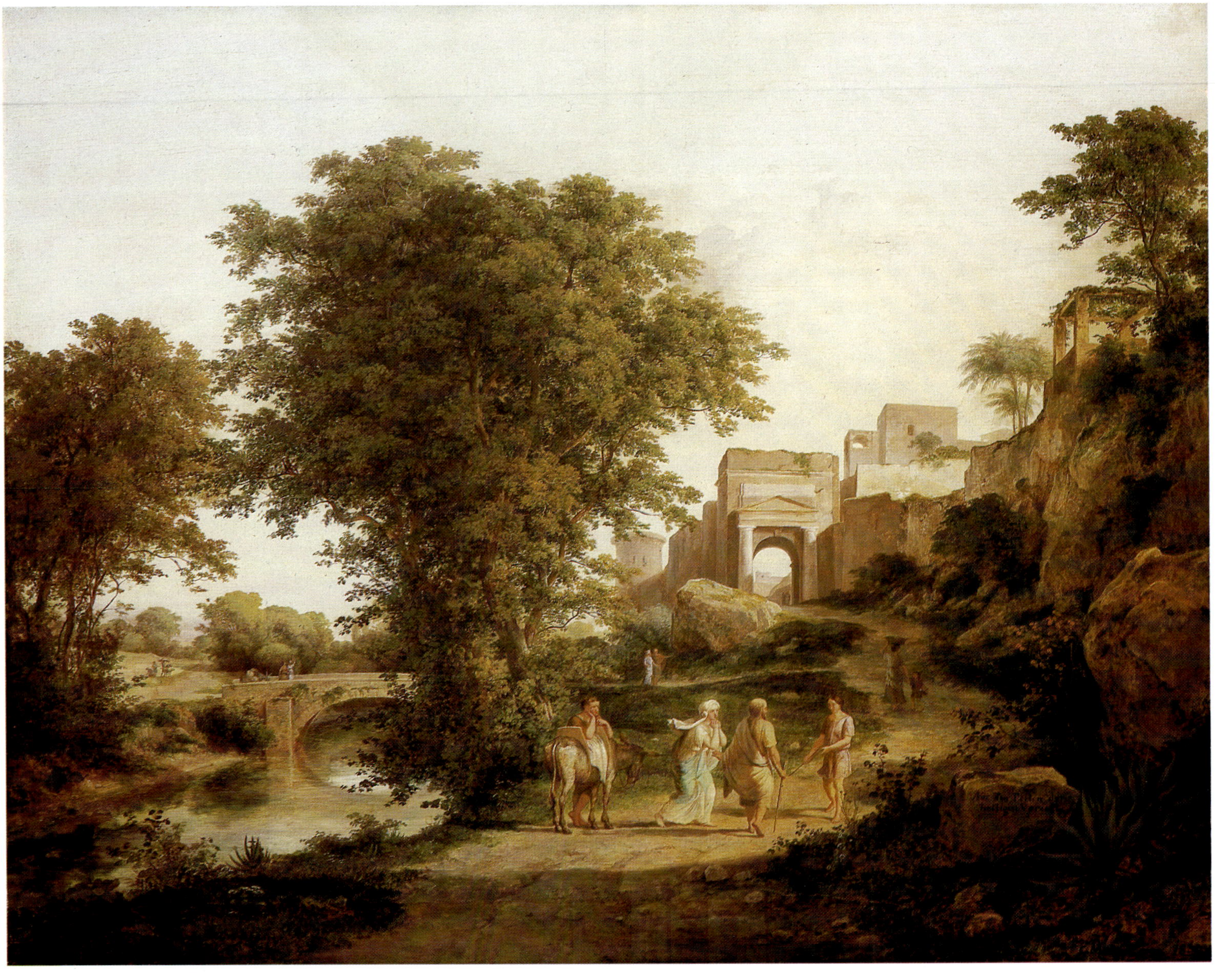

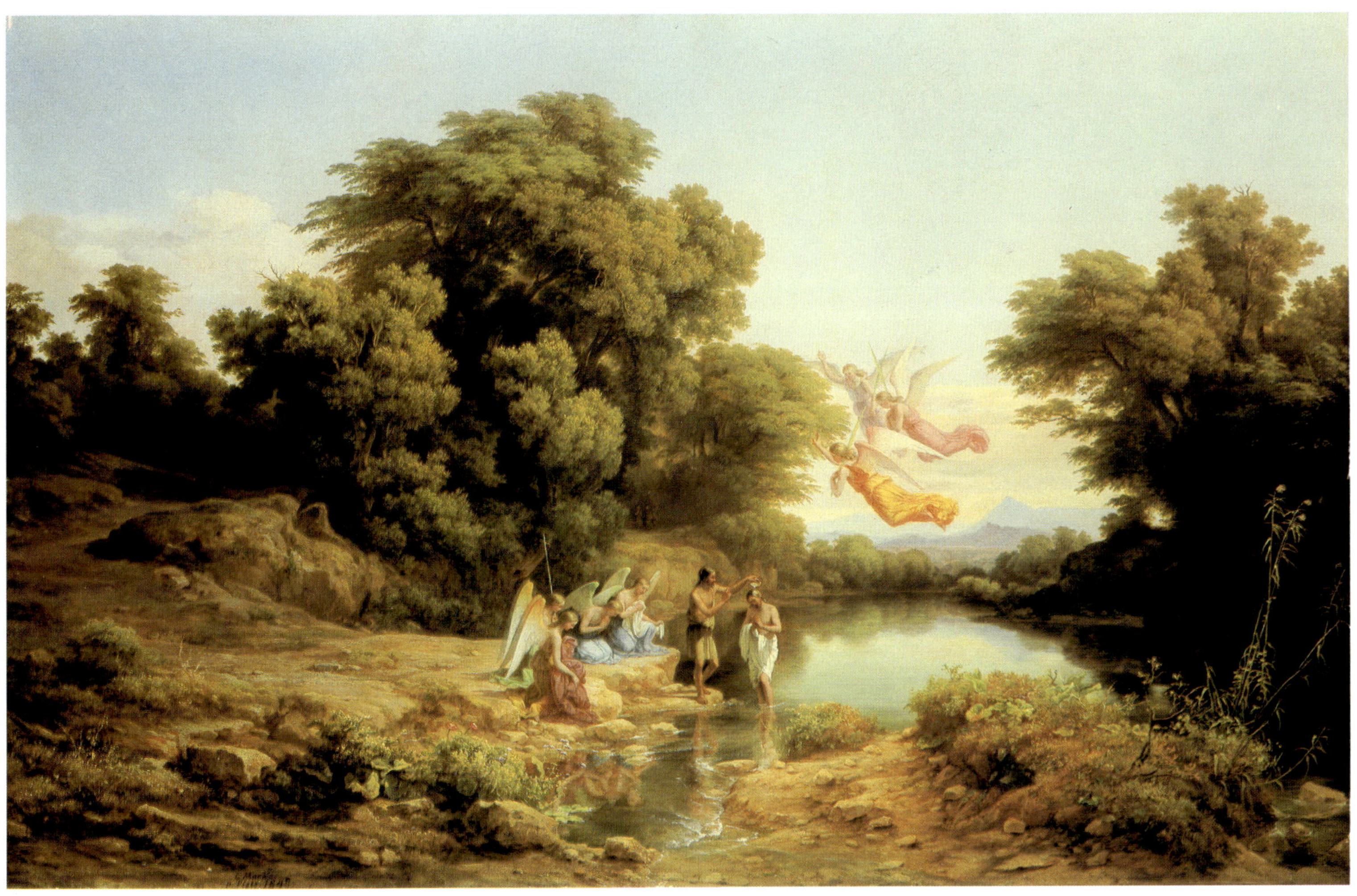

77. KÁROLY MARKÓ, the Elder
From "The Pearls of the Holy Past", 1833

Oil on wood, 43.5 × 55 cm
Inscription: "AUS DEN PERLEN DER
HEILIGEN VORZEIT
Vom C. Markó gem. 1833"
Budapest, Hungarian National Gallery
Inv. No.: 3076
From the collection of Archbishop János László
Pyrker

This picture illustrates a scene from János László Pyrker's poem, "Die Perlen der heiligen Vorzeit" (Buda, 1821). The painting was commissioned by Pyrker and was made by Markó during his stay in Rome. It represents Christ as a wanderer meeting other travellers on his way. The ancient ruins in the background evoke the age of Antiquity. The picture owes its existence to the determination of one of Hungary's cultured art patrons to have his Romantic literary efforts illustrated in a mythological landscape painting. In 1836 Archbishop János László Pyrker donated his collection of paintings, including this work, to the National Museum. Thus, this masterpiece by Károly Markó, the Elder became part of the national heritage.

78. KÁROLY MARKÓ, the Elder
The Baptism of Christ in the River Jordan, 1840–1841

Oil on wood, 44 × 64.5 cm
Signed bottom left: "C. Markó p. Pisis
184..."
Budapest, Hungarian National Gallery
Inv. No.: 3072
Donated to the National Museum by
Zsigmond Deáky,
Bishop of Caesaropolis, in 1842

The scene, favoured by the Nazarene painters, was also used twice by Károly Markó, the Elder. This painting was commissioned by Bishop Zsigmond Deáky, an admirer of the artist. The background is composed of familiar Italian landscape elements, creating an idealized valley with the atmosphere of a fairy tale, though the scene of the baptism is represented as described in the Gospels. Jesus Christ and St. John the Baptist are represented standing in the river, painted in brighter colours and on a larger scale than were the figures in any mythological scene painted by Markó. A choir of angels, in clear pink robes, kneeling on the river bank and hovering between the trees, symbolize heavenly approval of the baptism.

125

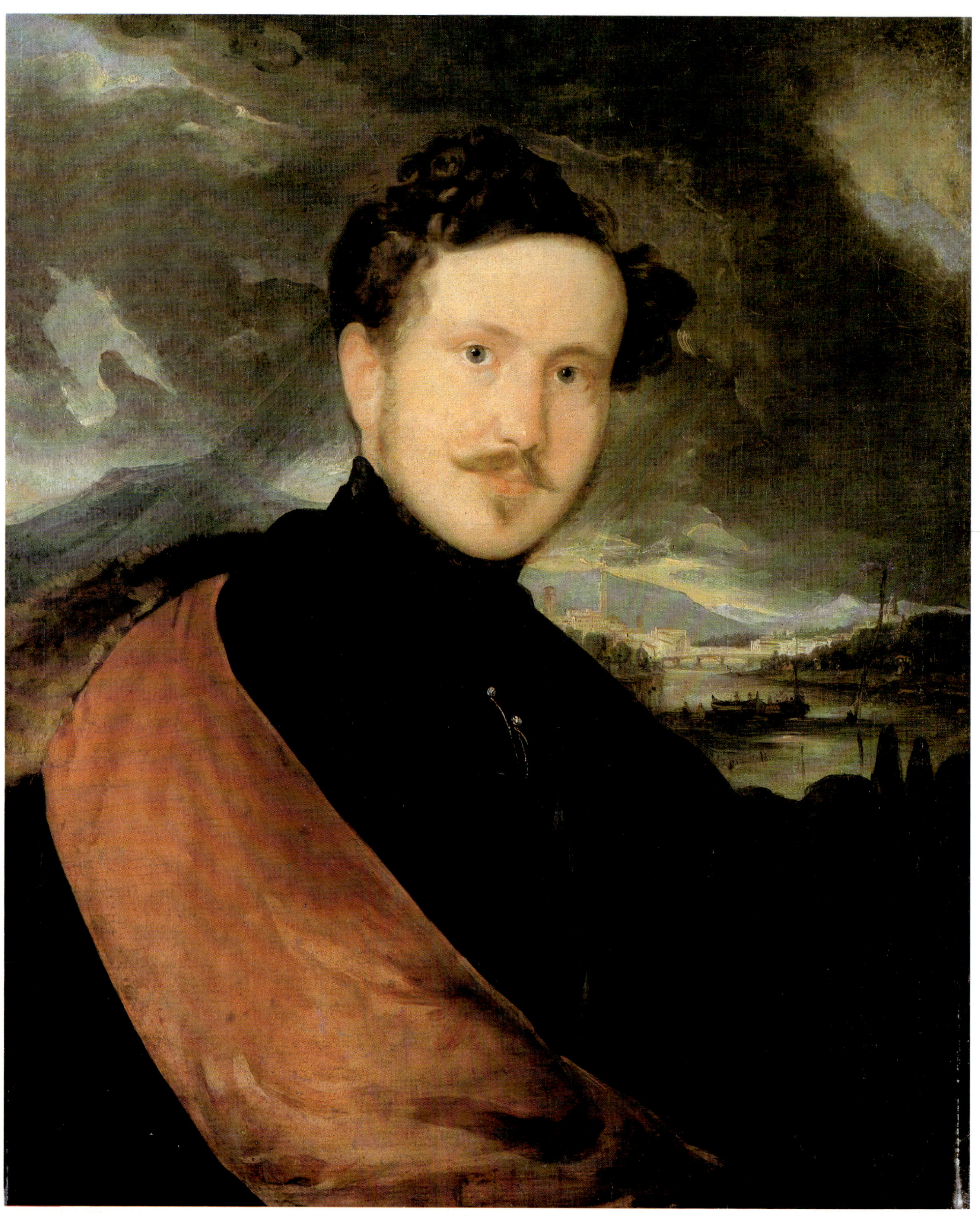

79. SÁNDOR KOZINA
Self-portrait, 1832

Oil on canvas, 73×58 cm
Unsigned
Budapest, Hungarian National Gallery
Inv. No.: 6097

This self-portrait was painted by Sándor
Kozina in Florence. It is an oil painting but
creates an effect more often produced by
water-colour. The painter is outlined against
a sky clearing after an evening storm, with
a distant townscape in the background. Experts of Kozina's works especially admire his
special skill in combining figures and landscape.

80. MIKLÓS BARABÁS
Portrait of William Leighton Leitch, Scottish Water-colourist, 1834

Sepia, 189×245 mm
Signed on the bottom: "Barabás en Florenz
1834 Noo. 16, Portrait de mon ami W. L.
Leitsch peintre anglais."
Budapest, Hungarian National Gallery
Inv. No.: 1903–68

As in previous centuries, Italy in the 1830s
was a mecca for painters from all parts of
Europe. After finishing their studies in Vienna, most Hungarian artists proceeded to Italy, which they subsequently revisited.
Miklós Barabás painted this sepia of his
friend Leitch, a Scottish water-colourist, on
their tour of Italy. He was not, however,
commissioned to make a portrait in oils.
From surviving water-colours of his it
would seem that Leitch was more skilled in
technique and more modern in his approach
than Barabás, but he was a less talented artist.

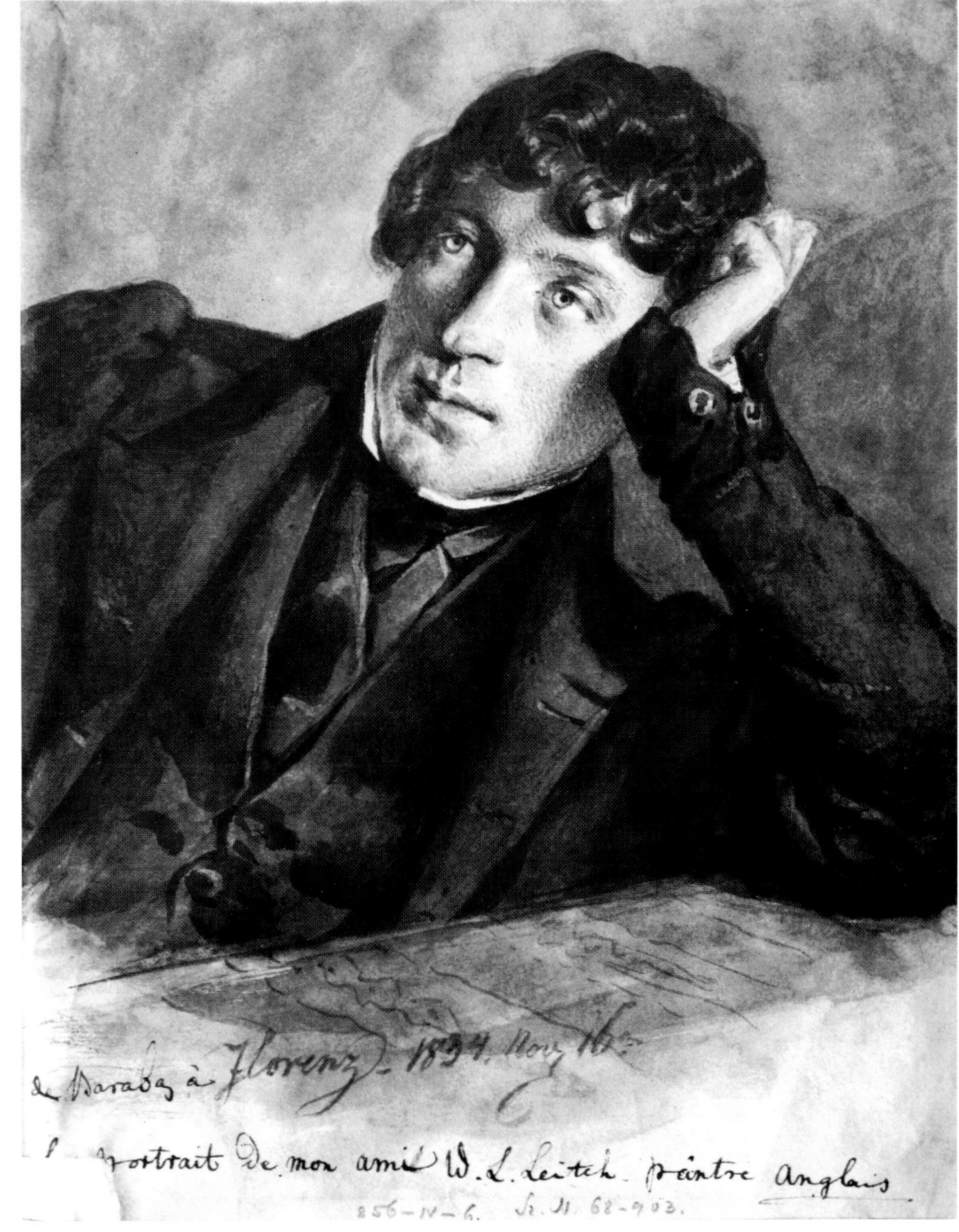

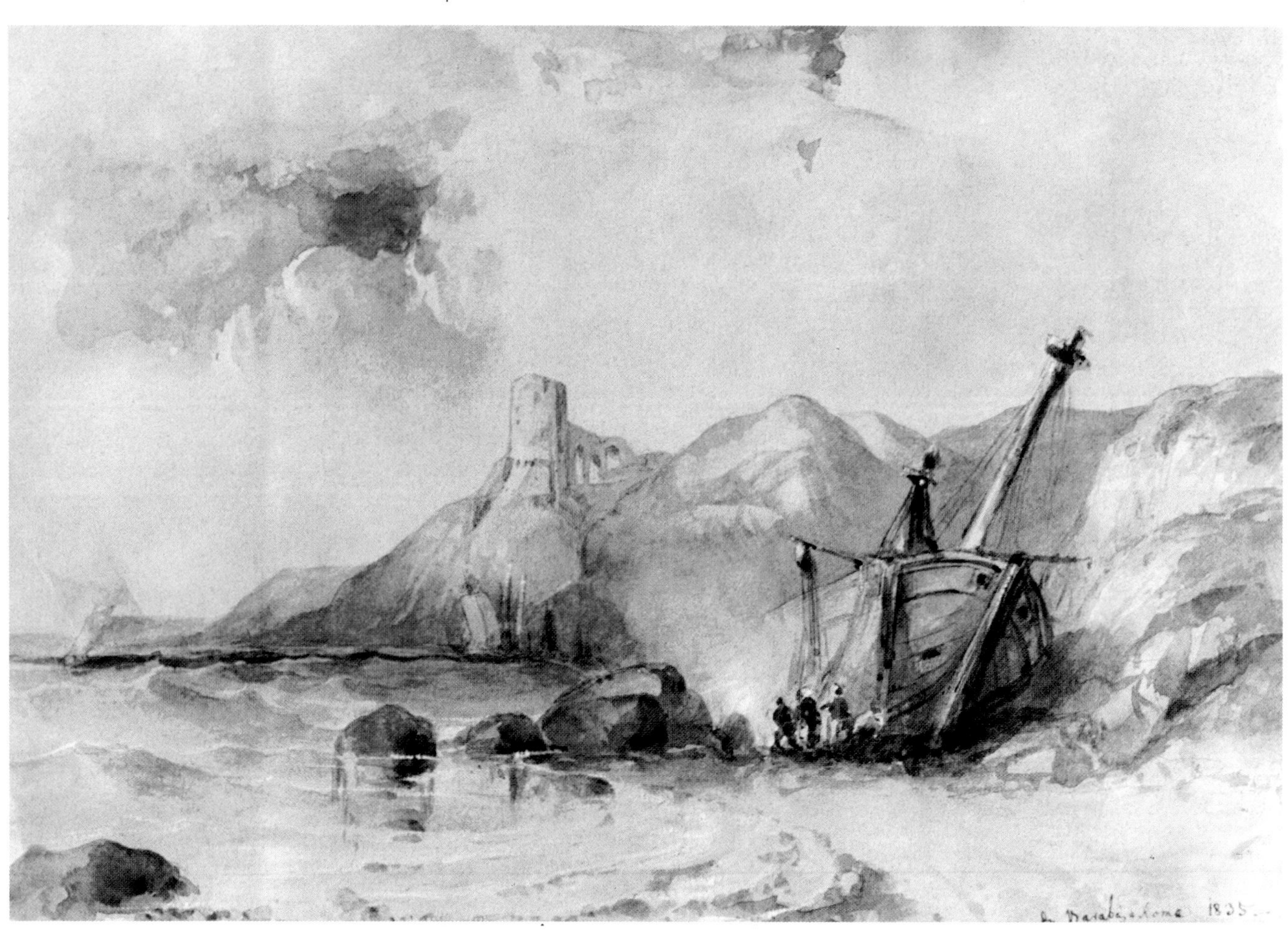

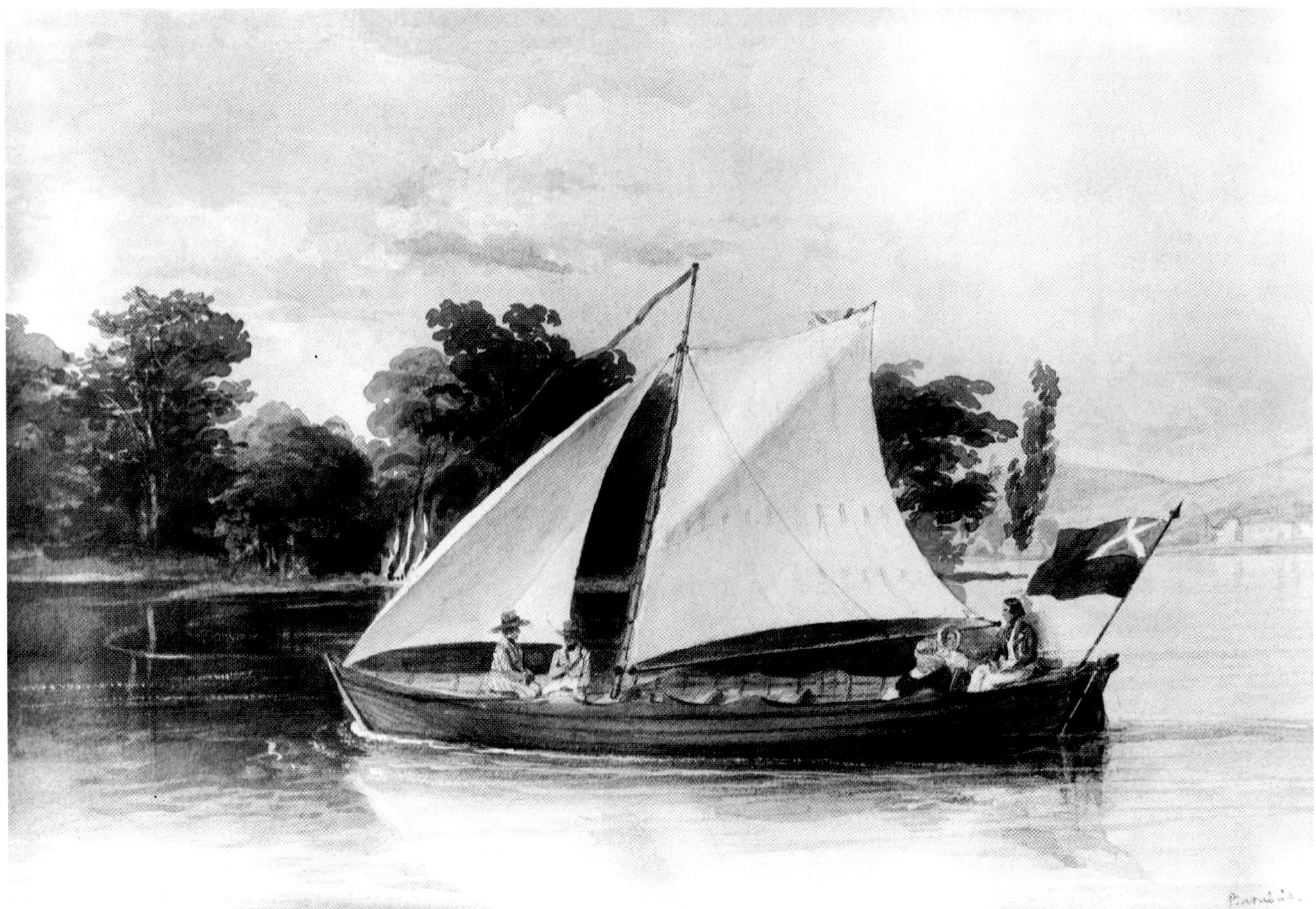

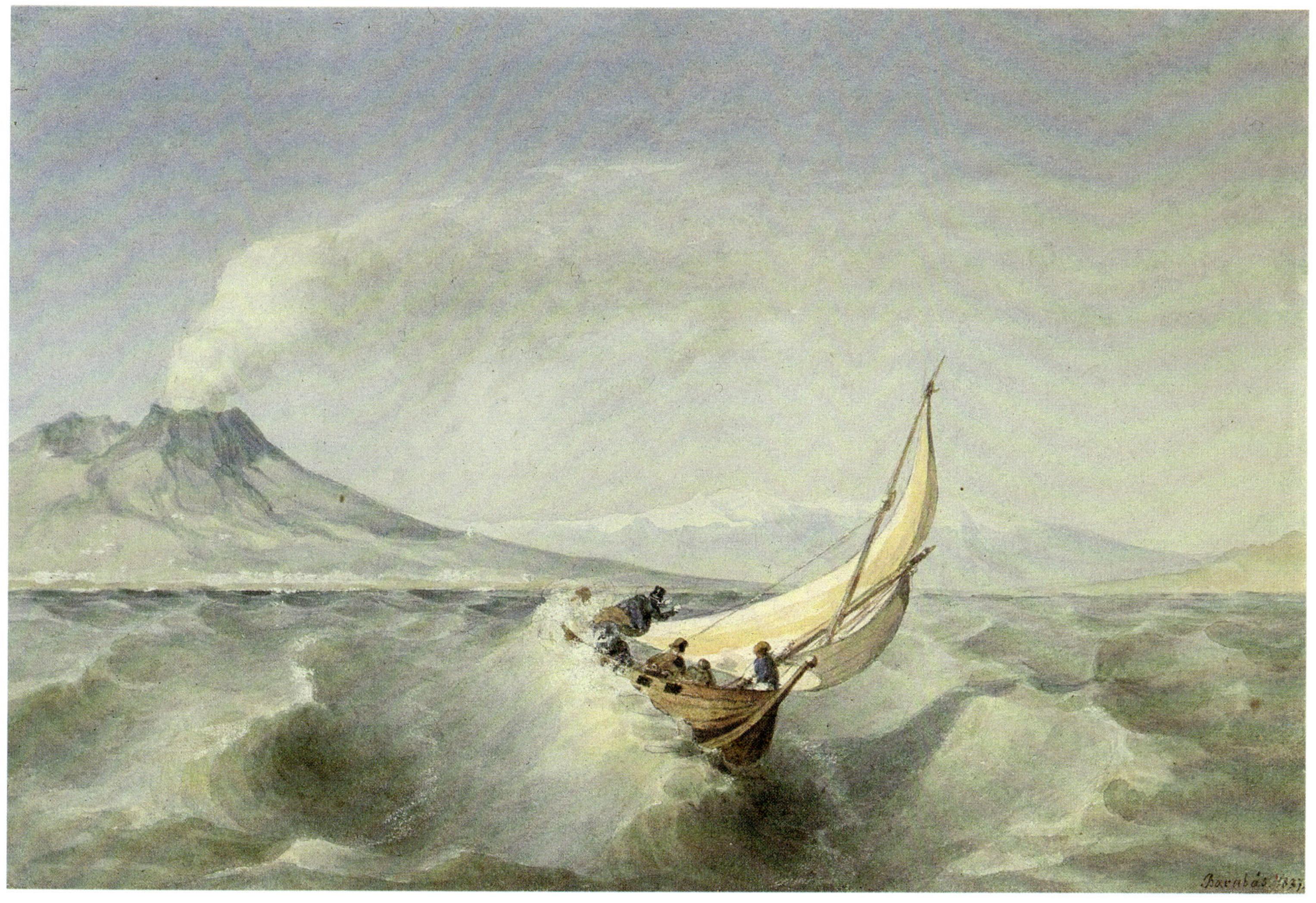

81. MIKLÓS BARABÁS
Shipwreck, 1835
Water-colour on paper, 149 × 215 mm
Signed bottom right: "Barabás/Róma, 1835"
Villány, private collection

Barabás made several versions of this composition and of others in which a shipwreck is the theme. In all of them we find the traditional motifs used for this subject of catastrophe: a ship in distress or actually sinking, a sailing boat tossed by the waves, cliffs by a seashore, and, for topographical precision, some indication of place, such as Vesuvius in smoke. These water-colours were not painted from nature, but were based on sketches of natural phenomena found in museums. The individual motifs were modelled after details seen in engravings, drawings and prints.

82. MIKLÓS BARABÁS
Adam Clark's Sail Boat, 1842
Water-colour on paper, 180 × 250 mm
Signed bottom right: "Barabás"
Budapest, Kiscelli Museum of the Budapest Historical Museum
Inv. No.: 581

Changing effects caused by the movement of air and water greatly interested Barabás, as shown in this painting of Adam Clark, the English engineer invited to Hungary by Count István Széchenyi to help him with his scheme for regulating the Danube. He is also well known as the engineer who, with his brother, designed the Chain Bridge which links Buda and Pest. In Barabás's water-colour Clark is shown in his sailing boat, measuring the depth of the Danube.

83. MIKLÓS BARABÁS
Boat in a Stormy Sea, I, 1837
Water-colour on paper, 149 × 215 mm
Signed bottom right: "Barabás 1837"
Budapest, Hungarian National Gallery
Inv. No.: 1903–93

Towards the end of the 1830s Barabás, having returned to Hungary, was still toying with the idea of producing a series of oil-paintings based on his small water-colour Italian seascapes. A few landscapes have been discovered by research workers but the seascapes survive only as a series of water-colours, providing a most beautiful souvenir of Barabás's journey to Italy.

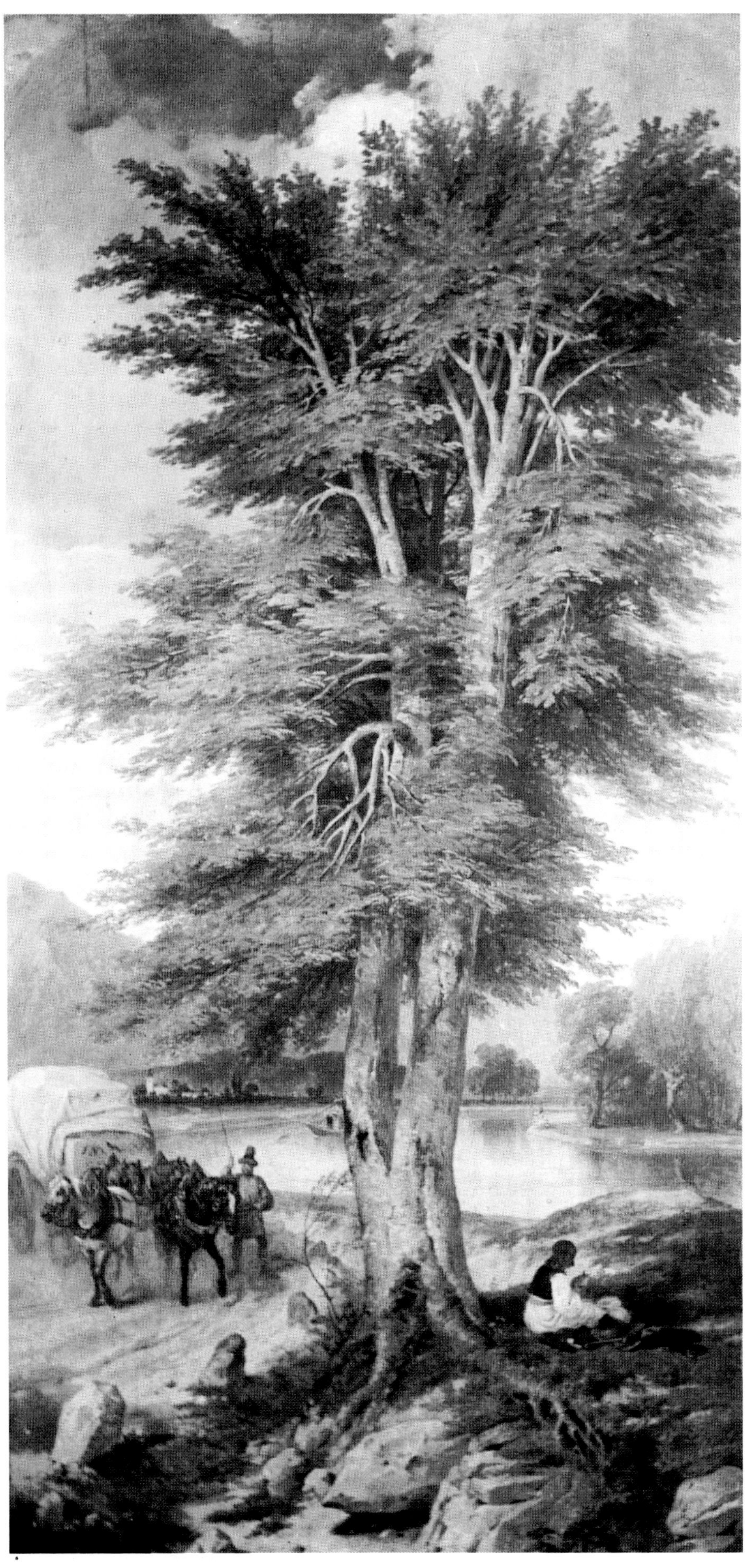

84. MIKLÓS BARABÁS
Trade-sign for the "Zöldfa" (Green Tree) Drapery Shop, 1838
Oil on wood, 192 × 94 cm
Signed bottom right: "Barabás, 1838"
Budapest, Kiscelli Museum of the Budapest Historical Museum
Inv. No.: 8865

In the 1830s Barabás was chiefly interested in drawing or painting landscapes. This might account for his readiness to undertake the painting of a trade-sign for the "Zöldfa" Drapery Shop in fashionable Váci Street in Pest. He was particularly interested in the lifelike representation of landscape detail and the creation of genre motifs. In this painting a weary traveller is shown resting in the shade of a large tree as a wagon waits nearby. The enormous tree offering shelter to a passerby is, as it were, an emblem of the shop.

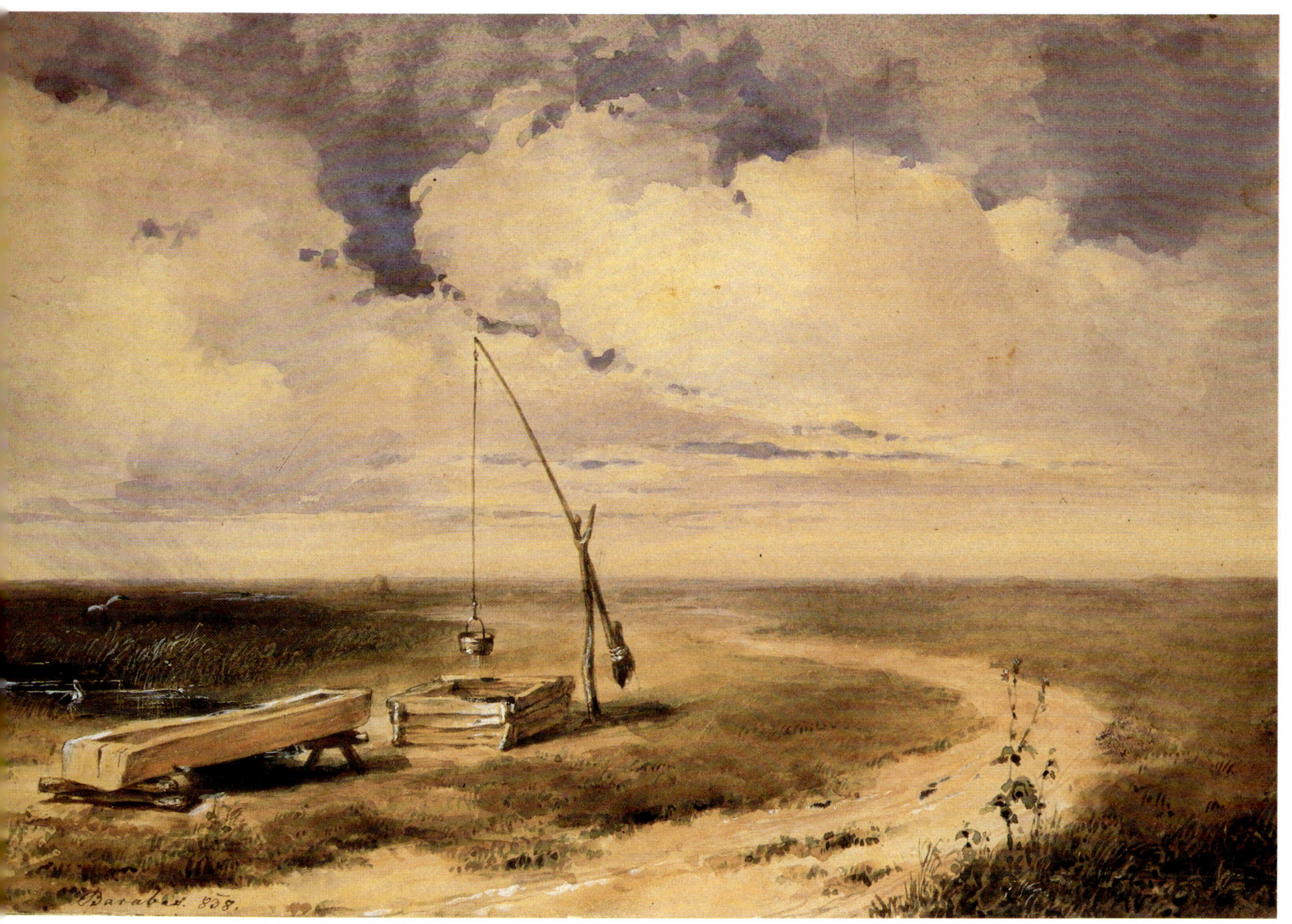

85. MIKLÓS BARABÁS
The "Puszta" (The Great Hungarian Plain with Beam Well), 1838

Water-colour on paper, with white body-colour, 200 × 290 mm
Signed bottom left: "Barabás 838"
Pécs, Janus Pannonius Museum
Inv. No.: 68.13

Barabás here applies his virtuosity as a water-colourist to evoke the mysterious atmosphere and beauty of the Great Hungarian Plain. This small painting was finished two years before Petőfi wrote his poem about the *Puszta* which was so widely acclaimed. Barabás's presents with unpretentious directness the seemingly endless plain which shares the canvas with a view of clouds scuddling across the sky, the two areas being divided by the line of the horizon. A cart track winds its way into the distance, the monotony relieved only by the storks in the rushes and the thistles turning yellow by the roadside. Attention is focused on the beam-well, without which there could be no life in the Puszta. The well is seen as the saviour of life as in the poems of Sándor Petőfi and János Arany, two great "folk" poets of 19th century Hungary.

131

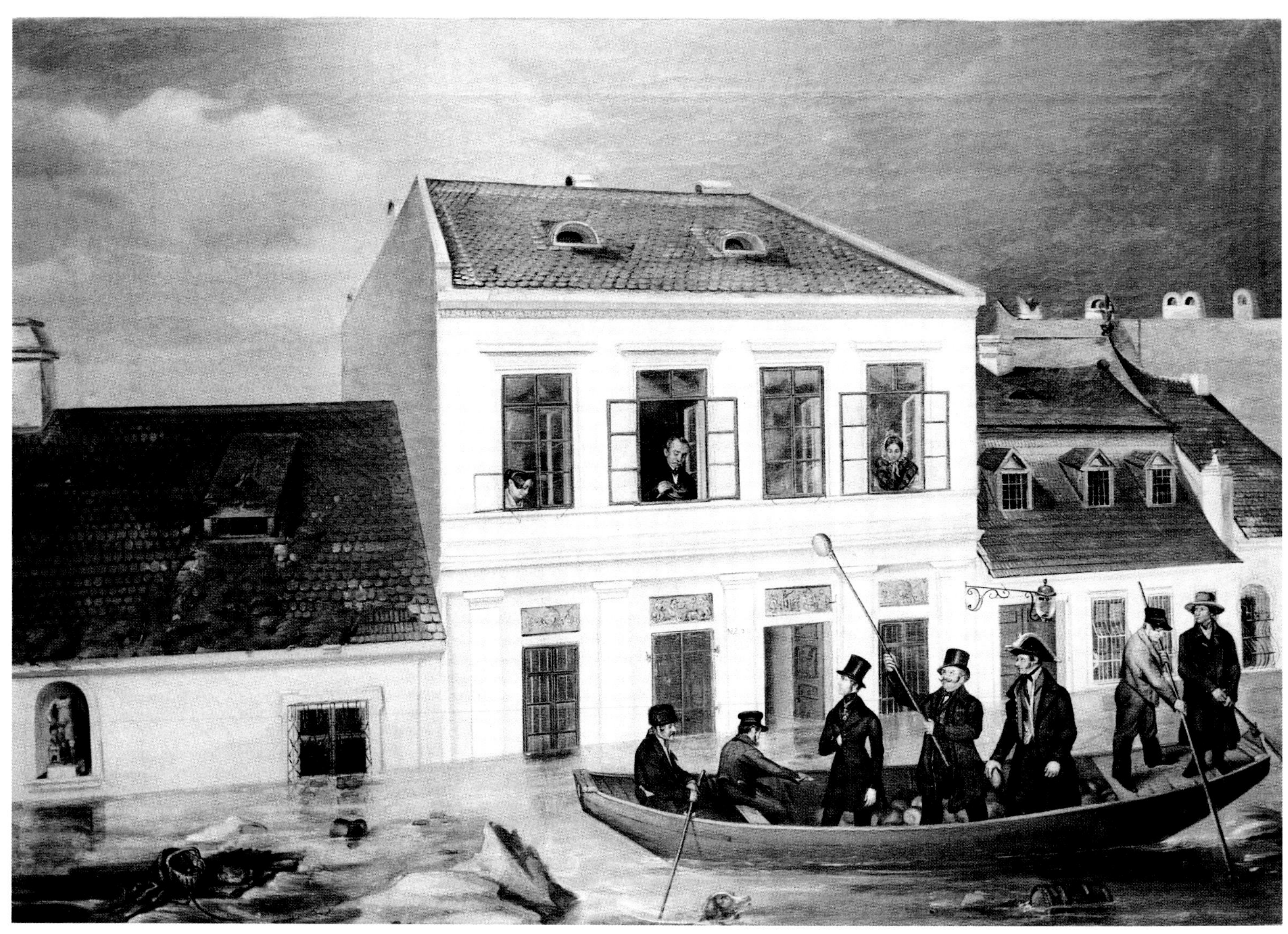

86. HENRIETTA KAERGLING
The Great Flood, 1840
*Signed bottom left: "Henrietta Kaergling
1840"*
Oil on canvas, 65.5 × 90.7 cm
*Budapest, Kiscelli Museum of the Budapest
Historical Museum*
Inv. No.: 81

Henrietta Kaergling, one of a well-known
family of artists living in Pest, was first
taught by her father before completing her
studies in Vienna and Munich. Exhibitions
were by now more frequently arranged in
Pest and it was there that her gift was recognized. Many artists recorded the Great Flood
of 1838 in Pest; for many years, in the József-
város district, a genre-type painting of the
flood by Jakab Warságh, was hung in the St.
Roche Chapel, as thanksgiving from those
who were rescued. Henrietta Kaergling
probably painted this scene of a rescue showing a house in Fő Street, Buda, after several
already existing compositions.

87. IVÁN FORRAY
The Flooded City, 1838
Water-colour on paper, 222 × 135 cm
*Budapest, Kiscelli Museum of the Budapest
Historical Museum*
Inv. No.: 17.066

Iván Forray was an aristocrat who though
only an amateur painter, produced works of
exceptional quality. He was recognized not
only for his sharply observed and technically
accomplished water-colours of the Great
Flood of 1838 in Pest but also for the sketches
he made while travelling in the East in 1842.
The flood, which was one of the great catastrophies of the 1830s, was depicted by
numerous artists.
In his water-colours, Forray vividly represents some of the dramatic incidents of the
scenes described in Mór Jókai's novels. In
the picture reproduced here, a gentleman in
top-hat and tail-coat rides through the flood,
seeking out people standing by open windows, waiting to be rescued.

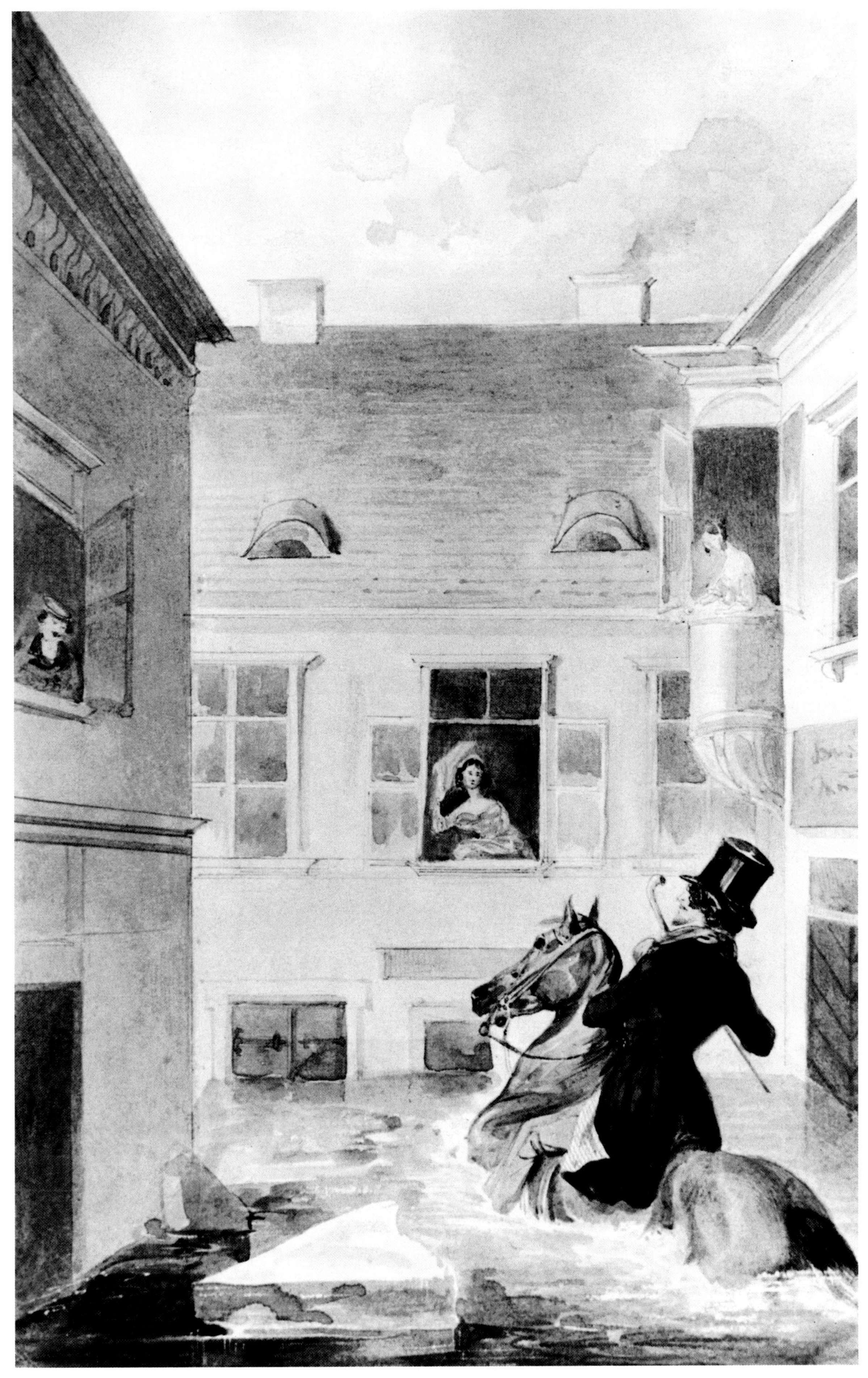

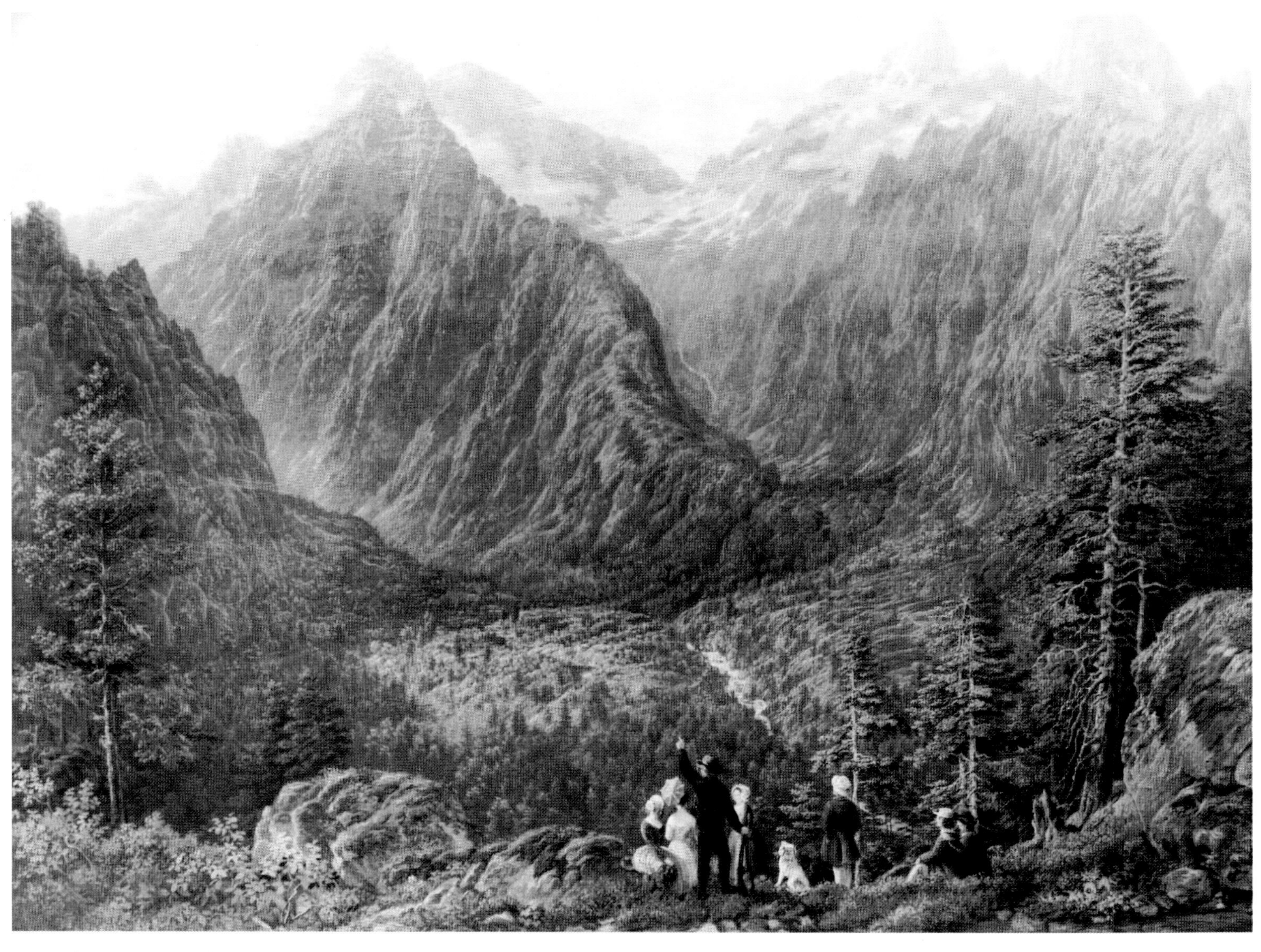

88. KÁROLY TIBÉLY
Landscape in the High Tátra, 1855
Oil on canvas, 49 × 65 cm
Košice, Východoslovenská Galeria

Károly Tibély was a portrait and landscape painter from Upper Hungary. There is a naive directness and freshness in this landscape which conveys the close relationship between man and nature. The mountain peaks and the happy party in the valley below are characterized in a vigorous Romantic style. There are earlier examples of this type of painting by the German Romantics, while later works in the same manner include Pál Szinyei Merse's *Picnic in May*.

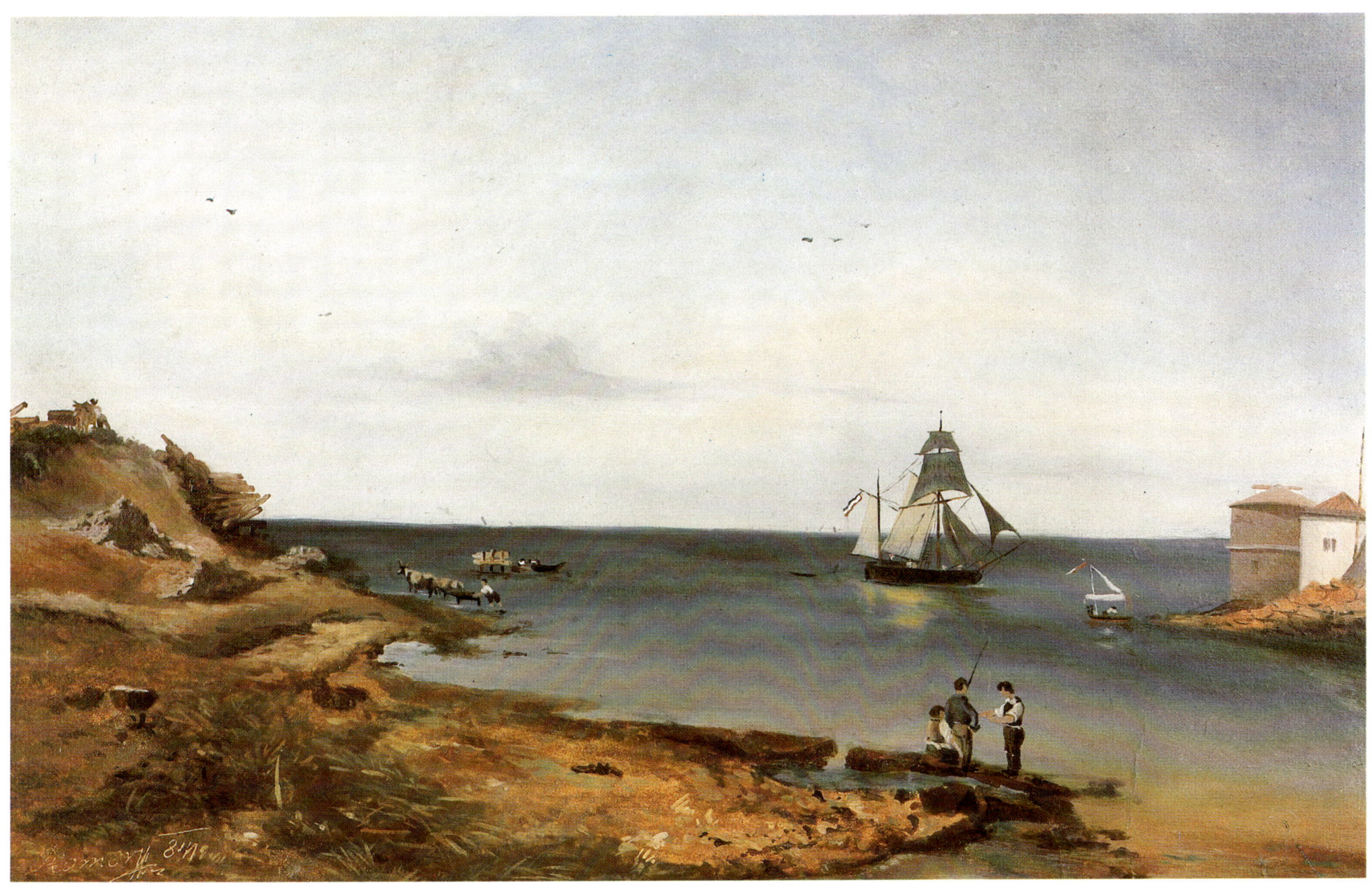

89. FLÓRIS RÓMER
Seascape, 1841
Oil on paper, 34.5 × 59 cm
Signed bottom left: "Rómer 841"
Bratislava, Mestská Galeria
Inv. No.: A. 2031

Flóris Rómer, born in today's Bratislava, was a scholar, art historian, collector and graphic artist. As a Benedictine monk, he became a professor of geography, geology and history in the grammar school in Győr until 1845 when he was offered the chair of Natural Sciences and Geography at the Faculty of Sciences in Pozsony. Some of his early series of pictures and drawings, completed during a period of travel, are now in the Bratislava City Gallery, and provide evidence of the skilful brushwork and talent for composition of a nature artist.

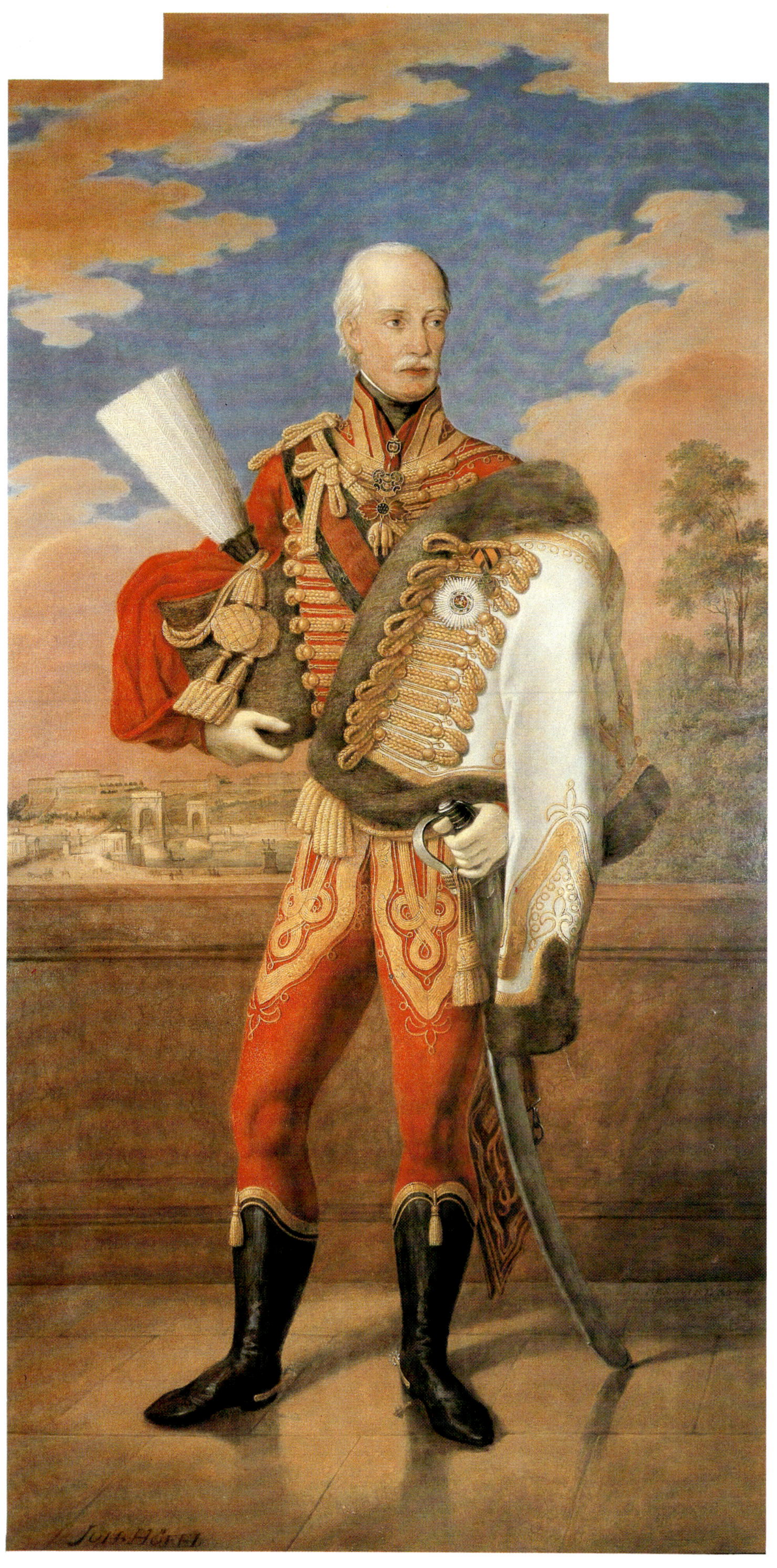

90. JOHANN NEPOMUK HÖFEL
Trade-sign depicting the full-length portrait of Joseph, Palatine of Hungary

Oil on metal, 242×125 cm
Budapest, Kiscelli Museum of the Budapest Historical Museum
Inv. No.: 56. 7. 1.

This full-length portrait of the Habsburg Palatine of Hungary, Joseph, wearing the uniform of a general of the Hungarian Hussars, was painted on metal. In the background we can see the Royal Palace on Castle Hill in Buda. The picture has obviously been retouched several times, a later addition being a representation of the Chain Bridge, (based on an engraving), erected some decades later. This addition may have been to show one of the Palatine's achievements, or it could have been added to supply a topographical detail of the site of his activity. Around 1850 trade-signs incorporated a variety of motifs from contemporary history with a view to publicizing the ideas and deeds of popular figures.

91. MIKLÓS BARABÁS
Trade-sign depicting Miklós Zrínyi, 1842

Oil on canvas, 242 × 99 cm
Budapest, Kiscelli Museum of the Budapest
Historical Museum
Inv. No.: 13.464

Art critics faulted the Austrian painter, Peter Krafft, Sr., for having deviated from historical truth by representing Zrínyi on horseback when he charged out of his fortress against the Turks. In Theodor Körner's drama, "Zrínyi or the Siege of Szigetvár", produced in 1833 in the Castle Theatre of Buda, and in 1837 at Pest's Magyar Theatre, Zrínyi makes his escape on foot, brandishing a sword and a club. It was probably in this play that Barabás found a model for his trade-sign, the costume being that worn by János Bartha in the role of Zrínyi, which he acted with great success. The sign may have been exhibited in the workshop of Ádám Kostyál, Chief Master Tailor of the National Theatre, or it may have been made for the Zrínyi Café opposite the theatre. The painting is notable for the precise detail of the dress, including the band which fastens the Hungarian style overcoat at the collar, the richly decorated belt and the feathered headgear. These details, however, in no way diminish the effect of Zrínyi's heroic stance.

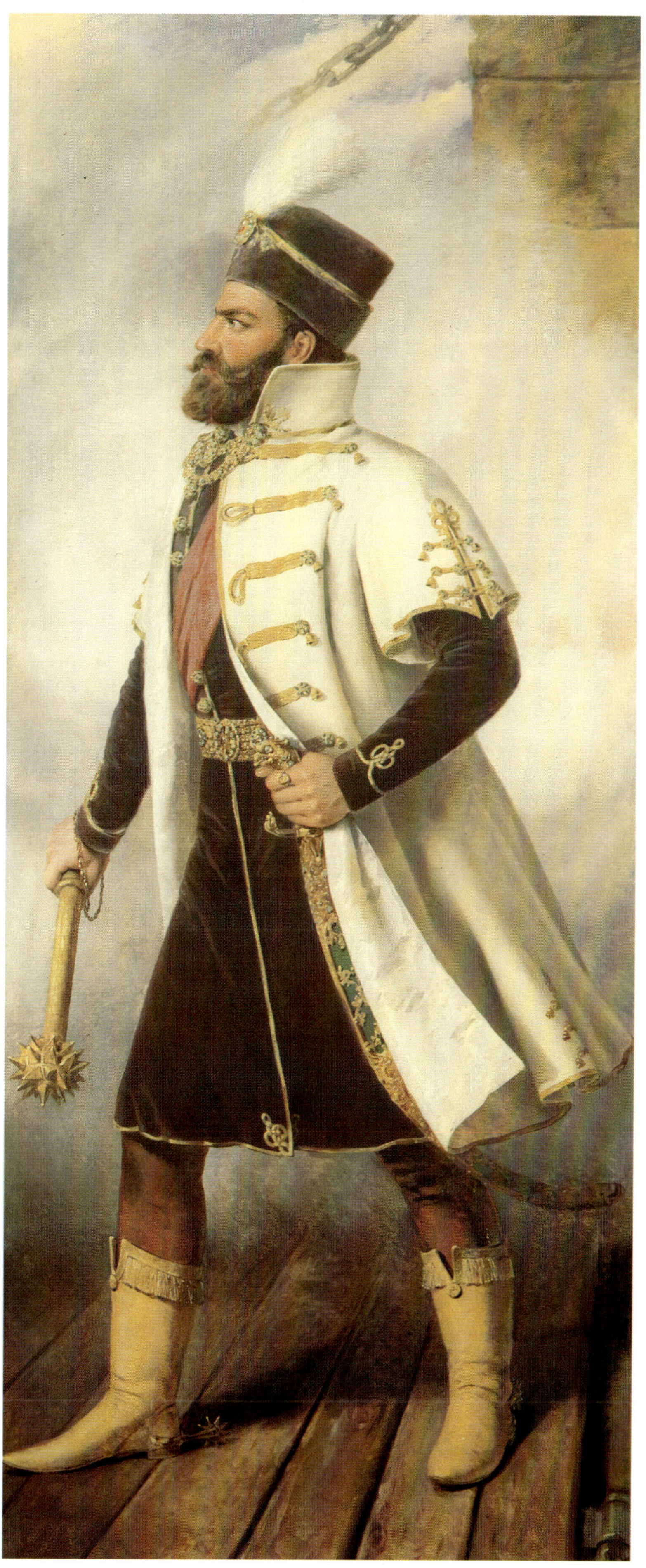

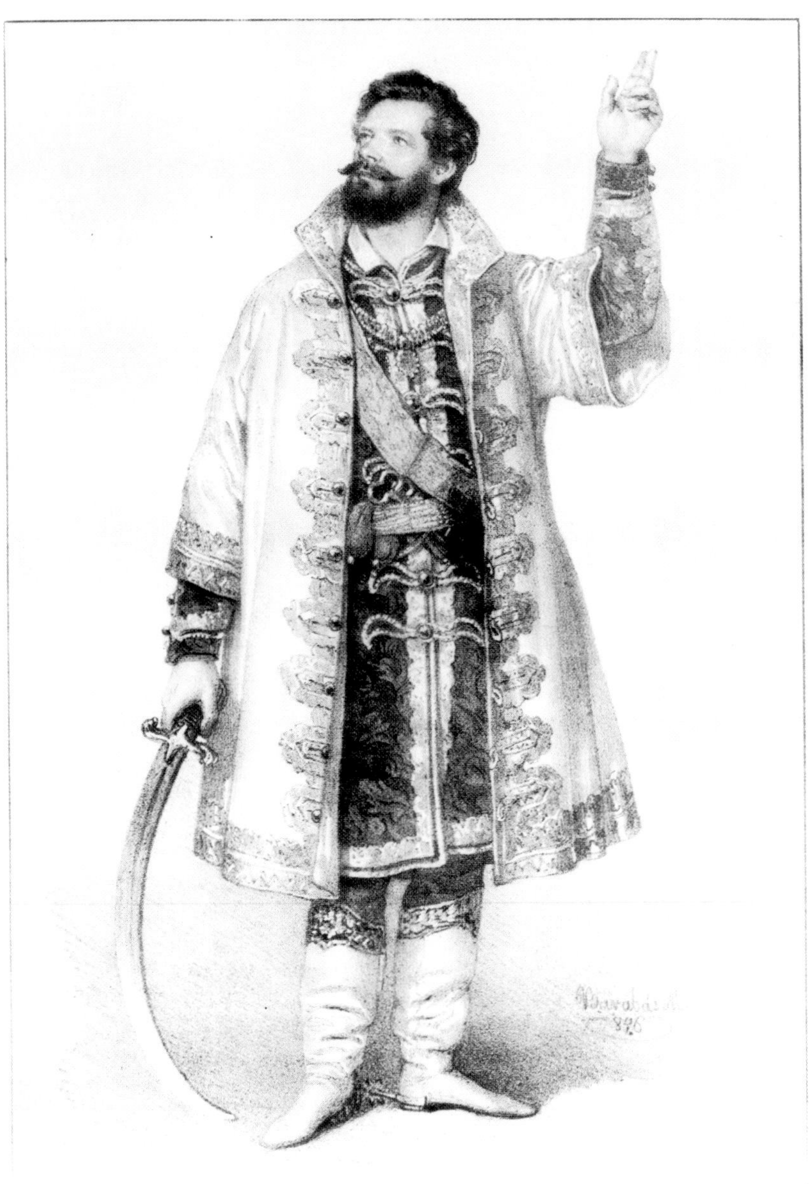

92. MIKLÓS BARABÁS–ÁGOST FRIGYES WALZEL
János Bartha as Miklós Zrínyi, 1836
Lithograph on paper, 314 × 233 mm
Signed bottom left: "Barabás M. 1836"
Inscription: "Bartha mint Zrínyi Miklós"
(Bartha as Miklós Zrínyi)
Published in the "Pesti Divatlap", a literary
and fashion magazine in 1845
Budapest, National Széchényi Library;
History of the Theatre Collection
Inv. No.: 55.5060/KE 3112

Graphic reproductions of János Bartha in the role of Zrínyi were being reproduced in the "Pesti Divatlap", a fashion magazine, even nine years after the opening of the play. (The play was first produced in 1833 in the Castle Theatre and again in 1837 in Pest's Magyar Theatre.) On his lithograph Barabás chose to portray the actor in a costume very similar to that on his trade-sign.

93. JÓZSEF SCHMIDT
The Death of János Hunyadi, c. 1837
Oil on canvas, 60 × 75 cm
Signed bottom left: "J. Schmidt pinx. 183"
Budapest, private collection

Few historical paintings were executed in Hungary in the 1830s. This work assumes a special significance in that it represents a subject frequently depicted not only then, but later as well. József Schmidt's painting was probably influenced by the poem about the death of Hunyadi written in 1837 by Gergely Czuczor. In this poem, the dying Hunyadi entrusts his children and his homeland into the care of his friends.
Period accuracy in the depiction of the architectural background apparently did not concern the painter. He places János Hunyadi's improvised bed in a Baroque church interior before a canopied altar in a similar Baroque style. A huge national flag, on which an elderly bearded warrior prepares to swear an oath, conceals much of the altar. His right hand clasps that of Hunyadi as he takes leave of him. The two central figures are surrounded by a group of noblemen. A youthful figure, presumably Matthias, Hunyadi's younger son and future king of Hungary, weeps on his father's shoulder while his elder brother, László, kneels at his father's feet. From the right, the white-haired Giovanni Capistrano, accompanied by two Franciscan friars, brings the chalice. In the right foreground a silver-bearded warrior comforts another child.
The main character of this crowded composition is undoubtedly the dying hero Hunyadi, the dreaded enemy of the Turks, who in his dying moments called upon his descendants to continue the struggle.

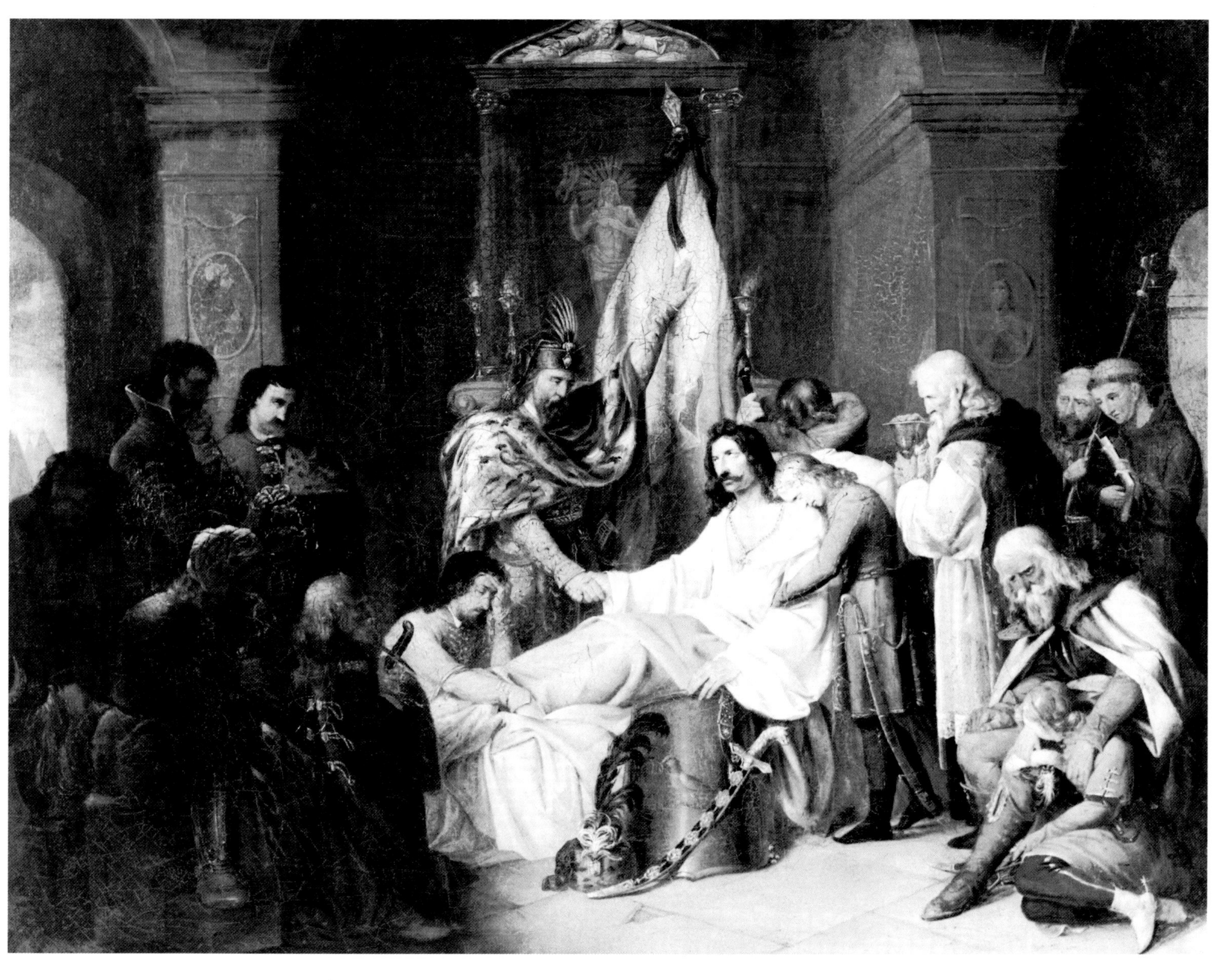

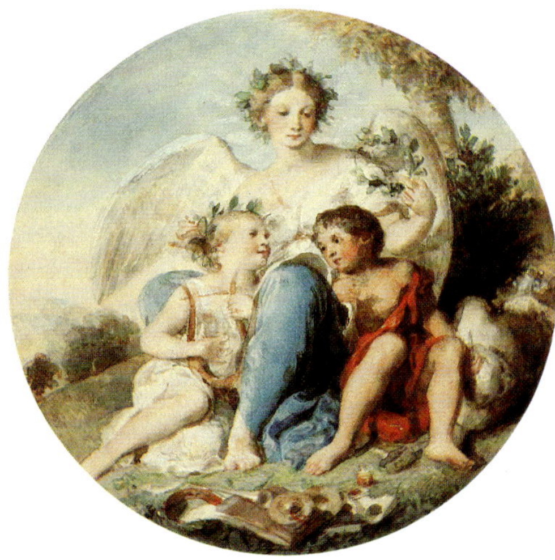

94. CHARLES (KÁROLY) BROCKY
Presentation and Crowning of Music and Painting by Poetry, 1853
Water-colour on paper, 167 mm in diameter
Unsigned
Budapest, Hungarian National Gallery
Inv. No.: 1909–2487

Charles Brocky was born in Temesvár, and in spite of his great poverty, succeeded in reaching Vienna where he studied assiduously before making a tour of Western Europe in 1837. In Paris he made the acquaintance of a Scottish art collector who invited him to England where he settled for the rest of his life. There, his portraits and mythological compositions brought him considerable social success.

This small water-colour, composed in the early 1850s, perpetuates the Viennese style of the 1830s, but the effect is less severe. It shows the influence of Gábor Melegh, Brocky's first teacher in Temesvár. The allegorical subject of this small but elegant picture is typical of 19th century allegories. Poetry is symbolized by the attractive elder sister, who is shown protecting her younger sisters and brothers, Music and Painting. However, this canvas, which was completed in England, could equally well be interpreted as representing the situation of the arts in Hungary, where poetry held sway over the younger, weaker and less educated music and painting.

95. CHARLES (KÁROLY) BROCKY
Christ and the Woman of Samaria. Copy of a painting by Paolo Veronese, 1840s
Water-colour on paper, 121×148 mm
Budapest, Hungarian National Gallery
Inv. No.: 1909–2482

It was customary in the 19th century for artists to copy old masters' paintings as a means of learning the methods used by, for instance, the Renaissance and Baroque painters. This practice was followed by Barabás, Brocky and, several generations later, Bertalan Székely and Károly Lotz as well.

It is quite possible that the Lutheran minister of Eperjes commissioned this painting with the approval of his parishioners for the church. Christ and the Woman of Samaria was frequently chosen for Lutheran churches, since it conveyed the belief that religious service had never been confined to one place or any specific ceremony, but was a matter of "the soul and the truth", as the Gospel says.

Brocky, on receiving the commission, would have been able to refer to his own copies of famous paintings and study from them how to solve problems related to this theme. He was interested in both landscape and figure drawing so that it was natural that he should have found a model in the work of Paolo Veronese.

96. KÁROLY STEINACKER
after Charles (Károly) Brocky
Christ and the Woman of Samaria (A contemporary copy of Charles Brocky's altar-piece in Eperjes), 1848
Oil on canvas, 71×47.5 cm
Inscription bottom left: "Steinacker 1848, nach Brocky"
Budapest, Hungarian National Gallery
Inv. No.: 59.161 T.

Charles Brocky's ambitious painting, which perished in a fire, is known to us only from this contemporary copy, which Brocky gave a totally new interpretation to the Biblical scene. The expression on Christ's face and the solemn and distant look in his eyes is reminiscent of holy pictures by the Nazarene painters. The Samarian woman is standing in front of Christ, dressed like a barefooted peasant girl. Their conversation is underlined by simple gestures. The disciples standing in the background are scandalized at seeing the Master speaking to a woman of Samaria.

Brocky made many preliminary drawings for this work. However, by the time he completed his altar-piece for the church in Eperjes, the priest who commissioned it had been transferred to the town of Sopron. The picture was first sent there, and was copied by Károly Steinacker, drawing master of the local Lutheran primary school, before it was forwarded to its final destination in the Eperjes church.

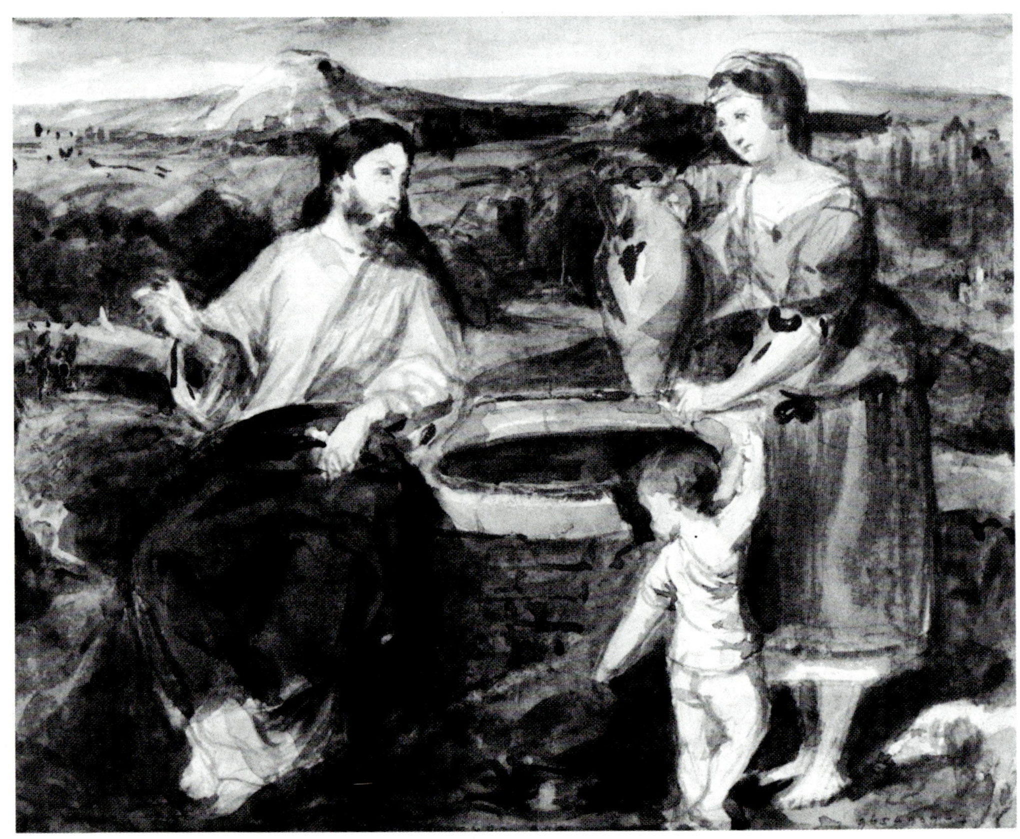

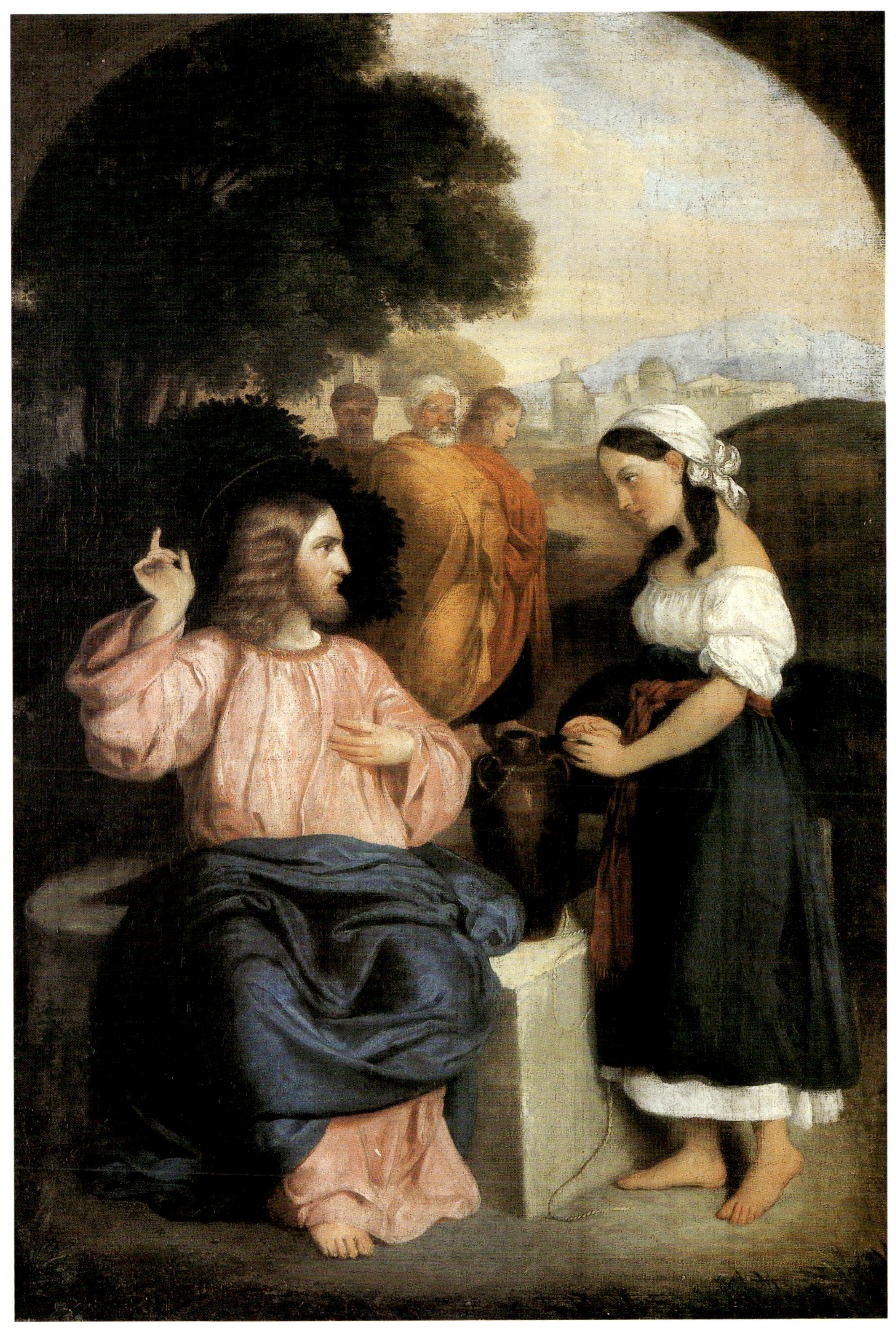

97. JÓZSEF BORSOS
Portrait of Kristóf Hegedűs, 1844
Oil on canvas, 126.5 × 82 cm
Signed bottom left: "Borsos 844"
Budapest, Hungarian National Museum,
Historical Picture Gallery
Inv. No.: 150

József Borsos studied painting as a youth
from József Schoefft, an elder member of the
Schoefft family. Later he attended Barabás's
studio, then enrolled at the Academy of
Vienna, proceeding thence, like so many
Hungarians, to a private school in Vienna.
This portrait, completed in the early 1840s,
excells with its meticulous figure painting
and the generous treatment of the background. It is undoubtedly one of the finest
achievements in the genre of portraits in
a landscape executed in the typical style of
the 1840s. Our only knowledge of the subject, Kristóf Hegedűs, is gained from notes
in a catalogue in which he is described as
a sailor whom Borsos probably met in Italy.
He is depicted sitting on a rock in calm meditation as clouds move all around his figure.

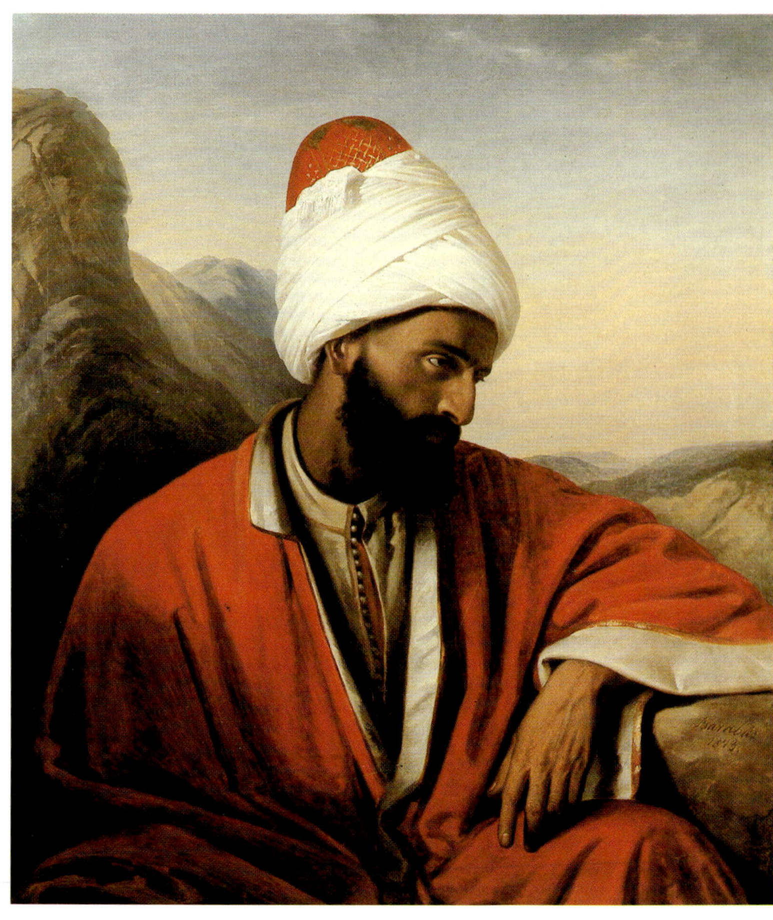

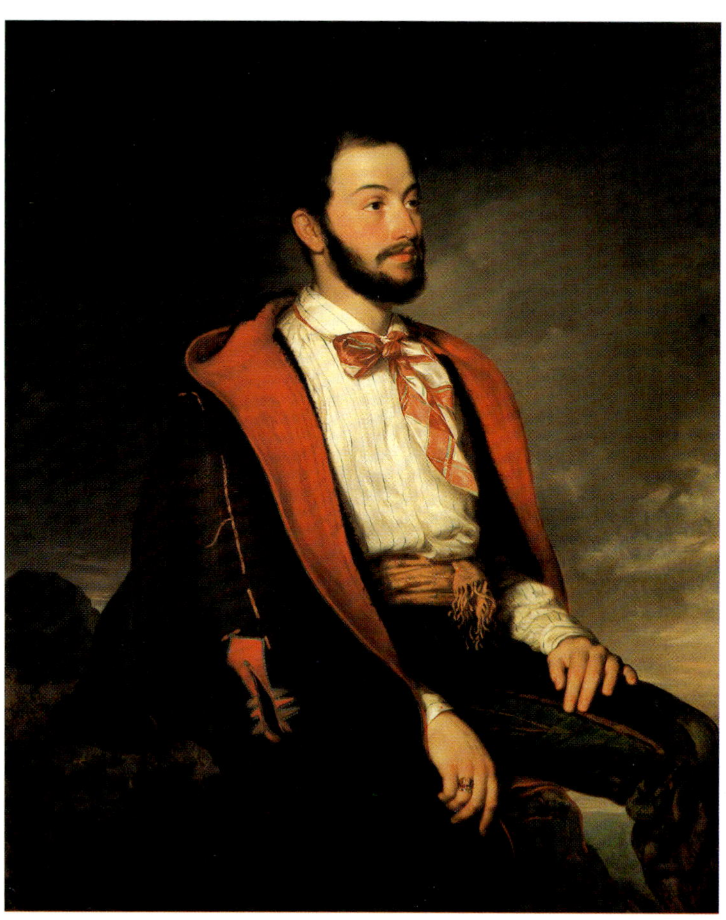

98. MIKLÓS BARABÁS
An Arab Man (A Dervish), 1843
Oil on canvas, 87 × 71 cm
Signed bottom right: "Barabás 1843"
Budapest, Hungarian National Gallery
Inv. No.: 9800

This painting is unlike the rest of Barabás's
work. An article in the contemporary literary journal, "Honderü", has been responsible for the belief held by Hungarian art experts that the painting is related to an Anton
Einsle canvas with a similar subject. In
Barabás's records, it is entitled "A Dervish",
which in those days indicated a Persian Mus-
lim who was either a scholar or member of
an order.
In the contemporary literature we also find
that the painting is associated with the prevailing theories about the Oriental origin of
the Hungarians. It is unique in Barabás's
oeuvre, an illustration of the artist's wide
range of interests.
The painting dates from 1843, the year
Barabás travelled to London. It was later that
he created his famous *Rumanian Family off to
the Fair*. The subject suggests a genuine
Oriental, yet we are tempted to see him as
a European traveller who has adopted an
Oriental philosophy of life reflected in his
choice of clothing and even in his meditative
expression.

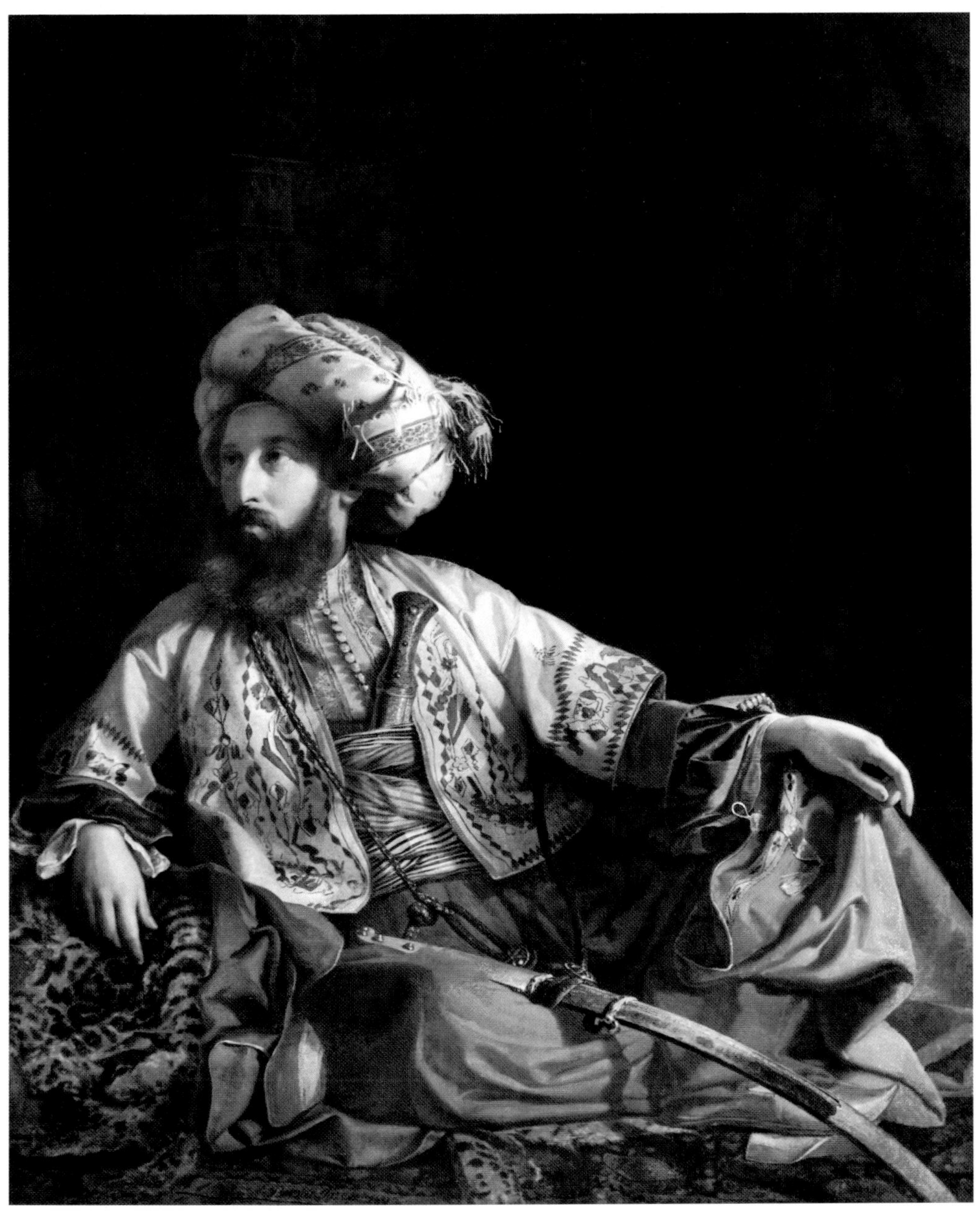

99. JÓZSEF BORSOS
An Emir from the Lebanon, 1843
Oil on canvas, 154×119 cm
Signed bottom left: "Borsos József 1843"
Budapest, private collection

Returning from the East in 1842, Count Edmund Zichy commissioned József Borsos, a young artist at the time living in Vienna, to portray him in his Oriental robes. He had worn these garments at a garden party given by Soliman pasha and obviously he had brought them back to Vienna. It is recorded that he also wore them when taking the part of a Turkish sultan in a *tableau vivant* presented at a reception at the Austrian Embassy in Dresden in 1857. Throughout his life Edmund Zichy was a keen patron of the arts and an avid collector, who worked tirelessly to foster the decorative arts and to establish museums in Austria and Hungary. This painting reflects one aspect of the cult of the Orient as manifest in the mid–19th century in Vienna and Hungary.

100. MIKLÓS BARABÁS
Portrait of a Lady, 1840
Oil on canvas, 83×67 cm
Signed bottom left: "Barabás 1840"
Budapest, Hungarian Academy of Sciences

Portraits by Barabás dating from the 1840s
are characterized by a certain maturity, more
detail and a skilful representation of fabrics.
Also, although Barabás idealized his sitters,
he recorded truthfully both age and indications of character. This likeness of a woman
in her middle age is more realistic than
Barabás's other works, and is reminiscent of
the intense pursuit of verisimilitude found in
Waldmüller's portraits.

The somewhat weary posture, the lowered
head and the broad scarlet shawl thrown
over a white dress are also in the style of the
Viennese master, whom Barabás emulated
in the 1840, though later he adopted different
views.

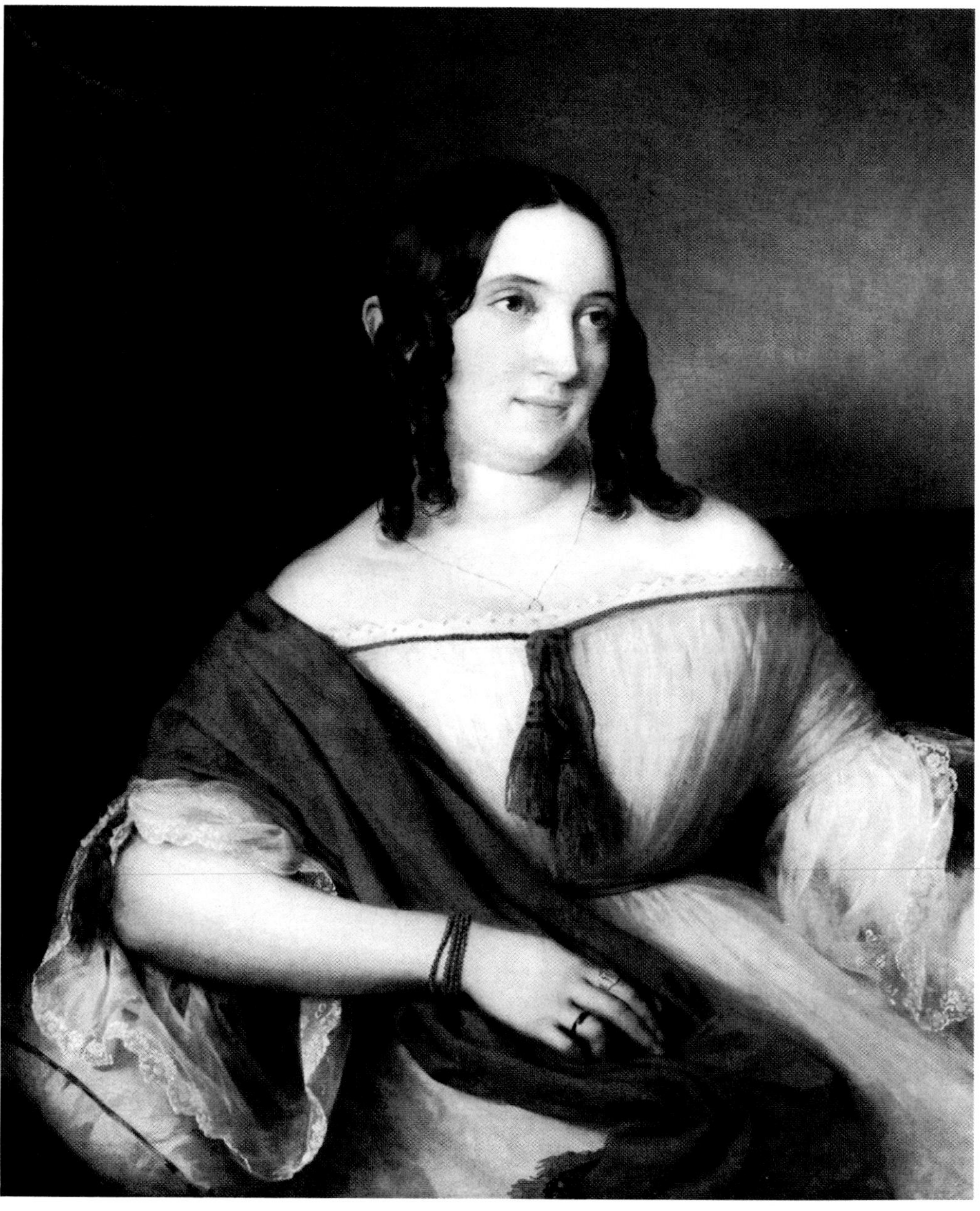

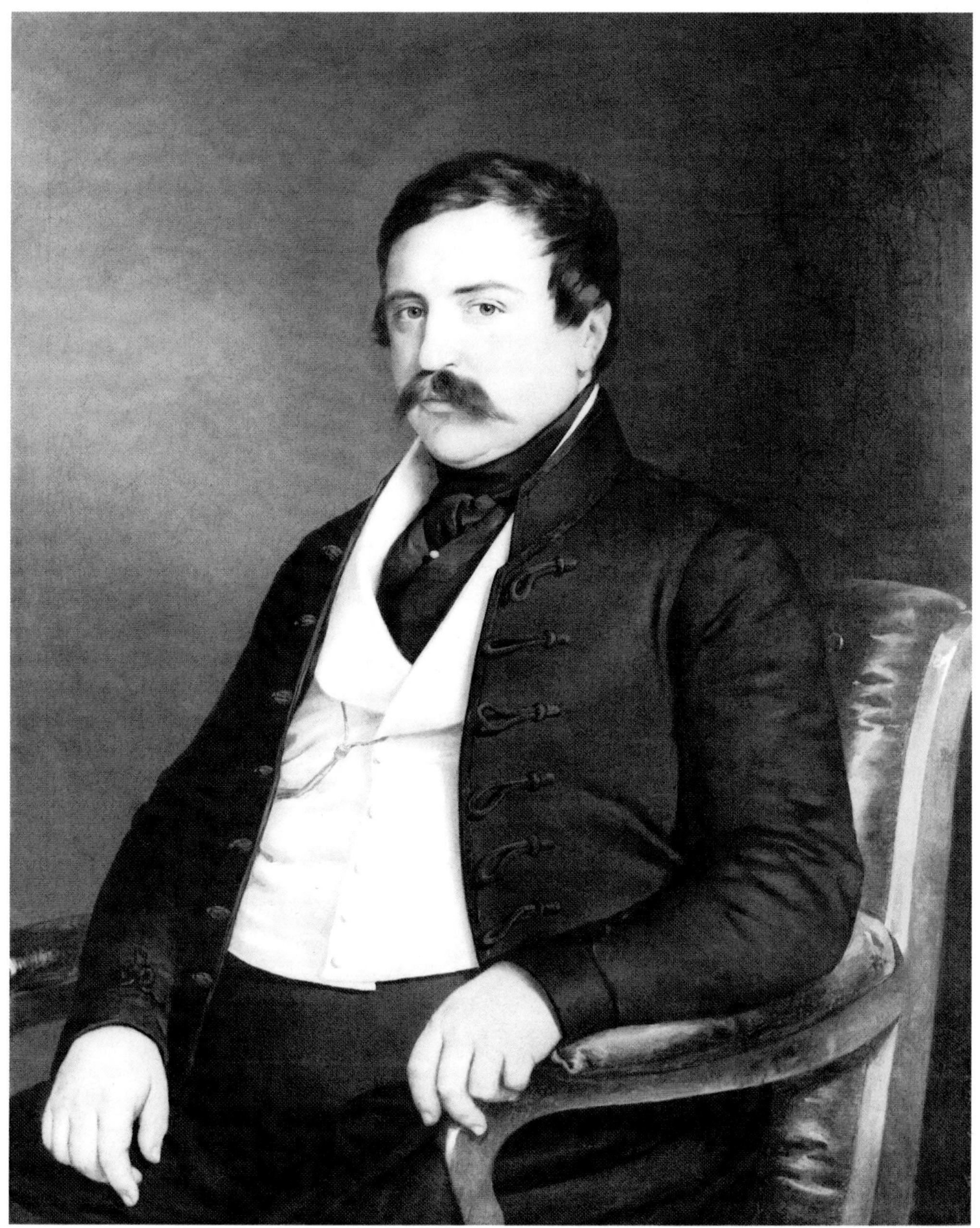

101. MIKLÓS BARABÁS
Portrait of Ferenc Deák, 1841
Oil on canvas, 98 × 79 cm
Signed bottom left: "Barabás 1841"
Budapest, Hungarian Academy of Sciences

In this portrait, Barabás portrays Deák at the outset of a political career in which he was to achieve great distinction. The character drawing is most effective, achieved through quite simple artistic means. A parliamentary deputy of County Zala, Ferenc Deák advocated a fairer tax system for which he became famous, and later several of his portraits were acquired by the Hungarian Academy of Sciences. This portrait was bequeathed to the Academy by a widow in 1860. It is interesting to find in this early work a motif that was to appear in later portraits of Ferenc Deák in which he is similarly depicted as somewhat corpulent, seated, thoughtful, one hand resting on the arm of his chair.

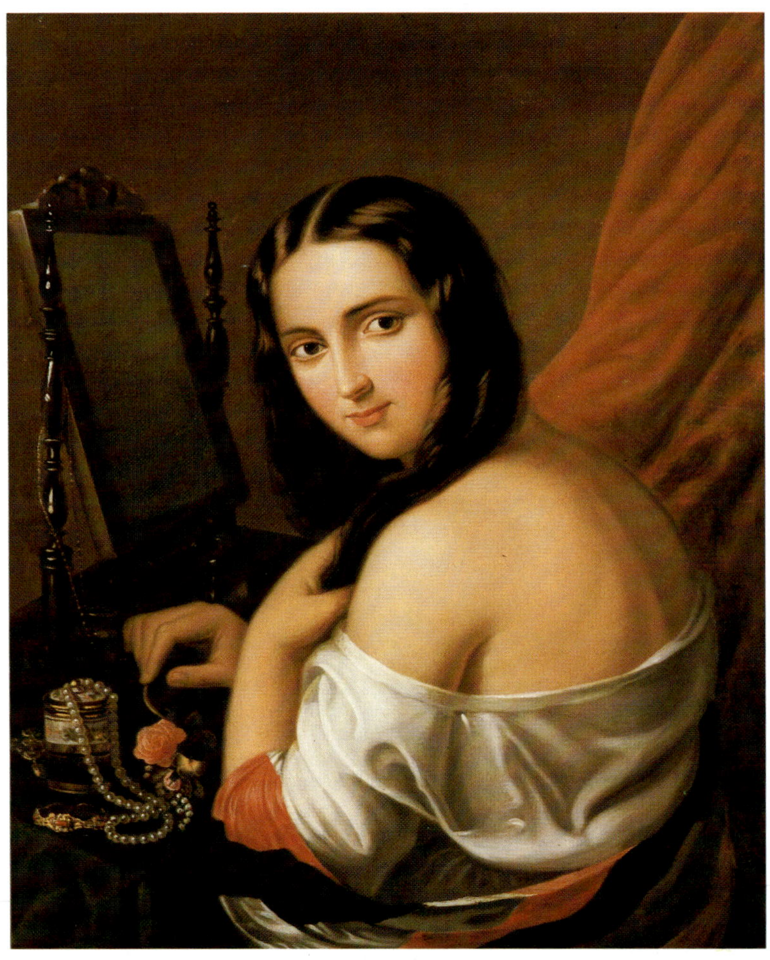

102. JAKAB MARASTONI
Woman Seated before a Mirror, 1840s
Oil on canvas, 77 × 60.5 cm
Bratislava, Mestská Galéria
Inv. No.: A 149

Marastoni, who was trained in Venice and
Rome, did not adopt the Viennese Neo-
Classical or Biedermeier style, which accounts for his use of an earlier more naive
technique. Nevertheless his work is closely
observed and his sensitive response to beauty is unmistakable. In the history of 19th
century Hungarian painting he was the first
to paint nudes or scantily dressed female figures, sometimes within a mythological context, sometimes without. In this picture
a woman is shown seated in front of a swivel
mirror on a finely carved wooden stand,
making her toilet. She reveals her naked
shoulder as she turns towards the viewer.

103. IMRE EMMANUEL RÓTH
Girl Leaning on her Elbow, 1841
Oil on canvas, 56.5 × 62.5 cm
Signed bottom right: "Róth 1841"
Košice, Východoslovenská Galéria
Inv. No.: 0–279

Little is known of Róth, who was active in
Kassa. This painting in the Biedermeier style
indicates that he was one of the Hungarian
artists trained in Vienna who, by the 1840s,
were active in Hungary and elsewhere. Róth
has achieved a seemingly unselfconscious
pose by introducing a rich interior with
a table on which the pretty girl rests her elbow. A velvet curtain ensures the sense of an
interior, completed by the representation of
a beautiful arrangement of flowers in an ornate china vase.

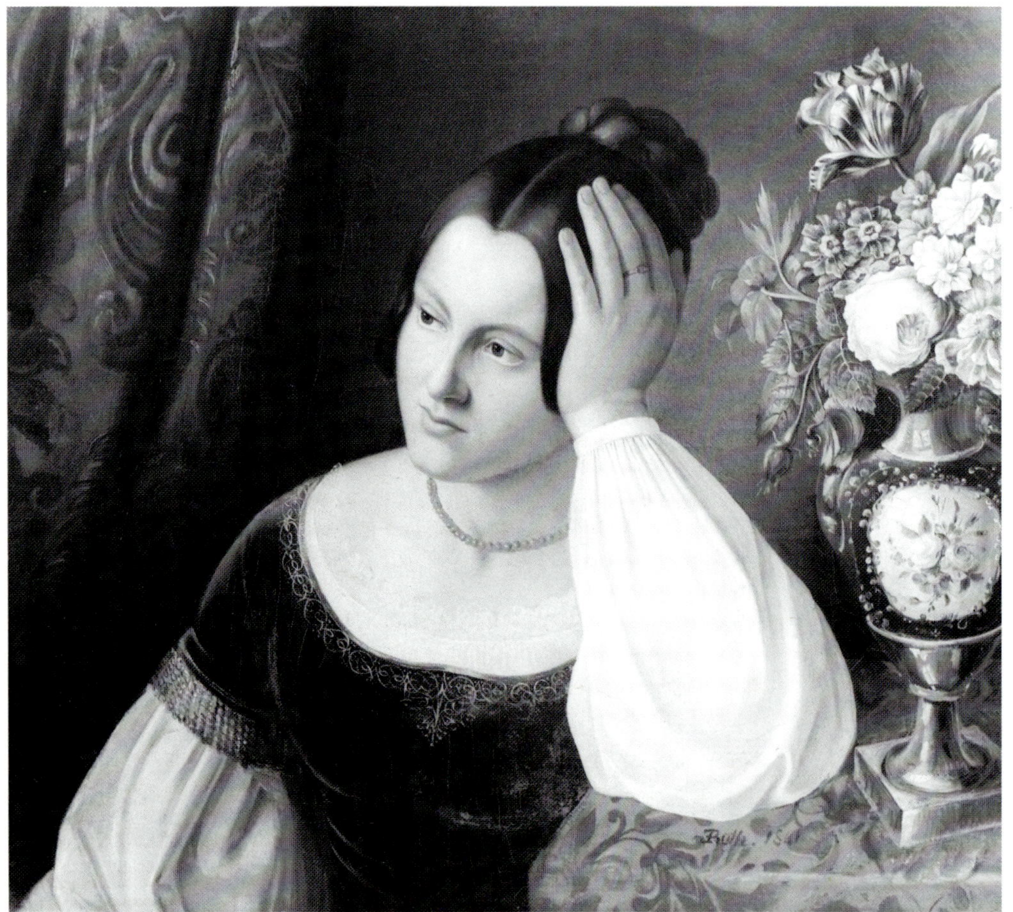

104. DAVID KONSTANTIN ROSENTHAL
Portrait of a Lady, 1844
Oil on canvas, 78 × 63 cm
Signed bottom right: "1844", bottom left:
"Rosenthal souvenir"
Bratislava, Mestská Galéria
Inv. No.: A 3028

This Biedermeier-style portrait of a distinguished and rich woman was probably composed in Pozsony where, because the Hungarian Parliament met there, life was con-
ducted in a high style. The Jewish painter,
David Konstantin Rosenthal, had previously received training at the Vienna Academy.
Well trained, he painted exquisitely the details of both face and dress. The woman is
represented wearing a fine blue and white
dress. The rose on her bosom was an even
more important attribute of female portraits
of the period than jewellery.

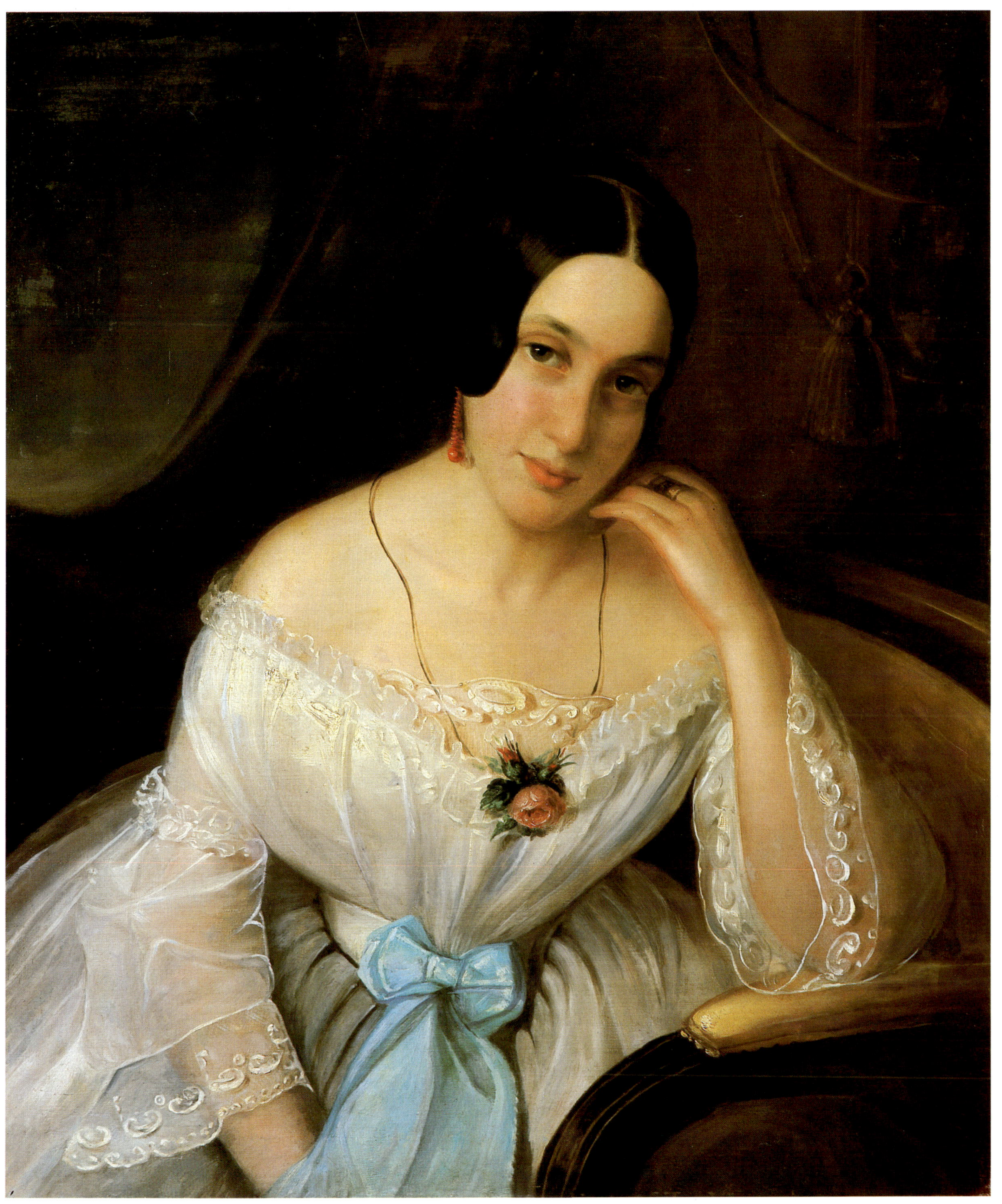

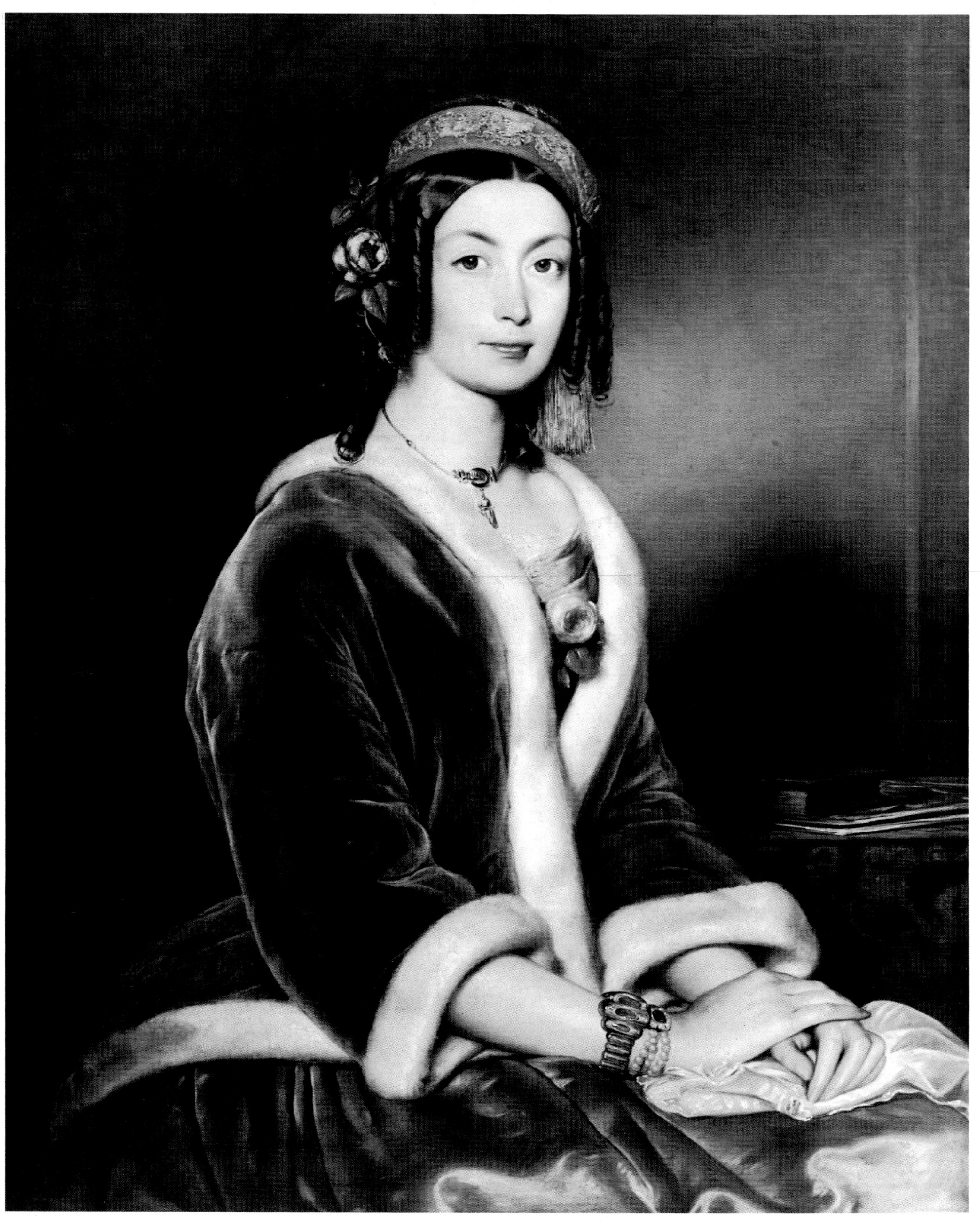

105. JÓZSEF BORSOS
**Portrait of a Lady in a Velvet Jacket,
1850–1855**
Oil on canvas, 102 × 82 cm
Unsigned
Budapest, Hungarian National Gallery
Inv. No.: 7449

Borsos excelled in a type of portraiture
which provided him with a major source of
income—the representation of ladies of
fashion. Such portraits were favoured by all
artists of the period. Descriptions of the features, the majestic presence and the elaborate
evening gowns of fashionable beauties were
a feature of contemporary magazines and
were illustrated by monochrome or coloured engravings. Celebrated painters were
engaged to draw life-like representations of
these ladies—noblewomen and wealthy
middle-class women—of the various
nationalities within the territory of the Austrian Empire and the Hungarian kingdom.
The velvet jacket and head-dress, the splendid necklace and bracelets all point to wealth
deriving from the East and it is probable that
the subject was the daughter of a Greek or
Serbian merchant. She reminds us of the
heroines in Mór Jókai's popular novels. The
flower in her hair and on her bodice may be
reminder of beauty's evanescence.

106. JÓZSEF BORSOS
Lady with a Lace Collar, 1845
Oil on canvas, 63 × 50 cm
Unsigned
Budapest, Hungarian National Gallery
Inv. No.: 7450

Simplicity and delicacy distinguish this portrait by Borsos from his more routine female
likenesses. Here we find the reserved refine-
ment of earlier Viennese and Hungarian
masters such as Friedrich Lieder, Anton
Einsle and their predecessor Gábor Melegh.
The sitter, whose self-conscious expression
is especially striking, is represented wearing
a simple travelling dress with a lace collar
and no jewellery.

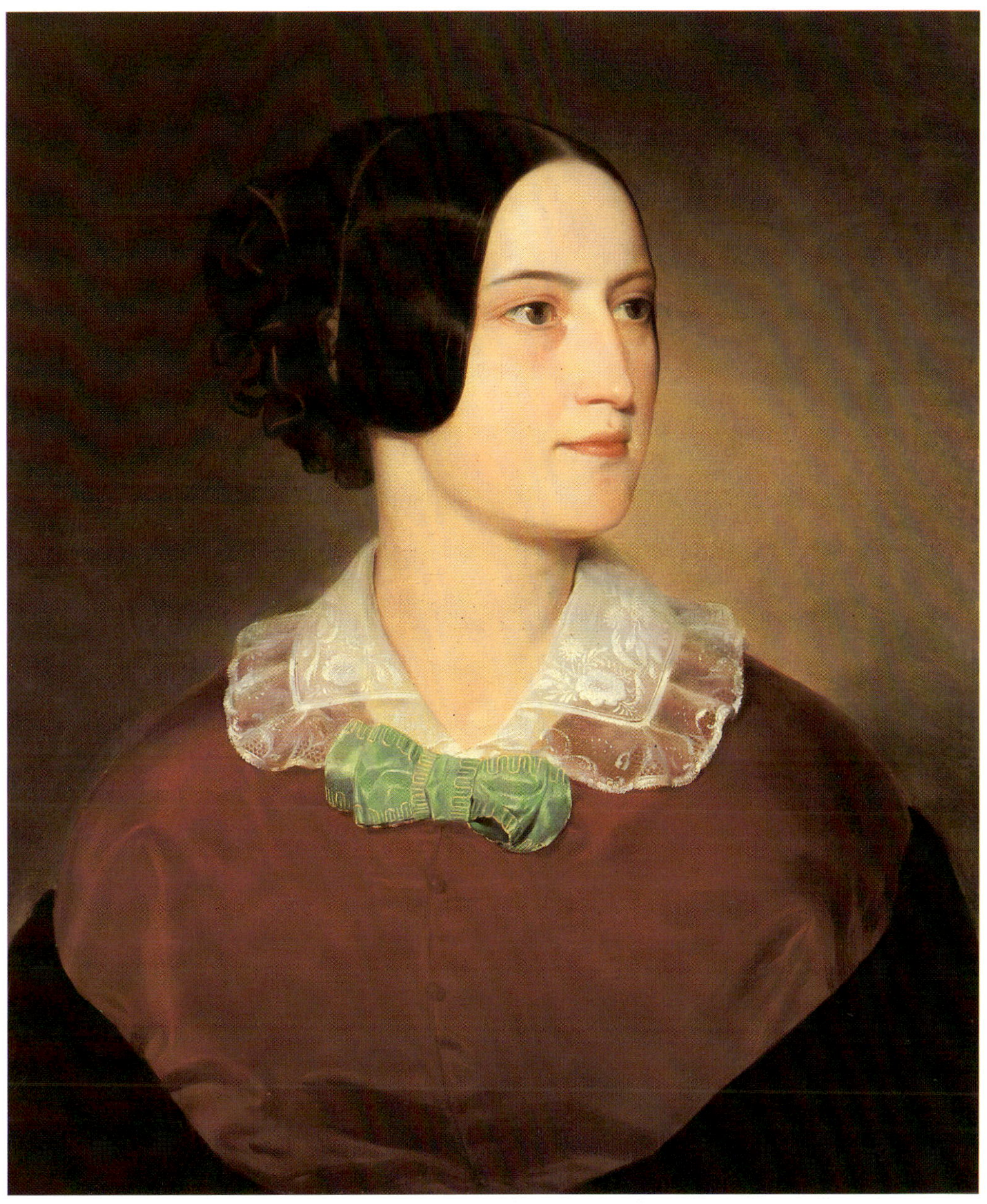

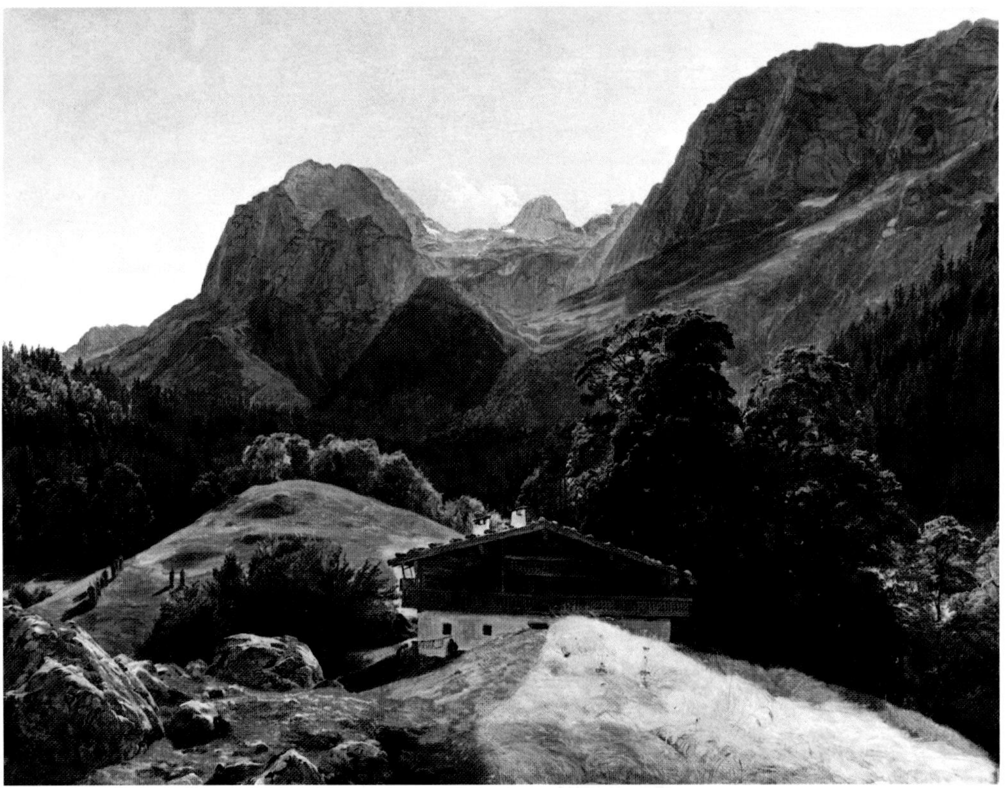

107. FERDINAND GEORG WALDMÜLLER
An Alpine Scene, 1836

Oil on wood, 44.5×55.6 cm
Signed below, on the rock: "Waldmüller 1836"
Budapest, private collection

In his later years, Barabás rejected his former idol, Johann Ender, as too narrowly Neo-Classical and too factual, and preferred Ferdinand Georg Waldmüller. As a young man Waldmüller had been famous for his Neo-Classical romantic portraits and had been admired for the accuracy and elegance of his landscape compositions. In the 1840s he created his most important works, peasant scenes in the Viennese style, which he also taught in his own school.

108. JOHANN ENDER
Greek Girl, 1821

Oil on canvas, 100×75 cm
Signed right: "Joh. Ender Rom. 1821"
Budapest, Hungarian Academy of Sciences

There has as yet been insufficient research to assess Johann Ender's place among Hungarian artists of the early 19th century. The most important collection of paintings from this period was that of the Széchenyi family, part of which was later donated to the Academy of Sciences. It is sure that Ender's water-colour sketches, pencil and other drawings made during his travels, as well as the oils and figure paintings he made in prep-

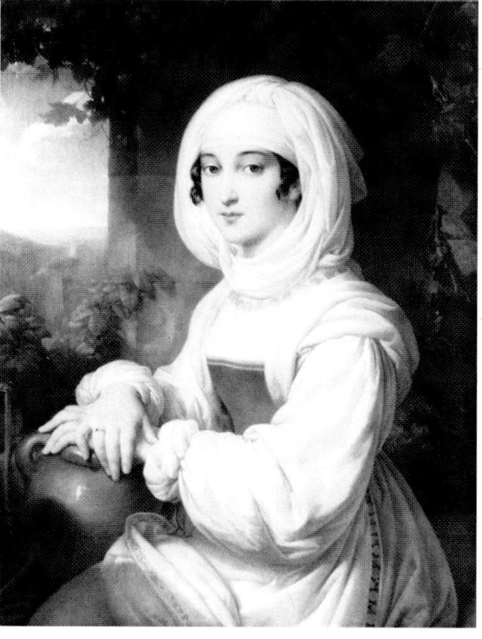

aration for later genre paintings, had a considerable influence on Hungarian art. In Italy, Greece and the Near East, Ender made many striking portraits, his subjects usually shown in fine costumes, and these studies were later elaborated into more detailed pictures. This half-length portrait representing a beautiful Greek woman wearing white dress and veil, exerted a marked influence on Miklós Barabás, who was affected by the character and style of the subject, and who assumed the task of developing the scope of contemporary genre painting.

109. MIKLÓS BARABÁS
Rumanian Family off to the Fair, 1843–1844

Oil on canvas, 138×109 cm
Signed bottom right: "M. vi Barabás Miklós 1843/4 Pesten"
Budapest, Hungarian National Gallery
Inv. No.: 2753

This picture was donated to the National Gallery by the Civil Rifle Club of Pest. It was shown at the 1845 Exhibition of the "Pesti Műegylet", an association founded in 1839 in the town of Pest to encourage artists and promote exhibitions (Catalogue No. 182). There are several versions and copies, one of them in the Oradea Town Museum in Rumania.

In the early 1840s Barabás received public encouragement to extend his range to genre painting. He had until then painted portraits and landscapes but he felt strongly attracted to genre painting. In his views of Pest and Buda he had already introduced groups of figures. But it was necessary for him to work on his large oil paintings with the aim of achieving more balanced and unified compositions. Before starting this picture, Barabás had already produced some genre paintings with one or two figures (*Pigeon-Post*, 1840; *Daffodil*, 1841). In 1843 he first painted the *Wandering Gypsy Family in Transylvania*. He followed this with the picture reproduced here, which became the most famous of all his genre-paintings. In fact it was so popular that Barabás himself made several copies.

The figures are placed in the middle ground forming a triangular group. They represent a wealthy Rumanian family in festive dress, and are shown advancing towards the viewer. Their proud bearing, especially that of the young woman on horseback, and the old man leading her horse, remind us of the noble gestures of their presumed Roman ancestors.

This presumption would explain why Ender's *Greek Girl,* which he painted in Italy, provided the female model for Barabás's Rumanian woman. The figures and the magnificent landscape background are both idealized, whereas the warm, life-like gestures show the artist's indebtedness to Waldmüller's genre-paintings.

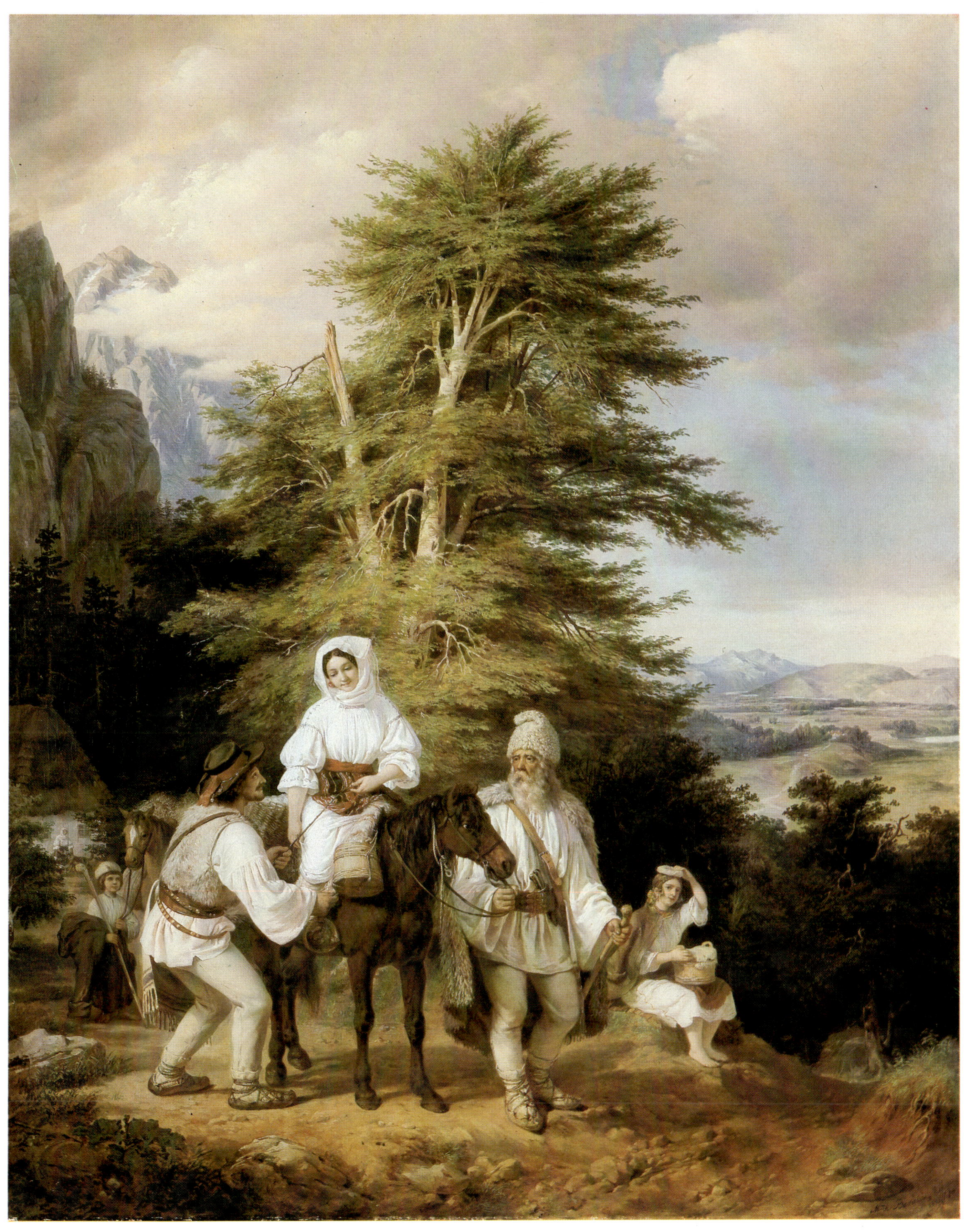

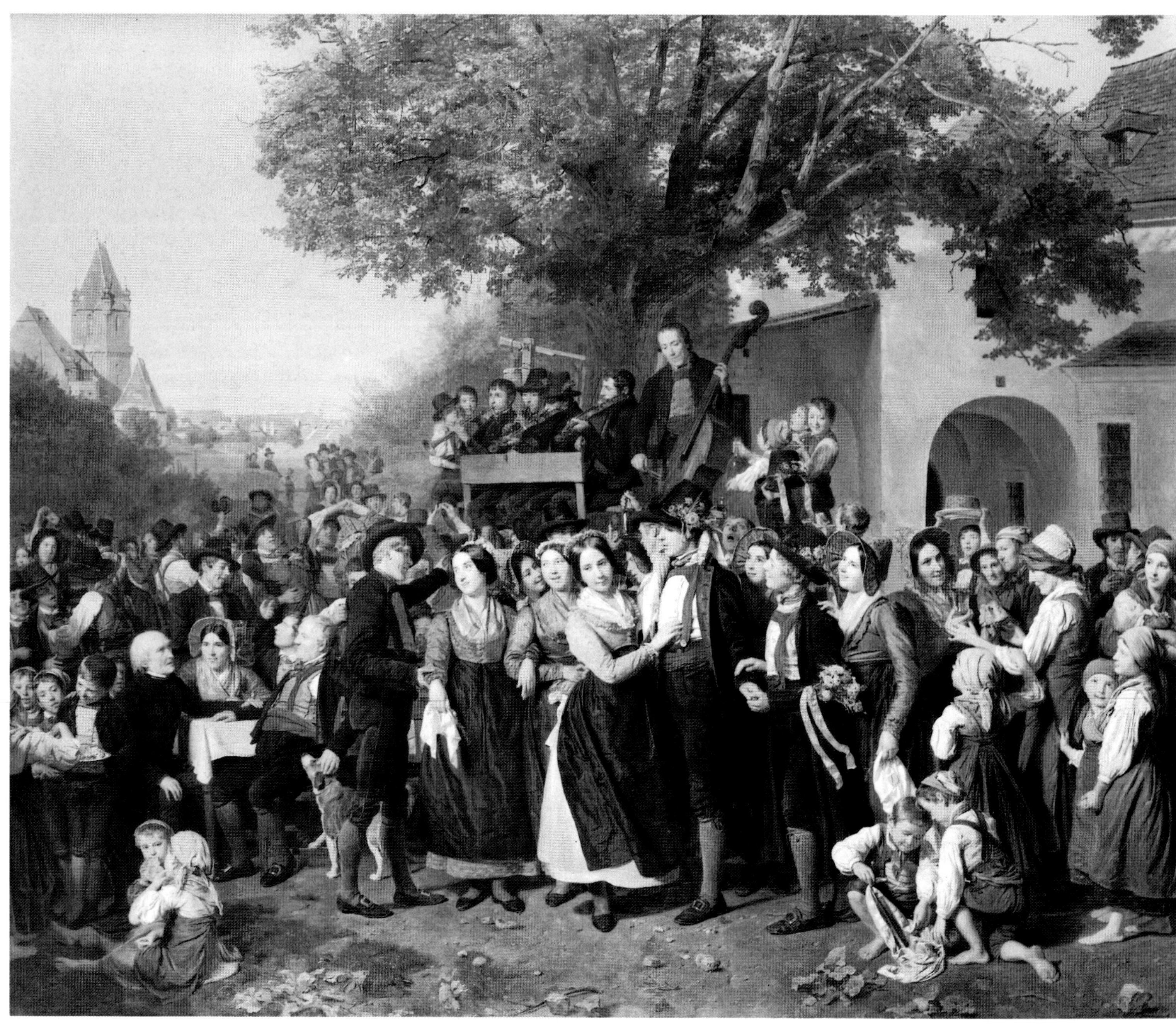

110. FERDINAND GEORG WALDMÜLLER
Peasant Wedding in Lower Austria, 1843

Oil on wood, 92 × 111 cm
Signed: "Waldmüller 1843"
Vienna, Österreichische Galerie
Inv. No.: 1122

This is one of Waldmüller's finest genre paintings, dating from the same year as the *Rumanian Family off to the Fair* by Barabás. It must have been well known to Barabás, since he also used the same subject some years later in a similar composition, though with typically Hungarian elements. This painting, dating from 1843, reveals Waldmüller's conscious rejection of the traditional style of classical compositions in which the action is usually depicted centrally in the middle ground and involves very few figures. Here, Waldmüller arranges the figures horizontally across the middle ground. The subject is a peasant wedding in Lower Austria. The bride and groom are about to open the dance; the village band can be seen on a raised platform children look on, and the young couple's parents sit with the priest. Houses and a Gothic church, all indicating the prosperity of the village, are visible in the background. Waldmüller wanted to create the impression of a true to life situation. This was in fact the major concern of European genre-painters in the 1840s. Here we see how the Viennese master tried to give unity to the composition, and devote attention to the minutest detail.

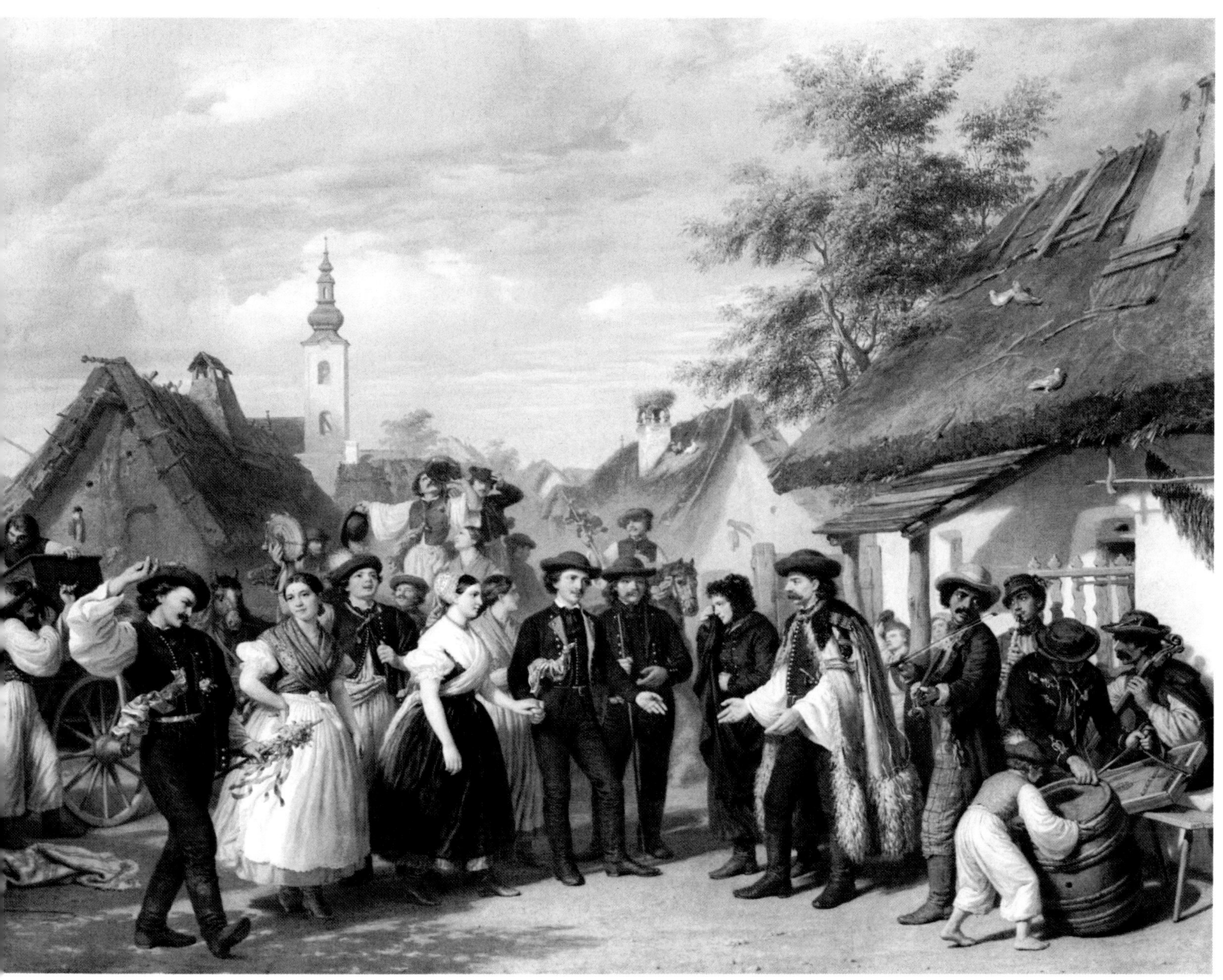

111. MIKLÓS BARABÁS
Arrival of the Bride, 1856

Oil on canvas, 127×157 cm
Signed bottom left: "Barabás Miklós 1856"
Budapest, Hungarian National Gallery
Inv. No.: 2762

In this painting, Barabás extends his solution to the problems of composition encountered in his *Rumanian Family off to the Fair*. By representing scenes from life and by studying the less formal genre-paintings with numerous figures painted in Waldmüller's style, Barabás was able to develop the technique seen in this picture.

By the 1850s he was already capable of arranging in this oil painting a large number of figures in a horizontal composition.

Barabás was interested in folk customs and took great care to reproduce accurately the details of the village weddings. One significant moment in the ceremony is when the bride's trousseau is carried into her new home and the groom's parents receive her into the family—a ceremony in which the whole village participates. The main figures are shown in festive garments, though Barabás is particularly careful to give a realistic rendering of the humble thatched houses and the simple village church. He is equally careful to make clear the social standing of the wedding guests, relatives and curious onlookers.

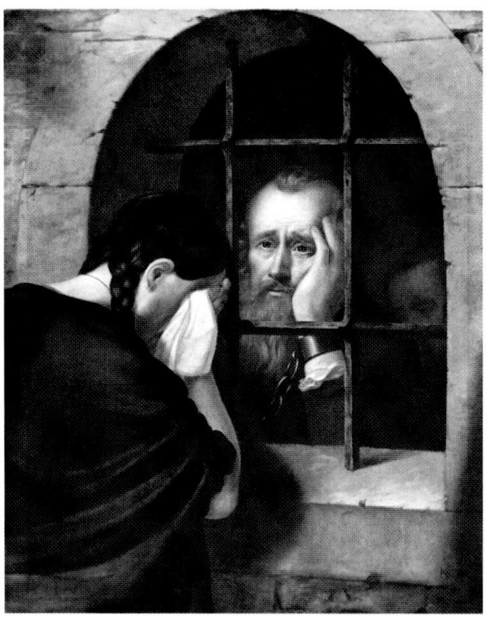

112. BÁLINT KISS
János Pethes Jablonczay's Farewell to His Daughter at the Window of Leopoldschloss Gaol, 1846
Oil on canvas, 95 × 75 cm
Signed at bottom: "KB 1846"
Budapest, Hungarian National Gallery
Inv. No.: 2749
Donated by Zsigmond Kovács to the National Museum in 1846

This painting is undoubtedly one of the most popular works of art to have survived from the Hungary of 1840s. Its influence extended to the years following the 1848 Revolution, which it so poignantly reflects. It portrays a Protestant minister who was imprisoned in 1674, during the Counter-Reformation. Bálint Kiss came from a Protestant family of clerics, and studied in Vienna, Italy, Switzerland and Germany. When the collection of pictures in the National Museum was rehoused and the new Gallery opened to the public in 1846, Kiss was appointed curator. There were in the collection very few genre-paintings representing country life or historical incidents. He therefore chose to paint a picture that very year on a historical theme which was part of Hungarian Protestant tradition. His work provided the Gallery with an authentic description of the sufferings of Hungarian Protestants, and at the same time, set a popular precedent for depicting prison visits.

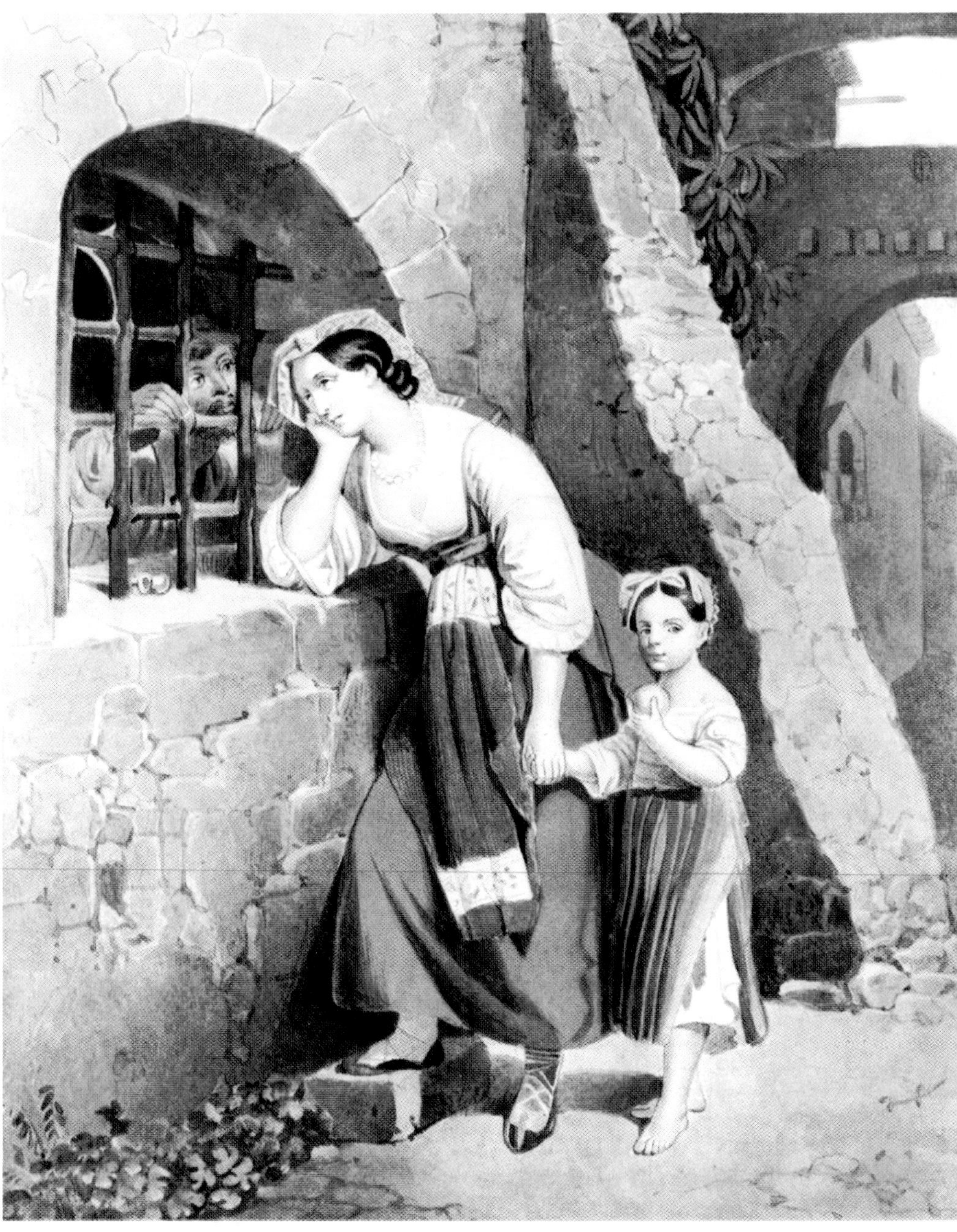

113. BORBÁLA SIGRAY
A Visit to the Prison
Water-colour on paper, 190 × 100 mm
Signed bottom right: "Gr. Sigray"
Keszthely, Balaton Museum
Inv. No.: 59.101

We cannot say with certainty from which model this sentimental episode was copied. It was one of the drawings, paintings and etchings depicting prison visitors which renewed the tradition of what was known as *Caritas Romana,* the Roman practice of philanthropy. The painter's identity—presumably an aristocratic amateur—can be inferred from the inscription on a drawing by Johann Ender in the Budapest Museum of Fine Arts, which may have encouraged the kind of genre paintings produced in Hungary from about 1840 onwards. Based on a variety of historical incidents or peasant situations, they appealed to humanitarian feelings, most of them being representations of middle class citizens or relatives visiting prisons to comfort and encourage the prisoners.

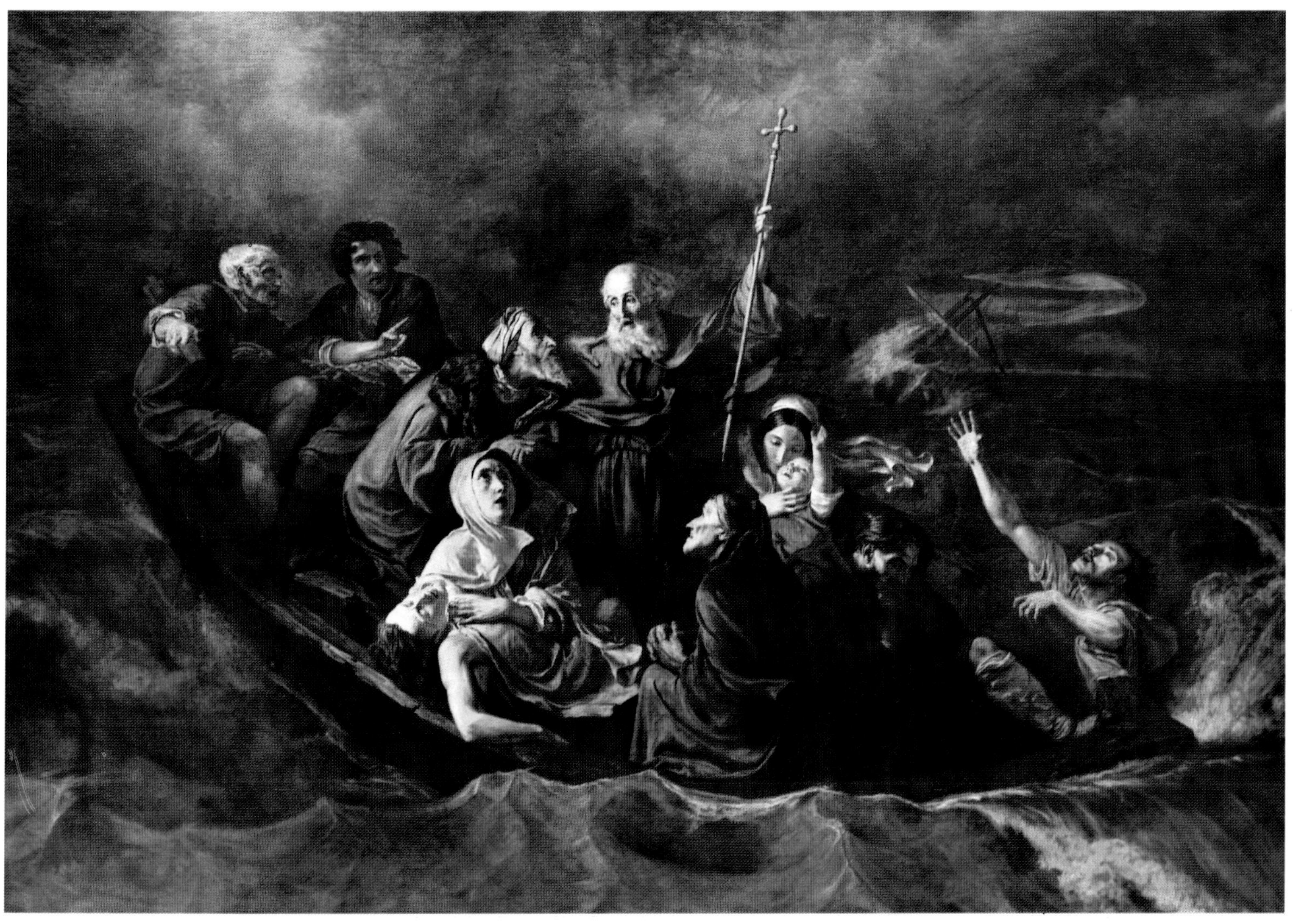

114. MIHÁLY ZICHY
The Lifeboat, 1847

Oil on canvas, 135×190 cm
Signed bottom left: "M. Zichy 1847"
Budapest, Hungarian National Gallery
Inv. No.: 2328
Purchased by the Museum of Fine Arts from
the artist in 1905

Count Mihály Zichy began to study art in Pest as a pupil of Jakab (Giacomo) Marastoni, proceeding later to Waldmüller's Free School in Vienna. Kiss, curator of the Picture Gallery in the National Museum, quickly recognized Zichy's talent, which was also acknowledged when he exhibited in Vienna. Kiss began to buy Zichy's genre-paintings and religious compositions, and was also glad to accept paintings donated by Zichy to the Gallery. This picture dates from 1847, when Zichy returned from a tour of Italy. The choice of the subject indicates the lingering influence of French Academic Romanticism, despite an outdated technique in the rendering of sentimental dramatic tension.

Following Géricault's large work, *The Raft of the Medusa,* the theme of shipwreck retained its popularity through the century. Zichy, a cultured man, was aware of contemporary trends and was ready to adopt them. However, as an artist who had learned to paint popular genre scenes in Vienna, and copied the old masters in picture galleries, in order to use them later in his own way, he made use of the most stringent traditional solutions when depicting these sentimental Romantic themes.

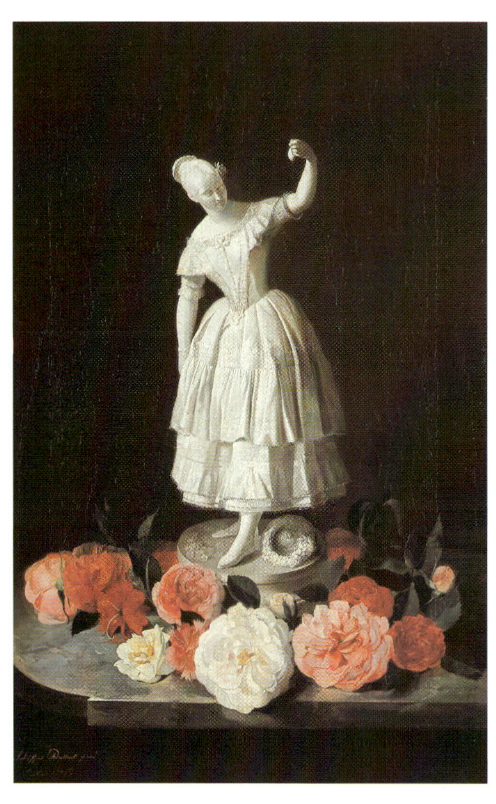

115. ADALBERT (BÉLA) SCHÄFFER
Still-life with a Statuette of Fanny Elssler, 1845
Oil on canvas, 56.5 × 34.5 cm
Inscription bottom left: "Schäffer Adalbert festé Pesten 1845" (Painted by Schäffer Adalbert in Pest 1845)
Budapest, Hungarian National Gallery
Inv. No.: 2790

The statuette, moulded in porcelain, represents Fanny Elssler, a famous ballet-dancer from Vienna. Soon it was very often painted and engraved and so distributed by fashion and theater magazines. The first time she danced in Hungary was in 1844. The artist made a new copy of his painting of the statuette with flowers arranged round the base, and gave it to the Hungarian National Museum in 1845.

116. JOSEPH CAJETAN
Fanny Elssler and Franz Opfermann in the Ballet, "The Painter's Vision", c. 1842
Coloured lithograph on paper, 20 × 26 cm
Inscription: "Des Malers Traumbild, N 99 Costume Bild zur Theaterzeitung"
Vienna, Museum der Stadt Wien

Joseph Cajetan is recorded as having left Hamburg for Vienna around 1850–1855, from which time onwards, he worked there as an illustrator and book publisher. He is likely to have noticed extravagant manners on previous visits to Vienna.

The present drawing, reproduced as a newspaper illustration, shows Fanny Elssler leaping suddenly out of a framed picture much to the astonishment of the painter. A curtain is drawn aside from the vast frame through which she leaps, revealing a stage set in the background. The lithographer pays homage to the ballet dancer through the Pygmalion theme, which he transposes into a genre painting.

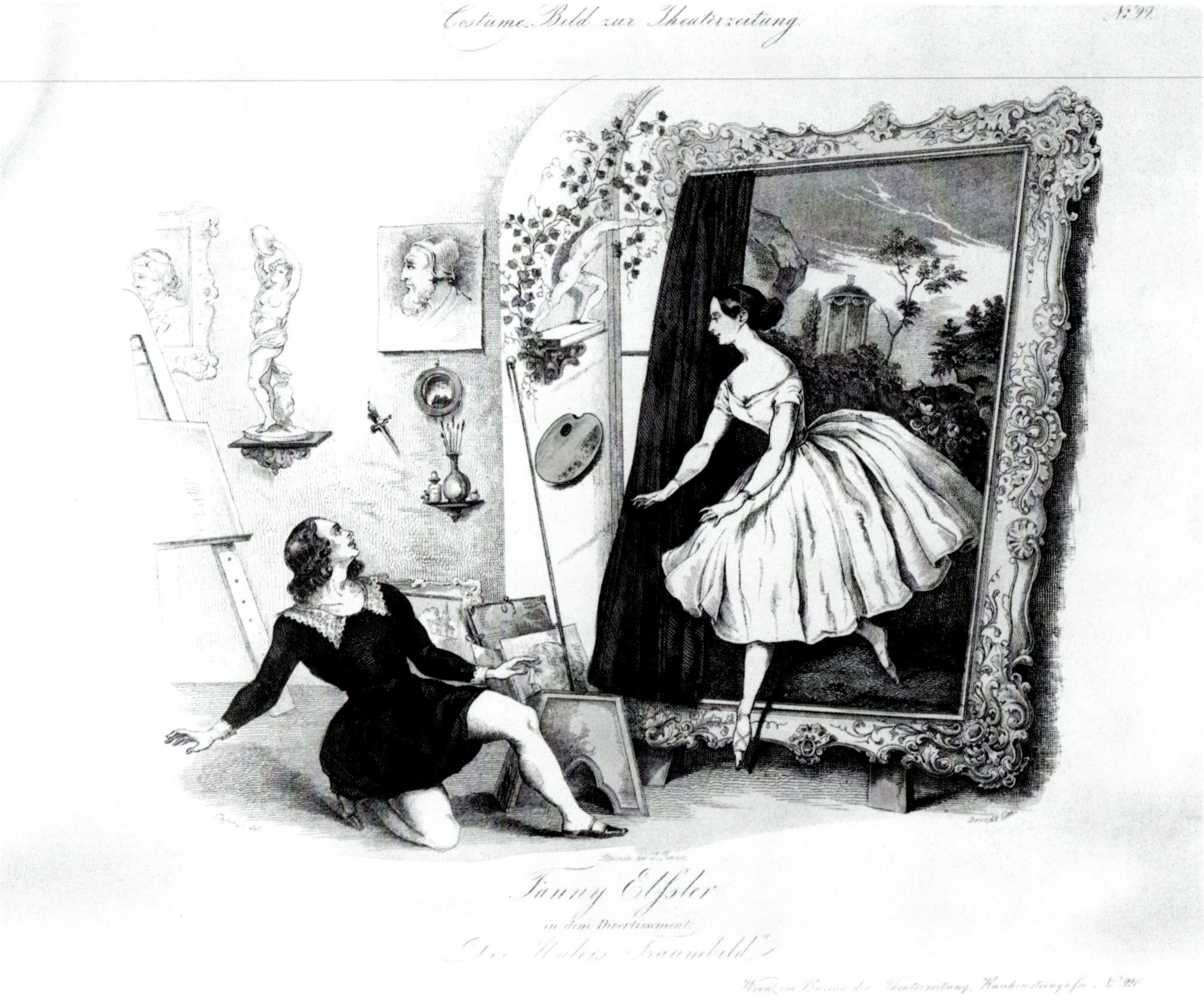

117. ADALBERT (BÉLA) SCHÄFFER
Still-life with Ornamental Vessels and Grapes (Historical Antiquities), 1852
Oil on wood, 79 × 62 cm
Signed bottom right: "Schäffer 852"
Budapest, private collection

Adalbert Schäffer, whose father was a
painter himself, began his career in Pest, but
from 1842 he exhibited his work in Vienna.
In 1845 he returned to Pest to take advantage
of the increased prosperity which promised
well for the sale of his work. He painted
chiefly still-lifes and objects of historical interest, especially Renaissance and Baroque
vessels, enhancing his compositions with
elaborate fruit and flower arrangements. He
made frequent use of the most beautiful
pieces from the National Museum and the
paintings composed in this way brought
him fame at home and abroad. When he
moved to Vienna in the 1850s he continued
to work in the same style, repeatedly depicting every detail of the same well-known
treasures of the museums. In this picture we
find an ostrich-egg mounted within the
frame of a goblet attributed to the Augsburg
master, Johannes Lencker (now in the
Budapest Museum of Applied Arts); also
a fine 15th century ornamental vessel from
the National Museum, encircled with a band
of spherical forms.

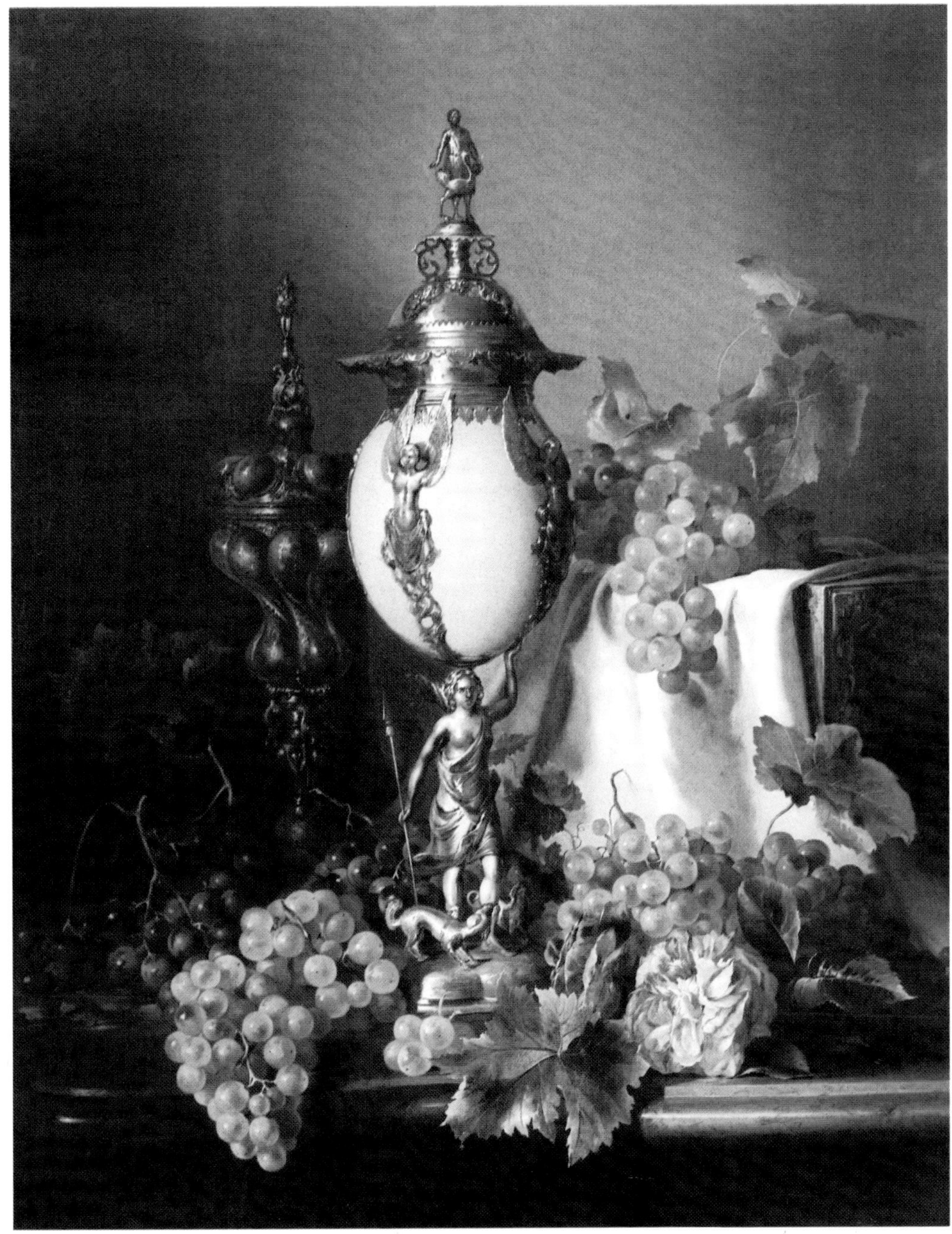

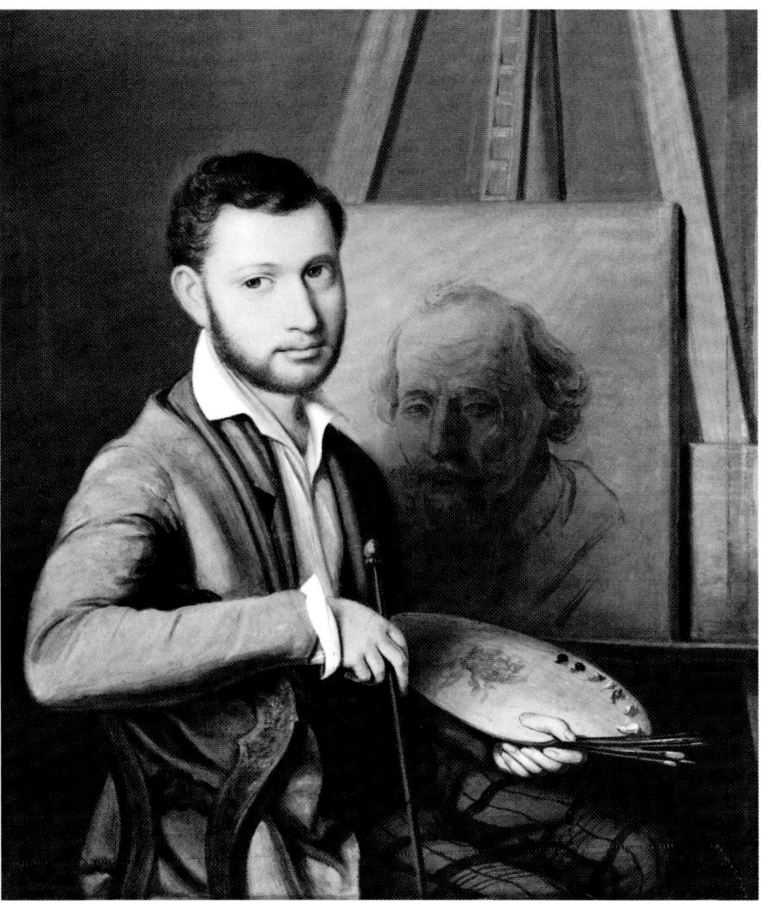

118. DAVID KONSTANTIN ROSENTHAL
Self-portrait, 1845–1850
Oil on cardboard, 35 × 29 cm
Unsigned
Budapest, Hungarian National Gallery
Inv. No.: 8888

This picture, formerly attributed to Lajos Mezey, was identified by Béla Biró as a self-portrait of David Konstantin Rosenthal. However, this identification is contested by those well acquainted with Mezey's portraits. It is unquestionably a self-portrait by an artist, and it is noteworthy for the presentation of the subject and the clarity of the details.

A young painter sits thoughtfully in front of his easel, which supports a canvas on which a head has been delineated.

The model is conceived in the unpretentious style of a serious artist indifferent to success. In both approach and technique there is therefore a reminder of the German Romanticism of the early 19th century.

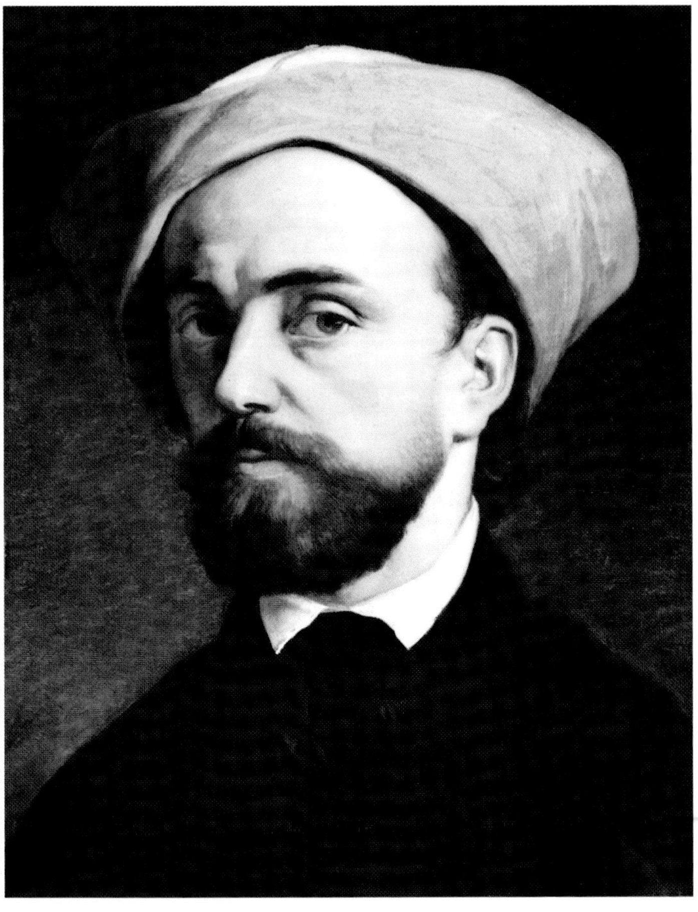

119. HENRIK WEBER
Self-portrait, 1847
Oil on cardboard, 46 × 36 cm
Signed top right: "H. Weber 847"
Budapest, Hungarian National Gallery
Inv. No.: FK 6780

Károly Lyka has listed two painters of the same name active in the late 1840s in Pest; they have also been recorded by Gyula Fleischer as students at the Vienna Academy. The present self-portrait was accomplished by the more qualified Weber, who visited Munich after studying in Vienna. He also stayed in Italy from 1845 to 1847, afterwards returning to Hungary where he completed this painting, notable for the precise drawing and choice of colours.

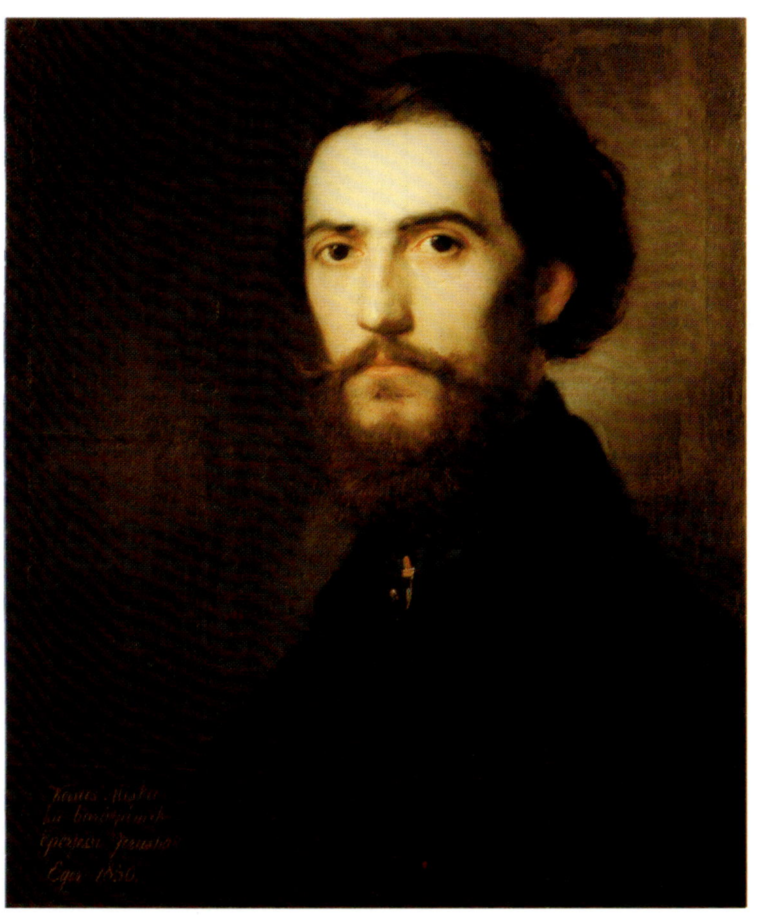

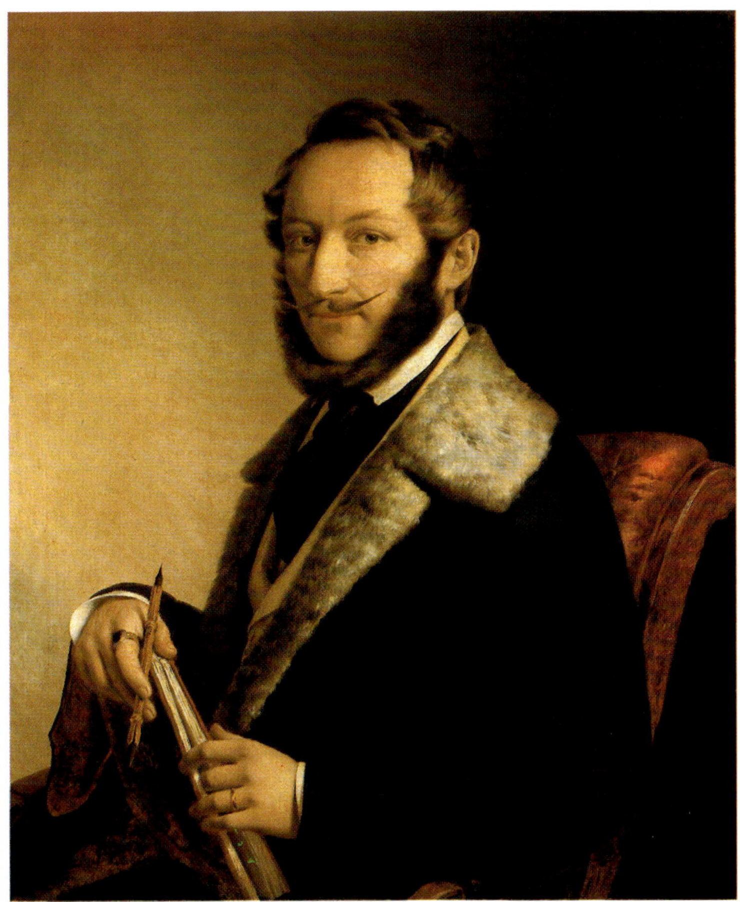

120. MIHÁLY KOVÁCS
Self-portrait, 1850
Oil on canvas, 54.5 × 45 cm
Inscription bottom left: "Kovács Miska hű
barátjának Eperjessi Jézusnak 1850. Eger"
(Miska Kovács to his true friend Jézus
Eperjesi 1850. Eger)
Pécs, Janus Pannonius Museum
In. No.: 74.34

Mihály Kovács was a talented peasant boy
who, thanks to the benevolence of a noble
patron, was able to attend the Drawing
School in Pest in 1833, and the Academy of
Vienna in 1835. In Vienna he was a pupil of
Leopold Kupelwieser, but Josef Danhauser
also influenced his development as an artist.
From 1842 to 1848 he studied in Italy. Yet he
never lost touch with artistic circles in Hungary and he even exhibited in Pest. When he
heard of the Revolution in 1848, at the beginning of the War of Independence, he returned home and volunteered to serve as
a soldier in the Revolutionary Army. This
self-portrait dates from after the War of Independence. It scarcely differs in style from
other self-portraits of the 1840s, though it is
characterized by a more intimate and un-
postured manner, and the artist's respect for
the great Renaissance portrait painters. The
dedication "to his true friend" reveals an undeniable element of the romantic in the
character of the artist.

121. MIKLÓS BARABÁS
Self-portrait, 1841
Oil on canvas, 83 × 65.5 cm
Signed bottom right: "M de Barabás 1841"
Budapest, Hungarian National Gallery
Inv. No.: FK 1890

This self-portrait by Barabás is like an elegant trade-sign, and reveals how the artist
thought of himself. By 1841 he was a celebrated painter, and a wealthy and honoured
citizen of Pest. He had also been a member of
the Academy of Sciences for some years.
After travelling extensively in Europe,
Barabás settled in the capital to commence
the task of founding a national school of
painting. Wherever he now travelled, he assumed the manner of one who has undertaken a sober and significant role in public
life. The sound traditionalism and rejection
of experimentation he upheld in his work
and in his teaching is perfectly expressed in
this self-portrait.

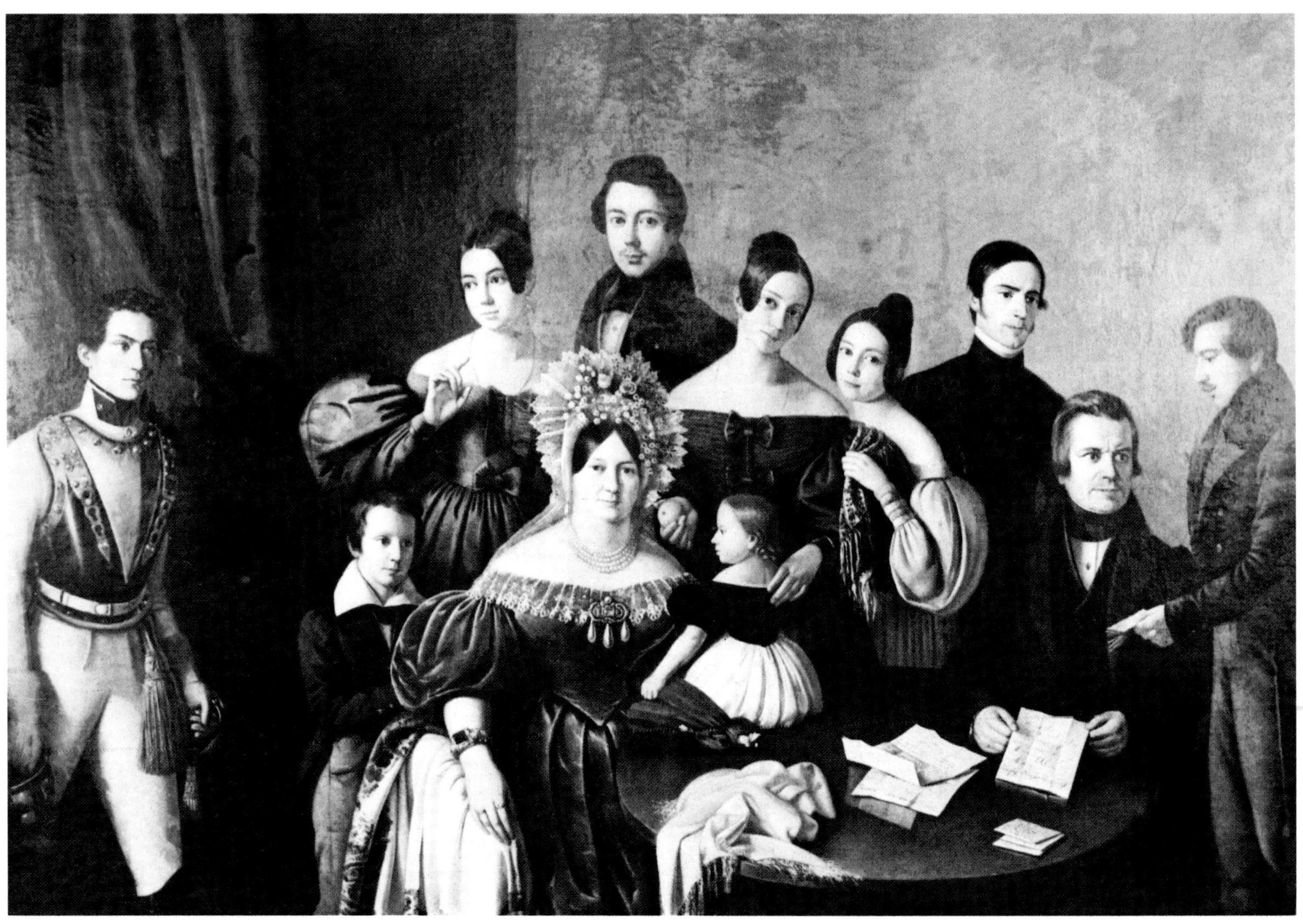

122. JAKAB (GIACOMO) MARASTONI
Family Portrait (Portrait of the Scherz Family), 1835
Oil on canvas, 191.3 × 283.5 cm
Signed. "G. Marastoni 835"
Bratislava, Mestská Galeria
Inv. No.: A 130

In the early 1830s, Marastoni made lengthy stays in Pozsony. Later, he returned occasionally to complete important commissions. One of these was a large family portrait, which Marastoni executed with the intention of depicting every detail to give complete satisfaction to the entire family. A narrative element is discernible. The mother has the central position; she is shown wearing an elaborate head-dress, looking unwaveringly at the viewer, while the head of the family, on her right, gravely receives a letter handed to him by a young man. Behind them a young girl waves timidly to a passing soldier. He may represent an absent son, present only in the minds of the others on this occasion. One son, like his father, stands behind his mother, a clerk. The dress worn by another son indicates that he is a seminarist. The social position, character and occupation of each member of the family is sensitively indicated.

123. HENRIK WEBER
The Weber Family, 1846
Oil on canvas, 210 × 160 cm
Unsigned
Budapest, the Kiscelli Museum of the Budapest Historical Museum
Inv. No.: 7136 F. 1596

This monumental family portrait is not a commissioned work; it represents Weber's own family and expresses his respect and love for his parents in particular, as well as the strong family feeling and intellectual affinity which creates a bond between the generations of large middle-class families. The head of the family, a cloth merchant, is shown holding a newspaper and reading from it to his granddaughter. The mother is knitting stockings, while another grandchild sits beside her, pouring over a picture book. The middle generation of men and women are seen ranked behind them, the men turning to each other, gesturing as they speak. We see only the back of the painter, yet he occupies a significant place in the composition and is portrayed showing his brothers and brothers-in-law a drawing which symbolizes his profession. His figure is balanced by that of his brother-in-law, the composer Mihály Mosonyi, who is depicted in a similar decorative posture.

The painting represents the varied, busy lives of citizens of Pest. Even political affiliation is indicated, for the Jacobin cap worn by one of the standing figures represents allegiance to revolutionary movements.

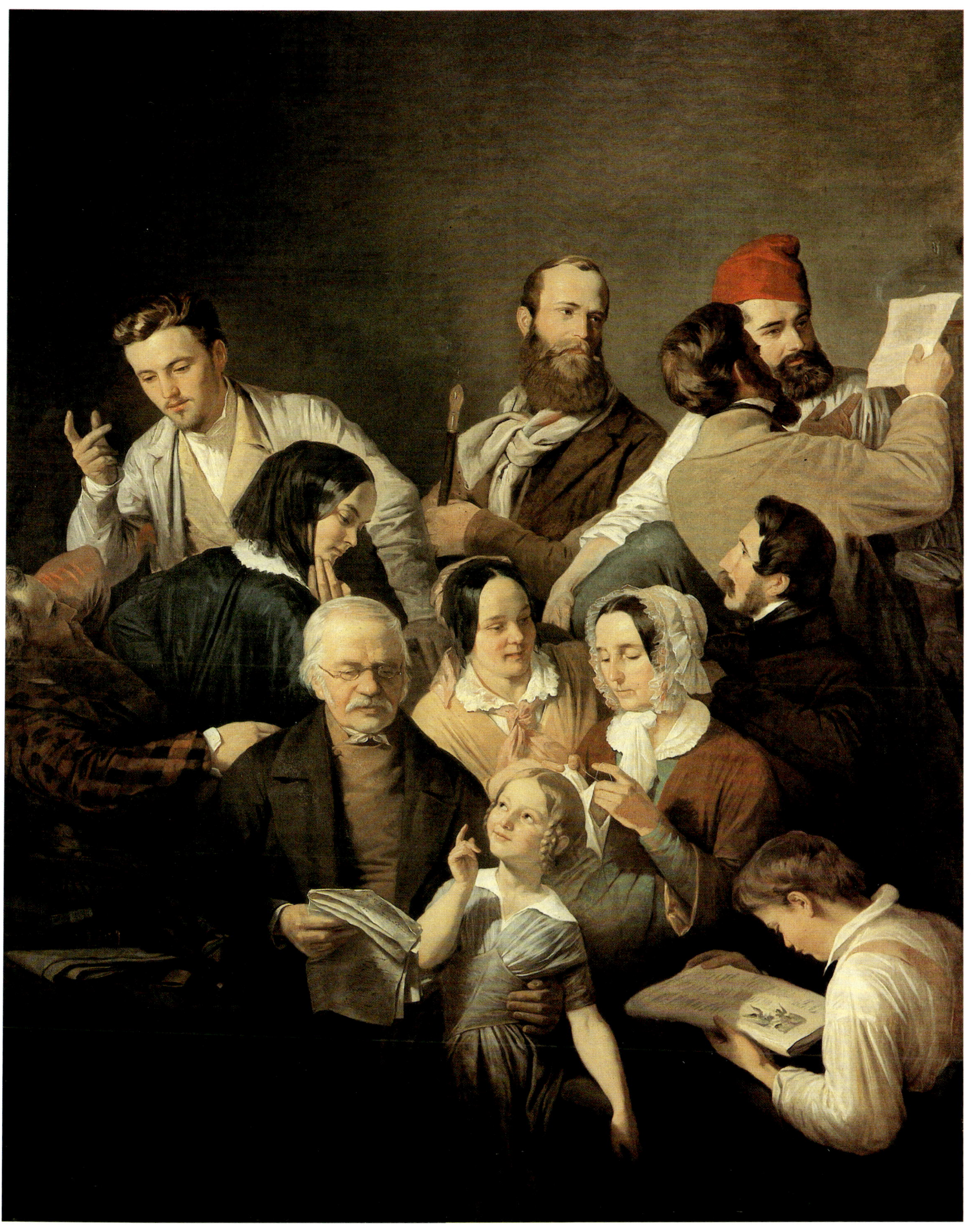

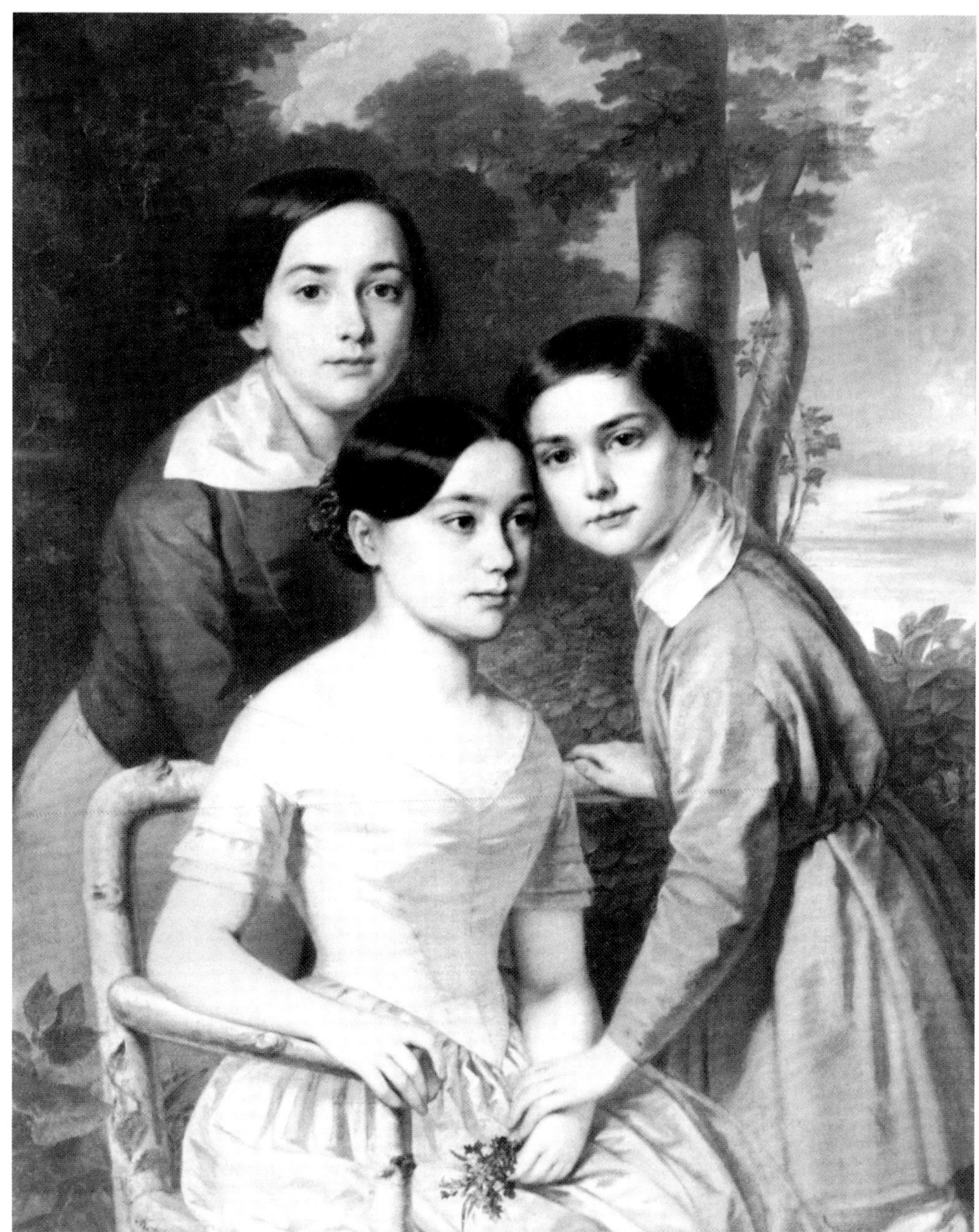

124. SÁNDOR KOZINA
Three Sisters, 1848
Oil on canvas, 104 × 82 cm
Signed bottom left: "Kozina 1848"
Budapest, private collection

This picture, generally believed to represent
the three Pejasevics children, has earned appreciative comments in art literature. The
little girl is sitting in a cane chair in a well-
tended garden with her two sisters. The
painter clearly conveys the sense of warm
family feeling between them. An exceptional quality of colouring is achieved by the
use of bright pinks, greyish violets and ivory
shades against very delicate warm browns.

125. MIKLÓS BARABÁS
Family Portrait (The Dégenfeld Family), 1854

Oil on canvas, 48.5 × 38 cm
Signed bottom right: "Barabás M 854"
Miskolc, the City Gallery of the Herman Ottó Museum
Inv. No.: HOM P77.12

Family portraits comprising numerous figures were much favoured by artists in the first half of the 19th century in Austria and Germany. In Hungary there was a similar vogue. In the 1840s and 1850s, most artists, known and unknown, produced such portraits, sometimes commissioned, sometimes from a wish to record members of their own families.

In depicting this family group, Barabás maintains the traditional style of the early 19th century, when portraits were introduced into landscape. The mother is shown in the middle of the group, dressed in white, wearing a necklace and earrings. Her three daughters stand beside her, simply dressed and without jewellery. The youngest holds a picture-book. The young father's elegance equals that of his wife. As in Barabás's single portraits and genre-paintings, so here the general impression is of an idealized vision of a family seen in a luxuriant landscape setting that serves to emphasize the warmth of family feeling.

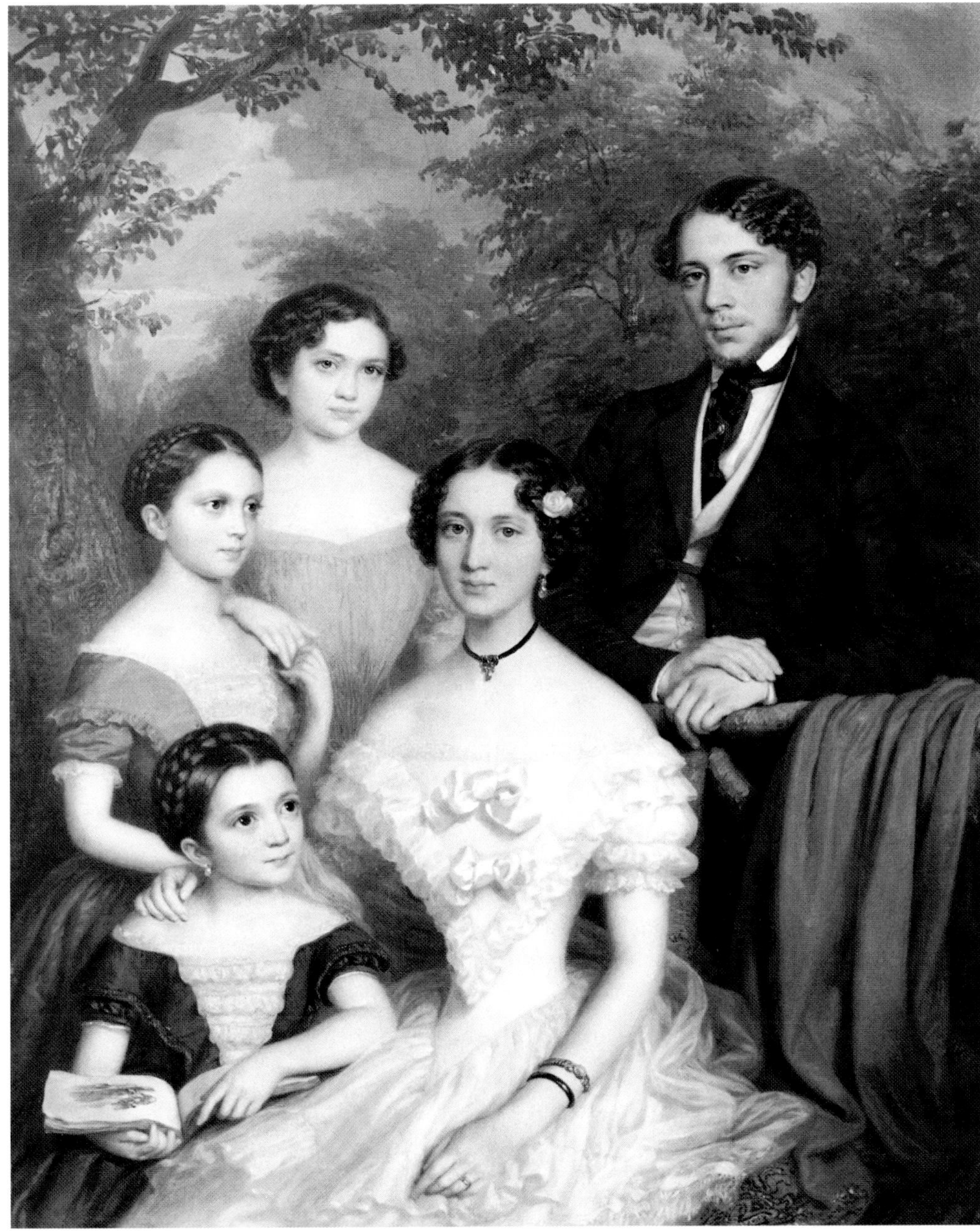

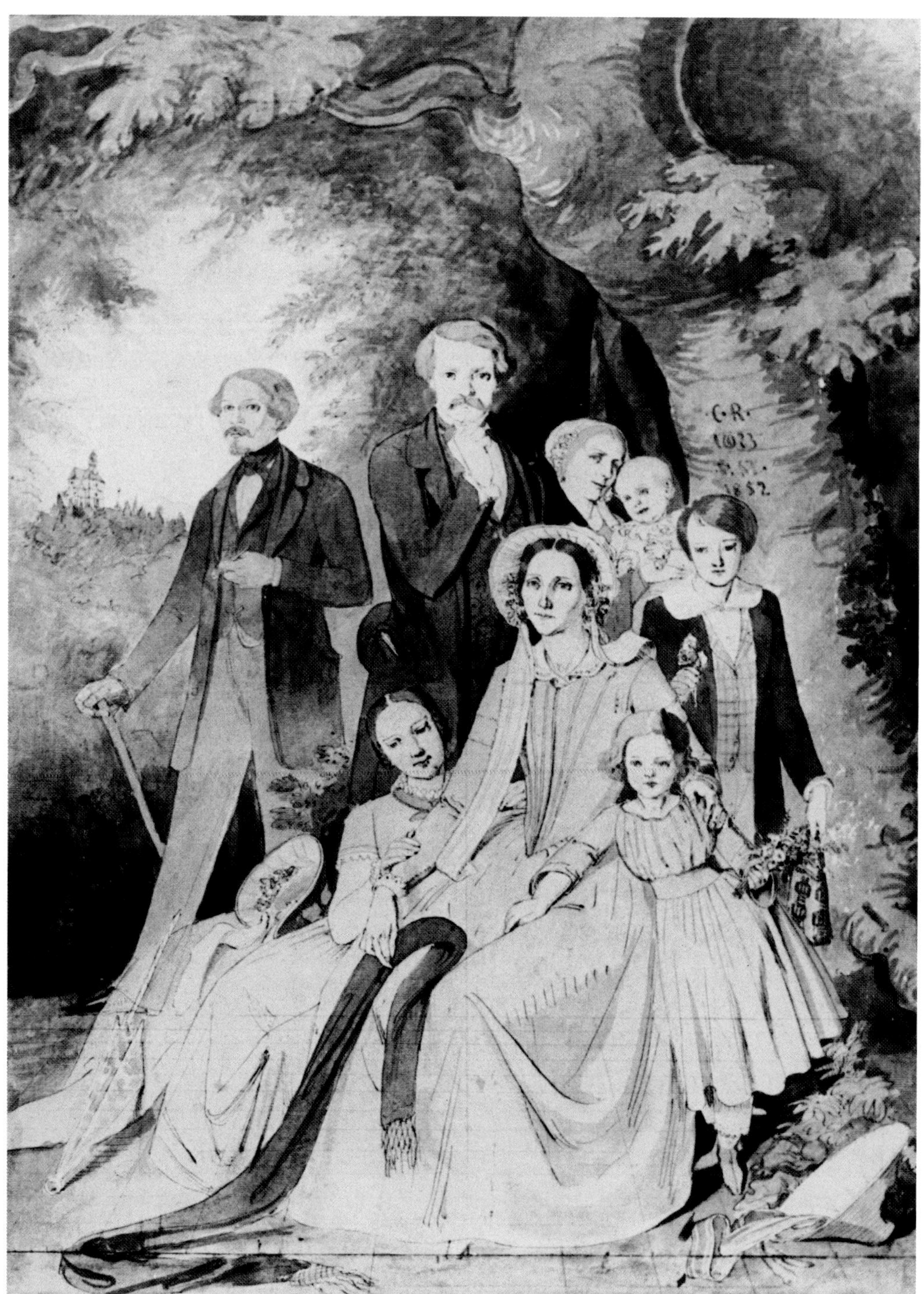

126. FERENC STORNO, the Elder
The Storno Family, 1852
Water-colour, ink, 60 × 25 cm
Signed on the right: "C. R. 1823 F.ST.
1852"
Sopron, Liszt Ferenc Museum, The Storno
Collection

Between 1840 and 1860 the vogue for family
portraits was at its height. The Storno family, some of whose members are portrayed
here, made a notable contribution to cultural
life in Hungary. The family produced architects, restorers, painters and sculptors.
Ferenc Storno. Sr. was born in Landshut and
studied in Munich and Vienna before opening a workshop in 1845 in Sopron, where he
was active as a church restorer and dec-
orator. He worked on the restoration of
most of the medieval churches in Hungary
and Transylvania. His drawings for glass
paintings and altars, and his sketches and collection of medieval buildings and objects
have been preserved by his descendants. By
1852, the date of this water-colour drawing,
Storno had become a wealthy citizen and the
father of several children. In this small picture, made for the family, every member of
this prosperous and cultured middle-class
family is depicted very correctly dressed,
against a landscape background. It is not impossible that the father was depicted twice:
once with a walking stick as though arriving
from far away, the second time in the central
position. The younger figure might, however, represent the eldest son, about to set
out on the period of travel traditionally required by the guilds.

127. HENRIK WEBER
Portrait of the Composer Mihály
Mosonyi and his Wife, 1840s
Oil on canvas, 84 × 68.7 cm
Unsigned. Budapest, Hungarian National
Gallery
Inv. No.: 5181

This is one of the most beautiful examples of
the double portrait, and the second made by
Weber, who had previously done a portrait
of a young couple, a work distinguished by
its unpretentious warmth. Here he portrays
his sister and her husband in their home, informally dressed and closely linked by the
bond of affection. Equal emphasis is given to
their individual characterization and the harmony of their relationship.

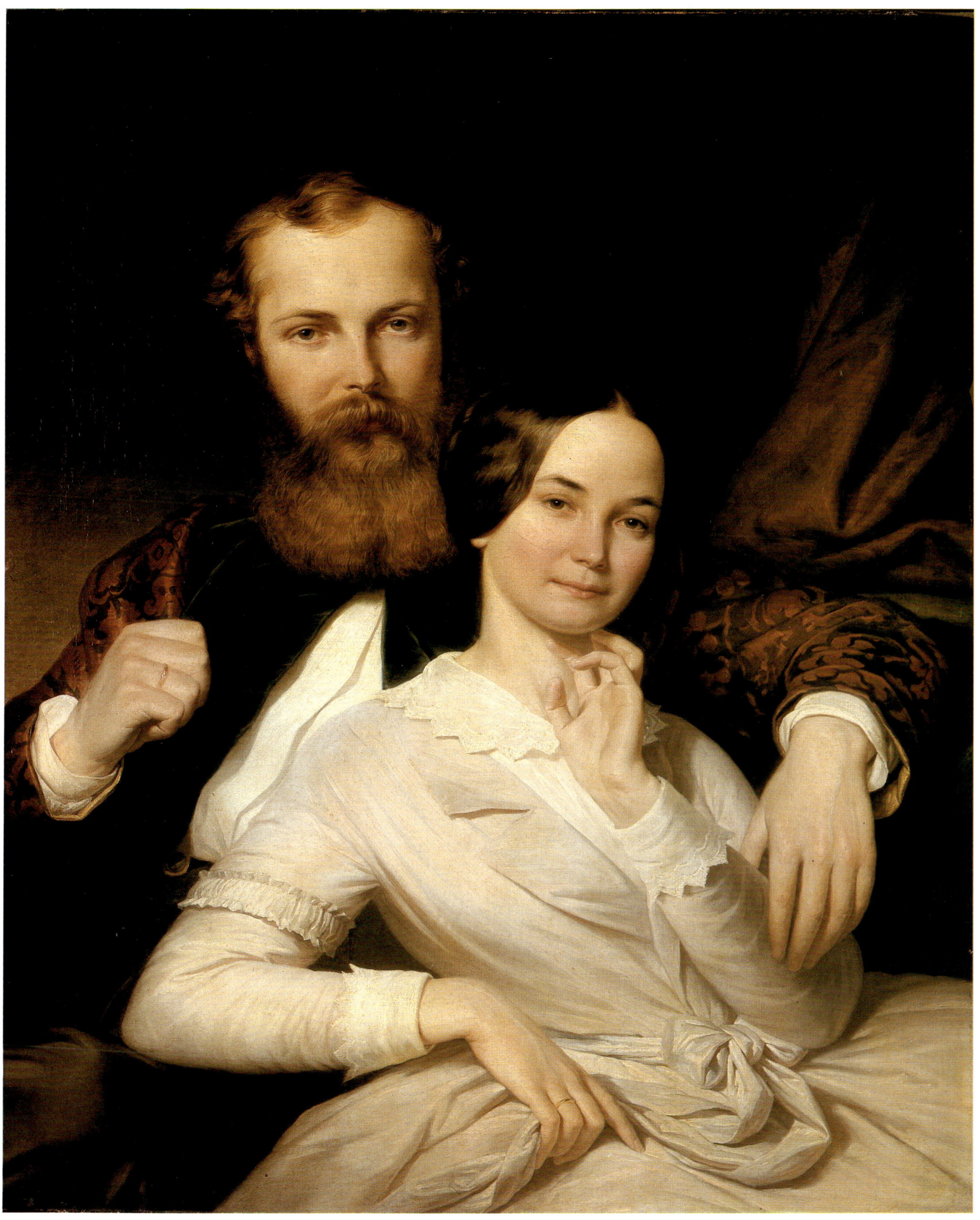

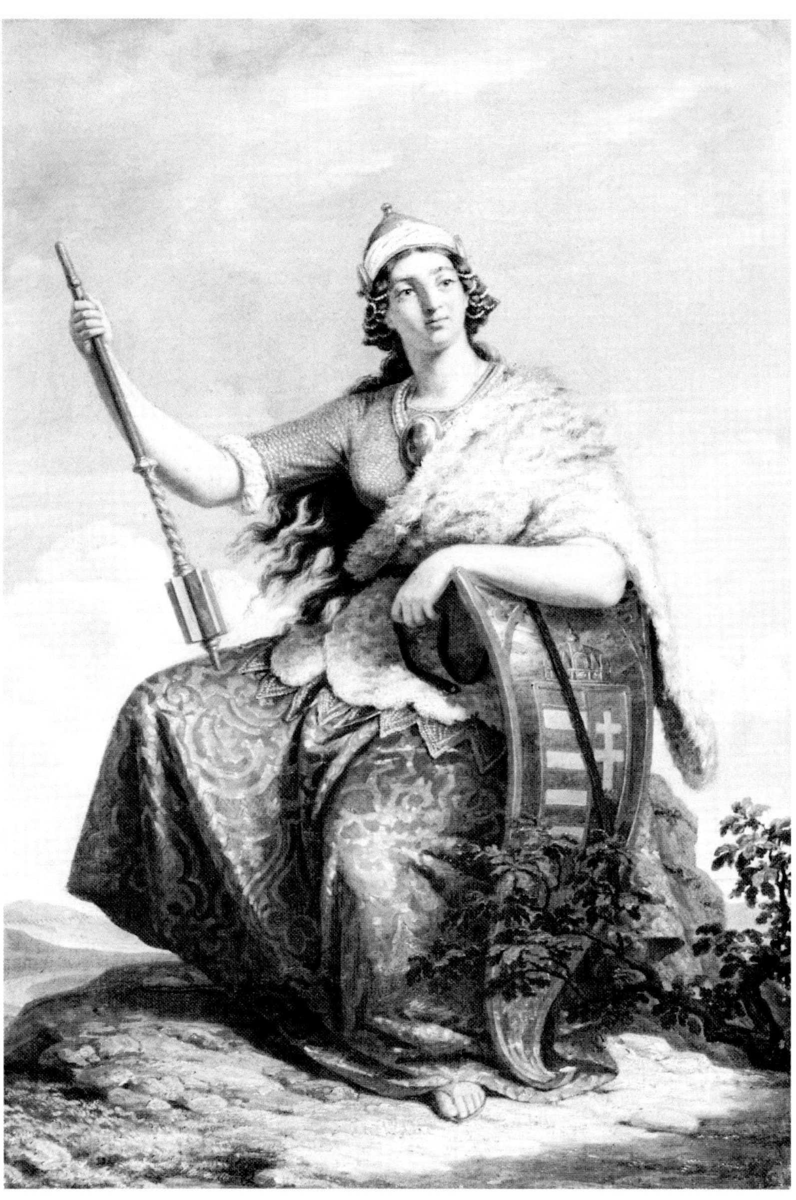

128. HENRIK WEBER
Hungaria, 1840s
Oil on canvas, 52×36 cm
Signed bottom left: "Weber H"
Budapest, private collection

This small picture differs both in style and in the way it has been signed from the other works by Henrik Weber reproduced in this volume. It is therefore most probably a work by the other Henrik Weber mentioned in the literature. His painting too indicates an Academic training. He paints with much heavier brush strokes and with less elegance than his more famous namesake.
This picture is yet another personification of Hungary, an individual artist's vision of the allegorical figure of Hungaria so frequently depicted at the beginning of the century.
Hungaria sits in triumph, holding a mace and wearing a coat of mail, an elaborate gown and a head-dress of Oriental style. Her shield bears the Hungarian coat of arms.

129. FERDINAND VIDRA
Pannonia, 1844
Oil on canvas, 225×185 cm
Signed bottom right: "Vidra Ferd. 1844
Romáb"
Budapest, Hungarian National Gallery
Inv. No.: 2672

Ferdinand Vidra's patrons were well placed to enable him to study in Rome from 1843 onwards. To show his gratitude he composed this large picture for exhibition in 1845 at the "Pesti Műegylet" art association and later he donated it to the National Museum.
His patrons were the Palatine and the Zichy family, and so the subject of the picture may have been suggested by an official of the Crown or a powerful member of the aristocracy.
It depicts a prosperous Hungary as an integrated part of the Habsburg Empire. A female figure, Pannonia, sits on a magnificent Renaissance throne wearing the crown of the Greek goddess Tyche or Cybele. She rests her left hand on a shield bearing the Hungarian coat of arms, while in her right hand she holds an open book, in which we can read verses by contemporary poet János Garay about the bloodshed of a past era and the dawn of a more promising future for Hungary.
On the semi-circular pediment of the throne the figure of the reigning Emperor and King of Hungary, Ferdinand V of Habsburg, is portrayed receiving eminent Hungarians who have come to pay homage at his coronation.

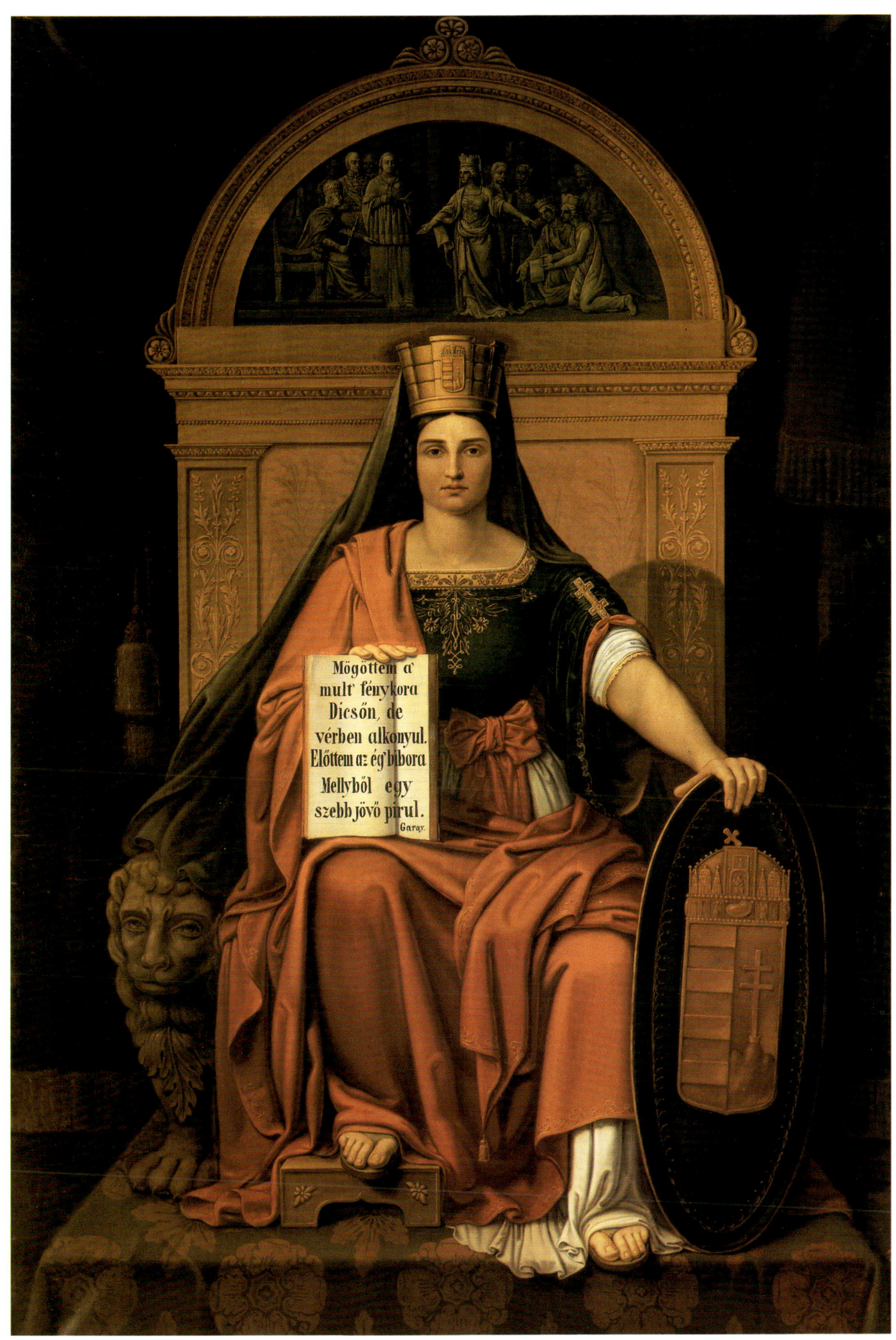
Mögöttem a'
mult' fénykora
Dicsőn, de
vérben alkonyul.
Előttem az ég'bibora
Mellyből egy
szebb jövő pirul.
Garay.

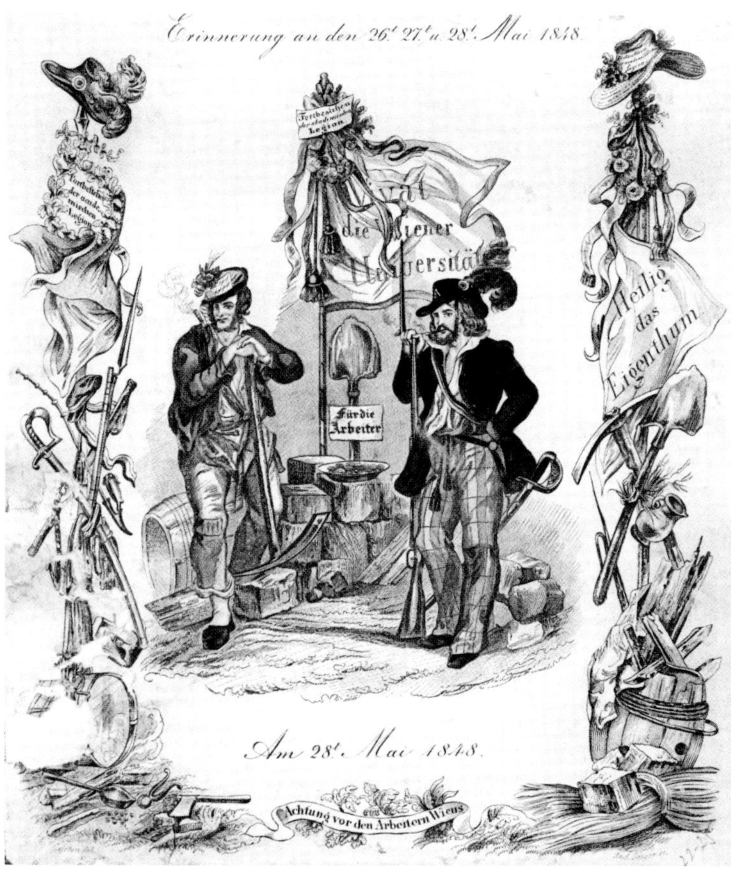

130. JOSEPH CAJETAN— ANDREAS GEIGER
Commemoration of May 26th, 27th, 28th, 1848

Copper engraving on paper, 250 × 220 mm
Signed bottom left: "Cajetan dal",
bottom right: "And. Geiger sc."
Bratislava, Mestská Galeria
Inv. No.: C 6983
Inscriptions: "Fortbestehen der akademischen
Legion. Vivat die Wiener Universität. Für die
Arbeiter. Heilig das Eigenthum. Am 28 Mai
1848. Achtung vor den Arbeitern Wiens."
(Continuation of the Academic Legion.
Vienna University for the Workers. Property
is sacred. Beware the Workers of Vienna. On
the 28th May, 1848.)

During the 1840s progressive bourgeois ideas gained influence in Vienna, and helped shape a new Austria. Many of these new ideas became manifest during 1848, when a series of revolutions took place throughout Europe. In Vienna, Klemens Metternich, the Conservative Chancellor, was ousted, Emperor Ferdinand V was forced to abdicate in favour of his nephew, and the Parliament of Austria was called into being. The revolutionary movement gained impetus above all through the action of the University students supported by the workers of Vienna. But this glorious period was short-lived. Within six months the only remaining traces of the events of May, 1848 were drawings of those events, some of them now in the Bratislava City Museum.

131. JOSEPH MATTHÄUS AIGNER
Self-portrait in the Uniform of a Commander of the Academic Legion, 1848

Oil on canvas, 73 × 54 cm
Long illegible inscription bottom right
Vienna, Museum der Stadt Wien
Inv. No.: 31.039

Aigner worked in Amerling's Studio and was already acknowledged to be a distinguished portrait-painter when in 1848 he joined the political movement in Vienna and became a commander in what was known as the Academic Legion. It was then that he completed his splendid, full length self-portrait in the uniform of a commander.
After the taking of Vienna by the troops of the Habsburg Emperor, Aigner was captured and condemned to death and it was only thanks to General Windischgrätz's intervention that he was pardoned. He subsequently changed his theme and painted portraits of the nobility, including those of Emperor Francis Joseph I and his wife, Elisabeth, Empress of Austria, and from 1867, Queen of Hungary.

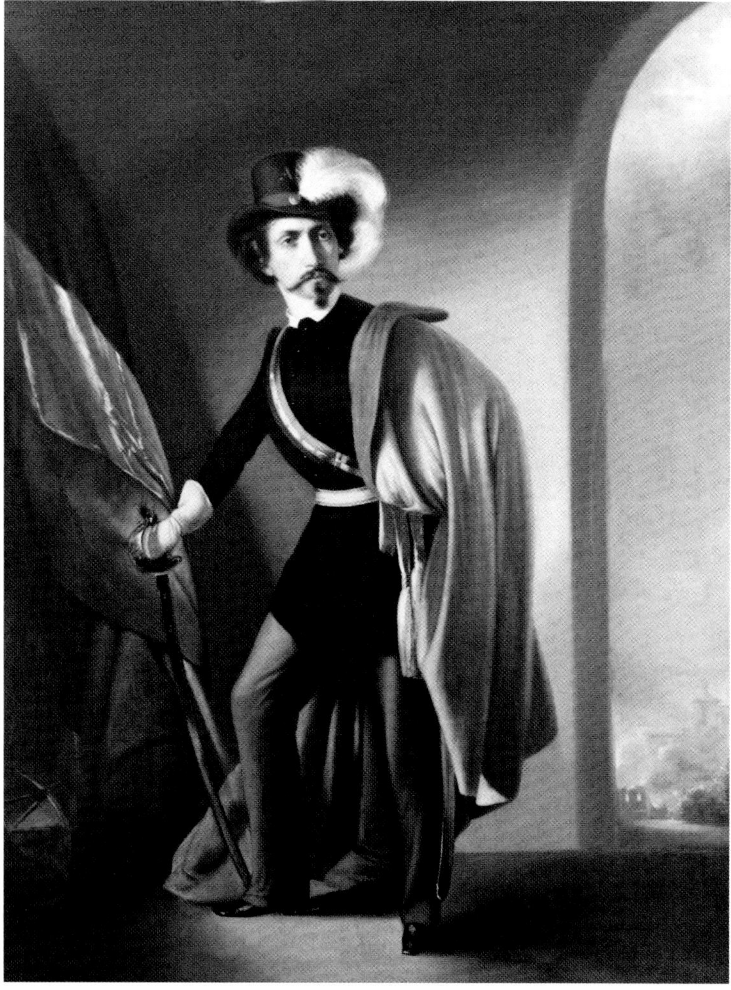

132. JÓZSEF BORSOS
A Hungarian National Guard, 1848

Oil on canvas, 110.6 × 86.8 cm
Signed bottom right: "Borsos J. Pest 1848"
Budapest, Hungarian National Gallery
Inv. No.: 923

This picture was completed in Pest as may be seen from the signature and from the uniform of the sitter. It is a Hungarian companion-piece to Aigner's self-portrait but is more daring and grandiose in its execution. Borsos often portrayed his subjects in a pose where head and body were turned in opposite directions, thus giving the figure more animation and enhancing the stateliness of the bearing.

The Guard, a man of middle age, wears a tricolour armlet, the symbol of his commitment to the ideals of liberty, equality and fraternity. It is one of the most mature works to come out of Pest in the year of the Revolution, comparable in its conception to pictures by Courbet and Daumier painted at around the same time in Paris, though the work of Borsos is in the Viennese style.

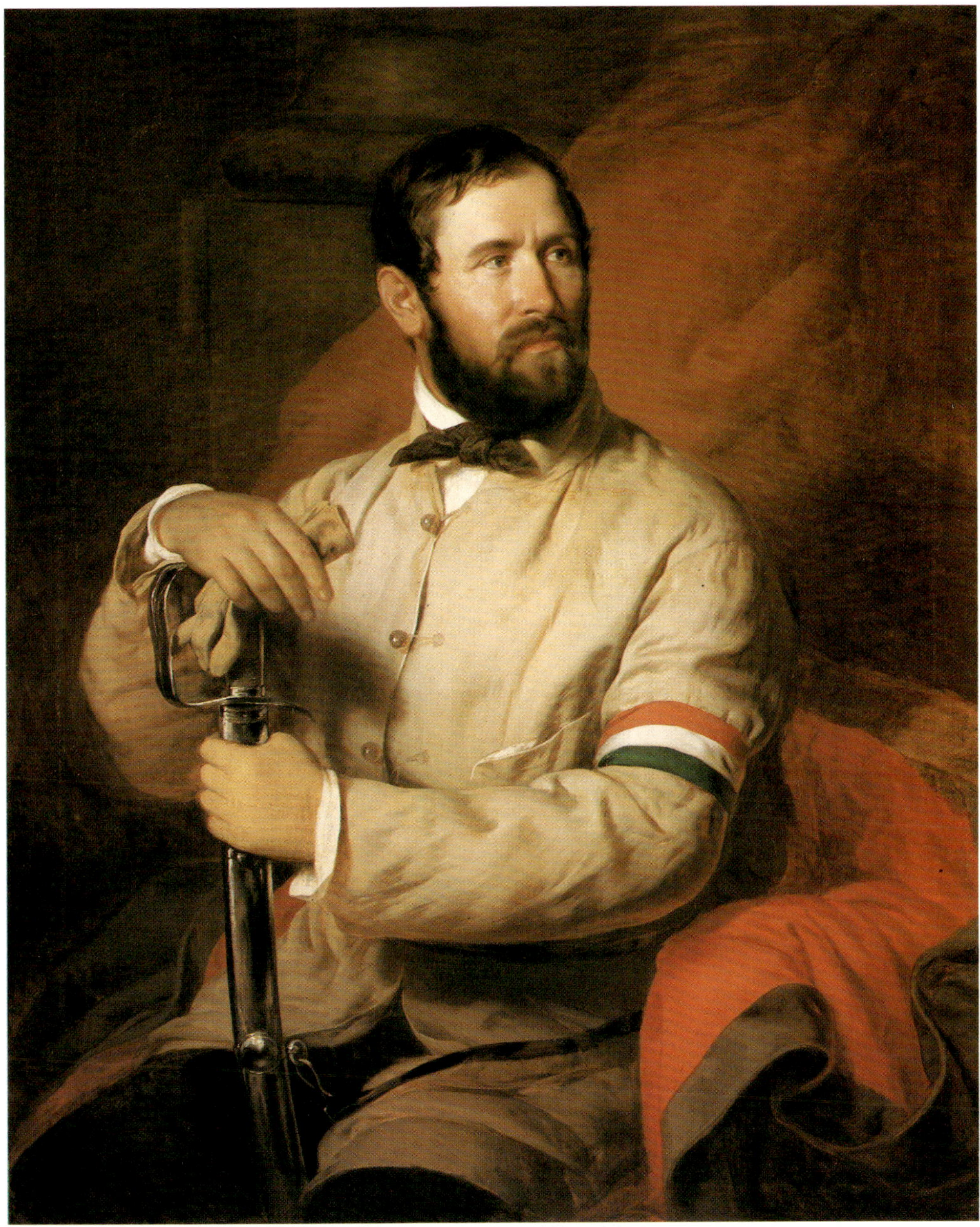

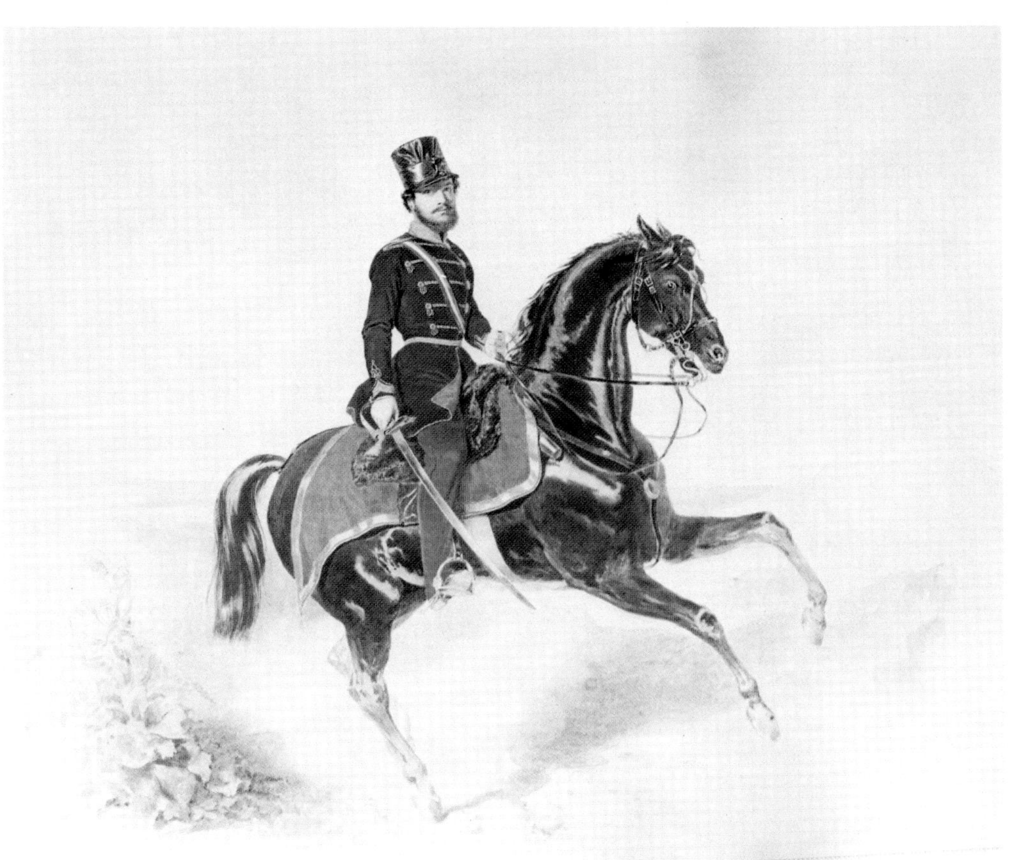

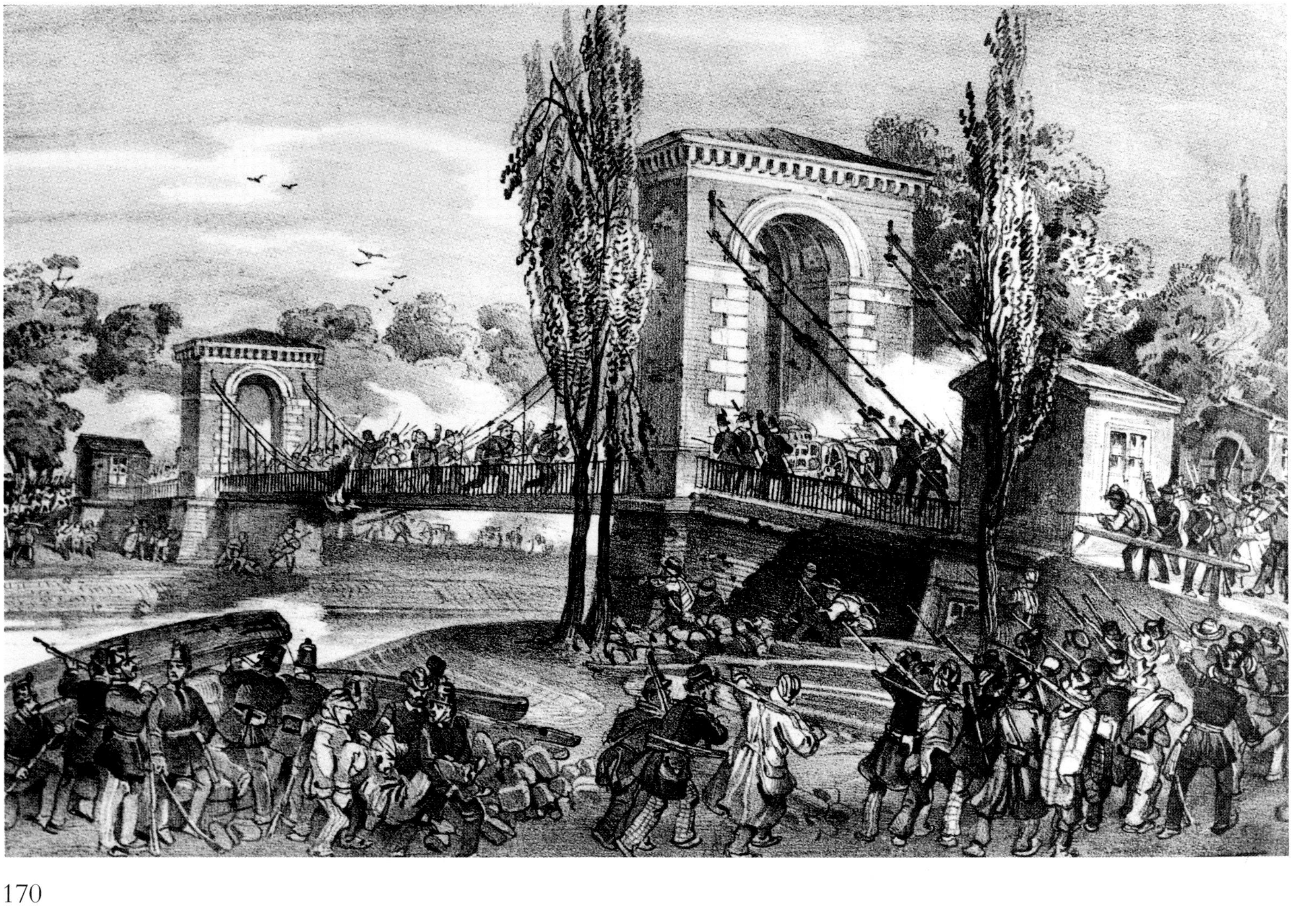

170

133. JÓZSEF BORSOS
A Hussar, 1849
Water-colour and gouache on paper,
345 × 428 mm
Signed bottom left: "Borsos 849"
Budapest, Museum of Military History
Inv. No.: 0980/Kp

Borsos depicted the First Parliament in Pest
and several scenes of revolution in Hungary.
It may have been his intention to use this
portrait of a Hussar for a lithograph or oil
painting, the execution of which was prevented by the course of events.
Not having committed his painting to the
cause of the Revolution in the years
1848–1849, Borsos was not molested on that
ground, and was able to return after the defeat of the Revolution to Vienna. There he
continued to paint portraits and other paintings acceptable to the Imperial authorities.

134. FRITZ FRIEDRICH
ALEXANDER WERNER
In Commemoration of the Glorious
Days of Austria: Capture of
Rasumofsky Bridge, Vienna, on the
24th October, 1848
Lithograph on paper, 280 × 400 mm
Bratislava, Mestská Galeria
Inv. No.: C-1704

This lithograph is one of a series of engravings completed at the time of the Vienna
Revolution. The events of those days were
immortalized for posterity by graphic artists. Their lithographs, first published in
newspapers and magazines, either on their
own or as accompaniment to articles, were
circulated in a series.

135. UNKNOWN ARTIST
Hungarian Flag and Coat of Arms,
1848
Oil on wood, 135.5 × 75 cm
Bratislava, Mestská Galeria
Inv. No.: A 2243

In this picture, the artist introduces a representation of the Hungarian flag into a landscape with a view of Pozsony. The revolutionary flag of the 1848 War of Independence dominates the foreground; the coat of
arms is seen beneath it.

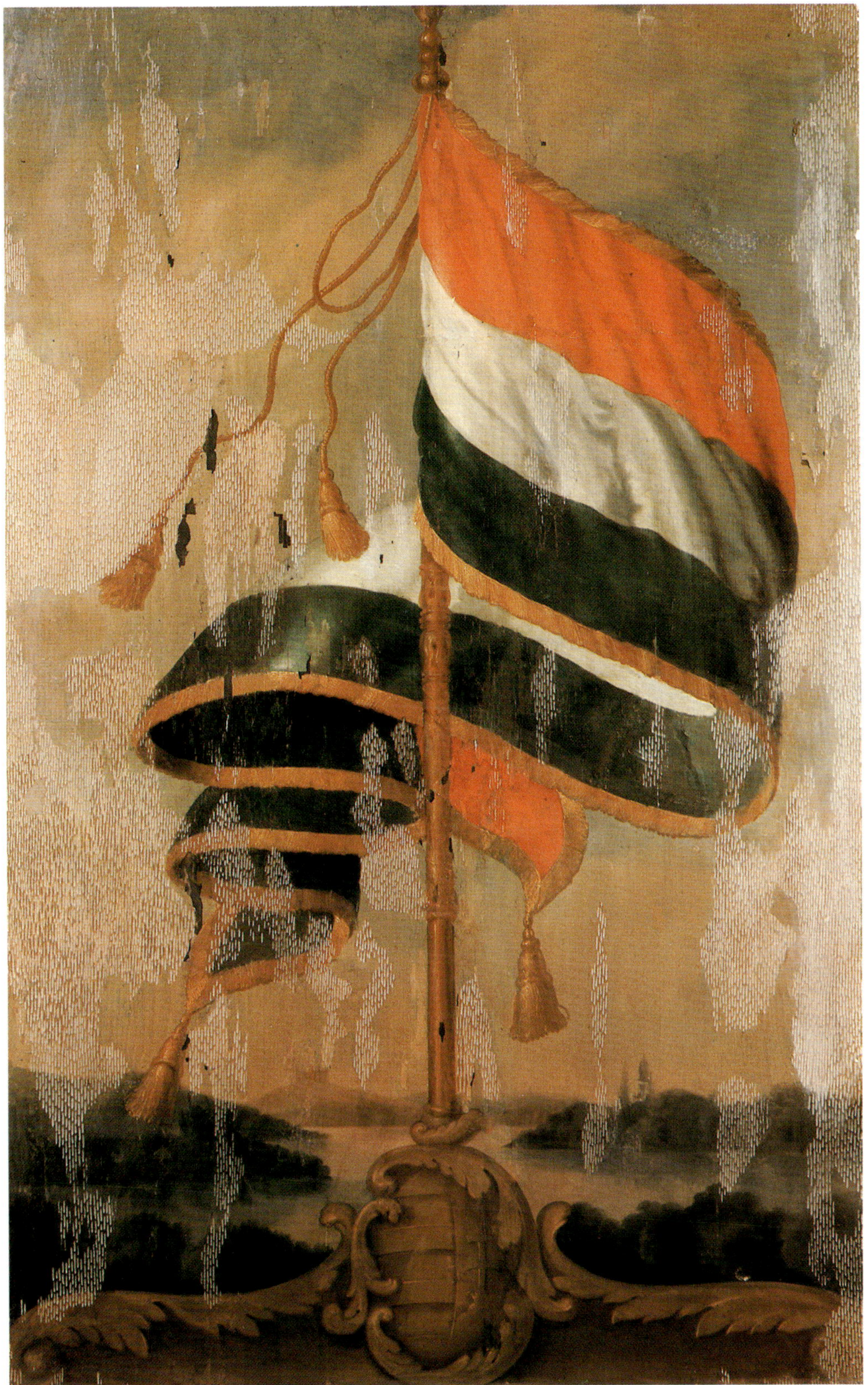

136. JOSEF ZABRATZKY AFTER JOSEPH LANZEDELLI
The Political Situation, 1848
Woodcut on paper, 231× 234 mm
Inscription: *"Osztria politikus helyzete."*
Képes Újság *(The political situation in Austria. Képes Újság, Kassa, Károly Werfer's Printing Office, Vol. I No. 27, 1st July 1848, p. 219)*
Budapest, University Library and National Széchényi Library
Inv. No.: H. 906

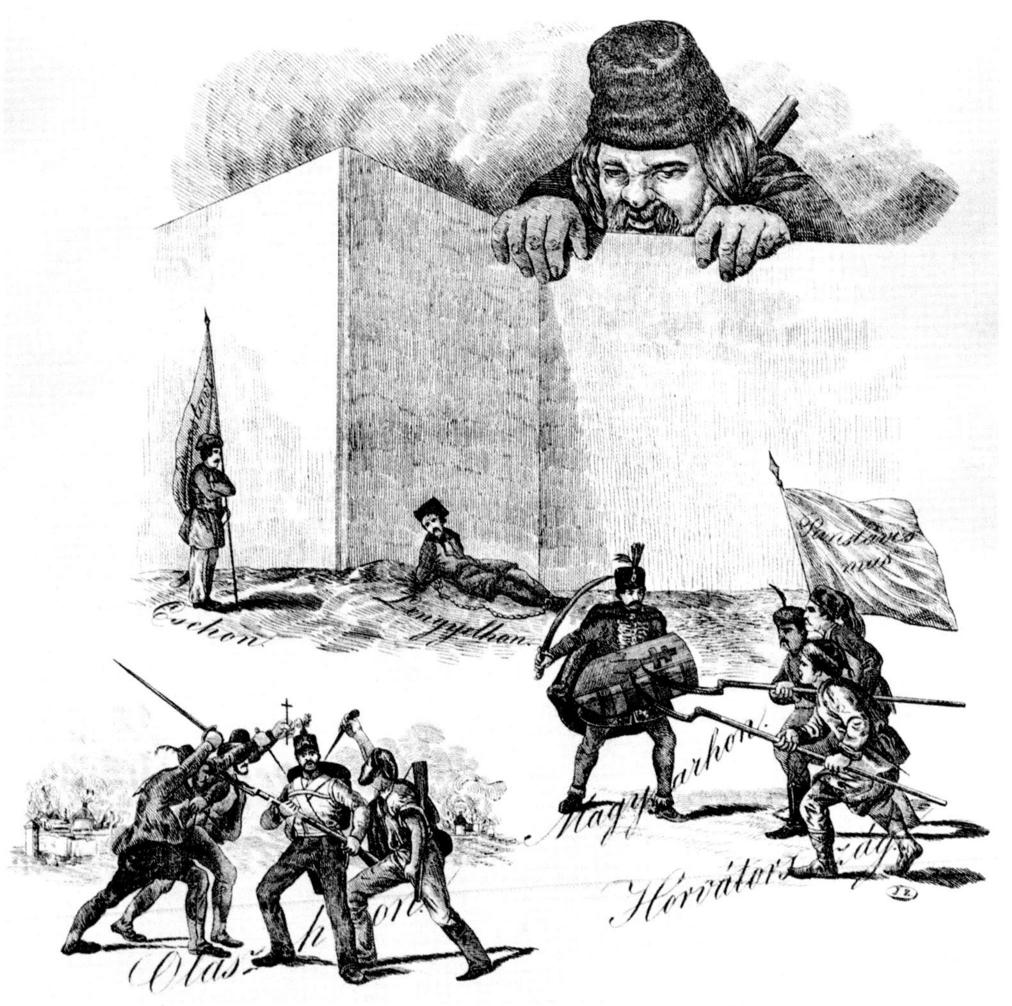

This woodcut was published in an illustrated periodical, which published many well informed articles about the general political situation in Europe. In this print, the artist caricatures the relations between member nations within the Habsburg Empire, and the general tension throughout Europe. Originally a much simpler woodcut, it was then made into a coloured lithograph to illustrate an article entitled "Our Hungarian Affairs". The intention of the writer was to warn the people against the belief that "the final act of the European drama has been played out… There is a strong reaction, a government plot afoot, aimed at forcing the nations back into the old rut".

The drawing is most likely the work of the younger Joseph Lanzedelli (Lanzedelly) who also depicted the 1848–1849 War of Independence in a series of lithographs. The woodcut was made by Josef Zabratzky, a permanent contributor for the "Képesújság" of Kassa.

137. MÓR THAN
The Battle of Tápióbicske, I–II, 1849–1850
Water-colour on paper, 284 × 401 mm
Unsigned
Budapest, Hungarian National Museum, Historical Picture Gallery
Inv. No.: T 6893. T 6894

As a young man Mór Than completed a series of colour sketches of battles in the War of Independence. The vivid colouring and the confident and animated drawing in his first pictures caused some astonishment. For the young painter had not yet studied in Vienna and although he had attended Barabás's studio, he had received no tuition in historical composition. It is possible, however, that Mór Than may have modelled his work on battle scenes composed in an earlier period.

There are two known water-colours of the Battle of Tápióbicske, which took place on the 4th April, 1849, in central Hungary. One of them depicts the encounter between two hussar regiments. Alajos Sebő, Lieutenant Colonel of the Hungarian Hussars, wearing the Hungarian uniform of the 1820s, confronts the Croatian Jellačič Hussars. The Hungarian leader is about to slay a robust Croatian Hussar, while officers and common soldiers clash with equal ferocity.

The other water-colour depicts two infantry battalions competing for possession of the Tápióbicske Bridge. This honourable rivalry almost ended in an armed skirmish, but Major Károly Földváry grasped the regimental flag and ran on to the bridge, an action which caused both the legendary Redcaps (a regiment in 1849) and their rivals to follow him into battle against the Austrian enemy.

This episode is reminiscent of the central motif in Napoleon's victory at Arcole (cf. Plate 58); in both battles opinions differed as to who had actually carried the flag. Mór Than supports both versions by depicting the flag twice—it is carried by a common soldier as his troop charges the bridge; it is also held aloft by a Redcap officer.

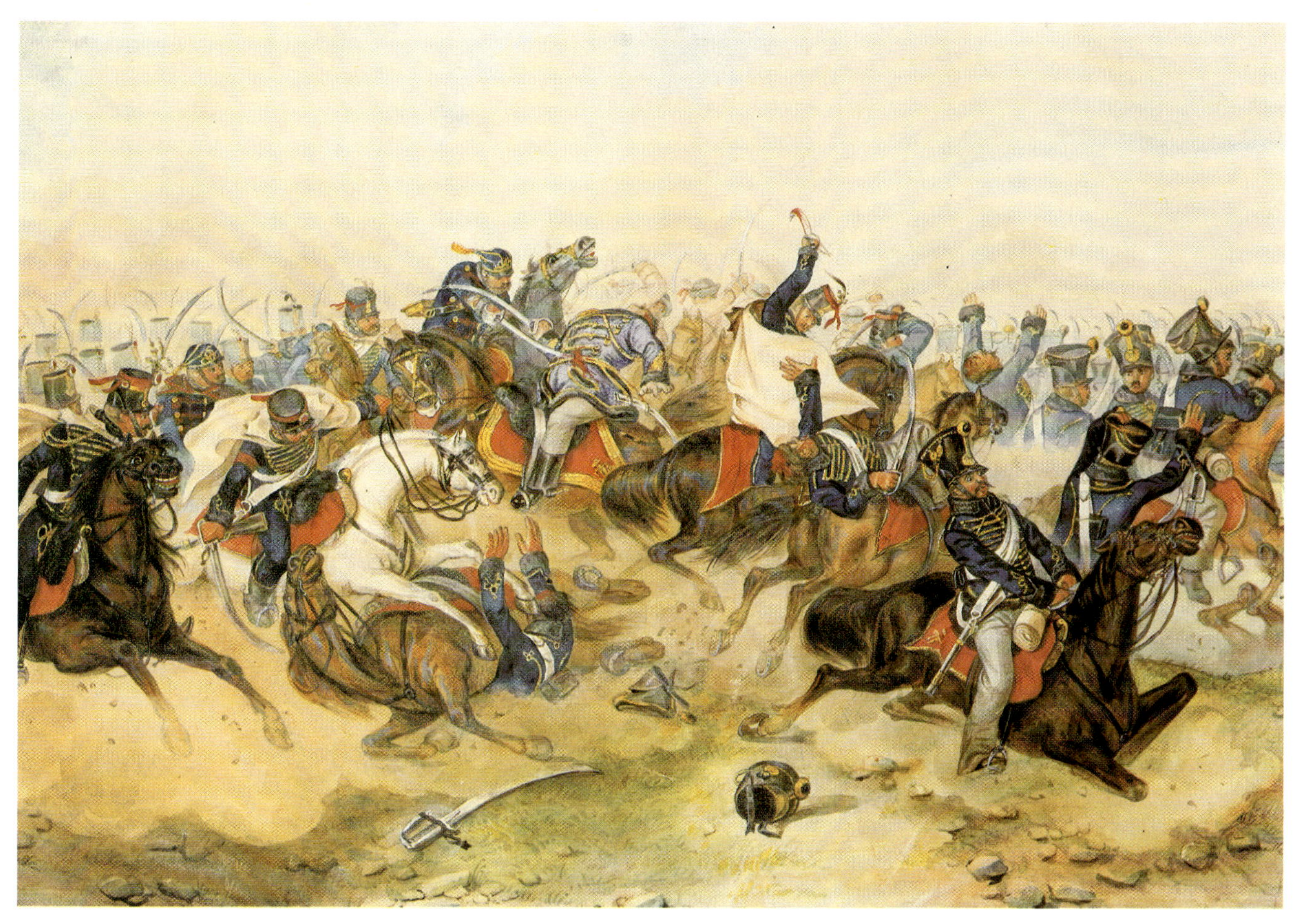

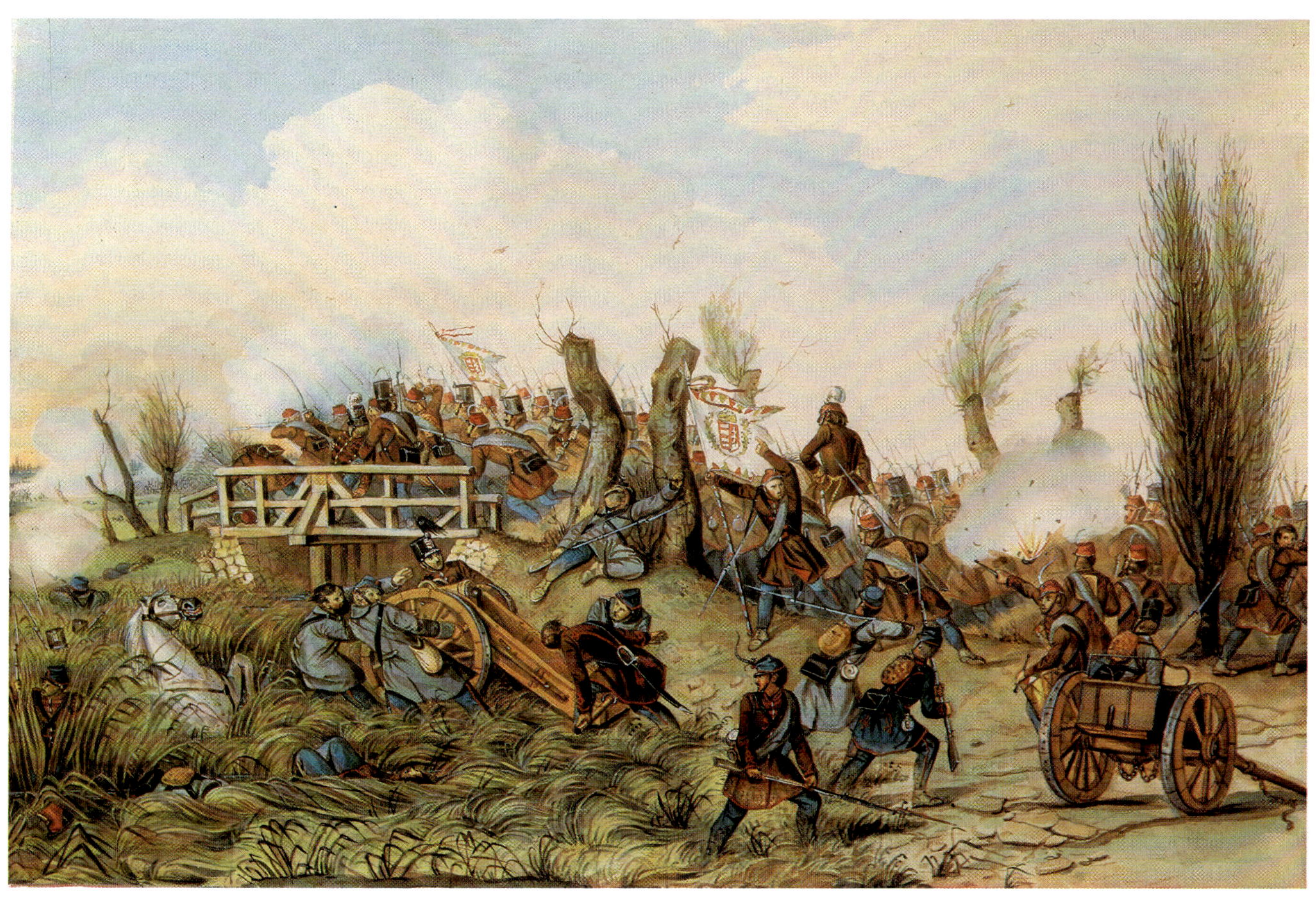

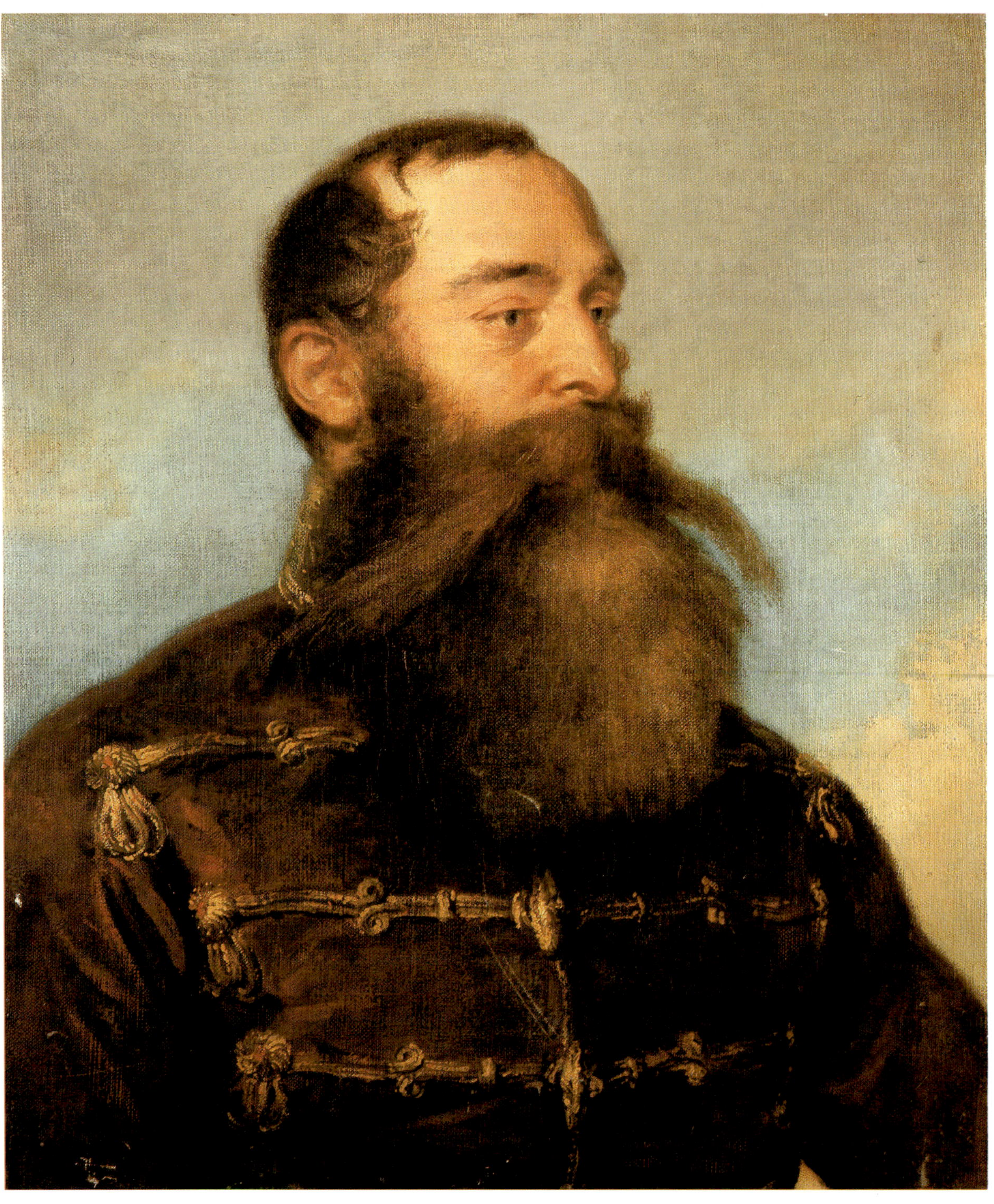

138. CHARLES (KÁROLY) BROCKY
Portrait of György Kmety as a Honvéd General, c. 1850

Oil on canvas, 61×51 cm
Unsigned
Budapest, Hungarian National Museum,
Historical Picture Gallery
Inv. No.: 432

In spite of failure, the War of Independence remains the memorable historical event of the 19th century in Hungary, for it appealed to the noblest aspirations, national pride, and met with general approval by progressives throughout Europe. After its defeat, Hungarian painters living abroad repeatedly sought out the heroes, soldiers and politicians of the War of Independence who were living in exile.

Charles Brocky's portrait depicts the Honvéd General György Kmetty in London, to which city the General had emigrated. He is depicted in his officer's uniform, calm and disciplined in appearance, his head held high, against a delicately overcast sky as if to convey the peace of eternity.

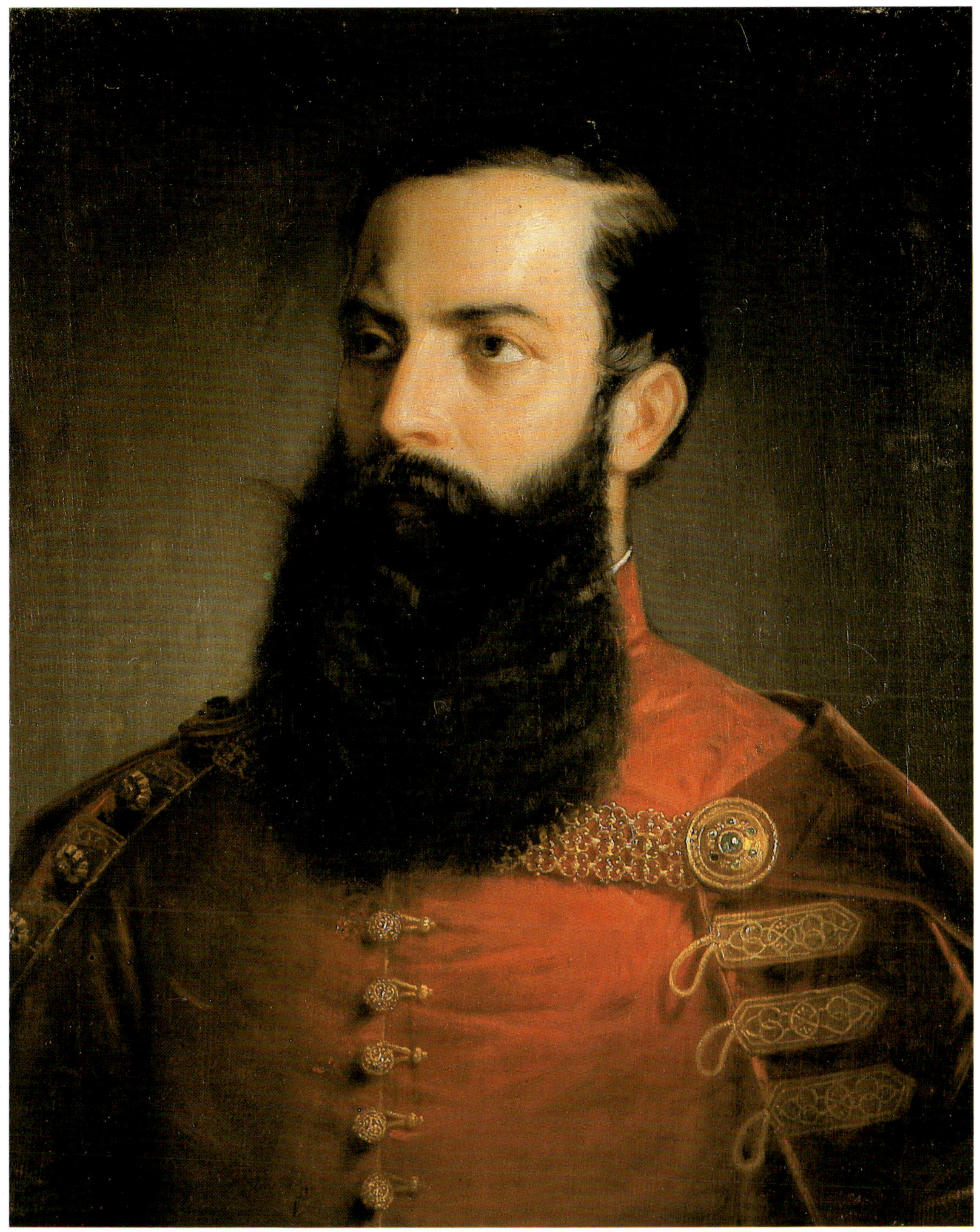

139. MIHÁLY KOVÁCS
A Hungarian Nobleman, c. 1850
Oil on canvas, 74 × 56 cm
Inscription on canvas stretcher, on paper:
"Előkelő magyar piros díszruhában. Pest,
Kovács Mihály" (A Hungarian nobleman
wearing red robes of state, Pest, [by] Mihály
Kovács).
Eger, Dobó István Castle Museum
Inv. No.: 55.106
Formerly in the Picture Gallery of the
Archiepiscopal Lyceum, bequeathed by Mihály
Kovács

The identity of the sitter is not revealed by the inscription nor indeed in any known documentary records. The painter depicts his subject looking seriously ahead. He wears a light red jacket and a splendid velvet cloak fastened with a delicately wrought clasp, all typically Hungarian. There is a certain quality of timelessness in the portrayal. The features have caused some art experts to believe that he could be one of the Batthyány family. In considering this possibility we have been tempted to think that the patriotic artist is here paying tribute to Lajos Batthyány, Prime Minister of Hungary, who was executed in 1849 by the Austrian government.

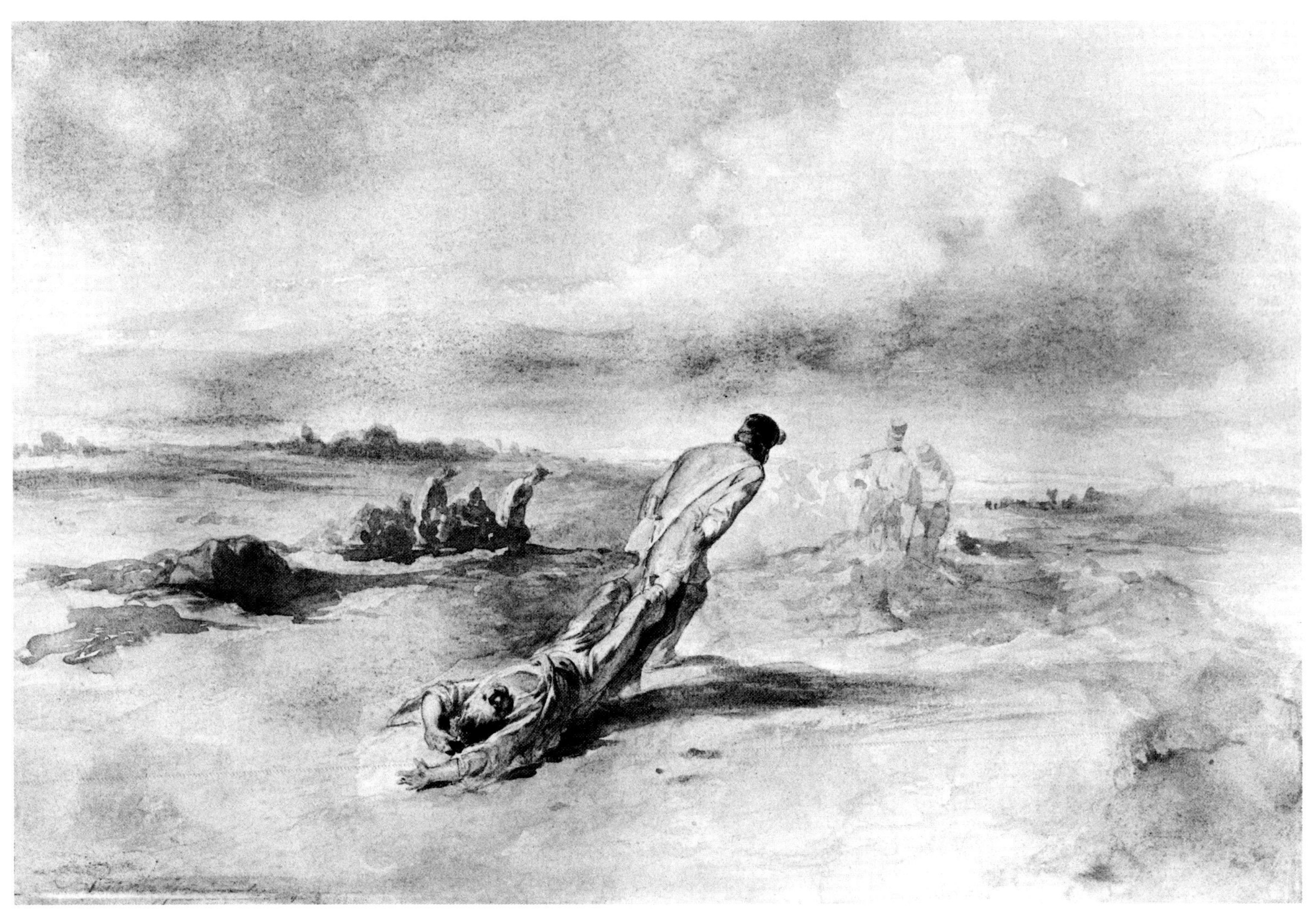

140. AUGUST VON PETTENKOFEN
Burial of the Fallen, 1849
Water-colour on paper, 235 × 345 cm
Signed bottom left: "Petenkofen"
Budapest, Museum of Fine Arts
Inv. No.: 1905–1984

The 1848–1849 War of Independence attracted to Hungary numerous Austrian artists wishing to depict scenes of battle to immortalize significant incidents or simply to record scenes of human suffering.

August von Pettenkofen's representations of the events of 1848 are far superior to his other water-colours and lithographs.

The artist also portrayed his close friend, József Borsos, and he executed a group portrait of the first Parliament in Pest in 1848, from which he made a lithograph signed with a pseudonym.

141. FERENC UJHÁZY
Grieving Honvéd, 1850

Oil on canvas, 50×64 cm
Signed lower edge: "Ujházy Ferenc, 1850"
Inscription on the tomb: "Your battle is the
battle of the people."
Budapest, Hungarian National Gallery
Inv. No.: 81

The Honvéd sits on the ground in the dusk of evening leaning against a romantic Neo-Gothic tombstone. The Hungarian flag droops to the ground beside him as he mourns his friend and the lost cause of the War of Independence. A long inscription is visible on the flat surface of the tomb, but so moved were those who saw the picture at the 1851 National Exhibition, that no words were necessary; everyone understood the meaning of the painting at first glance.

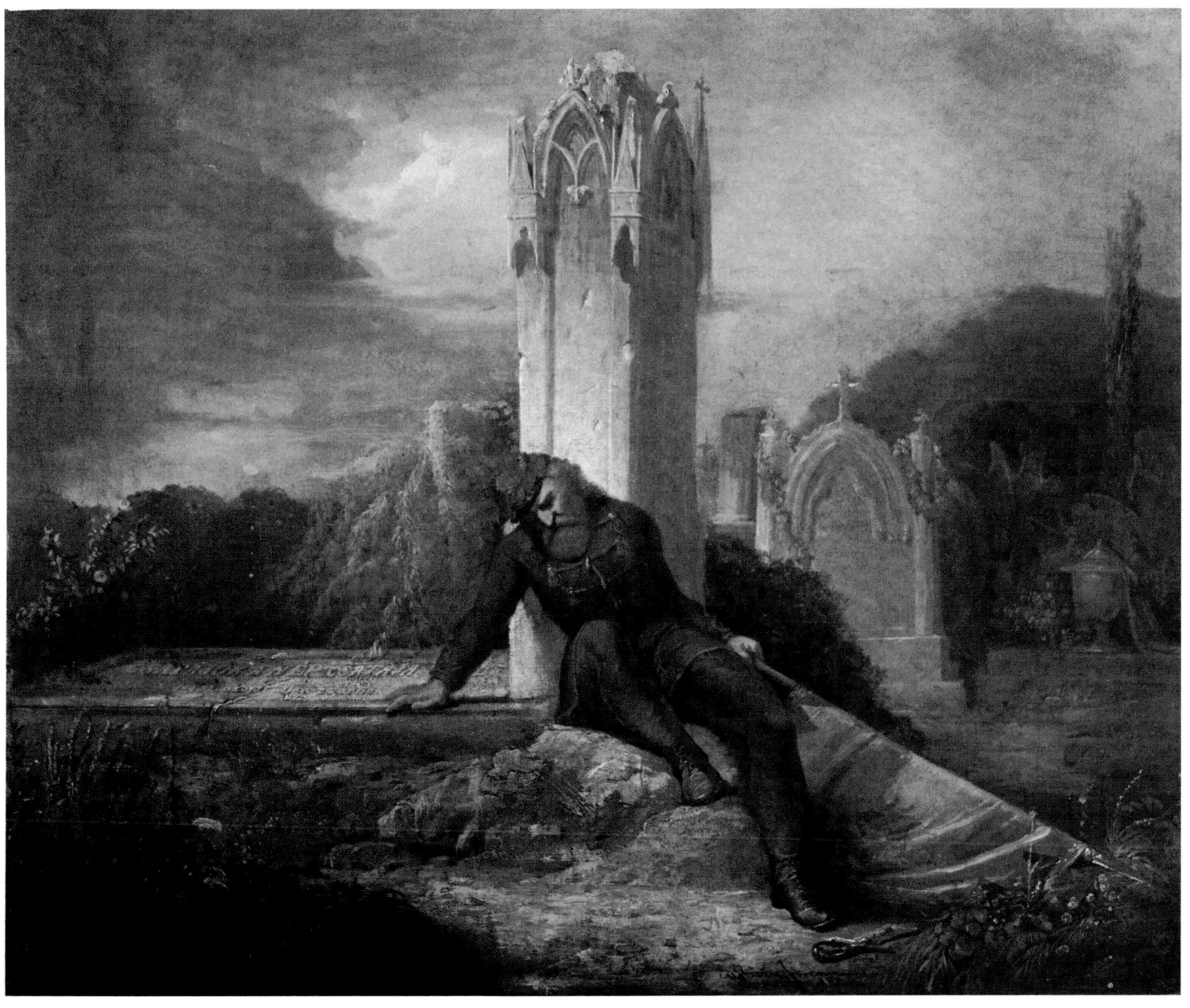

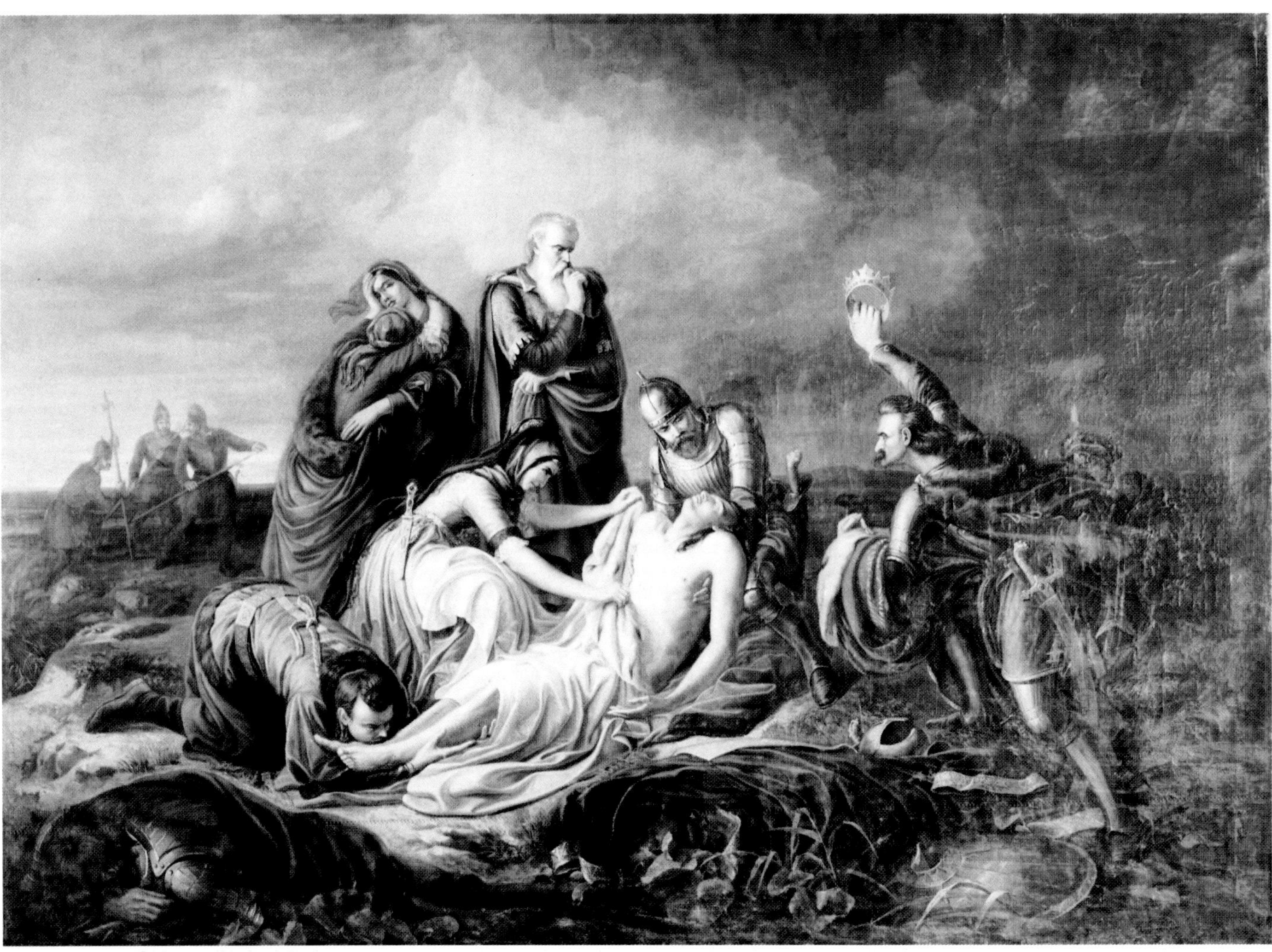

142. SOMA ORLAI PETRICH
The Discovery of the Body of King Louis II in 1526, c. 1851
Oil on canvas, 200 × 290 cm
Signed bottom left: "Orlay"
Debrecen, the Calvinist College
Bought from the artist in 1852

Orlai began this large painting in 1850 in Munich and completed it within two months, spurred on by his desire to exhibit at the 1851 Pest Art Exhibition where the picture eventually arrived with the help of Miklós Barabás.

Scenes of the Battle of Mohács had already been a subject for drawings and paintings by Hungarian artists in earlier periods. József Borsos based one of his paintings on István Dorffmeister's work which shows the influence of the Baroque style of the prints and paintings he copied. Earlier painters had been chiefly interested in the representation of dramatic battle scenes; the tragic historical episode which followed the battle—the discovery of the king's body—had previously been depicted only once, by a German graphic artist, who used it as an illustration in a history book. Orlai used earlier Pietà models for his composition. He depicts mourners grieving around the dead king in the central part of his painting. Despite the weakness of the figure drawing and the uneven colouring, the picture was favourably received by the general public and fellow artists alike.

143. MIHÁLY KOVÁCS
Lady Perényi Orders the Burial of the Dead after the Battle of Mohács, 1854
Oil on canvas, 38 × 53 cm
Signed top right: "fest. Kovács Mihály"
(painted by Mihály Kovács)
Eger, Dobó István Castle Museum
Inv. No.: 55.118

This episode at the Battle of Mohács, also depicted by Soma Orlai Petrich, shows Péter Perényi's widow, née Dorottya Kanizsay, with her followers as she orders the burial of her dead husband, together with the other victims. Kovács continued to use this subject for the next twenty years, during which period he composed several versions. It was thus born of the grief of a nation during the years after the 1848–1849 War of Independence.

The sense of horror is conveyed in a naive way as in the tragic works of the romantic "paintings of devastation" of the time.

144. SOMA ORLAI PETRICH
Lady Perényi Orders the Burial of the Dead at Mohács, 1860s
Oil on canvas, 48 × 81 cm
Unsigned
Budapest, Hungarian National Gallery
Inv. No.: 6825

This medium-sized picture was presumably a sketch in oil for a larger work to follow, which however was never painted. Orlai's composition, centred around the figure of Imre Perényi's widow as she cries aloud to Heaven, demonstrates a greater awareness of balanced symmetry than that of Mihály Kovács. Orlai composed his history pieces with the greatest possible care, giving much thought to balance, for he was aware of the weakness of his drawing; however, this often resulted in a stiff and formal effect.

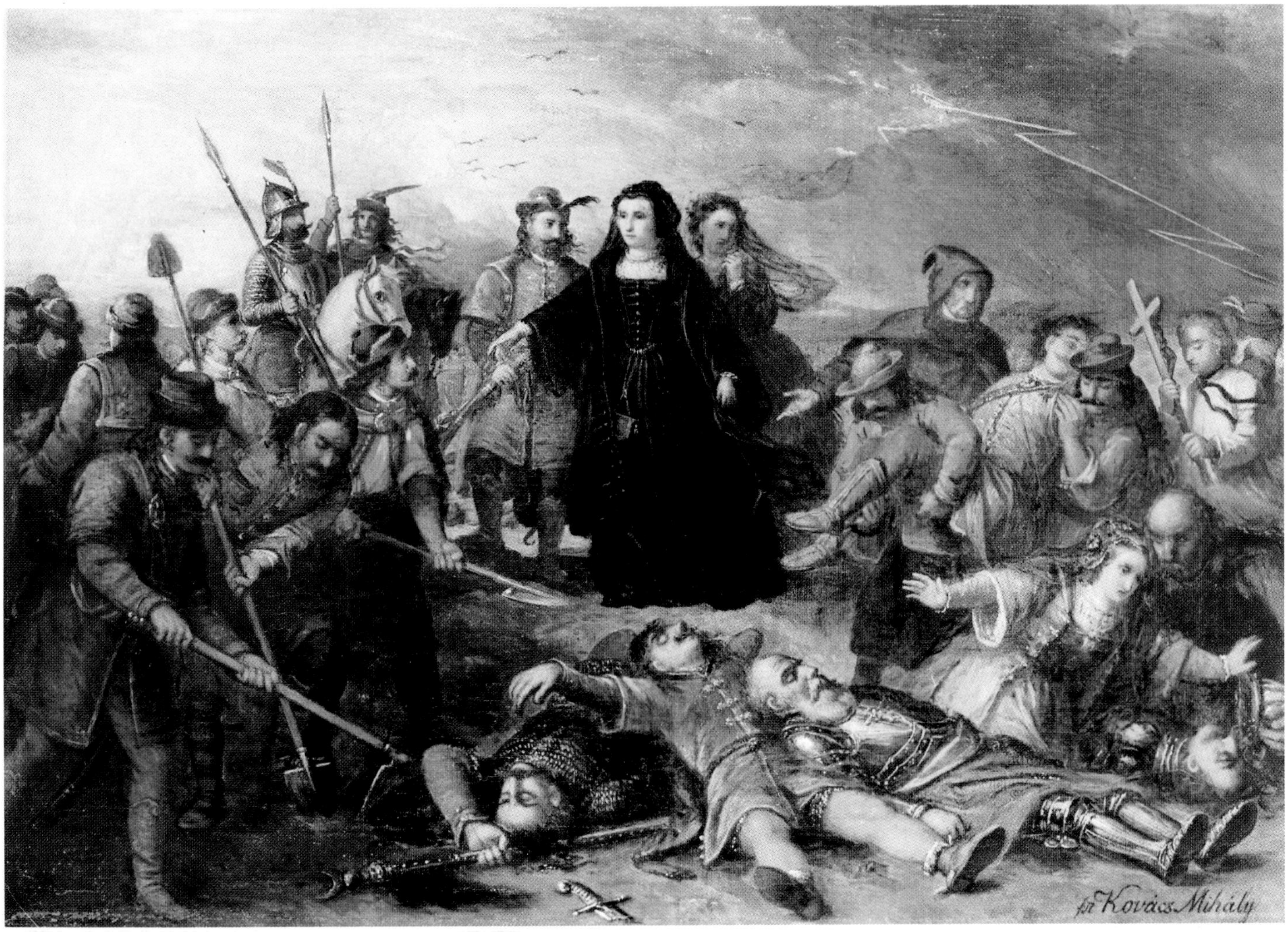

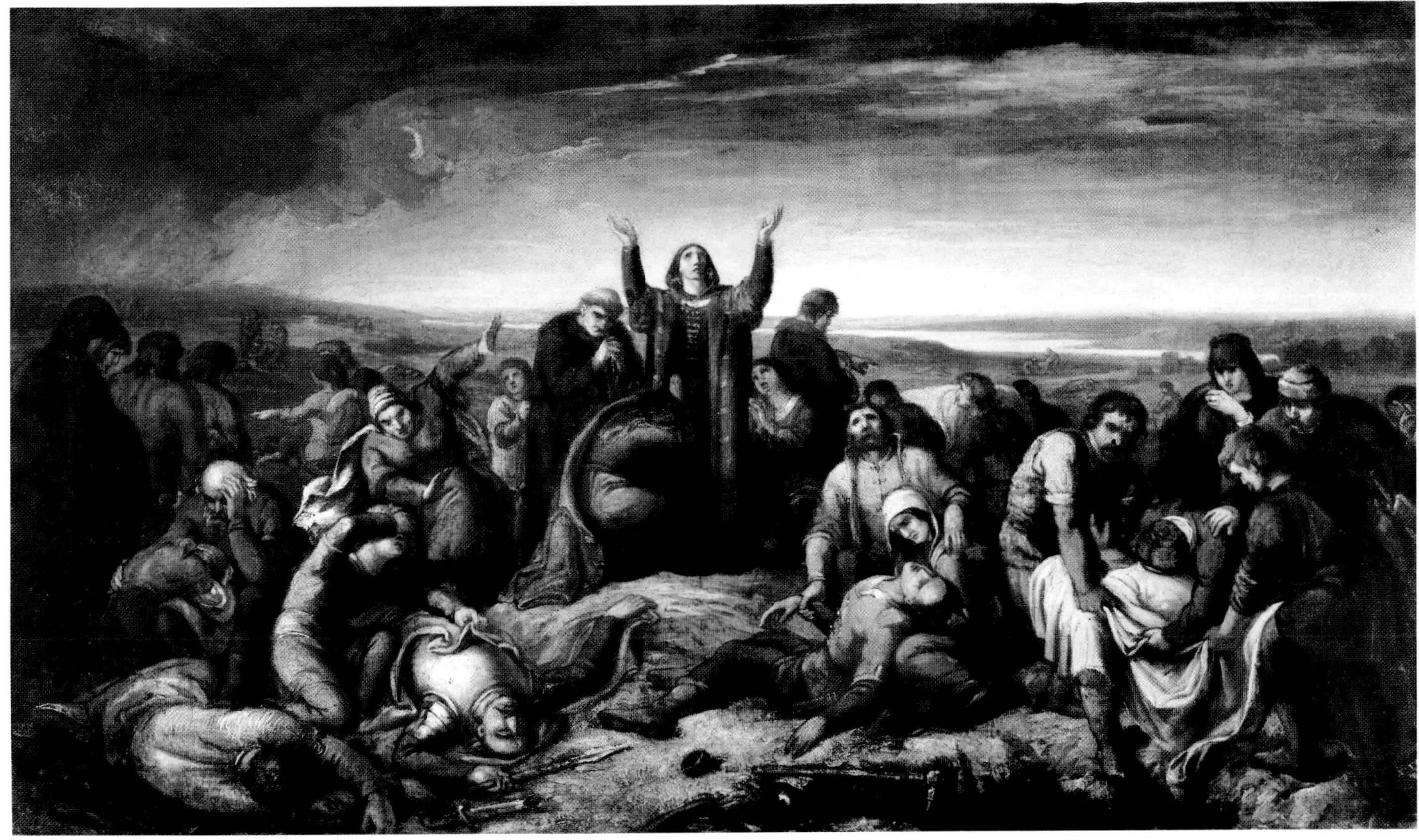

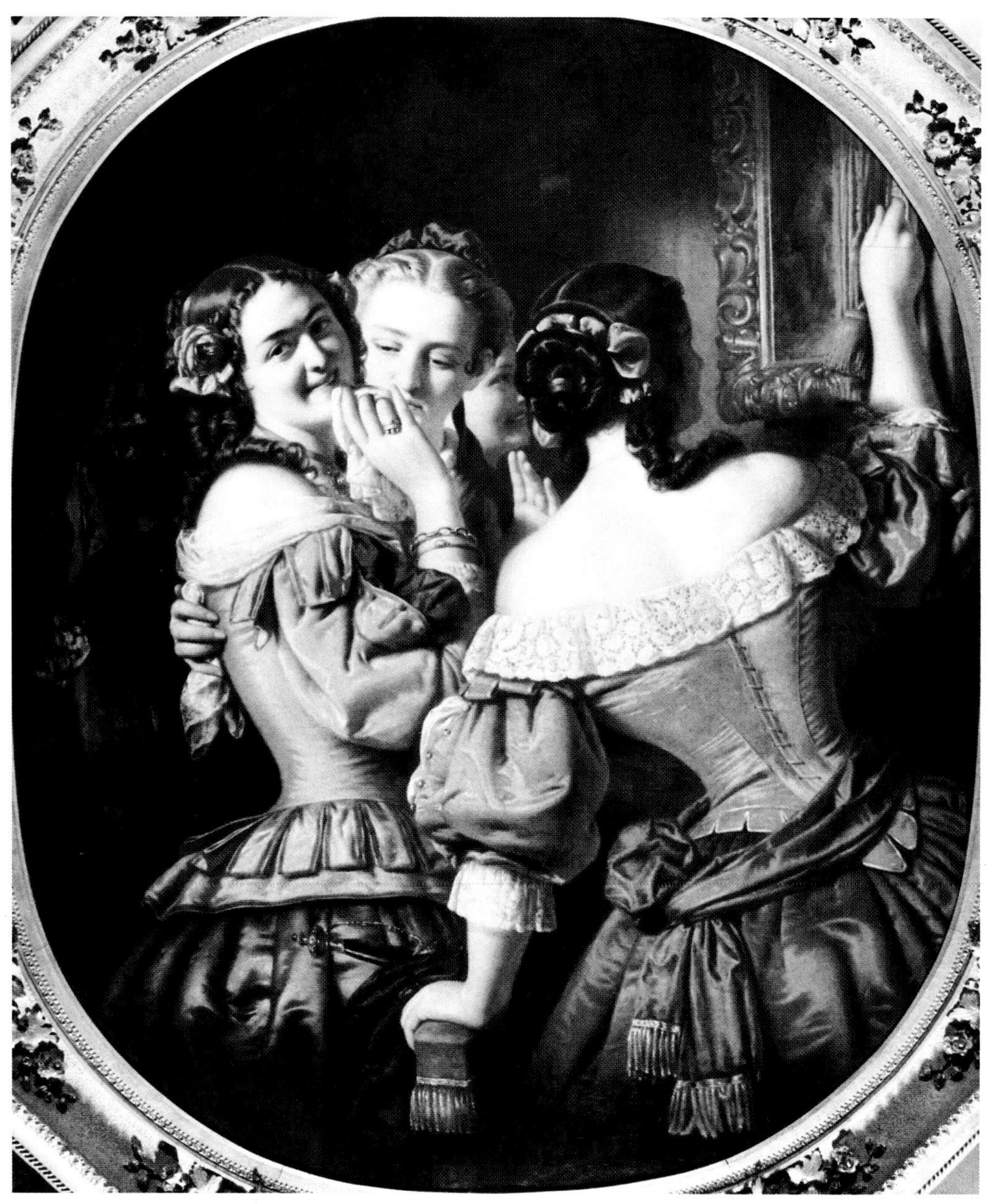

145. JÓZSEF BORSOS
After the Ball, 1856
Oil on canvas, 136×109 cm
Signed bottom right: "Borsos 856"
Austria, private collection
(There is a reproduction in the Archives of the
Art History Research Institute of the
Hungarian Academy of Sciences)
Inv. No.: 77/987-2

146. JÓZSEF BORSOS
Girls After the Ball (The Morning
After the Ball), 1850
Oil on wood, 121.5×125 cm
Signed bottom right: "Borsos J. 850"
Budapest, Hungarian National Gallery
Inv. No.: 1394

Genre-paintings of the Viennese private schools, and later works composed in the same style, frequently included the representation of preparations for a ball, elaborately trimmed evening dresses, fancy dresses, complicated hair styles and young ladies trying on jewellery. In József Borsos's oil painting of 1850, these popular motifs have been included, though there is more originality in the composition.

The three young ladies, no longer fully dressed, sleepily chat in the semi-darkness of their richly furnished boudoir with three lady visitors, whom they entertain with casual informality. The room is exquisitely furnished with velvet curtains and silver table appointments, while on the softly patterned carpet, art magazines with coloured engravings, can be seen lying where they have been tossed down.

The youth and beauty of the girls is equally revealed by the negligées they wear and the formal silk and velvet costumes of the visitors. The gestures of the girls enhance the harmony of the classical triangular composition.

In the Vienna of the 1850s Borsos's picture was inevitably overwhelmingly successful, so that the artist was obliged to make several versions of the same subject.

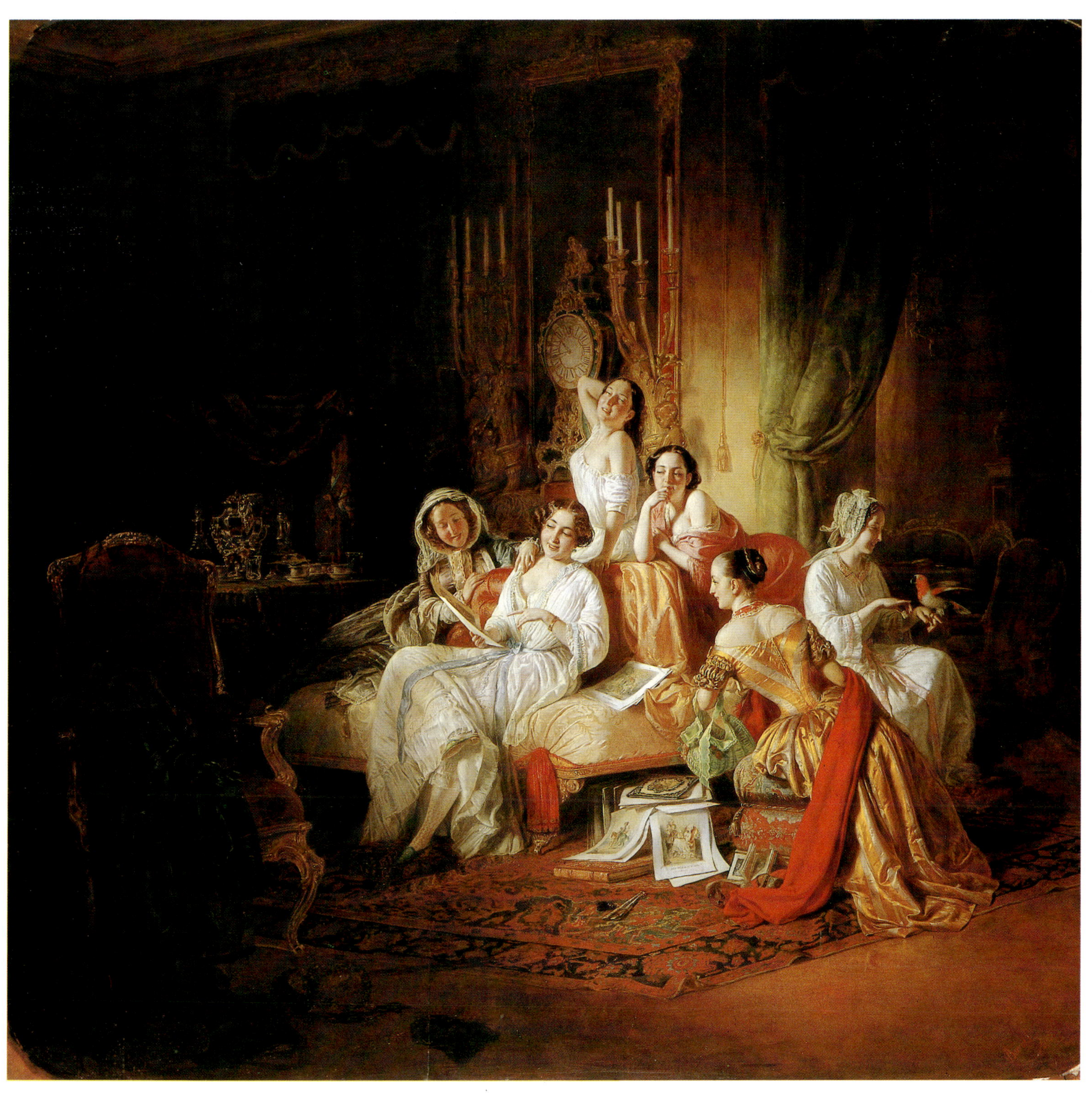

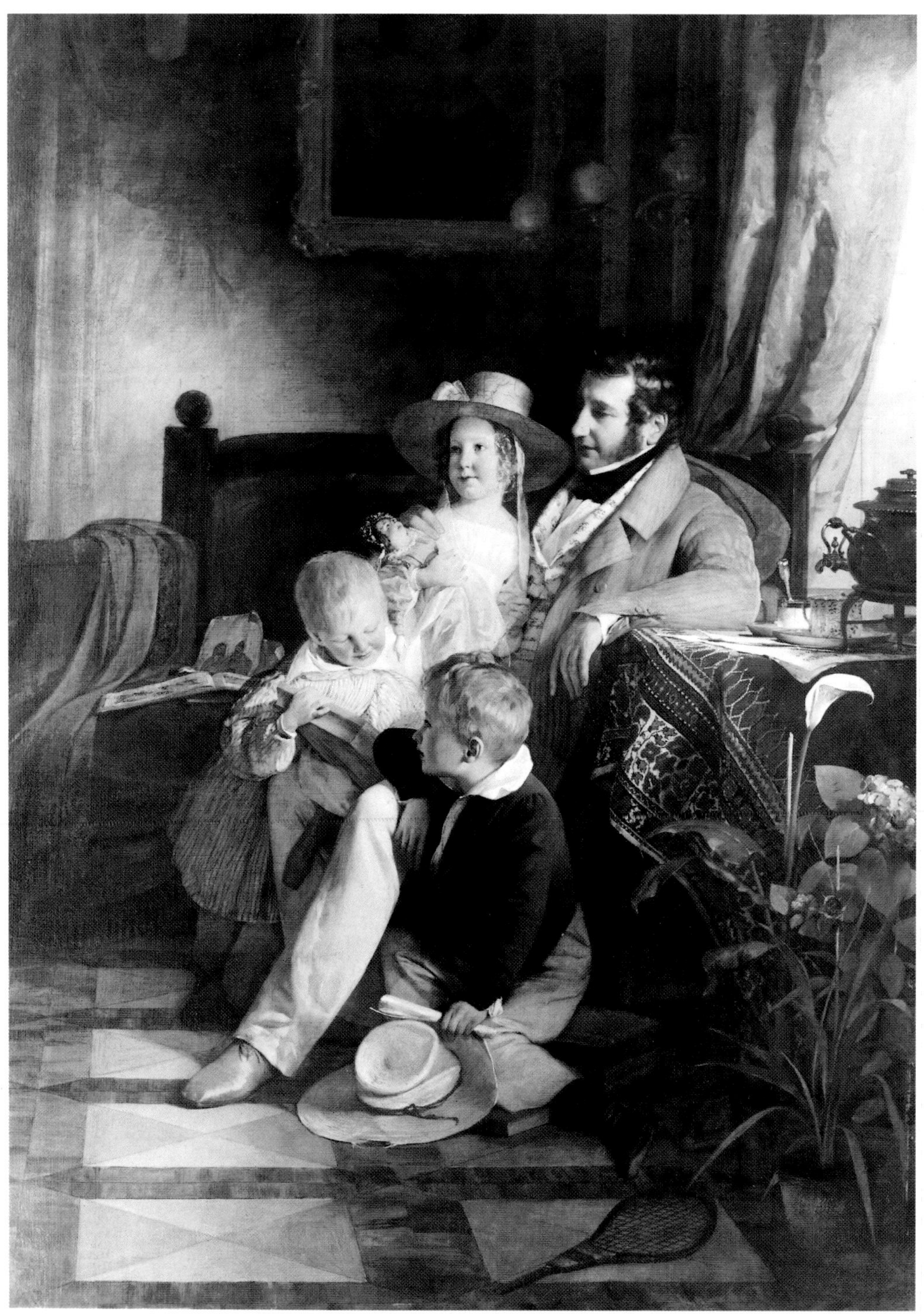

147. FRIEDRICH VON AMERLING
Rudolf von Arthaber with his Children, 1837

Oil on canvas, 221 × 155 cm
Signed bottom right: "Fr. Amerling 1837"
Vienna, Österreichische Galerie
Inv. No.: 2245

It is for the brilliance and elegance of his paintings that Amerling has most often been praised. Other characteristics of his art and no less worthy of mention are his keen powers of observation, his way of transposing group portraits into genre-paintings and his portrayal of character, comparable to that of the old masters. This picture exemplifies Amerling's transformation of a group portrait into a genre-painting. It represents Rudolf von Arthaber, an art collector and dealer, sitting with his children in a comfortable living room looking at a painting.

148. JÓZSEF BORSOS
The Dissatisfied Painter, 1852

Oil on paper, 97.5 × 81 cm
Signed bottom centre: "Borsos 1852"
Budapest, Hungarian National Gallery
Inv. No.: 3188

By around 1850, while in Vienna, Borsos had mastered the techniques of his art and was confident that he could supply paintings for exhibitions, complete his commissions for the aristocracy and satisfy his wealthy patrons. It was his aim to sell his work, and he therefore painted elegant still-lifes and genre-pieces. The exceptional quality of his work is seen in his sure draftsmanship, subtle characterization, his empathy for his sitters and his sensitive rendering of a variety of situations. His pictorial representation of luxurious fabrics and jewellery similarly demonstrate his skill.

In this painting, however, he expresses a growing dissatisfaction with the stylized manner which by now characterized all his work. Though his studio prospered, though he received all the commissions he needed, and in spite of a happy family and a wife who cared about his work, he felt that something was missing from his life, and he was at times driven almost mad by a sense of frustration. He sometimes raged against the impossibility of freeing himself from his all-absorbing world of painting; and it was no consolation to him that he was able to give expression to his frustration in his art. In the end, Borsos returned to Hungary and died as the proprietor of an inn.

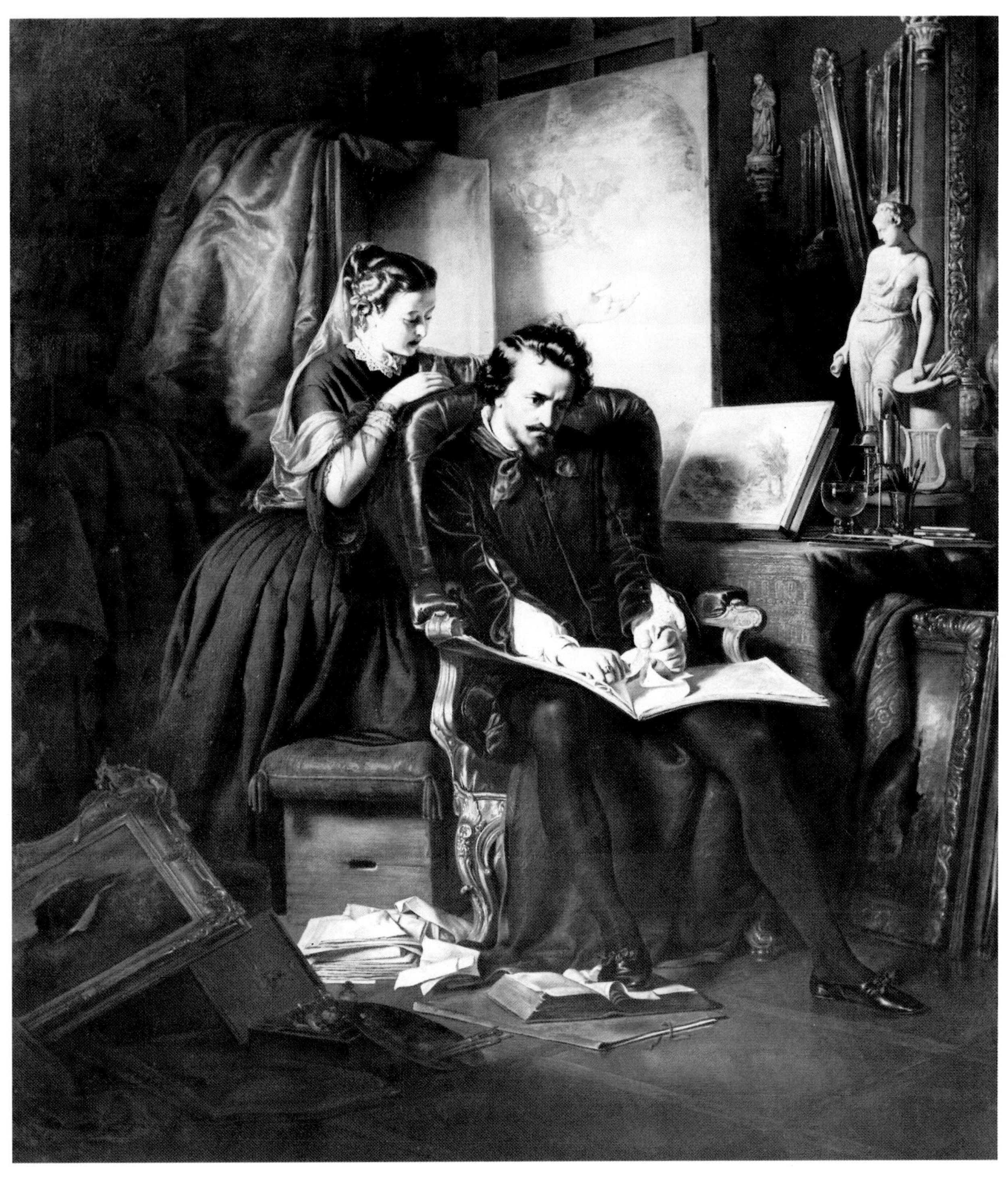

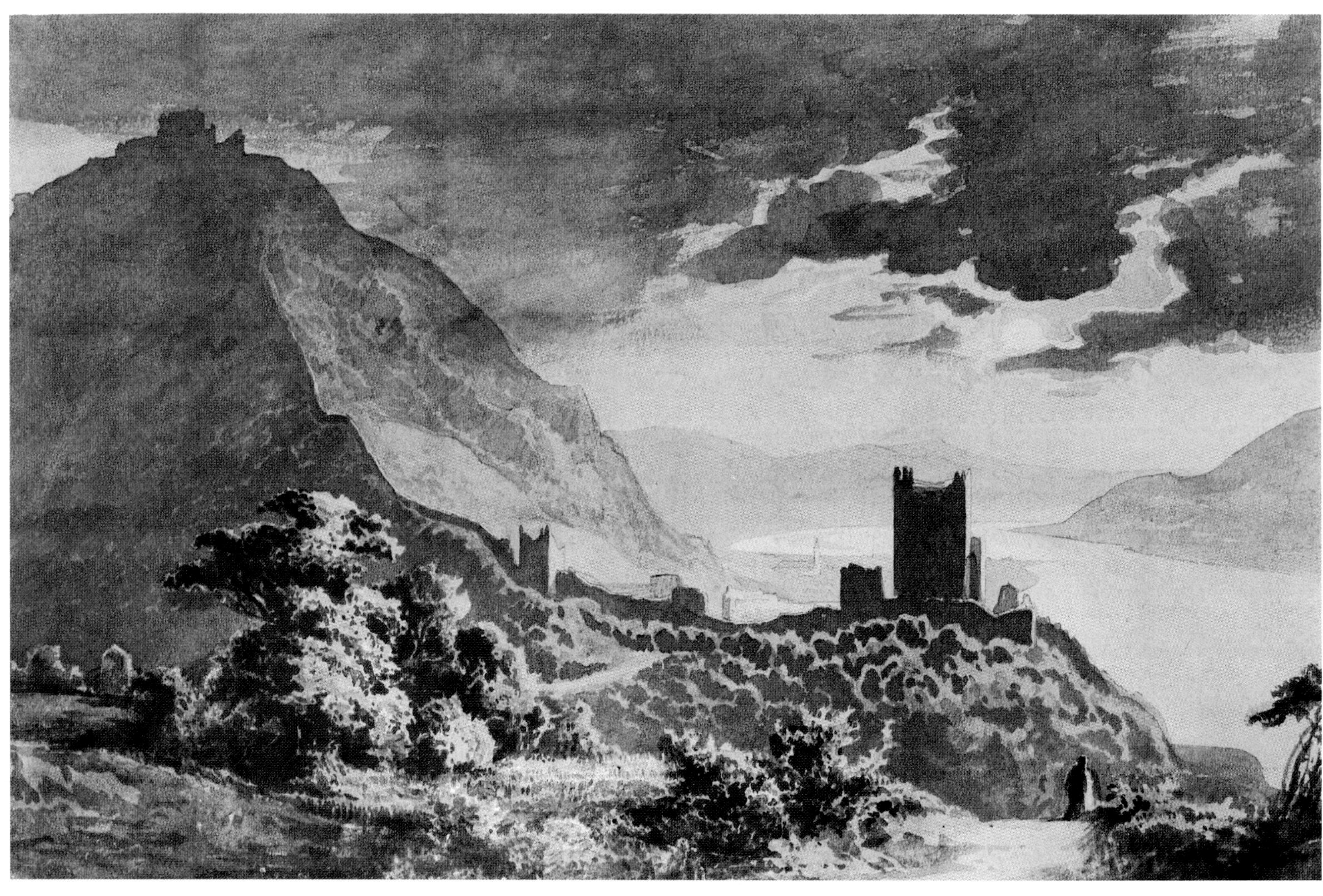

149. GUSZTÁV KELETY
Visegrád by Moonlight, 1860s
Ink wash on paper, 298 × 417 mm
Unsigned
Budapest, Hungarian National Gallery
Inv. No.: 1903-197.

Moonlight scenes are to be found among the
works of numerous painters, for instance
Czauczik, Kisfaludy, Markó and Gusztáv
Kelety, a very learned man with a great talent for landscape. Kelety's picture was completed nearly ten years after Markó's *Diana*
(Plate 150) yet it is similar in approach. The
painter's father, Károly Klette, was himself
a Romantic landscape painter who had come
to Hungary from Dresden.
Kelety had studied law in Pest and Vienna
before studying painting from Carl Rahl in
Vienna and then proceeding to the Academy
of Munich. His *Visegrád by Moonlight* shows
that he followed the finest Romantic traditions in his landscapes.

184

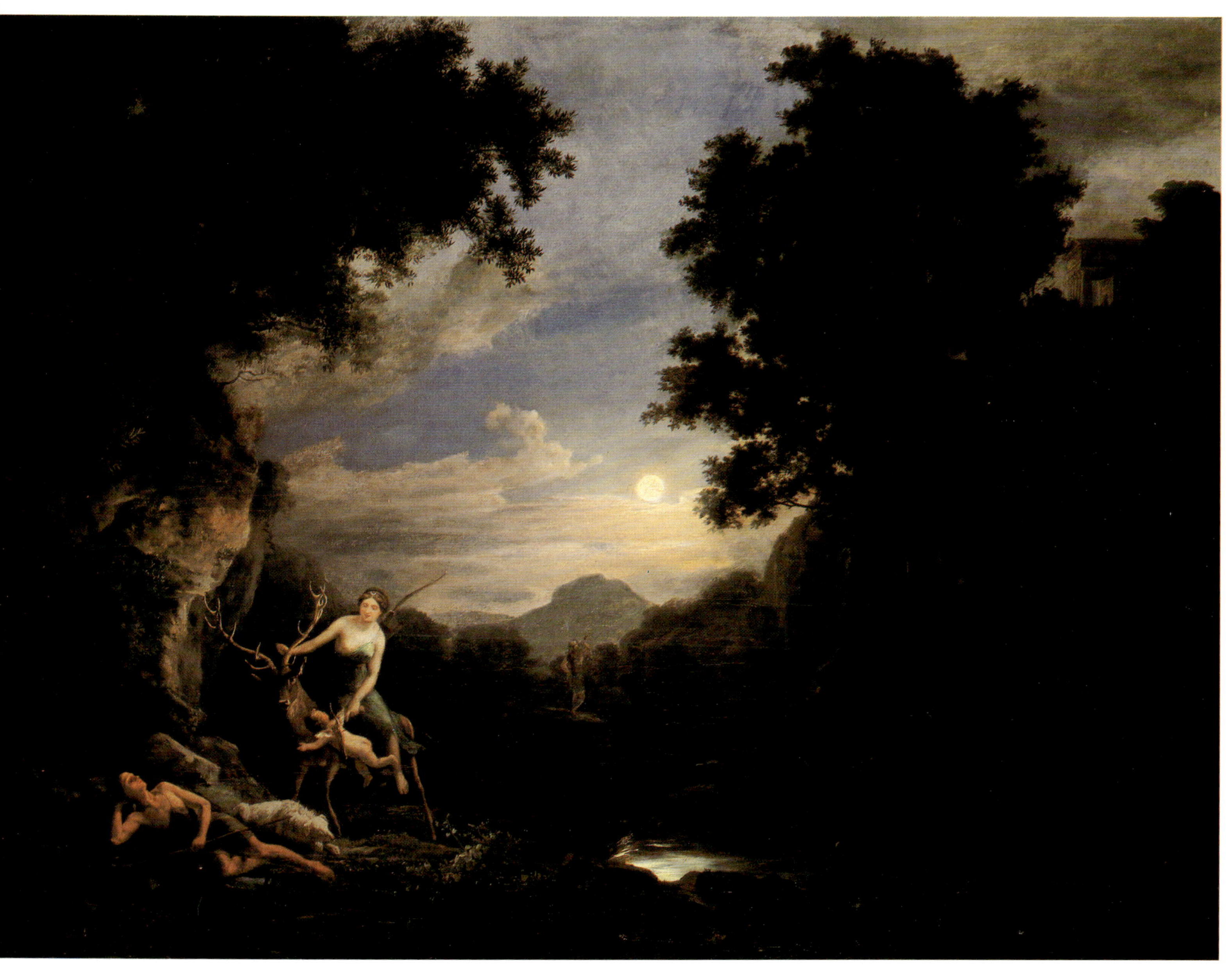

150. KÁROLY MARKÓ, the Elder
Diana and Endymion, 1853
Oil on canvas, 58 × 92 cm
Signed bottom left: "C. Markó S.p. Ap.
1853"
Budapest, Hungarian National Gallery
Inv. No.: 3086

Some Hungarian art critics, especially Emmerich Henszlmann, have criticized Károly Markó for his too frequent use of ochre tones which, they believe, "dazzle the eye", as well as for his habit of colouring very different objects with almost the same tones. In 1853, when Markó was thinking of returning to Hungary, he tried to create a new effect by means of a palette quite different from anything he had used previously. In this picture he was assisted in his endeavours by the subject, for this charming mythological scene takes place by moonlight. The sleeping Endymion is depicted in the foreground, while Diana, half naked and mounted on a stag, her bow and quiver on her shoulder, approaches him from behind. By experimenting with new light effects, Markó has created a work which is in many ways reminiscent of Czauczik's naive scene from the beginning of the century, the portrait of an aristocratic young lady dressed as Diana (Plate 7).

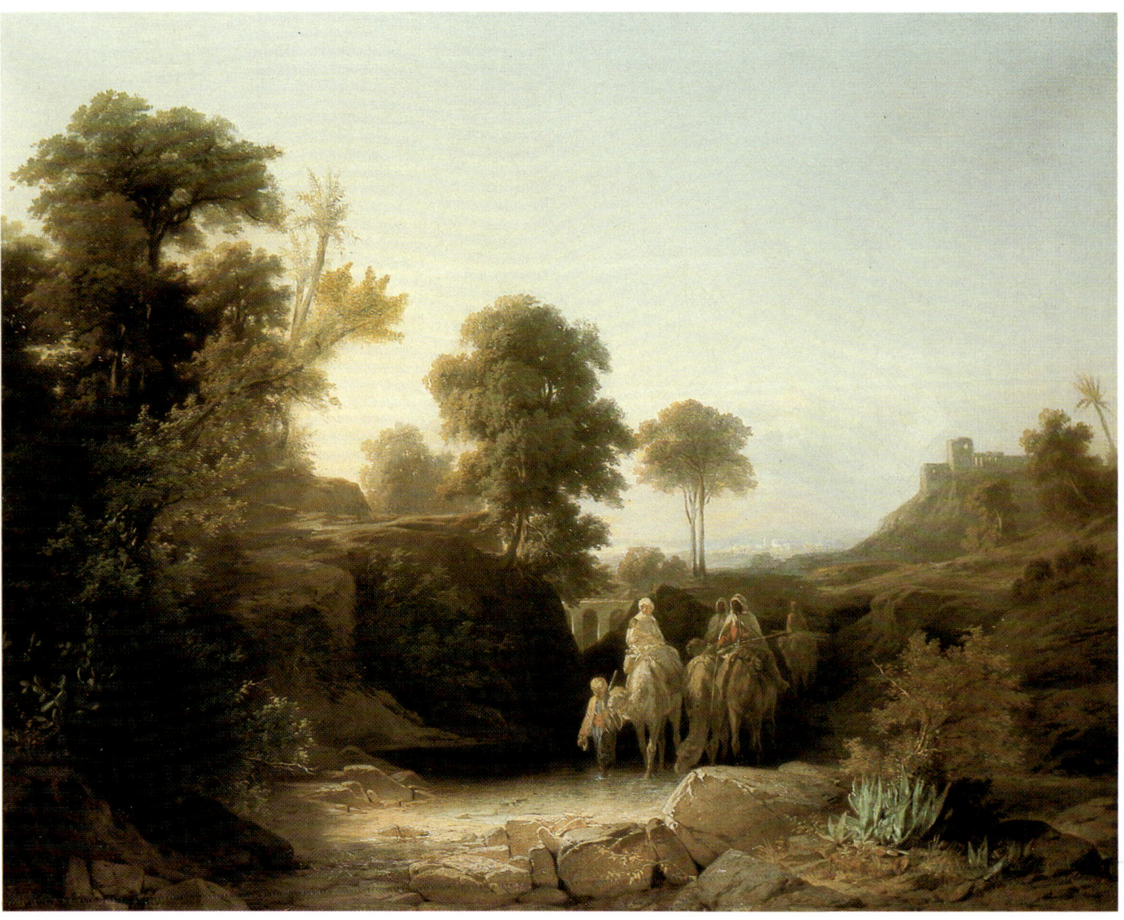

151. JÓZSEF MOLNÁR
Caravan, c. 1855

Oil on canvas, 72 × 90 cm
Unsigned
Budapest, Hungarian National Gallery
Inv. No.: 5015

József Molnár had already achieved a European reputation as a painter of landscape and religious compositions before his marriage in 1853, when he returned to Pest to settle there. He had however been exhibiting in Pest since 1841. This picture reveals his skill as a painter of Oriental landscapes.

A group of travellers emerge from the rich foliage of a romantic landscape; a camel driver leads three camels, one bearing a young woman and a child, the other two ridden by Arabs in a burnous.

Molnár's remarkable technique is exemplified by the way he achieves an effect of rippling water glistening in the level rays of the setting sun. The glow of sunset, painted in the ochres also used by Markó, and the townscape suggested in the distance.

152. KÁROLY MARKÓ, the Elder
The "Puszta" (View of the Great Hungarian Plain with Sweep Well), 1853

Oil on canvas, 39.5 × 52 cm
Signed bottom right: "C. Markó p. Vind 1853"
Budapest, Hungarian National Gallery
Inv. No.: FK 1571
From Jenő Zichy's bequest

Károly Markó regularly exhibited his work in Hungary and in 1853 he also visited his native land, and at about the same time chose the Puszta as the theme for two compositions. This oil painting was executed in Vienna; another, entitled *View of the Great Hungarian Plain with Sweep Well* was painted in Appegi. These two pictures are now in the Hungarian National Gallery. Markó's choice of subject confirms that for Hungarian artists, the Great Hungarian Plain had come to symbolize Hungary itself.

153. KÁROLY LOTZ
Clouds over the Great Hungarian Plain, 1850s

Oil on canvas, 32.5 × 41.5 cm
Signed bottom right: "Lotz"
Budapest, private collection

During the early 1850s, Károly Lotz began to paint genre-scenes of the traditional Hungarian way of life, and also landscapes. Among his works exhibited at the "Műegylet" were views of the Great Hungarian Plain.

Lotz had studied as a youth in Giacomo Marastoni's School of Drawing before progressing to Rahl's school in Vienna. In this early picture Lotz has tentatively tried to imitate Rahl's technique by employing the bright colours used by Rahl in his landscapes and genre-paintings. Lotz, who was only half Hungarian, now cherished an ambition to depict the Puszta with the enthusiasm of Barabás and Markó. He too concentrates on the stark line of the sweep well and the cumulus clouds so typical of the Puszta. But by introducing the group of figures near the well, Lotz cautiously attempts to transform a representation of the landscape into a genre-painting.

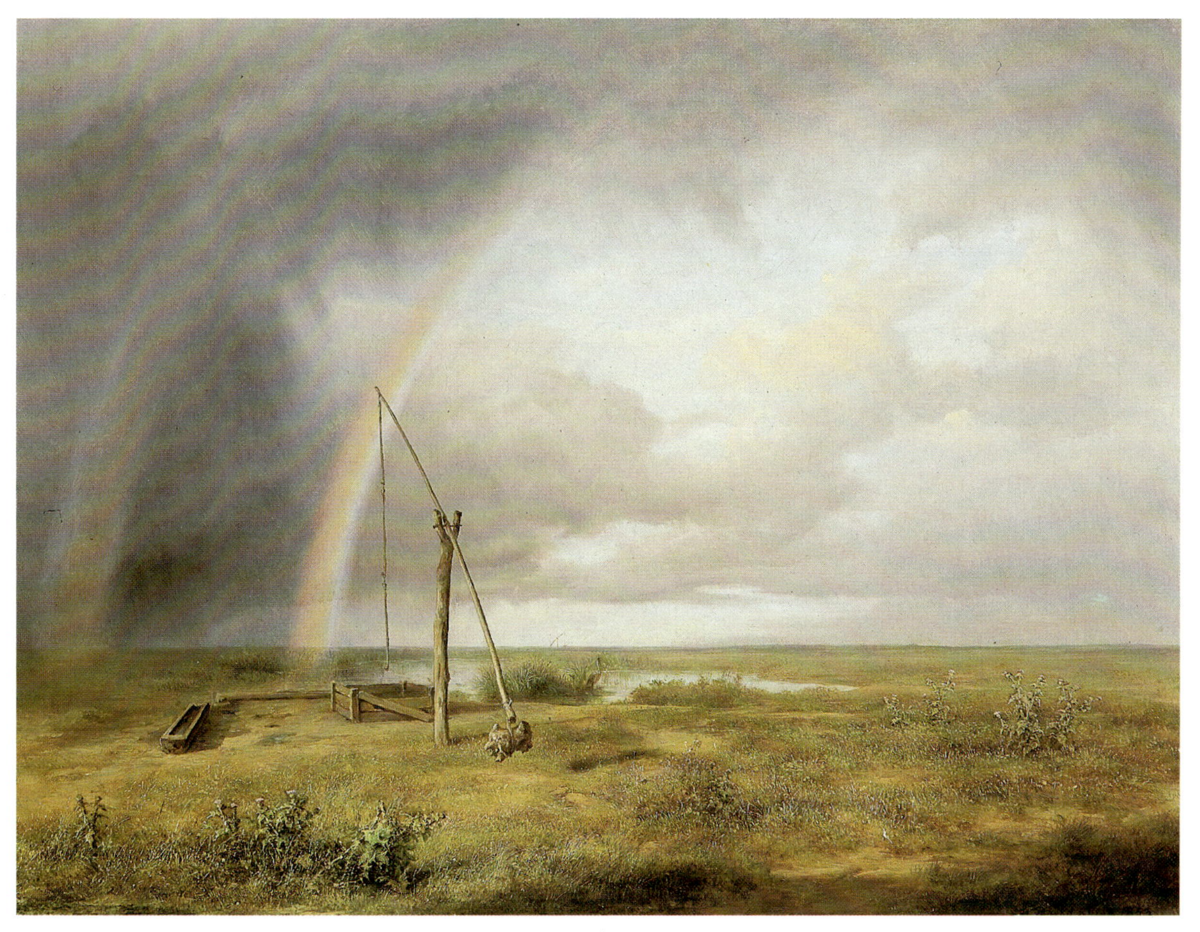

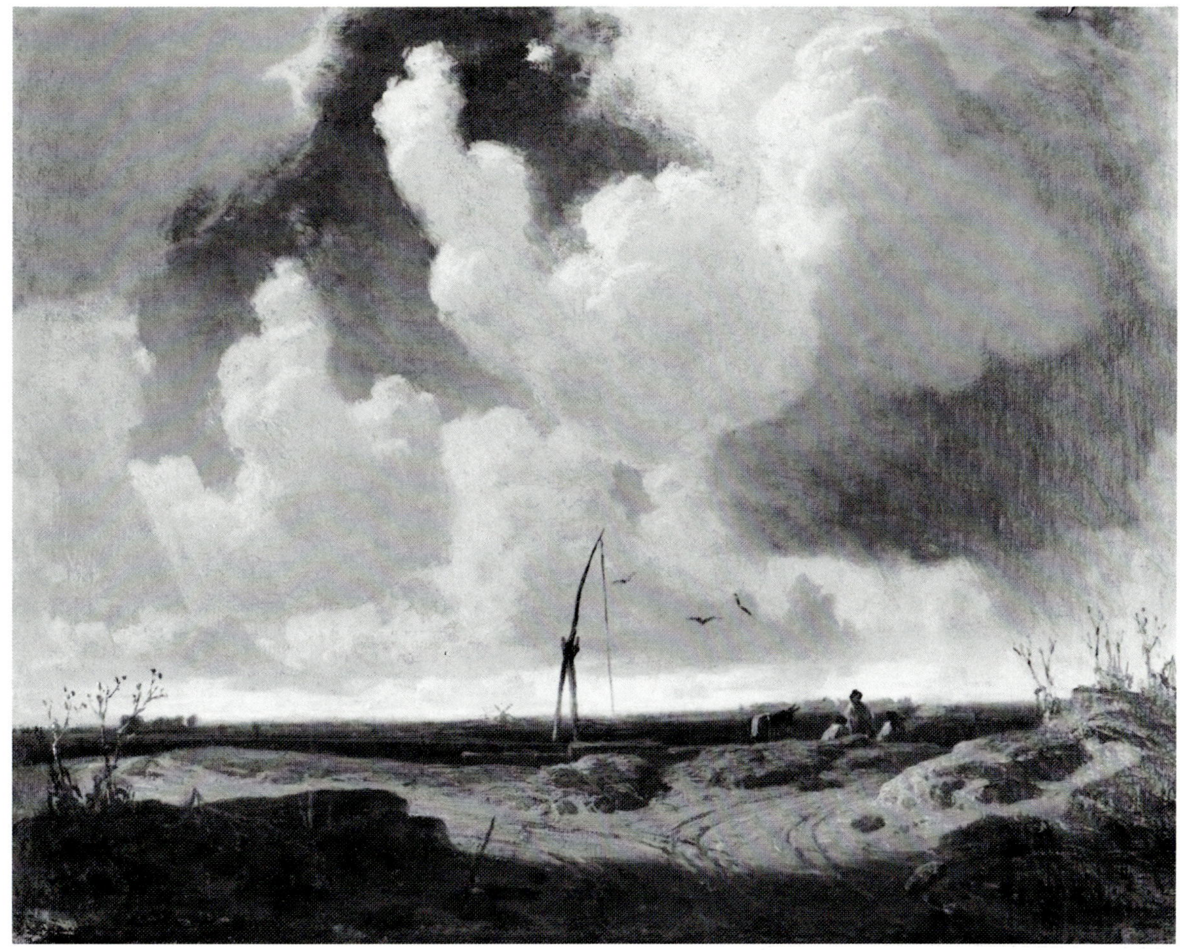

154. KÁROLY LAJOS LIBAY
Oriental Landscape, after 1855
Water-colour on paper, 218 × 302 mm
Unsigned
Budapest, Hungarian National Gallery
Inv. No.: F 65.61

Libay published some of his drawings as
a series of lithographs entitled *Oriental Travel
Pictures*. The series comprises a representative selection of drawings made while travelling in the Near-East in October 1855.
In this water-colour, the artist depicts
a group of ancient ruins in the middle of a
dense palm grove. He uses ethereal yellows
and oranges to convey the particular effect of
light in that region.
Libay was the son of a Besztercebánya gold-
smith. He first learnt his father's trade, then
left for the Vienna Academy and probably
studied later in Munich. He travelled with
his sketchbook throughout the whole of
Europe and the Middle East, continuing also
his systematic programme of depicting the
various regions of his own country. He became a master of the landscape and of the
Classicist-Romantic style.

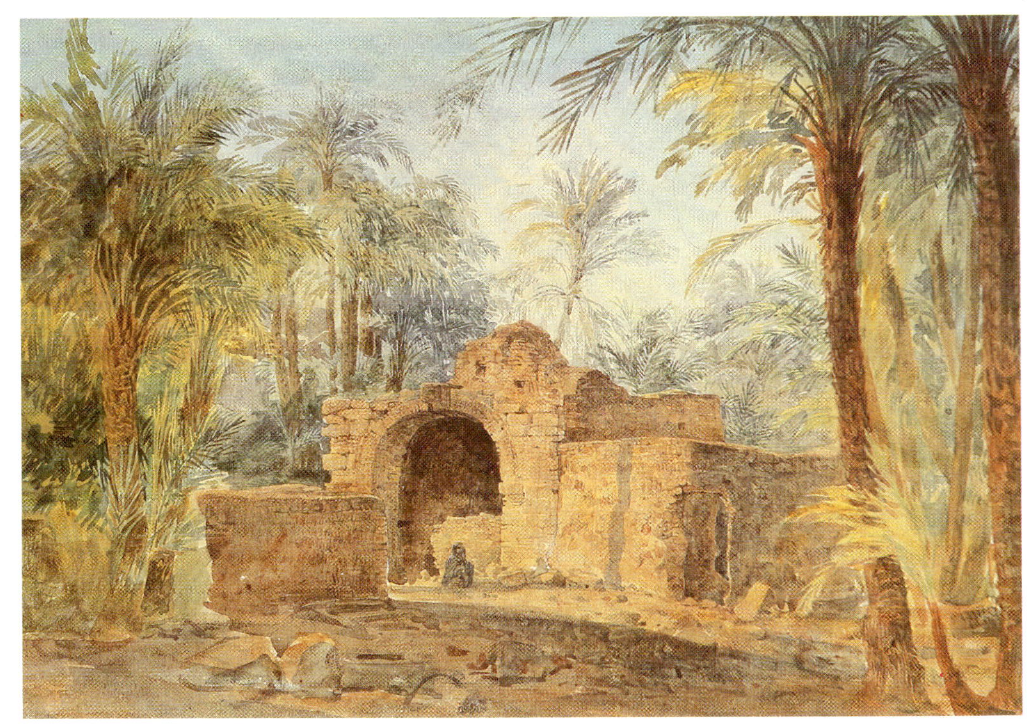

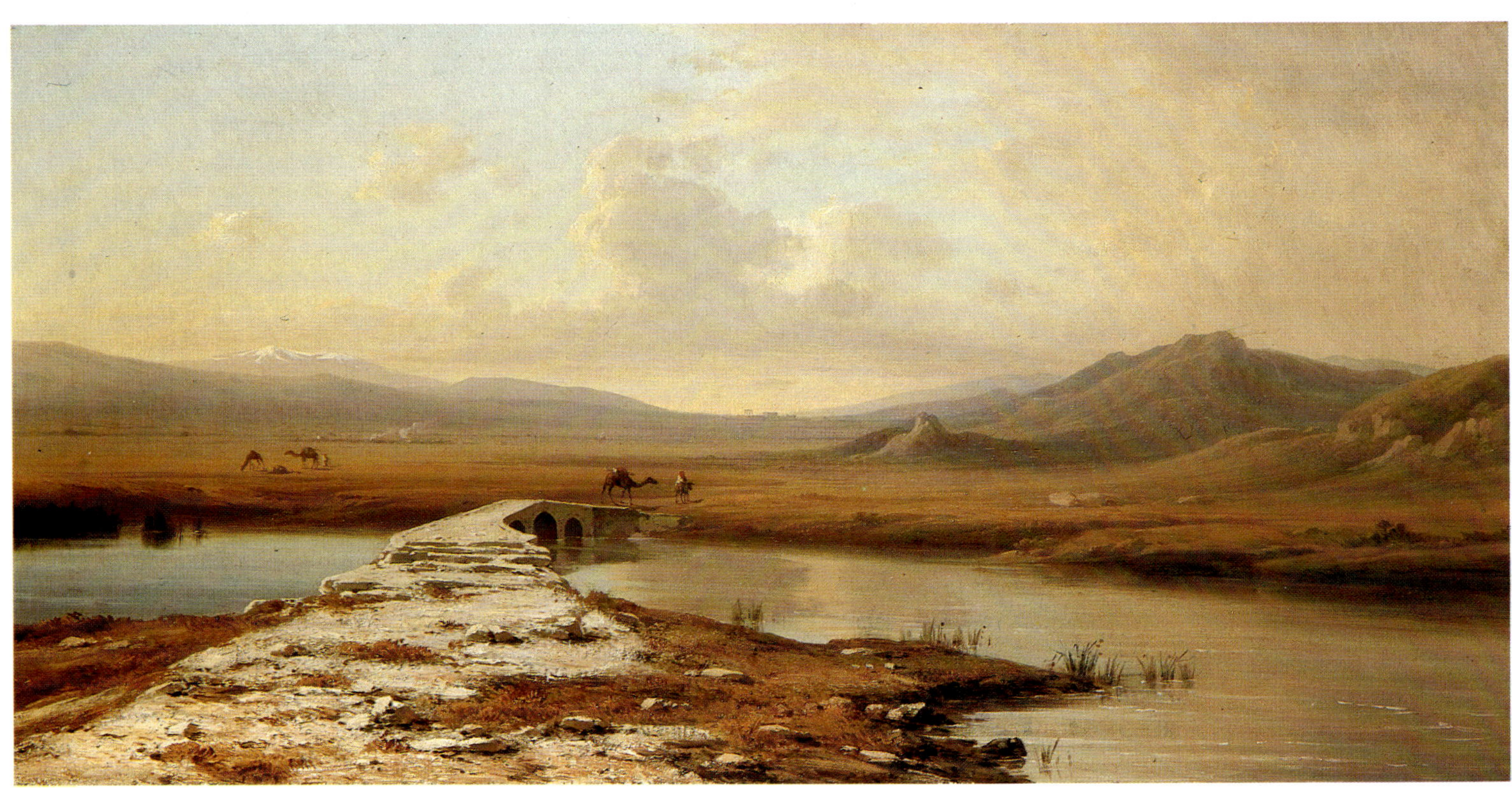

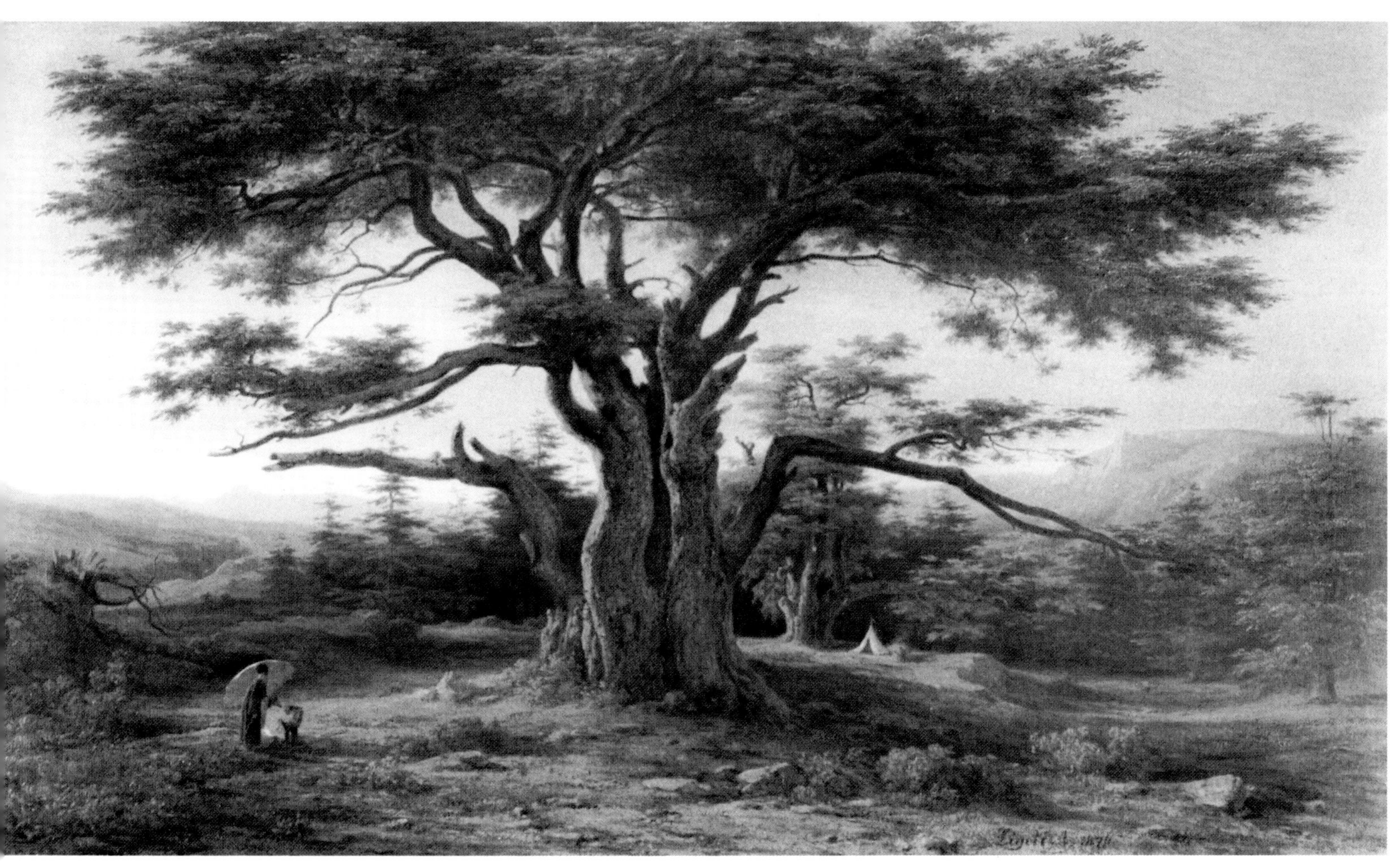

155. ANTAL LIGETI
The Mount Lebanon and Anti-Lebanon, 1855–1860
Oil on canvas, 32.2 × 65 cm
Unsigned
Vác, Episcopal Gallery
Inv. No.: 57.3

While travelling in Italy and the Holy Land, Antal Ligeti made hundreds of pencil drawings and water-colours on which he based his later compositions. His immediate response to colour and atmosphere can be felt in this picture, executed in exquisitely graduated shades and delineated with the utmost care. A sensitive feeling for nature characterizes his painting of the barren riverside in the foreground, the bridge that spans the river, the camel plodding over it, and details of the two famous mountains in the wide spaces of the background: the snowclad Lebanon, known as the White Mountain, on the left, and the gentle slopes of Anti-Lebanon on the right of the canvas.

156. ANTAL LIGETI
Cedar-grove on Mount Lebanon, 1876
Oil on canvas, 73.5 × 121 cm
Signed bottom right: "Ligeti 1876"
Budapest, Hungarian Academy of Sciences

In 1856 Ligeti spent several days on Mount Lebanon. He put up his tent in the ancient cedar-grove, close to the area called Ehden and there, in the open air, he set out to draw and paint the ancient trees, fearing neither the Bedouins nor the Moslem and Christian pilgrims who came to this sacred place. This oil painting was made twenty years later and is based on large ink drawings which Ligeti had made on the spot. Although colouring and light effects had somewhat faded from his memory, Ligeti was able to represent the living crown and the withered branches of the ancient tree in all its magnificence. His tent can be seen in the background, while in the foreground the painter and his assistant are at work under the shade of a parasol.

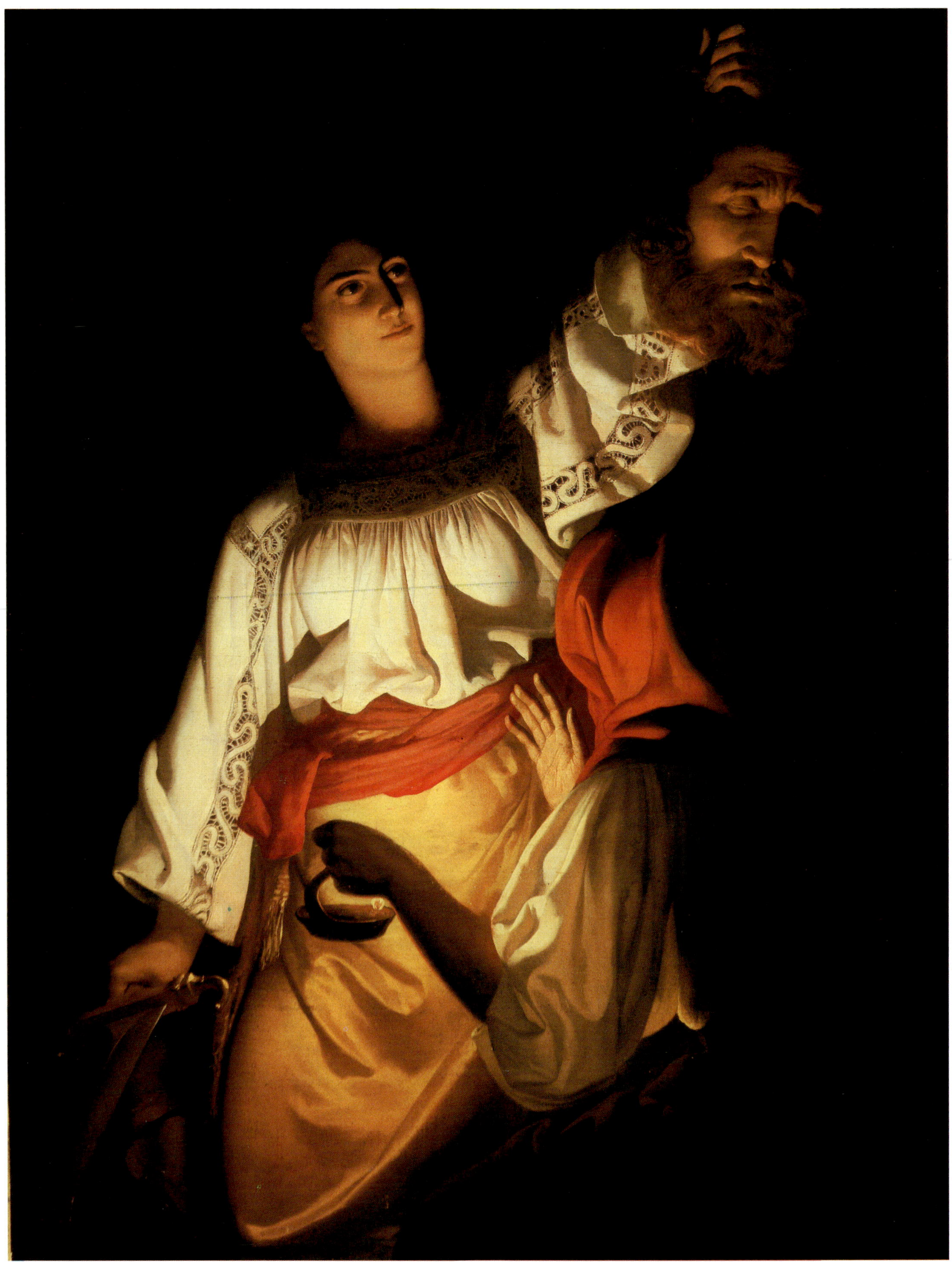

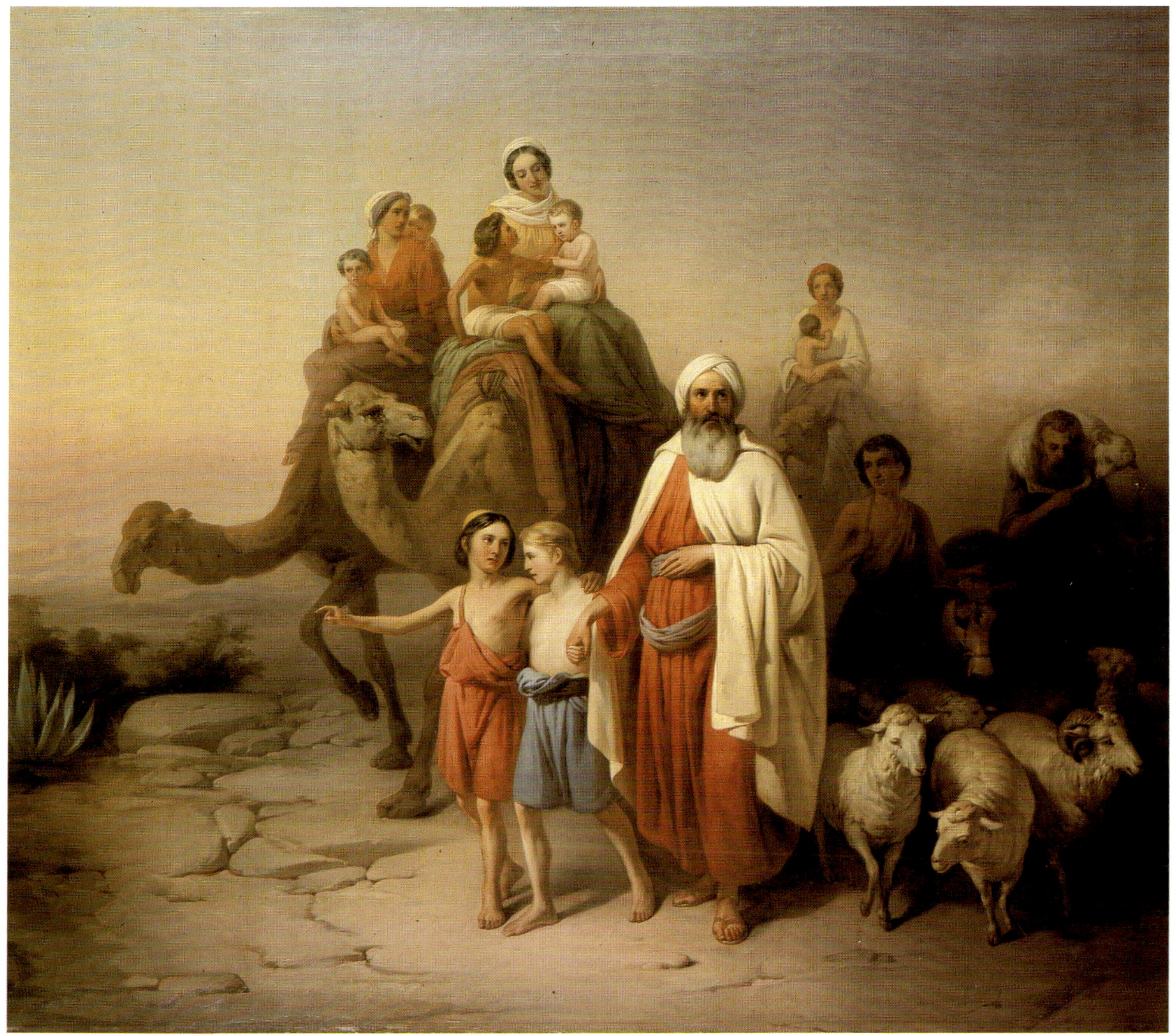

157. ANTAL HAAN
Judith and Holofernes, 1853
Oil on canvas, 135.5×100 cm
Signed bottom left: "Haan Antal fest.
Rómában. 1853"
(Painted by Antal Haan in Rome, 1853)
Szekszárd, Béri Balogh Ádám Museum
Inv. No.: 56267

This painting suggests Mannerist or early
Baroque precedents. The painter may have
seen Domenichino's work on a similar
theme in Rome, or another version now in
the Eger Lyceum.
The story of Judith and Holofernes as the illustration of a heroic act of defense was
much favoured by 19th century Hungarian
painters. The present painting may be
a composition created with a double intent:
to follow the examples of the Old Masters
and to appeal to the patriotism of the public.

158. JÓZSEF MOLNÁR
Abraham's Journey from Ur to
Canaan, 1850
Oil on canvas, 112×130 cm
Unsigned
Budapest, Hungarian National Gallery
Inv. No.: 2730
Donation of the Association of the Picture
Gallery, 1850

This genre-painting by József Molnár is
based on the Biblical story of Abraham who,
commanded by God, departed with Loth,
all his family and his animals to find Canaan
which the Lord had promised him. However, the representation deviates from the
Bible: the women and children on the camels
are probably a reference to Jacob, rather than
Abraham.
In his painting of the figures, the animals and
the garments, Molnár takes pains to convey
a truly Oriental style. In this he was no doubt
responding to immediate precedents, since
by mid-century he would have already seen
numbers of Biblical genre-paintings with
male and female figures richly dressed in
Oriental robes as well as scenes with camels.
There is a water-colour by Julius Schnorr
von Carolsfeld in the Museum of Fine Arts,
Budapest which is very similar to this
painting.

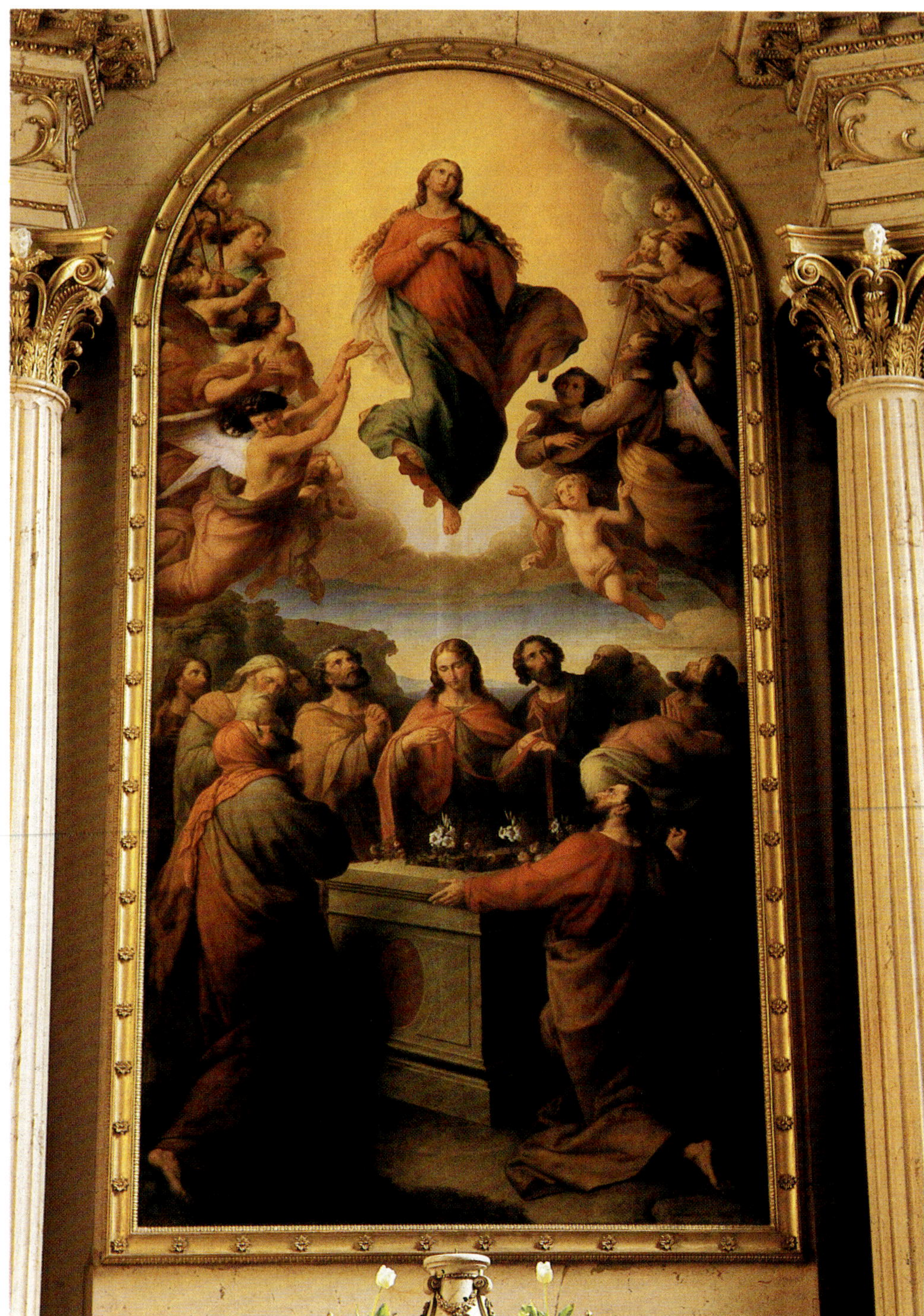

159. LEOPOLD KUPELWIESER
The Assumption of the Virgin, 1857
Oil on canvas
*Pécs, altar from the former convent church of
the Sisters of Our Lady*

In the opinion of art historian Károly Lyka,
Leopold Kupelwieser was one of the forerunners of the new "Romantic Catholicism". The painter, initially inspired by the
Nazarenes, was appointed to teach at the
Vienna Academy. Though he based his religious compositions on numerous earlier
examples, he worked with great empathy
for his subjects, and his paintings are notable
for their linear delicacy and etherealized and
sensitive colouring.
From the late 1830s until his death in 1862,
Kupelwieser painted many altar-pieces in
Hungary. He received commissions from
many church dignitaries including the
Bishop of Pécs and the Archbishop of Kalocsa and he produced paintings for the parish
church of Pest-Józsefváros. This painting
was probably commissioned in 1857 by Sci-
tovszky, Bishop of Pécs, for the small Neo-
Gothic convent church opposite the
cathedral.
The Assumption of the Virgin was a favourite theme in the 19th century, and was particularly suitable for a convent dedicated to
Our Lady.

160. MÓR THAN
The Assumption of the Virgin, 1855
Oil on canvas
Bečej, main altar-piece of the Parish Church

After completing his studies in Vienna, Mór
Than returned to his native town of Óbecse
where he painted this grandiose altar-piece
to replace an earlier one which had been destroyed. The work reflects not only his
knowledge of the Baroque and Renaissance
masters and his familiarity with paintings of
the Assumption by Raphael, Titian, Velaz-
quez and Murillo, but also the influence of
the heavier, earth-bound style of Carl Rahl
with its emphasis on realism. The detailed
rendering of the upper and lower parts of the
composition serves to link the two groups of
figures. The disciples gathered round the
tomb of the Virgin and the angels hovering
beside Mary are depicted in attitudes and
gestures that convey a human, earthly quality not previously found in religious paintings of this subject. The Virgin hovers above
a dark bank of clouds with arms outstretched, flanked by angels who either kneel
by her side or gently move towards her. Its
pictorial manner brings this composition
very near to the style of historical genre
painting.

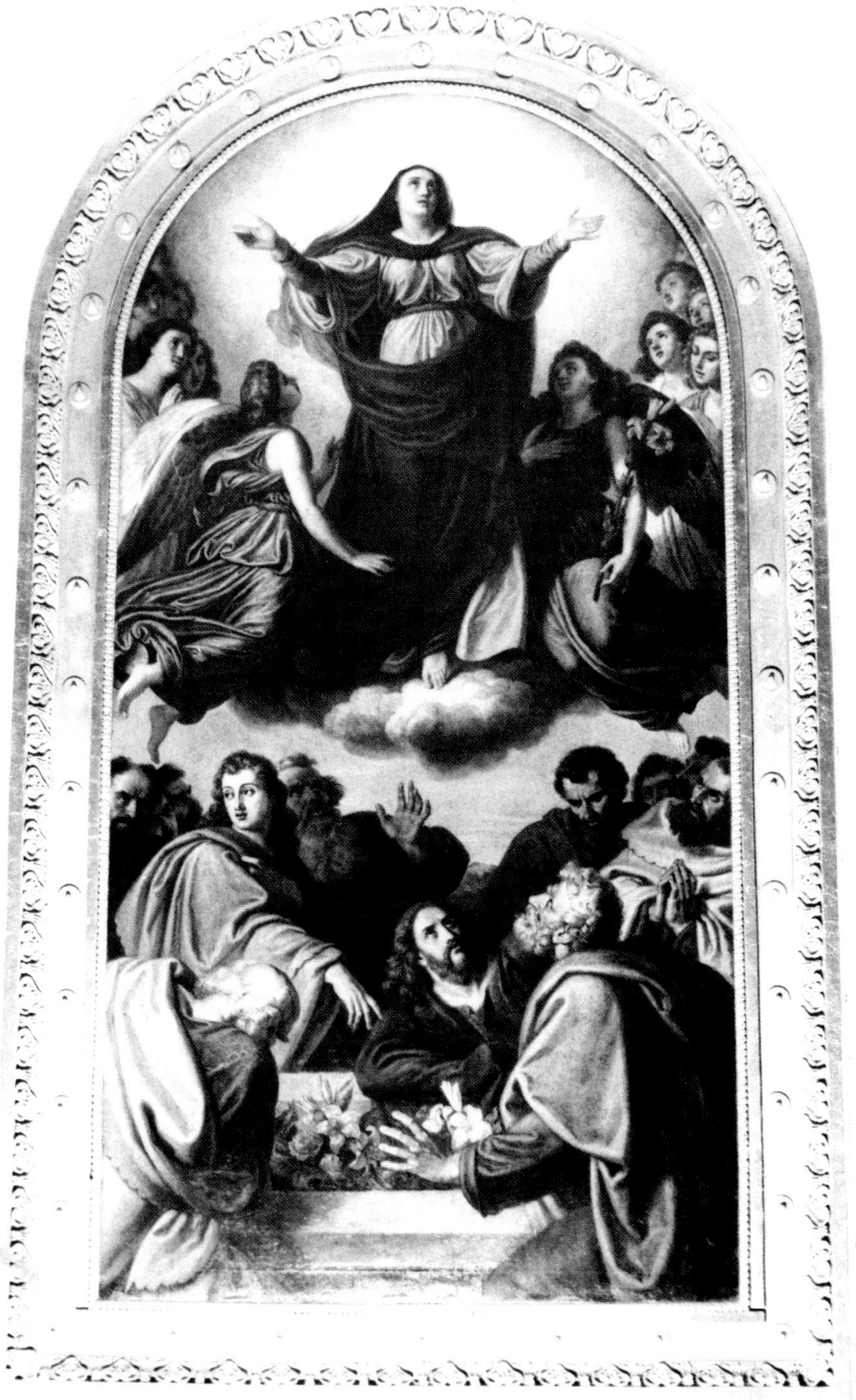

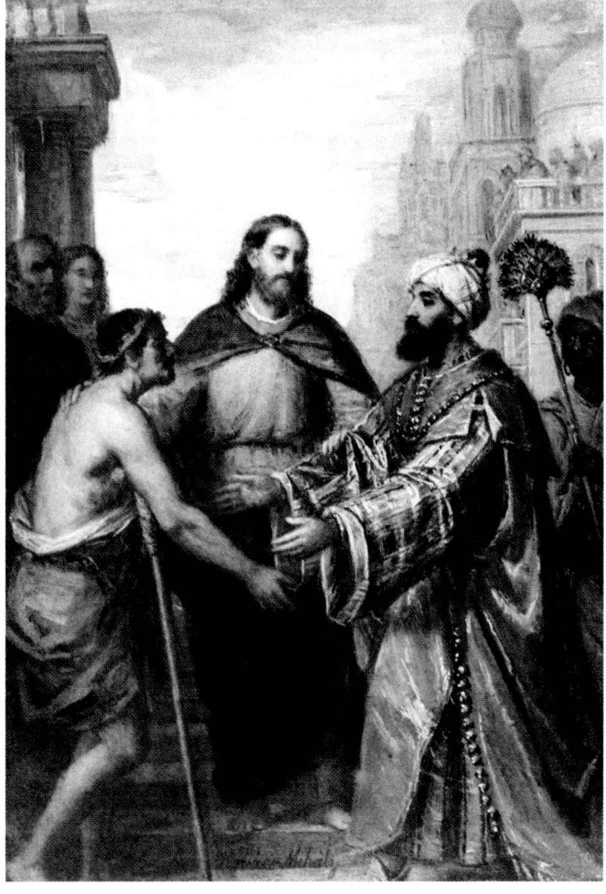

161. MIHÁLY KOVÁCS
"Thou Shalt Love Thy Neighbour as Thyself", 1872
Oil on wood, 45×32 cm
Signed in the middle: "Kovács Mihály"
Eger, Dobó István Castle Museum
Inv. No.: 55.60

Mihály Kovács, responsible for a great number of altar-pieces reflecting the influence of Renaissance and Baroque predecessors, brings his own personal touch to this scene from the New Testament, in which there is also a hint of the religious approach of the Nazarenes.

He executed the painting in several versions. Here the central figure is Jesus Christ as He encourages two men of very different origins, possibly also of different nationalities, to shake hands. The man wearing a turban may represent the Good Samaritan, and the youth stripped to the waist the Jew whom the Samaritan helped.

193

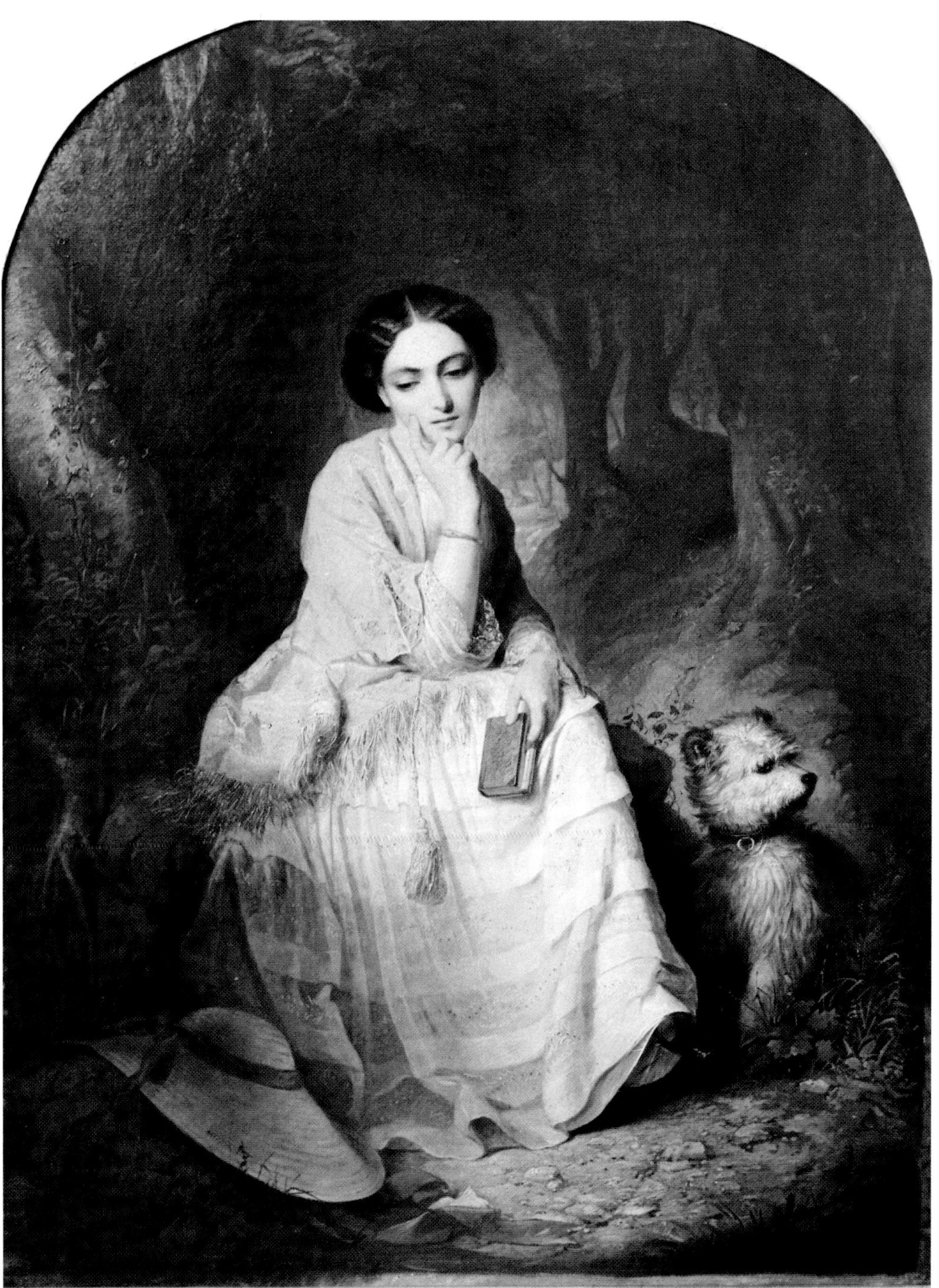

162. ALAJOS GYÖRGYI GIERGL
Woman Seated in a Woodland Glade, 1853
Oil on canvas, 93.5 × 70 cm
Signed bottom left: "A. Giergl 1853"
Budapest, Hungarian National Gallery
Inv. No.: 5256 T

We have here a popular portrait in a landscape by the celebrated painter of the 1850s
in which Romantic elements are blended
with the sweetness of the Biedermeier style.
A young woman is sitting in a woodland
glade, holding a book, her dog at her side.
The theatrical pose suggests an affectation of
weariness and grief.

163. GUSZTÁV KELETY
**Portrait of Loránd Eötvös as
a Young Man, 1858**
Oil on canvas, 95 × 79 cm
Signed bottom right: "F. Klette G. 858"
Budapest, Hungarian National Gallery
Inv. No.: FK 4176

The setting is typical of that found in landscape portraits dating from the late 18th century, usually associated in its early stages
with the philosophy of Jean Jacques
Rousseau.
Gusztáv Kelety was engaged as a tutor to the
children of József Eötvös, one of whom,
Loránd, was to become a great physicist.
Kelety (at that time known as Klette) gave
the children drawing lessons.
As revealed by this portrait, these excursions
also involved collecting butterflies and other
insects. The boy, still little more than a child,
sits down on the grass for a minute, tired by
the chase. His tutor either memorized his
pose or made a quick sketch to capture the
scene in order to reproduce it in a larger
painting intended for the boy's parents.

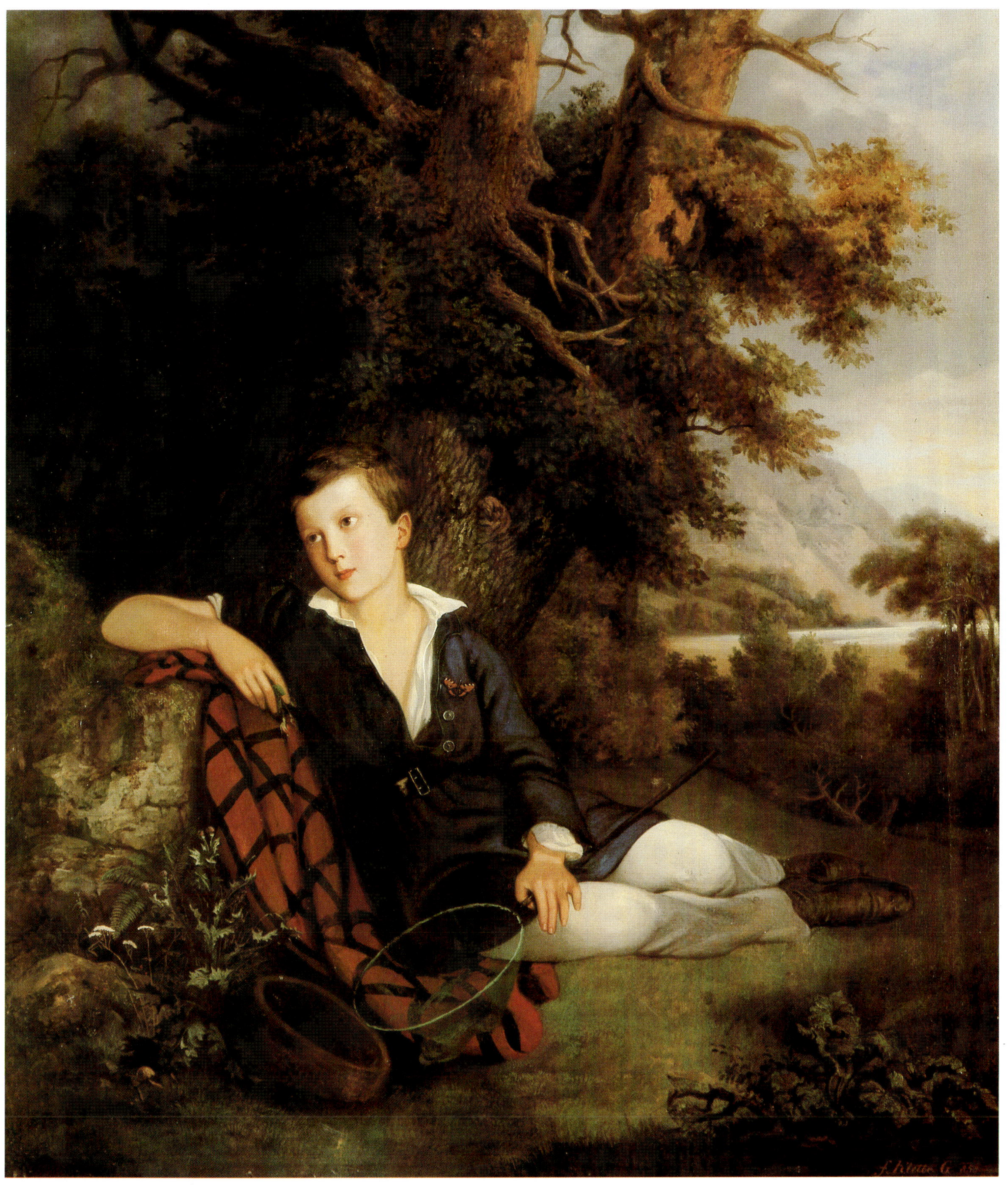

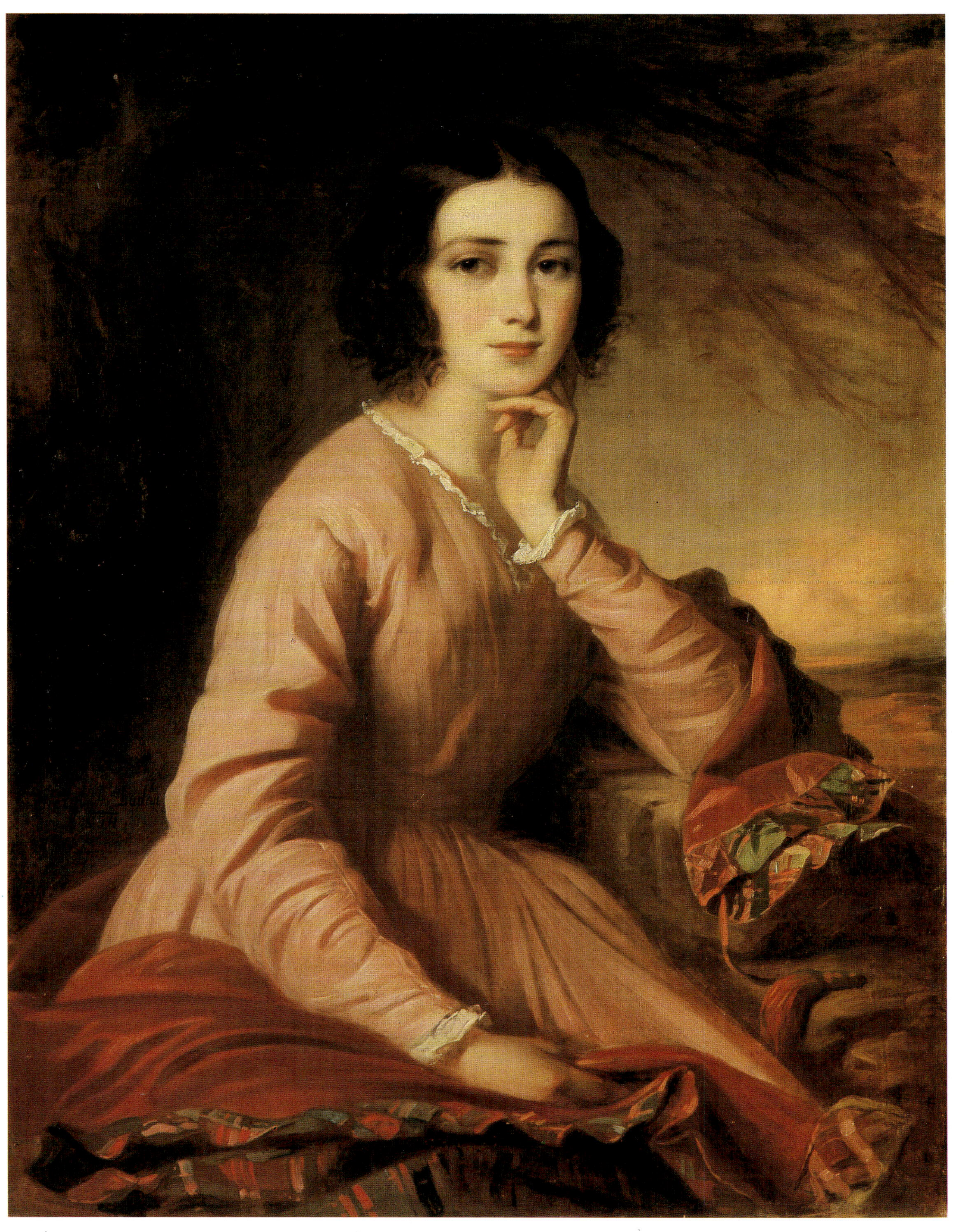

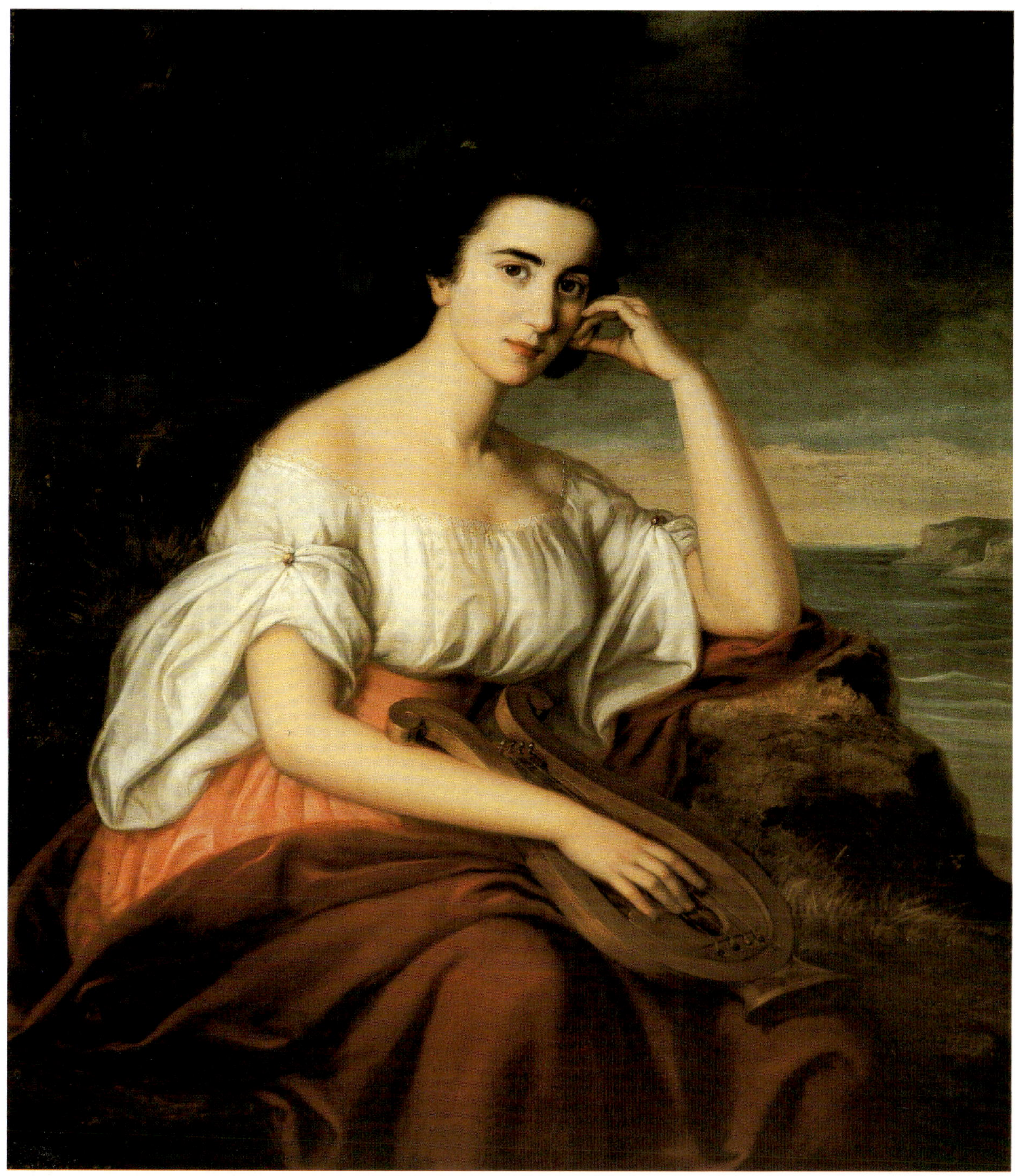

164. ALAJOS GYÖRGYI GIERGL
Portrait of Mária Bencsik, 1854

Oil on canvas, 98 × 77 cm
Signed bottom centre: "Giergl A. Budán 854"
(A. Giergl in Buda '854)
Budapest, private collection

Although Alajos Györgyi Giergl studied in Vienna, he seems to have been well acquainted with the pictorial qualities and the freshness and elegance of English portrait painting as characterized by Reynolds and Lawrence. This portrait of a young girl with delicately shaped face was painted from a miniature after her death. The girl is sitting in the twilight against a background of a tree painted in tones of greenish-brown. The easy pose, her chin resting on one hand, her serene expression and the casual drapery of her pale mauve dress and chequered shawl, all create a lifelike impression.

165. SOMA ORLAI PETRICH
Sappho, 1855–1860

Oil on canvas, 113 × 94 cm
Unsigned
Budapest, Hungarian National Gallery
Inv. No.: 2740

In the 19th century, in France and Hungary alike, the Greek poetess of Antiquity was frequently depicted in a superb landscape setting worked in a sentimental style. She was presented as an elegant lady wearing contemporary dress, often with a lyre in her hand.

Orlai's oil painting was probably prompted by the Pest première of Grillparzer's tragedy about Sappho, or it may have been the idealized portrait of a poetess living in 19th century Hungary.

197

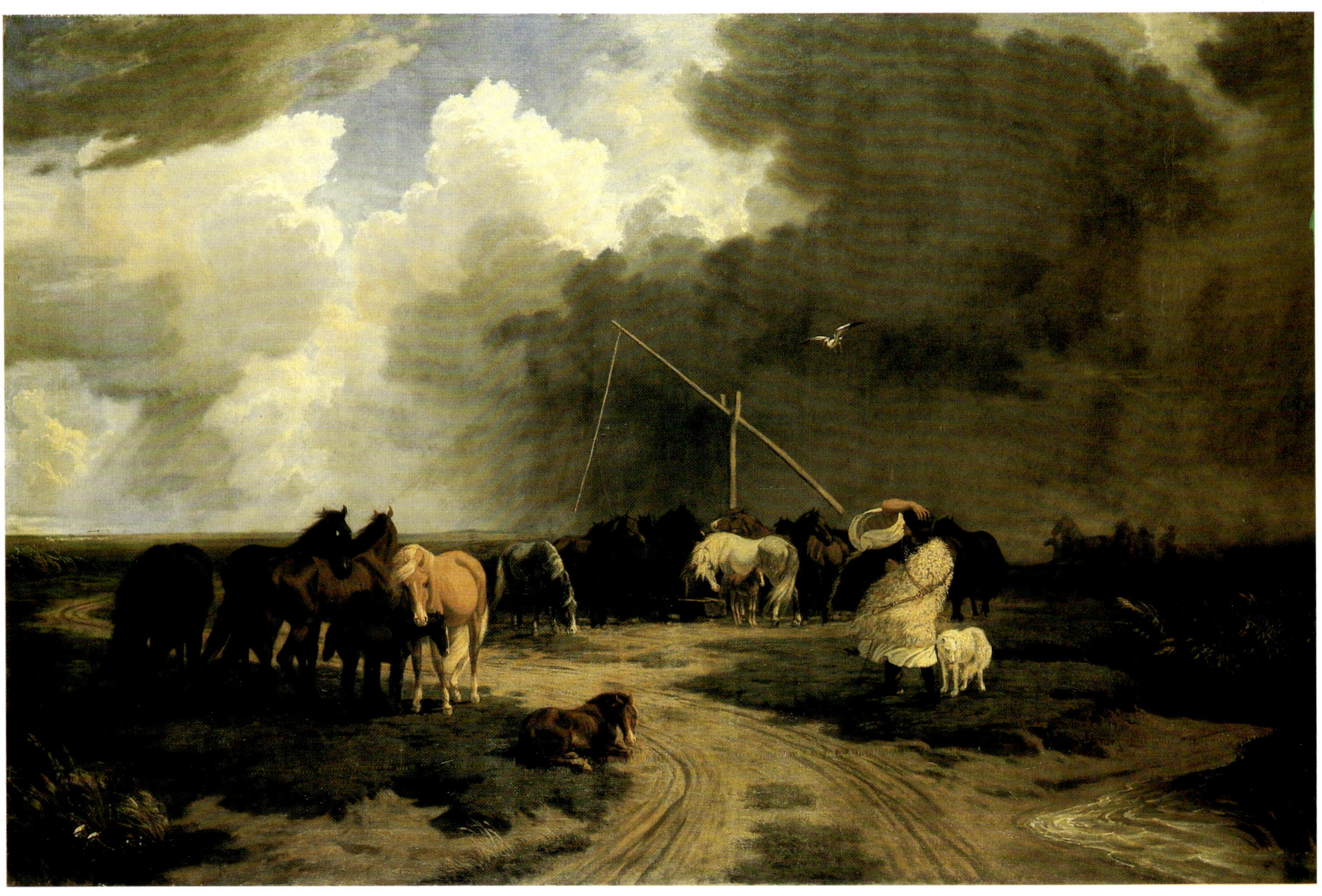

166. KÁROLY LOTZ
Stud in a Thunderstorm, 1862
Oil on canvas, 126.5×191.5 cm
Signed bottom left: "f. Lotz K. 862"
Budapest, Hungarian National Gallery
Inv. No.: 2742 T

Between 1850 and 1862 Lotz completed several versions of this subject in which the horses, frightened by the thunderstorm, rear in panic while the grooms struggle to quiet them. The dramatic quality of this scene is emphasized by the lightning and the startled birds.

We can certainly find parallels between the work of Lotz and that of contemporary Austrian painters of the Puszta, but the dramatic intensity achieved by Lotz while still a student in Carl Rahl's school of painting in Vienna had no rival, especially in its dramatic intensity.

167. ANTAL LIGETI
Visegrád, 1860
Oil on canvas, 28 × 42 cm
Signed bottom left: "Ligeti 1860"
Budapest, private collection

From the beginning of the 19th century Visegrád had been a popular subject for engravings and woodcuts, and there can be little doubt that Ligeti was familiar with them. Nevertheless, we believe that when Ligeti was commissioned to paint a Visegrád landscape he made no reference to earlier representations but visited the place personally and selected the aspect he judged to be most suitable. He depicted the hill surmounted by the citadel with the Danube behind the hill, the landscape being viewed from a point never previously selected by artists. The blue of the Danube and the sky clearing after a storm are evoked with animation and lively colour. This small picture was probably a sketch for a larger work intended for the decoration of a wall, such as, for instance, the four monumental landscapes hanging in the Assembly Room of the Hungarian Academy of Sciences.

168. ANTAL LIGETI
The Fortress of Trencsén, 1870
Oil on canvas, 148 × 220 cm
Signed bottom right: "Ligeti 1870"
Budapest, Hungarian Academy of Sciences

This is one of four Hungarian landscapes commissioned by the Hungarian Academy of Sciences for the Assembly Room of its residence. This painting represents a landscape with historic ruins, but Ligeti also introduces elements of genre-painting.

To emphasize the silhouette and the bulk of the fortification, Ligeti employs methods similar to those he used in the small picture of Visegrád. At the same time, because of the size and decorative function of the painting, he is as attentive to the need for historical accuracy as to the representation of space, distance and light.

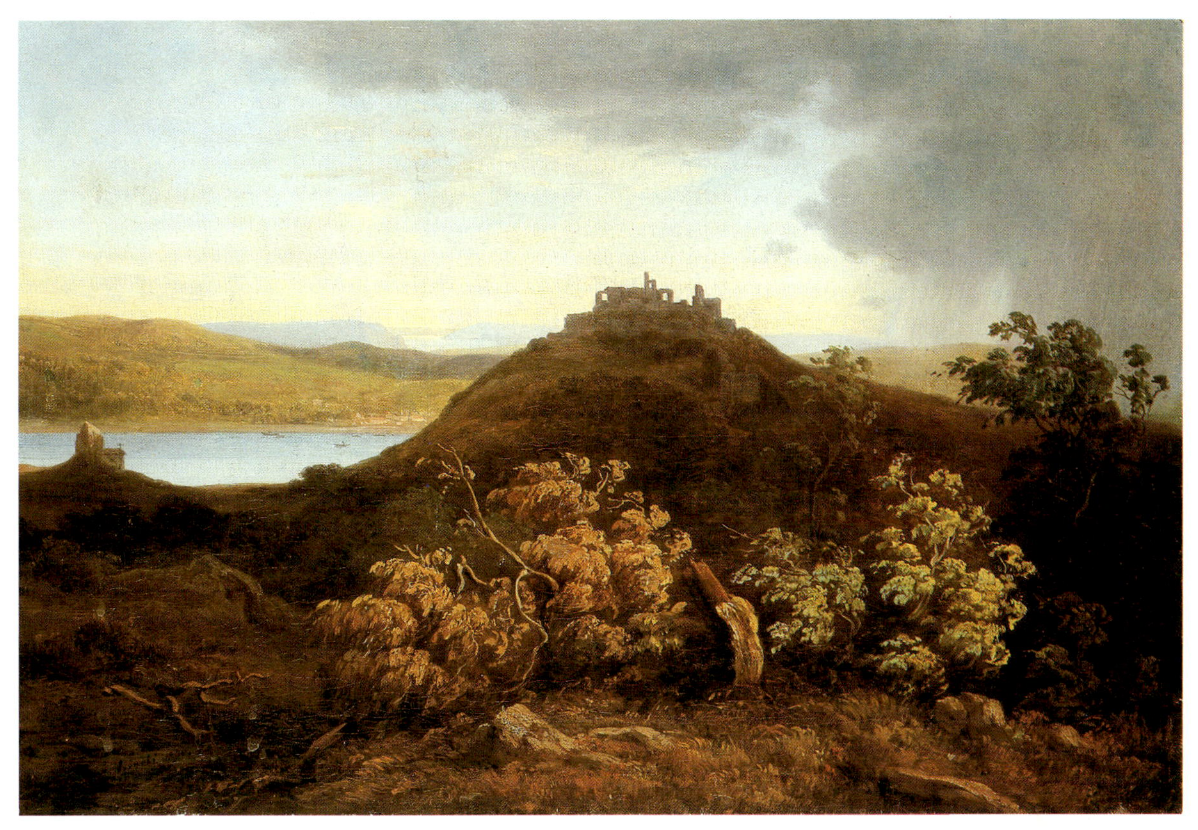

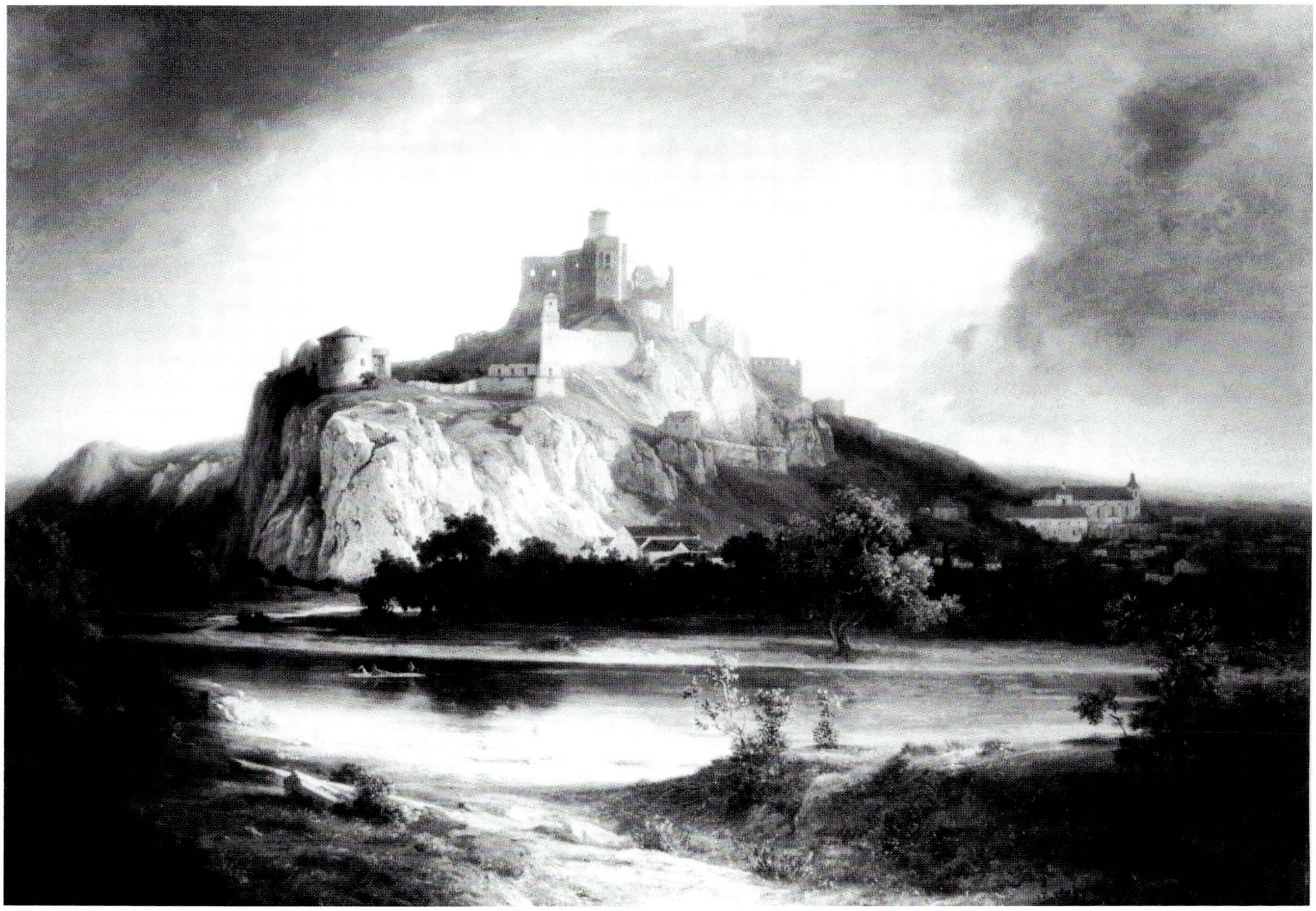

169. JÁNOS JANKÓ
Csokonai at a Wedding, 1859
Oil on canvas, 47 × 67.8 cm
Signed bottom right: "Jankó János 1859"
Debrecen, Déri Museum, on loan from the
Hungarian National Museum
Inv. No.: II. 132/1918

Mihály Csokonai Vitéz (1773–1805) was one
of the most popular poets in Hungary
throughout the 19th century. The esteem in
which he was held by his countrymen is expressed in the superb statue sculpted by Miklós Izsó in the 1860s.
In this painting János Jankó has blended literary illustration and folk scene. The poet is
depicted here as he is described in Sándor
Petőfi's poem entitled "Csokonai", at the
moment when, looking for a tap for a wine-
barrel, he finds himself in the midst of a wedding party, and stays there. Jankó puts a flask
covered with pony-skin into the poet's
hand, thus evoking the title of one of
Csokonai's own poems. To add a note of
authenticity, the wedding guests are depicted in the costumes of an earlier period.

170. JÁNOS JANKÓ
Genesis of the Hungarian Folk-song, 1860
Oil on canvas, 108.3 × 75 cm
Signed bottom left: "Jankó J. 860"
Budapest, Hungarian National Gallery
Inv. No.: FK 1379

With sketch-book and water-colours, János
Jankó wandered about Hungary drawing
and painting the country folk in their costumes and recording the regional types in
a manner similar to that of another contemporary painter, Mihály Szemlér. In 1860 he
used his early sketches as a basis for more
ambitious works—possibly using new
models for the figures, but copying the garments from his original drawings.
In this painting there is a hint of allegorical
significance, for it represents the birth of
a folk-song as a group of peasants listen to
the new composition played by a seated
youth. As the shepherd plays his flute the
peasants stand in the shade of a tree, posed in
pleasing attitudes, all wearing peasant finery.
Jankó elaborated each individual figure in
drawings and colour sketches before trans-
ferring them to the canvas. The colours are
vivid, the group carefully arranged and
spaced against an early autumnal landscape.

171. SOMA ORLAI PETRICH
Village School, c. 1860
Oil on canvas, 36.5 × 48 cm
Signed bottom left: "Orlai"
Budapest, Hungarian National Gallery
Inv. No.: 60.98 T.

Orlai liked to paint everyday scenes from
village life. Here he illustrates in a matter-of-
fact composition the development of public
education, so much urged by politicians.
Against the background of a bare school-
room simply furnished with wooden
benches and a map of Hungary, a young
mother is seen committing her child to the
care of the teacher. The teacher greets him,
stroking his head gently while the other
pupils look on, most of them with interest,
one of them seizing the chance to scribble on
the blackboard.

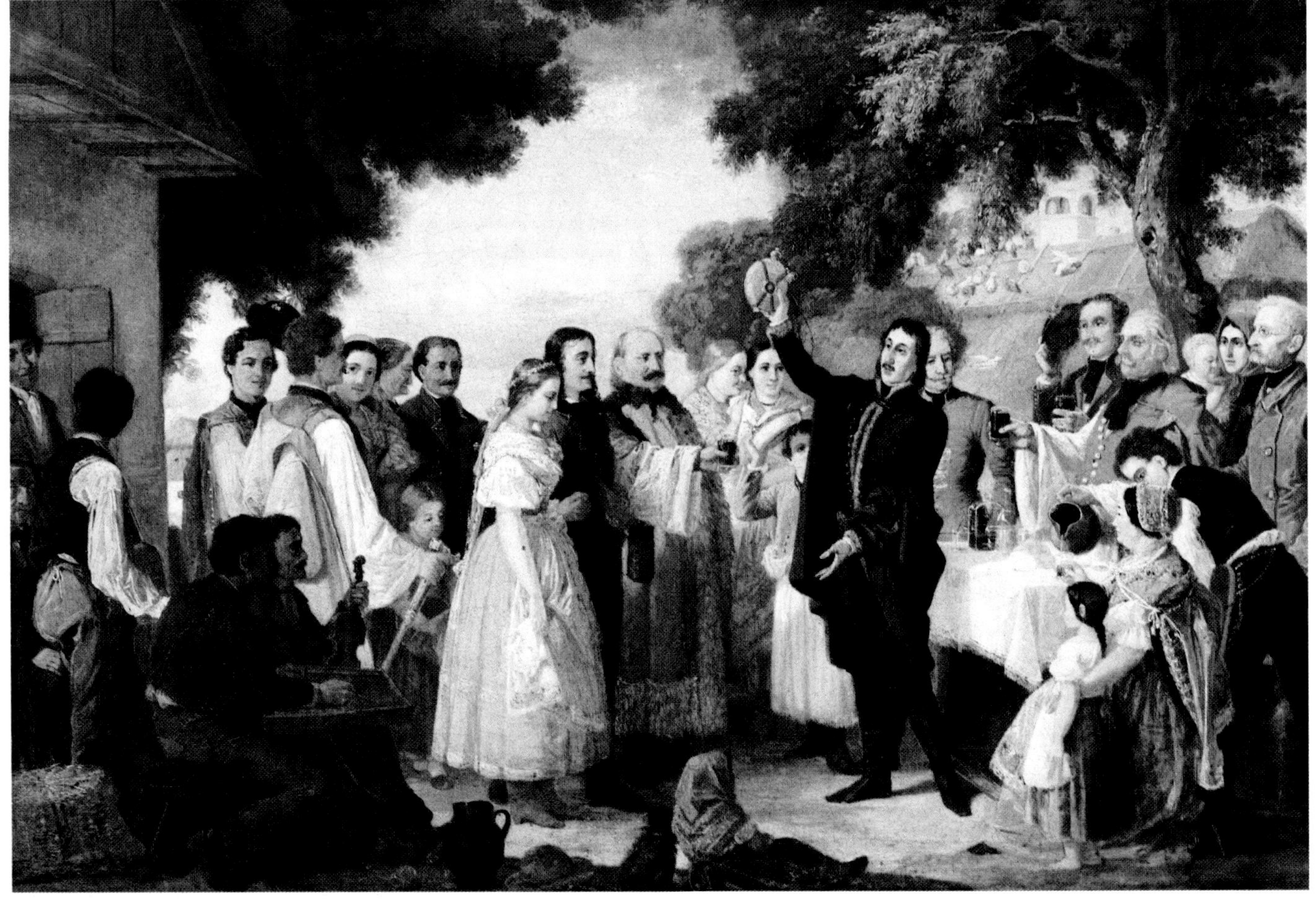

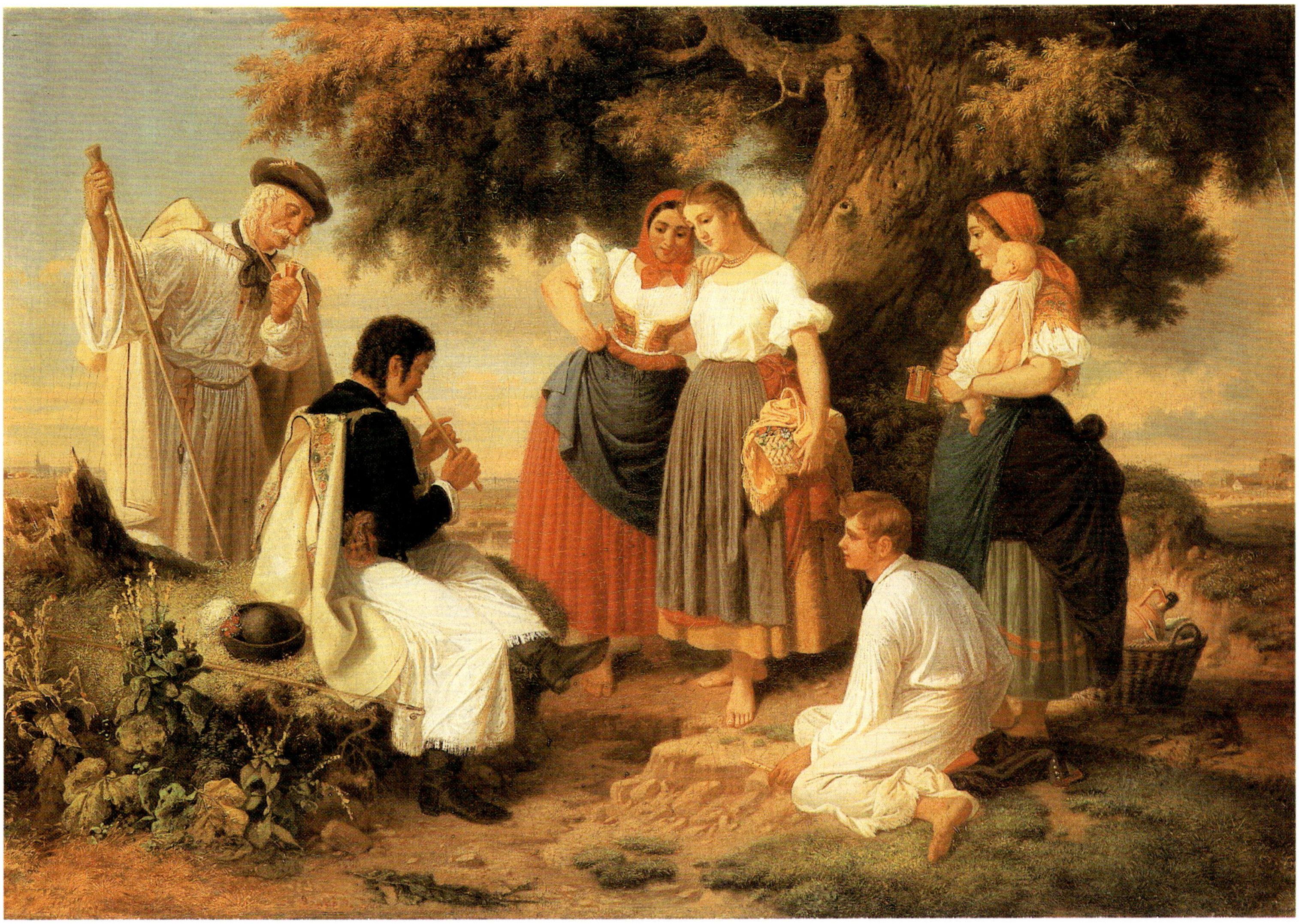

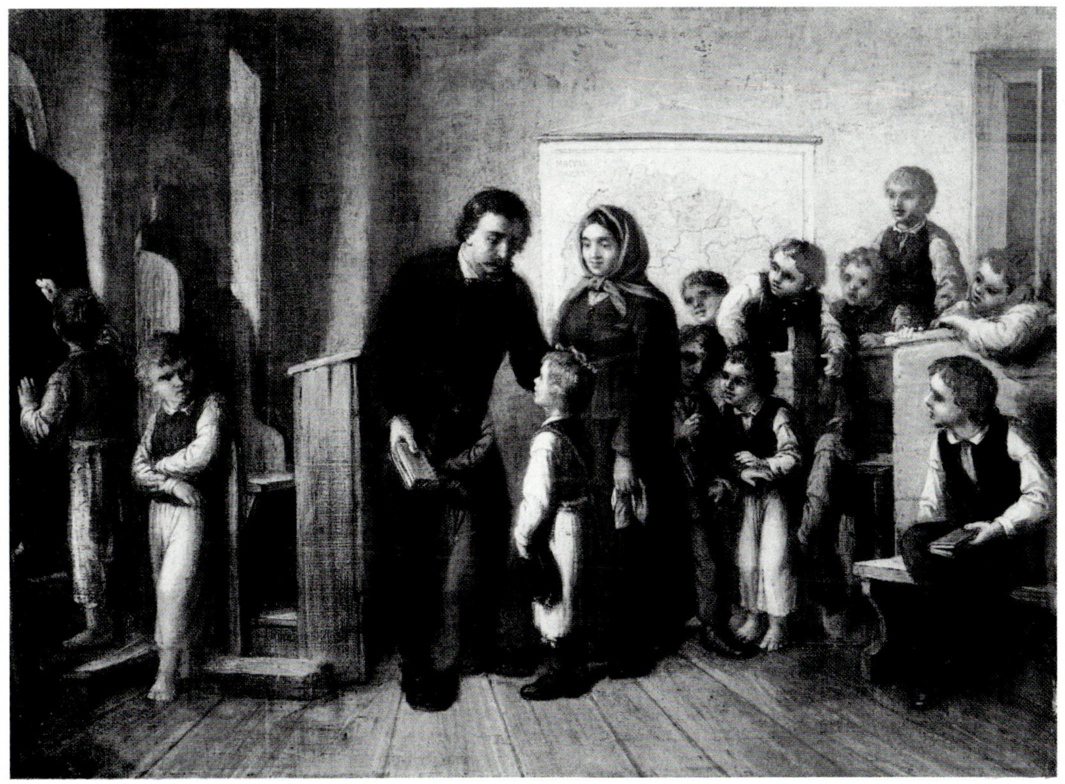

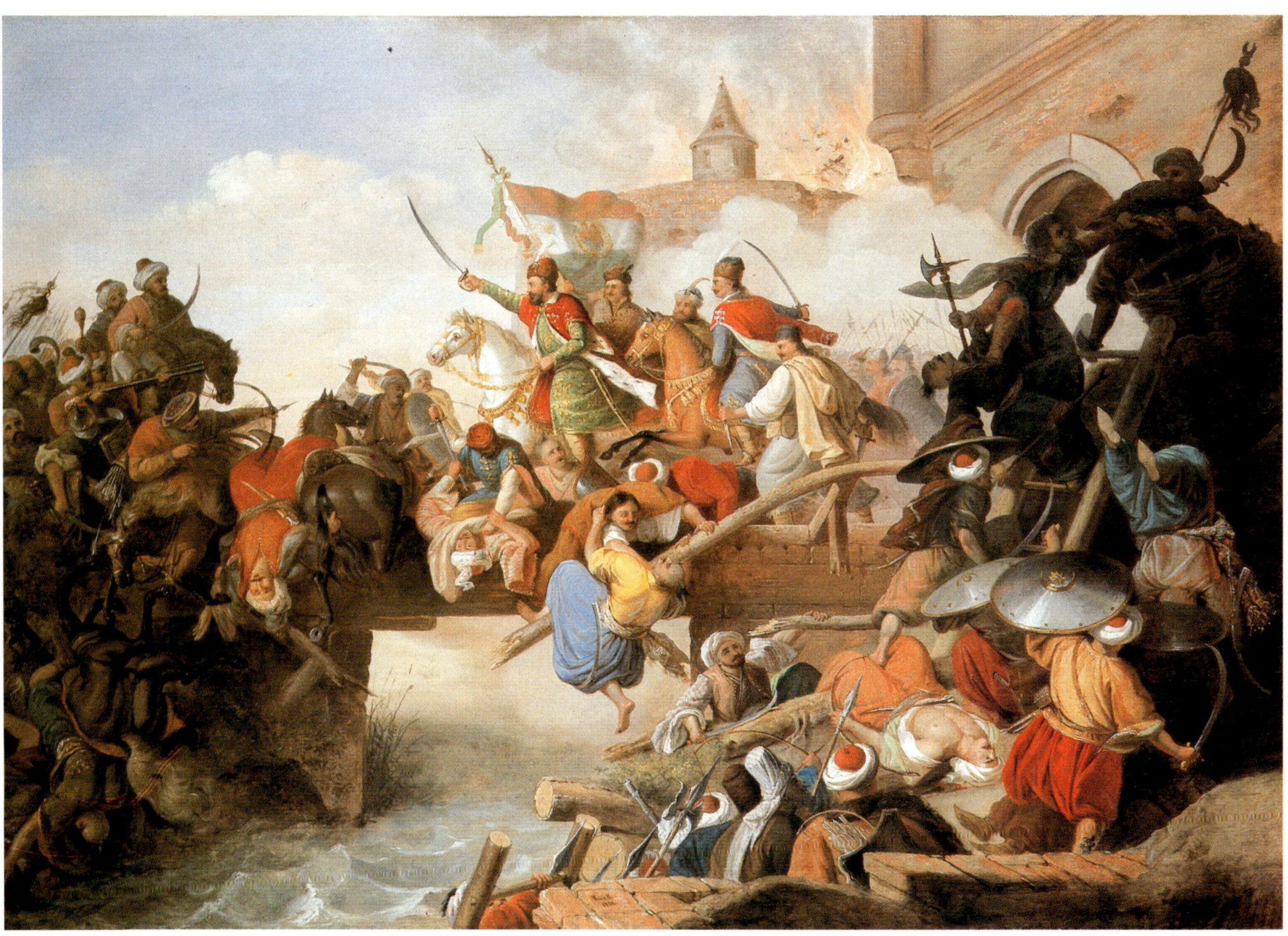

172. BÁLINT KISS
**After Zrínyi's Charge on the Turks
by Peter Krafft, the Elder, 1856**
Oil on canvas, 110×156.5 cm
Signed bottom right: "Kiss B. 856"
Szekszárd, Béri Balogh Ádám Museum

As curator of the Picture Gallery of the National Museum, Bálint Kiss was deeply concerned with the young generation of painters who frequently visited the museum to copy the works of Hungarian and Austrian painters and the old Masters, a method he himself practised diligently. In Krafft's large painting of this historic scene (Plate 59) Kiss must have seen a prototype for historical painting, for he copied it before beginning work on a new version for his own series depicting the history of Hungary. Yet, despite the careful reproduction of details, his imitation is more naive than the model. It reveals, nevertheless, a degree of technical skill lacking in the scenes painted after engravings of Krafft's work made for clock faces.

173. MÓR THAN
**The Arrest of Nyáry and Pekry
(Original title: The Arrest of Lőrinc
Nyáry and Lajos Pekry, 1552), 1853**
Oil on canvas, 138.5×213.5 cm
Signed bottom right: "Than Mór Bécs 853."
(Mór Than, Vienna, 853)
Budapest, Hungarian National Gallery
Inv. No.: 2713
*Donated by the Art Gallery Association to the
National Museum, 1854*

While still a student in Vienna, Mór Than was already recognized as a talented artist. One of his fellow students, George Mayer, mentioned this painting in his memoirs of Rahl and Rahl's school of painting. It was there that Than learned historical composition in which the main protagonists were distinguished from the minor figures by their more energetic gestures. Fortunately, the painter followed his own instincts and his own sense of pictorial quality and was thus prevented from overworking this principle.

The painting records the battle of Szolnok in 1552, when the fortress was besieged by the Turks and Captain Lőrinc Nyáry and his companions were in great danger. Here the Turkish commander prevents a Turkish soldier from killing the captain as he lies wounded. The scene is repeated on the left-hand side of the canvas.

174. MÓR THAN
The Battle of Mohács, 1856
Oil on canvas, 200×400 cm
Signed bottom left: "f. Than M. Páris 856"
(Painted by Mór Than in Paris, 1856)
Košice, Východoslovenské Museum
Inv. No.: 52660–8599 (R)

This picture is one of the largest works conceived by Mór Than as a young artist. It is an elaborate composition inspired by Carl Rahl's *Battle at the Lajta*. The elongated shape indicates that the artist intended it for some specific room in a large building. The figures are arranged along two horizontal lines of the rectangle, the movements being skilfully composed to bring the action from the sides to the centre, and so draw the eye into the background. Along the vertical axis stands the purposeful figure of the standard bearer, his eyes raised towards heaven. Kneeling before him is a warrior praying to the image of the Virgin Mary with the Infant Jesus seen on the flag. Adjacent to the flag a white-bearded prelate, the Archbishop of Esztergom, fights with drawn sabre. In the right foreground the body of another prelate, Pál Tomori, Archbishop of Kalocsa, is rescued by his men. In the background, half concealed by the flowing black mane of a horse, is the King as he escapes with one of his companions. The painting commemorates the heroic resistance of the Hungarian nation.

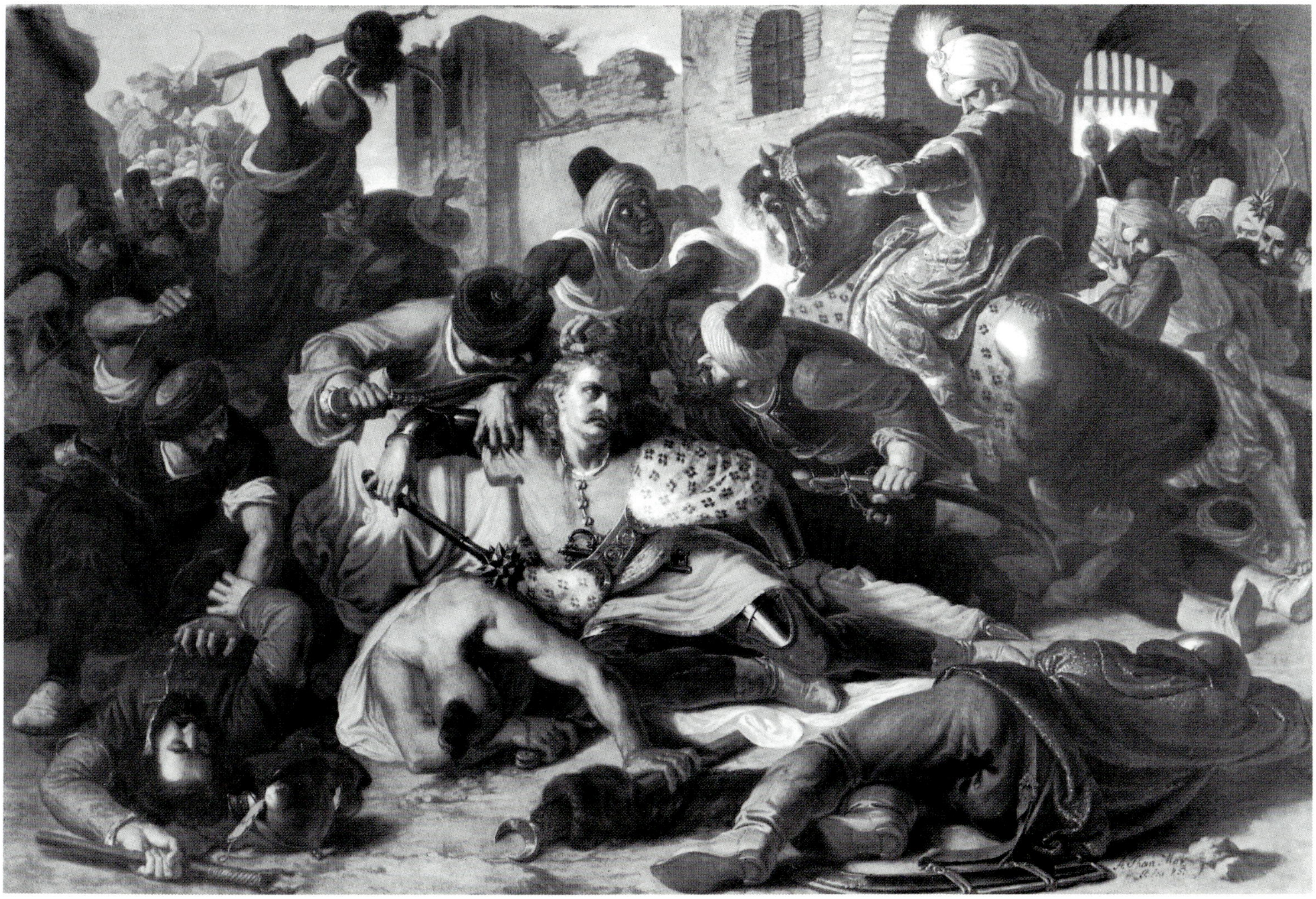

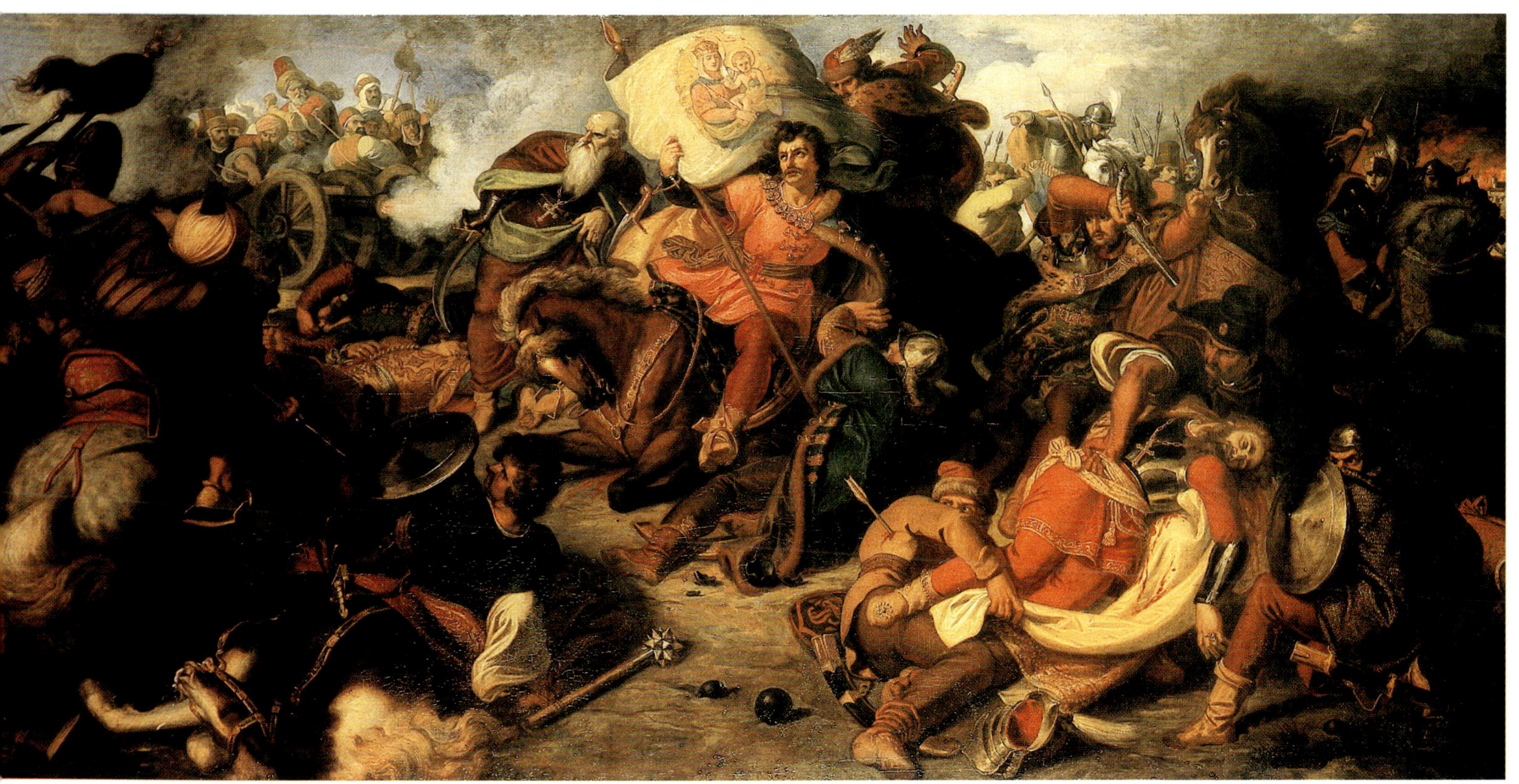

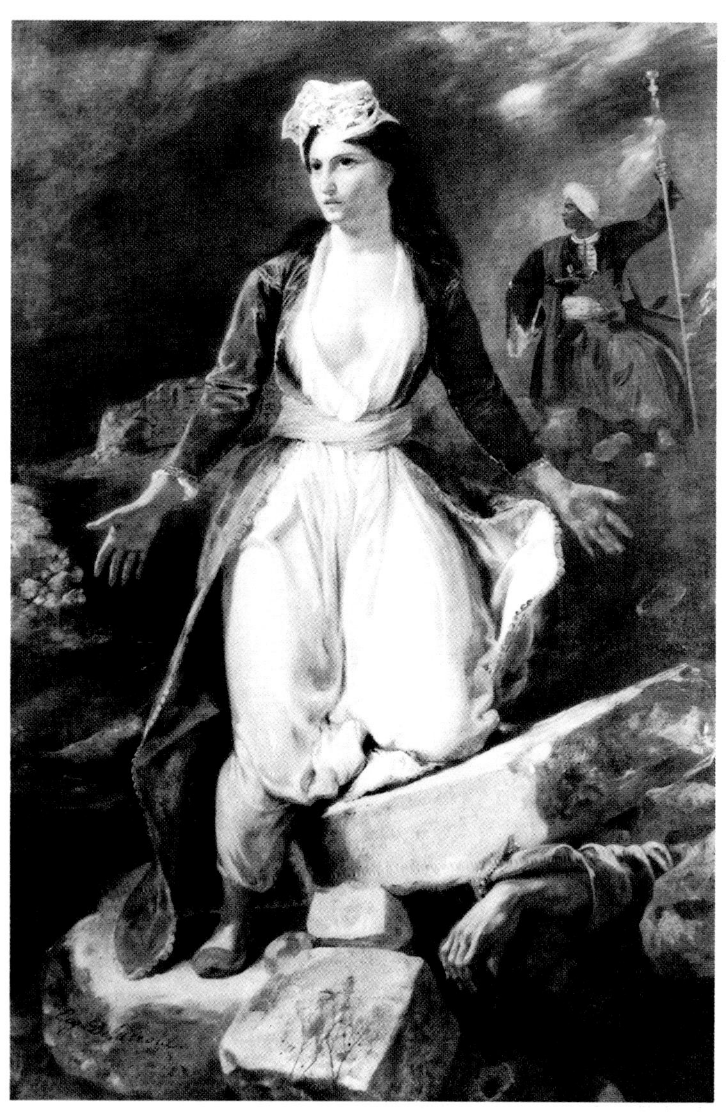

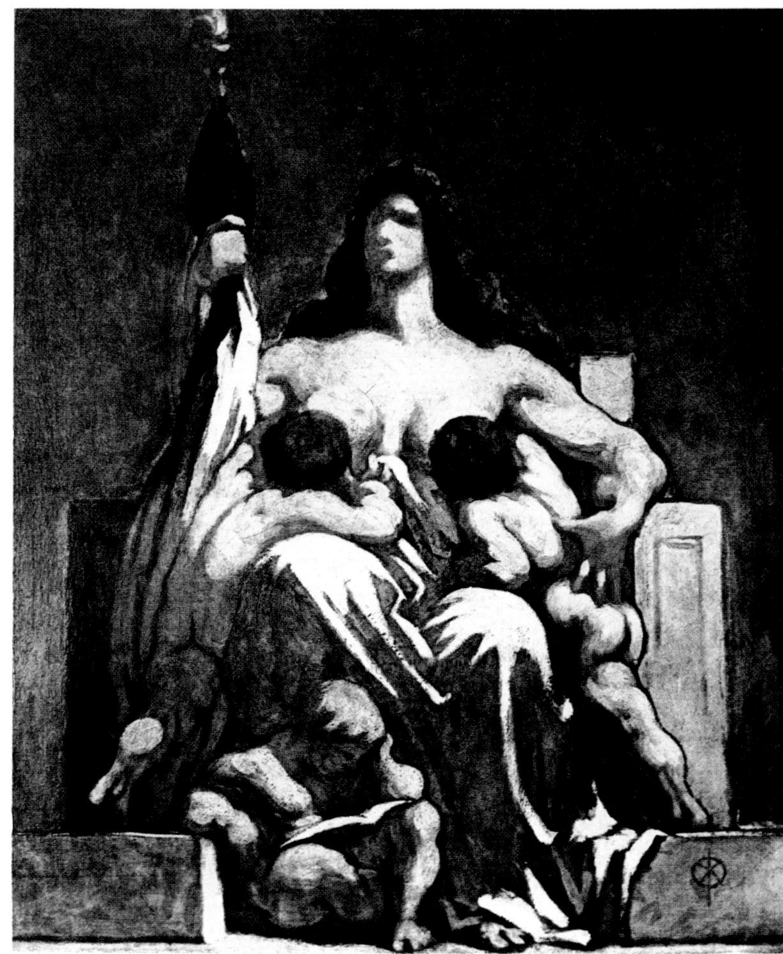

175. EUGÈNE DELACROIX
The Allegorical Figure of Greece
Expiring on the Ruins of Missolonghi,
c. 1826
Oil on canvas, 209 × 147 cm
Signed bottom left: "Eug Delacroix"
Bordeaux, Musée des Beaux Arts

The reverence for the Greek War of Independence (1822–1829) in the first half of the 19th century symbolized the artists of Western Europe the fusion of Neo-Classicism and Romanticism—on the one hand reverence for the ancient world, and on the other, a passion for national independence. In this painting Delacroix represented Greece as a richly apparelled female figure kneeling by a dead body protruding from under a stone slab. In the background is the triumphant figure of a Turk.

176. HONORÉ DAUMIER
Allegory of the Republic, c. 1849
Oil on canvas, 73 × 60 cm
Paris, Louvre

In this allegorical painting, the symbolic figure representing the nation is quite unlike the elegant female figure seen in Academic compositions. Daumier has chosen to symbolize the Republic in the figure of a poor woman in ragged clothing suckling her two standing children, who represent the citizens and workers. Her third child—perhaps symbolizing the new intellectuals, the spiritual basis of the new born state—sits at her feet, absorbed in a book.

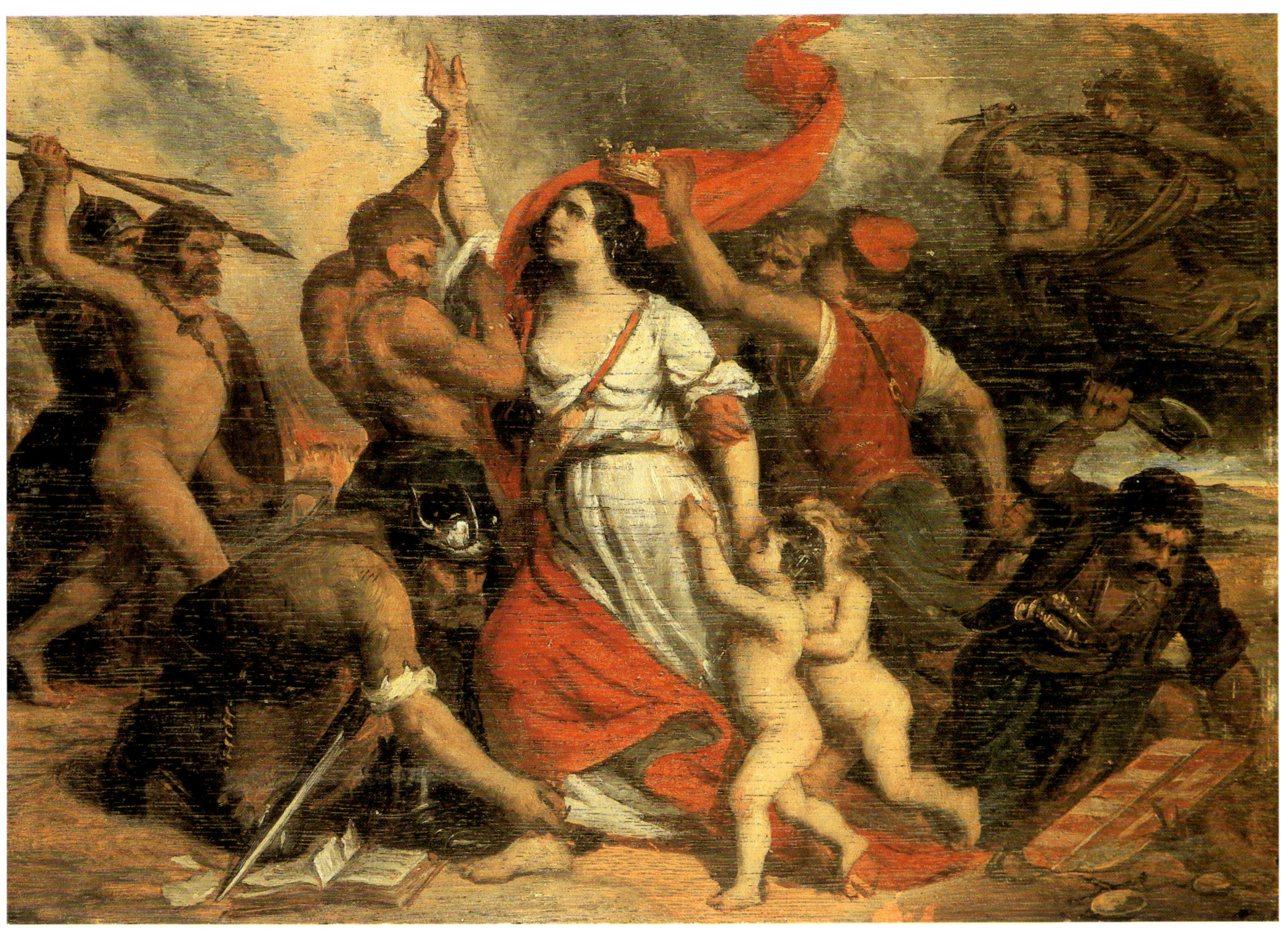

177. MIHÁLY KOVÁCS
The Oppression of Hungary in 1849, 1861

Oil on wood, 32.5 × 43.5 cm
Inscribed on canvas stretcher: "Magyarország
leigázása 1849-ben, allegóriai vázlat. Pest.
Kovács Mihály." (Oppression of Hungary in
1849, allegorical sketch. Pest. Mihály Kovács)
Eger, Dobó István Castle Museum
Inv. No.: 55.119

This painting was inspired by a visit to Paris
in 1857 where the painter saw the work of
Delacroix and Daumier. At the centre of the
composition is the figure of a woman wear–
ing a loose red and white robe. The two chil–
dren holding her skirt may well represent the
Sciences and the Arts, as in Mór Than's
mural in the National Museum (see Plate
224). All are attempting to escape from the
armed men who surround them. A male fig–
ure in the right corner attempts to smash the
Hungarian coat of arms. Three Furies are
approaching in a turbulent sky. The woman
represents Hungary, and the menacing male
figures represent oppressive neighbouring
countries and minorities within Hungary.

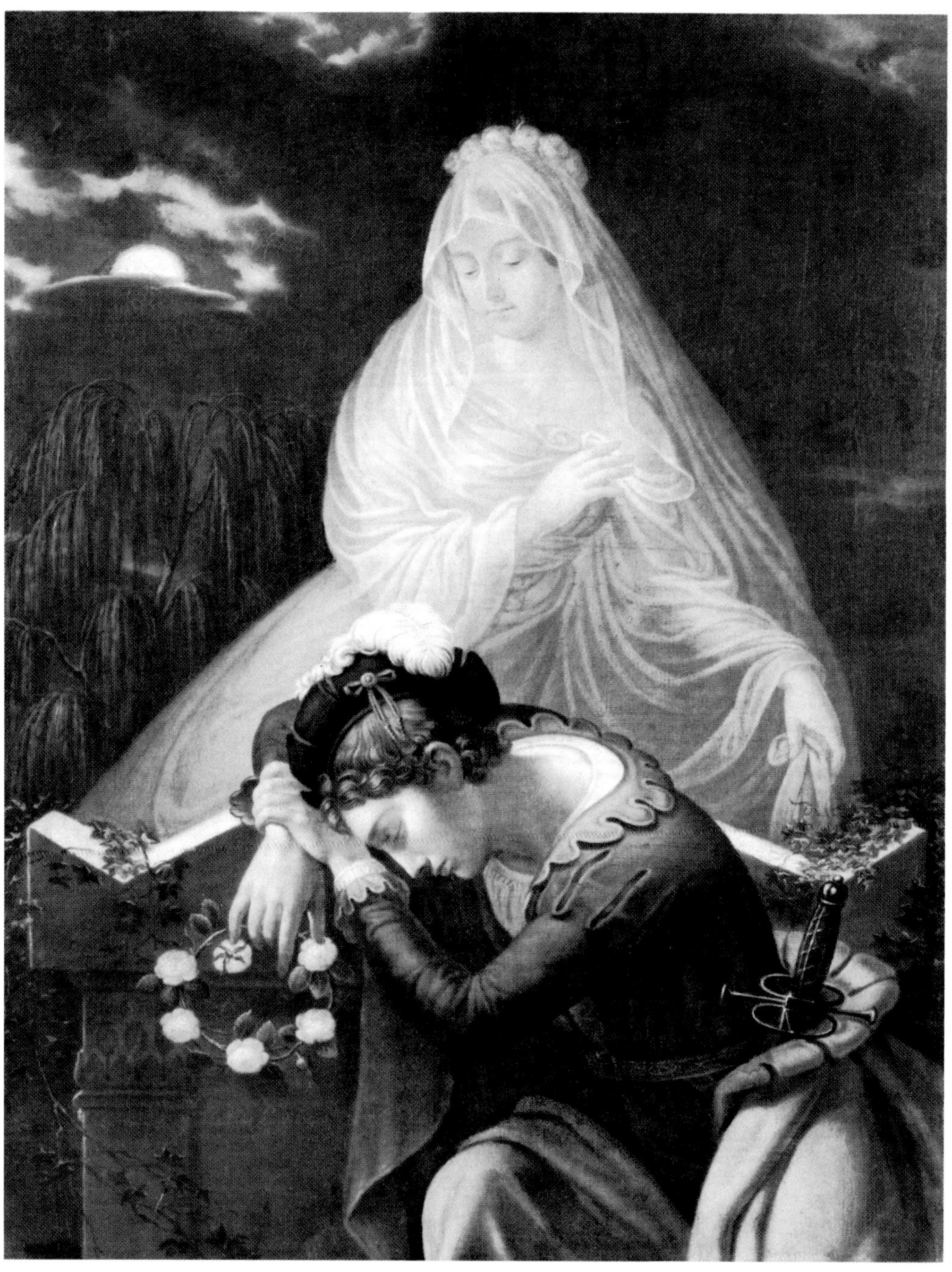

178. ALAJOS LANDAU
Apparition, 1858
Oil on canvas, 44.5×48 cm
Budapest, Hungarian National Gallery
Inv. No.: FK 6168 T

Alajos Landau came from a family of painters. His father, Lenárt Landau, studied at the Academy in Vienna from 1814 to 1818 and was well known for his historical paintings and drawings; he was also from 1820 a teacher of drawing, including architectural drawing, and free-hand drawing in Pest, by which he meant the drawing of flowers, landscapes and figures in chalk and water-colours, a practice strongly condemned by his rivals.

Although Lenárt Landau was regarded mainly as a painter of historical scenes, it seems that he also taught composition technique; he trained his son to become a "true" painter, and may have sent him to Vienna, where he himself had spent his youth.

This painting by Alajos Landau appears to be an illustration to a literary work: a young man is depicted grieving by his lover's tomb, lost in reverie, while the apparition of his fiancée, wearing her bridal gown and wreath, hovers over him. The white-grey tonality is intended to give a nocturnal atmosphere. The theme is related to *The Fugi-tive's Dream* (Plate 179) by Viktor Madarász, which suggests that the twenty-five-year old artist may have created this painting during, or after, his stay in Vienna.

179. VIKTOR MADARÁSZ
The Fugitive's Dream (Original title: Thököly's Dream)
Oil on canvas, 252.5×189 cm
Signed bottom right: "Madarász Viktor 1856 Bécsben" (Viktor Madarász 1856 in Vienna)
Budapest, Hungarian National Gallery
Inv. No.: 5244

After the War of Independence, Madarász was obliged to go into hiding. Later, while studying in Vienna between 1853 and 1856 and searching for a powerful historical sub-ject, he painted this picture which represents Imre Thököly, a famous Hungarian prince who had to go into exile in the seventeenth century because of his anti-Habsburg feel-ings and policy. It is not the type of composi-tion he would have seen at the Academy in Vienna nor in Waldmüller's School. Prob-ably it is his own conception of the scene with added details taken from antecedents. The young Imre Thököly is depicted sleep-ing in a small clearing in the midst of a juniper thicket. The figure is in a position similar to Correggio's *Danae*. By his side we see his companion, also overcome by sleep, his head resting on his battle-axe. Thököly's moonlit face suggests that in his dreams he is looking upon an apparition of his father. The apparition, eyes closed, seems to approach the youth from above, the chains falling from his wrists. Beside him is the shadowy figure of a winged skeleton wrapped in a shroud. The painting conveys the mes-sage, transferred in a dream from father to son, that the father has been freed from the slavery he endured in his earthly existence.

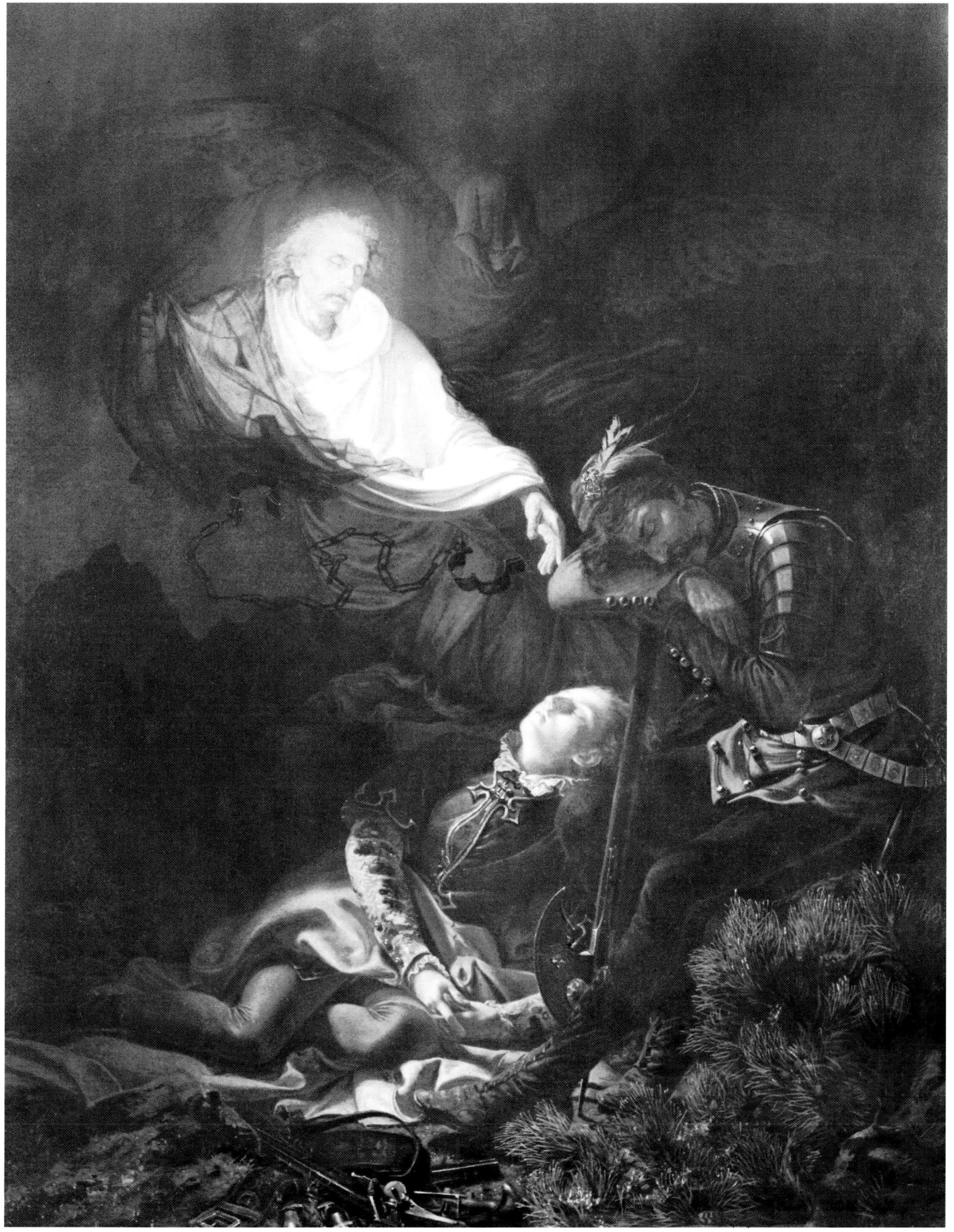

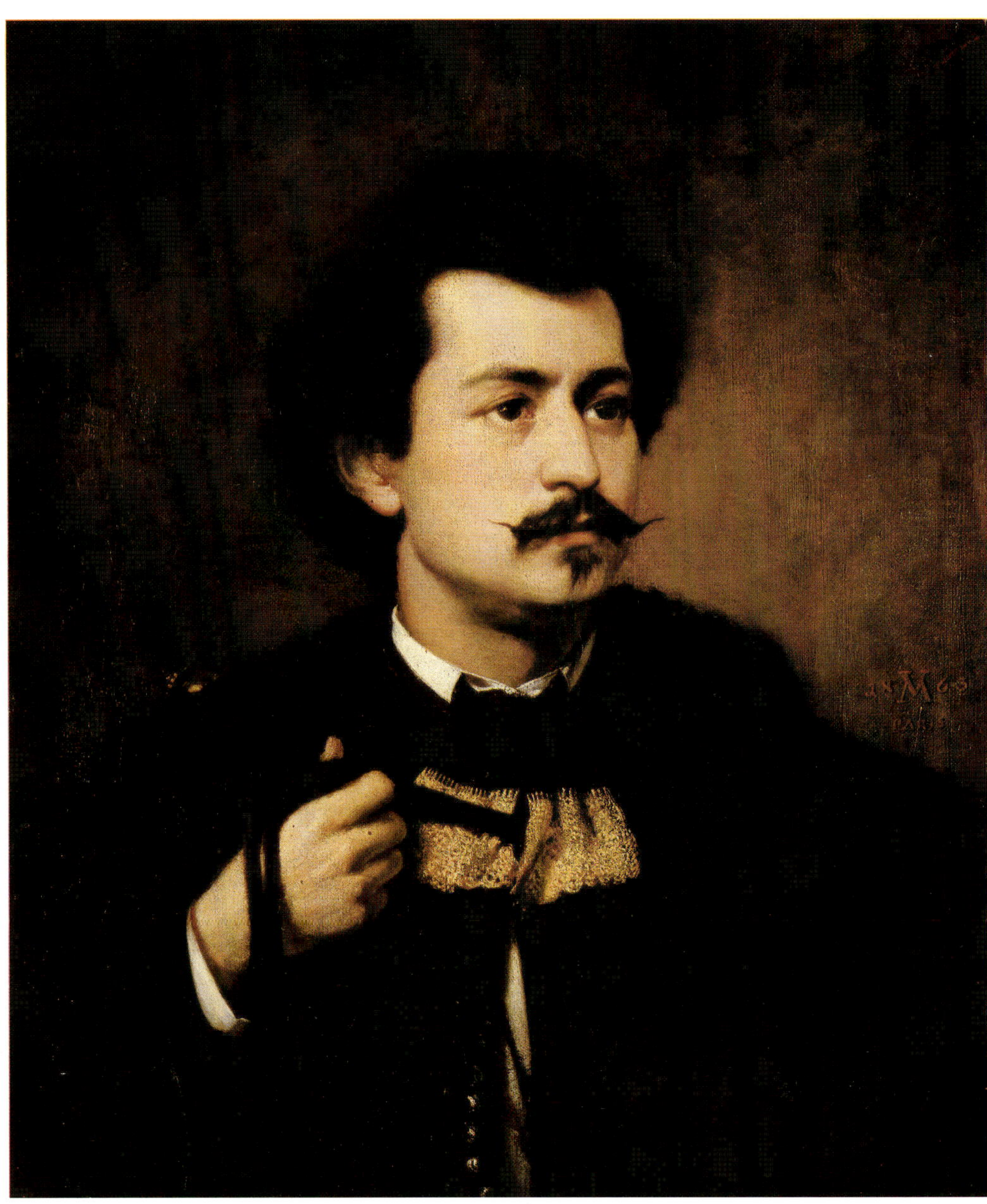

180. VIKTOR MADARÁSZ
Self-portrait, 1863
Oil on canvas, 73 × 60 cm
Signed by right shoulder: "18M63 PARIS"
Budapest, Hungarian National Gallery
Inv. No.: 7585

The dandified self-portraits executed by painters of the Romantic period may have been the source of inspiration for this work. Madarász, however, has chosen to paint a half-length portrait, as generally favoured in Hungary. He portrays himself as an earnest gentleman, dressed with the utmost care. One possible Hungarian antecedent might be Mihály Kovács's self-portrait of 1850 (Plate 120). The fine scarf and brilliant jewellery in that painting is echoed here by the black "attila" (a tight-fitting, typically Hungarian pelisse of the period), the white shirt and, above all, the gold lace scarf. The expression suggests concentrated attention. We are given a strong impression of the artist's pride in his Hungarian nationality and his sense of the importance of his artistic calling.

181. VIKTOR MADARÁSZ
Felicián Zách, 1858
Oil on canvas, 152 × 112 cm
Signed bottom right: "Madarász Viktor Paris 58"
Budapest, Hungarian National Gallery
Inv. No.: 66.74 T

In this painting Madarász illustrated an historical event also much favoured by writers. In the 14th century, Clara Zách, the daughter of the Hungarian magnate Felicián Zách, was seduced at the court of Charles Robert I, whereupon the father plotted to kill the king. The plot failed, the father was killed while fighting, and his family cruelly persecuted. There are poems by Sándor Petőfi and János Arany describing the tragedy, which Madarász approached through the Romantic medium of historical painting. He chose to depict Clara Zách as she tells her father that she was seduced by a member of the Queen's family.

Father and daughter are seen in a rather theatrical setting, richly dressed and wearing splendid jewellery. The father, furious and despairing, thinks of vengeance, while his broken-hearted daughter sobs bitterly beside him. In this work the artist is also clearly concerned with the problem of depicting natural light.

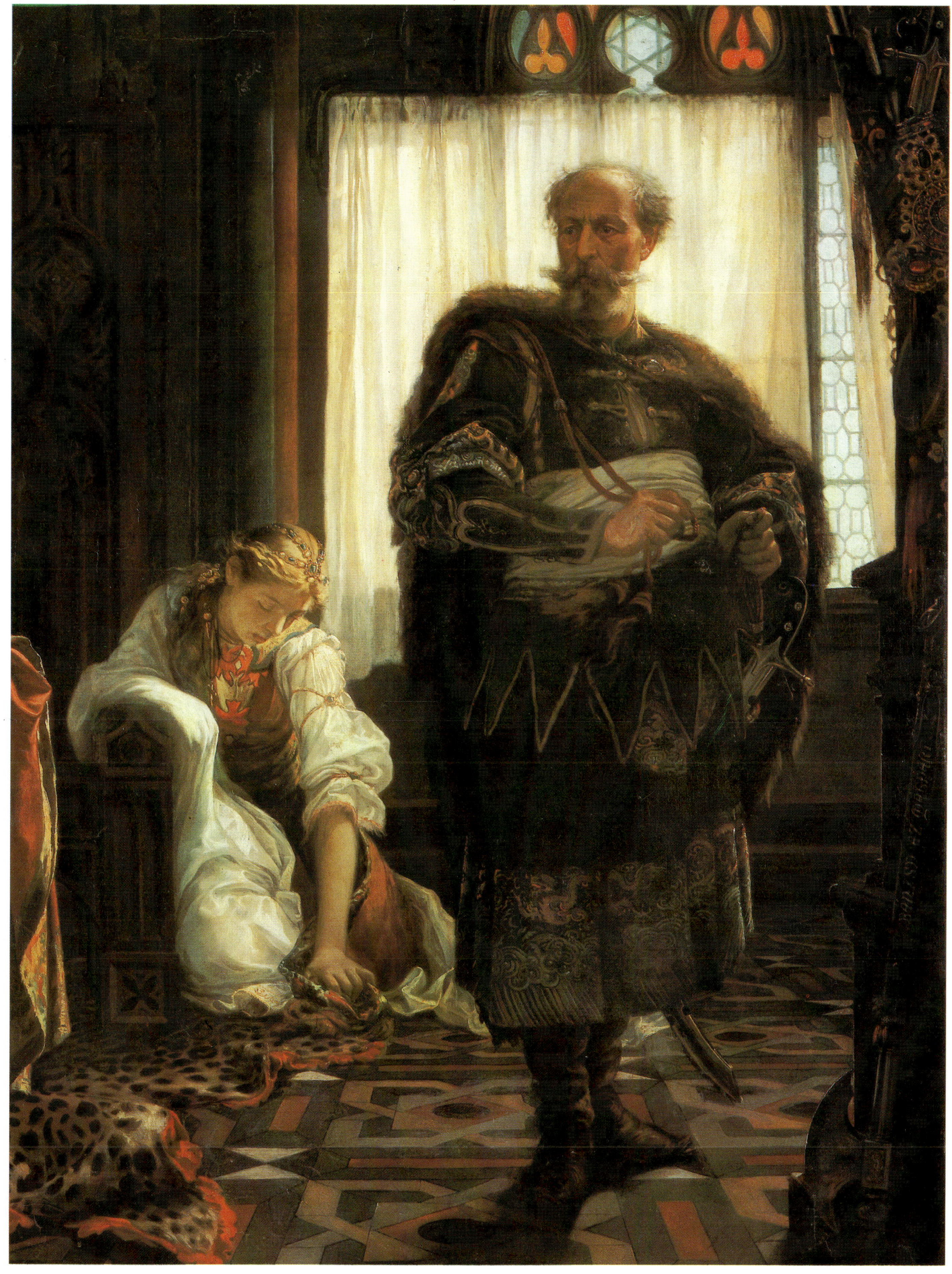

182. JEAN JACQUES HENNER
Adam and Eve Mourning the Dead Abel, 1858

Oil on canvas, 30 × 24.5 cm
Signed bottom right: "J. Henner"
Paris, École des Beaux Arts, from 1923
Musée National J. J. Henner
Inv. No.: JJHP90

This is a preliminary sketch for a painting that was awarded the Gold Medal of the Paris Academy. Soon afterwards, the final composition was also awarded a prize. Although today the French painter Henner is not well known and his name only figures in books on academic art, this was not the case when he completed this painting. Numerous writers praised his bold style, especially his treatment of Abel's nude body lying on the ground exposed to the viewer's gaze, also his ability to convey emotion by means of gestures, in this case the grief of Adam and Eve.

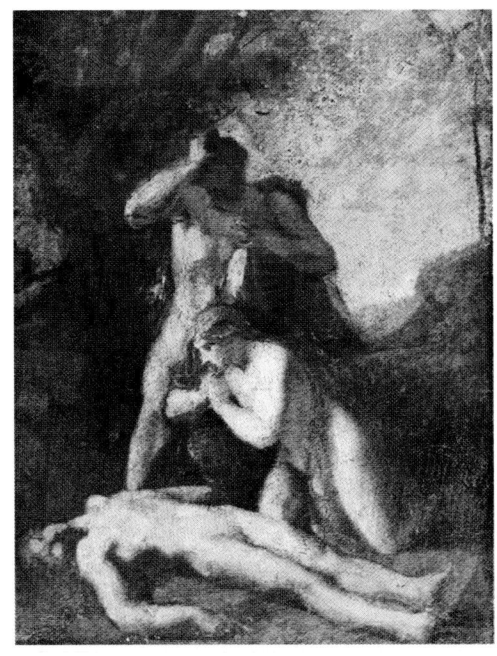

184. VIKTOR MADARÁSZ
Sketch for The Mourning of László Hunyadi, 1859

Oil on wood, 34 × 48 cm
Unsigned
Budapest, Hungarian National Gallery
Inv. No.: FK 4933

By the 1850s, the theme of Hunyadi's death had already been popularized by Ferenc Erkel's opera *László Hunyadi* produced in 1844, as well as Sándor Petőfi's poem recording the same event—the execution of Hunyadi on charges of high treason by the order of King Ladislas V in 15th century Hungary. Yet the subject was still uncommon in this form in Hungarian painting, though Orlai's *Discovery of the Body of King Louis II* (Plate 142) might have served as a model for Madarász. László Hunyadi, described in Petőfi's poem as a handsome youth who died by the executioner's sword, is not represented in the painting, but only his shrouded corpse. The principal motifs in the final composition are all present in the sketch: on the ground in front of the altar, the body of László Hunyadi lies wrapped in a white shroud, stained with blood around the neck. At his feet, two kneeling female figures, his mother and his bride, cling to each other for consolation. The two candles in tall candlesticks are rather startling, since they rank in importance with the other details. Nevertheless, this sketch introduces a painter of genuine talent.

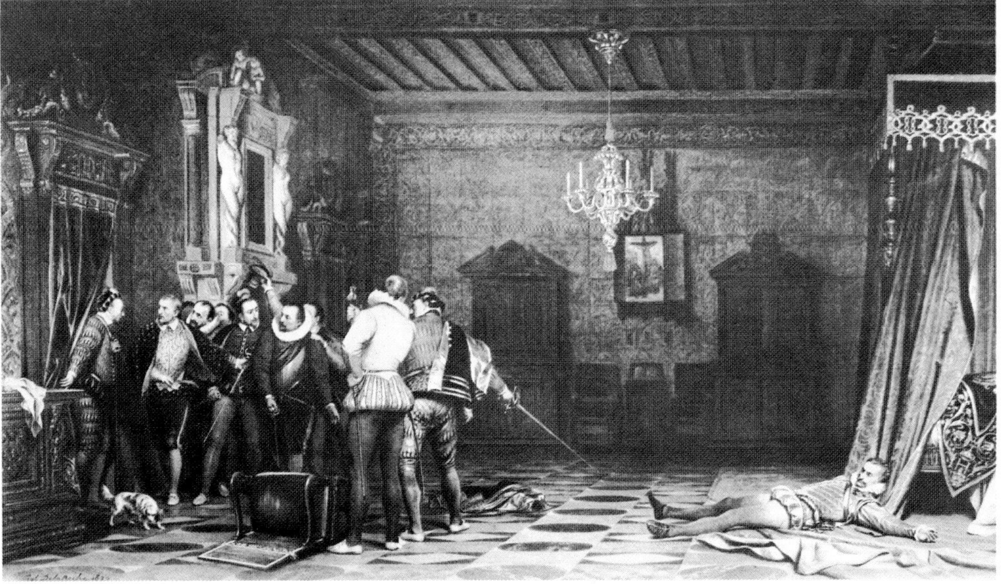

183. PAUL DELAROCHE
The Death of the Duc de Guise, 1834

Oil on canvas, 57 × 98 cm
Signed: "Paul Delaroche 1834"
Chantilly, Musée Condée

Henry III of France, fearing the Duc de Guise's lust for power, ordered his courtiers to lure him into the court and assassinate him. Some contemporary critics dismissed the Delaroche painting depicting the death of the Duke as a mere illustration of an event, but others praised it for its dramatic impact. The painting shows the Duke's body lying where he fell, left for all to see on the orders of the King. Grouped at a distance, the courtiers whisper to each other. The facts as related here and the artist's approach to his subject are both similar and yet different from the theme and approach seen in *The Mourning of László Hunyadi*, painted by Madarász (Plate 185). This may have been the reason why Madarász based his *Hunyadi* painting on it, the representation of a political murder. Hungarian painters would often paint a historic event in such a way as to illustrate that in Hungary any event might end very differently from a similar event in another country.

185. VIKTOR MADARÁSZ
The Mourning of László Hunyadi, 1859

Oil on canvas, 243 × 312 cm
Signed bottom right: "Madarász Viktor Párisban, 1859"
Budapest, Hungarian National Gallery
Inv. No.: 2800

In the final version of the painting, the setting is more concrete than in the sketches (Plate 184). The entrance and windows suggest a Gothic chapel, which can be identified as a chapel in the Church of Holy Mary Magdalene in Buda. Period accuracy did not much concern Madarász, the two candlesticks and the candelabra are of a shape and size typical of the 18th and 19th centuries, but not of the 15th century, when Hunyadi lived and died. The women express their grief in slow and dignified gestures. Hunyadi's bereaved bride places the wreath of roses (tribute to a hero) beside the sword above the shrouded body. The mother's grief is evident in her profile, pale against the surrounding darkness. Each detail expresses one of the great themes of the century—heroic death and the ceremonious exaltation of the hero.

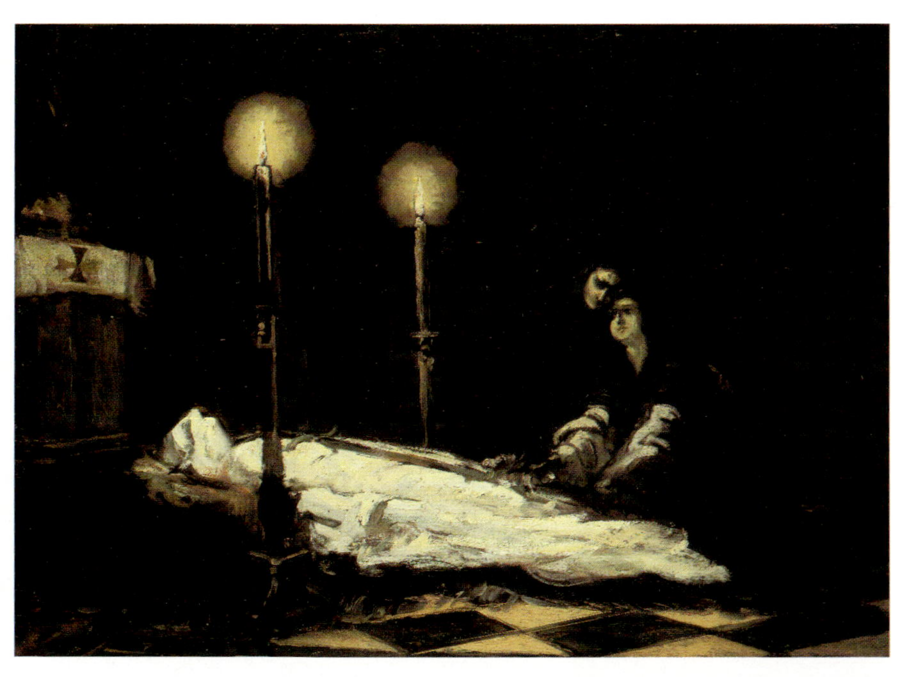

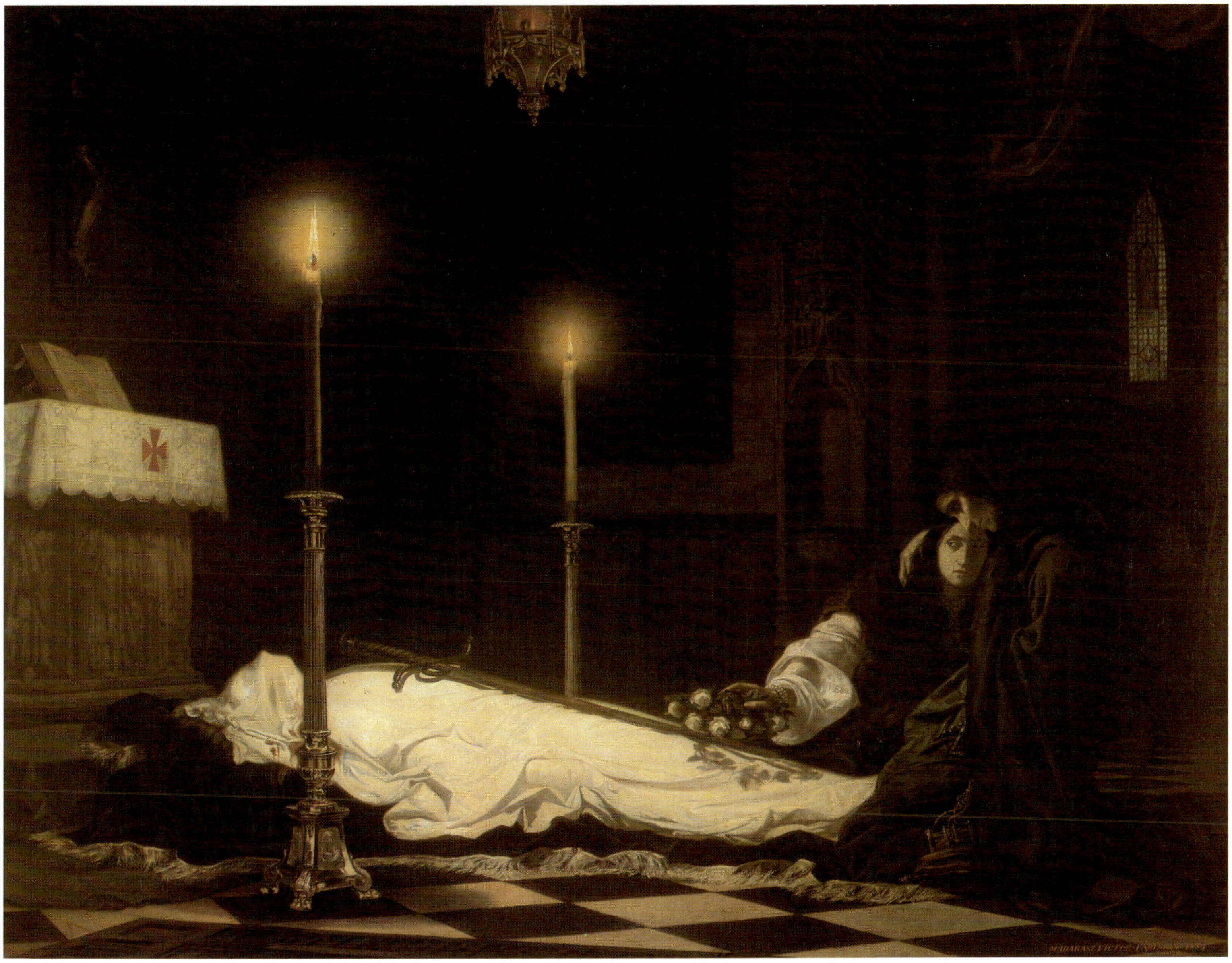

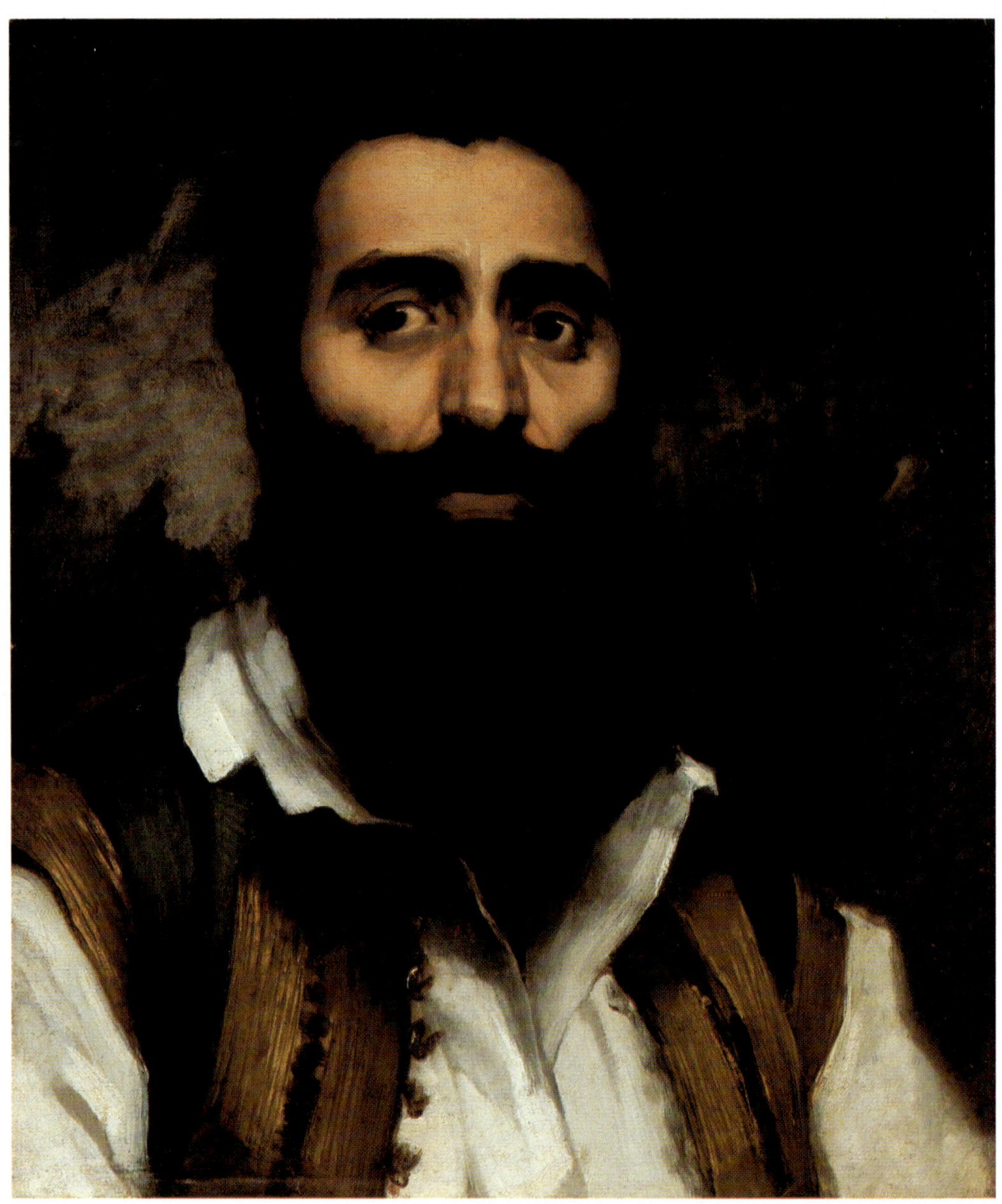

186. VIKTOR MADARÁSZ
Zrínyi, 1858
Oil on canvas, 55.5 × 48 cm
Unsigned
Budapest, Hungarian National Gallery
Inv. No.: 4882 T

It is not possible to identify with certainty
who this painting is meant to represent. It
could represent Miklós Zrínyi, the defender
of Szigetvár against the Turks, his grandson
of the same name who was a poet, or Péter
Zrínyi, the poet's younger brother, leader of
a conspiracy against the Habsburgs.
Madarász completed several idealized portraits of heroic figures from Hungarian history. Two of them portray György Dózsa,
the legendary leader of a Hungarian peasant
rebellion executed in 1514, with the Temesvár Fortress where he was defeated burning
in the background. There is something for-
bidding about this bust-portrait of a man
with a black beard; he calls to mind our image of Dózsa rather than any one of the three
Zrínyis mentioned above.

187. VIKTOR MADARÁSZ
**Péter Zrínyi and Ferenc Frangepán in
the Wiener-Neustadt Prison, 1864**
Oil on canvas, 65 × 81.5 cm
Unsigned
Budapest, Hungarian National Gallery
Inv. No.: FK 4110

In Christian iconography the parting of St.
Peter and St. Paul before their martyrdom
has similarities with Madarász's subject—a
favourite among painters of the early 19th
century. The solemnity of the occasion and
the characterization are reminiscent of the religious precedent, but Madarász presents the
scene less harshly by placing the main
characters in the foreground. In previous
works—religious paintings and an earlier
engraving—the parting of the Apostles or of
noblemen was represented with the same
gestures.
Madarász conceived the parting of Zrínyi
and Frangepán as a long discussion between
a frightened youth and a more resolute man
before their deaths, as yet undisturbed by the
soldiers and officials in the background. In
spite of the authentic historical details, the
painting thus becomes primarily a stage on
which the leading characters exchange their
ideas and feelings in a long dialogue.

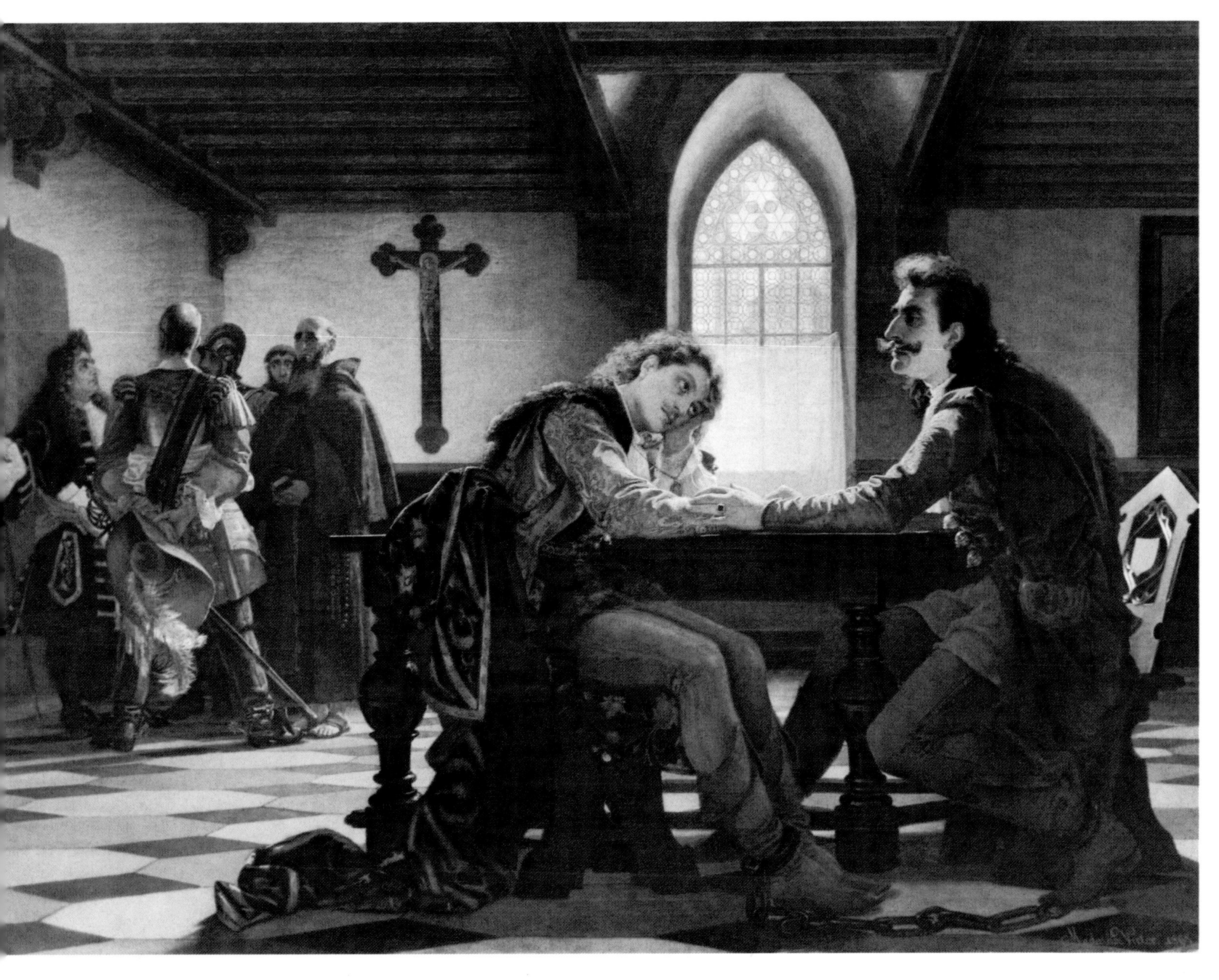

213

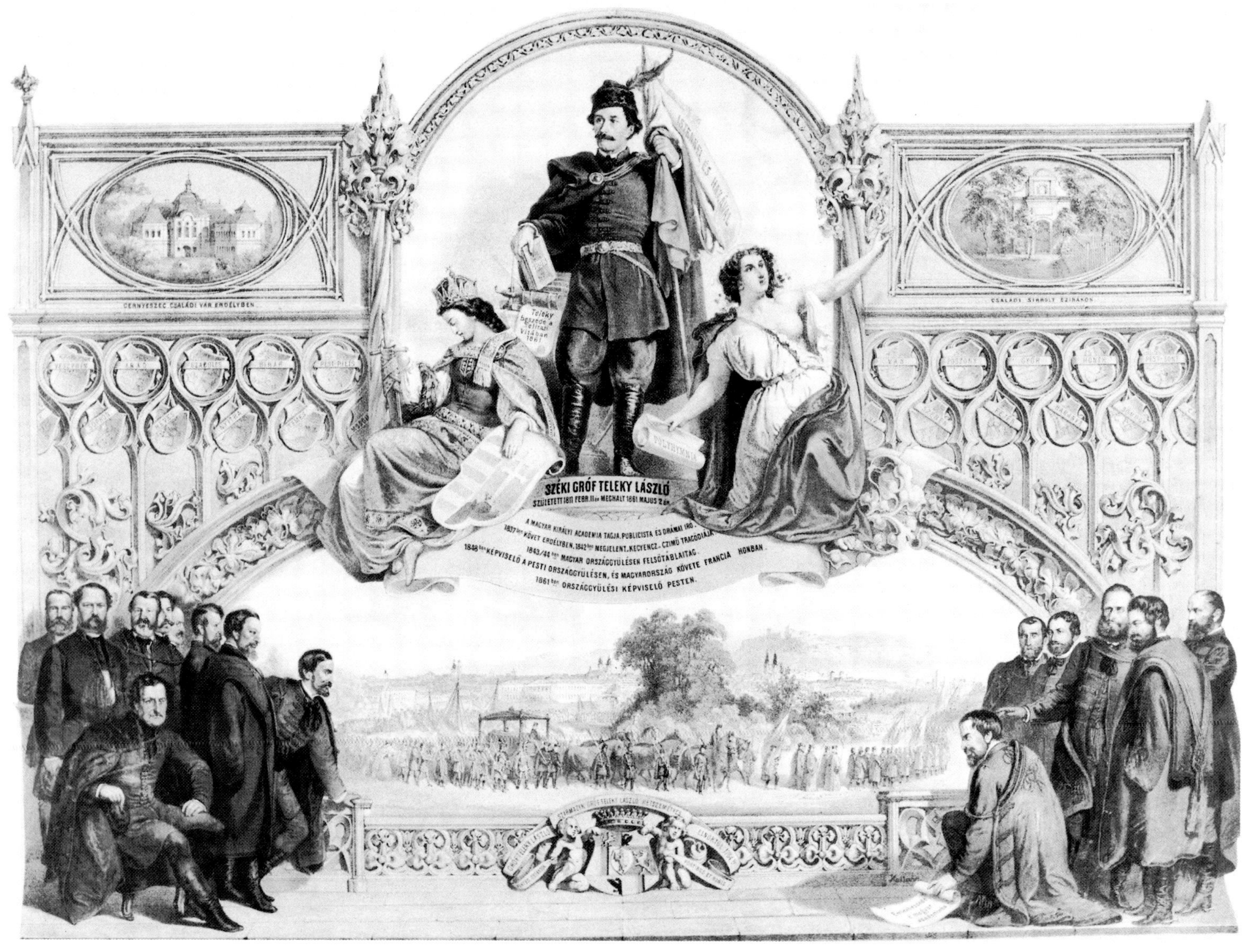

188. FERDINAND TEVELY (TEVELE)
Symbolic and Historical Memorial for Count László Teleki, 1861

Coloured lithograph on paper, 471×544 mm
Inscription bottom right: "Tevely Ferdinánd tanár rajz. – Kőre metsz. Kollarz Ferenc. — Reich és Rösch" (Drawing by teacher Ferdinánd Tevely. — Lithograph on stone by Ferenc Kollarz. — Edited by Reich and Rösch)
Budapest, Hungarian National Museum, Historical Picture Gallery
Inv. No.: 55.1069

By placing the figure of Count László Teleki in the upper arch of the Neo-Gothic architectural framework, the artist symbolically places him among the immortals. Symmetrically arranged in the two upper corners are the view of his native castle and that of the family vault; arranged below these are the coats of arms of all the Hungarian counties. The two mourning female figures accompanying Teleki are the crowned Hungaria on the left, and on the right, a half naked Polyhymnia, the muse of oratory and sacred poetry. In the lower part of the geometrical lattice-work is the scene of Teleki's funeral, an occasion of national mourning. The two foreground groups represent either his fellow politicians mourning over his death or prominent members of the two major political parties, likewise grieving. The inscriptions on the memorial indicate the various activities of the deceased politician: member of the Academy of Sciences, playwright, member of Parliament and ambassador to France.

189. MIKLÓS BARABÁS
Portrait of László Teleki, 1861

Oil on canvas, 254×159 cm
Signed bottom left: "Barabás 1861"
Eger, Dobó István Castle Museum
Inv. No.: 55.274

Barabás completed this portrait in 1861, shortly before Teleki's death. Teleki at this time was one of the most honoured patriots and, for all too short a period, the greatest hope of his fellow-countrymen. The painter did not sense the inner struggle of a man who was soon to put an end to his life. (Following defeat in the War of Independence, Teleki was pardoned in return for a promise not to engage in politics again. He nevertheless became involved in parliamentary life, which led eventually to mental conflict and suicide.)

Barabás executed his work in the style of Amerling's portraits of kings and emperors. The setting is strongly reminiscent of that in the portrait of István Széchenyi (Plate 65). The figure stands in an open portico beside symbolic representations of a writing desk, open books and books with markers. The scarlet drapery behind a pillar might symbolize universal freedom. Teleki is depicted with arms crossed and a sword at his side, clad in the dark Hungarian gala dress, worn by revolutionary Hungarians in exile, seen also in Viktor Madarász's *Self-portrait* (Plate 180).

214

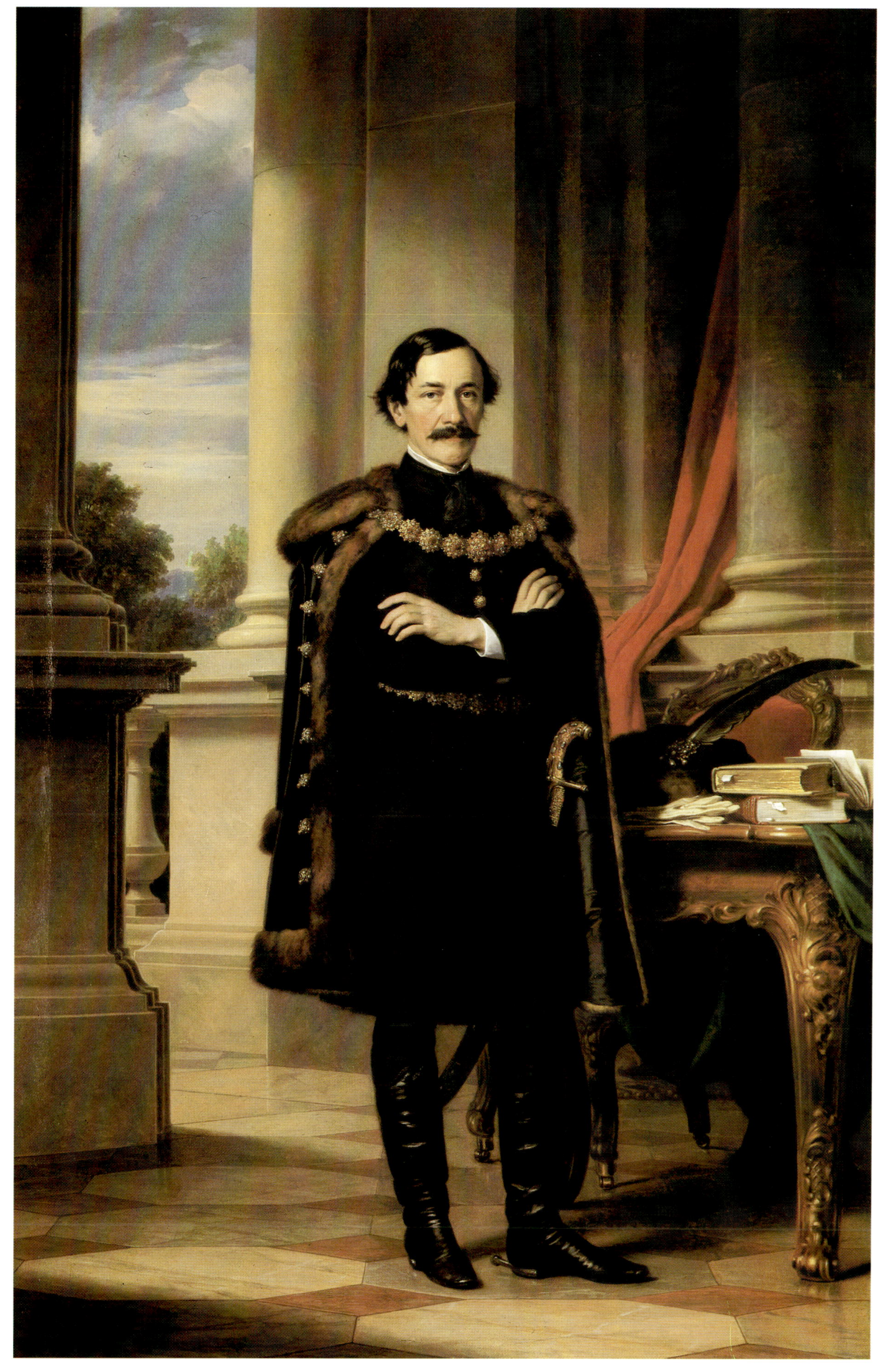

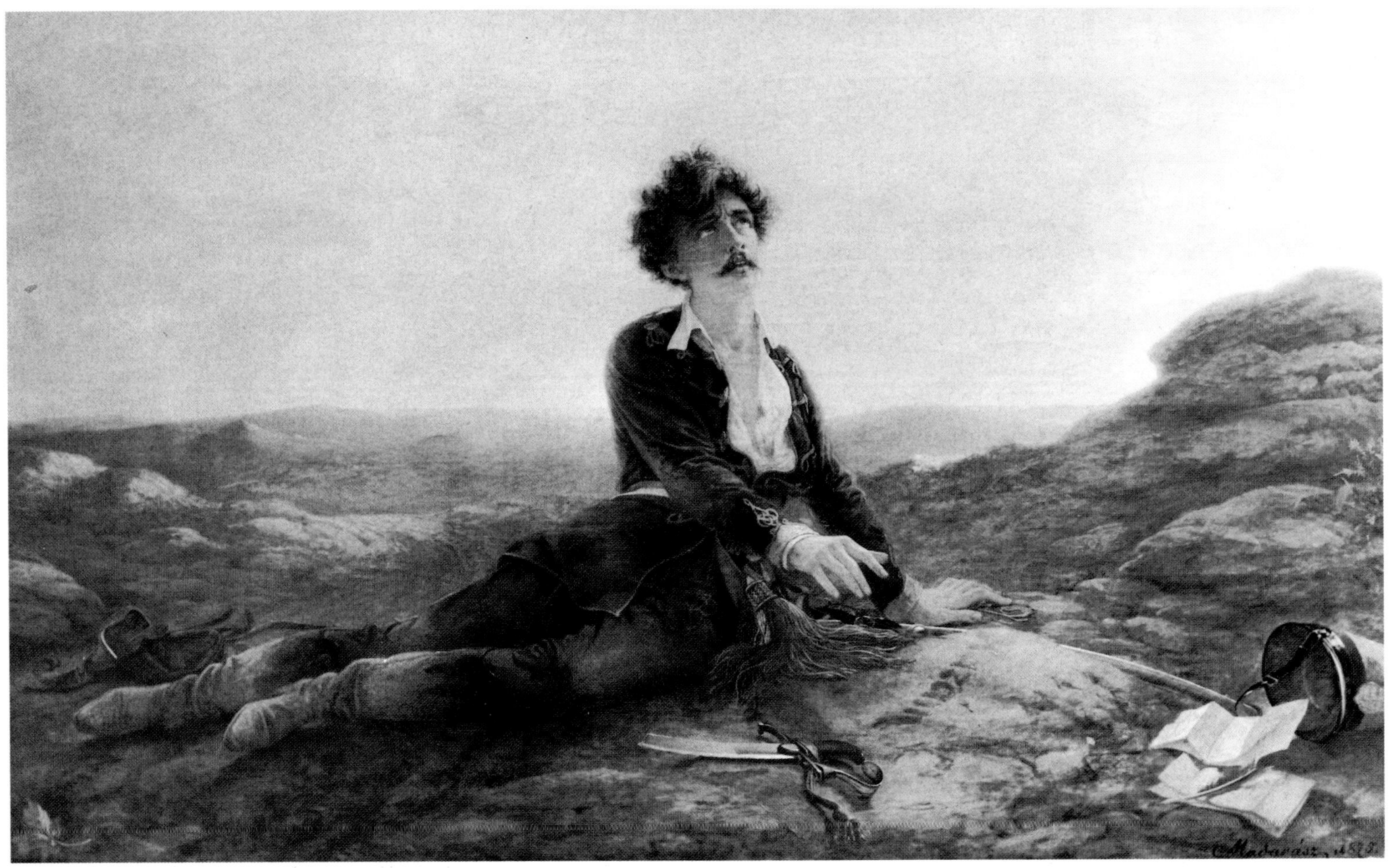

190. VIKTOR MADARÁSZ
Petőfi's Death ("My Homeland"), 1875

Oil on canvas, 138 × 230 cm
Signed bottom right: "Madarász V. 1875 (8)."
Budapest, Petőfi Literary Museum
Inv. No.: 57.3321.

In this painting, Madarász portrays his own imaginative reconstruction of the last moments of Sándor Petőfi, one of the greatest Hungarian poets, alone on the barren slopes of a mountain in the battle of Segesvár. Although there is documentary evidence that Petőfi preferred civilian clothes and did not carry a sword in the last, fatal battle, he is depicted here in uniform, a broken sword by his side, his helmet abandoned. His quill and some pages of his poetry lie in the ground within his reach, yet for him, too far. The word "Hazám" (My Homeland), written in the dust with his blood, has been traced with his finger. His shirt is unbuttoned, his unnaturally large eyes turned to the sky. The painting is a naturalistic parallel to the kind of allegorical composition employed by Károly Lotz for his graphic work entitled *Petőfi's Apotheosis*. It does not claim historical accuracy, but offers instead a life-like representation of the poet's last movements before his death.

The painting tells more of the 1860s and 1870s than of 1848 and expresses the artist's passionate concern for the fate of his country.

191. SOMA ORLAI PETRICH
The Poet Petőfi in Debrecen, 1867

Oil on canvas, 121 × 93 cm
Signed bottom right: "Orlai Petrich 867"
Budapest, Hungarian Academy of Sciences

Orlai was related to Sándor Petőfi, and was a close friend of the poet since their school days in the Protestant college of Pápa. He painted several portraits of Petőfi both in his lifetime and after his death, representing him at different stages of his life. This large oil painting from the year of the Compromise with Austria (1867) gives us a vivid impression of how Petőfi passed the winter of 1844 in Debrecen. The painter shows his friend as a young poet living under miserable conditions, at work in an unheated room. All the objects mentioned by the poet in his poems and prose dating from this period have been given a place on Orlai's canvas.

216

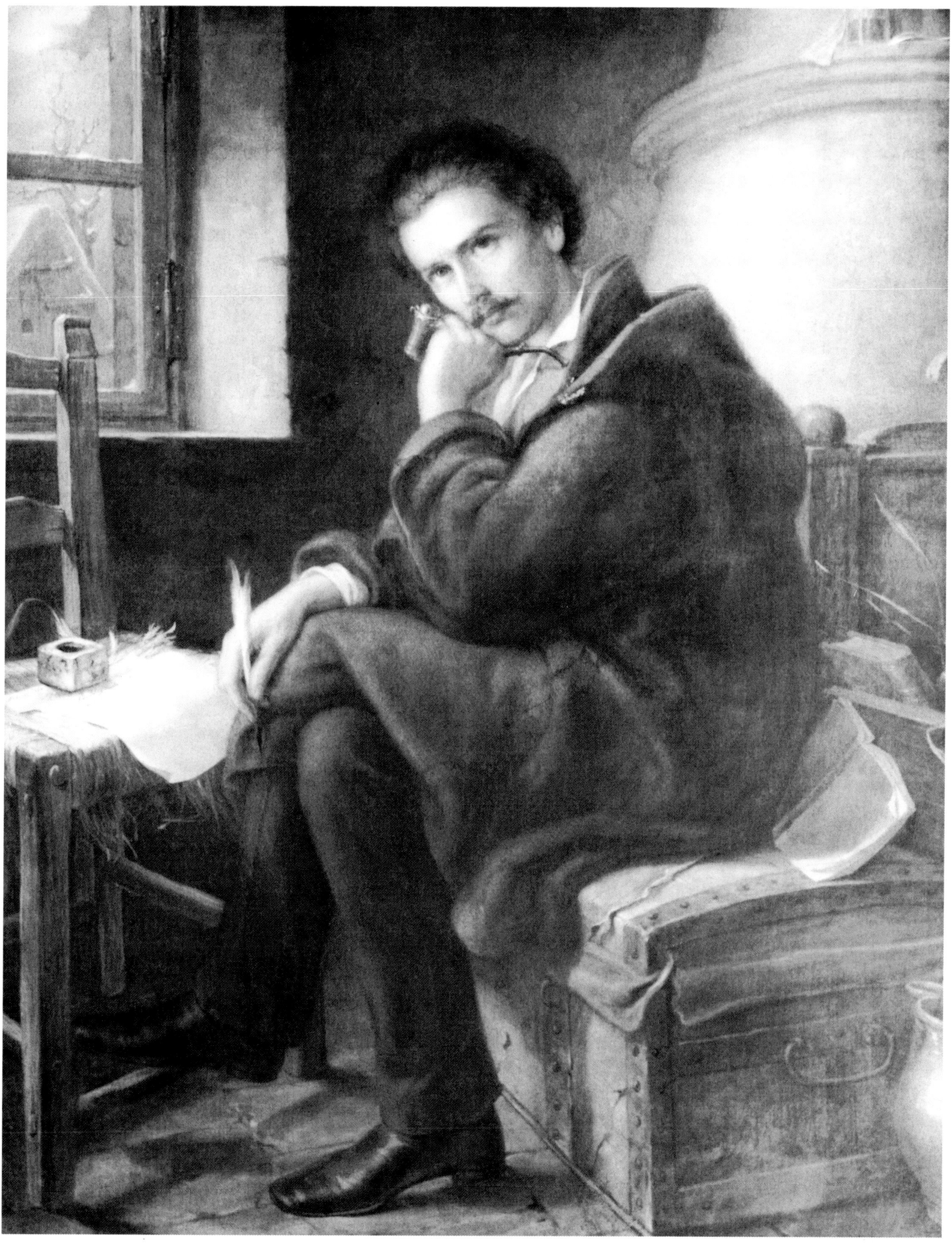

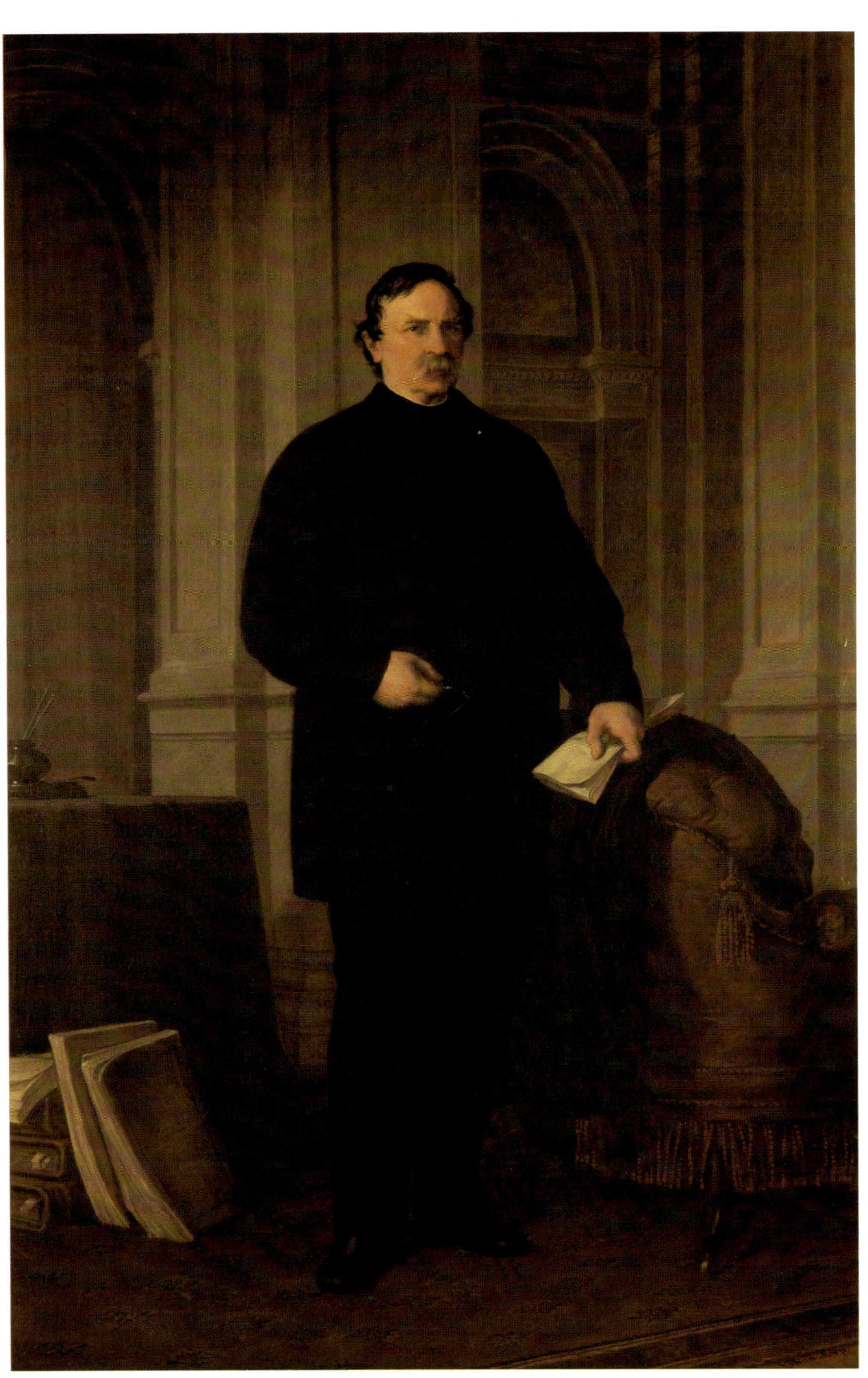

192. MÓR THAN
Portrait of Ferenc Deák, 1870
Oil on canvas, 280×160 cm
Signed bottom right: "Than 1870"
Budapest, Hungarian Academy of Sciences

The portrait of Ferenc Deák as a young man,
painted by Miklós Barabás, was already in
the Academy of Sciences by 1841 (Plate
101). Deák, an eminent political figure in the
history of Hungary, played an important
role as a deputy of Zala County at the time of
Kossuth's imprisonment from 1837 to 1839.
After the 1867 Compromise, for which he
was partially responsible, he became even
more powerful and it seemed appropriate to
commission a full length portrait. It was intended as a companion piece to Amerling's
Széchenyi portrait (Plate 65) and Bertalan
Székely's likeness of József Eötvös. It was to
meet the requirements of the commission
that Mór Than painted the great politician in
an open colonnade dressed in the sober black
clothes of the period.

193. MIKLÓS BARABÁS
Portrait of János Arany, 1884
Oil on canvas, 158×118 cm
Signed: "Barabás 1884"
Budapest, Hungarian Academy of Sciences

János Arany, the great 19th century poet,
made a unique contribution to the cultural
development of his age. He was largely responsible for the revival of the Academy following the defeat of the War of Independence and he was active in the Kisfaludy
Society, an independent literary association.
He taught at the Nagykőrös Grammar
School until 1860, when he moved to Pest.
When elected to the Academy, he made it his
duty to promote the best literary activities in
Hungary. He even edited a review called first
"Szépirodalmi Figyelő" (Literary Observer)
and later "Koszorú" (Wreath). This unpretentious but indefatigable member of the
Academy was also its Secretary General
from 1869.
Barabás, who had made a smaller portrait of
Arany in his lifetime, was commissioned to
paint this full-length likeness two years after
the poet's death. He depicts the poet as the
author of the long epic poem "Toldi", a remarkable example of Realistic–Romantic
Historicism in Hungarian literature. Just like
in his earlier portraits, the careful and detailed rendering of the poet's humble surroundings and the painter's close attention to
face and clothes are typical of the stylistic
means adopted by the painter throughout
most of his career.

194. MÓR ADLER
Allegorical Portrait of Baron József Eötvös in a Still-life Composition (Original title: Apotheosis of Baron József Eötvös), 1872

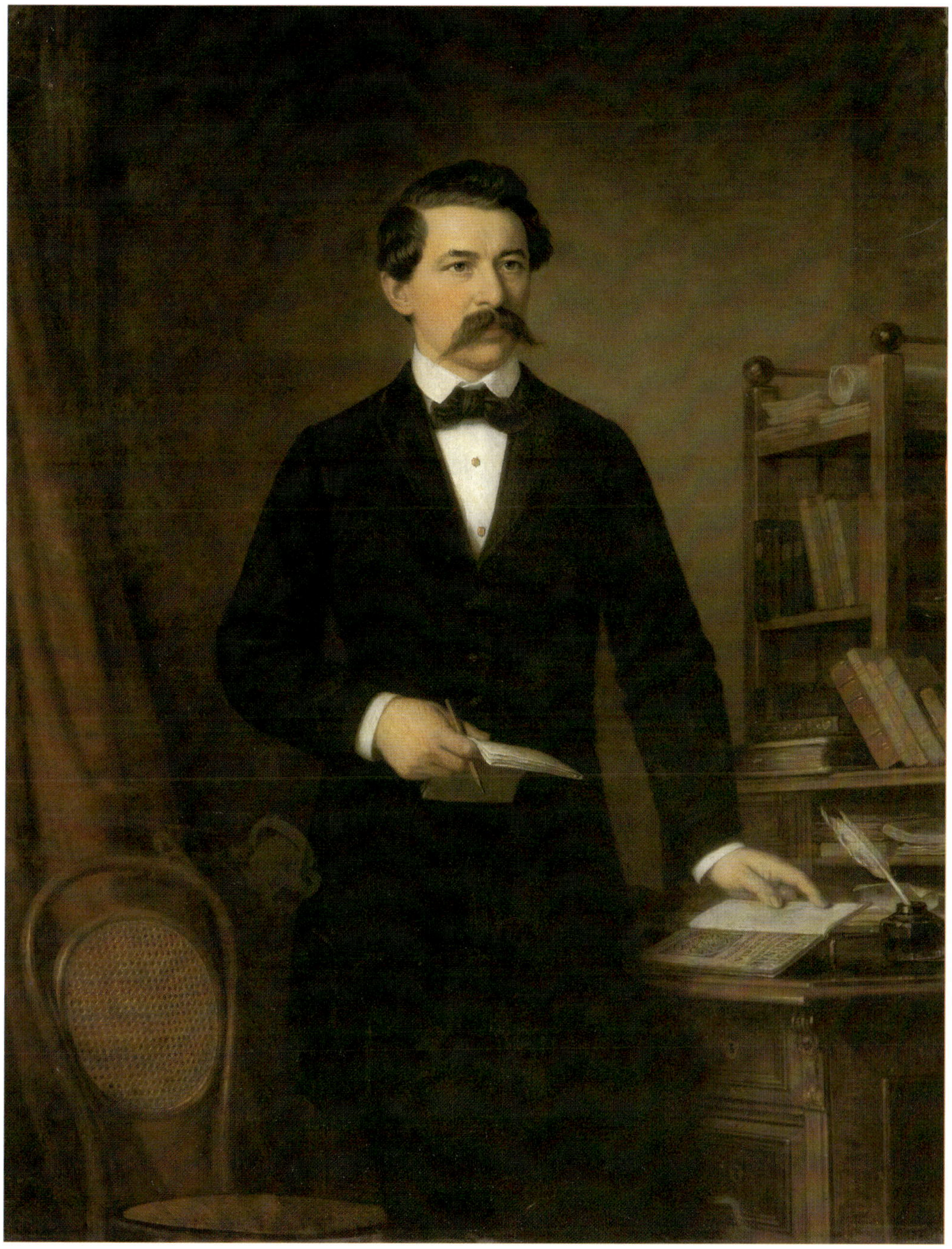

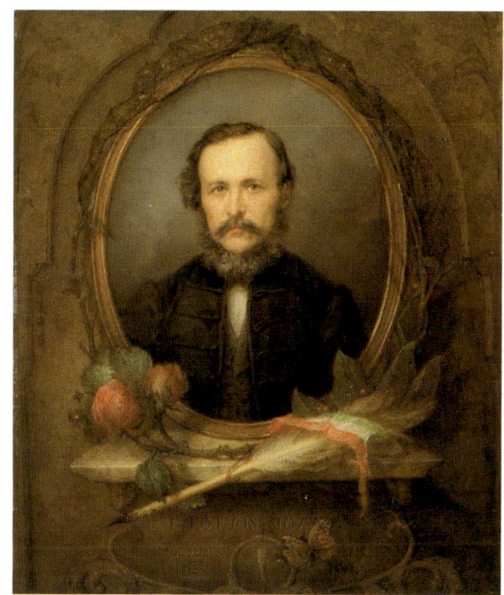

Oil on canvas, 42 × 35.3 cm
Signed left: "Adler Mór fest. 1872" (Painted by Mór Adler in 1872)
Inscription: "B. Eötvös József, szül. szept, 3. 1813 februar 2. 1871" (József B. Eötvös, born Sept. 3, 1813, Feb. 2, 1871)
Budapest, Hungarian National Gallery
Inv. No.: 2811
Purchased in 1890

Eötvös was Minister of Religious Affairs and Education in the Batthyány Government of 1848 and, although he was less active in the later periods of the War of Independence, he contributed greatly to educational reforms. After 1867, as a politician and philosopher, he had a clear insight into the problems of the minorities within the territory of the Austro–Hungarian Empire and created realistic plans to pave the way for a reform towards a democratic monarchy.

In this posthumous painting, József Eötvös's portrait stands on a small marble table decorated with a laurel branch and sprays of roses. The goose-feather quill and the tricolour ribbon in Hungarian colours are symbols of a writer who serves his country. The standing portrait itself shows József Eötvös in the second half of his life. It is not impossible that Mór Adler who also made a replica of this painting, tried to express the tragedy that not all the ideas of this great politician could be put into practice in his lifetime.

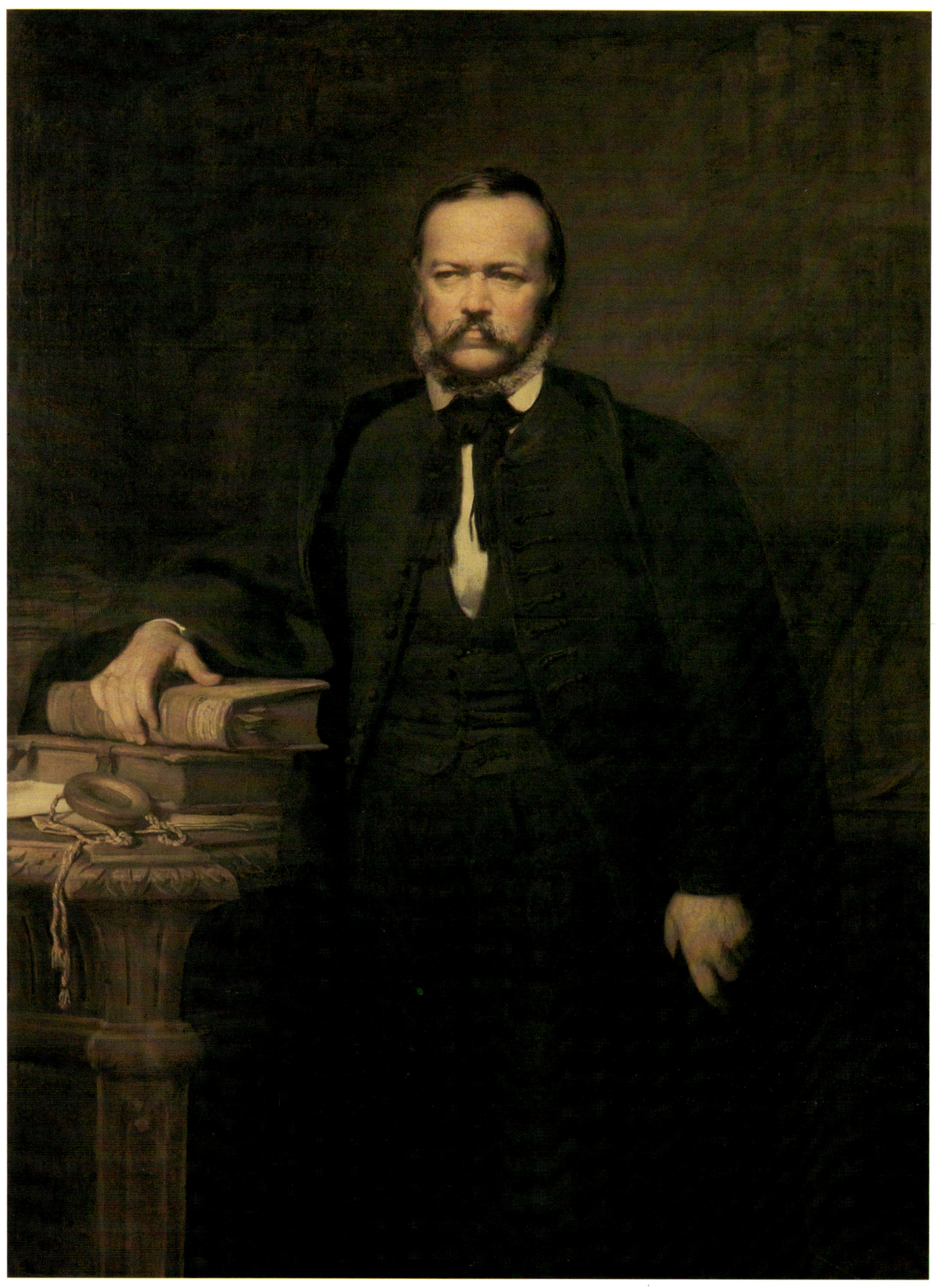

195. BERTALAN SZÉKELY
Portrait of Historian László Szalay, 1864

Oil on canvas, 153×110 cm
Signed bottom right: "Székely"
Budapest, Hungarian Academy of Sciences

In 1848, László Szalay was sent by the Batthyány government to report to the Frankfurt Parliament the state of affairs in Hungary. When, under Austrian pressure, he
was forced to leave, Kossuth sent him for
support to London where he was no more
successful than in Frankfurt. After the defeat
of the War of Independence, he lived in exile
until 1855 when he returned home to engage
in scientific work and to write the history of
Hungary. From 1861–1864 he was Secretary
of the Academy. It was his ambition to
transform the Academy into a modern
scientific institution. He made a name for
himself among historians by publishing
a work on historical sources, and a standard
history of Hungary. He started work on his
book while in exile and the first volume was
published in Leipzig, but he died after completing his account of the years up to Rákóczi's War of Independence (1703–1711).
This portrait, by Bertalan Székely, painted
after Szalay's death, shows the politician at
work in his study. The face is represented
after a half-length likeness painted by Mihály
Kovács some years earlier for the Academy
of Sciences.

196. BERTALAN SZÉKELY
Self-portrait, 1860

Oil on canvas, 60×47.5 cm
Unsigned
Budapest, Hungarian National Gallery
Inv. No.: 7588

This self-portrait, completed when the
painter was in Munich, is a self-examination
after ten long years of study. He gives us no
flattering image of himself, nor the customary attributes of a painter, such as brush,
palette or canvas. Rather, he aims at objectivity, analyzing himself as if observing and
painting someone else. For Székely, painting
and drawing had to reflect reality more accurately than mere photography, for which he
had little regard. Furthermore, he believed
that the essence of painting consisted in precise drawing and careful application of light
and shade rather than an immediate translation of vivid colour effects.

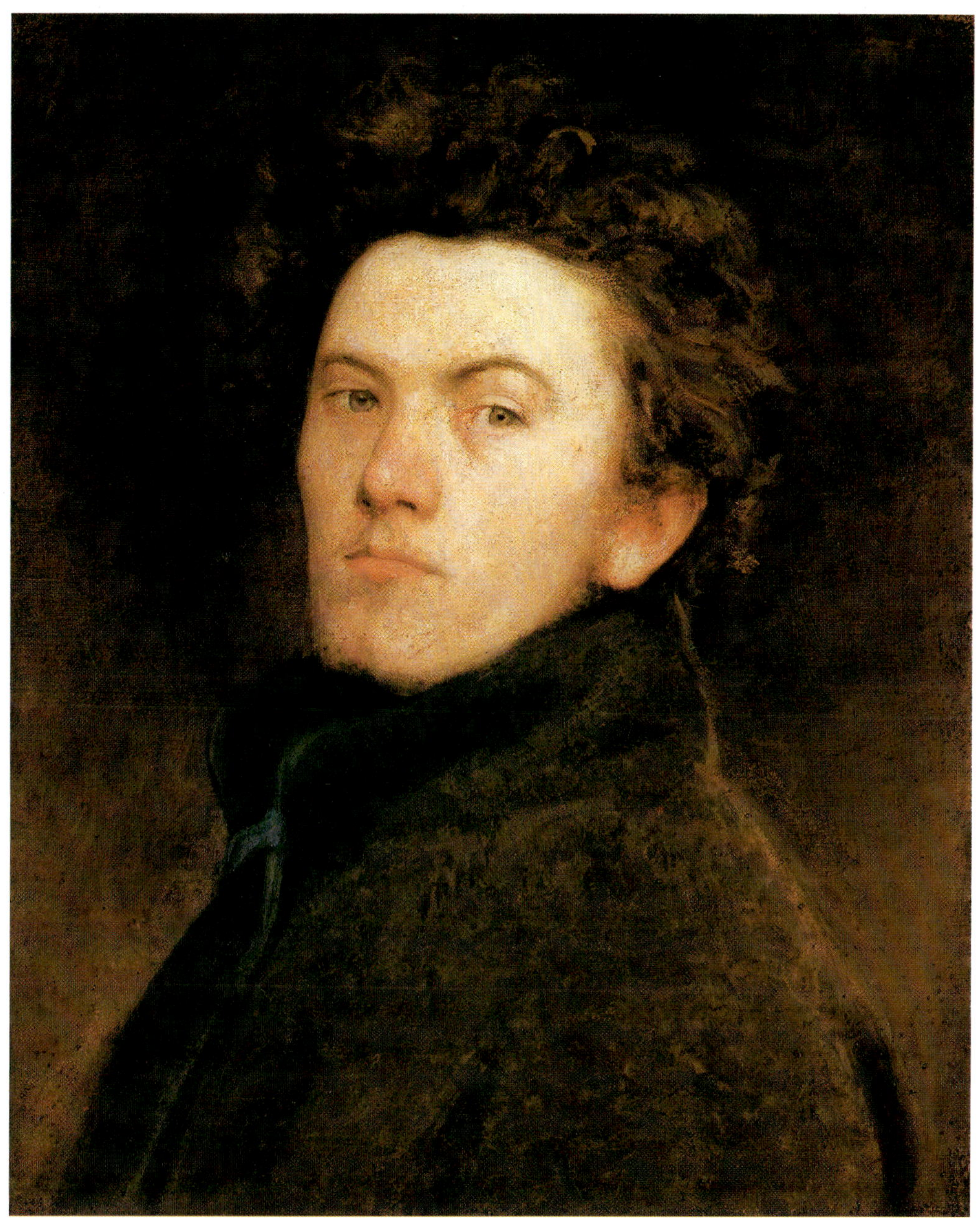

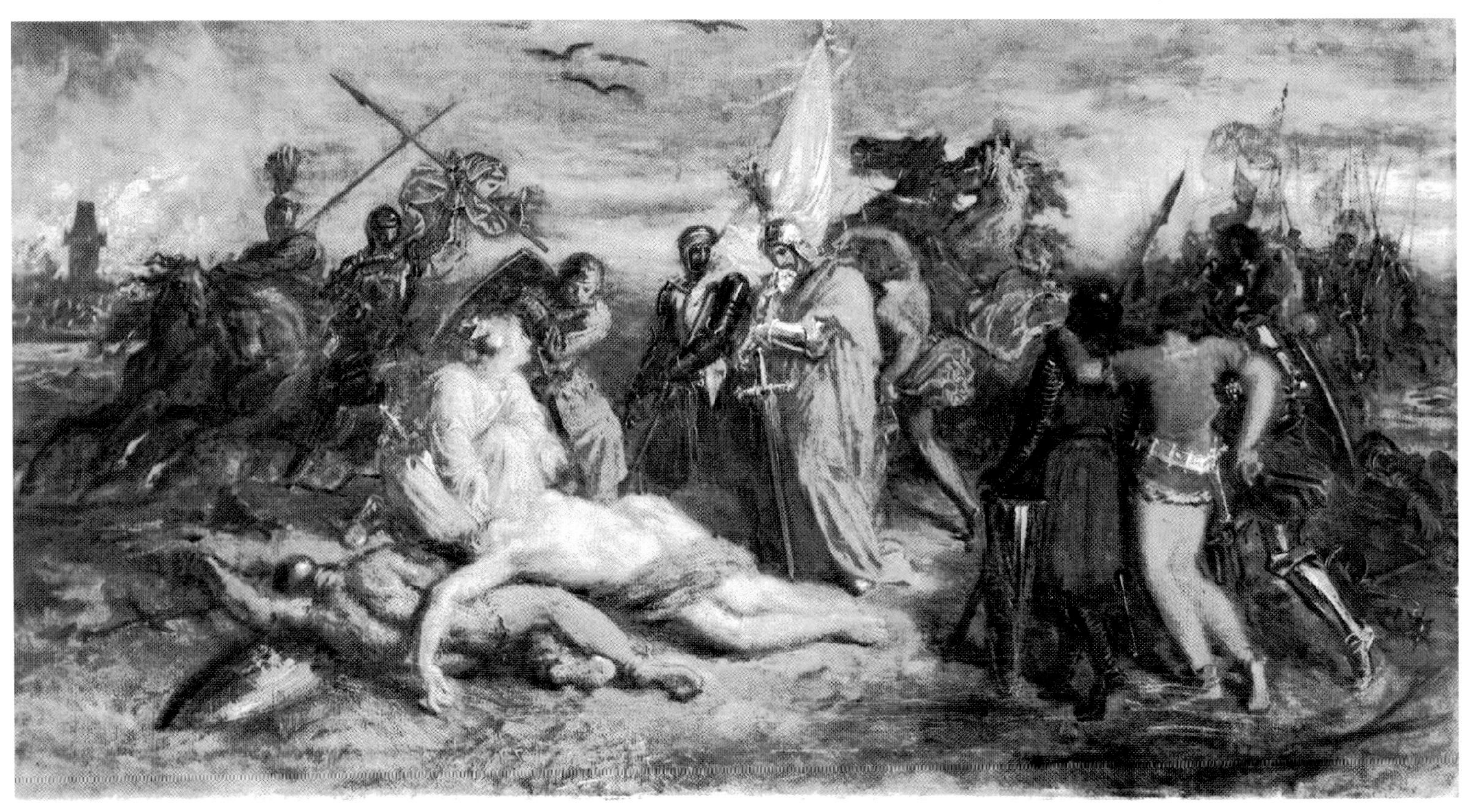

197. ANTON ROMAKO
Prince Rudolf of Habsburg Contemplating the Body of Ottocar Přemysl, 1855

Oil on canvas, 40 × 72 cm
Unsigned
Vienna, Österreichische Galerie
Inv. No.: 4425

Rudolf Habsburg led his army into battle against Ottocar Přemysl and his troops on the 26th August, 1278, at Morvamező (Dürnkrut, Marschfield, Austria). He was supported by Ladislas IV, the "Cumanian", king of Hungary and his troops, while Moravian and Silesian soldiers supported Ottocar Přemysl. It was a long and heroic struggle which ended when Ottocar was captured. In the end he was killed by one of his personal enemies, his body plundered and left on the battle-field. Rudolf Habsburg showed his respect for a valiant enemy by ordering the body to be conveyed to Vienna and at Easter in the following year he allowed it to be returned to Ottocar's widow, Kunigunda.

In this small painting, the young Anton Romako depicts both the final moments of the battle and the events following it. Our attention is drawn to the figure in the centre ground of the painting: Ottocar's plundered body and the kneeling figure of a young woman, probably his wife. She makes an imploring gesture towards the helmeted Rudolf, who stands visibly moved, leaning on his upright sword above the body of his former enemy.

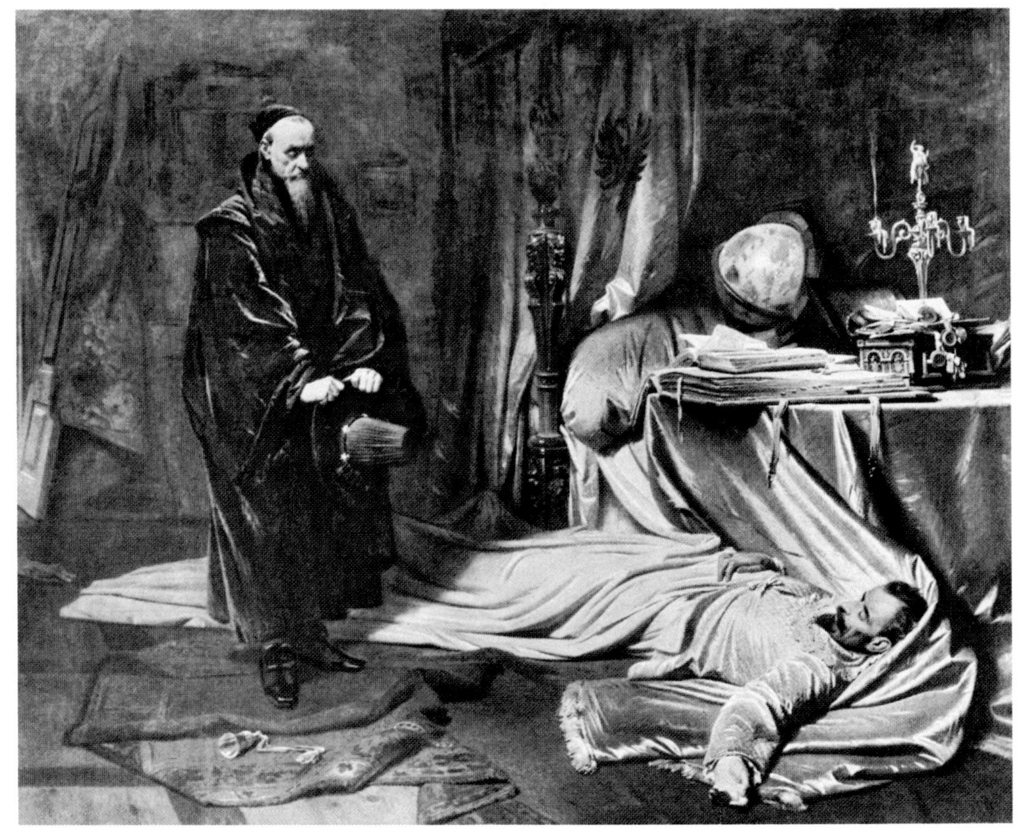

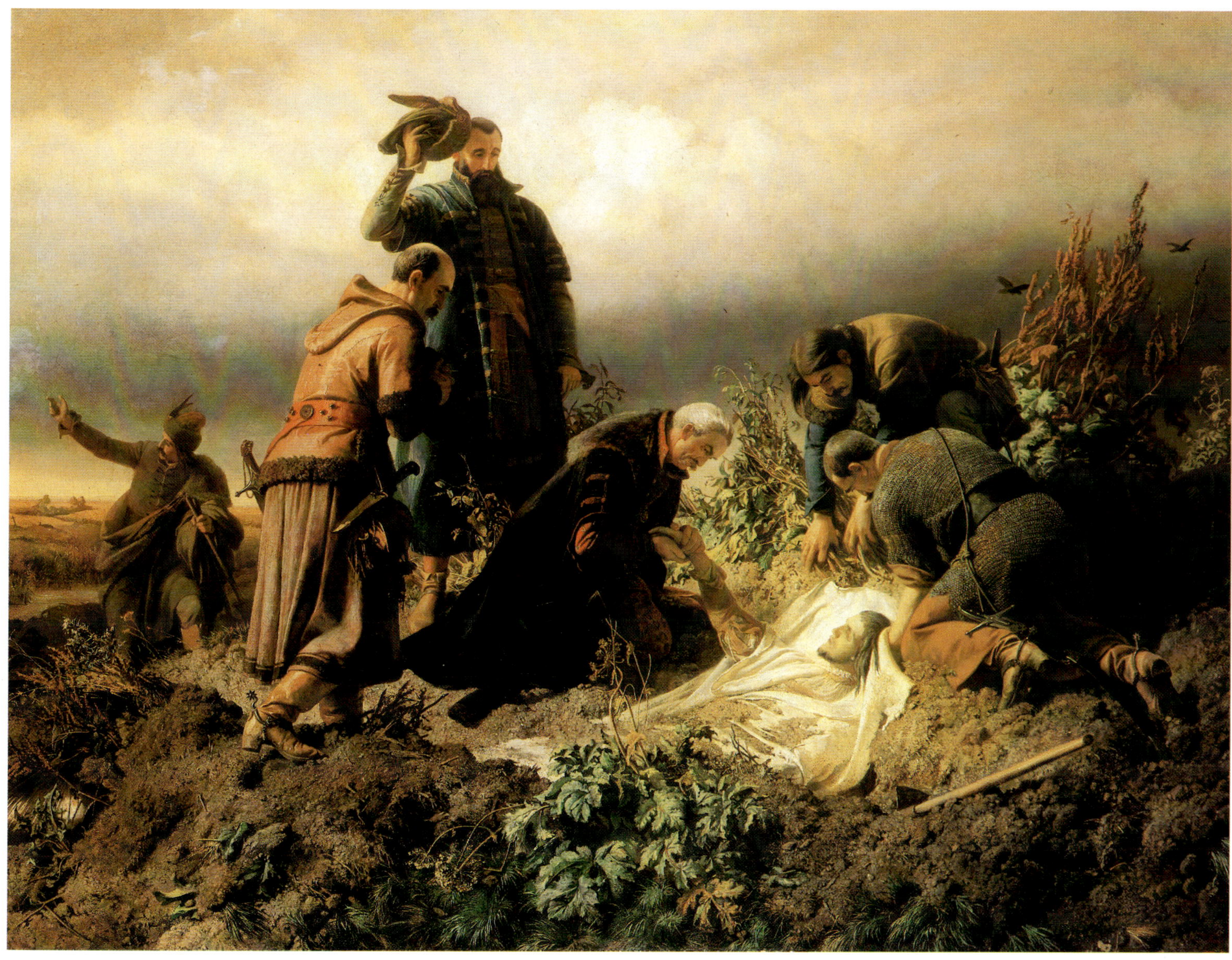

198. CARL THEODOR VON PILOTY
Giovanni Baptista Seni Standing by Wallenstein's Body, 1855
Oil on canvas, 365×411 cm
Unsigned
Munich, Neue Pinakothek
Inv. No.: WAF 770

Von Piloty uses the description of the scene from Schiller's tragedy as a basis for this portrait of the great military leader of the Thirty Years' War.

Wallenstein's corpse lies stretched out on the ground, the head resting in the folds of a sumptuous cloth. On the table is a globe with the signs of the zodiac, a candelabrum with the figure of Fortuna and two smouldering candles. These details do not, however, divert our attention from the two main figures of the composition, the lifeless body lying on the cloth and his friend, the old astrologer, who stands, visibly moved, gripping the broad brim of his hat.

199. BERTALAN SZÉKELY
The Discovery of the Body of King Louis the Second (Original title: King Louis II in the River Csele), 1860
Oil on canvas, 140×181.5 cm
Unsigned
Budapest, Hungarian National Gallery
Inv. No.: 2807

Székely made numerous sketches and studies in preparation for this fine large oil painting, which he intended for the National Art Gallery, as revealed in a letter to József Eötvös in 1862. It portrays the dramatic moment when the young king's body was discovered and the spontaneous tribute accorded him by men of all ranks as the body was lifted out of the river. Székely's aim in representing the dead king was to avoid both excessive sentimentality and excessive realism. He limits his description to an idealized rendering of the pale young face and the white silken shroud—unlike earlier compositions on this theme where the body is lifted naked out of an improvised grave. He also omits the lamenting women of the earlier composition by Orlai (Plate 142). The characters display great reserve—three noblemen, dressed simply but in accordance with their social status and three humble men, two of whom are helping to lift the body out of the grave, while the third calls to the following escort. Rich and realistic detail characterizes the foreground vegetation and displaced soil.

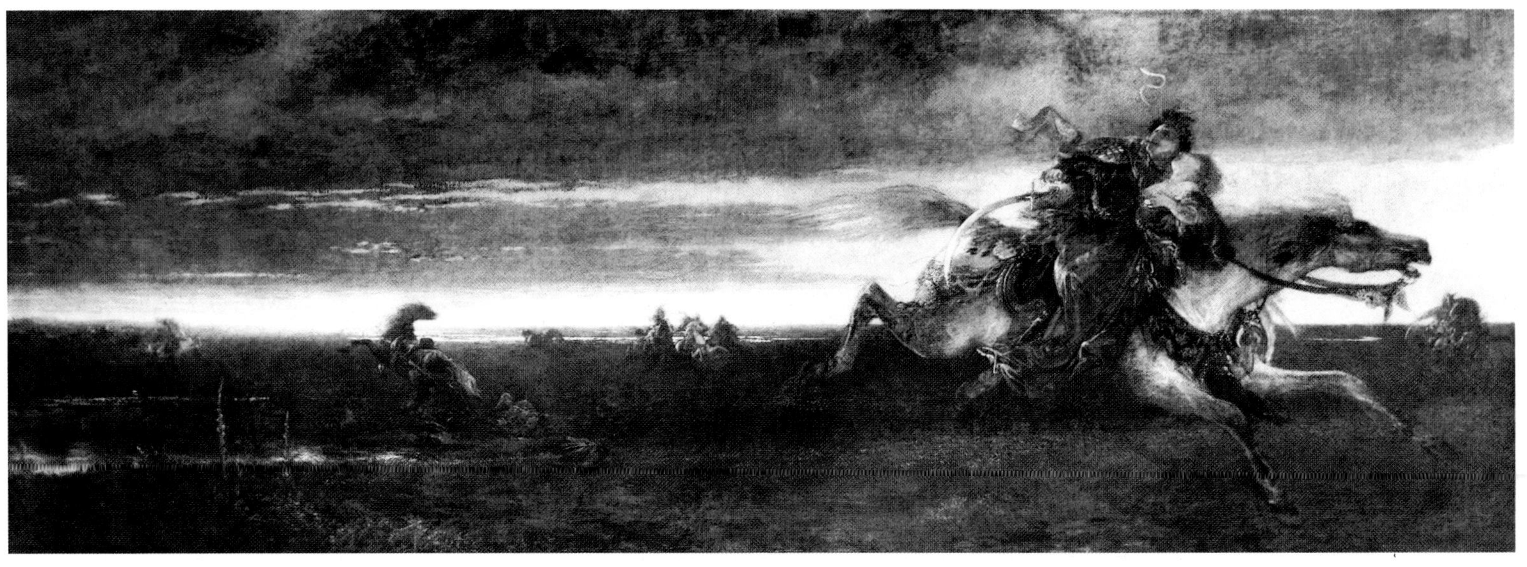

200. VIKTOR MADARÁSZ
Dobozi, 1868
Oil on canvas, 112×308 cm
Signed bottom left: "Madarász Viktor"
Budapest, Hungarian National Gallery
Inv. No.: 59.153 T

The style of this painting based on a popular theme reflects the influence of Delacroix and the French Romantics. Madarász chose this subject from Hungarian history, one much favoured in the 1830s, where escape and pursuit provide dramatic intensity, but his work is less naive than its forerunners. The composition covers a bold rectangular plane. The movement of Dobozi and his pursuers is echoed by the reddish-yellow clouds and the swirling dust of the plain. Particularly remarkable is the representation of the magnificent fleeing horse, a masterly execution testifying to the painter's knowledge of Delacroix's portrayal of horses in action.

201. BERTALAN SZÉKELY
Dobozi and His Spouse, c. 1860
Water-colour on paper, pencil, 137×169 cm
Unsigned
Budapest, Hungarian National Gallery
Inv. No.: 1954–5210

When Bertalan Székely conceived his composition on the Dobozi theme, he first fixed the main outlines in this rough sketch dated 1860. He then made a number of water-colour and sepia drawings of each section of the composition, defining these areas or "groupings" according to colour effect. In this dramatic colour sketch, the centre of interest is the embracing couple, their moral courage being, in Székely's eyes, the essence of the theme. The dark cloud moving towards them from the left upper corner symbolizes their imminent fate.

202. BERTALAN SZÉKELY
Dobozi and His Spouse, 1861
Oil on canvas, 133×155 cm
Unsigned
Budapest, Hungarian National Gallery
Inv. No.: 2757
Presented by the Women of Székesfehérvár to the National Museum in 1862

After making numerous preliminary drawings and colour sketches, striving for perfection in each detail, Székely eventually composed this large oil painting. He depicted Dobozi and his wife as idealized hero and heroine of the Roman type. This conception was, in fact not unlike the customary representation of them in historical sources and in literature. As in double portraits painted in the early years of the 19th century, the lines and colours of the two figures merge, forming a harmonious unit. Thus the viewer feels the strength of character of both husband and wife,—a unity of purpose not to be demonstrated in the devotion of a lifetime as in the case of Mihály Mosonyi and his wife in the painting by Henrik Weber (Plate 127). Here, the decision is to die together.

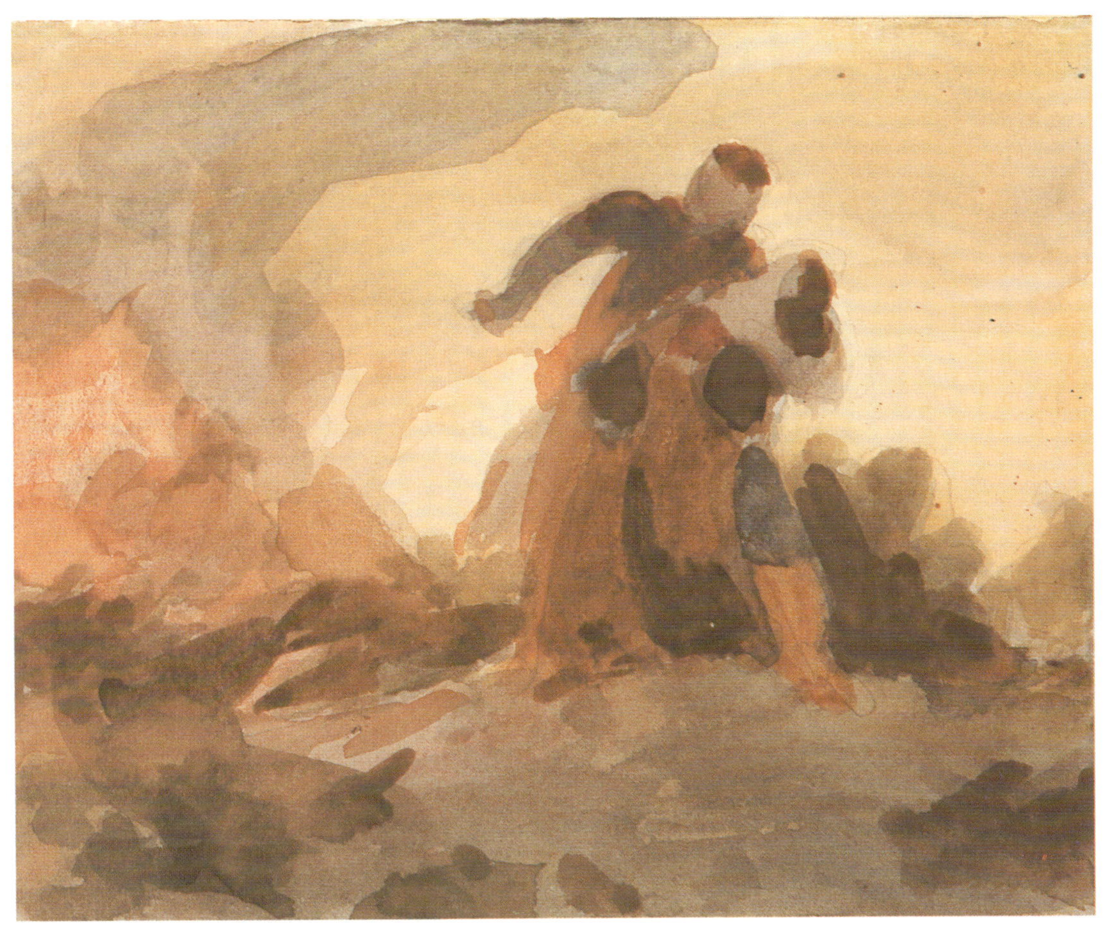

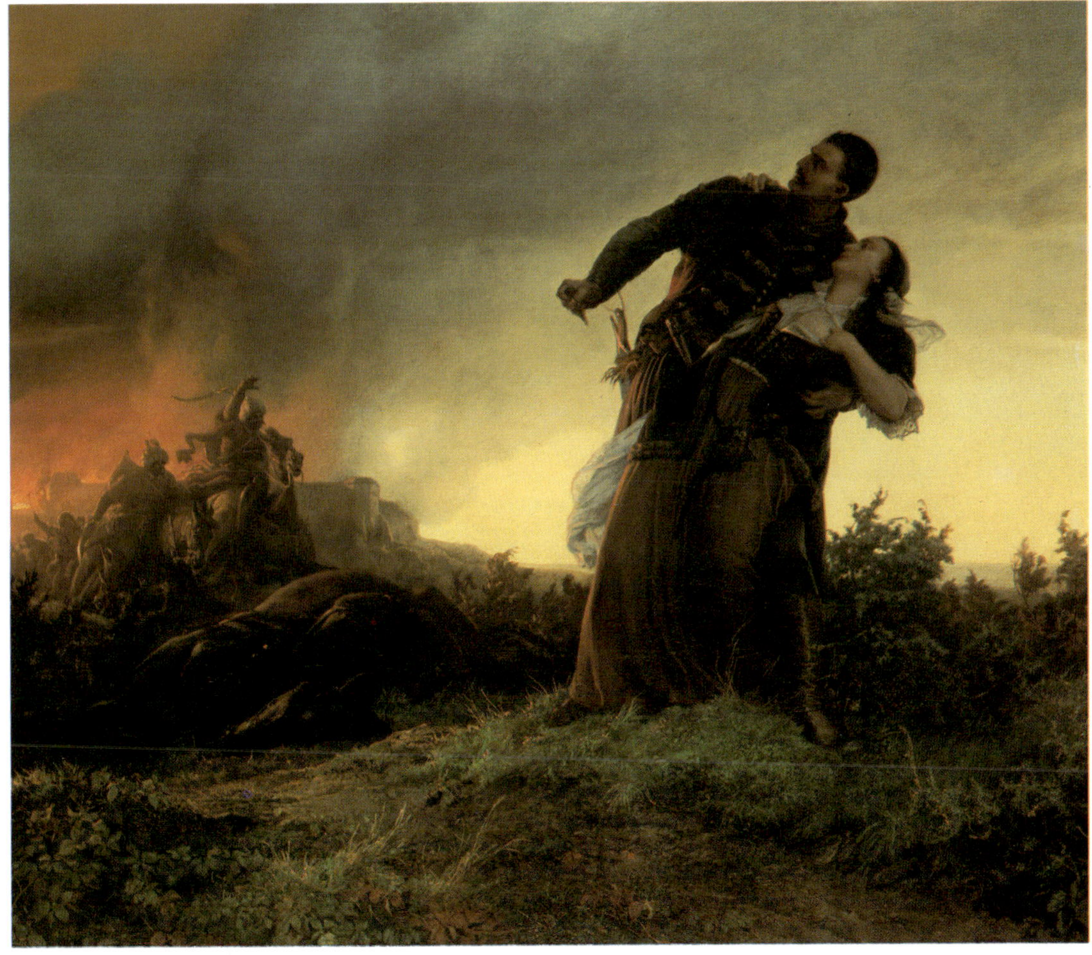

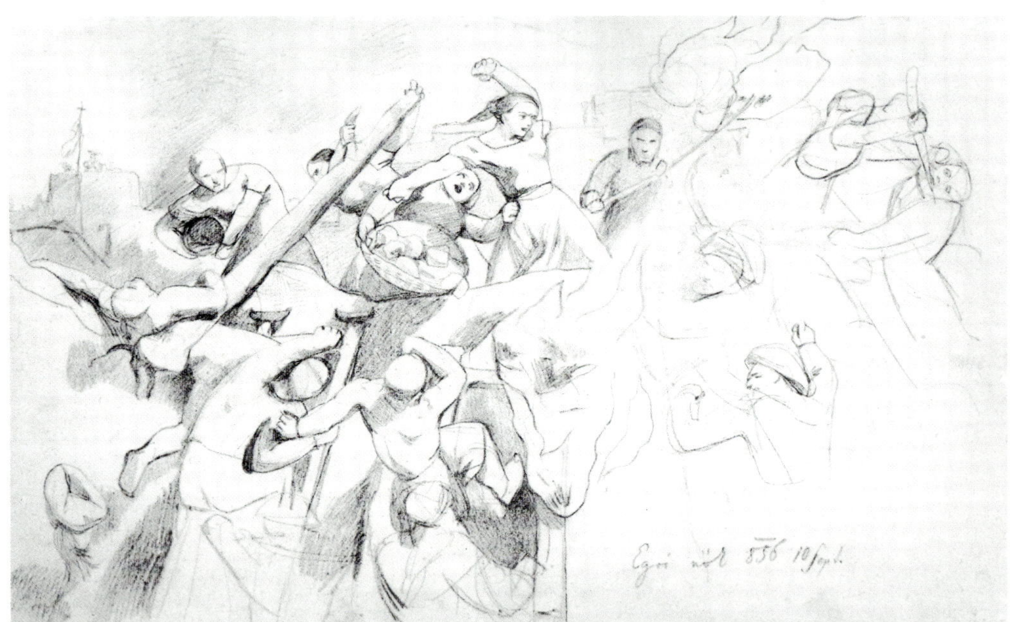

203. BERTALAN SZÉKELY
The Women of Eger, 1856
Pencil on paper, 223 × 198 mm
Inscription bottom right:
"Egri nők 856. 10. sept."
(Women of Eger 1856, 10. Sept.)
Budapest, Hungarian National Gallery
Inv. No.: 1967–351

This small sketch shows that Székely was already interested in the story of the legendary heroines of the Turkish–Hungarian wars ten years before he actually composed an oil painting of it. He may have been inspired by scenes of resistance to the Turks painted by Karl von Blaas and Johann Till.

204. BERTALAN SZÉKELY
The Women of Eger, 1861
Sepia on paper, 252 × 213 mm
Signed top right: "1861. Nov."
Budapest, Hungarian National Gallery
Inv. No.: 1917–362

By 1861 Székely finalized the vertical composition of his work. In this sepia sketch a fortification interrupts the castle wall from the top of which a flag is flying. In the midst of the fighting, a monumental female figure is depicted as she raises her sword to slay a giant Turk, while with her left arm she continues to support her wounded husband.

205. BERTALAN SZÉKELY
The Women of Eger, 1866–67
Oil on wood, 42.5 × 33 cm
Unsigned
Budapest, Hungarian National Gallery
Inv. No.: FK 4929

The heroine of this colour sketch is brought into relief by means of colour applied by broad brush strokes. The woman's posture gives the impression of rhythmic dancing as she thrusts her sword towards her victim, who falls backwards. Her posture dominates the whole composition. The same rhythm prevails in the arrangement of ladders and the figures of the Turks attempting to climb them. To achieve this rhythm, the artist made several preliminary sketches.

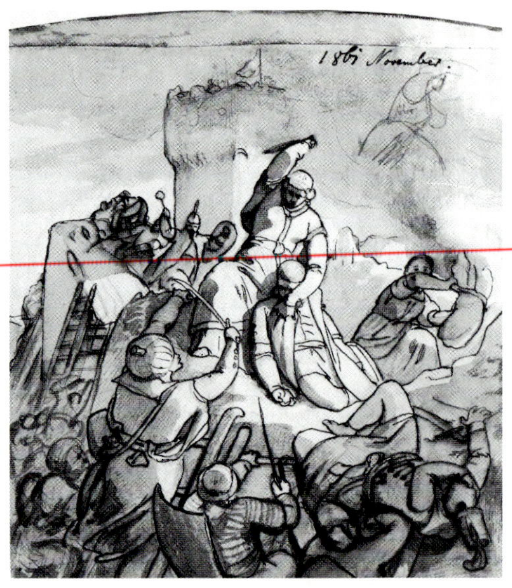

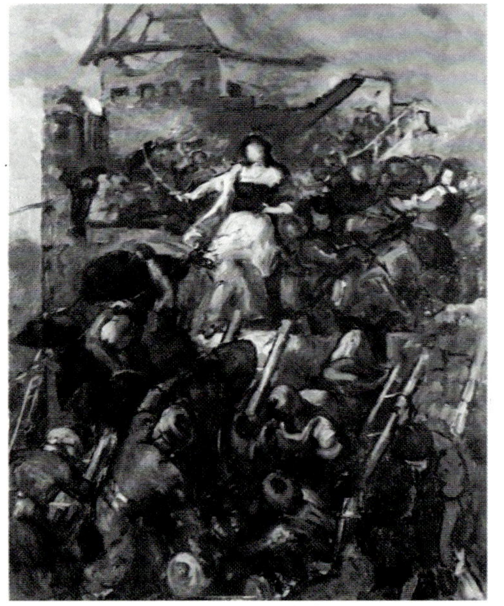

206. BERTALAN SZÉKELY
The Women of Eger, 1867
Oil on canvas, 226.5 × 176.5 cm
Unsigned
Budapest, Hungarian National Gallery
Inv. No.: 2795

By the time he made the final large oil painting, Székely's historical composition had become almost a votive offering. The scene of the most exciting moment of the siege has been worked out to the last detail. Yet the emphasis remains on the idealized figure of the chief of the women, depicted fighting with a tenacity expressed in her solemn expression and the tautness of her muscles. The wall of the fortress is laid open to the enemy, and only three women continue the defence. Beside the monumental female figure in the centre supporting her wounded husband, two other women are seen on the wall, one resolutely charging the enemy, the other, rather frightened, holding a basket full of stones. As the first line of Turks fall back defeated, the second line scramble up the ladders. It is the climax of the drama that Székely deliberately chose to depict—the moment when the outcome is still uncertain. Yet the rather grotesque features and purposeful attitudes of the women of Eger leave no doubt that they are activated by a passionate belief in their own cause.

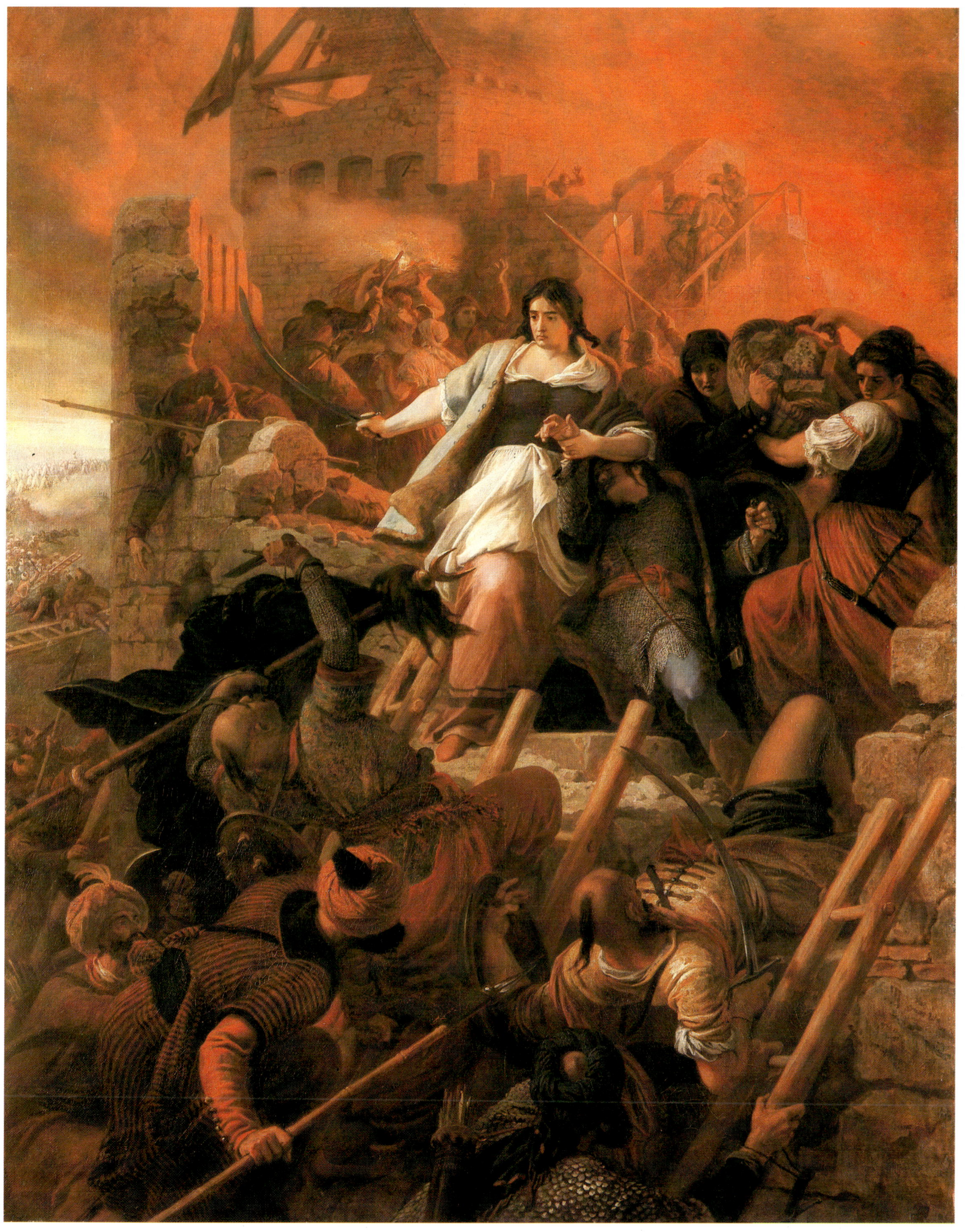

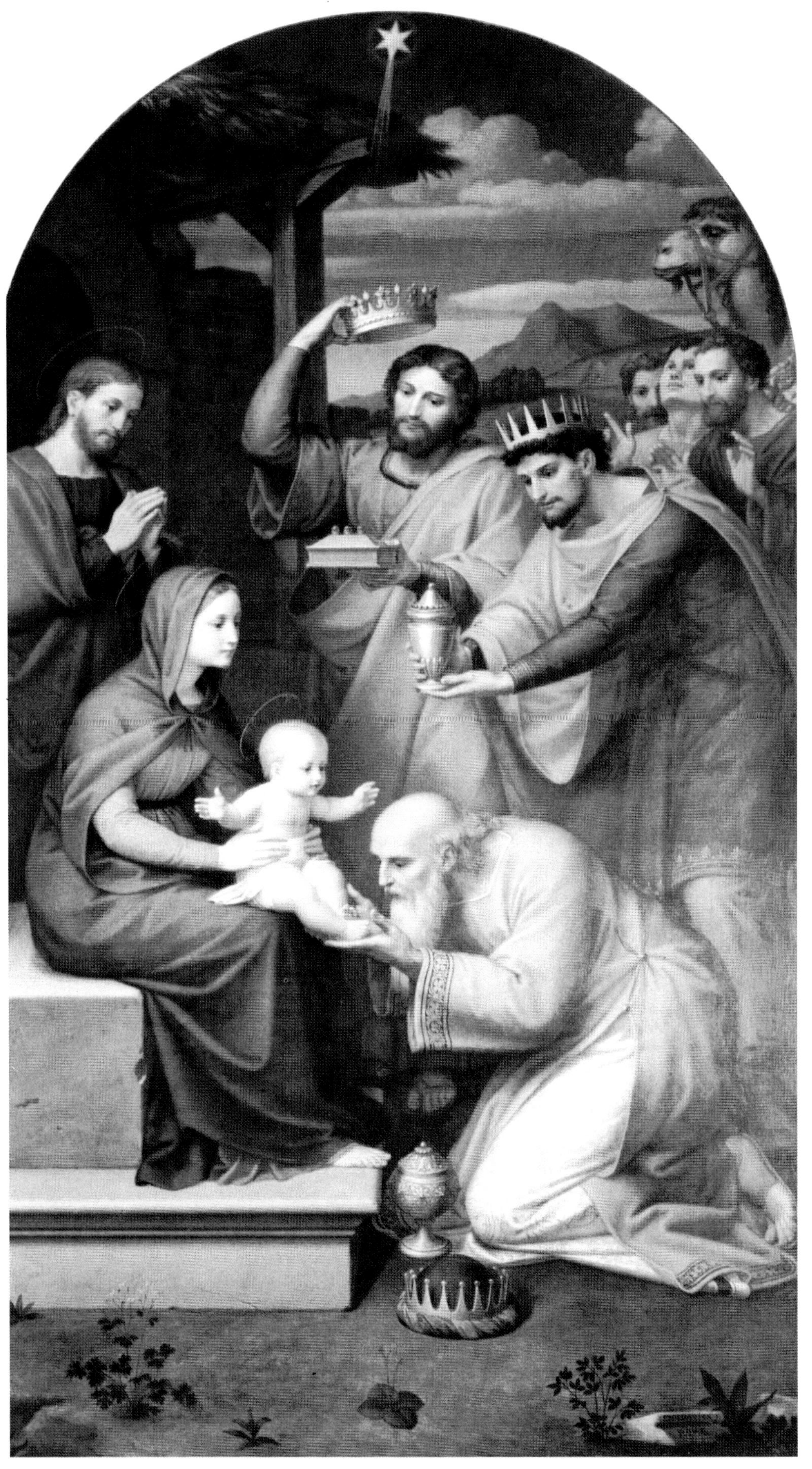

207. FERENC SZOLDATICS
Adoration of the Magi, 1868
Oil on canvas, 210×114 cm
Signed bottom right: "Szoldatics F Romae
1868"
Esztergom, The Archbishop's Office

Szoldatics was a pupil of Joseph Führich
and Leopold Kupelwieser at the Vienna
Academy. In 1853 he entered a religious order in Rome. He seldom accepted commissions from Hungary, but his altar-pieces,
though few in number, are all notable.
Szoldatics's treatment of the subject is traditional. The Virgin Mary, reminiscent of
a Madonna by Raphael or Perugino, is
shown seated on a finely hewn stone block;
Joseph, his hands folded in prayer, stands in
adoration of the Infant who receives the
homage of the Magi with open arms and
a lively expression of interest. The kneeling
sage has removed his crown and the others
press forward to present their offerings.
Above the heads of their followers, in the
background, a camel's head can be seen. The
work evokes the atmosphere of a fairy tale,
yet the drawing is of academic excellence, as
is the smooth, careful application of the colours.

208. BERTALAN SZÉKELY
**Christ Walking on the Water ("O thou
of little Faith where fore didst thou
doubt?"), c. 1864**
*Copy of the Altar-piece in the Protestant
Church of Modor*
Water-colour on cardboard, 37×24 cm
(the upper edge curved in an arch)
Unsigned
Hungary, private collection

This small, delicate water-colour sketch
shows with what meticulous care Székely
handled all his motifs, religious or otherwise. In the water-colour sketch Christ
seems to walk on the water like an apparition, light, ethereal, almost floating,
a miraculous feat which convinces even the
doubting Peter, who is nearly sinking.
In its delicate colours, the precision of the
drawing and the interplay of light and shade
in the translucent blues, violets and whites
which combine to create a harmonious masterpiece, there is something reminiscent of
Viennese models. In the altar-piece itself,
Székely, instead of preserving this visionary
quality chose to create a more dramatic representation: the storm seems to be more
menacing with St. Peter in greater danger of
being drowned by the waves and even
Christ's gesture, leaning towards Peter,
seems less ethereal and more powerful. This
different treatment removes some of the
miracle from the incident and renders it
more human.

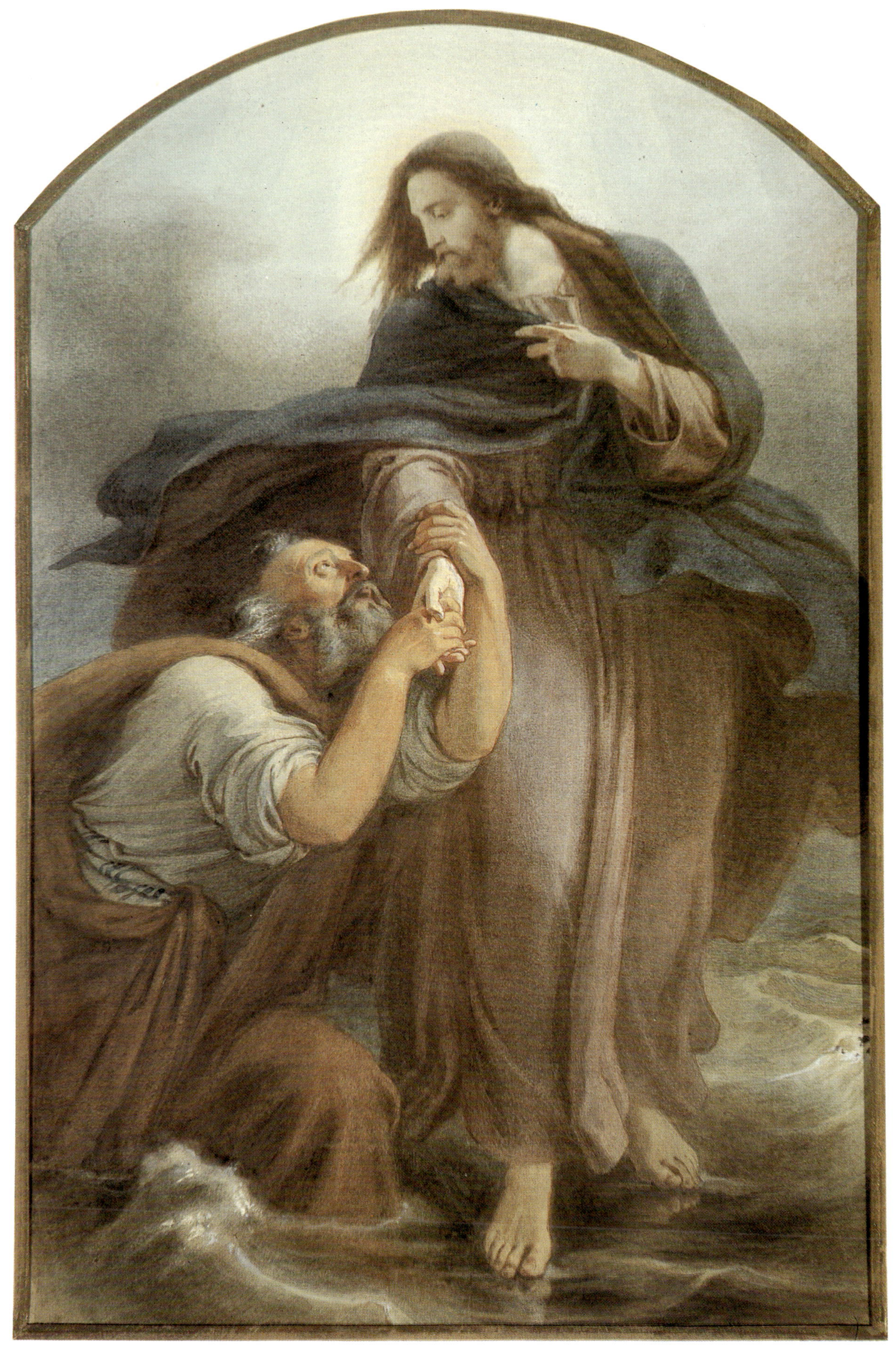

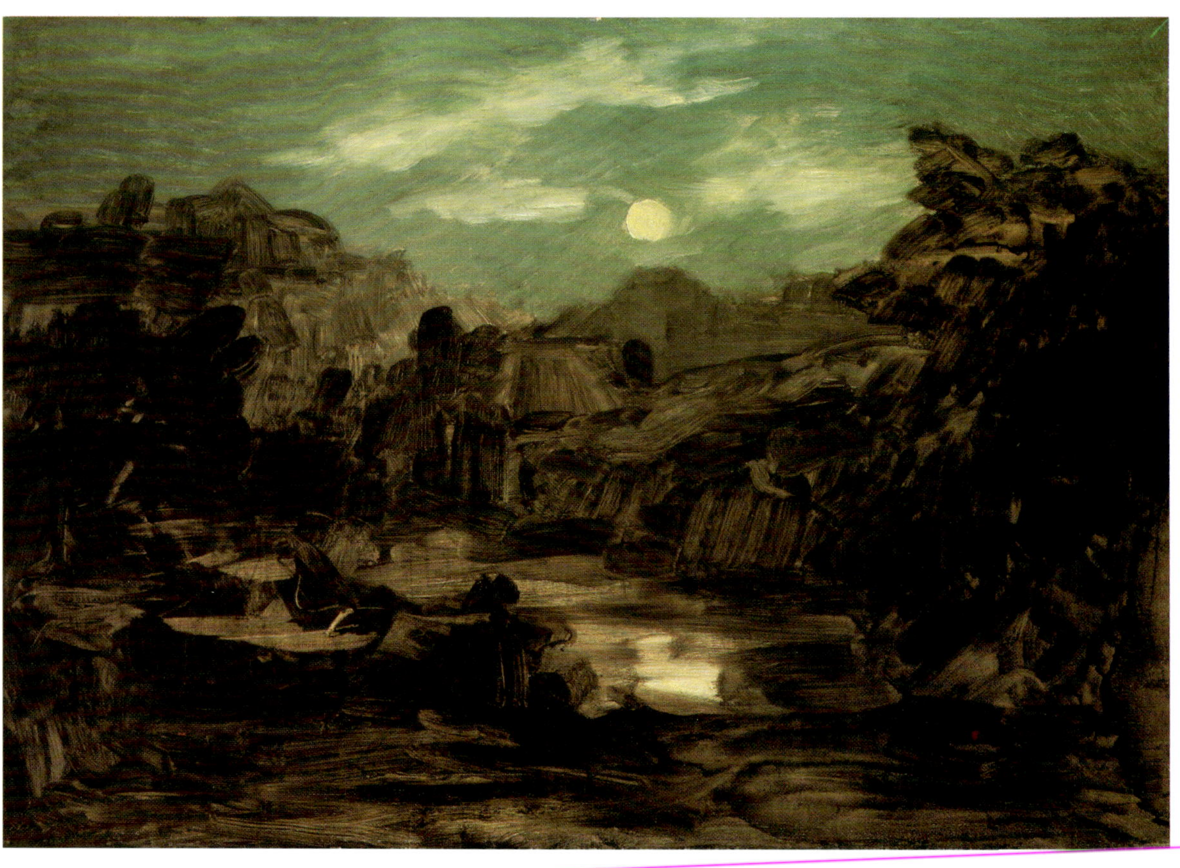

209. BERTALAN SZÉKELY
Landscape (sketch), 1840s
Oil on canvas, 66 × 95 cm
Unsigned
Budapest, Hungarian National Gallery
Inv. No.: FK 4242

At the beginning of his career Bertalan Székely usually chose landscape backgrounds to reinforce the message of his paintings. He tried out every means and technique with which to depict a landscape, but only a few of his early works can qualify as descriptive or topographical. He did not concern himself with abstractions resulting from a keen observation of nature, nor did he aim at precise and objective representation of observed details. What mattered to him was to create the appropriate mood for his chosen subject by means of carefully grouped landscape elements. Yet in his less formal landscape compositions, dramatic and romantic elements are introduced in a more direct style than is generally found in academic landscape backgrounds.

Székely's individual approach to landscape can be observed in his series of brush drawings and oil sketches depicting the effect of light at different times of day and in different seasons. This concern dominates especially the pure landscape paintings dating from the later years of his career.

210. BERTALAN SZÉKELY
The Dancer, 1875
Oil on canvas, 61 × 51.5 cm
Signed upper right: "Székely B."
Budapest, Hungarian National Gallery
Inv. No.: 55.312

In his *Ladislas V and Ulrik Cillei* (Plate 211) Székely represented beautiful girls dancing before the king. Here again he represents a dancer, this time in contemporary attire. Although it is a colour sketch, Székely signed it, proof that he thought enough of it to want to exhibit or sell it.

According to Zsuzsa Bakó, Székely's monographer, this work was one of a series called *The Lives of Women*. She supposes it to represent a woman of doubtful morals, resigned to her fate, albeit regretfully. In his study of "Hungarian masterpieces" (Magyar mestermüvek), the art historian Elek Petrovics affirms that the mature final version of this sketch is one of Székely's finest works. It was produced after numerous colour sketches; when Petrovics pronounced his verdict, it was in a private collection.

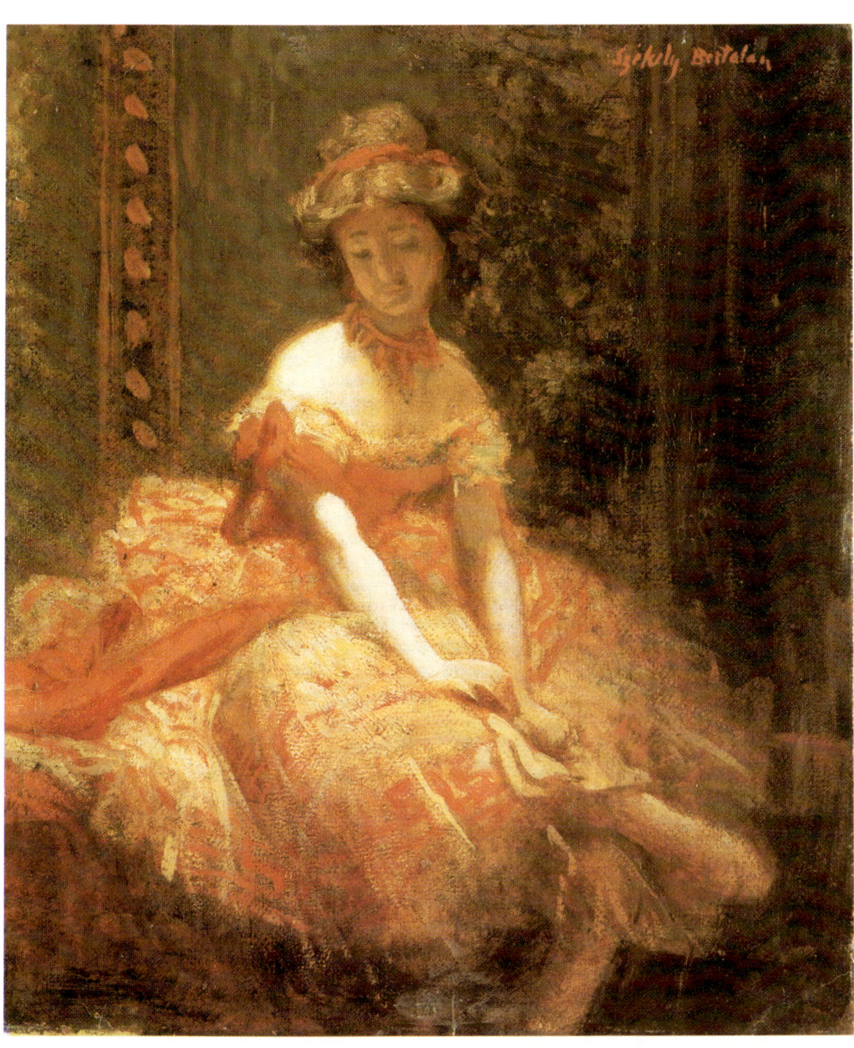

211. BERTALAN SZÉKELY
Ladislas V and Ulrik Cillei, 1867(?), or 1870–1875

Oil on canvas, 123 × 222 cm
Unsigned
Budapest, Hungarian National Gallery
Inv. No.: 2796

Székely's biographers date this painting from 1870–1875, though the first sketch for it was made in 1861, and therefore it was created no later than 1867. In the sketch Ladislas V, the youthful King of Hungary is depicted in a reclining pose, holding out his cup to be refilled with wine as he watches the dancers. (He is the same person who later sentenced the young László Hunyadi to death.) The young king is represented as ignoring the fate of his country. He relaxes in sensual contemplation of the dancers and listens to the music as his evil counsellor, Ulrik Cillei, a well-known figure from Ferenc Erkel's opera "László Hunyadi", entices him by suggesting vicious crimes against his country.

The portraits of former kings, hanging on the wall seem to register stern disapproval. The King's jester alone expresses in his attitude a suitable apprehension of danger.

It is an arresting scene, the dominant red tones, heightening the beauty of the moment and projecting the sense of underlying menace.

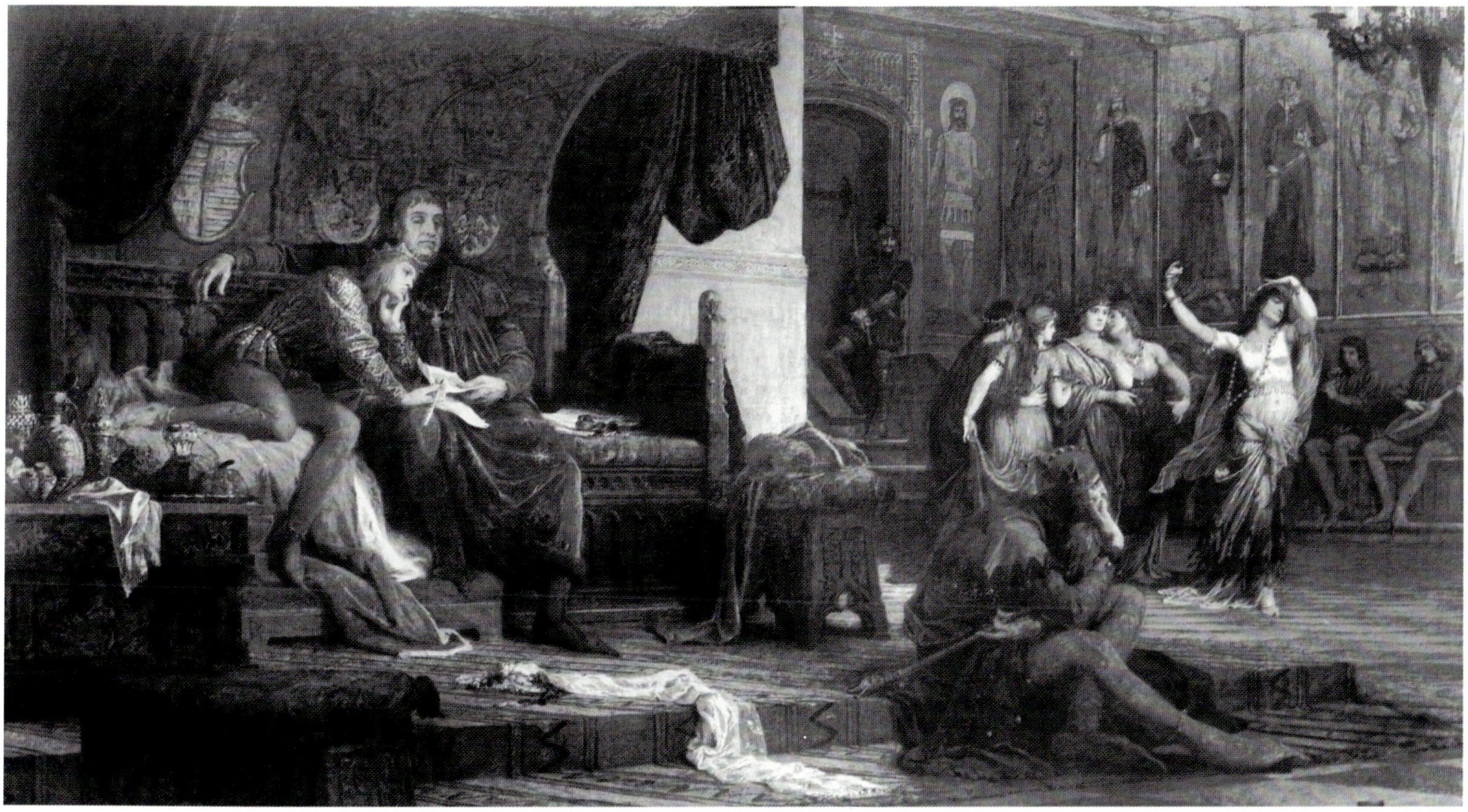

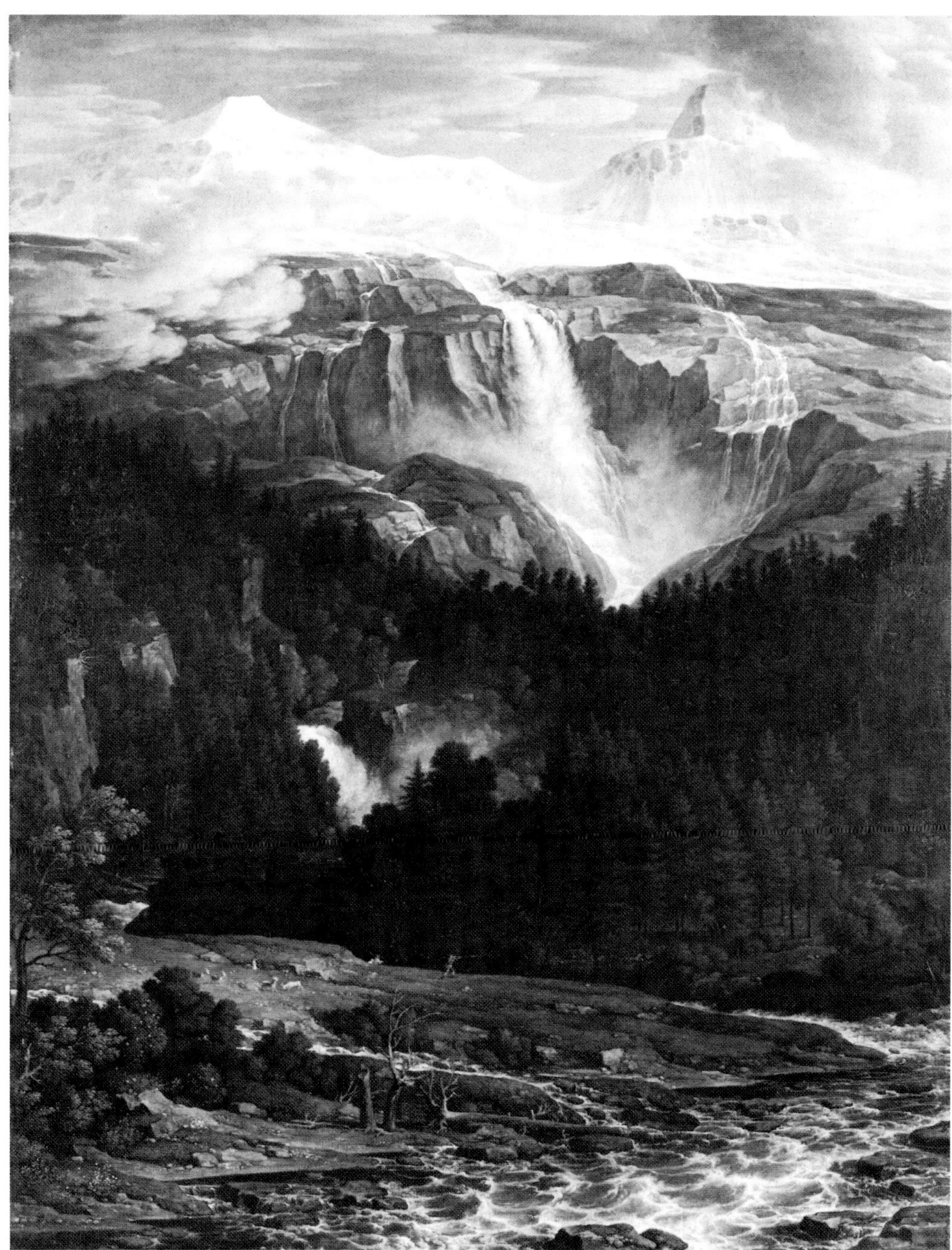

212. JOSEPH ANTON KOCH
Waterfall, 1805–1812

Oil on canvas, 123 × 93.5 cm
Signed bottom right: "J. Koch 18…"
Leipzig, Museum der Bildenden Kunst
Inv. No.: I. 121

Joseph Anton Koch became well-known as a landscapist around 1800. He had studied at the Academy in Stuttgart but left for Switzerland during the Napoleonic wars. There he worked industriously, drawing and painting the Alpine scenery. Though from 1794 onwards he visited Italy on several occasions, he still favoured the mountains of the Alps.

In 1805 he produced his *Heroic Landscape with Rainbow,* now in Karlsruhe. This impressive painting of the Schmadribach Waterfall in the Lauterbrunner Valley followed soon afterwards. It is in fact Koch's second most important work, now in Leipzig.

Koch's paintings became known to artists and to the public at exhibitions in Vienna and Munich as well as in his studio in Rome. Experts saw in him the father of 19th century heroic landscape painting, and his pieces served as models for several generations of landscapists.

213. GUSZTÁV KELETY
Landscape in the Tatra Mountains with Waterfall, c. 1860

Oil on canvas, 126 × 105 cm
Signed bottom right: "Kelety"
Miskolc, Herman Ottó Museum
Inv. No.: 77.217

The format and proportions of this painting are very similar to that of Joseph Anton Koch's famous *Waterfall.* It represents a scene in the Tatra Mountains, probably part of the waterfall of Tarpatak.

Kelety produced this work after a thorough study of the site: the creek in the foreground and the mountainous rocky background which leads from the zone of vegetation to the realm of eternal snow. Kelety acquired the technique of transforming majestic scenery into a coherent composition from the works of such Neo-Classical Romantics as Joseph Anton Koch. Large shapes fill out the space, broken only by the delicate inter-play of sunshine and mist.

Half a century passed between Koch's *Waterfall* and the creation of this painting. Here, Kelety surpasses the great landscapist of the early 1800s; both the surface of the water and the snow capped rocks are painted with more power and movement than in the work of his forerunner.

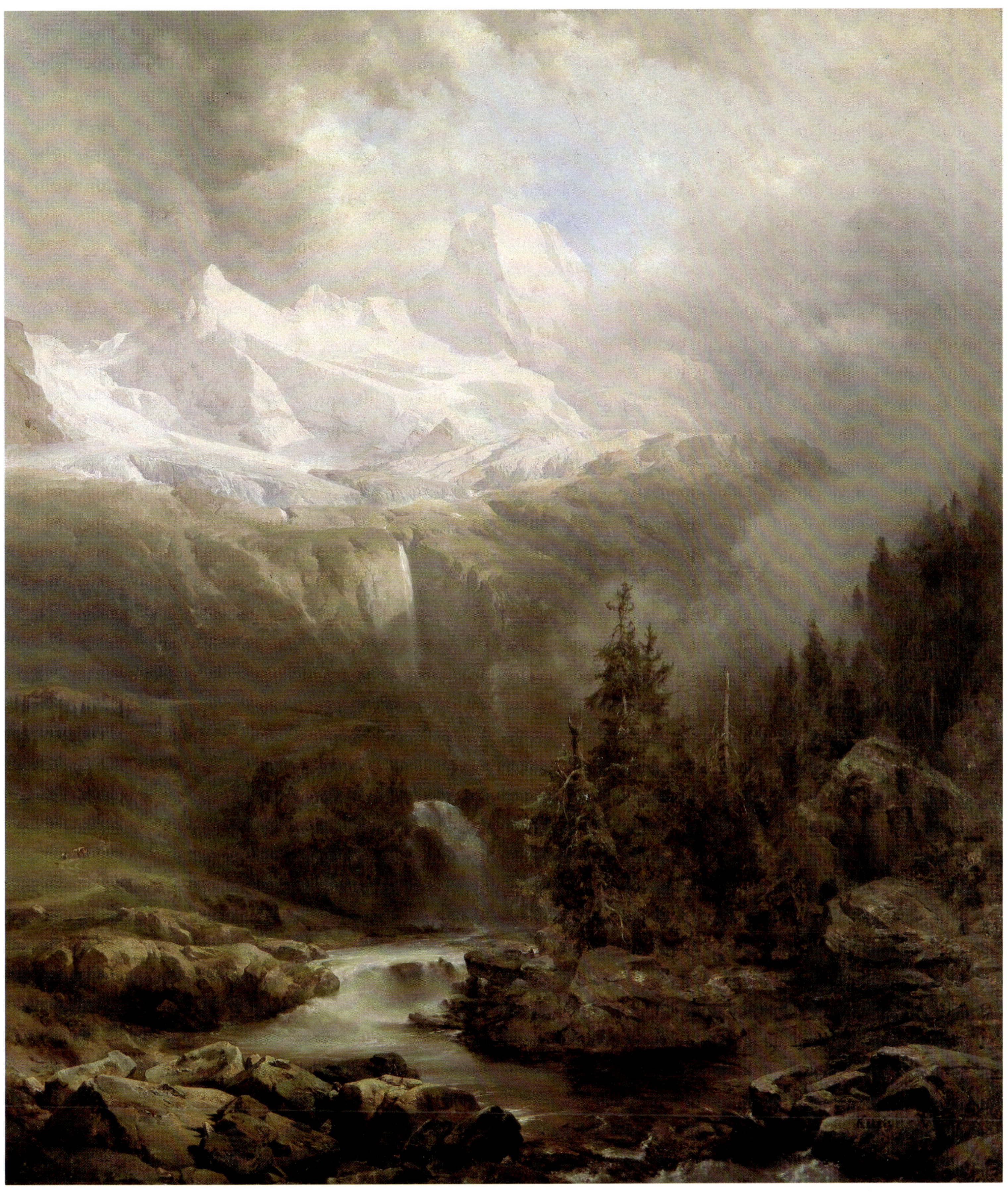

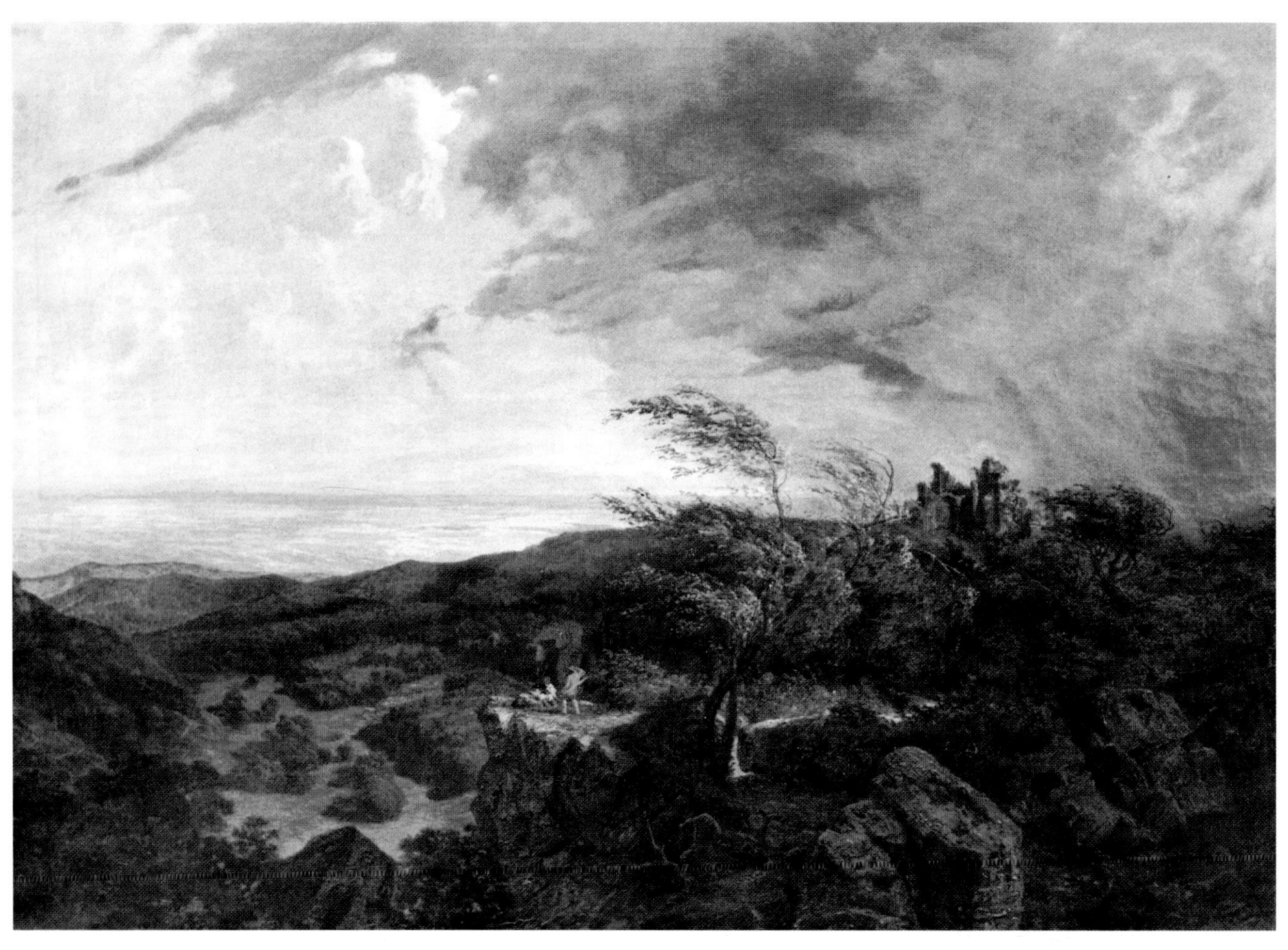

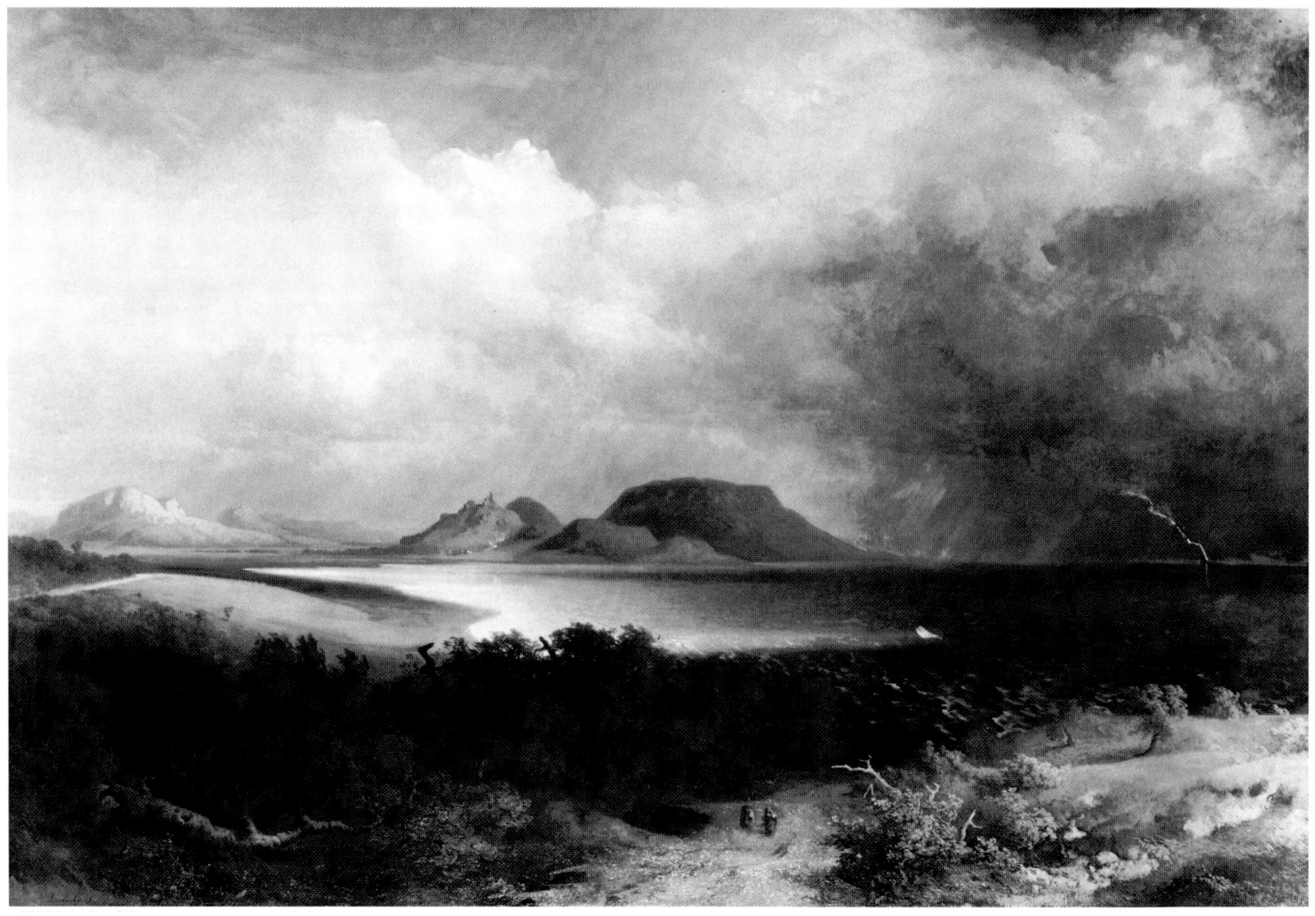

214. KÁROLY TELEPY
Storm on Lake Balaton, 1881
Oil on canvas, 112×150 cm
Signed bottom right: "Telepy K. 1881"
Budapest, private collection

Károly Telepy was one of the most gifted
Hungarian landscapists of the second half of
the 19th century. He studied in Munich and
Venice and spent several years in Rome. At
home, his Hungarian landscapes painted
after 1861 were the most highly appreciated.
This painting represents a storm on Lake
Balaton, though some of the motifs and the
dynamics of the composition relate it to
Johann Schirmer's *Roman Campagna*,
painted twenty years earlier. Telepy ob-
serves landscape according to a system
which he learned in Italy and which he made
his own. He only differs from the classical
balance in placing the horizon somewhat
higher in the painting, and in linking the individual elements of the whole painting less
closely.

215. SÁNDOR BRODSZKY
View of Lake Balaton, c. 1874
Oil on canvas, 143×206 cm
Signed bottom left: "Brodszky S"
Budapest, Hungarian National Gallery
Inv. No.: 2776
*Purchased by the National Picture Gallery in
1874. Inaugurated in 1865, this collection was
transferred in 1906 to the new Museum of
Fine Arts*

Both Sándor Brodszky and József Molnár
were Gusztáv Kelety's elders by more than
ten years. Of the two, Brodszky continued
painting mainly in an already outdated Neo-
Classical and Academic style. Except for the
format and size, this view of Balaton in its
classical approach might well date from the
1840s and bears a resemblance to works
made by Joseph Rebell in Vienna, and by
Johann Schirmer and his contemporaries in
Munich.

216. JÓZSEF MOLNÁR
Carpathian Landscape, 1874
Oil on canvas, 170×140 cm
Signed bottom right: "Molnár 1874"
Budapest, private collection

This monumental landscape of the Tatra
Mountains painted by József Molnár who
had studied in Vienna and Munich, is closely
related to Gusztáv Kelety's *Landscape in the
Tatra Mountains with Waterfall* (Plate 213).
Yet the rocks, pine trees and the mountain
torrent tumbling into a pool give the impression of a rather theatrical conception,
whereas Kelety's work is undoubtedly an
expression of personal experience.

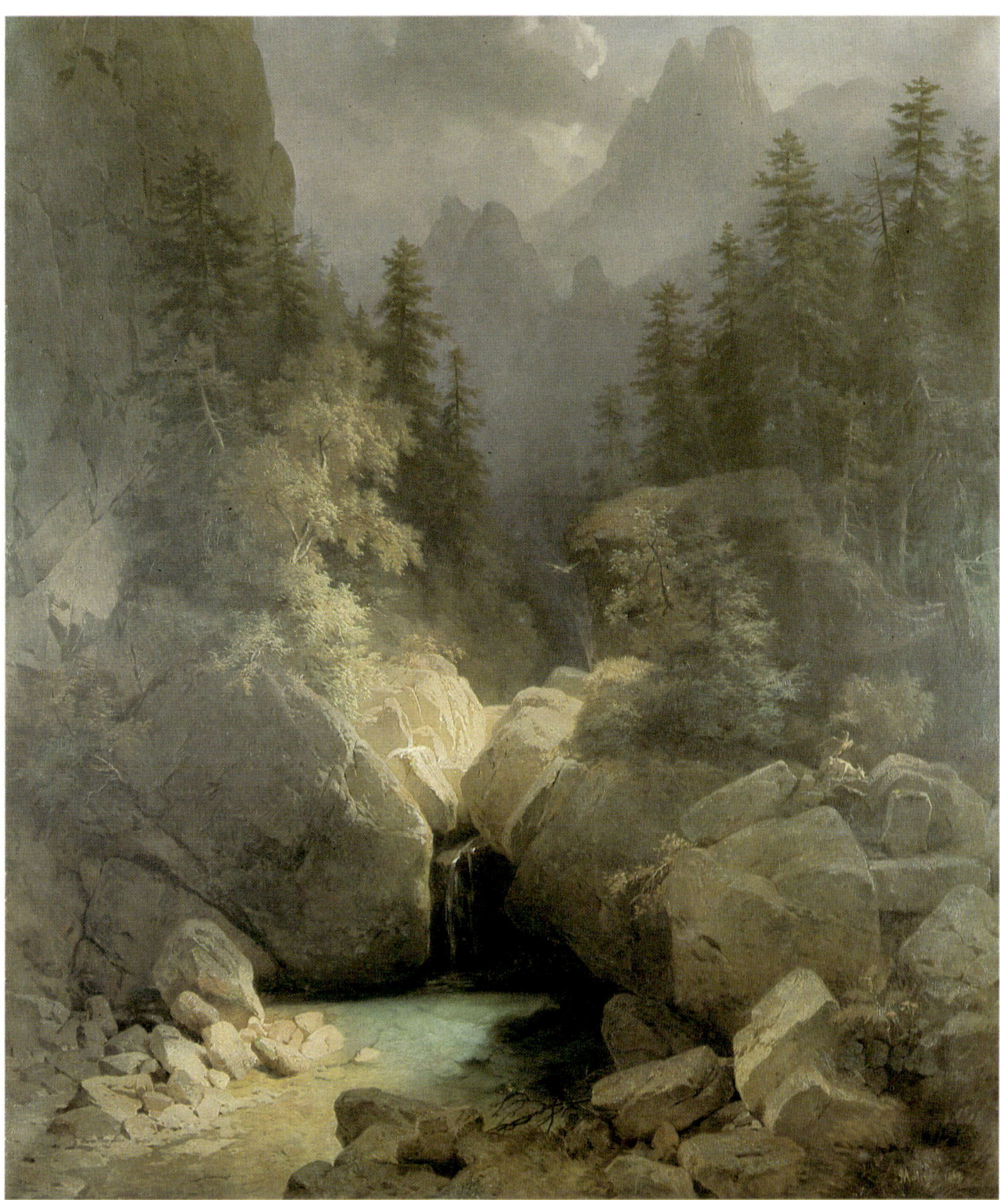

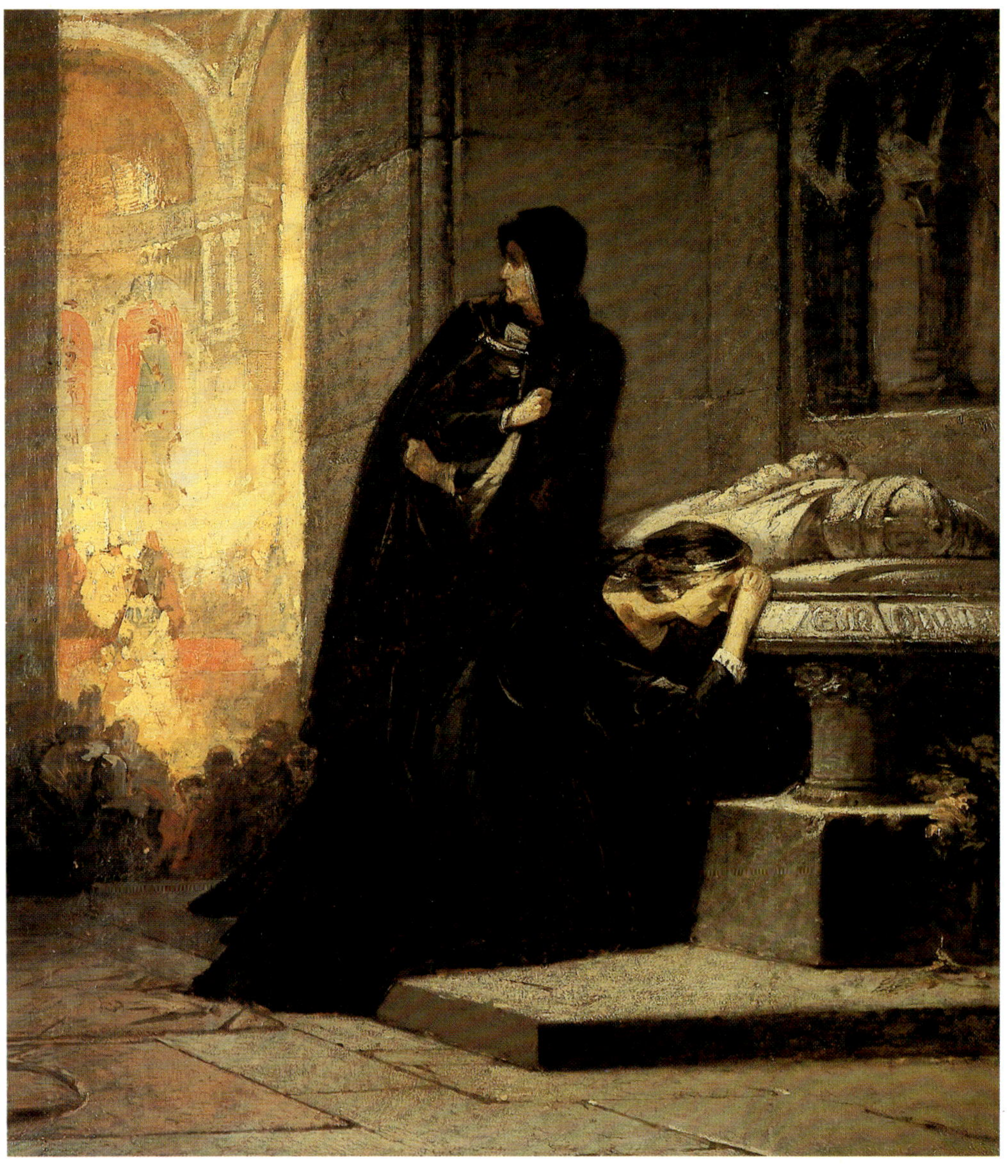

217. SÁNDOR LIEZEN-MAYER
Queen Elizabeth and Queen Mary at the Sarcophagus of Louis Anjou the Great, 1864
Oil on canvas, 77.7 × 65.5 cm
Budapest, Hungarian National Gallery
Inv. No.: 1611 T

Although Hungarian historical painters relied on a variety of sources when composing historical scenes, they did not always follow their sources closely, but instead hinted at the aftermath of the events they depicted. Here Sándor Liezen-Mayer has used János Thuróczy's chronicle as his source for this oil sketch.

According to Turóczy, at King Charles's coronation in Székesfehérvár two Queens were present—Mary, the daughter, and Elizabeth, the widow of Louis Anjou the Great. "First they go round the holy altars, then they enter King Louis' chapel. Upon catching sight of the deceased King's statue, their hearts nearly break. They embrace the cold marble and cover his sad likeness with

kisses." In the painting we see the two women in mourning. Mary is wholly abandoned to grief, resting her forehead on the tomb. Elizabeth, the widowed Queen, gazes into the distance, as if stunned by the enormity of the tragedy. Her pose also suggests that she is resolving to seek vengeance upon the newly crowned King.

This decision to seek revenge inaugurated a period of royal strife and bloodshed in which both King Charles and Queen Elizabeth were killed.

218. SÁNDOR WAGNER
Queen Isabella Taking Leave of Transylvania (sketch), after 1858
Oil on canvas, 322 × 507 mm
Unsigned
Budapest, Hungarian National Gallery,
Department of Graphic Arts
Inv. No.: 1933–2484

219. SÁNDOR WAGNER
Queen Isabella Taking Leave of Transylvania, 1863
Oil on canvas, 128 × 167 cm
Signed bottom right: "Wagner S. 1863"
Budapest, Hungarian Academy of Sciences,
deposit with the Hungarian National Gallery

Sándor Wagner painted several historical works, the most important being *Titusz Dugovics,* a hero from the Turkish–Hungarian wars, *Saint Ladislaus's Struggle with the Cumanian* and *Matthias Corvinus's Victory over Holubar,* a Czech warrior. Of these *Titusz Dugovics* is the most famous. Nevertheless, Queen Isabella's leave-taking is possibly the most popular of his pictures. The painter made several versions of this painting in which Isabella, János Zápolyai's widow, is depicted taking leave of her country, now vanquished by the Turks.

In the present oil sketch the tall female figure virtually becomes one with the majestic oak in colour, tone and proportion. She looks out over a vast landscape of low-lying watery plains. Even the uninitiated viewer feels drawn to share her grief.

In the final version, there is more detailed drawing and more highly accentuated colouring.

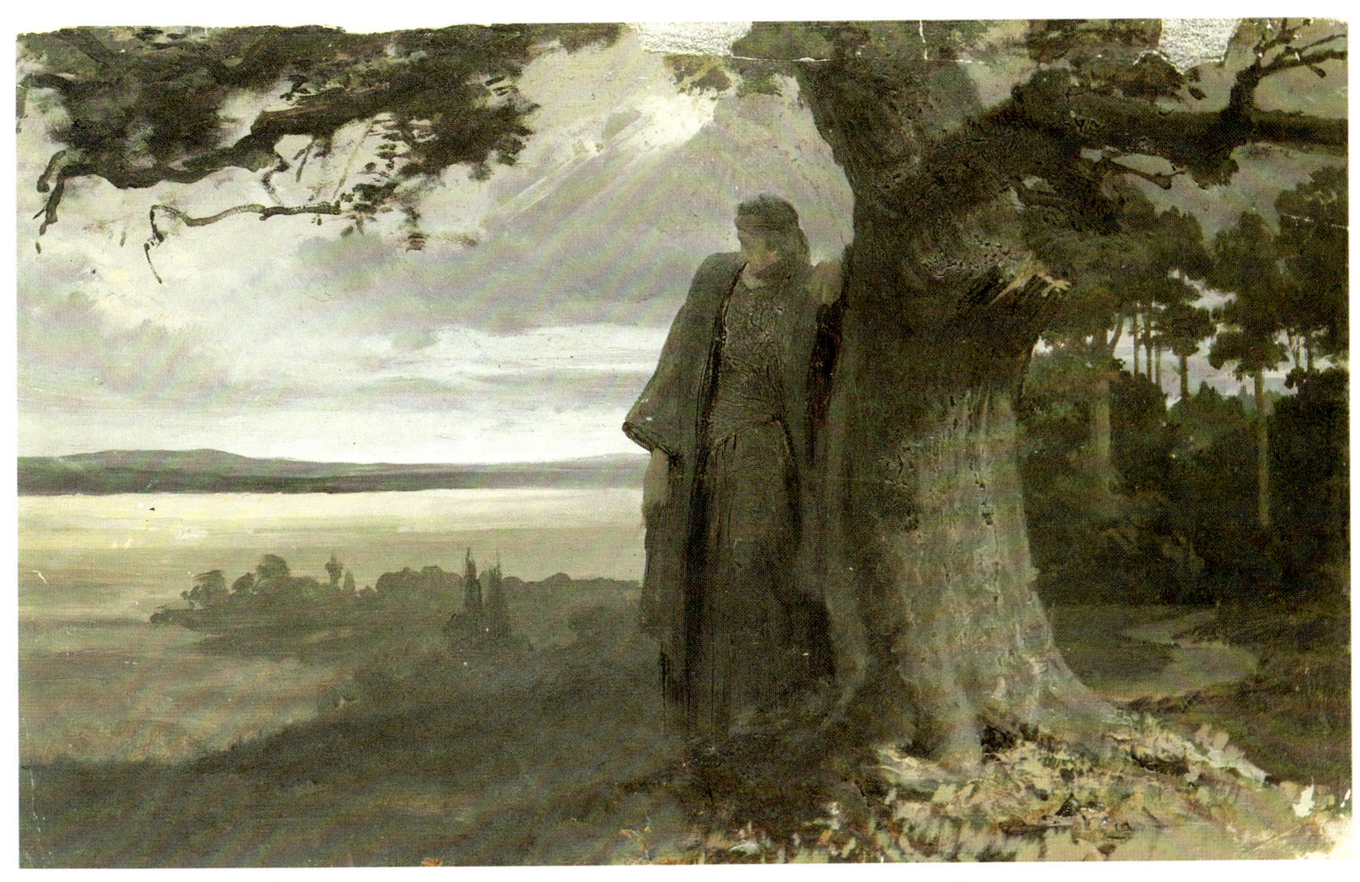

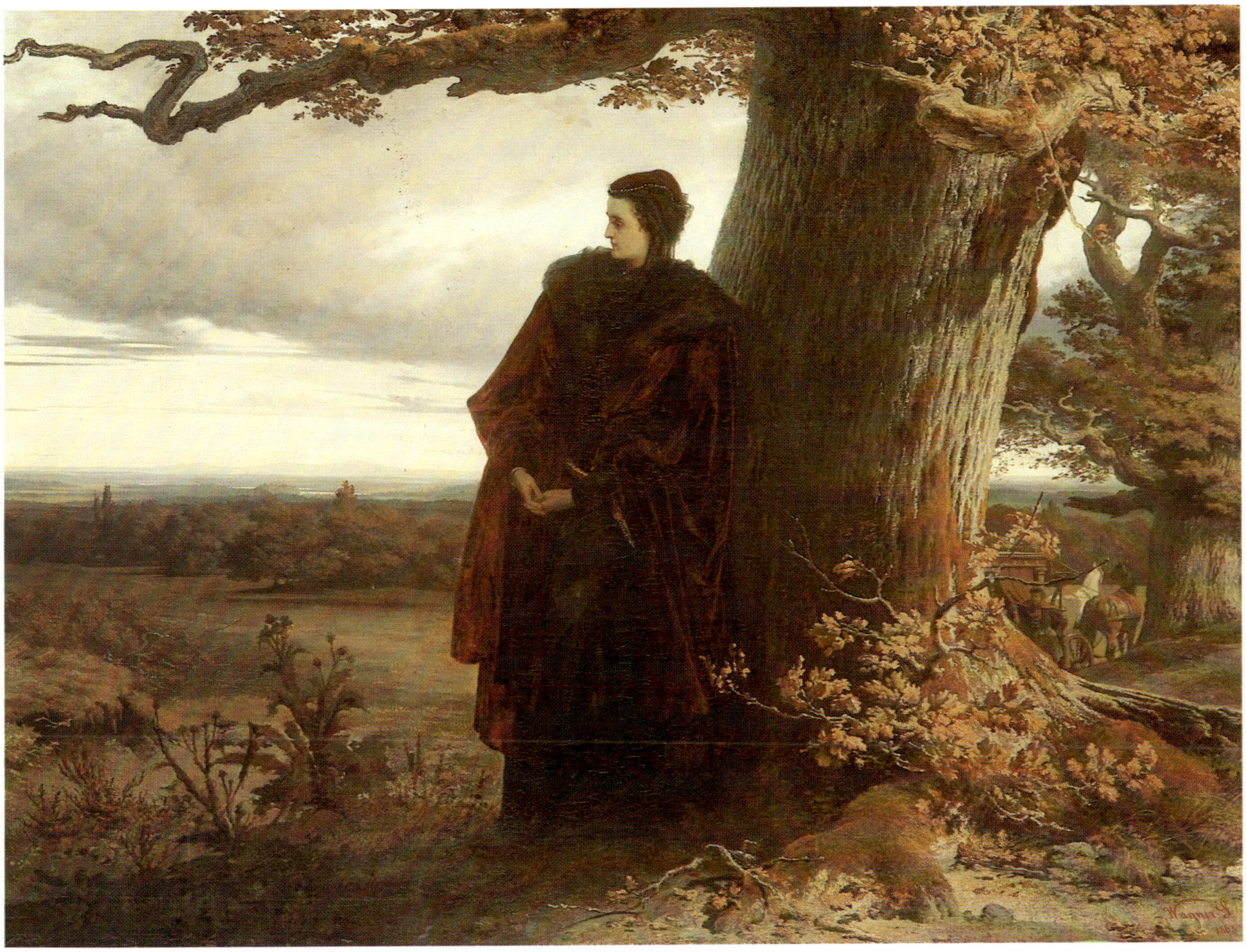

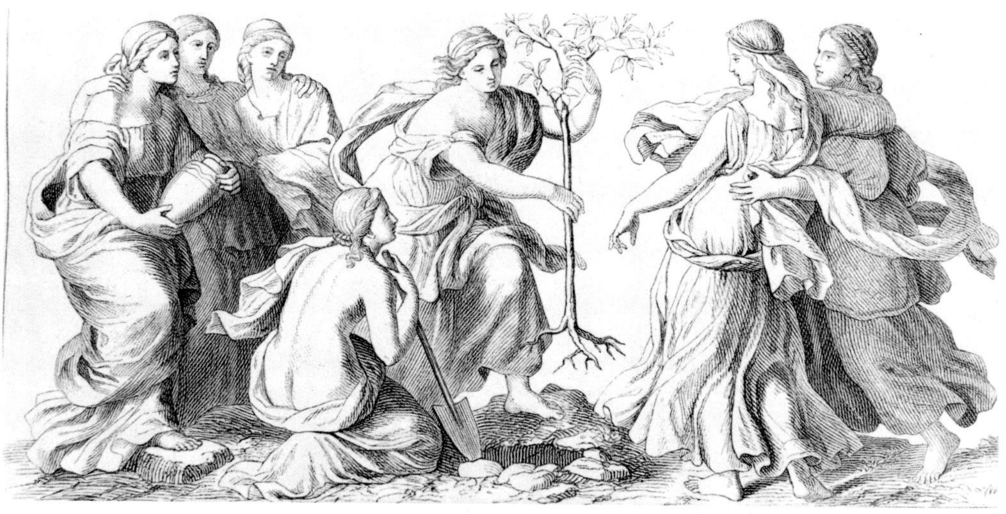

220. KÁROLY LOTZ
Planting the Golden Apple. The Story of Fairy Ilona and Argyrus, I, 1866
Charcoal on paper; size unknown
Unsigned
Original sketch on cardboard for the series of wall-painting in the Pesti Redoute (Municipal Concert Hall)
Published in the "Zeitschrift für bildende Kunst"
(Leipzig) Vol. 1866, p. 204

This is one of twelve small scenes executed by Károly Lotz for the main staircase of the Redoute. These represent, together with a large composition by Mór Than, the popular story of Fairy Ilona and Prince Argyrus.
The theme was chosen for them by Arnold Ipolyi who borrowed it from a romance written by Albert Gergei (Gyergyai) from 15th century Italian sources, which he felt held elements adoptable to Hungarian folklore. Lotz painted these scenes on rectangular panels between the pillars which support the ceiling above the staircase. He gave the wall-paintings a mosaic-like gold background.
The place chosen for them is unfortunate because the paintings can only be seen clearly through opera glasses. The composition is thus best appreciated from the surviving sketches and reproductions.
The first of the twelve paintings represents Fairy Ilona with six of her fairy companions as she plants a tree in the king's garden, whose son is Prince Argyrus, later her lover.
According to Friedrich Riedl, a Hungarian critic and man of letters, Lotz's paintings have not only an illustrative but also a symbolic value. If we accept this premise, the planting of the tree symbolizes Spring. As Lotz painted twelve pictures, it may be that there is a new type of representation of the months in this interpretation of the fairy-tale.

221. MÓR THAN
Fairy Ilona Meets her Lover, 1860–1865
Pencil on paper, 387 × 760 mm
Inscribed: "Than Mór eredeti rajza..."
(Original drawing by Mór Than...)
Budapest, Hungarian National Gallery
Inv. No.: 1900–303

222. MÓR THAN
Fairy Ilona Meets her Lover, 1865–1870
Wall-painting for the Main Staircase of the Pesti Redoute (Municipal Concert Hall)

Mór Than conceived the composition for his large wall-painting while making this pencil sketch. He describes a scene in a romantic landscape, creating a style that is livelier and more picturesque than that of Lotz.
Nymphs and mermaids play on a fairy isle surrounded by a narrow stream. Prince Argyrus flies over the stream on his winged horse led by one fairy who holds a wreath intended for him. Above them a small cherub lights the way with his burning torch. Fairy Ilona is shown seated on a throne. One of the fairies is combing her hair while another is about to drape her with a star-spangled shawl. Behind her stands the apple tree. In the tree a youth plays his lyre, to the sound of which the fairies dance in a semi-circle round the apple tree.
In some details, the painting differs from the sketch. The winged cherub with the torch is replaced by an older child who lights the way in the foreground. Also, in the wall-painting the magic steed turns towards us, and while Prince Argyrus is shown as a youth, Fairy Ilona's ladies-in-waiting are older. The starry black shawl over the fairy Queen's head, symbol of godliness and immortality, receives more emphasis. The apple tree and its immediate surroundings are more luxurious; the gesture of the youth playing his lyre is especially gracious, while the dancing fairies' rhythmical steps become almost audible.
Mór Than painted several of the characters after the inspiration of Classical models, especially Raphael, yet he managed to depict the scene with all the animation dictated by the theme.

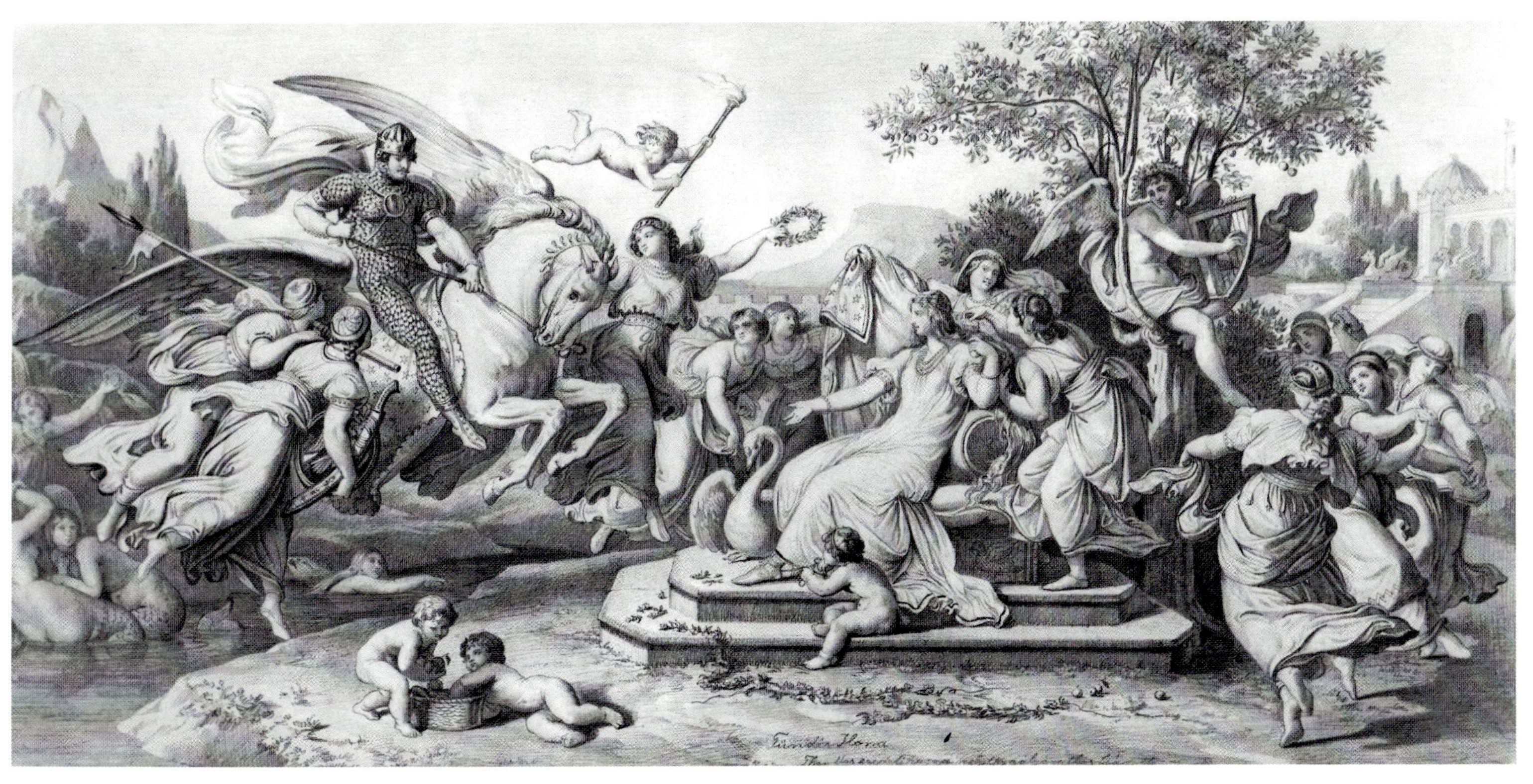

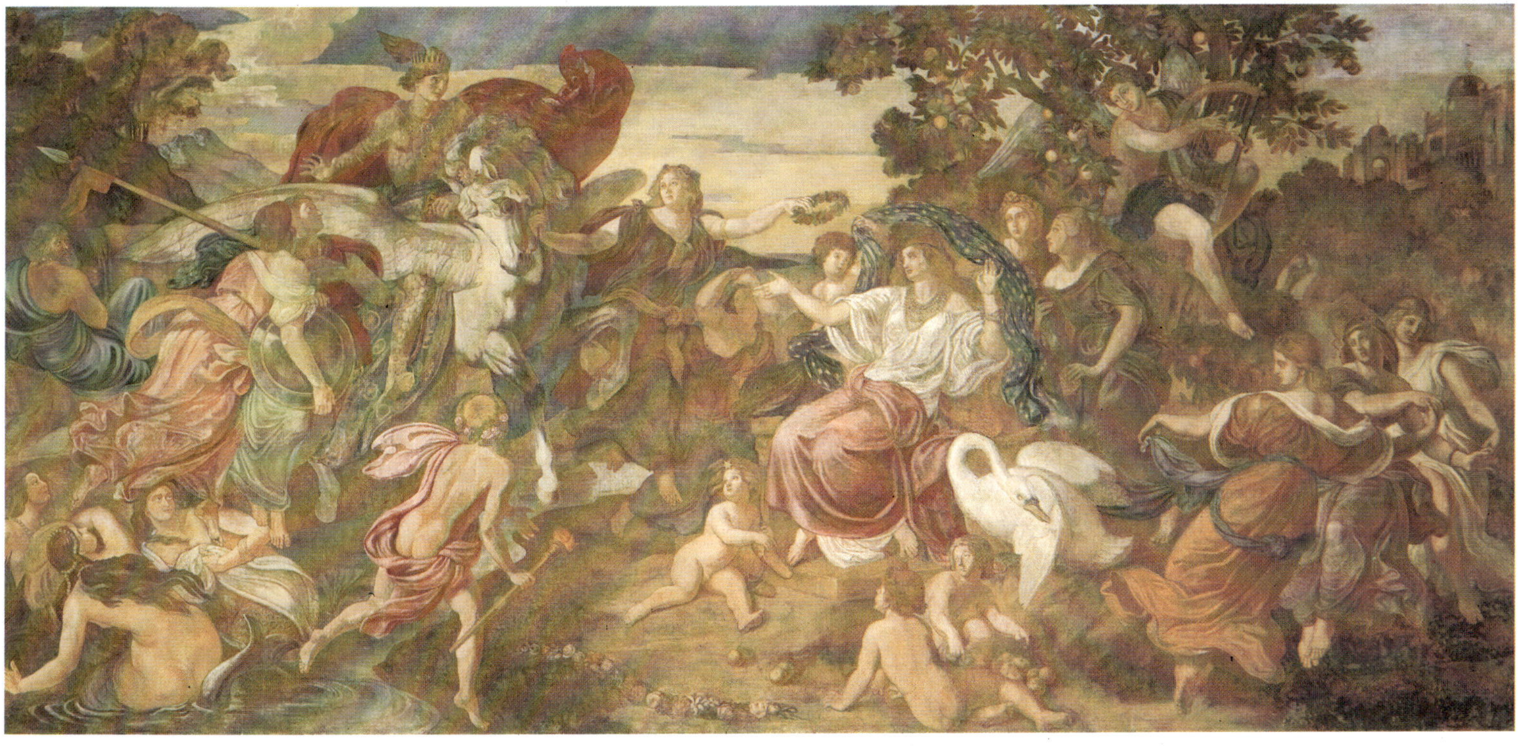

223. CARL RAHL AND HIS PUPILS

The Judgement of Paris, Nemesis and Themis, 1864

(Mural on the ceiling of the dining room in the Édouard Todesco Palace)
Unsigned
Vienna, Kärtnerstr. 51

The Todesco Palace (later called Oppenheimer Palace) faces one side of the Viennese Opera. In the spring of 1864, Carl Rahl undertook to create wall-paintings for its third storey apartment. For this he asked Károly Lotz to return from Hungary to assist him. According to art historian Ervin Ybl, the series, which shows the influence of Titian and Michelangelo, was painted by Rahl himself in the marble hall facing the courtyard. The halls facing the street, with the allegorical figures of Science, Trade and Industry, are attributed to Lotz, who must have painted them from Rahl's sketch on cardboard. More recently, Austrian art historians have come to believe that the series

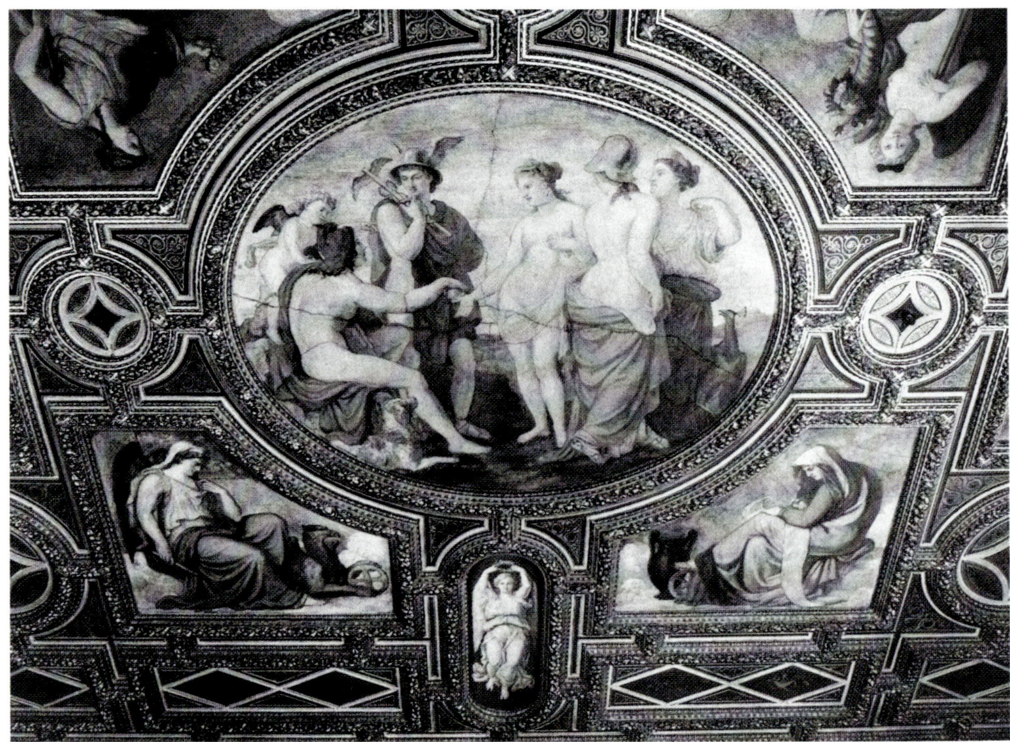

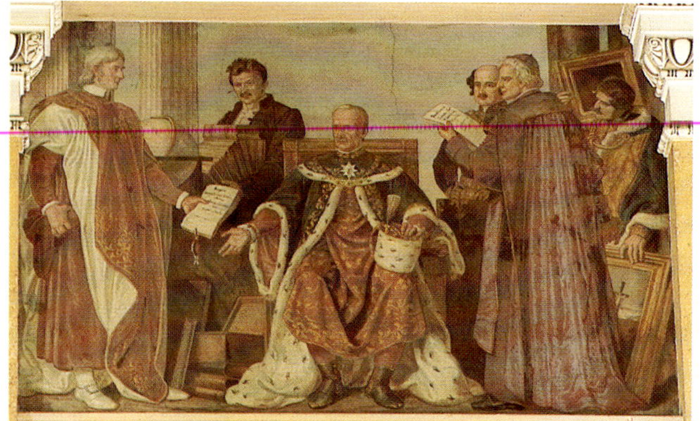

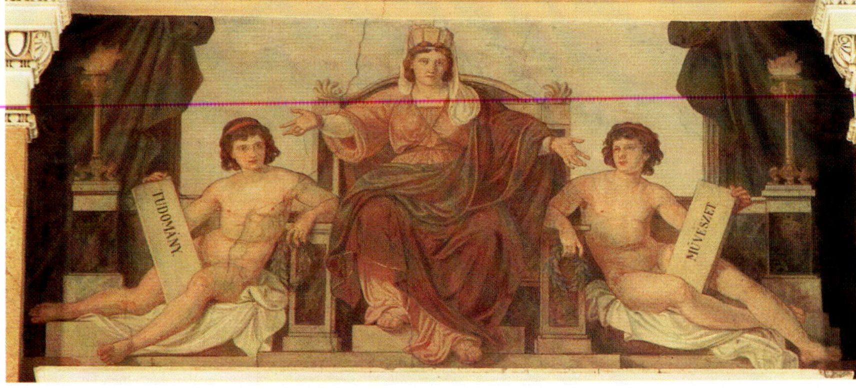

depicting the story of Paris was executed by Rahl and his pupils in collaboration.

In some of its details and general layout, the painting on the Todesco Palace ceiling served as a model for the staircase ceiling in the National Museum. If we search for elements that may have come from Lotz, they are perhaps to be found in the four corner compositions.

224. MÓR THAN

Joseph, Palatine of Hungary's Patronage of Arts. Pannonia and the Allegory of the Arts and Sciences (Pannonia, the Genius of Hungary, Crowns the Anointed Symbols of Science and Art), 1875

Budapest, Hungarian National Museum, murals on the first floor of the main staircase

In 1875 Gusztáv Kelety published in the "Fővárosi Lapok" (Metropolitan Journal) a project for wall-paintings for the National Museum. The project was largely conceived by Mór Than, who reserved for himself the task of painting an allegorical composition indicating the function of the building.

Mór Than chose to place his painting in a dominant position above the entrance at the top of the staircase. Pannonia, the Genius of Hungary, is depicted pointing towards two youths, personifying the Sciences and the Arts, each holding a wreath.

To the left and right of the entrance, numerous scenes illustrate the history of the Hungarian nation from the time of Attila to the mid-19th century. In the composition on the left of the main entrance, the painter commemorated the great art patrons of the early 19th century. In one group we see "Palatine Joseph between Ferenc Széchényi and Archbishop Pyrker, those distinguished sons of our nation whose generosity made possible the foundation of our museum", as Mór Than wrote.

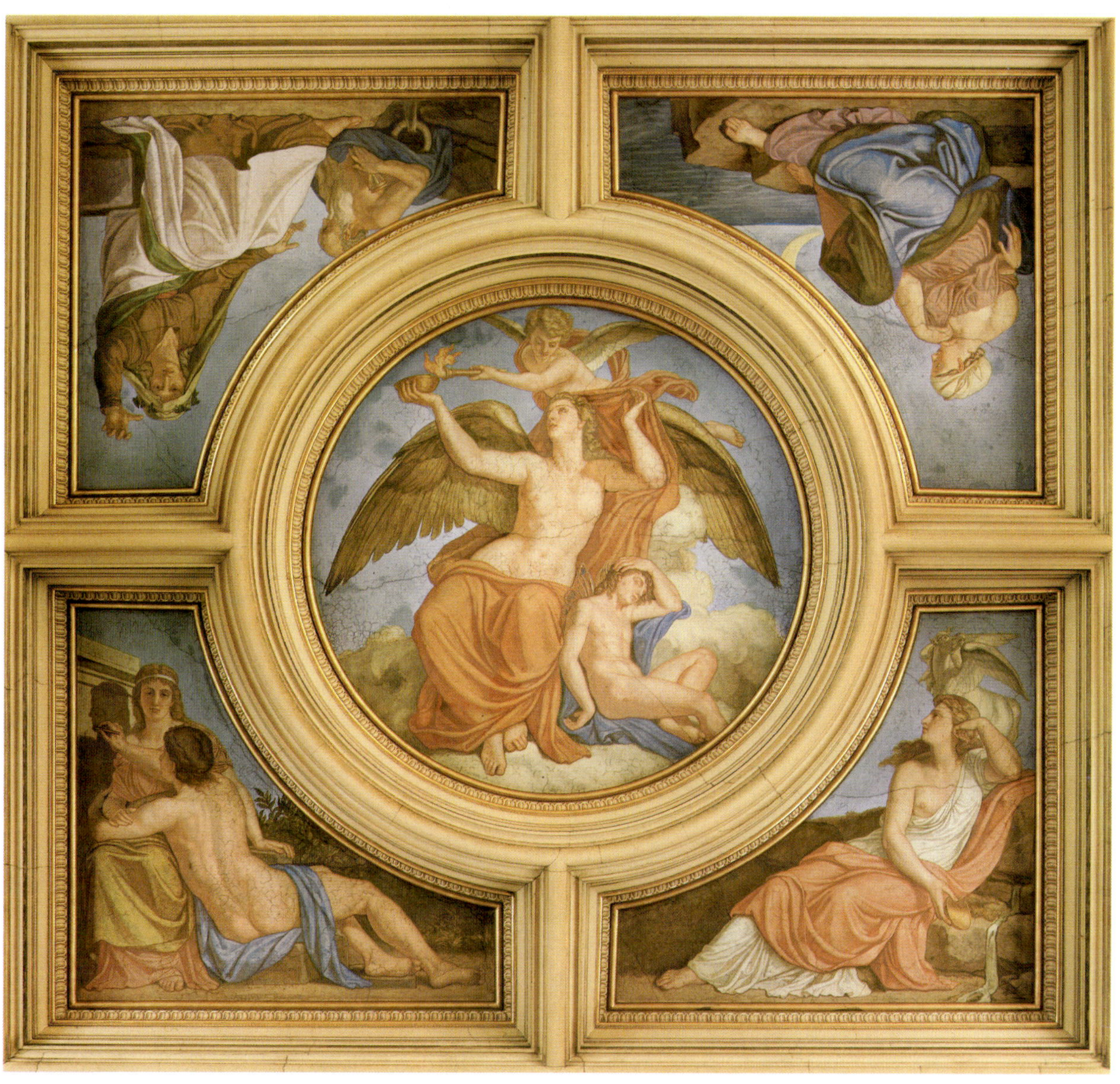

225. KÁROLY LOTZ
Allegorical Figures (mural), 1875
Budapest, Hungarian National Museum,
on the ceiling above the staircase
Centre medallion

The frescoes on the ceiling of the National Museum were intended to commemorate not only the most remarkable events in Hungarian history, but also "the greatest spiritual qualities of mankind". In the circular composition called *Genius Inspiring Phantasy,* Lotz borrowed some details from Raphael. For right-angled projections the circular frame extends into a square which determines an outer frame. In the four areas of the square thus created outside the circle, Lotz painted allegorical figures.

They all can be interpreted in different ways. Love of Beauty or Painting is symbolized by a youth who tries to catch the shadow of his beloved and trace it on the wall in accordance with Greek mythology. At the same time he also symbolizes Noon and the brightness of day. In the opposite corner, a female figure sits by the Castalian fountain. She symbolizes Poetry and Inspiration as well as Dawn, the beginning of the day. In the upper right corner we see a woman posed as in a work by Michelangelo (Medici chapel); she is the symbol of Meditation, and of evening by moonlight. The companion-piece on the left represents an old woman, meditating on the past, and thus she personifies Tradition, Legend or the Night. Beside her we see the bearded white-haired figure of Cronus, God of Time. The composition perfectly embodies the idea of a museum as the temple of the arts.

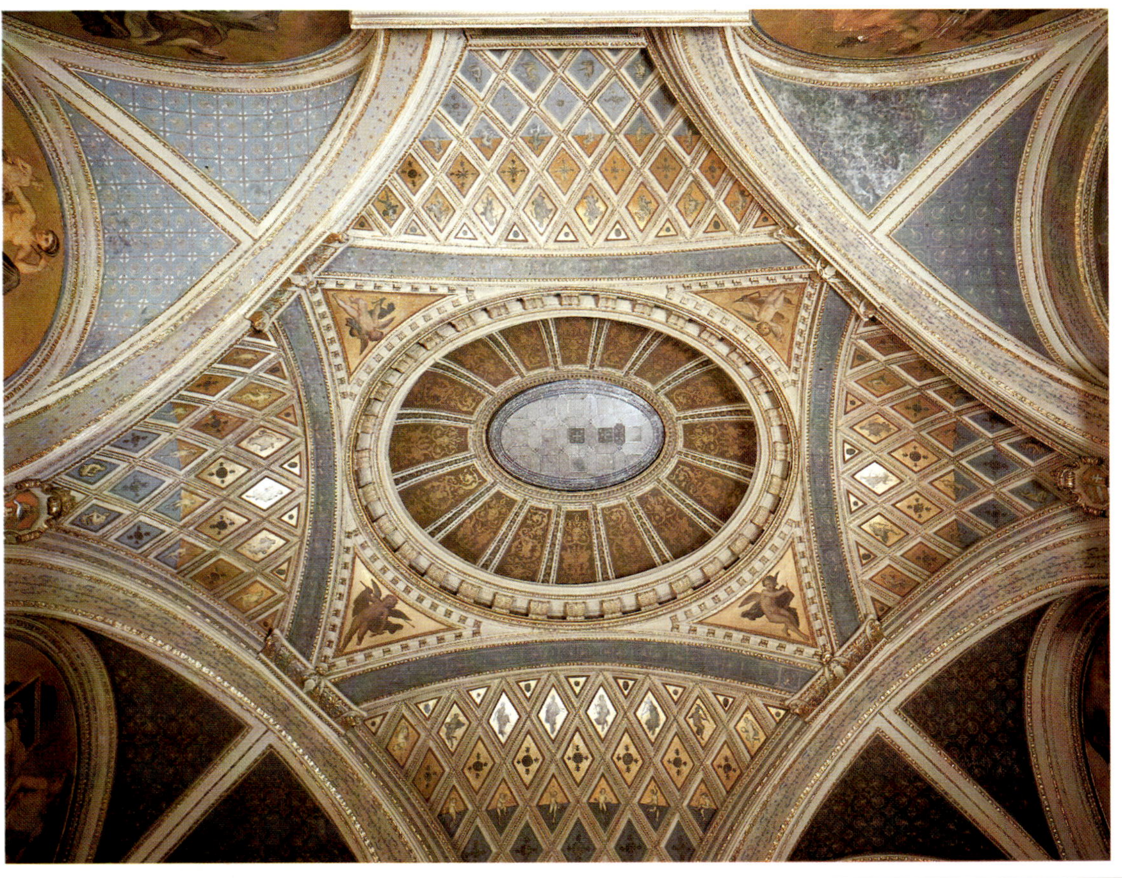

**226. KÁROLY LOTZ—
ADOLF LÁNG**
**Ceiling above the staircase of
the former Art Gallery,
after 1877**
Tempera on gold mosaic ground

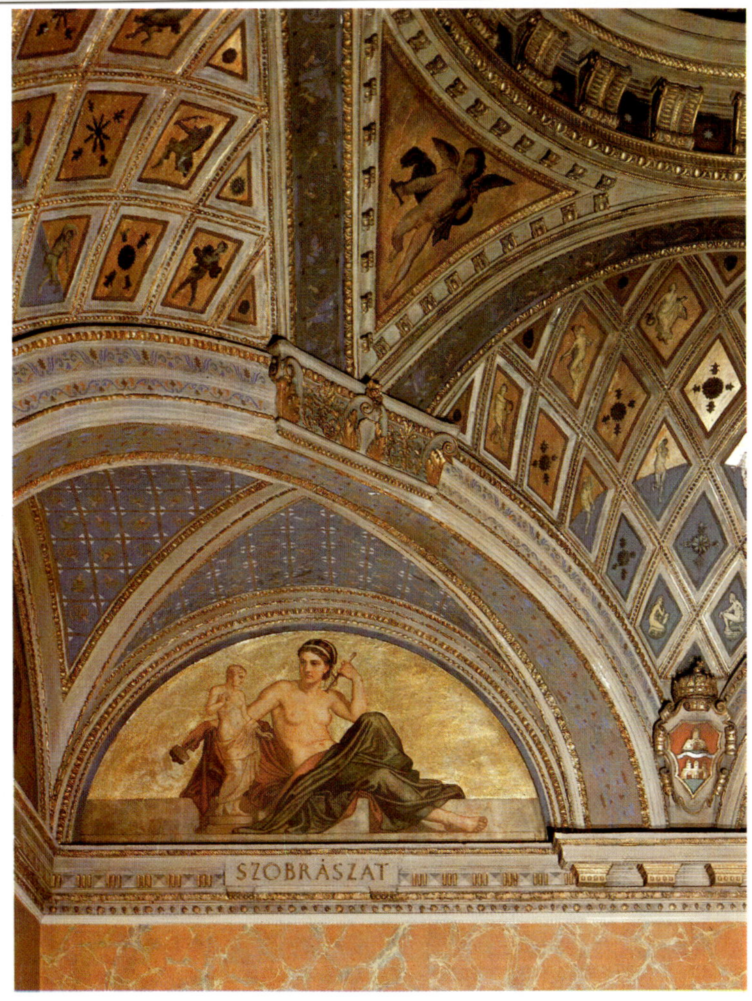

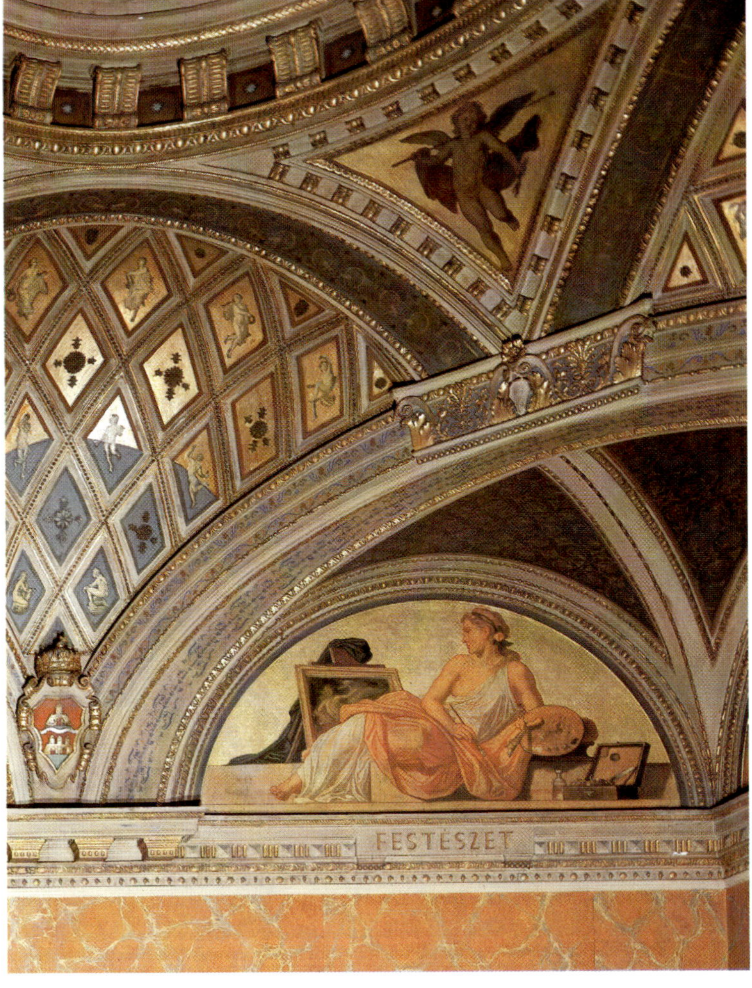

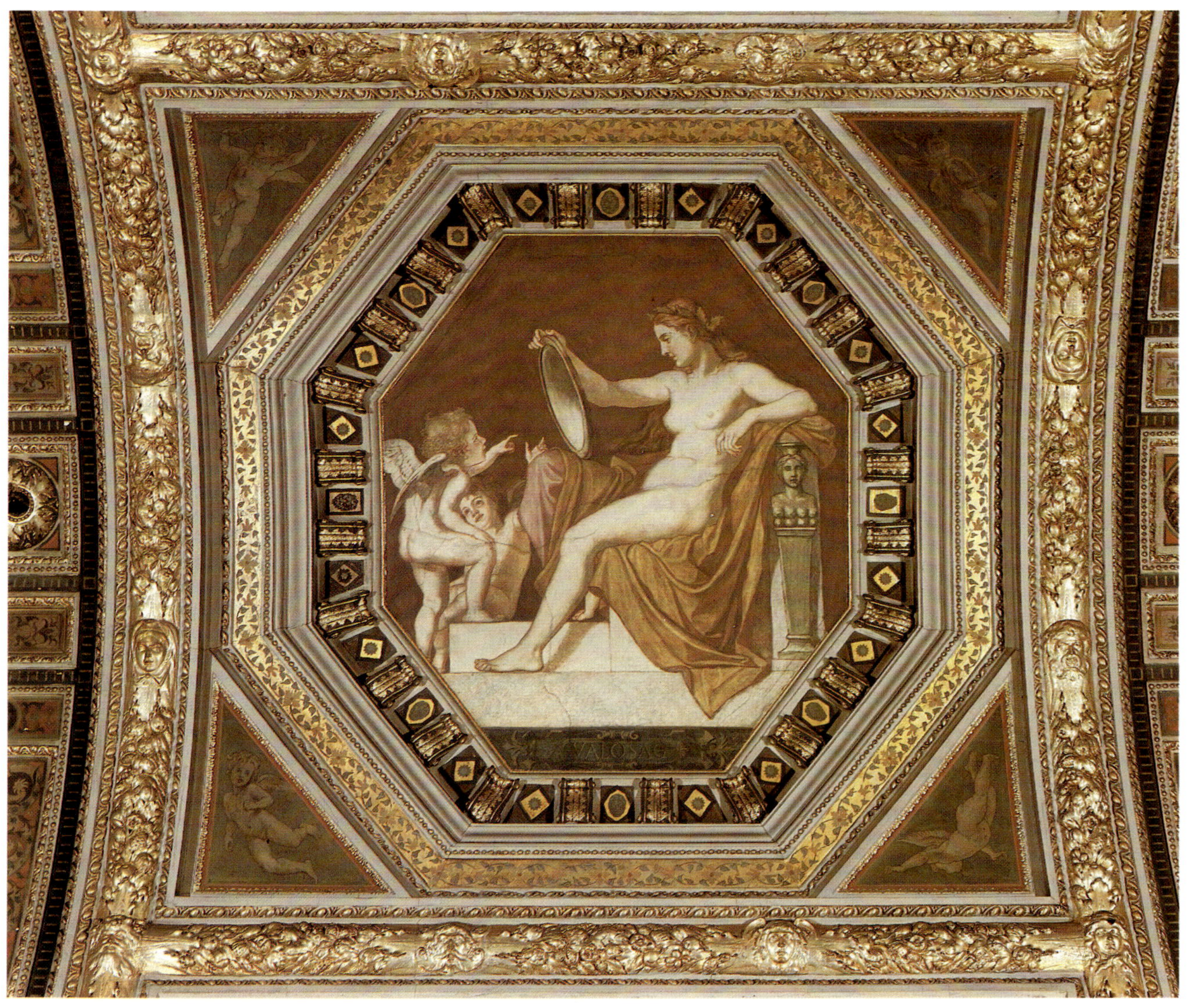

227. KÁROLY LOTZ
Details with allegorical figures of
Painting and Sculpture from the
painted ceiling of the former Art
Gallery, after 1877
Tempera on gold mosaic ground
Budapest, today the Academy of Fine Arts

The former Art Gallery (Műcsarnok) was
designed by the architect Adolf Láng. For
a period this building also housed the Képzőművészeti Társulat (Association for the
Development of Fine Arts).
The small figures painted on a gold background in the vaulting of the magnificent
staircase are the work of Adolf Láng. He
himself decorated the interior with grotesque ornaments. Károly Lotz placed his allegorical composition in the lunettes in the
lower half of the ceiling. The female figures
represent painting, the decorative arts,
drawing, copper engraving, the history of
art, handicrafts and sculpture. Painting is
symbolized by a female figure draped in
white and pink robes studying a canvas on
an easel. Sculpture is personified in the half-
robed figure of a young woman holding
a hammer in her right hand and a chisel in
her left.

228. KÁROLY LOTZ
The Allegorical Figure of Reality,
after 1877
Painting in tempera on the ceiling of the upper
hall on the first floor of the former Art
Gallery. Detail.

Lotz also painted the decorations of the ceiling of the hall opening out from the ornate
corridor on the first floor of the former Art
Gallery (Műcsarnok). There are four
allegorical pictures within octagonal frames
set against a background of dark Pompeian
red. Small angels painted in grisaille decorate
the triangular corner spaces, while in the
curves of the windows muses can be seen.
The figures represent Harmony, Beauty,
Imagination and Reality, perhaps the most
remarkable being the latter. In contrast to
a figure who symbolizes Beauty, the figure
in the opposite corner is of a serious-looking
female nude shown seated on a stone seat covered with yellow drapery; the arm of the
seat is decorated with a bust of Diana of
Ephesus. This female figure, far removed
from the Classical style, is reminiscent of
Rembrandt's nudes.

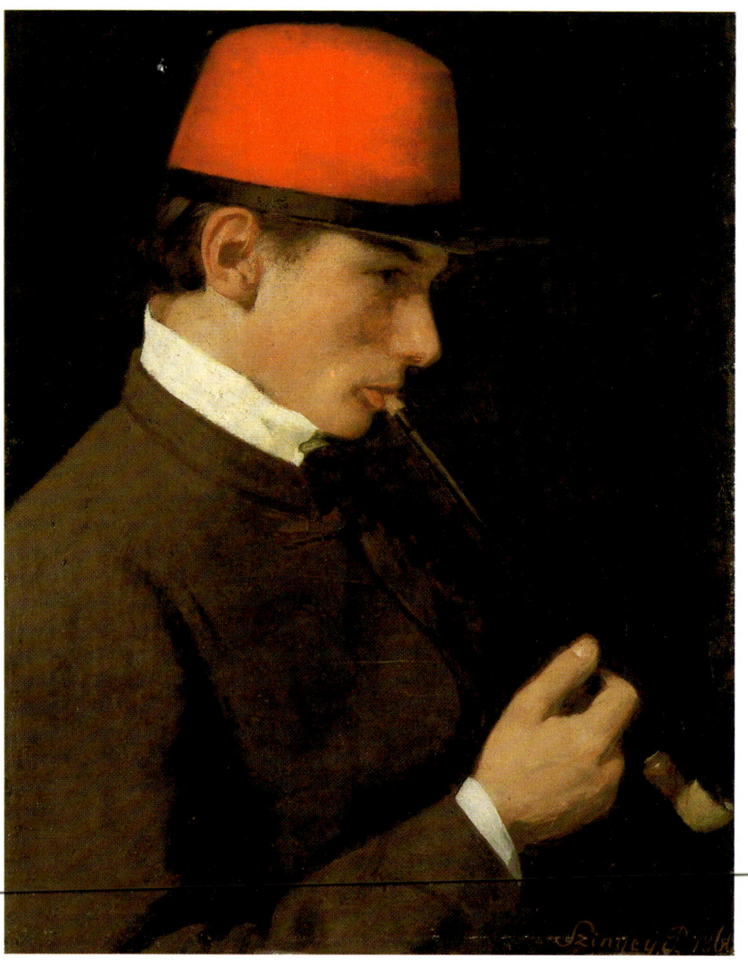

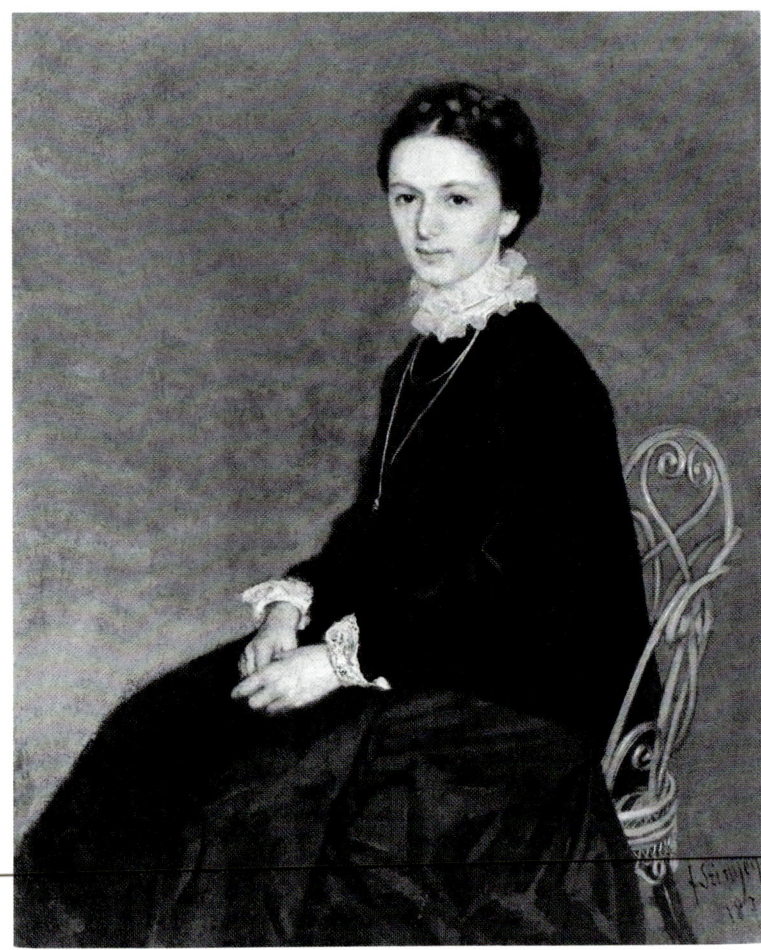

229. PÁL SZINYEI MERSE
Portrait of Zsigmond Szinyei Merse with a Turkish Pipe, 1866
Oil on canvas, 64.5 × 49 cm
Signed bottom left: "Szinyei Pál"
Budapest, Hungarian National Gallery
Inv. No.: FK 9236

As a young man Szinyei painted several portraits of his brothers and sisters, initially in the style then prevalent in Hungary with the average portraitists but later in more innovative styles. He portrayed his elder brother, László, in Hungarian gala dress; here he portrays his younger brother Zsigmond, in everyday dress, in a casual pose, smoking a long-stemmed pipe. Portraits in this style, which might be classified as single figure genre paintings, are frequently found among the works of young painters active in Munich in the 1860s.

230. PÁL SZINYEI MERSE
Portrait of Mrs. Edmund Berzeviczy, née Ninon Szinyei Merse, Sister of the Artist, 1870
Oil on canvas, 61.5 × 48.3 cm
Signed bottom left: "f. Szinyei P. 1870"
Budapest, Hungarian National Gallery
Inv. No.: 5987

This small portrait of the artist's sister may have been painted from an earlier drawing or it may date from the period when Szinyei was at home in 1870. Ninon is shown seated on an elegant garden chair in an interior where the entire background is of the same grey colour. She is dressed in black relieved only by a lace collar and cuffs and a fine silver necklace. Her hair is braided in the Madonna fashion. It is a likeness of great simplicity, reflecting the painter's warm love and respect for his sister, without becoming overly sentimental. It is the model's gentle but composed bearing, her warmth of expression and fine open brow that impress the viewer most of all.
This likeness reflects Szinyei's individual approach to the representation of visual impressions.

231. GÉZA DÓSA
Portrait of Two Girls, c. 1870–1871
Oil on canvas, 162.5 × 121 cm
Unsigned
Budapest, Hungarian National Gallery
Inv. No.: 6637

This painting of two young women was among the last works of Géza Dósa, who died at the age of twenty-five. After studying in Kolozsvár, Pest and Vienna, he went to Munich, where he was greatly influenced by the exhibition which summarized the artistic innovations of Courbet, the Barbizon painters, and the direct forerunners of French Impressionism. He consequently left the Academy of Munich to open an atelier of his own. However, his parents, fearing his experiments in the French style, and even more strongly objecting to his going to France during the Franco-German war, summoned him home to Marosvásárhely. There he painted likenesses and studies. According to experts, this delicate portrait is of the two daughters of a Marosvásárhely merchant called Wittich. It is especially striking for the harmonious colours and the enigmatic atmosphere projected by the earnest, pensive expressions of the two sisters.

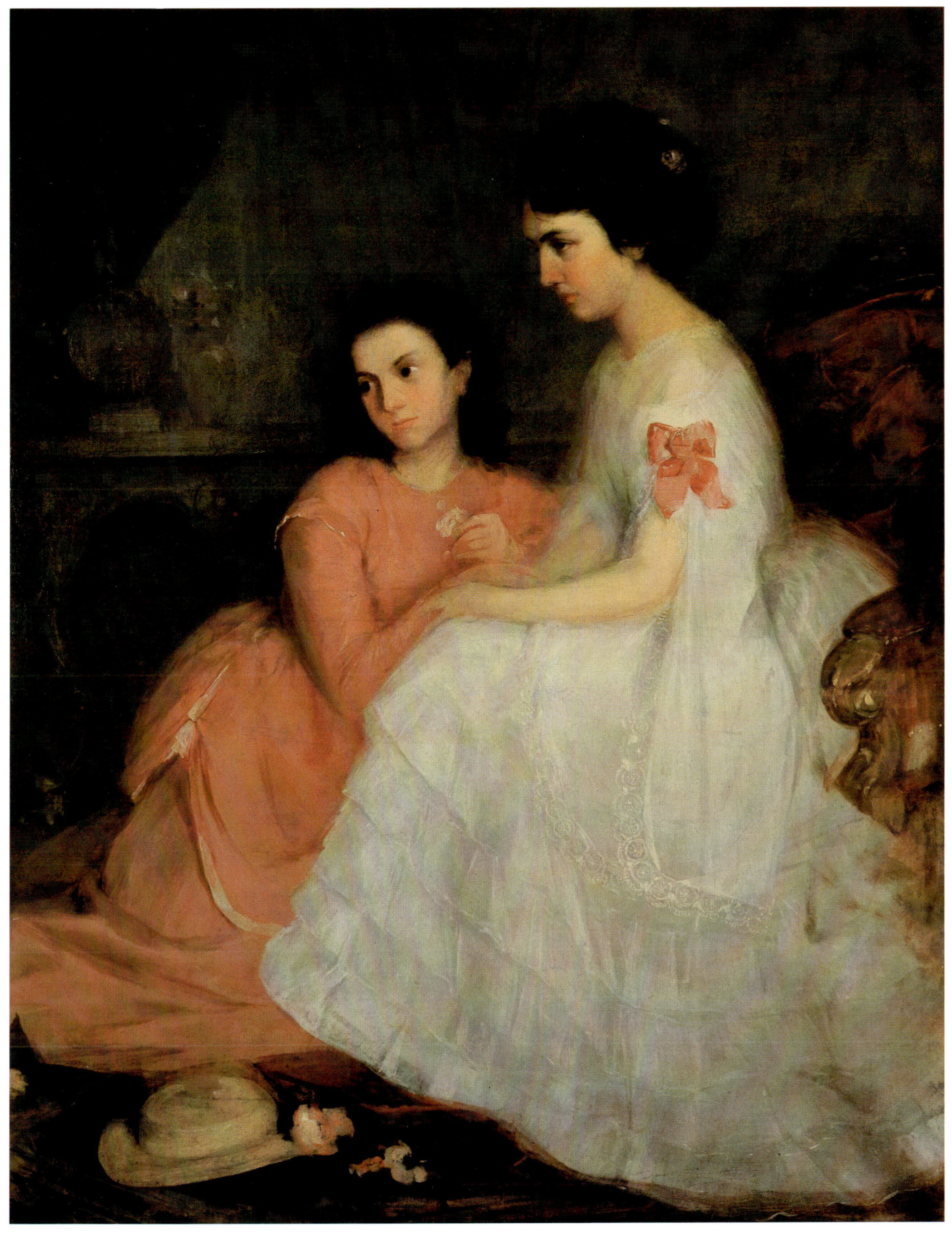

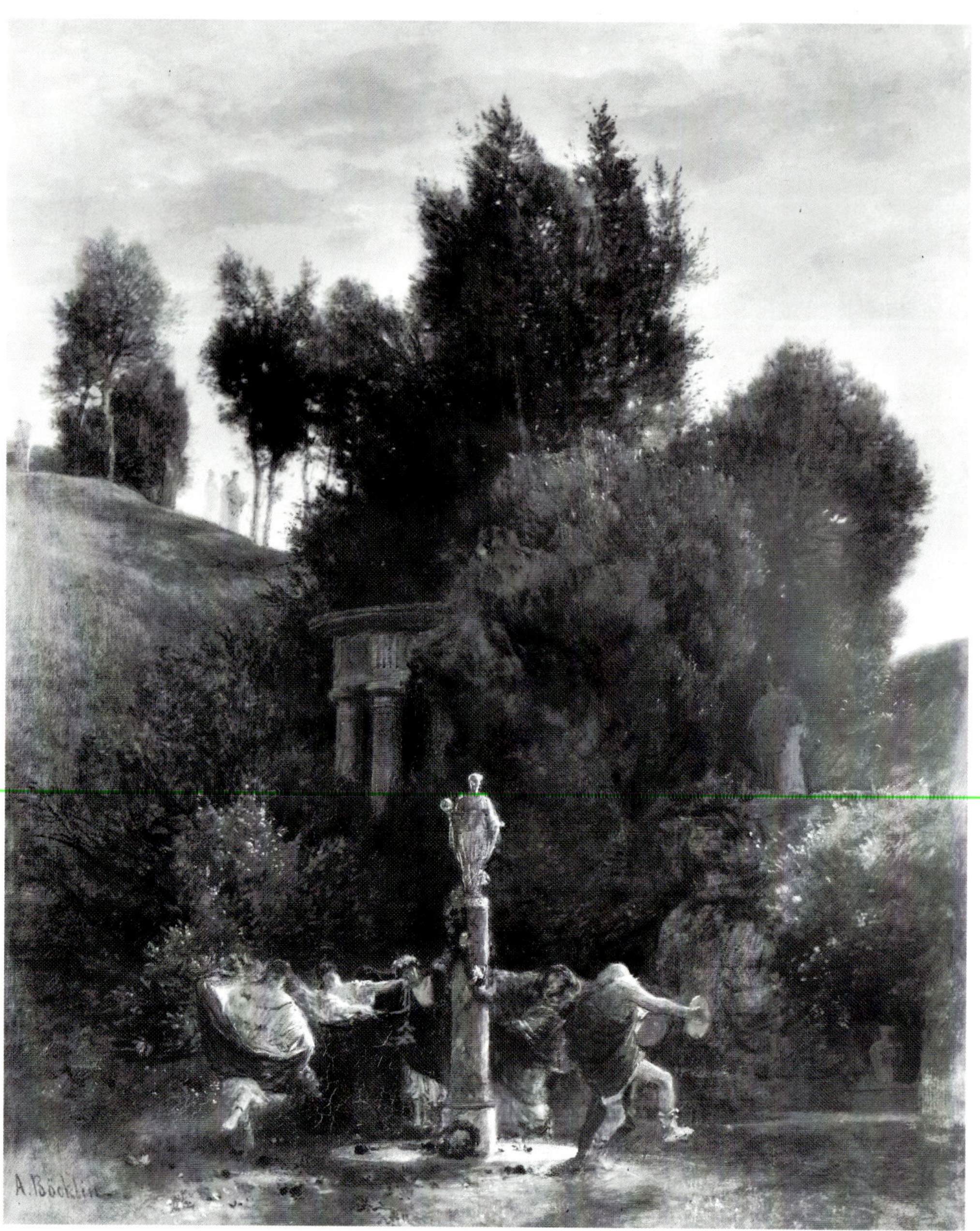

232. ARNOLD BÖCKLIN
A May Festival in Ancient Rome, c. 1877

Oil on wood, 75.5 × 61.6 cm
Signed bottom left: "A Böcklin"
Munich, Neue Pinakothek
Inv. No.: 9335

Ancient Romans dancing in the open air or offering a sacrifice in accordance with their cult are a recurrent theme in Böcklin's work. This interest in mythological themes was a new element introduced in the latter part of the 19th century into German painting. In fact, Böcklin had personal experience of just such a scene as this, for sometime in the 1850s he had taken part in a performance of dances of the Roman cult in front of the grotto of the nymph Egeria. Later, Böcklin created a painting from this scene, imaginatively transposing it to the time of the myth, while retaining the earthy vitality and immediacy of his own experience.

233. PÁL SZINYEI MERSE
Bacchanalia, 1869

Oil on canvas, 66 × 88 cm
Budapest, Hungarian National Gallery
Inv. No.: 5612

Szinyei's friend, Arnold Böcklin, was already painting themes such as this in the 1850s, and Hans Makart executed several similar paintings in the 1860s. Scholars have seen a link between the work of both these painters and this sketch by Szinyei, which exemplifies his search for his own special style. The possible relationship between mythology and nature interested Szinyei more than Böcklin. But unlike Böcklin, Szinyei was not interested in personally experiencing and re-enacting mythological scenes, nor did he wish to create a new sys-

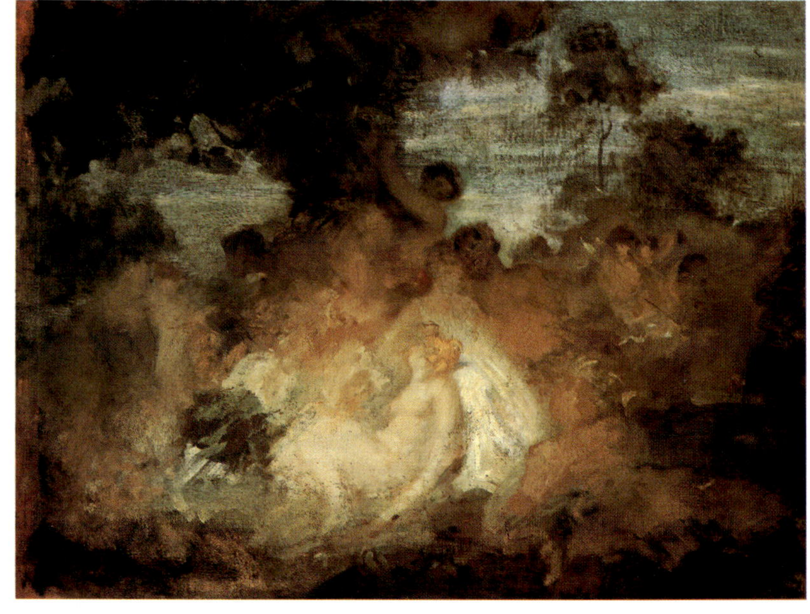

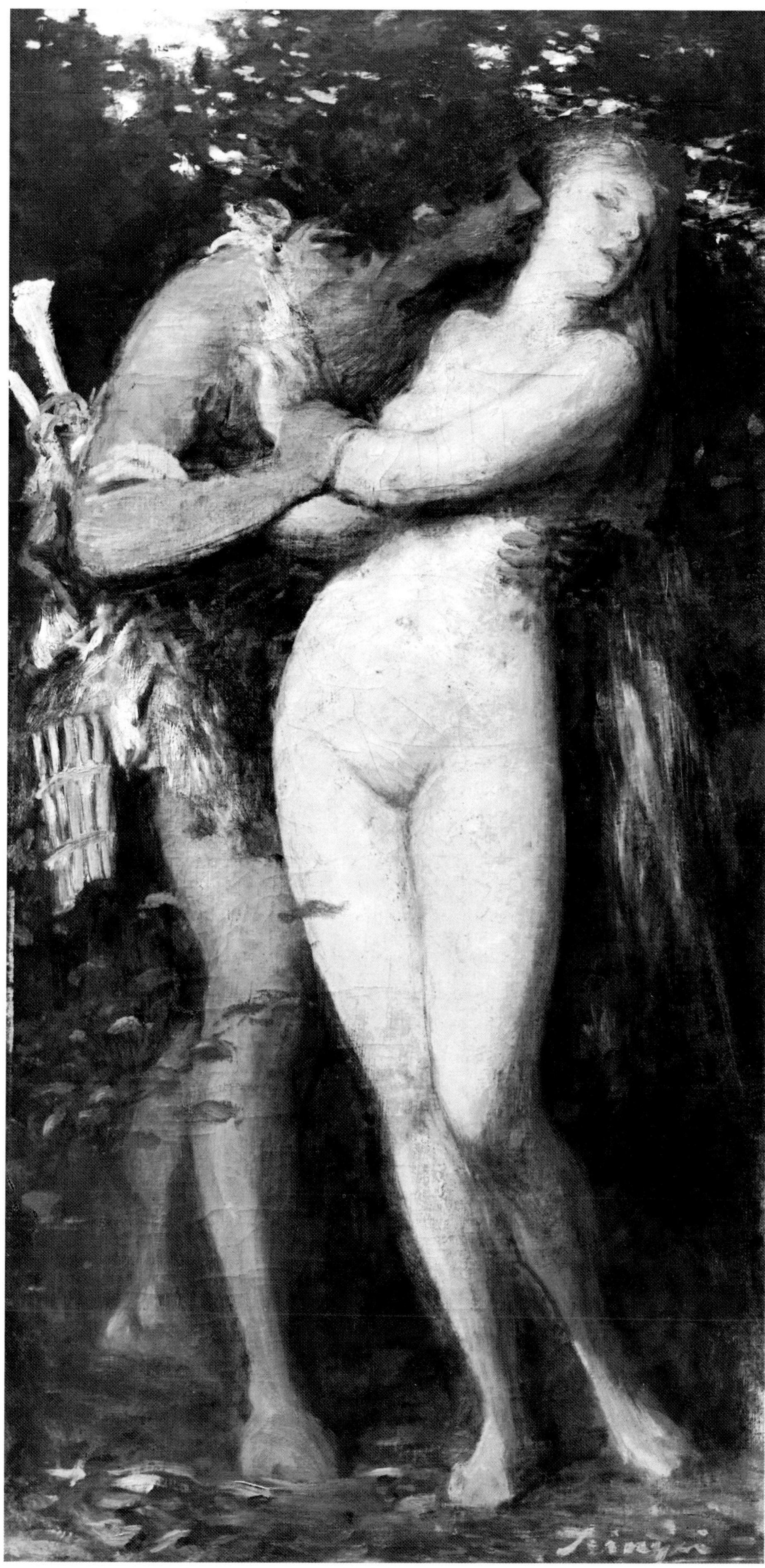

tem of symbols. In this painting, his aim was simply to evoke a popular mythological scene, in an autumnal setting of leaves swirling in the wind. Though this pictorial problem of representing bacchanalia recurs from time to time in his work, from 1860 onwards it was only one of many interests of the painter.

234. PÁL SZINYEI MERSE
Paganism, II, 1869
Oil on canvas, 86.5 × 39.8 cm
Signed bottom left: "Szinyei M. Pál"
Budapest, Hungarian National Gallery
Inv. No.: 2636

In a series painted in 1869 Pál Szinyei Merse experimented with compositions in which mythological figures are depicted together with humans. In this painting, an attempt to synthesize several of his areas of interest is obvious. For Szinyei, an encounter between mythological and human figures could be best expressed in an outdoor setting, in scenes of heightened eroticism. In this painting a faun—reminiscent of those painted by Böcklin—attempts to embrace a young girl who, although naked, gives the impression of a well bred young lady rather than a mythological figure. In another sketch the roles are reversed: a well dressed man embraces a nymph. Indeed, Szinyei painted every possible variation of this theme.

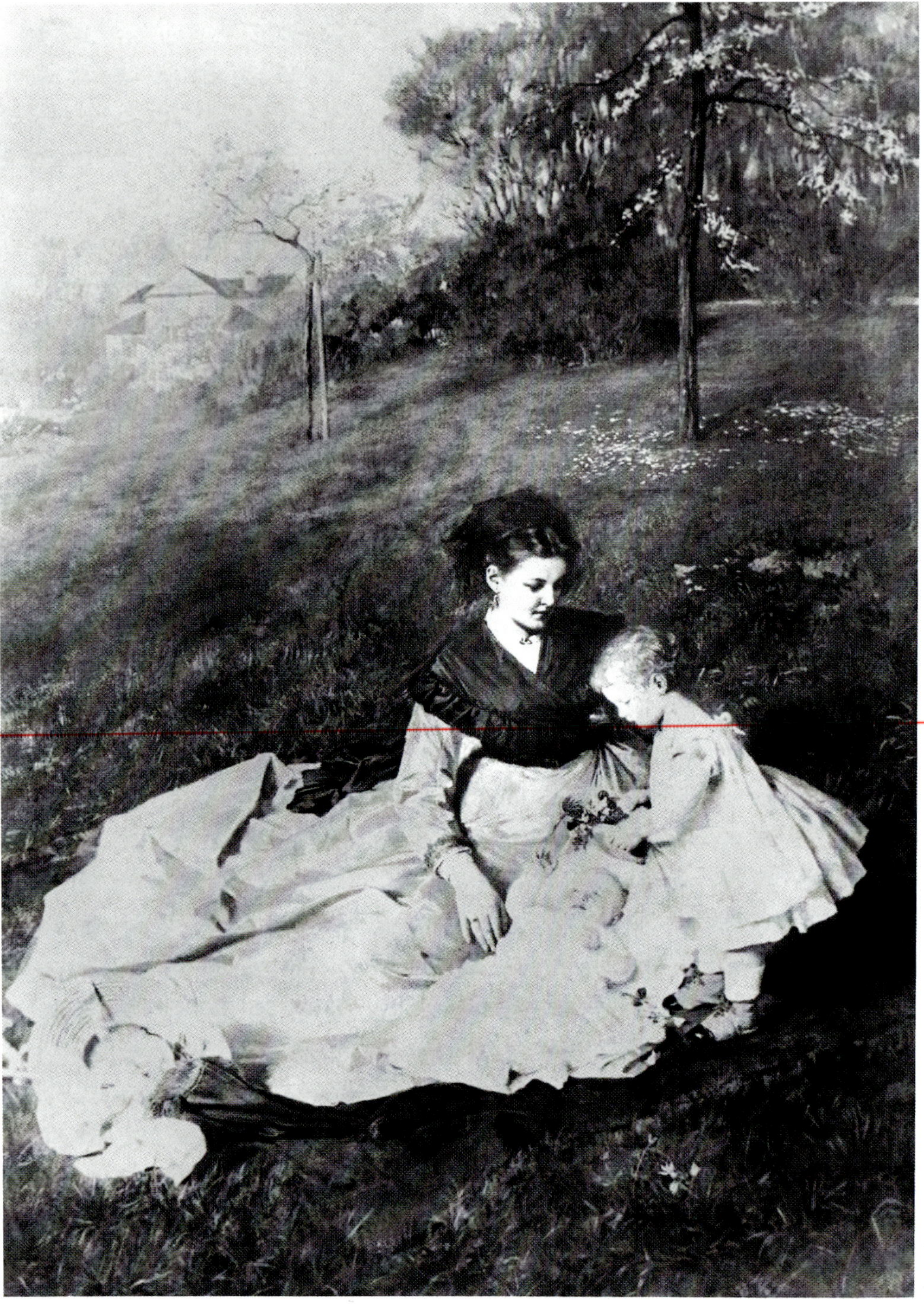

235. PÁL SZINYEI MERSE
Mother and Child, Version I, 1869
Oil on canvas, 137 × 98 cm
Signed bottom right: "Paul V. Szinyei 1869"
USA, private collection

In 1870 Szinyei painted a second version of this genre piece, but it was not exhibited. His art dealer, realizing the novelty of the subject, presumably wanted a series of such paintings before making them public. However, he must have lost contact with Szinyei who was eventually richly compensated financially for this initial loss. His pleasure, however, was marred by his frustration in not being able to satisfy public demand for similar works. It may be that these circumstances led to his painting the famous *Picnic in May*.

236. PÁL SZINYEI MERSE
Lovers, 1870
Oil on canvas, 53.5 × 63.5 cm
Signed bottom left: "Paul v. Szinyei 1870"
Budapest, Hungarian National Gallery
Inv. No.: 6533

This painting is one of a number of informal works which are antecedents to Szinyei's *Picnic in May* (Plate 243). The lovers rest by a haystack. The young woman, half-sitting, half-lying, leans on her elbow, while her lover, reclining at her feet, stretches his left arm behind his head and so touches his beloved's hand. The girl's yellow hat and pink frilled skirt show many fine pictorial details, but in marked contrast to the rapt expression of the young man her face remains as expressionless as that of a professional model. The background landscape unites the details of an unremarkable stretch of country. The evening light reveals a row of haystacks and greyish-brown details which become less defined as they recede into the distance, thus suggesting the effects of the play of light and perspective.

237. GYULA BENCZÚR
A Woman Reading in a Wood, 1875
Oil on canvas, 92 × 73.5 cm
Signed bottom right: "Benczúr Gyula, München, 1875"
Budapest, Hungarian National Gallery
Inv. No.: 61.121 T

In the early 1870s, Benczúr and Szinyei worked in Munich as close friends. This work by Benczúr, who later became an Academic painter, demonstrates his understanding of the essence of *plein-air*, possibly the result of seeing Courbet's 1869 exhibition in Munich.
The style and setting of the painting is similar to that of Szinyei's *Mother and Child* (Plate 235) and *Lovers* (Plate 236). There is also an identical detail in all three—the chequered scarf.
This painting inaugurated a period of promise for Benczúr. The simplicity achieved here and the naturalness of the pose were nevertheless not to become features of his later work.

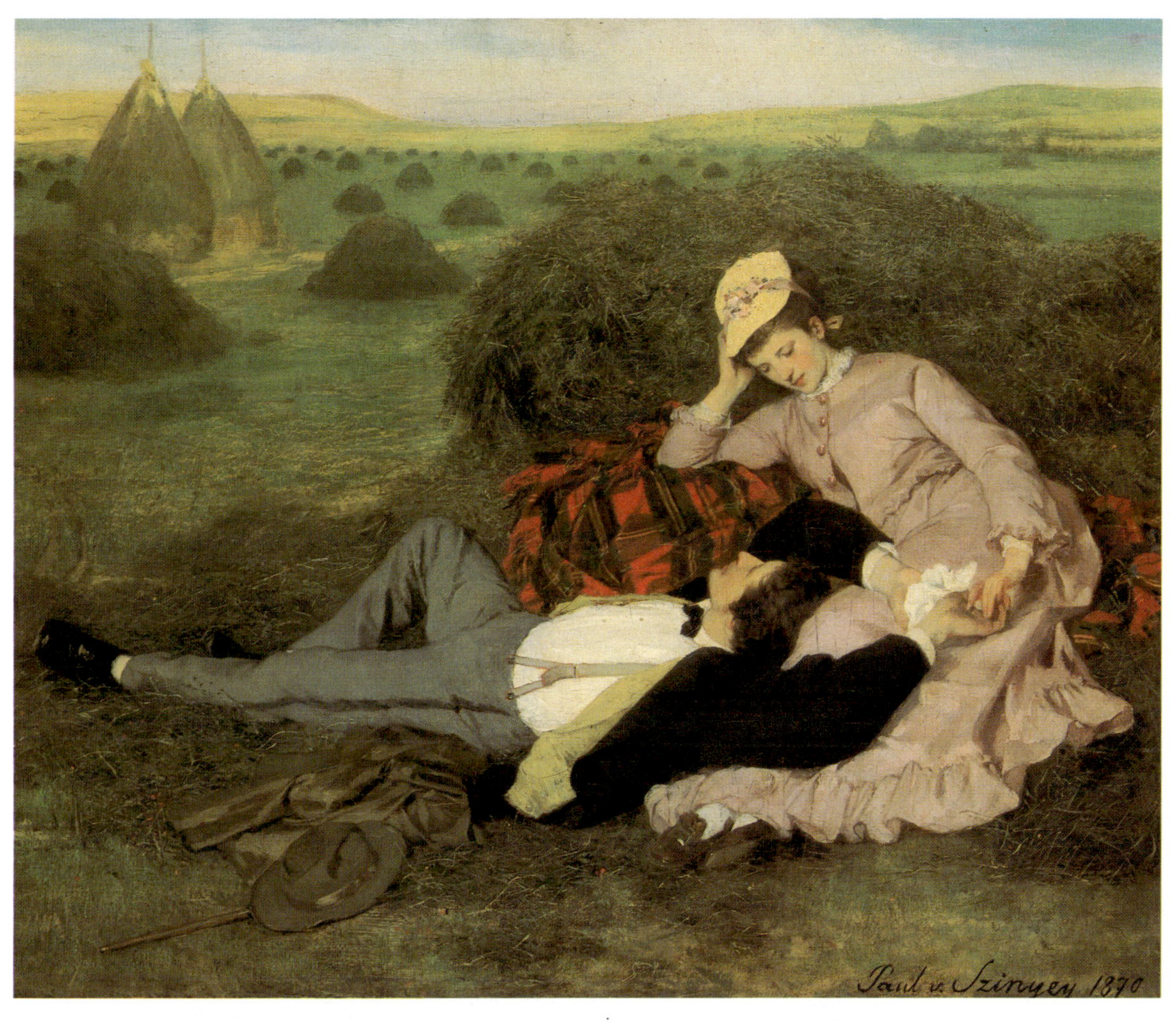

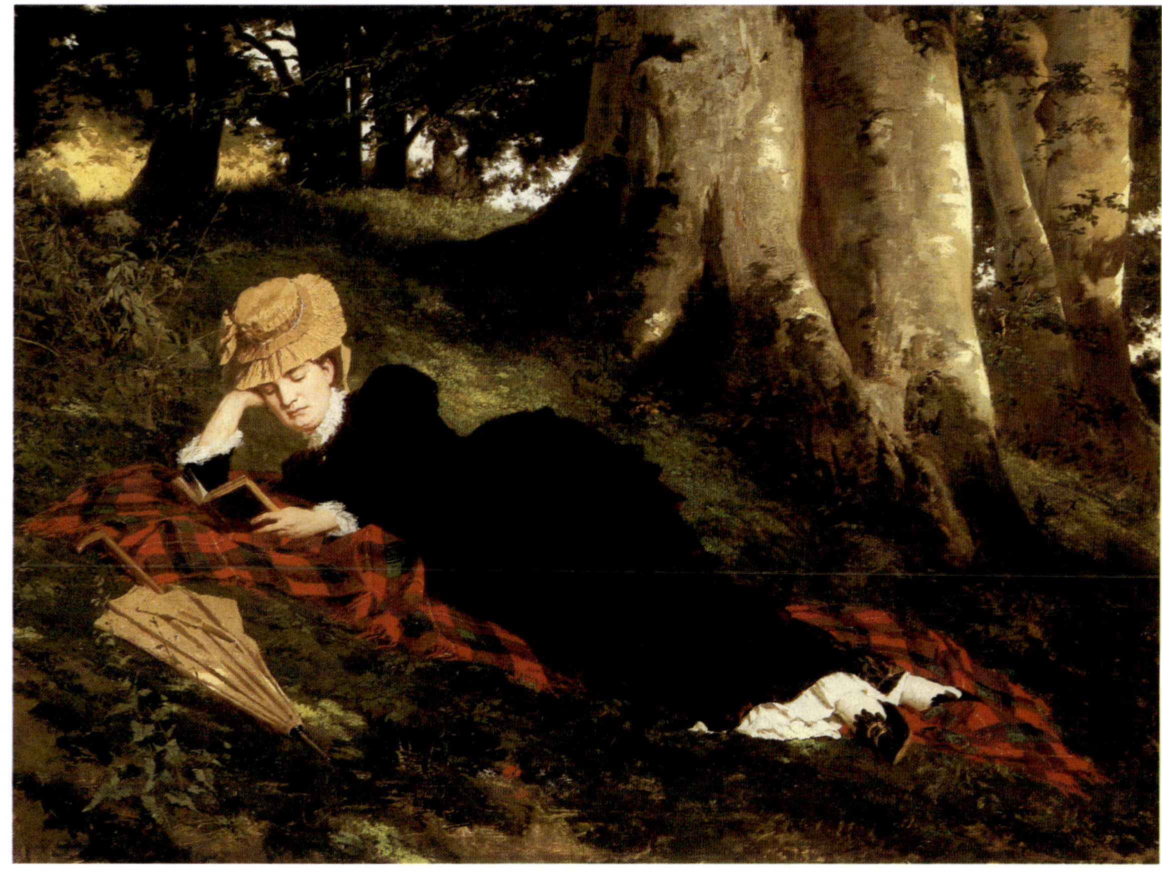

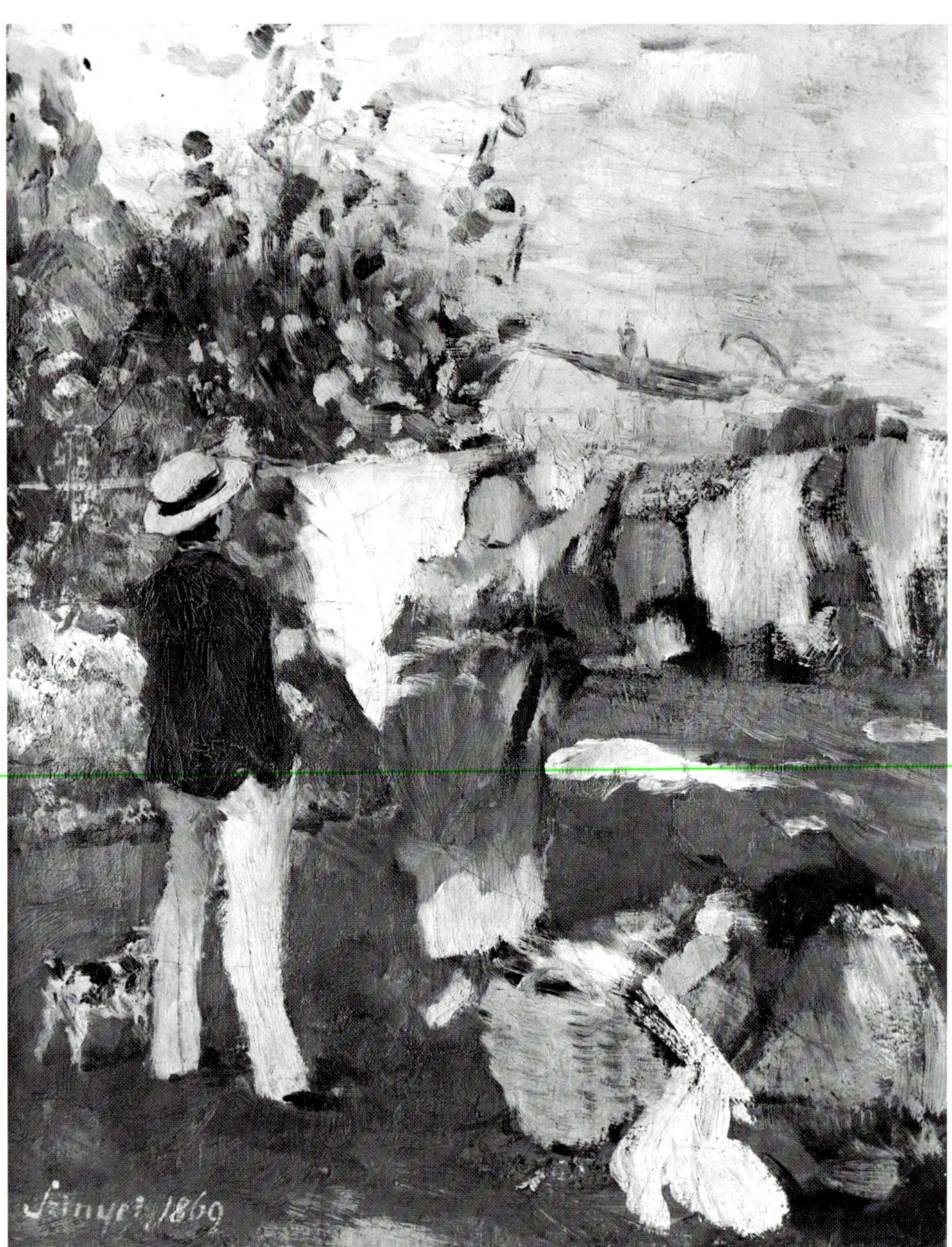

238. PÁL SZINYEI MERSE
Hanging Out the Wash, 1869
Oil on canvas, 30.5 × 31 cm
Signed bottom left: "Szinyei, 1869"
Budapest, Hungarian National Gallery
Inv. No.: 56.167

Between the years 1869 and 1872, when Pál Szinyei Merse was active in Jernye and Munich, his work can scarcely be recognized as coming from the hand of the same artist. In this painting, believed to have been composed at Jernye, the artist uses brush strokes and fresh, bright colours to capture a commonplace, everyday event. At Jernye, Szinyei did not concern himself with making literary allusions, nor with painting mythological figures.

239. PÁL SZINYEI MERSE
The Swing (Vacationers, In the Garden), 1869
Oil on cardboard, 54.2 × 41 cm
Signed bottom left: "Szinyei"
Budapest, Hungarian National Gallery
Inv. No.: 68.55

Although it appears to be taken at random from a larger slice of life, this composition in fact comprises three small, loosely connected groups. The first group is composed of a young lady in violet sitting on a swing, and her companion, who pushes the swing. Nearby, a mother sits on the ground, playing with her little child; in the baby carriage beside her lies her baby. The third group is arranged around a garden bench on which two ladies are seated while three others are standing nearby, one of the latter holding a violet parasol. In front of this group is a wicker picnic basket covered with a red cloth. The painting achieves cohesion through the delicate play of light and shade on the faces as the sunshine filters through the foliage.

This work is more loosely composed than Manet's *Déjeuner sur l'herbe* of 1863 (Plate 240), yet Szinyei does not achieve the same natural linking of the groups, nor the relaxed and spontaneous arrangement seen in Claude Monet's sketch of 1866 for his *Déjeuner sur l'herbe* (Plate 241).

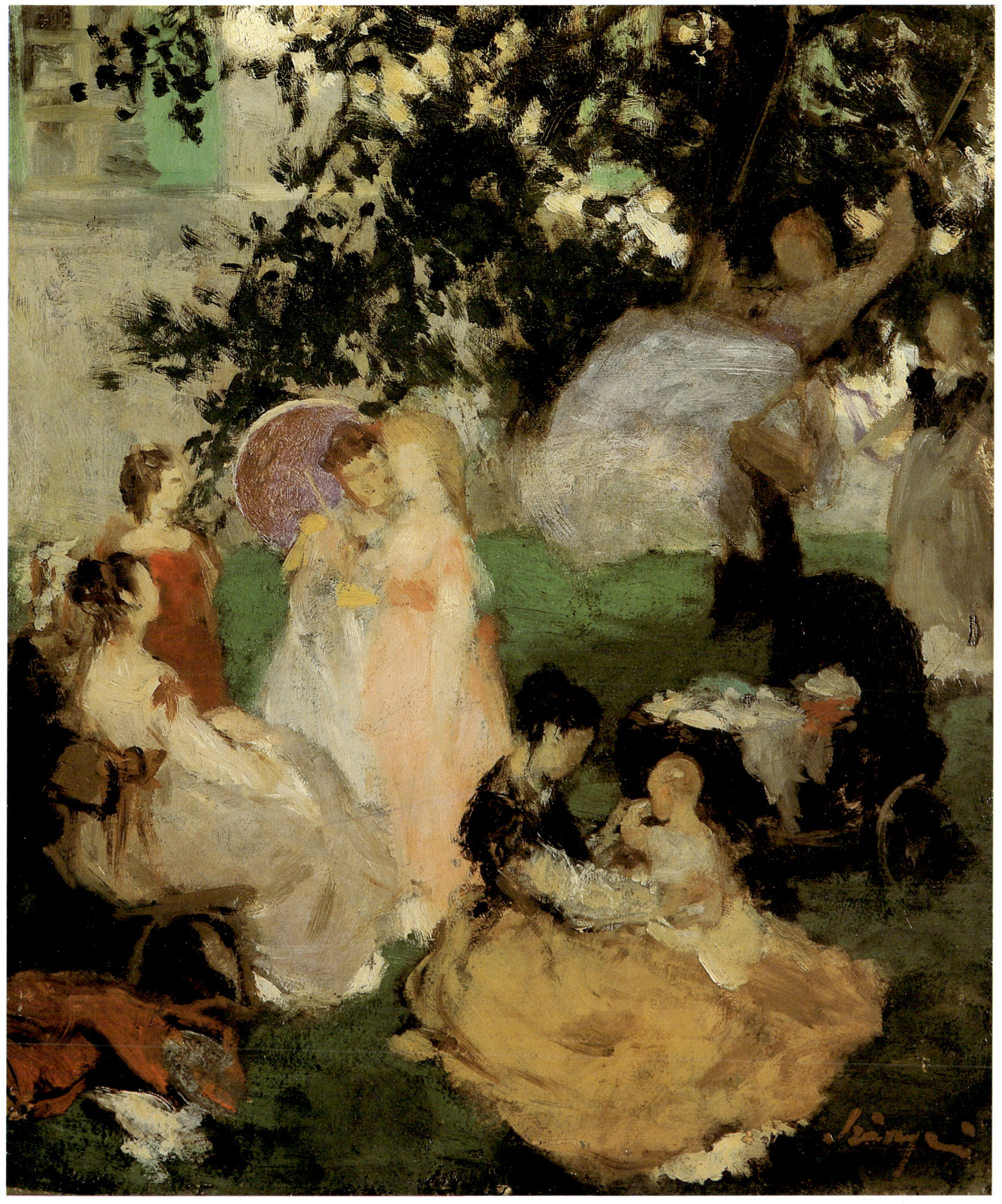

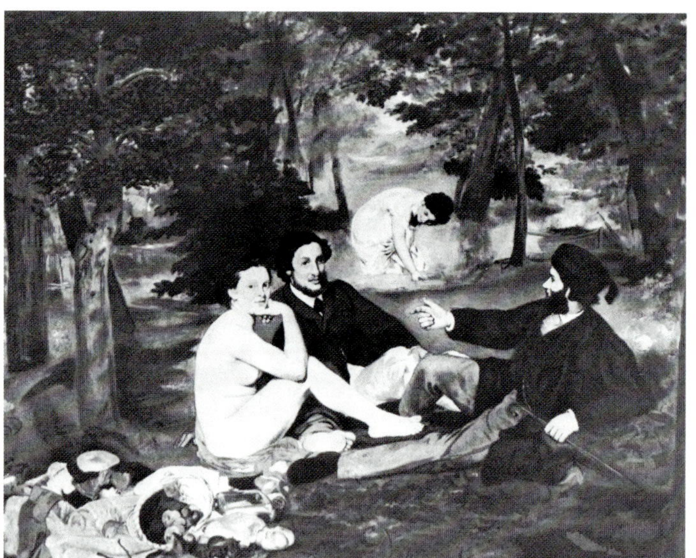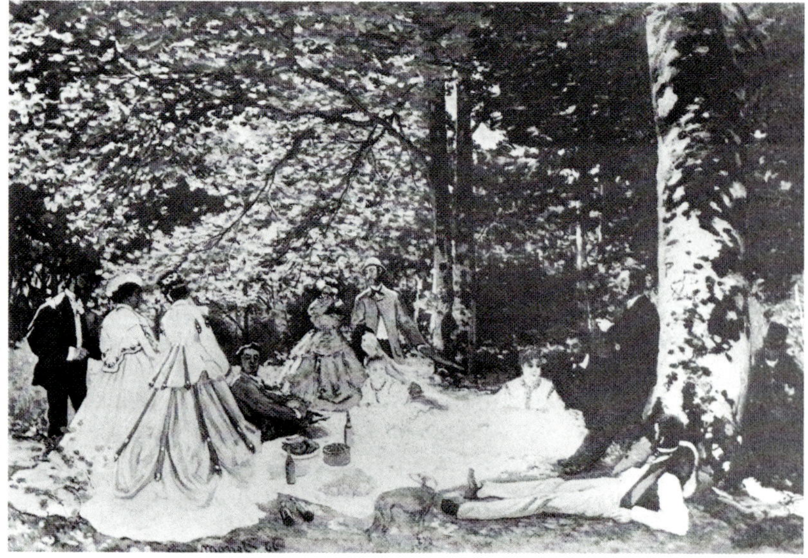

240. ÉDOUARD MANET
Déjeuner sur l'herbe, 1863
Oil on canvas, 214 × 270 cm
Signed bottom right: "E Manet 1863"
Paris, Louvre

This masterpiece by Manet is generally believed to have exercised a decisive influence on European painting in the 1860s and 1870s. In turn, art historians have rightly pointed out that in numerous details in his composition Manet modelled his work on the great classical works of the past, notably an engraving by Marcantonio Raimondi which is reminiscent of a composition by Raphael. Nevertheless, contemporary artists and the public were disconcerted by the unaffected spontaneity of a scene in which artists picnic together with their models, one of them a nude.

Szinyei was undoubtedly appreciative of the still-life details in Manet's painting, but he could not accept a representation, unless in a mythological context of clothed artists together with a naked girl. Consequently, despite all its informality, his *Picnic in May* (Plate 243) still projected the atmosphere of middle class society in Munich, unlike Manet's painting in which the artist pointedly ignored all such manners.

241. CLAUDE MONET
Déjeuner sur l'herbe (sketch), 1866
Oil on canvas, 124 × 181 cm
Signed: "Monet, 1866"
Moscow, Pushkin Museum

After the success and scandal caused by Manet's painting of the same title, Claude Monet decided to depict the same scene himself, and to do so without the classical references still evident in Manet's work. He wanted to create a large composition so that he could paint full-length portraits of the picnickers. He planned to offer the large version, similar in composition to this sketch, for exhibition at the 1866 Salon, but he was not able to finish it. Monet based his sketch and oil painting on previous landscape studies painted out of doors, which he then completed in his studio, inserting the figures painted individually from models. It was Monet's aim to create figures in contemporary dress who would convey the sublime and heroic qualities of men and women in the modern world (cf. Baudelaire).

242. PÁL SZINYEI MERSE
Sketch for Picnic in May, I, 1872
Oil on canvas, 28.8 × 34.3 cm
Signed bottom right: "Szinyei"
On reverse side, bottom right: "Szinyei 1872"
Budapest, Hungarian National Gallery
Inv. No.: 70.83

Szinyei made several small-colour sketches for his *Picnic in May*. This, believed to be the first, differs from the final, large painting only in some of the background details. The six figures are centrally placed on a gentle slope; of the four upper figures each couple is engaged in conversation, one man lies face downwards and in the foreground the man wearing a hat reaches forward to take something out of a hole which, in the final picture, is seen to be a bottle. The painter shows an equal interest in the relationship between the large coloured patches of skirts, gowns and rugs scattered on the grass, the various shades of the dark green hillside, the sunlit background, and the middle ground shaded by huge areas of shadow. On the left in the distant background figures can be seen walking up the hill. In this sketch their relationship with the figures in the foreground has not really solved the problem of perspective, and contemporary painters put forward the view that Szinyei, in his final painting, should have placed the walking figures partially behind the hillside.

243. PÁL SZINYEI MERSE
Picnic in May, 1873
Oil on canvas, 123 × 163.5 cm
Signed bottom right: "Szinyei Merse Pál 1873"
Budapest, Hungarian National Gallery
Inv. No.: 1547

After making several preliminary pencil and colour sketches, Szinyei took half a year to complete this famous masterpiece in his studio. The figures are those of Viotti, an architect, the wife of Gyula Gundelfinger, a Hungarian painter who worked in Munich and was a friend of the artist, Maria Probstner (dressed in white), a professional model (in pink), Baron Zsigmond Luzsénszky, Heinrich Max and, lying face downwards, the artist himself. These figures were painted from life in the studio, each of them being added to the composition in turn.

In his *Picnic in May*, Szinyei attempted a more modest task and one easier to carry out than Monet's heroic vision which involved full-length figures, twelve models in all. At the same time there are certain similarities between Szinyei's working method and that used by Monet in his early Impressionistic work, which, however, Szinyei could not have known, since it was never finished. In creating his composition, Szinyei's first concern was the form of the subject matter. In terms of the painted surface of his canvas, he did not achieve the same homogeneous effects of colour and light as did the French master; rather he applied large, even shapes of colours boldly contrasting with each other. Thus, instead of following the Impressionists' way of solving the problem of light in painting, he tended rather toward decorative colourism.

This famous painting, analyzed by many European art historians, nevertheless defies the intellect, like masterpieces in general.

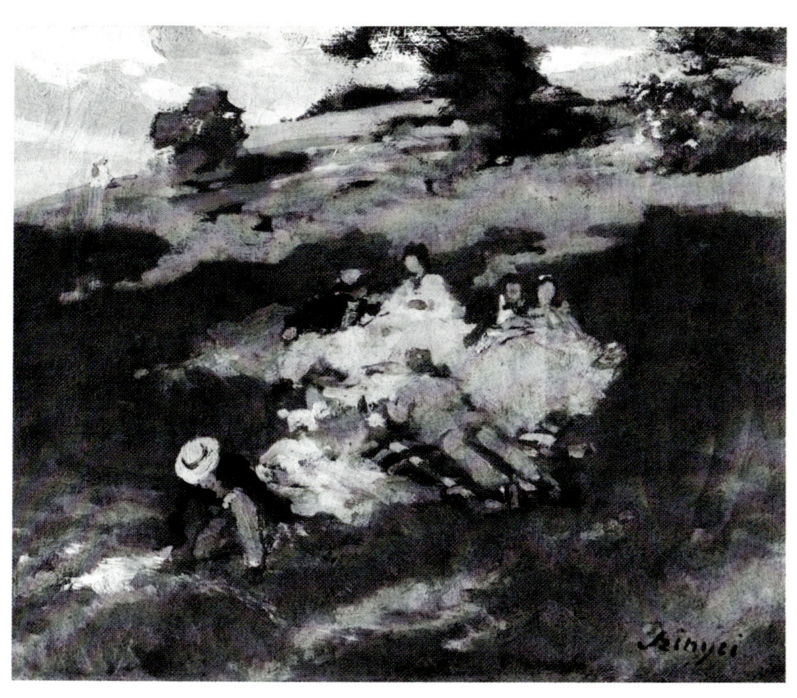

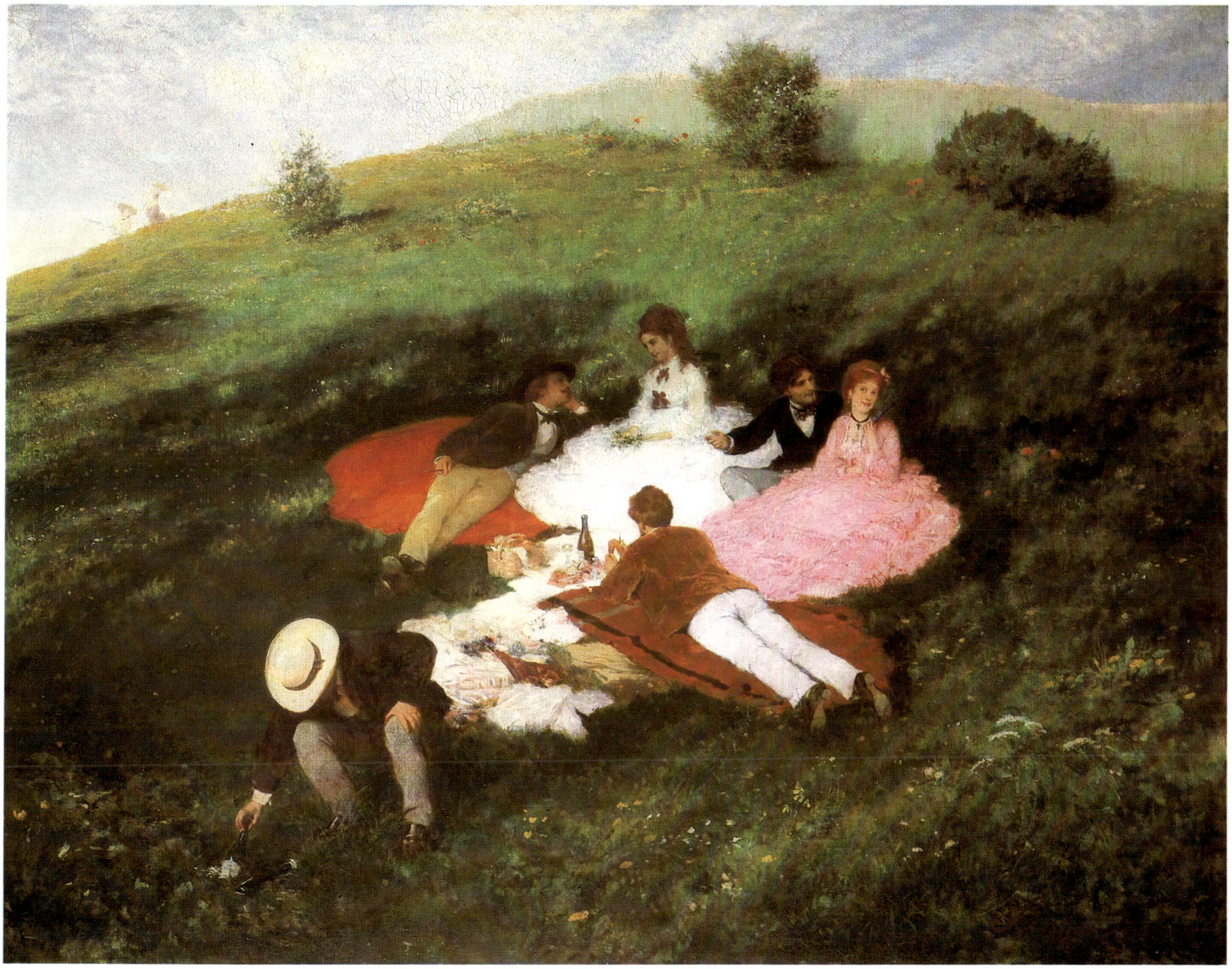

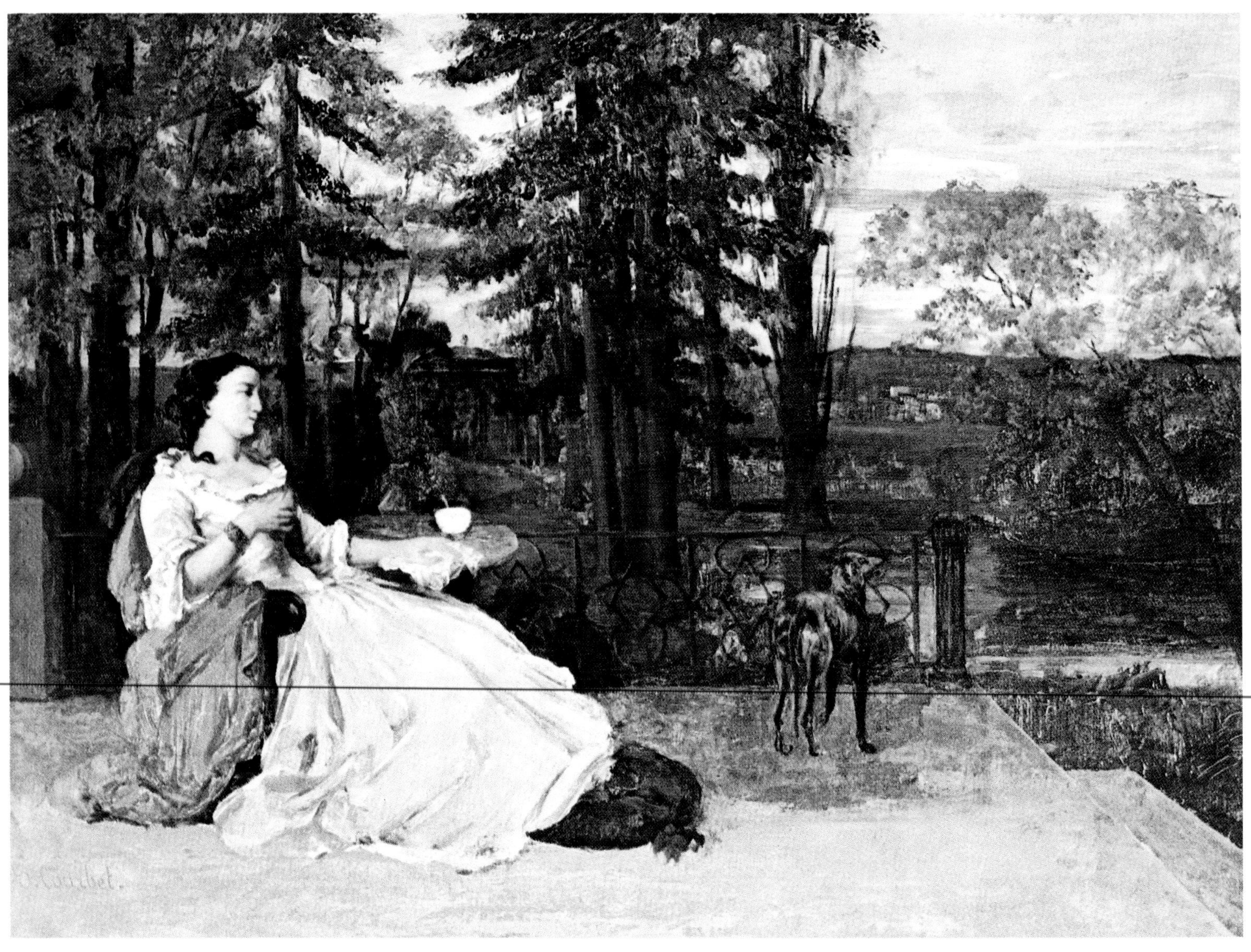

244. GUSTAVE COURBET
Lady on a Terrace (Lady from Frankfurt), 1859
Oil on canvas, 604 × 140 cm
Signed bottom left: "G. Courbet"
Cologne, Wallraf Richartz Museum
Inv. No.: WRM 2635

In Courbet's work the pursuit of natural simplicity alternates with a striving for the monumental, which was a consequence of his following the Classical ideal. The duality of his artistic aims showed itself first in one way then in another. This painting of a woman sitting on a terrace was completed in 1858, when the artist was staying in Germany. By then Courbet had made Realism his precisely defined artistic style, which he expressed in a concise manifesto and also in his exhibited works. In this picture, sharply observed details of the natural setting combined with the subject's dignified pose impart a quality of classical timelessness. This painting was one of his favourites, and was exhibited at his big show of 1867 in Paris.

245. PÁL SZINYEI MERSE
Lady in Violet, 1874
Oil on canvas, 102.5 × 77 cm
Inscribed bottom left: "1874, Szinyei Merse P"
Budapest, Hungarian National Gallery
Inv. No.: N. 5078

This portrait of his young wife was completed by Szinyei at Jernye, in the drawing room of their country home, although he has given her a landscape setting. Because of the questionable rendering of the play of light on the face of the lady it cannot be classed as a *plein-air* painting.

The interplay of colours in Szinyei's *Lady in Violet* is linked with the decorative problems of his painting entitled *The Artist's Studio* (Plate 248). Szinyei's biographers saw in the characterization of the model the timeless Classicism and Symbolism seen in Feuerbach's paintings of Iphigenia. Although the setting and the proportions of the figure related to the landscape differ in this work from those in Courbet's *Lady on a Terrace* (Plate 244), Anna Szinyei Merse's observation about the two paintings is relevant: she said that both Courbet and Szinyei realized that the relation between model and landscape is not solely dependent on the effect of light, but also on the equality of emphasis and the use of complementary colours.

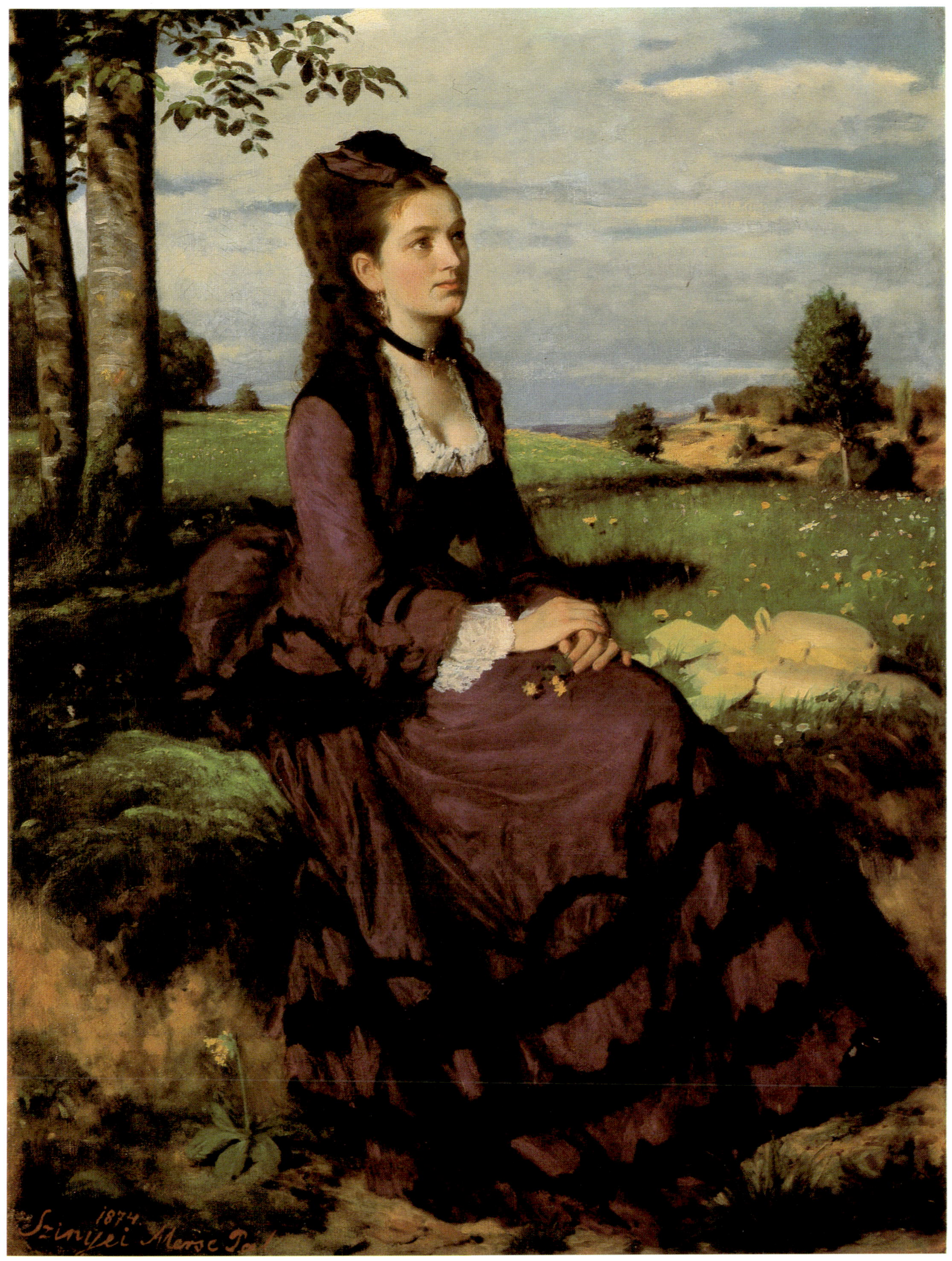

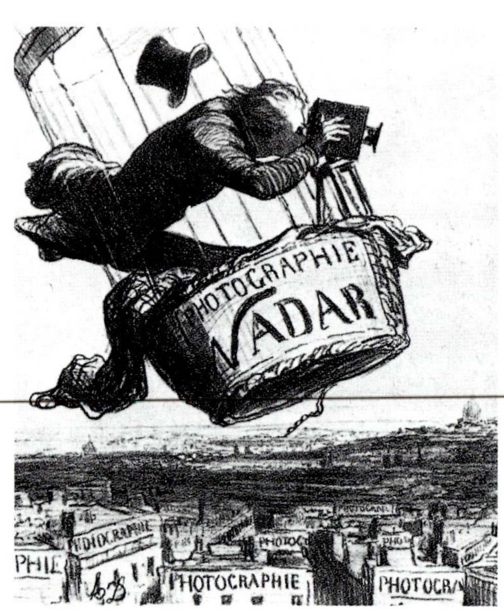

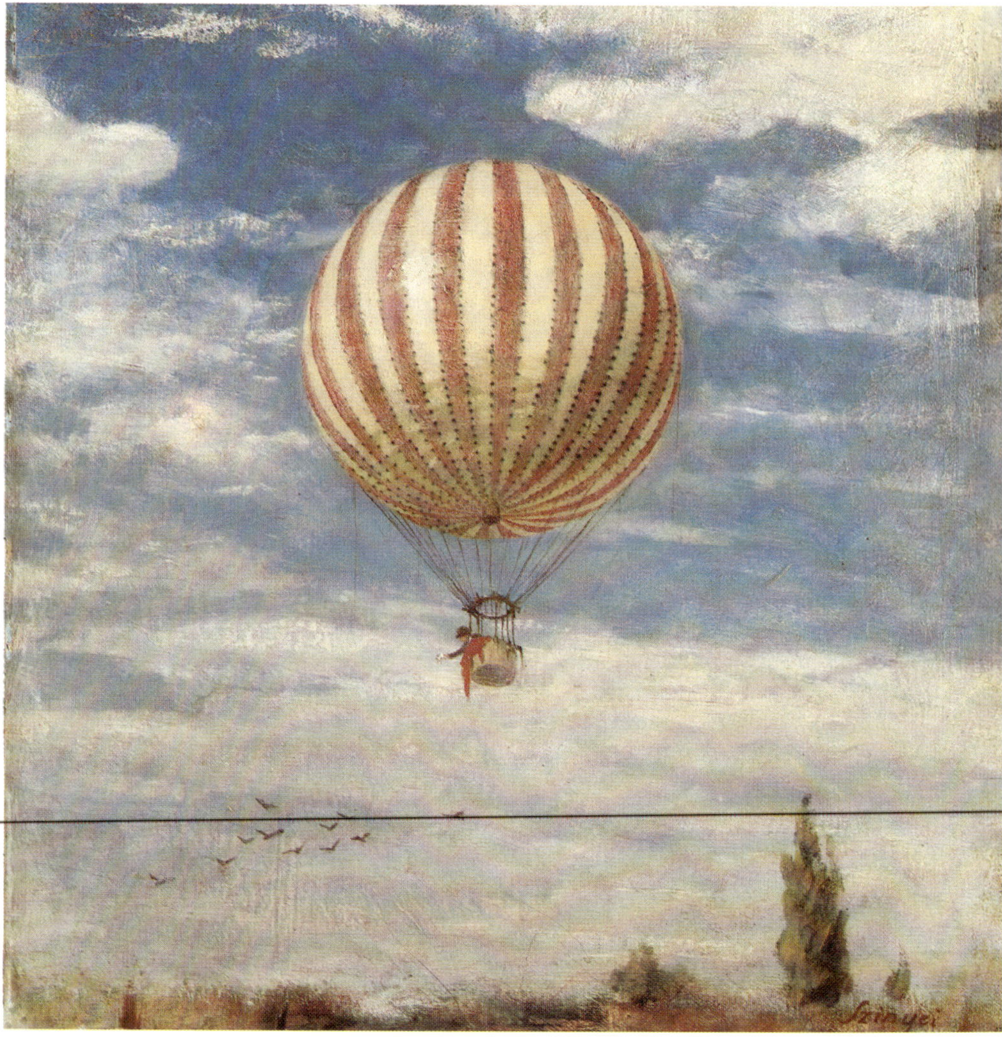

246. HONORÉ DAUMIER
The Photographer Nadar in his
Balloon over Paris, 1862
Lithography on paper, 272 × 222 mm
Signed bottom left: "D."
Paris, Louvre, Cabinet des Estampes. L.
Delteil 3248

In this lithograph Nadar (the photographer
who espoused the cause of Impressionism) is
shown floating in a balloon over Paris trying
to photograph the panorama below. He represents a new type of artist, interested in the
broader aspects of a view. Nadar was the
first to organize an exhibition for the Impressionists, who tried to explore the connection between sight and time according to
a new visual understanding; he was one of
a new generation interested in painting ever
changing colours and the effect of light.
Nadar attempted to solve the same problem
by means of the new technical invention of
the 19th century—the camera. Honoré
Daumier, who made this lithograph, rightly
understood the importance of Nadar's experiment and its significance at that time.

247. PÁL SZINYEI MERSE
The Balloon, 1882
Oil on canvas, 42 × 39 cm
Signed bottom right: "Szinyei"
Budapest, Hungarian National Gallery
Inv. No.: 4648

Szinyei painted this amusing scene while
staying in Vienna. He probably saw a balloon in the Prater, where it was exhibited as
an object of curiosity. The figure of his
brother-in-law, who was about to set off on
a long journey, was added by way of a joke.
Szinyei could not compete with Daumier
when it came to rendering the airborne motion of the balloon although, while Daumier
solved the problem in a bold drawing,
Szinyei used colour. Yet, as on so many
other occasions, he showed his awareness of
a new theme, which was to remain with us
to the present day.

248. PÁL SZINYEI MERSE
The Artist's Studio, 1873
Oil on canvas, 35.7 × 43 cm
Signed bottom left: "Szinyei 1873"
Budapest, Hungarian National Gallery
Inv. No.: 5130

In this picture Szinyei shows his large *Picnic
in May* half-finished on the easel. However,
his intention went beyond the story of his
creation of a genre painting with landscape
background painted in the studio. Displayed
on the walls in horizontal rows are details of
decorative wall paintings and scenes from
nature. The ceiling is embellished with
a green garland of leaves, beneath it a frieze
composed of patches of pure colour, and below it another band of brilliant blue representing the sky trellised with branches of the
same green as the hillside in the painting on
the easel. The lower wall is divided into
fields in which Japanese actors or Pompeian
dancers can be seen against a very vivid red
background, a patch of the same pure red being repeated in the as yet unfinished composition on the easel. This small patch eventually became the red cape spread on the
ground in the final version (Plate 243).

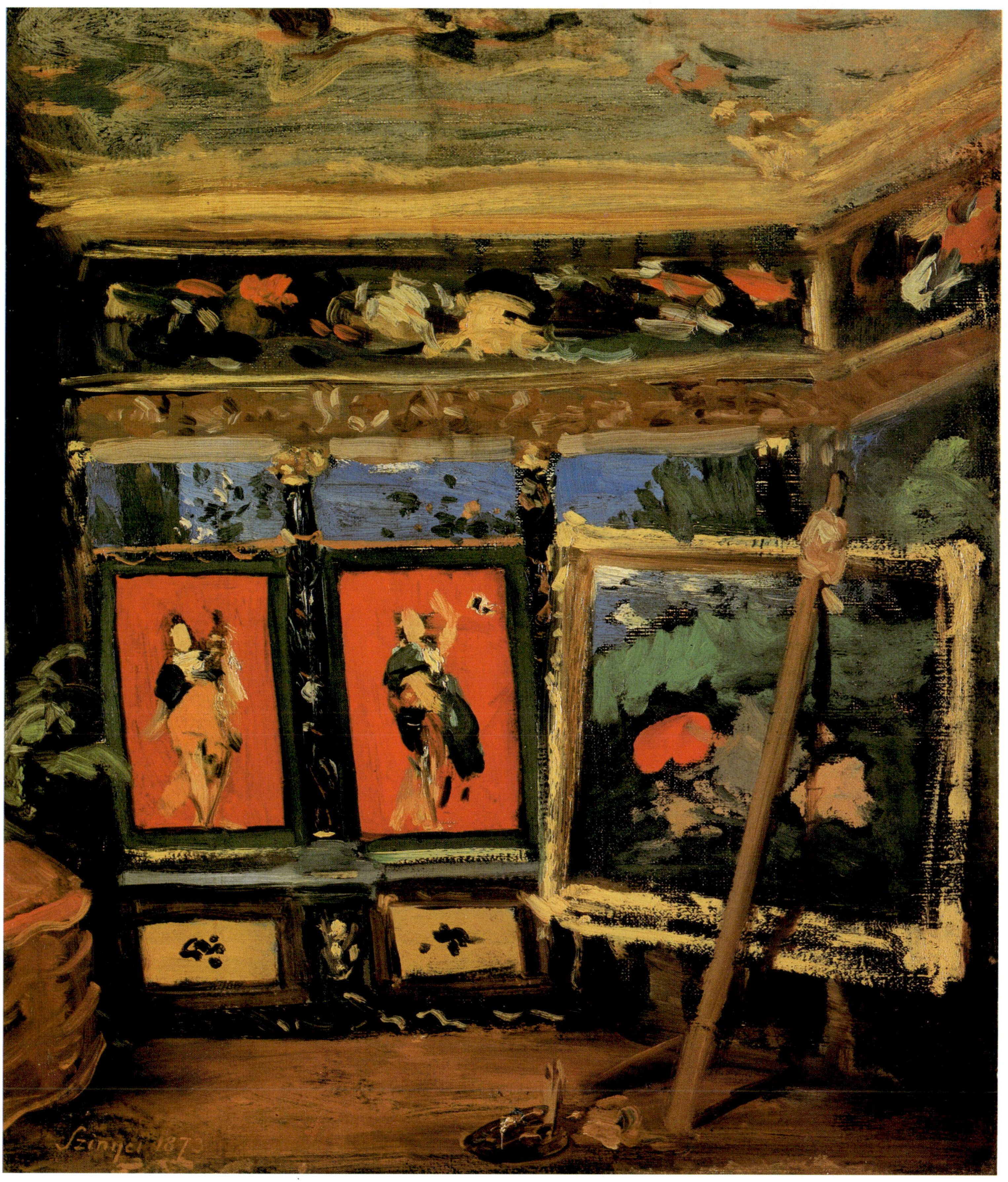

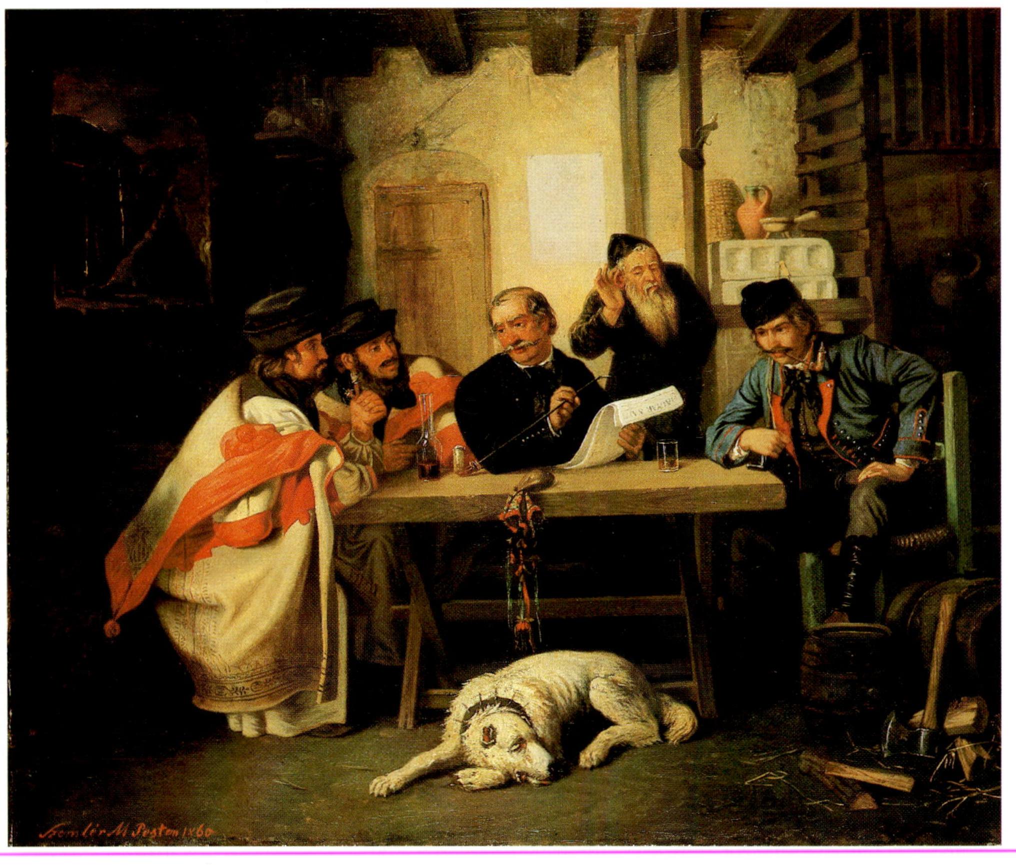

249. MIHÁLY SZEMLÉR
The Council, 1860
Oil on canvas, 50×60 cm
*Signed bottom left: "Szemlér M. Pesten
1860"*
Budapest, Hungarian National Gallery
Inv. No.: 58.294 T

Though the signature indicates that the painting was executed in Pest, it is well known that in the 1850s Szemlér spent a good deal of time in the country, especially in Transdanubia and the Great Plain. When travelling he carefully observed the shepherds and peasants in their national dress and the life in the village inns, so that he could later use these subjects for water-colour drawings. This scene is authentic in every detail—the interior of an inn with an earthen floor, plain beams, white-washed walls, wooden partition and the stove with the obligatory sour-milk jug, earthenware vessel and water tub.

The customers sit round a trestle table in the middle of the room. An elderly nobleman reads a political newspaper called "Magyar Sajtó", a hunter in a blue suit and two swineherds sit beside him, while an old man listens to their conversation. Szemlér obviously enjoyed painting every detail from the red border on the shepherd's long felt cloak to the wreath on the table with a band around it.

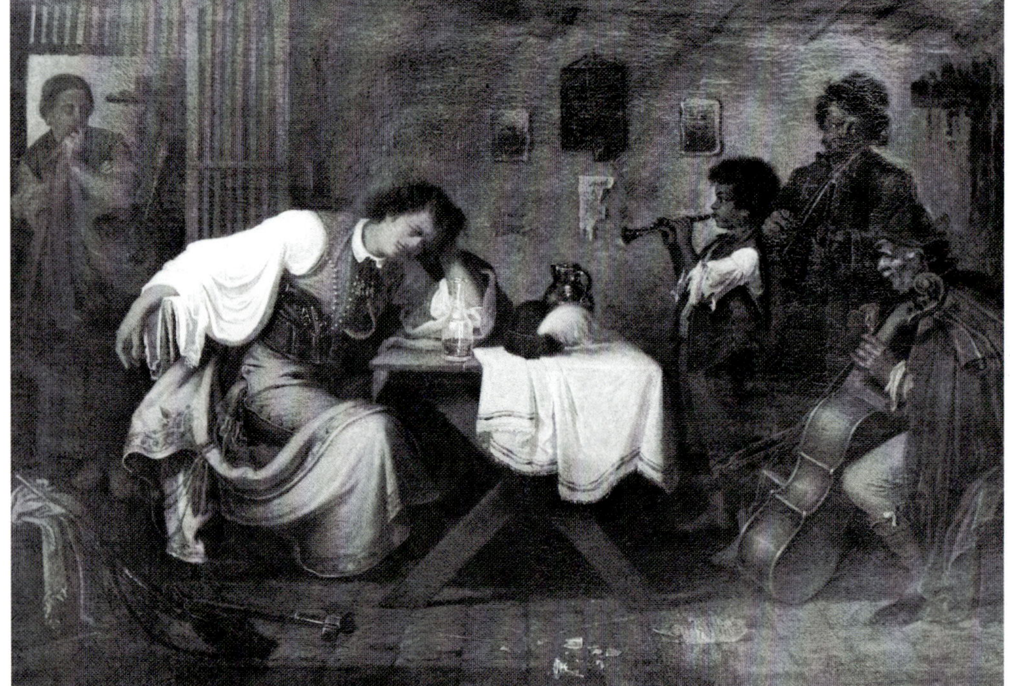

250. MIHÁLY MUNKÁCSY
Lovesick Lad (Grieving Betyár), 1865
Oil on canvas, 70.5×98 cm
Unsigned
Debrecen, Déri Museum
Inv. No.: DF 205.9.3

Mihály Munkácsy follows the Hungarian tradition in his representations of peasant scenes. He tried his hand at illustrations for magazines, using themes from everyday life and history, like those used by Mihály Szemlér and Mór Than. Later he used these themes for large oil paintings.

There is a drawing by Szemlér in which a *betyár* (outlaw) is seen sitting in an inn, supporting his head with his elbow on the table. In this painting by Munkácsy, however, the *betyár* is neither revelling nor resting. He is grieving, his mood expressed in every line of his body. Some musicians play for him, so that he breaks down under the strain of his misery. The woman in the background stands rather at a loss, curious but unable to understand why the *betyár* is grieving.

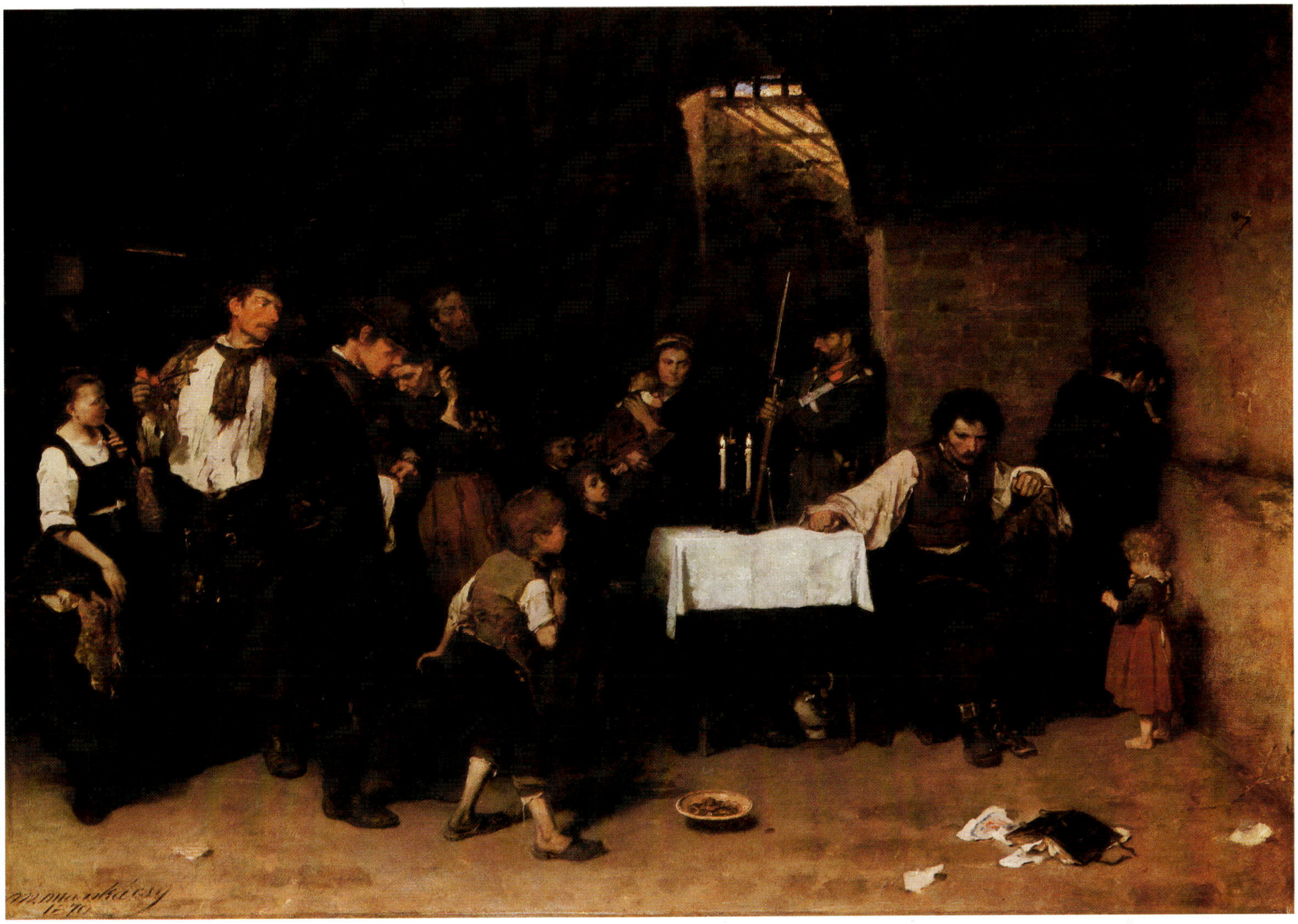

251. MIHÁLY MUNKÁCSY
The Condemned Cell, I, 1869–1870
Oil on wood, 139×193.5 cm
Signed bottom left: "M. Munkácsy 1870"
Budapest, Hungarian National Gallery
Inv. No.: 65.54 T

From 1865, when Munkácsy painted his
Lovesick Lad (Plate 250) until the time he
composed this scene, he made repeated
sketches. In two oil sketches the setting is already a condemned cell. In both sketches the
young *betyár* (outlaw) is seen alone in his cell.
By 1869 Munkácsy had conceived a more
ambitious composition. Having observed
how thoroughly Ludwig Knaus had studied
the character of each figure in his genre-
paintings, Munkácsy decided to represent
a group of contrasting characters, the prisoner and his visitors.

The painting was awarded the Gold Prize in
the Paris Salon of 1870; from there the painting was taken to America, and it was only in
1968 that it was re-sold to the Hungarian
National Gallery.

252. MIHÁLY MUNKÁCSY
**A photographic study for the main
character of the Condemned Cell,
Düsseldorf, 1869**
Photograph: 20×13.5 cm
Békéscsaba, Munkácsy Mihály Museum
Inv. No.: Hd 58.26.103

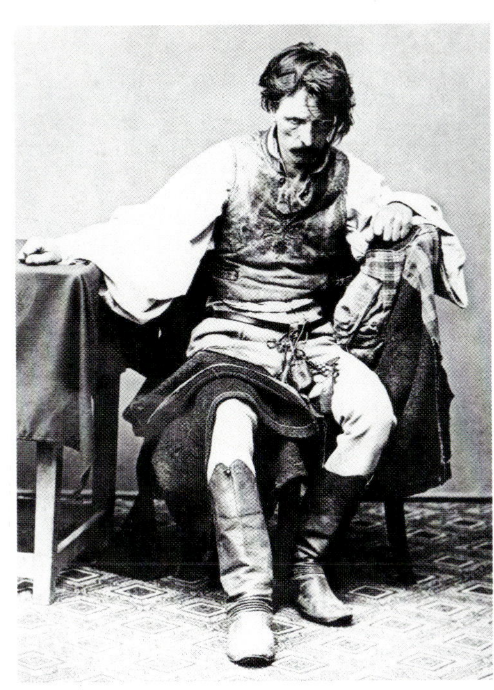

By the 1850s the practice of using photographs as a basis for composition was customary among French Realist painters, especially Gustave Courbet. How Munkácsy
actually worked can only be guessed. He
probably first "staged" the entire scene in his
imagination, made sketches of the setting
and the main characters, figured out the relationship of the various visitors to the condemned man, then dressed his models to suit
their characters. The next step probably consisted of several stages: the models would be
photographed and sketched in pencil; the
pencil sketches would provide a base from
which colour sketches would be made; the
figures would then be placed within the setting and thus the final composition was
achieved.

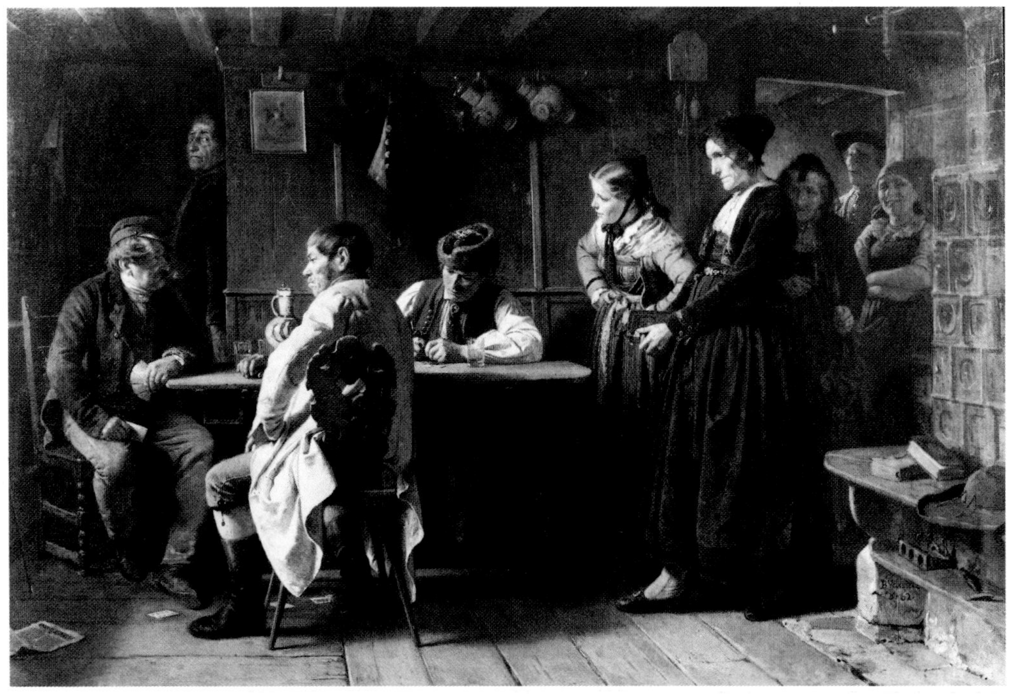

253. BENJAMIN VAUTIER
Peasants Playing Cards at Church Time, 1862

Oil on canvas, 62×90 cm
Signed right, under bench: "B. Vautier 1862"
Leipzig, Museum der bildenden Künste
Inv. No.: I. 268

Benjamin Vautier was a Düsseldorf painter whose work is linked by numerous art historians with that of Munkácsy. At an art dealer's in Düsseldorf, the *Condemned Cell* was exhibited for some time next to a painting by Vautier, and visitors remarked that its juicy colours made those of Vautier look "grey and dull".

This picture reflects a confrontation between two worlds. Some of its motifs were later used again in the background of the *Condemned Cell*. The interior of the inn is minutely rendered. Three peasants, who are playing cards instead of attending the Sunday service in church, are confronted by three scandalized women who clearly hold strong views about church-going. Behind them stand two laughing servants.

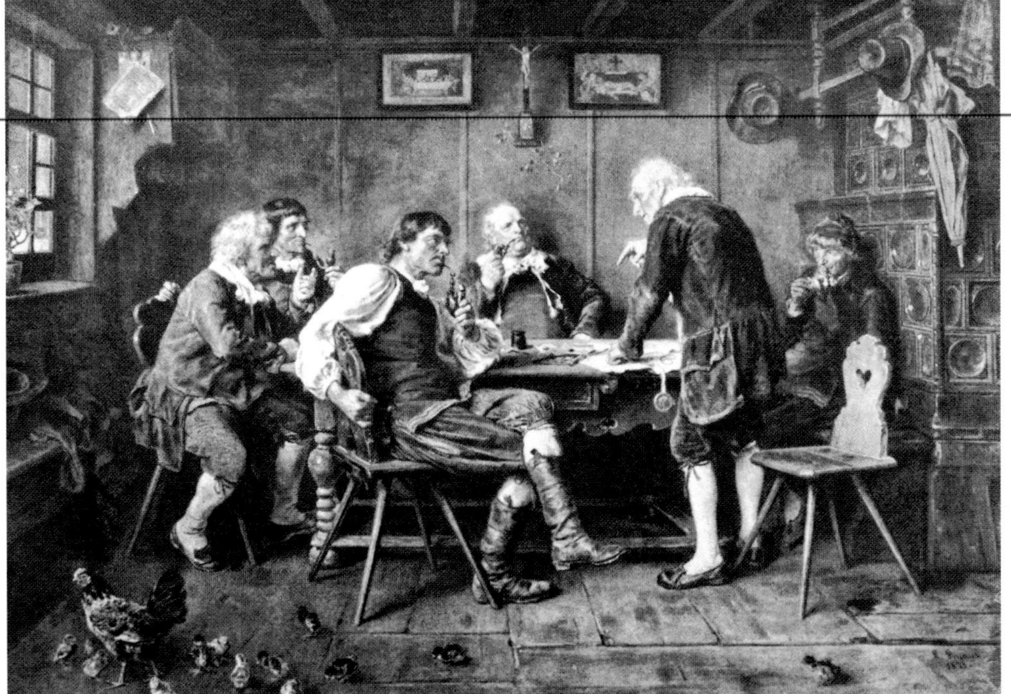

254. LUDWIG KNAUS
The Aldermen of Hauenstein Debating a Breach of the Law, 1873

Oil on canvas, 106.5×144.5 cm
Düsseldorf, Kunst Museum
Inv. No.: 1288

In some respects Knaus's career is not unlike that of Munkácsy. He too took his first lessons in the craft of painting from an itinerant painter before going to Düsseldorf where he became a pupil of Karl Sohn. The influence of the French Realist school can be felt in Knaus's works as early as the 1840s and 1850s; moreover he actually worked in Barbizon. This painting is considered to be his masterpiece—a representation of an everyday scene in a German village in which the characterization of all the figures is masterly. It was completed several years after Munkácsy's most important works, and though lacking the intensive dramatic element of those works, equals them in every other respect.

255. MIHÁLY MUNKÁCSY
Study for the principal figure of the Lint-Makers, 1871
Pencil on paper, 240×313 mm
Unsigned
Budapest, Hungarian National Gallery
Inv. No.: 1935–2812

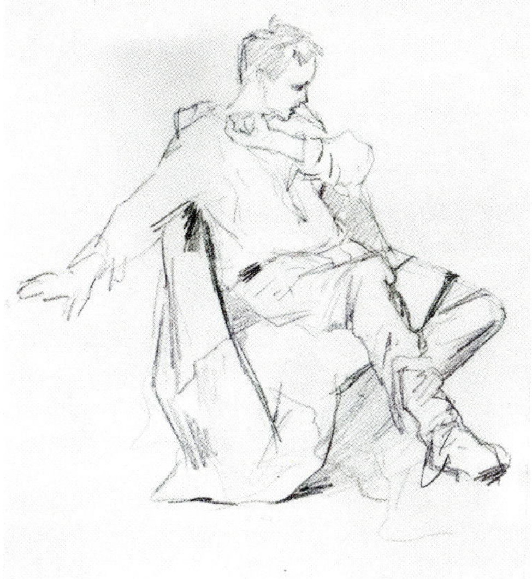

256. MIHÁLY MUNKÁCSY
The Lint-Makers, 1871
Photographic study, 30×17.5 cm
Békéscsaba, Munkácsy Mihály Museum
Inv. No.: 58.26.106

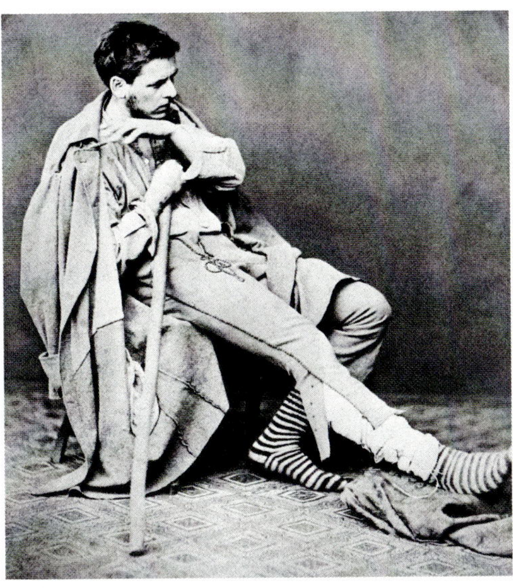

257. MIHÁLY MUNKÁCSY
The Lint-Makers, 1871
Oil on canvas, 141.3×196 cm
Signed bottom left: "Munkácsy M. 1871"
Budapest, Hungarian National Gallery,
deposited by István Károlyi

A sense of nobility, characteristic of great works of art, permeates this picture in which the figures are so beautifully grouped, the women engaged in their merciful task of ministering to the wounded.

Munkácsy also contributed a fine drawing to the 1868 Honvéd album, in which, as in this painting, he commemorates the War of Independence and the traditions perpetuated in small towns and village communities. In a dark peasant interior, women young and old give their full attention to a wounded man. The old peasant wives are seated like the Fates who know the Law of Time and preside over Destiny, while the young ones are Penelopes in mourning, or bringing up a new generation. The injured man gravely supporting his arm was created from preliminary studies and photographs.

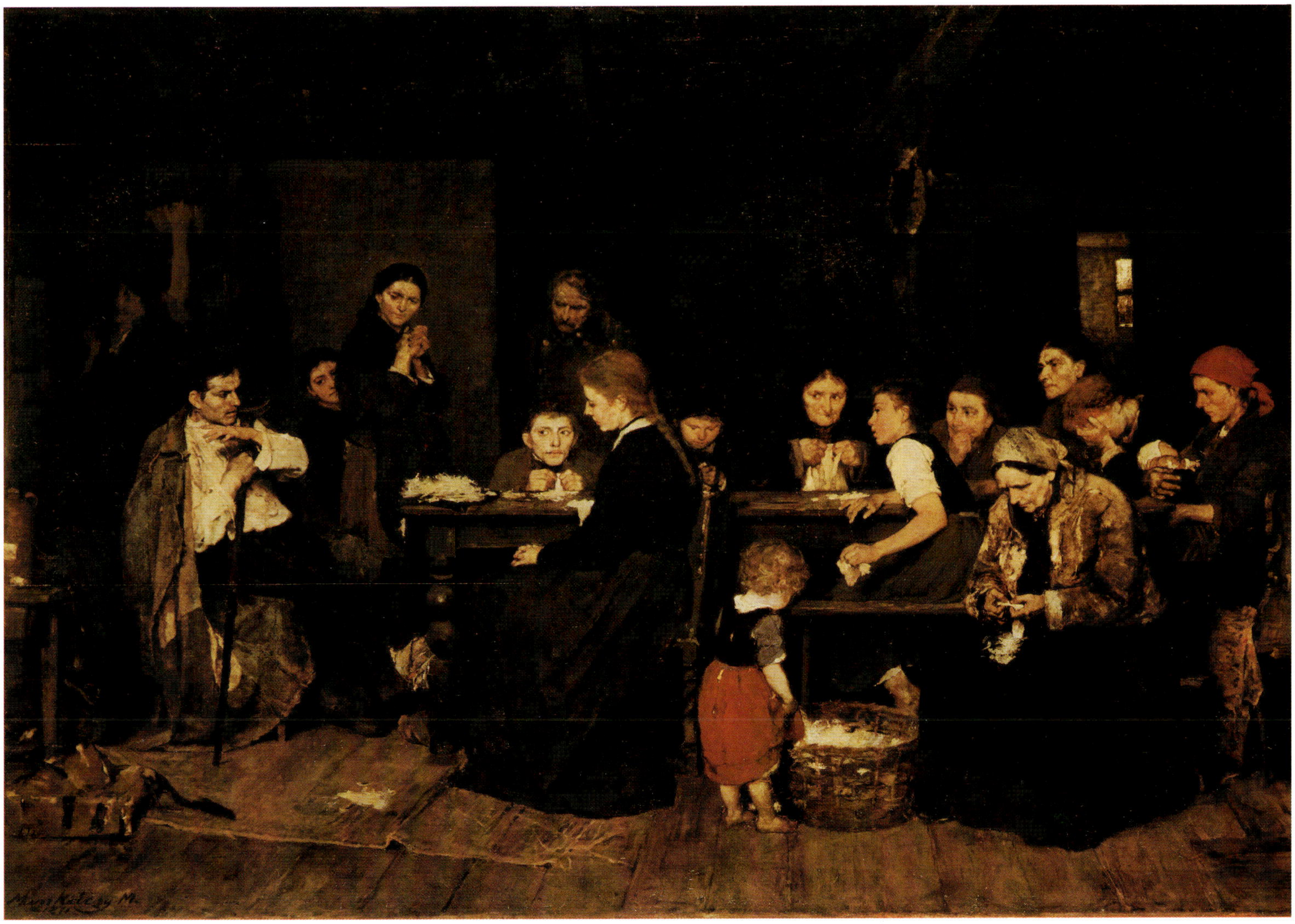

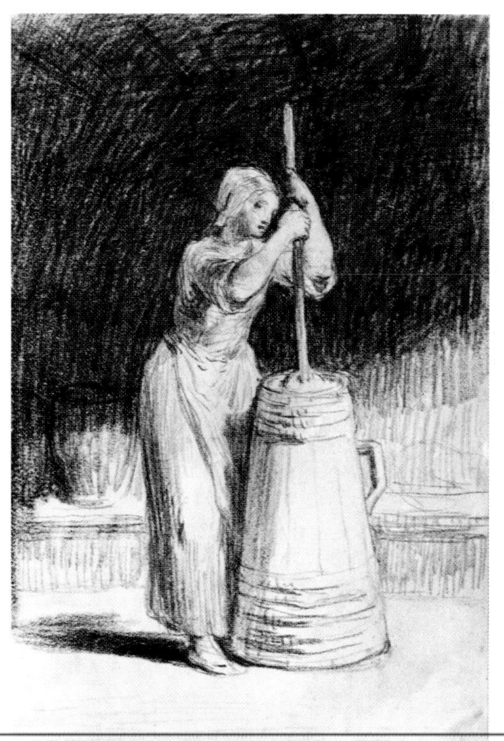

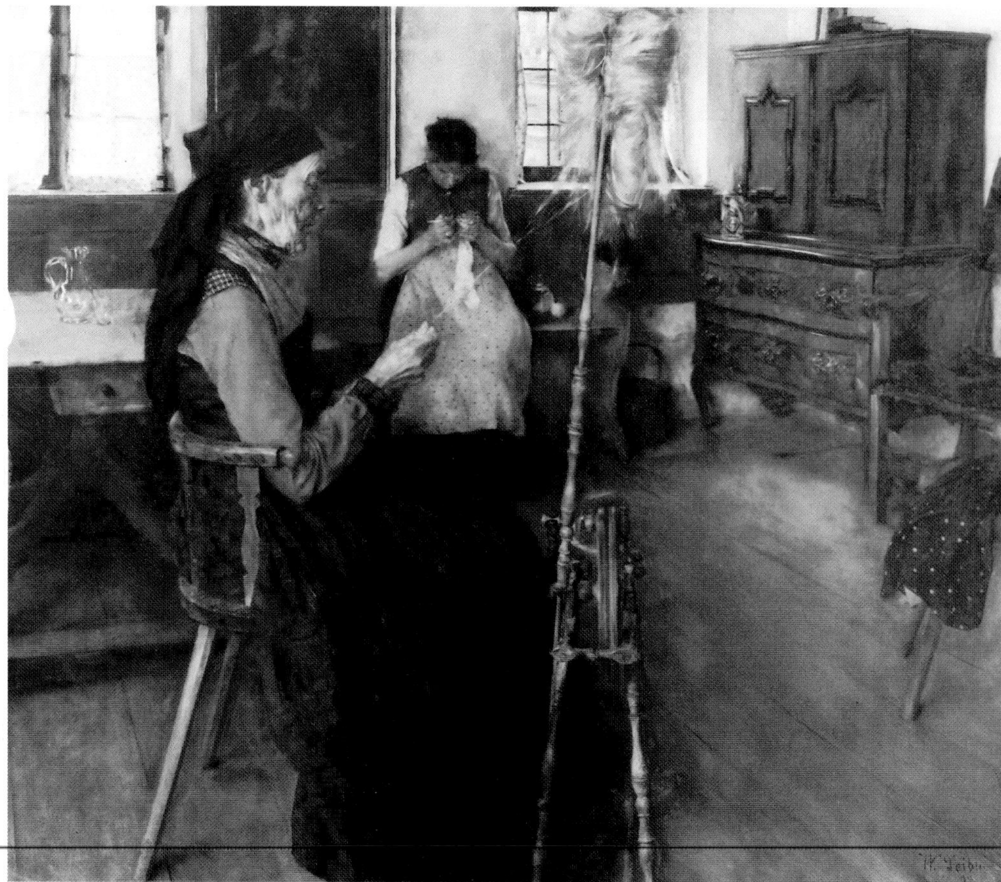

258. JEAN FRANÇOIS MILLET
Peasant Woman with a Butter Churn, 1840s

Chalk on paper, 39 × 24 cm
Signed top right: "Millet"
Budapest, Museum of Fine Arts
Inv. No.: 1935–2742

Jean François Millet's drawing represents with noble simplicity an ordinary event in the working life of a woman, just as Courbet made work the subject of his paintings in the late 1840s.

In 1871, when Munkácsy moved to Paris, he tried to achieve the realistic descriptive quality of the French School. This influence is especially marked in some of his genre-paintings in which there are only a few figures—this restraint being exercised when he felt the "need for rest".

259. WILHELM LEIBL
Spinning Woman, 1894

Oil on canvas, 65 × 74 cm
Signed bottom right: "W. Leibl 94"
Leipzig, Museum der bildenden Künste
Inv. No.: I.928

Leibl's painting is not related through its composition to Munkácsy's *Woman Churning Butter* (Plate 260), which was completed in another decade, nor is it characterized by the black and white impasto seen in both Munkácsy's and Leibl's early paintings. The two paintings are related because of the similarity of their conception. In a wider context, they can also be classed together with those paintings by Millet and some of the Barbizon painters, in which the subject is work and working men and women; and there is a similar link with Courbet whose prodigious working class figures greatly influenced both painters. (Indeed, from the early 1870s, both Munkácsy and Leibl belonged to the circle of solemn Realists.)

260. MIHÁLY MUNKÁCSY
Woman Churning Butter, 1872–1873

Oil on canvas, 120.5 × 100 cm
Signed bottom left: "Munkácsy M. 1873"
Budapest, Hungarian National Gallery
Inv. No.: 9639

The first sketch for this painting, which Munkácsy executed in Paris, was made in Düsseldorf, since Munkácsy had been pondering over the theme before he went there. In the summer of 1868 he made a drawing on a similar theme in which there are numerous figures and which has only survived in the form of a wood cut. Munkácsy finally painted it in Paris after experiencing the liberating influences of the city, where he could visit the great art collections repeatedly. This experience enabled him to give up his attempts to compare his work with the intricate, artificial, dramatic compositions of Knaus and Vautier and to depict instead such simple and yet noble subjects as this elderly woman at work, with her grandchild looking on.

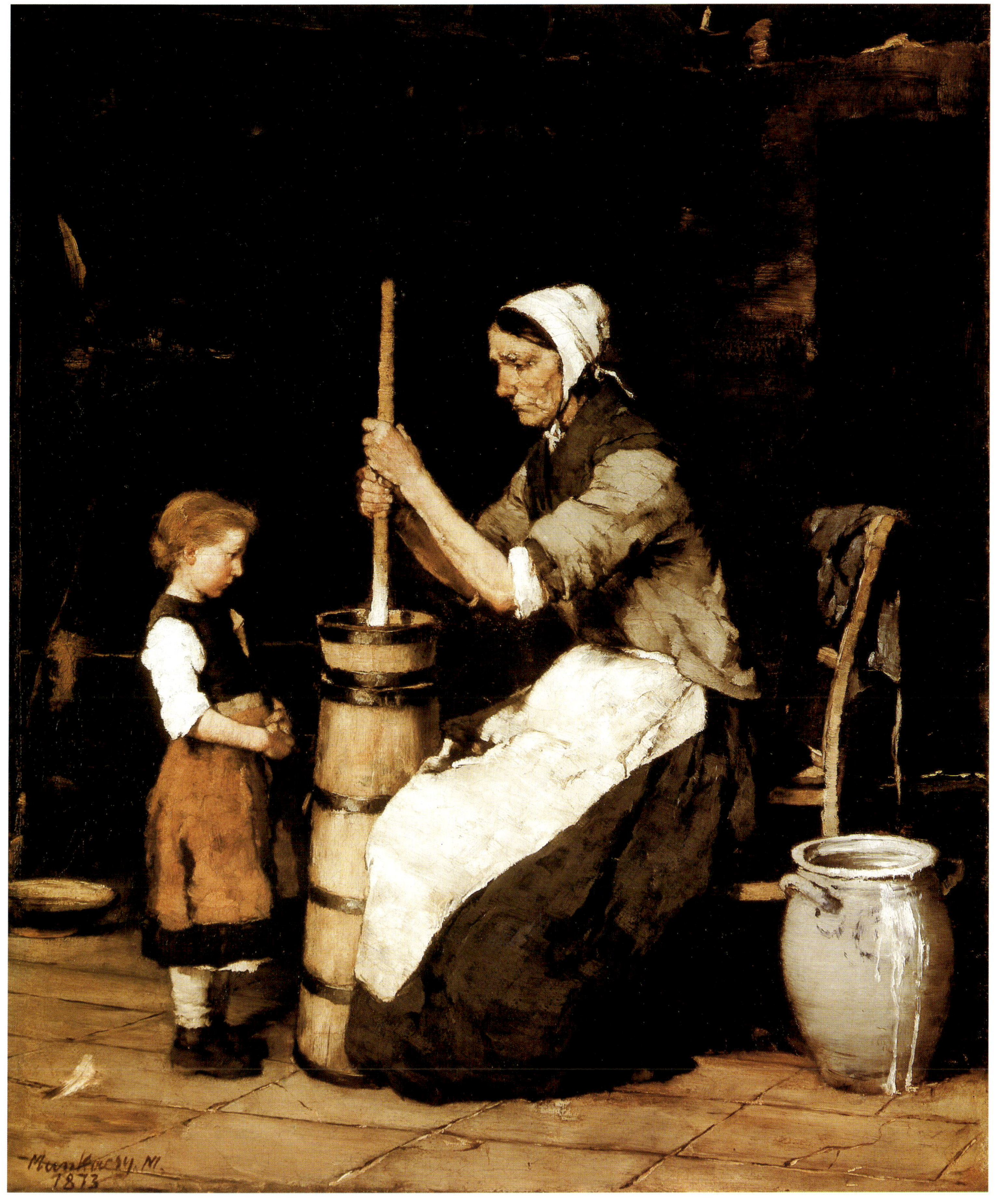

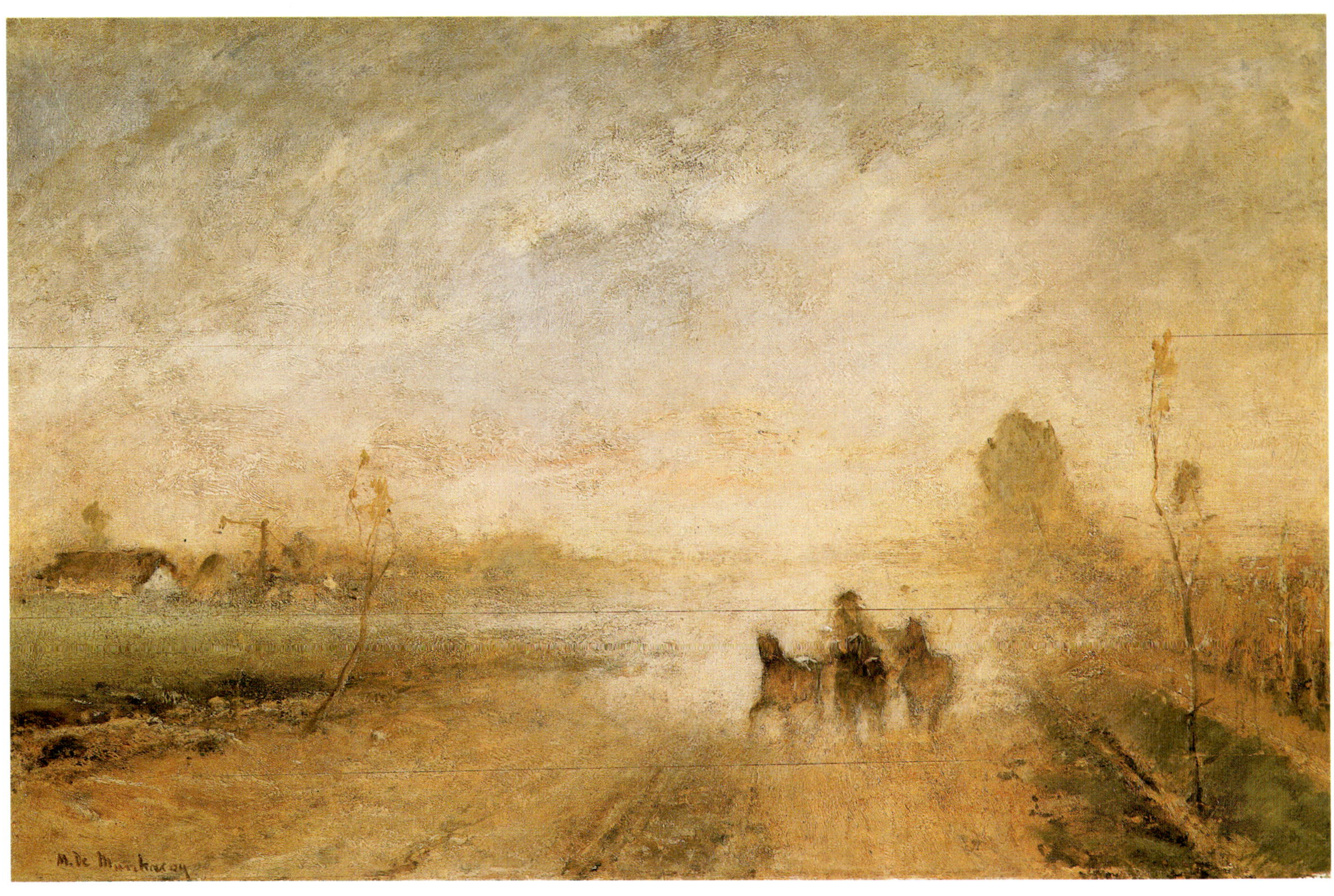

261. MIHÁLY MUNKÁCSY
Dusty Country Road, 1874
Oil on wood, 77×117.5 cm
Signed bottom left: "M. de Munkácsy"
Budapest, Hungarian National Gallery
Inv. No.: 2536

By the end of the 1860s Munkácsy had made several lively drawings in which he experimented with the theme of a cart driving at breakneck speed along a dusty road of the Great Hungarian Plain. In the 1870s and again a decade later, he painted two different but equally ambitious compositions on this theme. The pictorial solution he then chose brings him nearer to Impressionism.
Having married the widow of one of his friends from Düsseldorf, Baron De Marches, Munkácsy returned to Hungary for a period so that his wife could see the Hungarian countryside. The present painting was completed either during his stay or shortly afterwards.

This was not the artist's last painting of a dusty road in the Great Plain. There is another dating from 1881, in which pink tones rather than grey predominate; once again he represents the clouds of dust stirred up by the cart and by the wind.

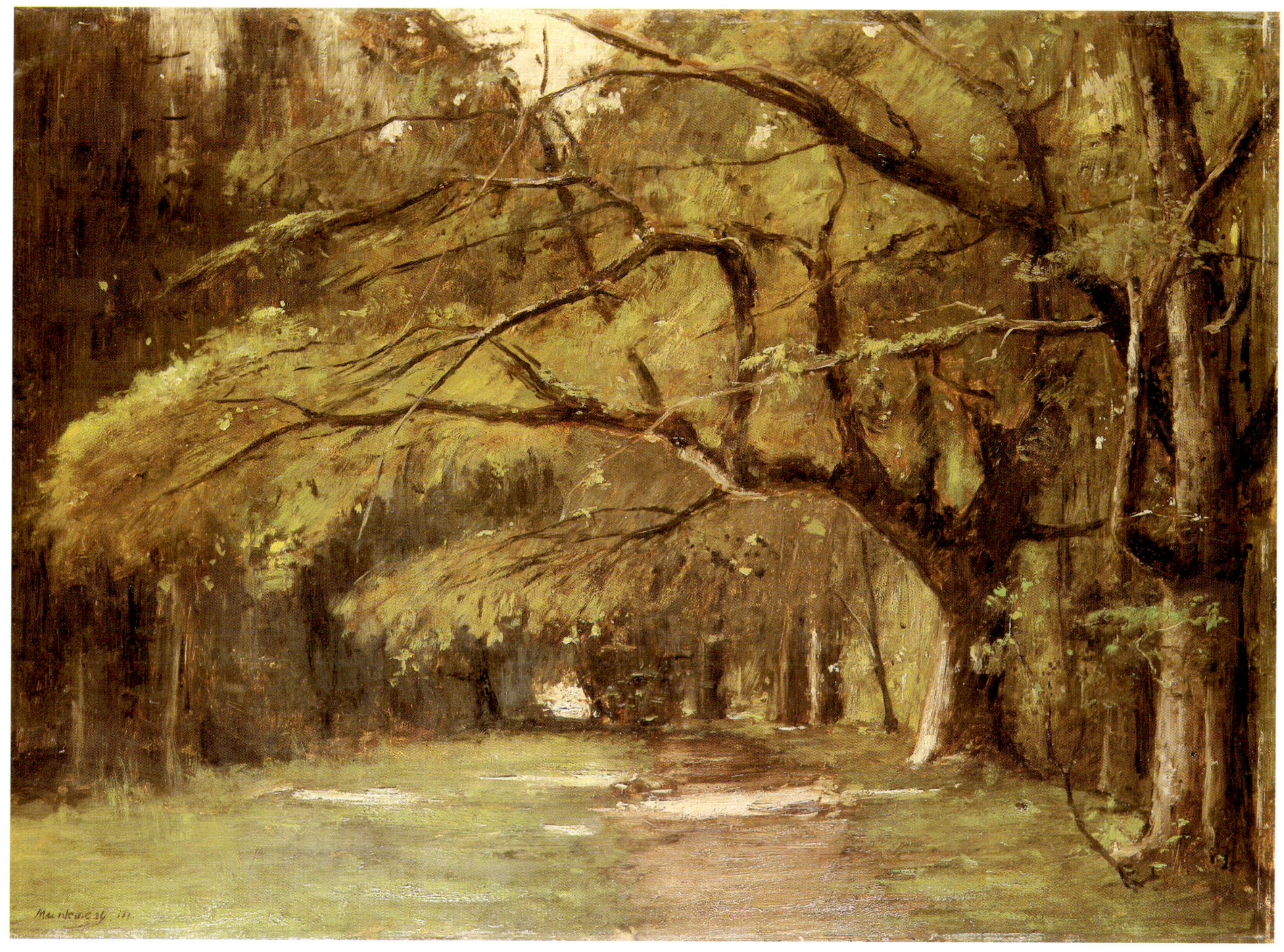

262. MIHÁLY MUNKÁCSY
The Park in Colpach, 1886
Oil on wood, 96.5×130 cm
Signed bottom left: "Munkácsy M"
Budapest, Hungarian National Gallery
Inv. No.: 2571

One finds relatively few landscapes in Munkácsy's oeuvre. In the sketch for this painting he included two prone figures no longer present in the final version, which bears witness to the artist's creative drive in the late 1880s.

In the words of 20th century art critic Géza Feleky: "The trunks of these giant trees soar majestically towards the sky, while the fresh green foliage dances playfully over the branches. No detail is superfluous, the entire surface of the painting being enlivened by light and easy brushstrokes, the tree trunks are articulated in a clear, precise way to project the individuality of each tree."

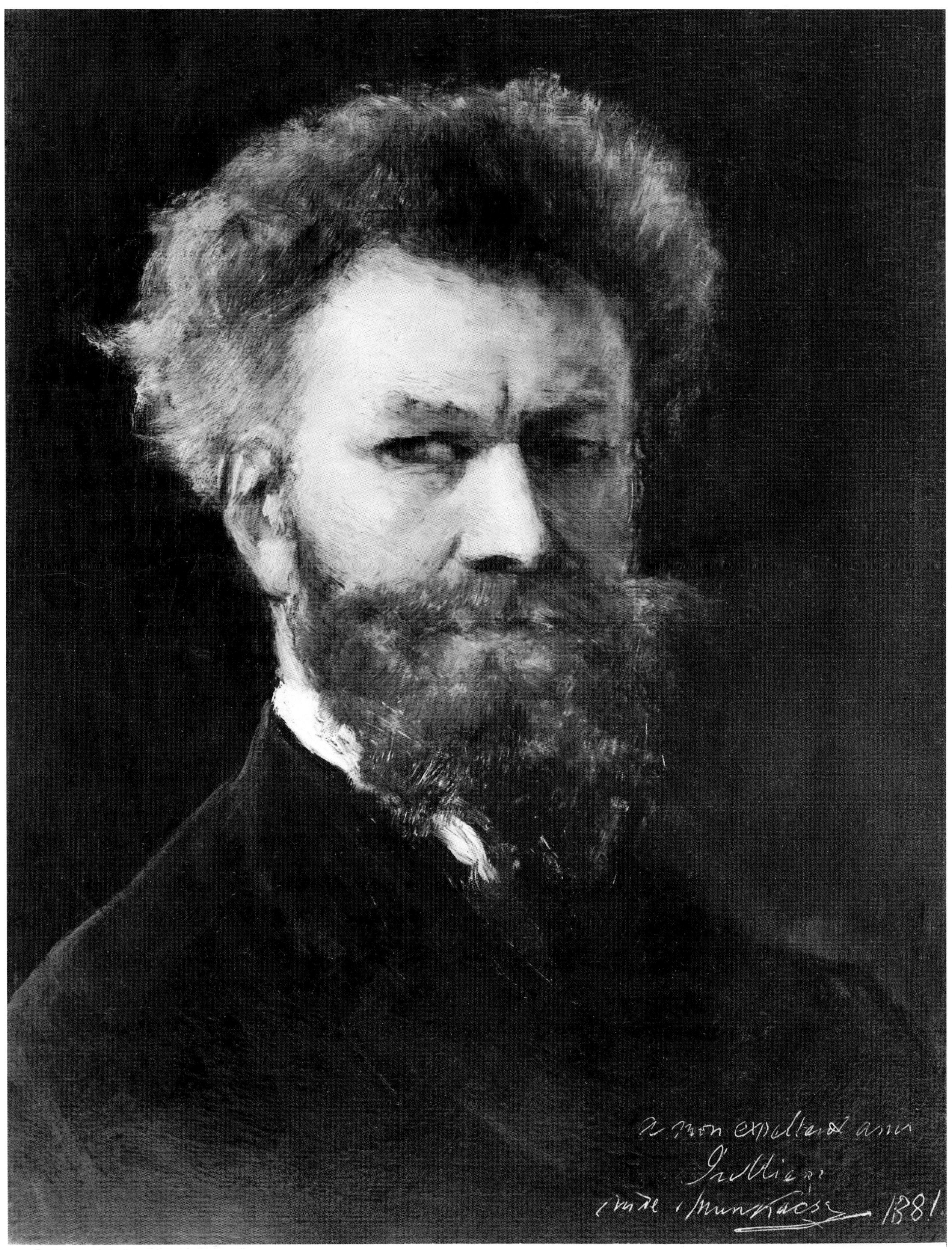

266

263. MIHÁLY MUNKÁCSY
Self-portrait, II, 1881
Oil on wood, 41.9 × 32 cm
Inscribed right: "A mon excellent ami Jullien,
M de Munkácsy, 1881"
Budapest, Hungarian National Gallery
Inv. No.: 1881

Munkácsy painted very few self-portraits.
When he did so, whether a small portrait or
a self-portrait as a detail in a larger composition—his chief concern was not self-
analysis. Rather, he tried to represent his features, or some aspect of his life and work,
thus creating a picture which would be an
appropriate present for his friends or admirers. This masterly self-portrait, based on different hues of brown, depicts the painter as
a very serious, dignified character who
nonetheless struggles with the contradic-
tions of his inmost self.

264. MIHÁLY MUNKÁCSY
Portrait of László Paál, 1867–1877
Oil on canvas, 45.8 × 37.7 cm
Unsigned
Budapest, Hungarian National Gallery
Inv. No.: 2224

During his brief life László Paál, a realistic
landscape-painter with a European reputation, was one of Munkácsy's closest friends.
They first met in Arad as boys and worked
together during several significant phases of
their lives. It was to László Paál that Munkácsy turned when he was oppressed by an
emotional illness in Düsseldorf. He asked
László Paál to come and stay with him, and
later he was equally dependent on his friend
during the period of concentrated hard work
which brought him his first taste of success,
and also in Paris where, though celebrated,
he found life at times unbearable.
In contrast to the versatile Munkácsy, László
Paál worked with the modesty and assurance of a painter concentrating on one task.
Though according to his friends Paál was
both charming and adaptable, his paintings
emanate a feeling of utter loneliness and suggest much suffering, which he humbly accepted in the manner of a Dostoevsky hero.
This is the impression conveyed in this
quietly sad portrait, painted by Munkácsy.

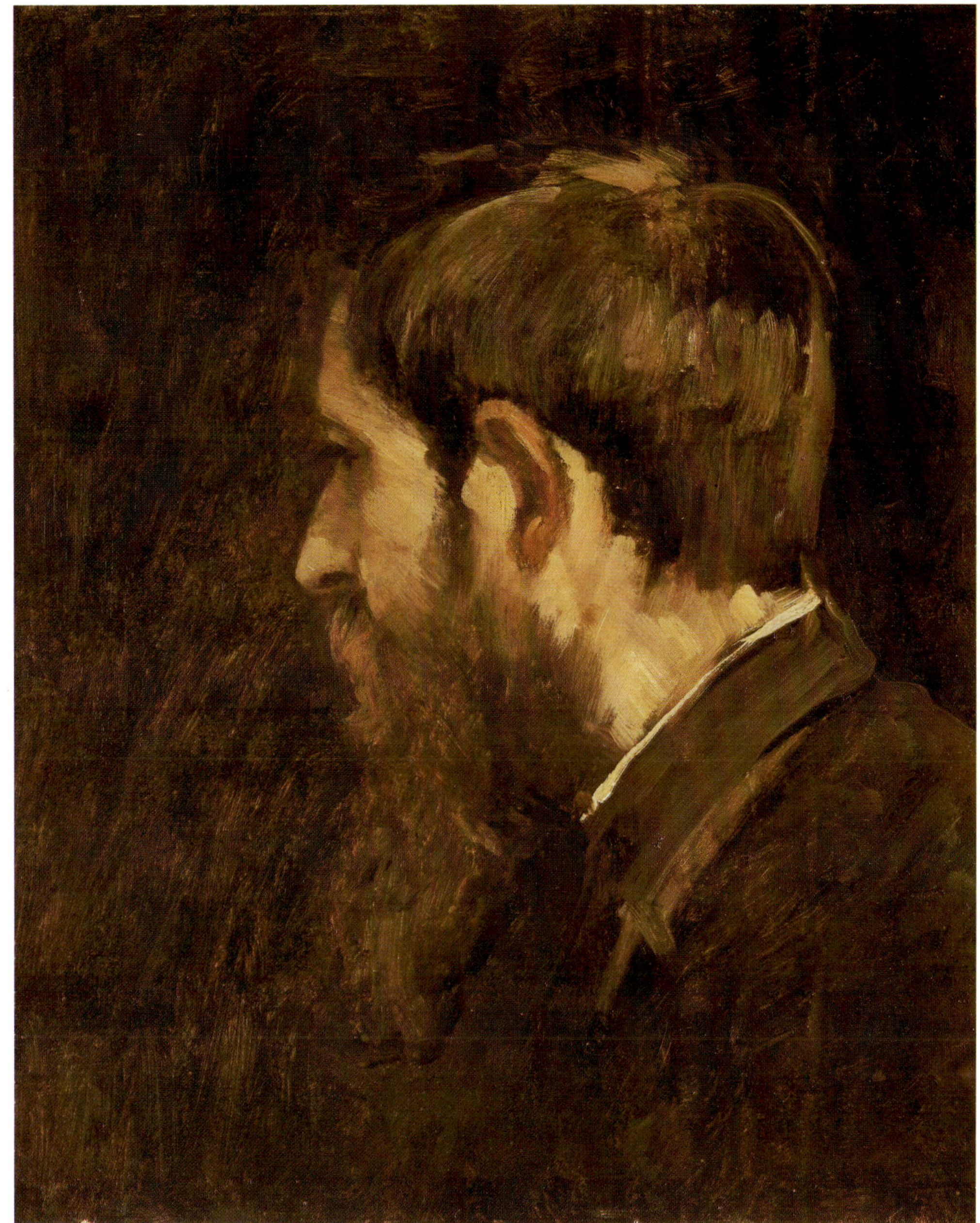

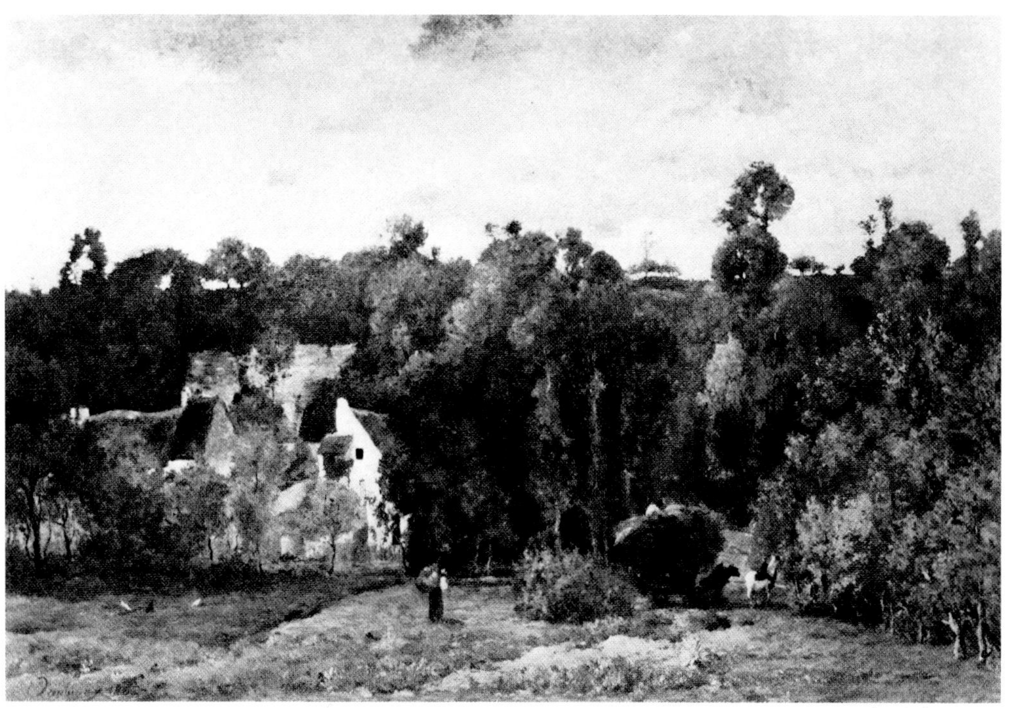

265. CHARLES FRANÇOIS DAUBIGNY
Landscape near Pontoise, 1866
Oil on canvas, 112×161 cm
Signed bottom right: "Daubigny 1866"
Paris, Louvre

Daubigny came from a family of painters. He took his first lessons from his father who was, like him, a landscapist. In 1840 he began to exhibit regularly and from the 1850s onwards was a prominent member of the Barbizon School. As one of the younger generation, he liked to paint out of doors, thus becoming, with his later pieces, a harbinger of Impressionism. He exerted a considerable influence which extended even to Claude Monet. László Paál, active in Barbizon, was one of the young artists most strongly influenced by the immediate forerunners of Impressionism.

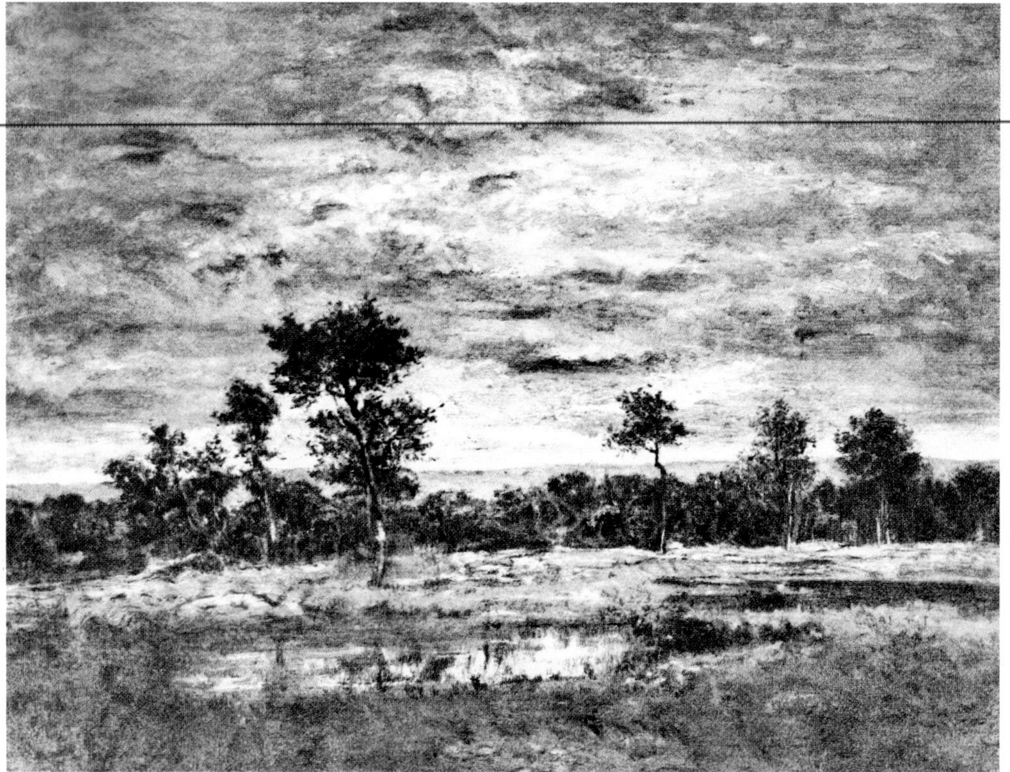

266. THÉODORE ROUSSEAU
Pond at the Edge of the Forest, c. 1863
Oil on canvas, 61×81 cm
Paris, Louvre

Rousseau worked in Barbizon as early as the 1830s and eventually he settled there. He painted in the Barbizon forest almost fanatically, from morning till night, and from spring to autumn, concentrating on pure landscape. Figures are rare in his paintings.
In 1863 he composed this painting synthesizing the movement of every detail in the landscape. By now he was no longer painting "emotional" views under the influence of Dutch landscape-painting; his aim was to analyze the scene objectively in terms of time. The work of Rousseau and his friends in Barbizon—Daubigny, Dupré and Diaz—provided models of the kind of delicate, serene landscape paintings which László Paál hoped to create with the help of similar artistic methods.

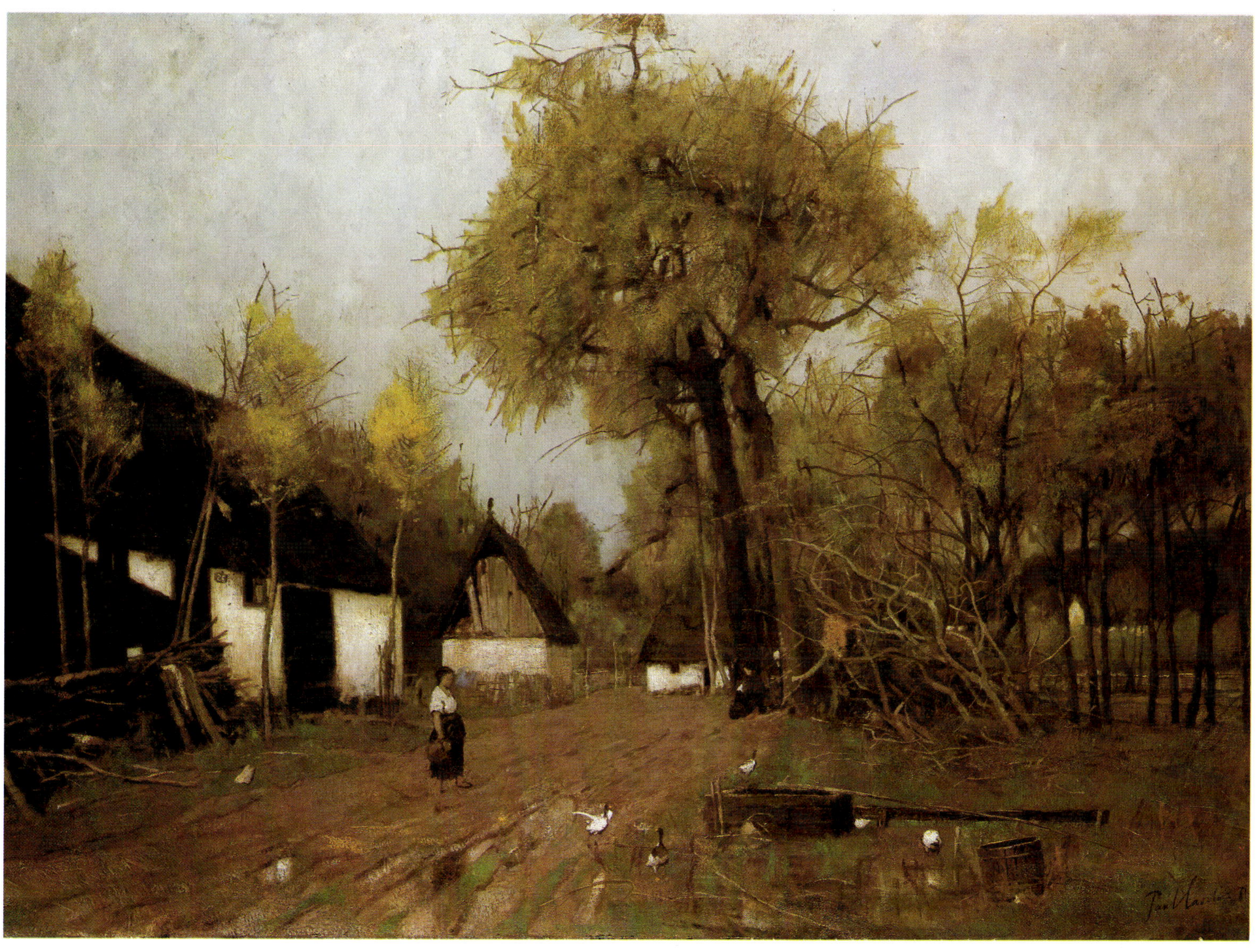

267. LÁSZLÓ PAÁL
A Road in Berzova, 1871

Oil on canvas, 27.6 × 130.4 cm
Signed bottom right: "Paál László 71"
Budapest, Hungarian National Gallery
Inv. No.: 2230

In the 1860s László Paál took drawing lessons from Albert Zimmermann in Vienna.
In the summer months he worked with
Eugen Jettel, who later also came to the artists' colony at Szolnok. Thus he was able to
study the solutions to compositional problems found by other painters, for instance
Emil Jakob Schindler. His early paintings
show similarities with Géza Mészöly's
works (Plates 271, 272). In 1869, not only
did Paál become acquainted with Academic
artists in Munich who had been inspired by
the Barbizon School, such as Eduard
Schleich, the Elder who taught at the
Academy, but he was also able to study the
actual works of the Barbizon painters, including some by Courbet. It is interesting to
note that after this encounter with French
art, Paál still went first to Holland and from
there, upon Munkácsy's insistence, to Düsseldorf rather than Paris. Before setting out
on these journeys, however, he returned
home to visit his parents. It so happened that
he found the main motif for his first significant landscape in the village of Berzova, near
Arad. Scholars believe that he executed his
Road in Berzova in Vienna and in Düsseldorf,
in which case he must have memorized
every detail in this view of his native country. Each motif in the painting—the tower-
ing tree, the leaning bush, the high, shingled
roofs and the white-washed houses—are
vividly portrayed with a strength of feeling
greater than any details in Paál's Dutch landscapes.

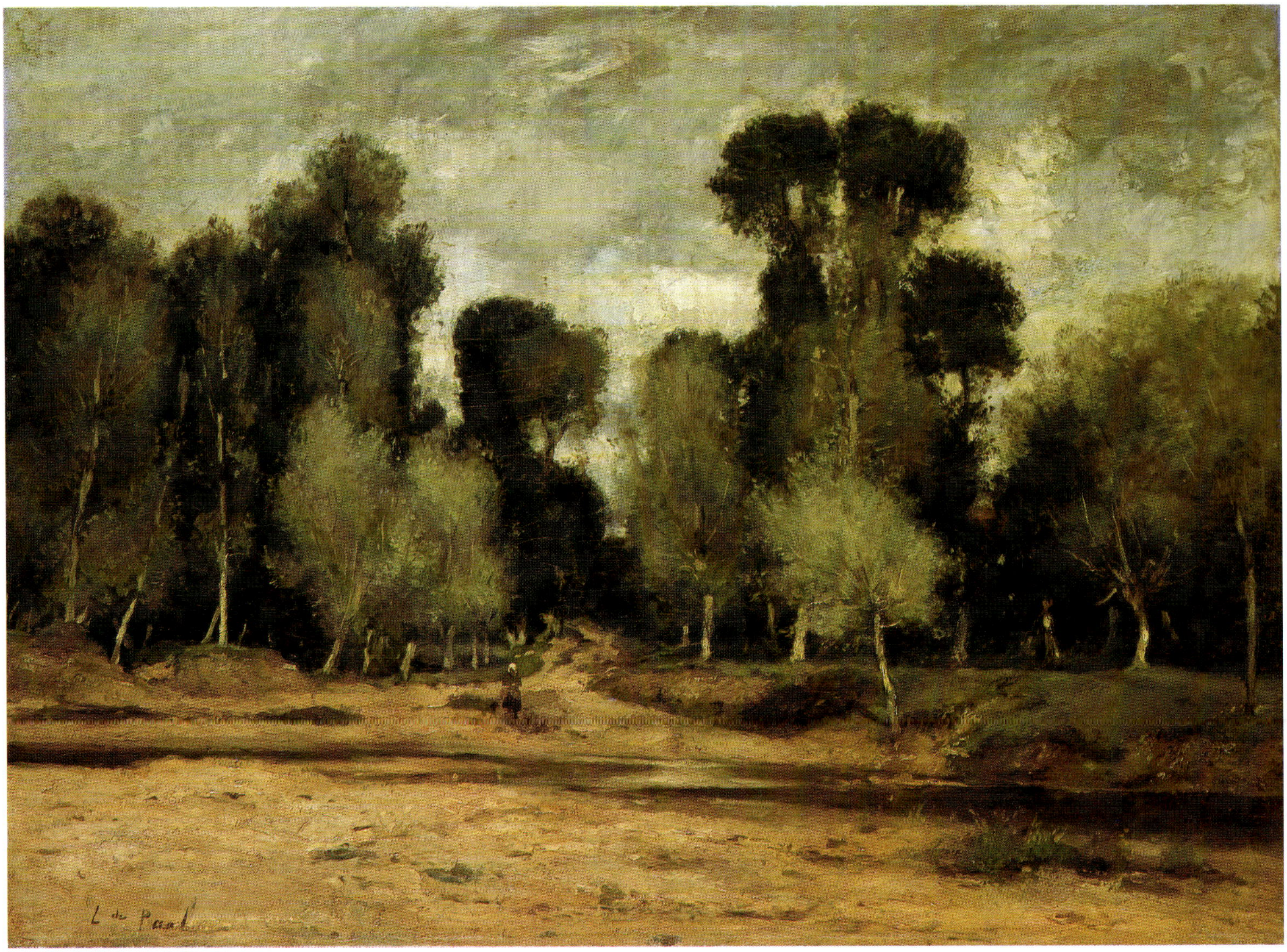

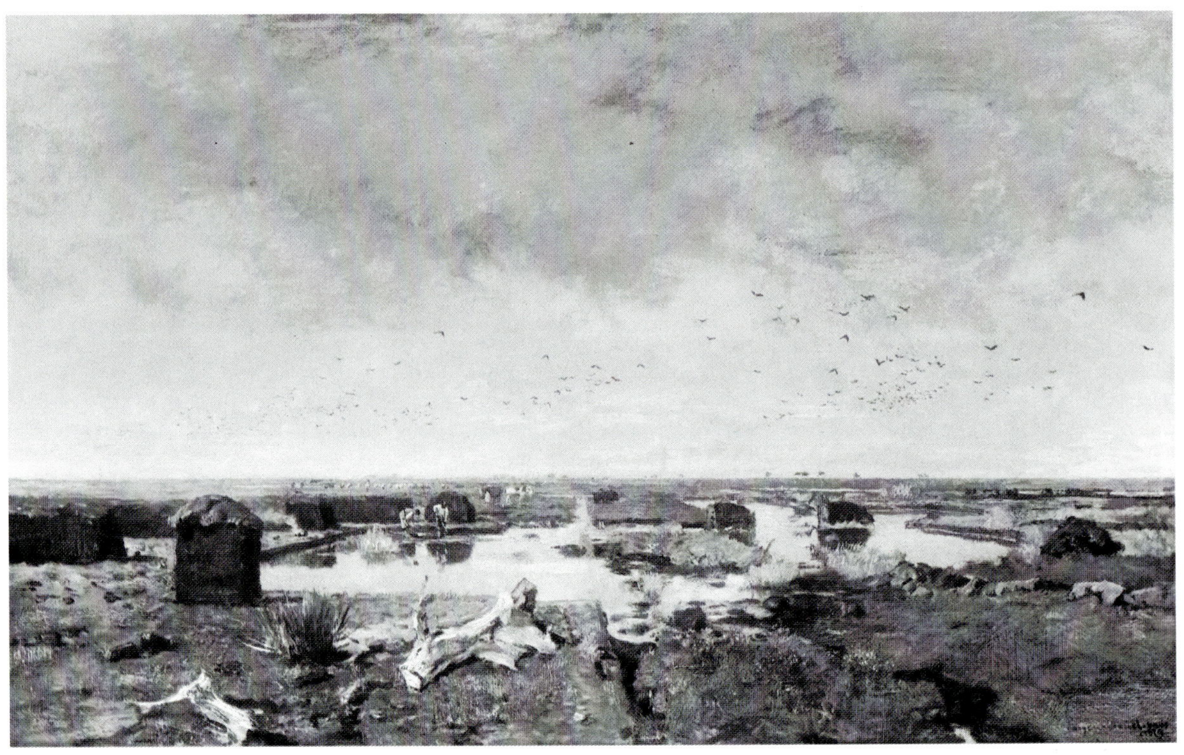

268. LÁSZLÓ PAÁL
The Edge of a Forest (Poplars), 1876
Oil on canvas, 53.3 × 72.6 cm
Signed bottom left: "L. de Paál"
Budapest, Hungarian National Gallery
Inv. No.: 5077

While in Holland, László Paál had already
experimented with the horizontal format. In
Barbizon he repeatedly chose this solution.
His work is based on careful observation of
the poplars in the forests near Barbizon, their
shapes and size, the shapes of pools in the
clearings, the effect of light on the surface of
the water, the shape of the massed trees and
the clouds. He painted in all weathers, fine or
overcast, regardless of the season or the time
of day and from different view-points. His
Barbizon poplars are reminiscent of the
crooked, restless trees on the side of the
street in Berzova; they reach up to the
clouded sky in the same bent and mournful
way. Unconsciously, the painter allows his
search for accurate observation to be influenced by his own essentially romantic tem-
perament.

269. EUGEN JETTEL
Marshland, 1879
Oil on wood, 71 × 112 cm
Signed bottom right: "E. Jettel, 1879"
Vienna, Österreichische Galerie
Inv. No.: 2543

Eugen Jettel had been friendly with László
Paál for about ten years when around 1870
they went to Holland where they wandered
about and painted. Jettel was closely connected with August Pettenkofen and other
artists of the Szolnok Artists' Colony. On
one occasion he travelled to Hungary when
he certainly visited Szolnok. This landscape
of a marshland occupies an intermediate position between László Paál's romantic Realism and the *plein-air* paintings of the Szolnok
artists.

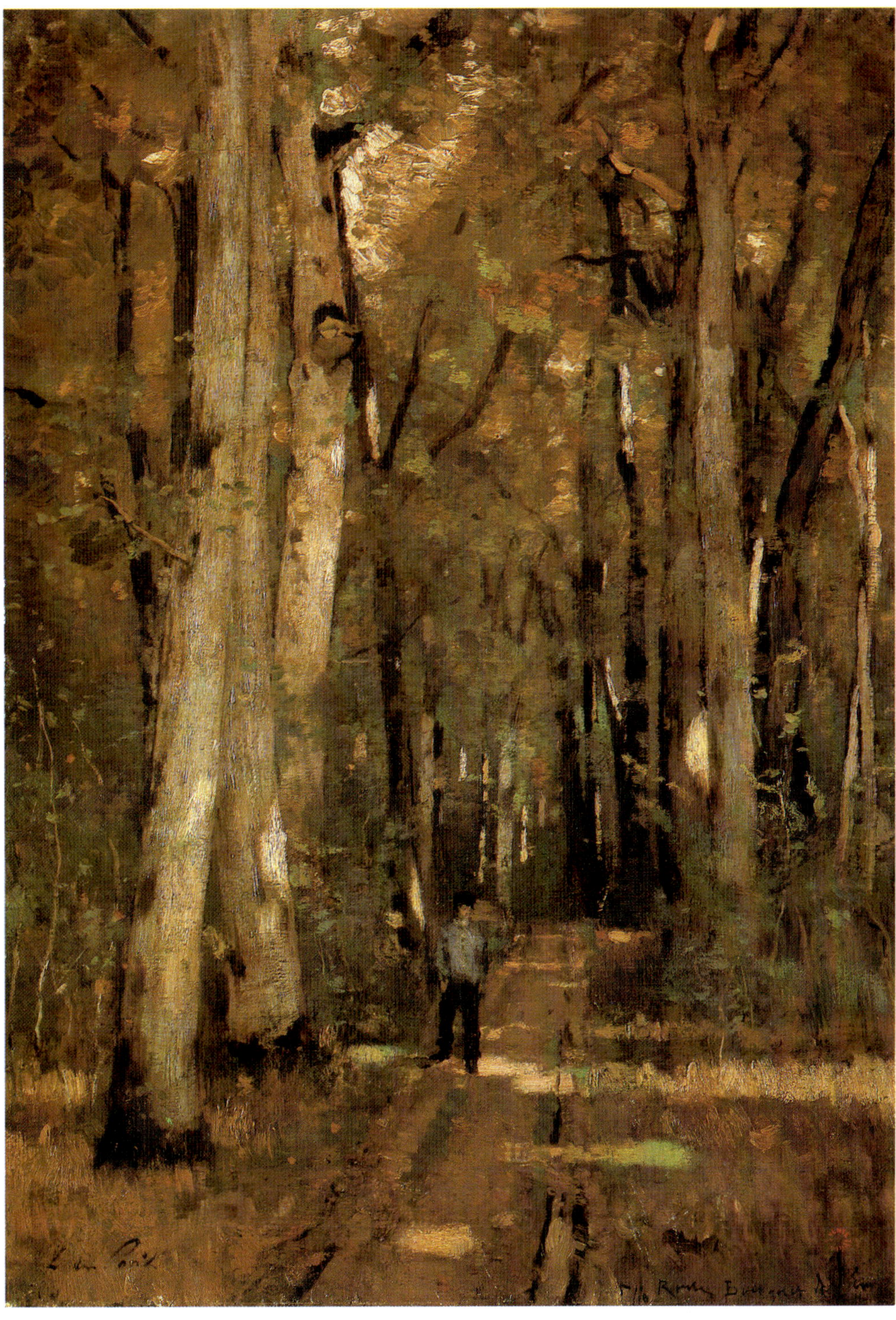

270. LÁSZLÓ PAÁL
Foot-path in the Forest of
Fontainebleau, 1867
Oil on canvas, 91.5 × 63 cm
Signed bottom left: "L. de Paál"
Budapest, Hungarian National Gallery
Inv. No.: 3722

In some of his dramatic landscapes, Paál
achieved the freer style of the Barbizon
painters, producing delicate landscapes
without ever neglecting the individuality of
the forest he depicted.
This outstanding forest scene is one of the
painter's most accomplished works. The tall
trees bordering the narrow forest path form
a well-ordered yet uninhibited pattern as the
branches reach towards each other, with
broad shafts of sunshine penetrating the
foliage. The figure of a man can be seen in
a shaft of sunlight crossing the path.

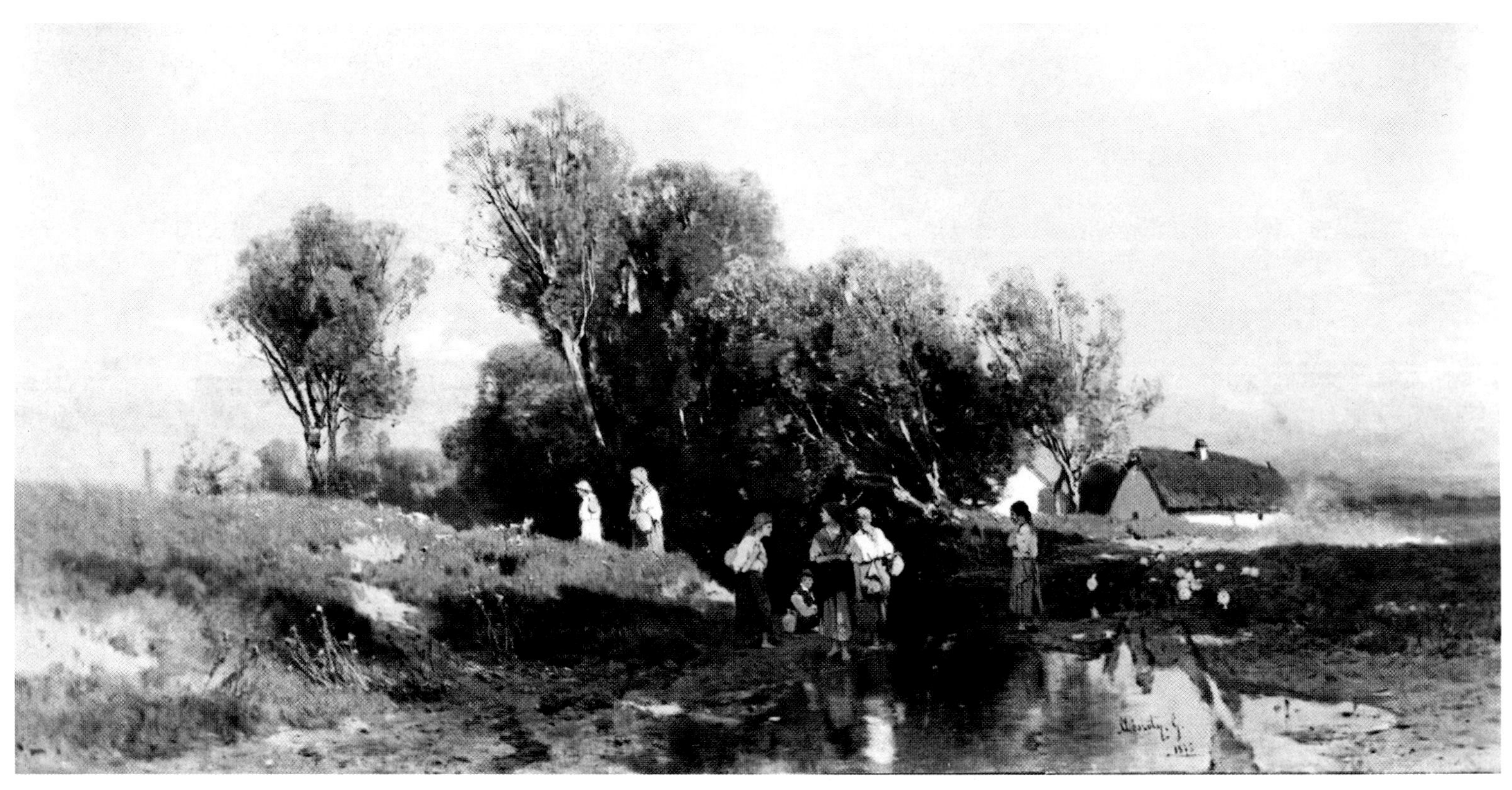

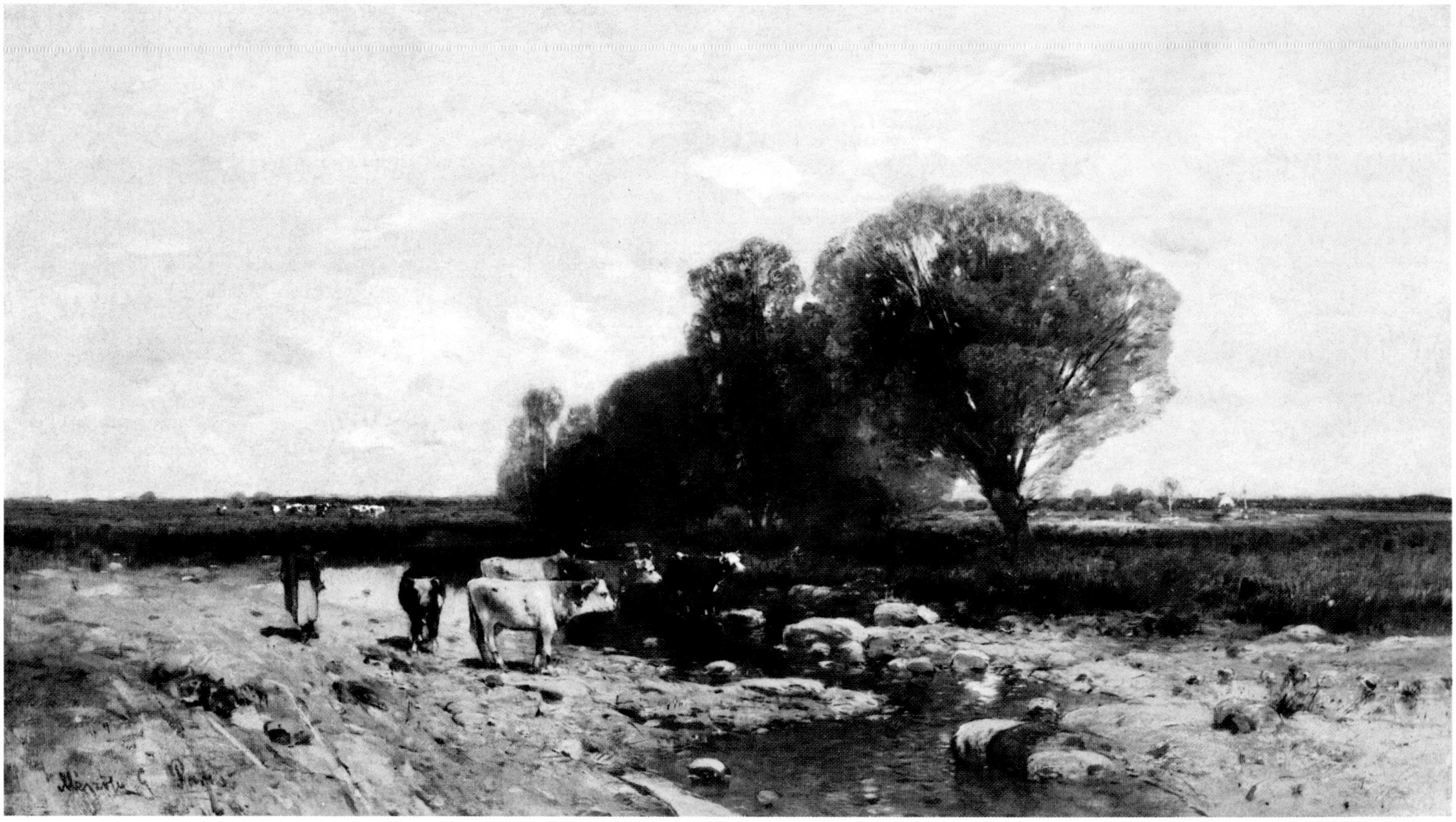

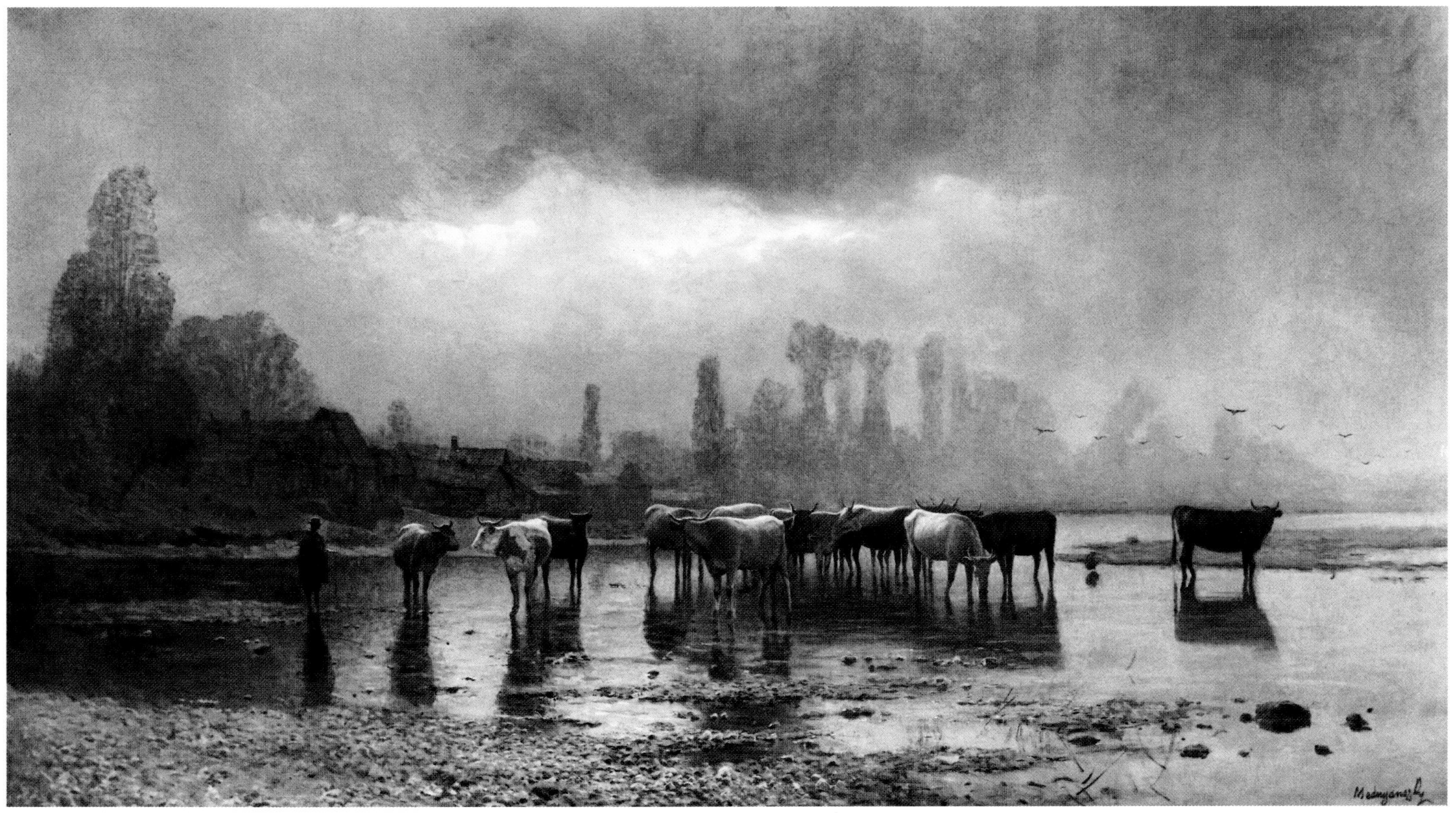

271. GÉZA MÉSZÖLY
The End of the Village, 1875
Oil on canvas, 40 × 78 cm
Signed bottom right: "Mészöly G., 1875"
Budapest, Hungarian National Gallery
Inv. No.: FK 68

Géza Mészöly was a pupil of Albert Zimmermann until 1869. Later he moved to Munich where he settled, returning to Hungary only for the summer months. Gusztáv Kelety, artist and art-critic, describes his paintings as follows: "Mészöly renders nature in all its freshness. This seeming spontaneity, however, conceals a careful choice of subject which enables the artist to create an illusion of naturalness in the composition." Kelety names this method "refined Realism".
If we compare Mészöly's painting with Paál's work from about 1875 or the landscape by Jettel reproduced in this book (Plates 268–269), it becomes apparent how far all these "casual" elements are part of an ordered composition. Women and girls, singly or in groups, make their way to a spring, hardly visible in the picture, which is situated at the end of the village. Another group is shown chatting together in the middle ground. In this genre-painting the painter depicts familiar everyday tasks and introduces them into a landscape.

272. GÉZA MÉSZÖLY
Cows by the Stream (Landscape with Cows and a Tree), 1882–1883
Oil on canvas, 38 × 67.5 cm
Signed bottom left: "Mészöly G. Paris"
Budapest, private collection

Mészöly completed this landscape in the summer of 1882 in Paris, from sketches made in Hungary. Once again we see how he incorporates observed details into a careful composition. In the foreground a shallow ribbon of water meanders through stony ground between dried-out banks where thirsty cattle are standing forlornly. In the middle ground a group of trees provides shade beyond which the flat plain stretches into the distance. The treetops, the skyscape and the animals are all more stereotyped in this painting than in sketches made on the site.

273. LÁSZLÓ MEDNYÁNSZKY
Watering-place with Cattle, 1888
Oil on canvas, 115 × 200 cm
Signed bottom right: "Mednyánszky"
Budapest, Hungarian National Gallery
Inv. No.: 55.849

László Mednyánszky learned the rudiments of landscape drawing as a young man from Thomas Ender of Vienna and later he studied at the Academies of Vienna and Paris. Like Géza Mészöly he too went to Barbizon and by the 1880s he was depicting nature with the same assurance as Mészöly or Eugen Jettel.
In this painting, the accuracy of the motifs and the light effects suggest the influence of Dutch art, whereas the group of houses in the background and the shepherd's clothing are typically Hungarian.
Mednyánszky first went to Szolnok in 1877. This town by the river Tisza, with its artists' colony, was a new inspiration to the artist after Paris and Barbizon. In 1880 he again stayed in this area which provided him with a wealth of motifs which possibly influenced even his later landscapes.

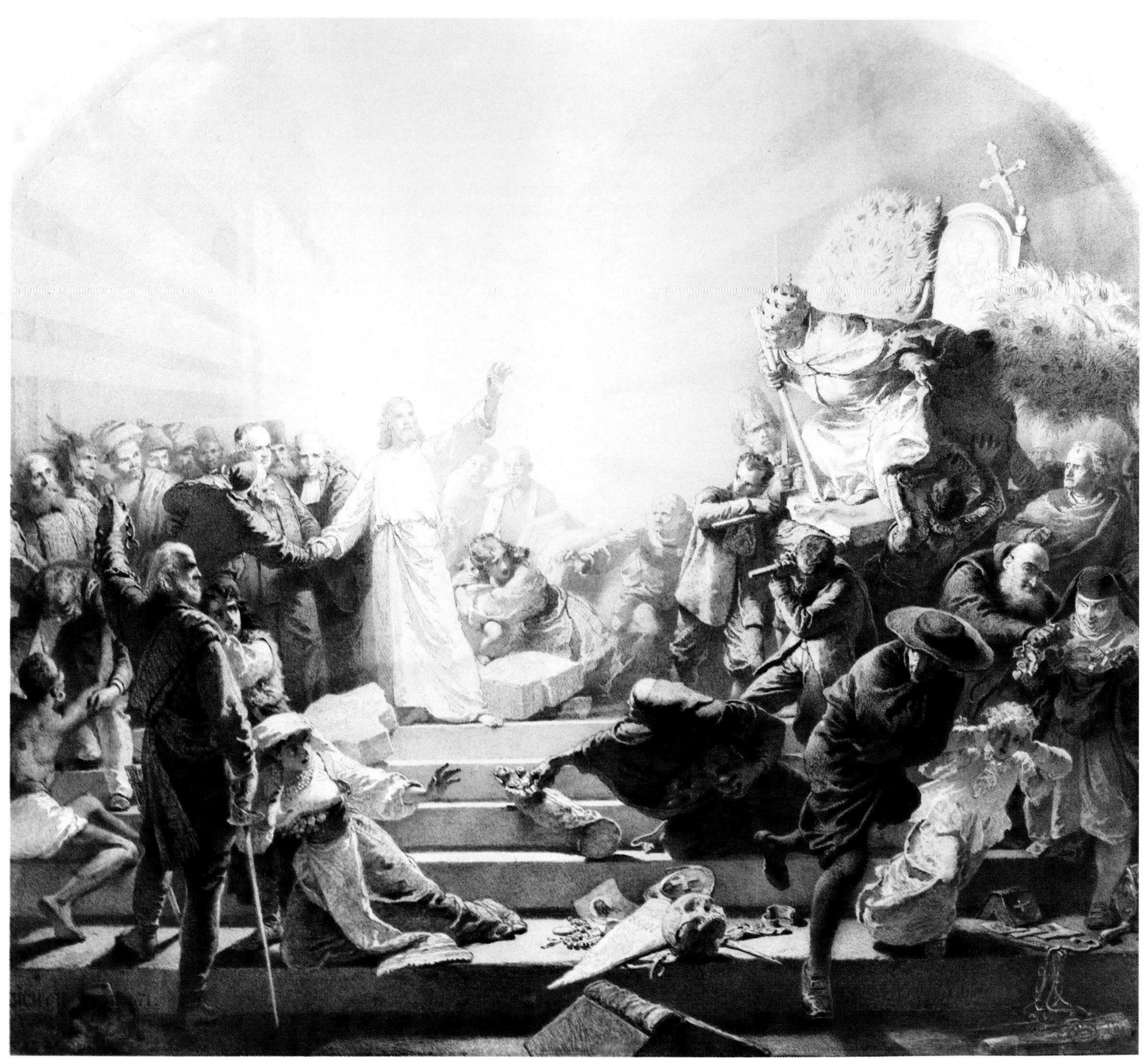

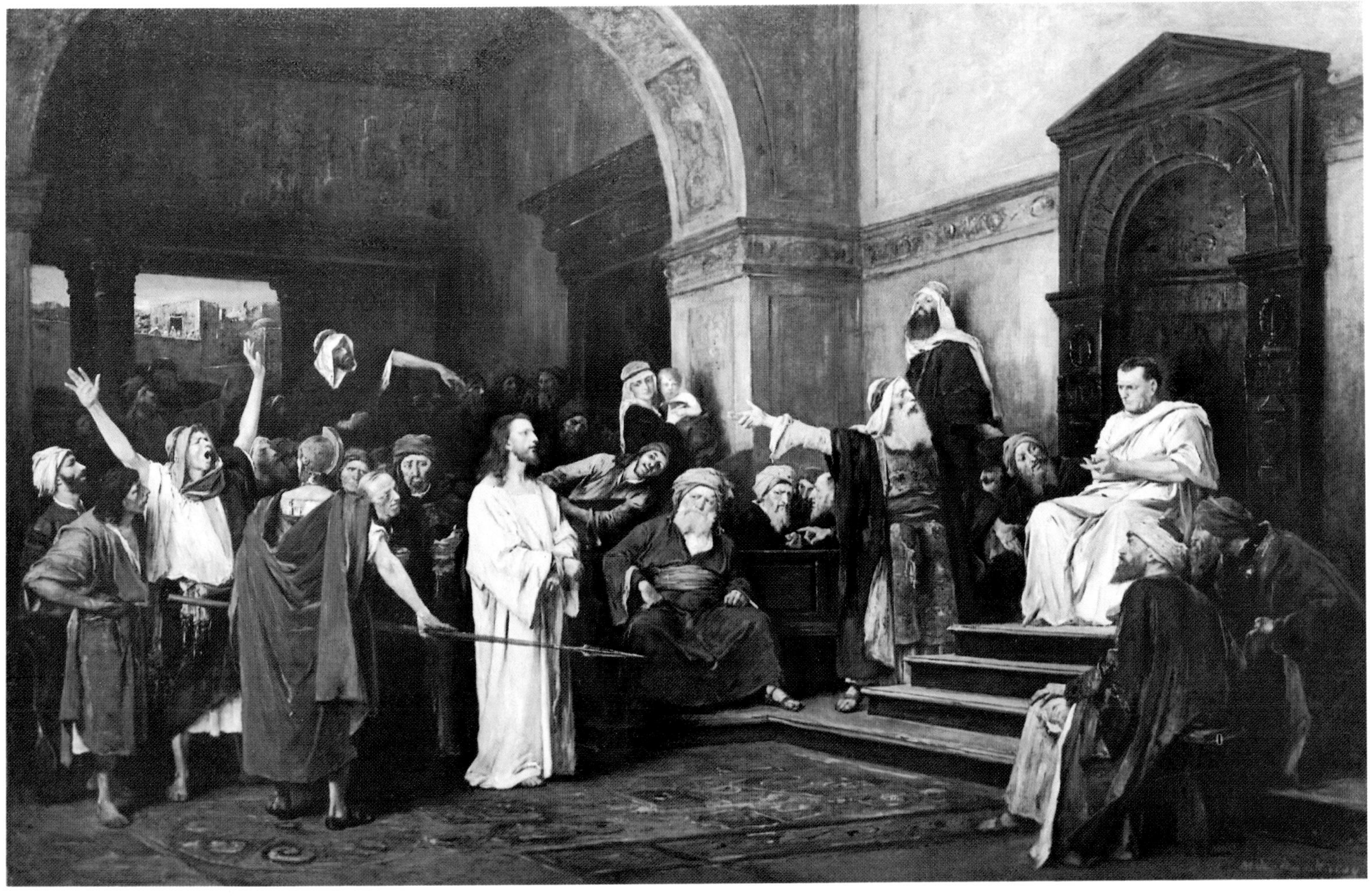

274. MIHÁLY ZICHY
Christ and the Pope (The Messiah), 1871
Charcoal and zinc-white on cardboard,
112×124 cm
Signed bottom left: "Zichy 1871"
Debrecen, Library of the Calvinist College

The drawing indicates Zichy's deep faith in Christ, his piety and independence from the teachings of any particular religious denomination or sect.

Two main figures dominate the composition which includes also numerous meticulously drawn minor figures. The Head of the Catholic Church, seated on his throne, is brought forward by bearers so that he can see more clearly the figure of Christ, portrayed in white robes, transfigured. Christ holds up his left arm in a gesture of greeting, while with his right hand he grasps the clasped hands of four priests, thus demonstrating his desire for unity between the Protestant, Catholic, Greek Orthodox and Jewish Churches. The Pope's panic-stricken escort tries to leave hurriedly, scarcely daring to look back at the gentle but stern figure of Christ. A mother, on the contrary, approaches Him with her child. A crowd of curious onlookers, representing the other religions of the world, has gathered in the background.

275. MIHÁLY MUNKÁCSY
Christ before Pilate, 1881
Oil on canvas, 218×324 cm
Signed bottom right: "M. de Munkácsy"
Budapest, Hungarian National Gallery
Inv. No.: 4812

After the warm reception given to his *Condemned Cell,* Munkácsy repeatedly made use of historical or literary themes. Around 1880, he was considering with his agent the subject for a new work which might be equally popular. For this, the figure of Jesus Christ seemed the most appropriate. The life and teachings of Christ and His attitude to the powerful rulers who opposed His doctrines absorbed the thoughts of many artists and writers of the 19th century.

Though Munkácsy first feared the difficulties inherent in such a great task, he embarked on the project with growing enthusiasm, producing many preliminary sketches and studies.

The composition is centred around the figure of Christ, depicted in white robes and somewhat related to Zichy's simple but determined Christ-figure, although the incidents shown in the two paintings are different. In this picture Christ stands alone, the hostile crowd at his back, his hands bound with rope as he calmly faces His Roman judge. Pilate too is robed in white, which serves to emphasize the contrast in character. Pilate's uneasy bearing and confused expression scarcely reflect the intellectual and spiritual superiority appropriate to one who wears the Roman toga. Spiritual strength rests with Christ, as He ignores the mob and proclaims the Truth of the Kingdom of God. Ignorance, indignation and rage are all expressed by the figures in the background who are demanding Christ's death, since they fear Him as a dangerous prophet.

This painting, which differs from other traditional religious works, has been variously interpreted, the strangest suggestion being that Christ represents the Hungarian nation, abandoned and solitary, during and after the War of Independence.

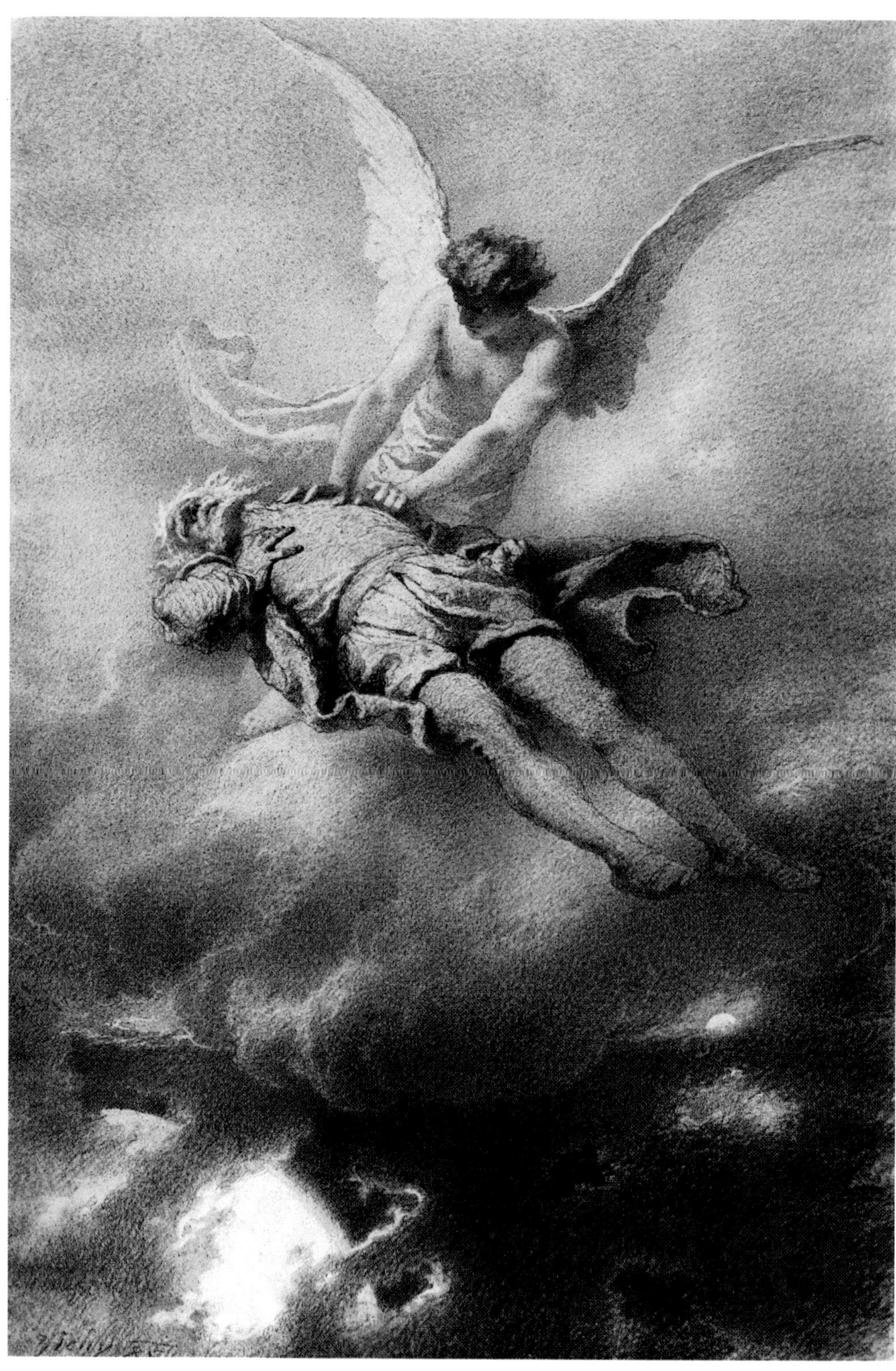

276. MIHÁLY ZICHY
In Space. Illustration to Imre Madách's "The Tragedy of Man", 1885
Charcoal on paper, 790 × 503 mm
Signed lower left: "Zichy 85."
Budapest, Hungarian National Gallery
Inv. No.: 1905–1760

This is one of a series of illustrations completed by Mihály Zichy for Imre Madách's famous epic drama, "The Tragedy of Man", which traces the history of mankind from its genesis to a visionary scene when Lucifer carries away Adam, who has sinned, into the infinite void. Lucifer is represented as a winged demon, tearing Adam, a weary old man, out of his mortal domain, bearing him away from the earth into space. The manner in which Lucifer is represented is similar to that of the main figure in *The Triumph of the Genius of Destruction* (Plate 277).

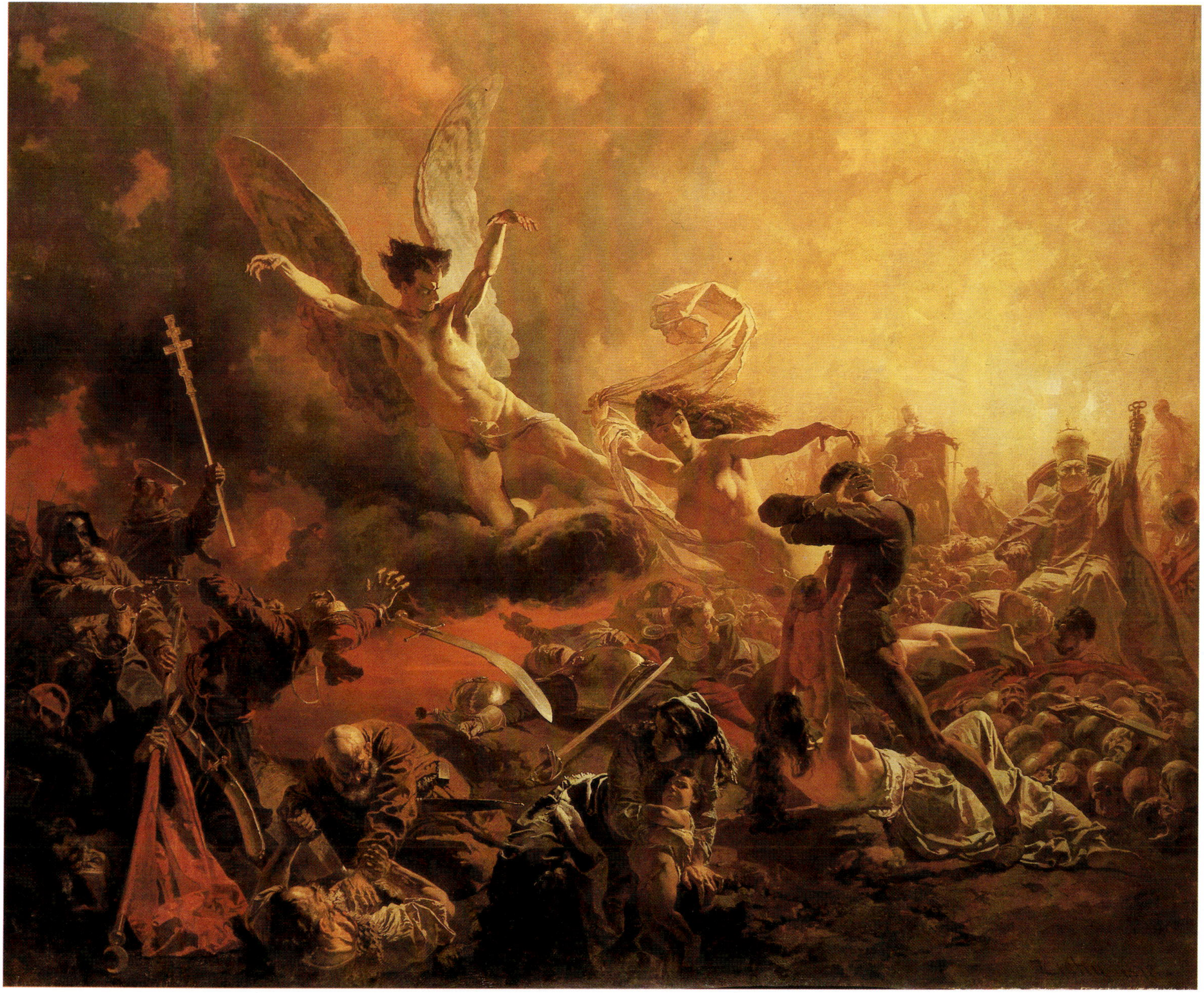

277. MIHÁLY ZICHY
The Triumph of the Genius of Destruction, The Demon 1878

Oil on canvas, 447 × 550 cm
Signed bottom right: "Zichy 1878"
Budapest, Hungarian National Gallery
Inv. No.: 2337

Wings and arms outstretched, the Demon is shown soaring into a blood red evening sky towards the storm clouds above, disseminating devastation, death and cruelty as he goes. In depicting the demon's powers of destruction, Zichy refers to concrete and topical political events: the wars fought by Tsarist Russia against Turkey and Bulgaria, the Franco–Prussian War and the defeat of the Paris Commune (1871). In spite of all these concrete historical references, the painting is an ideological rather than a historical work. The Pope is shown encouraging this bloodshed as he sits enthroned above the sculls of French and German soldiers while in the background we see the contrasting figure of Christ, benign and radiant. On Christ's left the German Emperor can be seen receiving homage from the German princes, at his feet the trampled body of Napoleon III. In the sunlit background, behind the Emperor and the Pope is a proud allegorical figure representing the French Republic. When the painting was exhibited for the first time, this figure also symbolized the Paris Commune. To the left a Russian Grand-Duke resists two attacking Turks. Tsar Alexander II, standing behind him with a patriarchal cross, spurs on his Russian soldiers against the Turks. Beside him is a scene of mass slaughter. With a movement of his owl-like wings the Devil passes over all these atrocities accompanied by an alluring female figure who mockingly entices a young man to leave his wife and child and go with them.

According to the artist himself, the theme concerns the triumph of Destruction, but the contemporary critic Gusztáv Kelety saw in it the triumph of the republic, a message subtly hidden in the painting, as discreet as the figure of Christ depicted between those representing the Republic and the Commune. Kelety saw a contradiction between these motifs. But bearing in mind Zichy's drawing, *Christ and the Pope* (Plate 274), there seems no contradiction between Christ as Zichy understands Him, and the personification of the Republic and the Commune.

The allusion to the Future is nevertheless much weaker. The painting is more obviously a symbolic representation of the tragic wars in Europe and Asia during the second half of the 19th century.

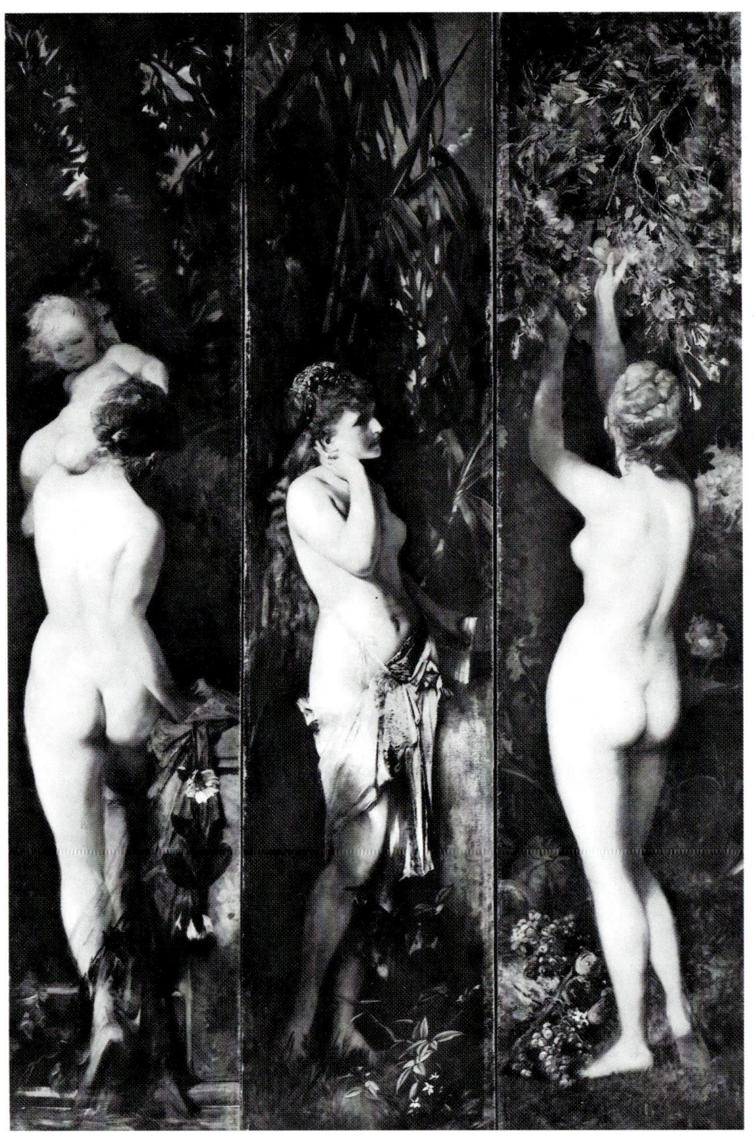

278. HANS MAKART
**Touch, Hearing and Taste, from
a composition depicting the Five
Senses, 1872–1879**
Oil on canvas, (319×70 cm each)
Signed: "H. M."
Vienna, Österreichische Galerie
Inv. No.: 427

By 1869 Hans Makart had become so famous that he was summoned from Munich
to Vienna by the Emperor Franz Joseph I.
His paintings are vivid and highly decorative. In the series called *The Five Senses,*
possibly part of a larger group, he depicts
female nudes symbolizing the senses, against
a background of luxuriant vegetation. One
of them, Touch, balances her child on her
shoulder; Hearing, the second figure, lifts
one hand to her ear; Taste, the third figure, is
about to pluck an apple. This series enabled
the artist to depict the same model viewed
from different angles. He did not follow the
Antique or Renaissance examples, but instead painted directly from his models.

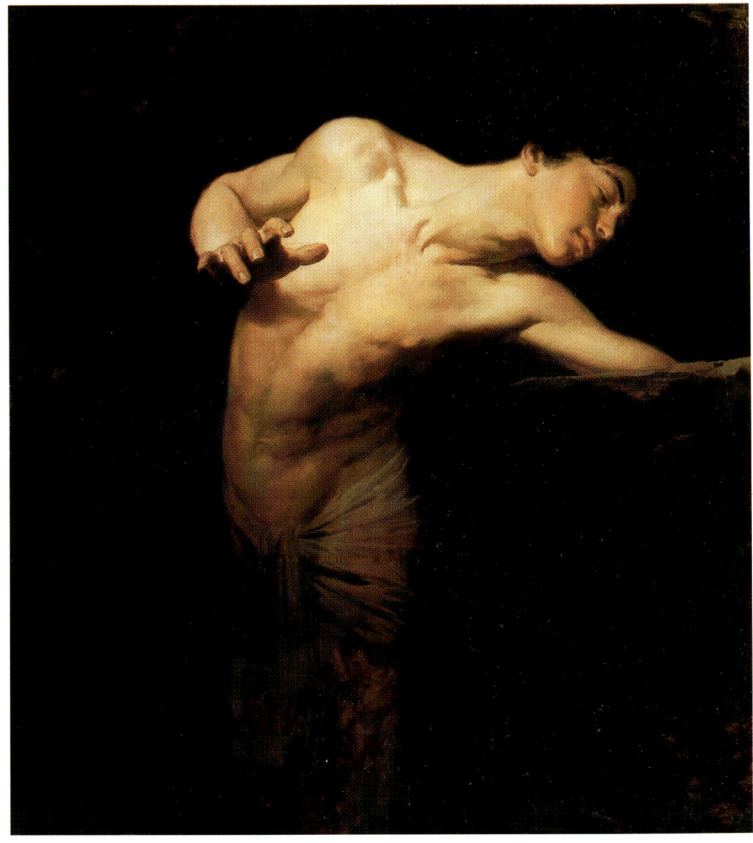

279. GYULA BENCZÚR
Narcissus, 1881
Oil on canvas, 115×100.5 cm
*Signed bottom right: "Benczúr Gyula 1881
München"*
Budapest, Hungarian National Gallery
Inv. No.: 6164

In the 1880s Gyula Benczúr made a study of
the interpretations of mythology currently
fashionable in both Vienna and Munich and
he made use of some of them in his own
work. Similar attempts were made in the
period of European Mannerism; but in later
Academic art it became customary to give
a new interpretation both emotional and
sensual to figures and motifs of Greek
mythology as well as the Christian religion
once painted by Caravaggio and his followers. Benczúr's mythological compositions
were mostly rather trivial, but in Narcissus
he managed to balance sensuality and lyricism without reference to a living model.

280. MIHÁLY ZICHY
Falling Stars, 1879
Oil on canvas, 400 × 200 cm
Zala, Zichy Museum (on loan from the
Hungarian National Gallery)
Inv. No.: 2331

Towards the end of the 1870s Zichy completed several large paintings suitable for exhibition in large houses and institutions.

In this painting, three beautifully painted female figures are represented clinging together in the dark firmament, while a fourth dives into the depths. These figures personify stars. One of the three reaches out to support her falling friend, but her own fear of falling prevents her from rescuing her companion.

In terms of his pictorial conception Zichy is related to Hans Makart, who painted from experience, rather than to Gyula Benczúr, who referred to earlier models. This particular painting is closely linked, stylistically and iconographically, with those painted by Makart for the living room ceiling of a house built by the architect Oetzelt in Vienna. These ceiling paintings date from 1870 and represent the four different periods of the day.

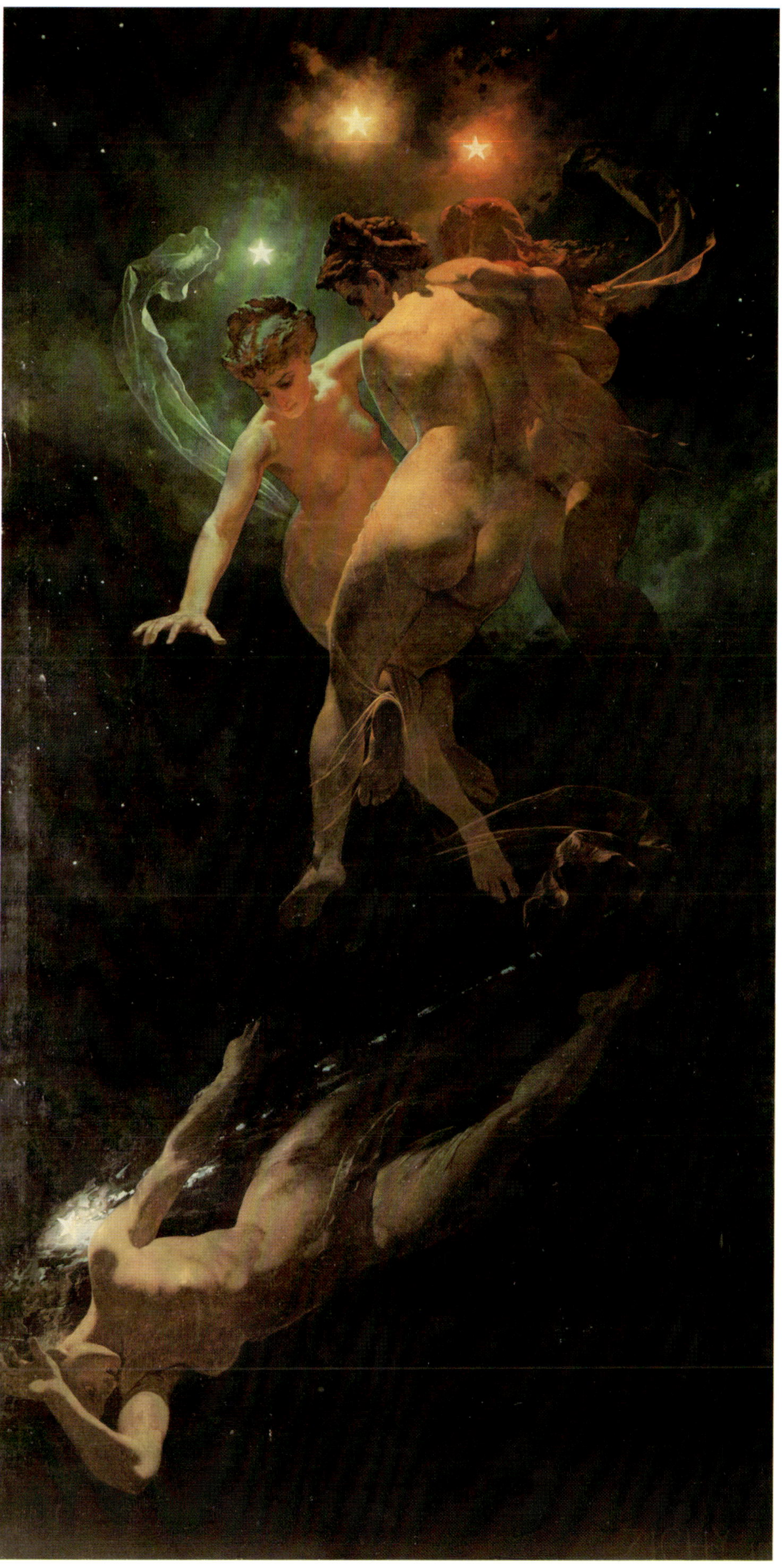

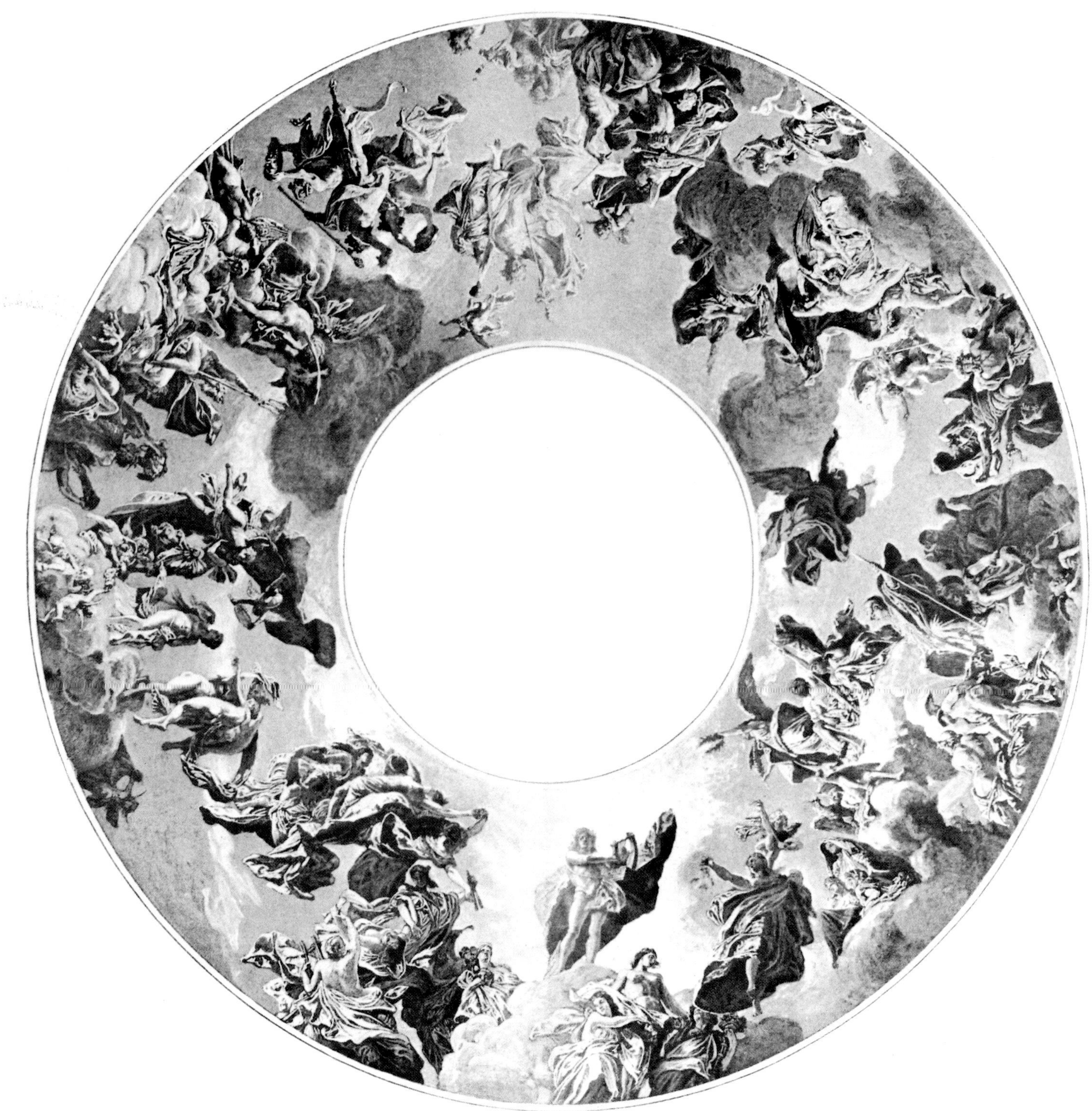

281. KÁROLY LOTZ
Paintings for the ceiling of the Budapest Opera House, 1844
Reproduction of the original cardboard drawings made from Antal Weinwarm's photographs by members of the Budapest Institution of Robert Aust, Gyula Háry and Sándor Papp
Published in Frigyes Riedl: Lotz Károly falfestményei (Károly Lotz's wall paintings), Budapest, 1890

The painting on the ceiling of the Budapest Opera represents the gods of Olympus arranged in groups. The principal figure is that of Apollo, shown holding a lyre. On his right hovering in the clouds are Zeus and Hera and numerous figures surrounding Hermes. Close to Zeus stands Ganymede. On Apollo's left the Muses dance towards their leader. The dancing figures of the three Graces are followed by the Nereid Amphitrite, the queen of the sea, waving and stretching; Poseidon, her husband, sitting in the midst of naiads, tritons and genii, watches her from nearby. The next group is formed by the Bacchantes who are depicted dancing wildly around Dionysus. Then come the three Fates from Hades, and the Greek gods, Sleep and Dreams, resting by the side of Death. In the literature this painted ceiling is referred to as a symbolic representation of all the different movements in music from *maestoso* to *allegro*. The structure of the composition is based on the antipodean groups around Apollo and Dionysus. This contrast can also be found in 19th century philosophy (Nietzsche), and, in the field of music, in Wagner. Here the composition is so precisely calculated that it seems likely that the subject was specified by those who commissioned the Opera House ceiling.

280

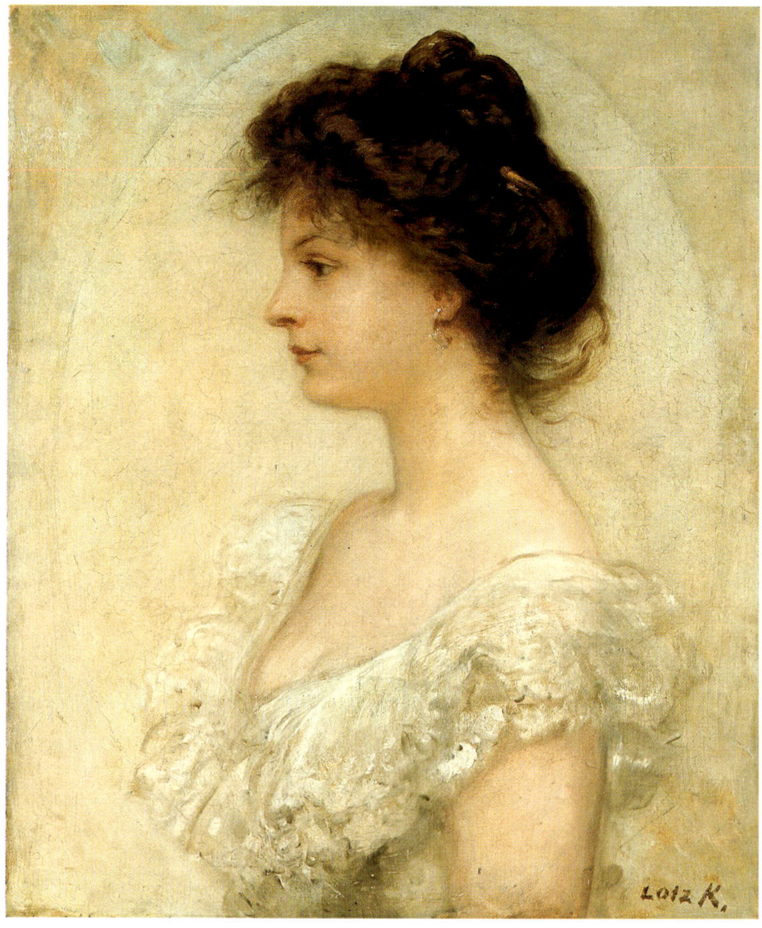

282. KÁROLY LOTZ
Portrait of Kornelia Lotz, 1890s
Oil on canvas, 68.5 × 55.5 cm
Signed bottom right: "Lotz K"
Budapest, Hungarian National Gallery
Inv. No.: 3511

Károly Lotz often painted his step–daughter
in profile. He captured her elegant bearing
and usually painted her wearing a white
dress. His portraits are notable for standard
Academic stylistic traits and a range of palette which earned him a comparison with
English painters. Certainly, in the refined
portraits of Alma Tadema and Lord Leigh-
ton, beautiful women are depicted in a similar style.

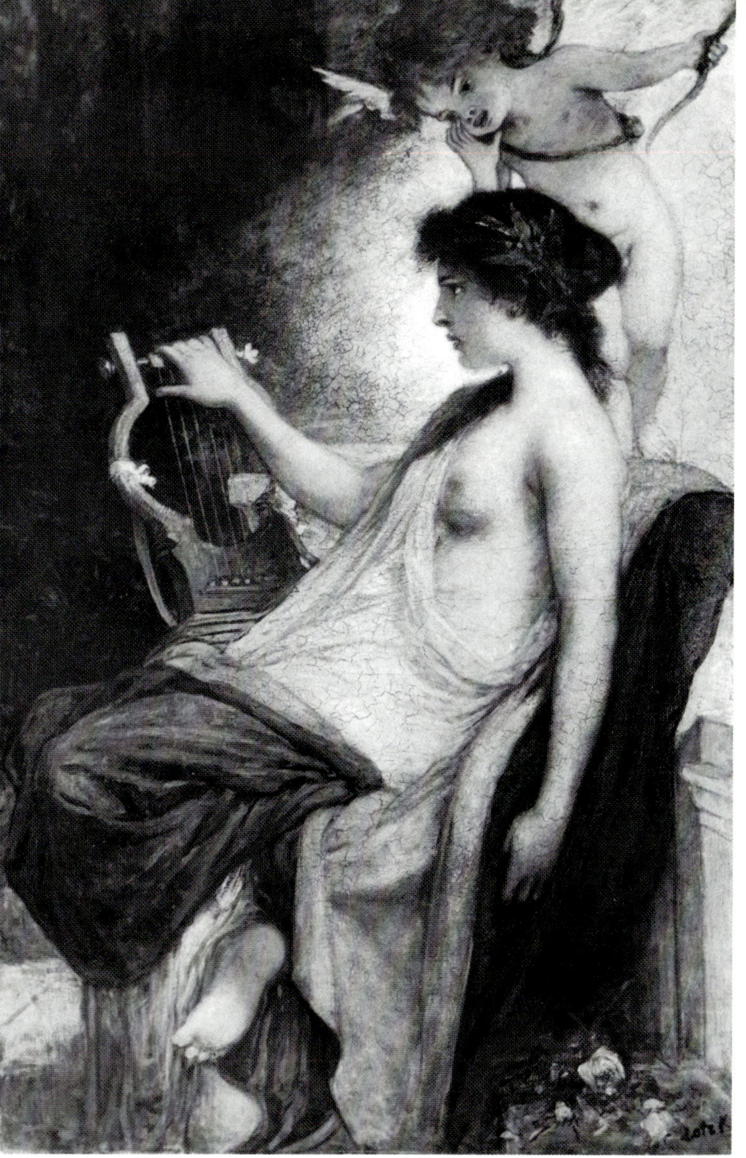

283. KÁROLY LOTZ
Muse, 1890s
Oil on canvas, 144.7 × 95 cm
Signed bottom right: "Lotz K."
Budapest, Hungarian National Gallery
Inv. No.: 2163

This Muse, loosely robed to reveal one
breast and arm is related to the "Allegory of
Sculpture" in the National Museum; the lyre
nevertheless indicates that she is the Muse of
Poetry. This is confirmed by the laurel
wreath in her hair. On the back of her chair
stands a small, playful cherub, about to
whisper something in her ear. The Muse,
however, pays no attention to him; she gazes
into the distance like a Sibyl, one of the
priestess of Apollo, her lips slightly parted;
but she is not a tragic figure. Lotz could not
realize in his mythological scenes that accuracy which only results from close study of
the mythology and of its precise implica-
tions. He was much more interested in the
representation of beautiful female models.

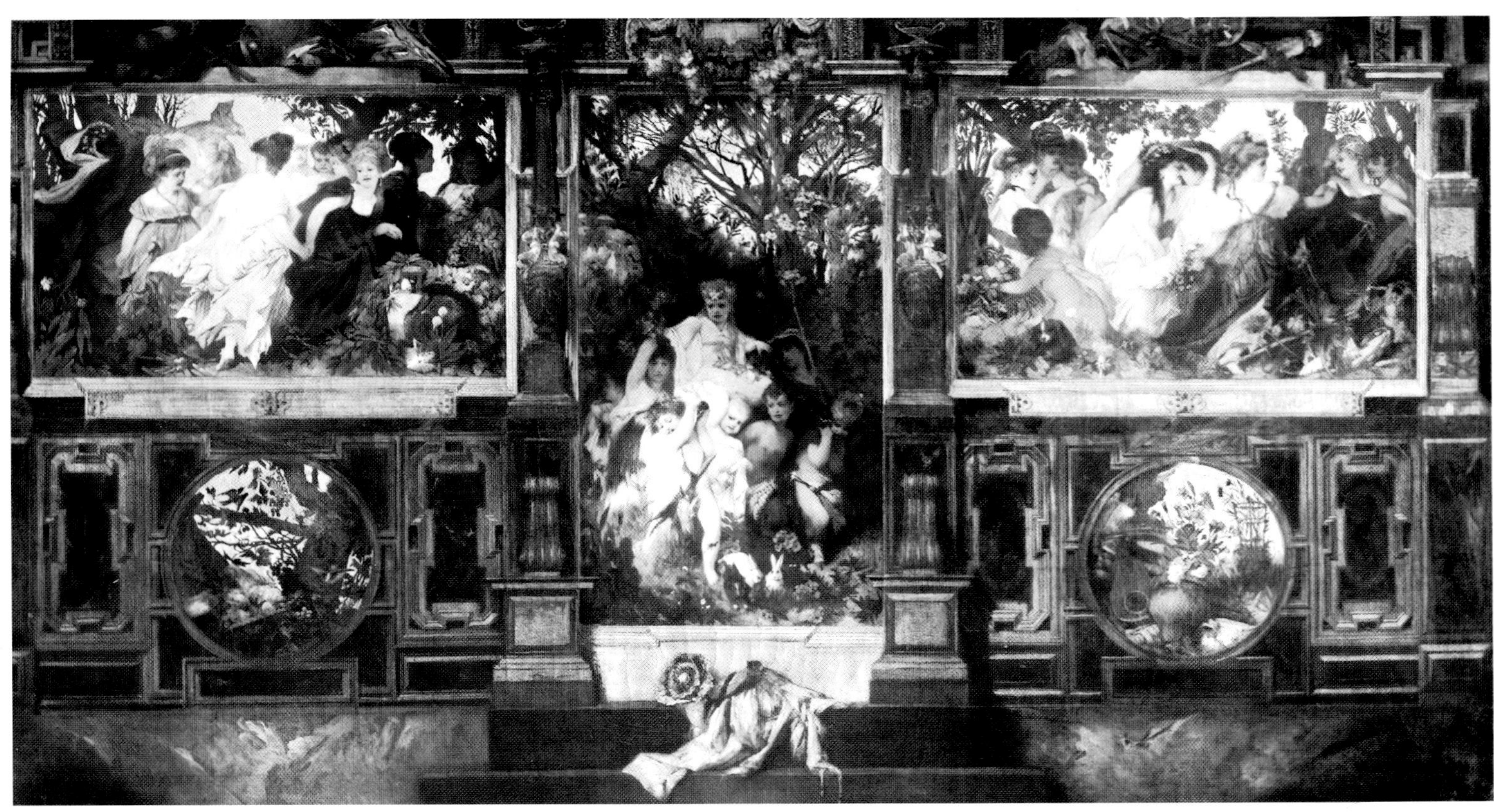

284. HANS MAKART
Scheme for a wall painting (Modern Cupids), 1868
Oil on paper and wood, 81×149 cm
Vienna, Österreichische Galerie
Inv. No.: 264

Hans Makart's decorative painting, made in 1868 in Munich, surprises by its light touch, imaginative qualities and sensuality. The celebrated painter divided the surface into panels by means of a heavy, Neo-Baroque wooden framework. He then stuck his paintings, made on paper, onto the panels. The central panel of the triptych represents six small cupids frolicking under a tree in full bloom. To the left and right, fashionable society women are seen dancing. In the lower part of the composition are two circular panels, one showing a gloomy winter scene with bare-branched trees—the other a summer field full of flowers. Makart thus openly combines the themes of an ancient mythology with those of his own age.

285. JENŐ GYÁRFÁS
Sketch for a decorative painting for a restaurant, 1879
Oil on canvas, 85×160 cm
Unsigned
Budapest, private collection

In style, this sketch by Jenő Gyárfás for a wall-painting in a restaurant—never realized—is similar to that of Hans Makart. Gyárfás placed his paintings in panels formed by the frame of an open Neo-Renaissance fireplace. Above the fireplace he planned to paint two figures as background for a Baroque clock—possibly intended to symbolize Time. The whole area would have been divided by pillars shaped in the form of statues, thus providing five large and two small panels on which Gyárfás planned to paint many-figured mythological scenes. The lower right-hand composition may represent a scene from the life of Dionysus.

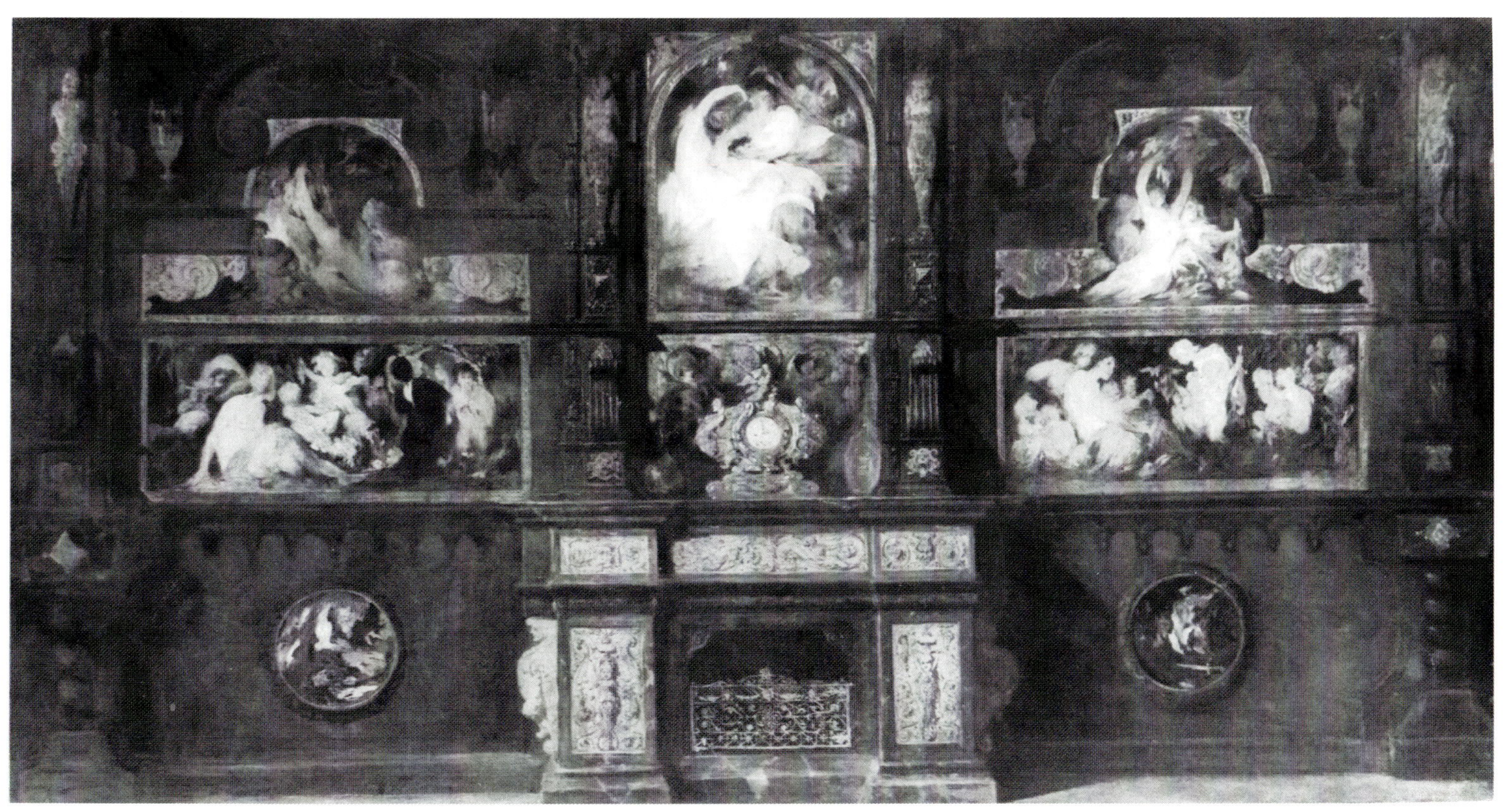

286. JENŐ GYÁRFÁS
Portrait of Simon Hollósy and study for a hand, 1880s
Oil on canvas, 38 × 43 cm
Signed bottom right: "Gyárfás Jenő"
Budapest, Hungarian National Gallery
Inv. No.: 6871

In this work Gyárfás was moving away from Academic portraiture towards an expressive Realism. Like all his finest portraits this sketch testifies not only to his understanding of the personality of his subject, but also to his method of depicting people.

Simon Hollósy had an attractive, romantic personality. Fellow painter István Réti remembered him from the 1880s as a man who "wore his dark wavy hair combed onto his forehead… [and] his usual expression was rather sad. He had a slight squint, and when he smiled, his large eyes glinted with moisture. As a painter he was a firm advocate of the cult of nature, feeling and spontaneity."

Gyárfás portrays Hollósy as a gay, strong, flexible and active person, who nevertheless lived in his dreams. He never painted a representative portrait of him, but this sketch precisely expresses his understanding of Hollósy's enchanting personality.

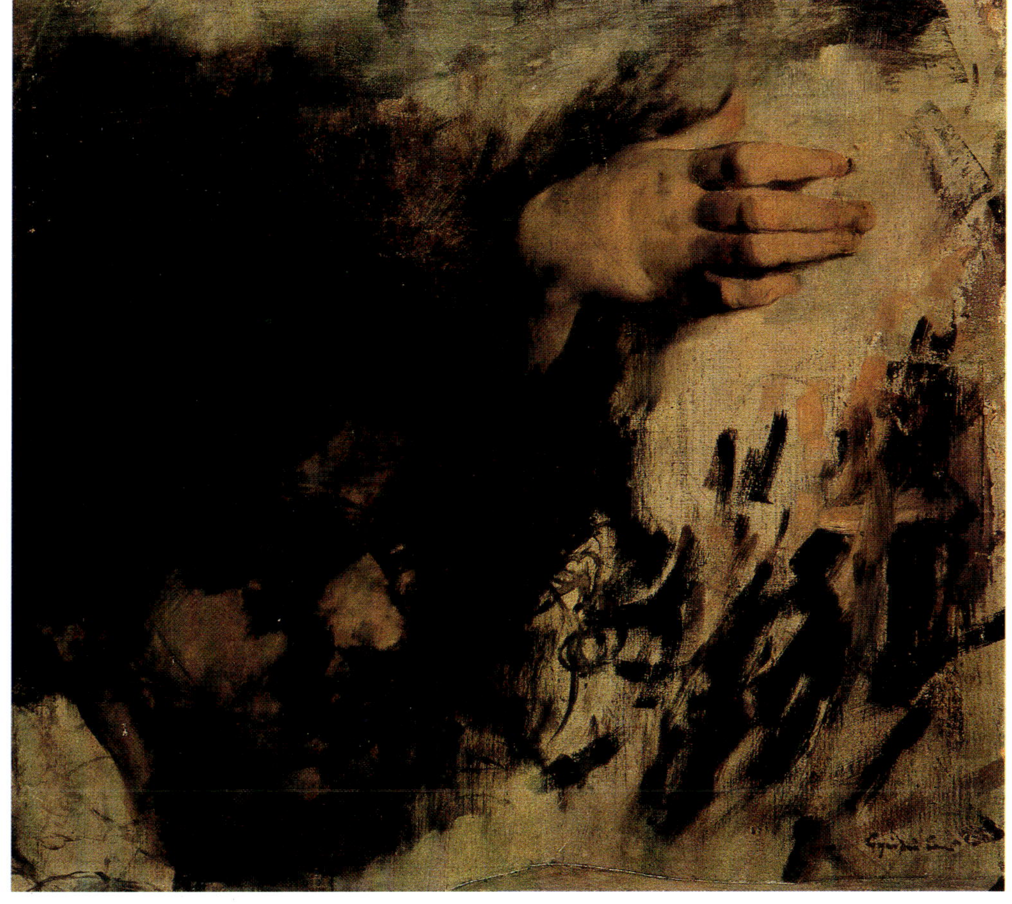

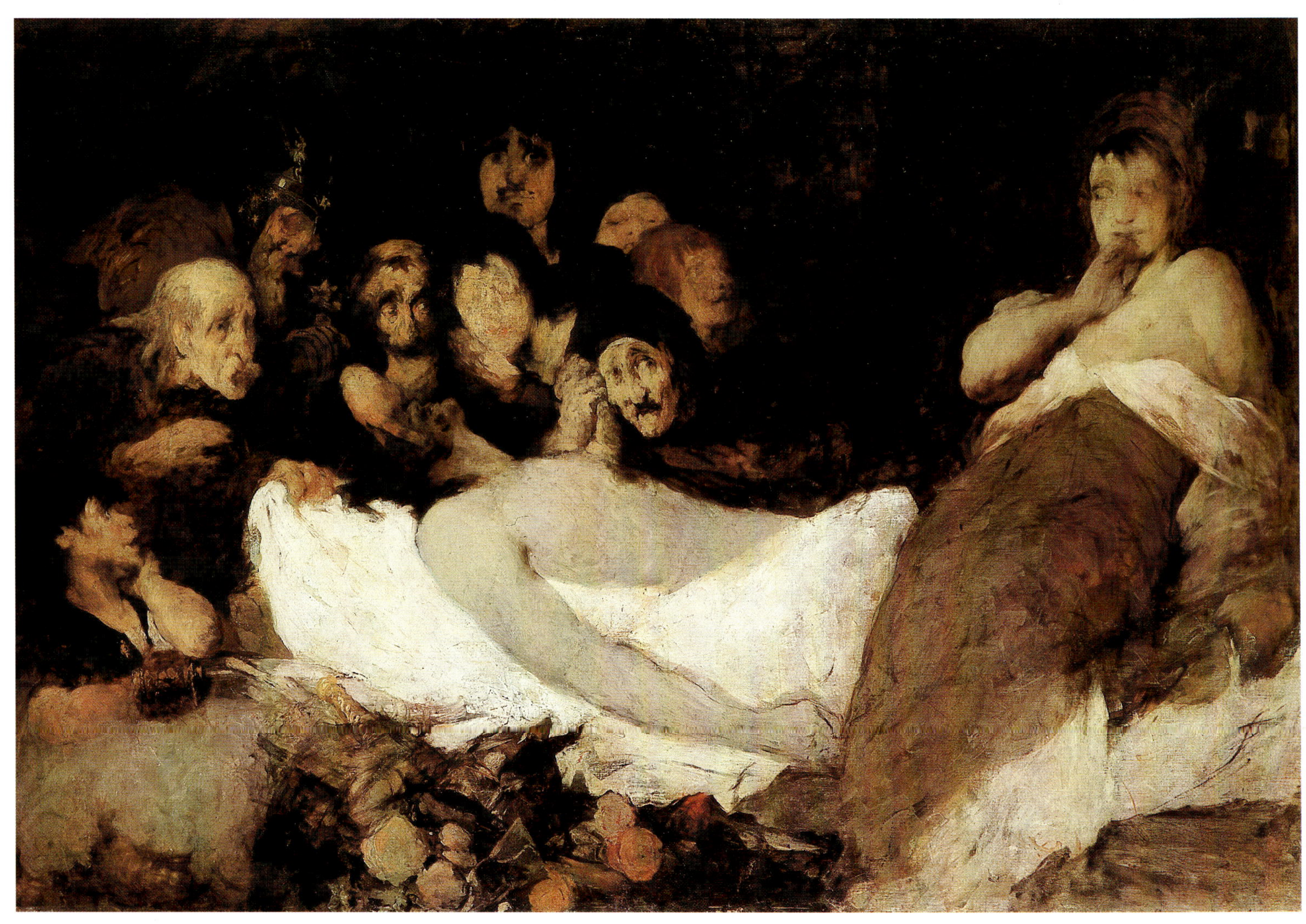

287. JENŐ GYÁRFÁS
The Ordeal of the Bier (sketch), 1881
Oil on canvas, 109×158.9 cm
Budapest, Hungarian National Gallery
Inv. No.: 56.416

Jenő Gyárfás had the sensitivity and artistry
which enabled him to paint in a decorative,
sensuous style reminiscent of Hans Makart.
But the compulsion of Hungarian literature
drew him in another direction. Thus, one of
his chief works was to be a vivid, almost
Naturalistic piece, intended as an illustration
of a ballad by the great poet János Arany
(Plate 288).

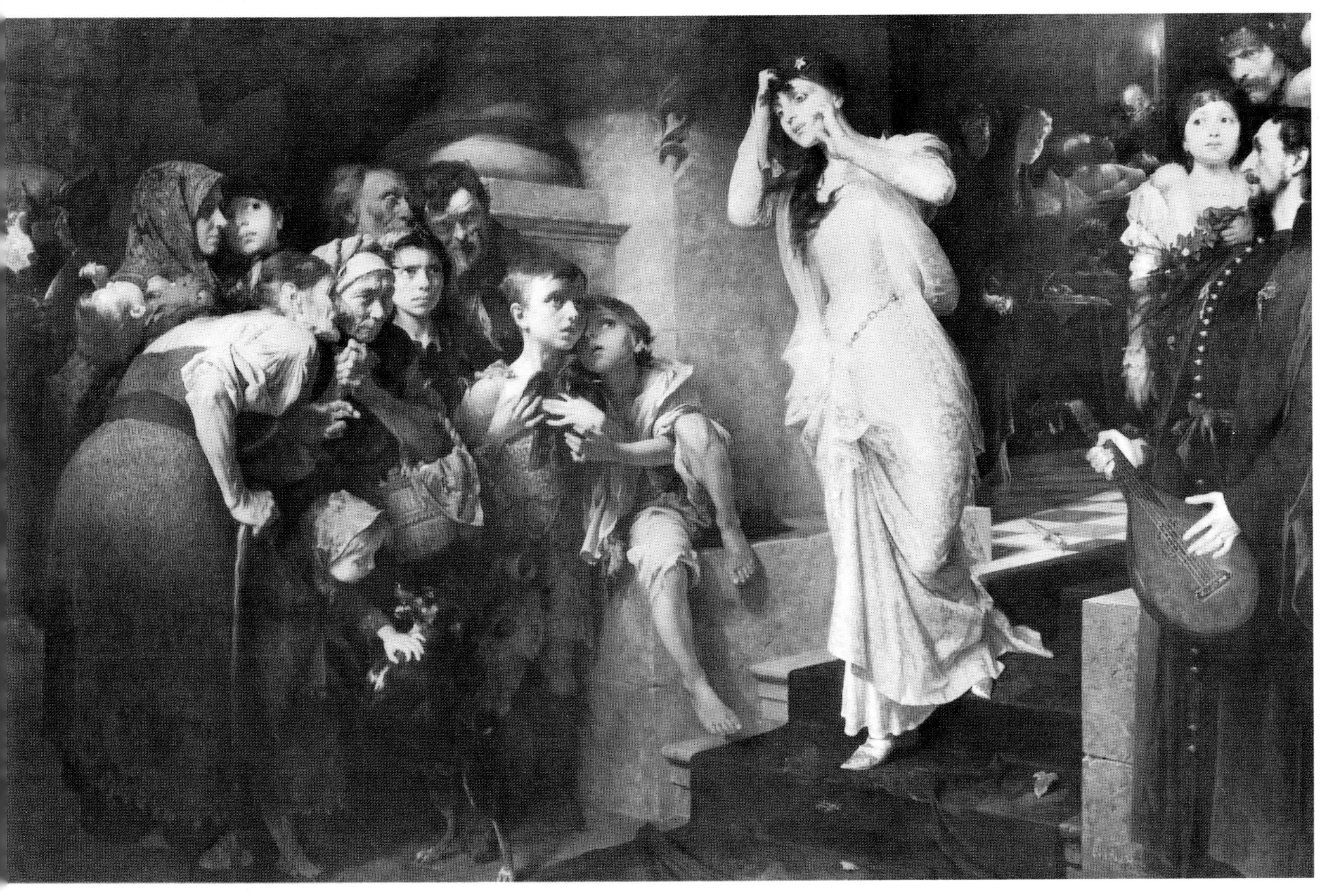

288. JENŐ GYÁRFÁS
The Ordeal of the Bier, 1881
Oil on canvas, 192.5 × 283.5 cm
Signed bottom right: "Gyárfás Jenő,
Sepsiszentgyörgy, 1881"
Budapest, Hungarian National Gallery
Inv. No.: 2777

This is one of the most representative paintings of the period. It illustrates the ballad of the same title written by János Arany in 1877. The poem and the painting alike project the tension and intellectual disquiet of that time. Looking for other examples of this kind, one could relate this painting to those of the Pre-Raphaelites, for instance, Millais' *Ophelia*. In France, Gustave Moreau's bloodthirsty visions and in Germany several eerie paintings by Alfred Rethel, Arnold Böcklin and Franz von Stuck were all based on literary inspiration and offered scenes of horror and bloodshed to exhibition visitors. Yet Gyárfás's Academic painting method renders the horror less poignant, so that to a certain extent the painting must be deemed a failure. Gyárfás possibly realized this himself, for he soon turned to other themes.

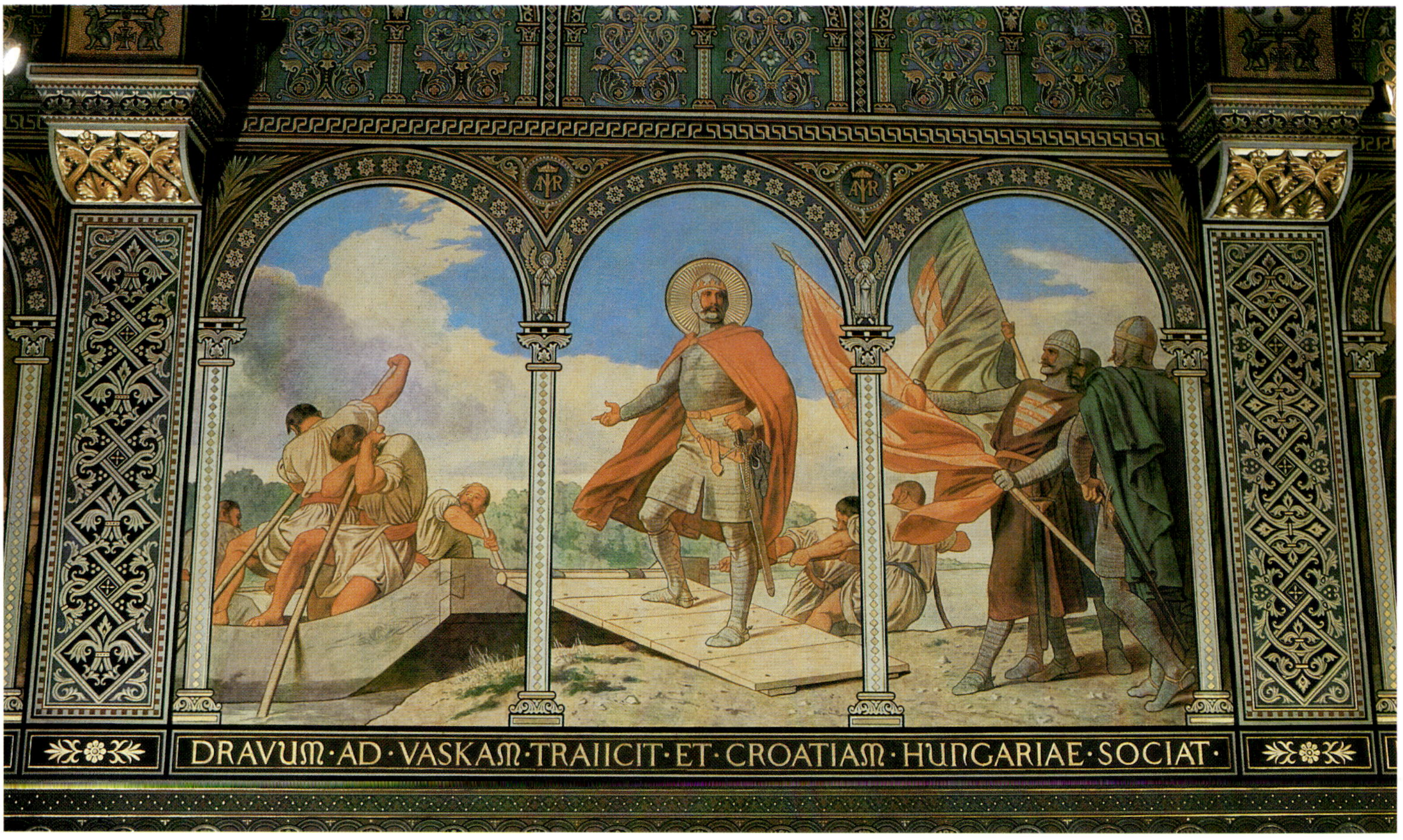

289. BERTALAN SZÉKELY
Saint Ladislas Crosses the River
Drava, 1887–1889
*Pécs, the Chapel of the Holy Virgin in the
Cathedral (second composition to the right of
the altar)*
*Inscription: "DRAVUM AD VASKAM
TRAICIT ET CROATIAM
HUNGARIAE SOCIAT" (He crossed the
river Drava and united Hungary with
Croatia)*

Székely was commissioned to paint two side
chapels in the newly rebuilt Cathedral of
Pécs. It was perhaps not pure chance that his
choice fell on those chapels which required
historical paintings. Though one of the
chapels opens from the left side-aisles, and
the other to the right of the sanctuary, they
are linked through the themes of the wall-
paintings. The Chapel of Saint Maurice
commemorates the heroic nature and historic deeds of the former Bishop of Pécs.
The paintings in the Chapel of the Holy Virgin represent the chief events of the first centuries after the foundation of the kingdom of
Hungary. Székely did not emphasize the
scene depicting the presentation of the
crown, painted just above the altar; he concentrated rather on the scene depicting St.
Ladislas' campaign in Croatia, an historical
event not previously painted in a church.

290. GYULA BENCZÚR
The Baptism of Vajk, 1875
Oil on canvas, 89×114 cm
*Signed bottom right: "Benczur Gyula,
München 1875"*
Budapest, Hungarian National Gallery
Inv. No.: 2798
(In the National Picture Gallery from 1876)

Gyula Benczúr was twenty-two years old
when he completed his first major historical
work. Soon afterwards he won the Hungarian Government's open competition for
historical compositions with his *Baptism of
Vajk*. It is a dramatic composition evoking
the confrontation between heathen Hungarians and Christian missionaries headed by
the newly baptized Prince Vajk (later King
St. Stephen). By 1875 Benczúr had completed the final version of this theme. In this
painting the Christening ceremony, attended by several princes, takes on a symbolic character. In the foreground the young
black-haired Vajk kneels before Bishop (St.)
Adalbert. Vajk's red cloak leaves his shoulder uncovered as he is baptized by the mag-
nificently robed bishop. The splendour of
the scene is further enhanced by the solemnity of the gestures, the jewelled cross, the
crosier and the richly embroidered ecclesiastical vestmens.

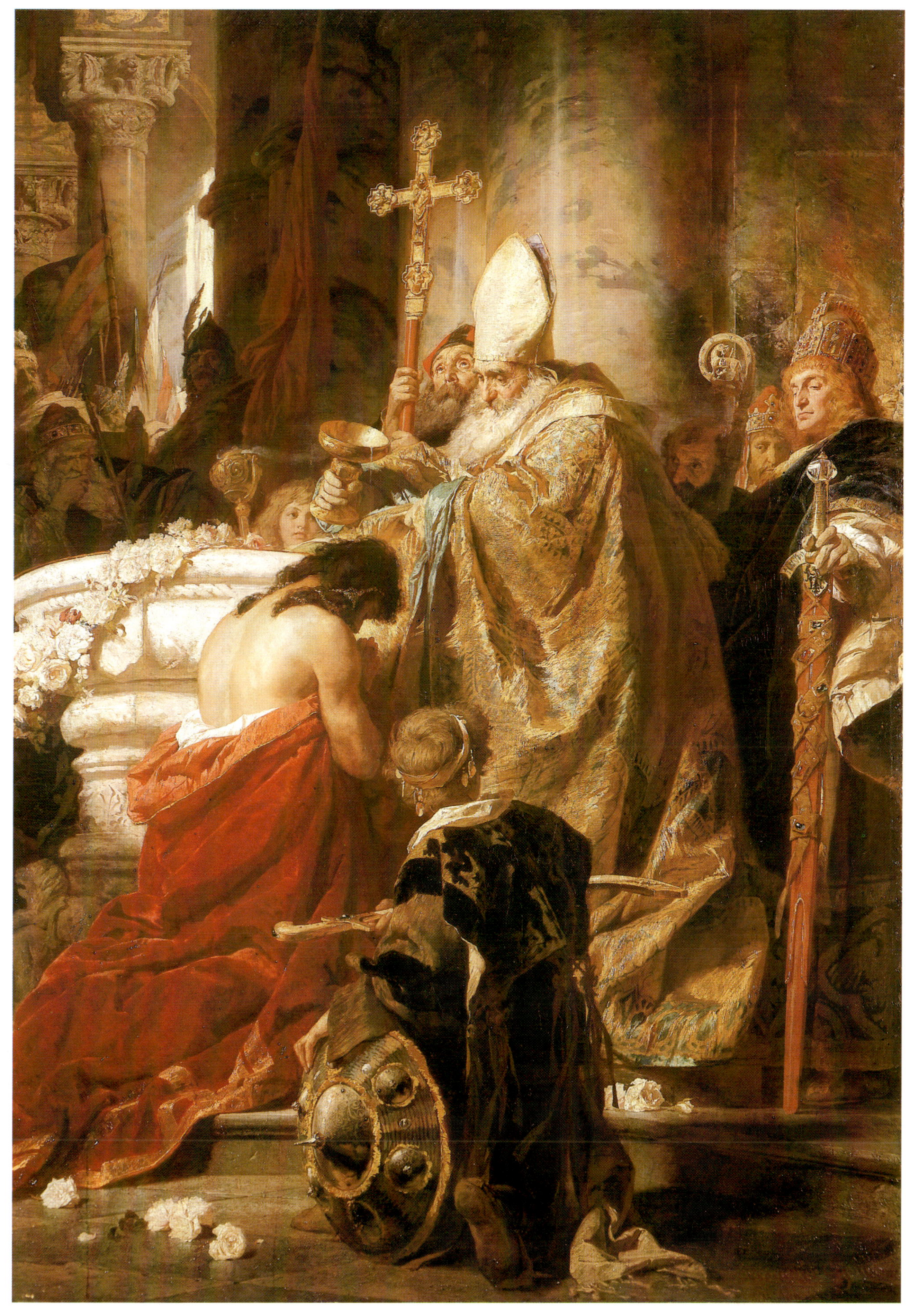

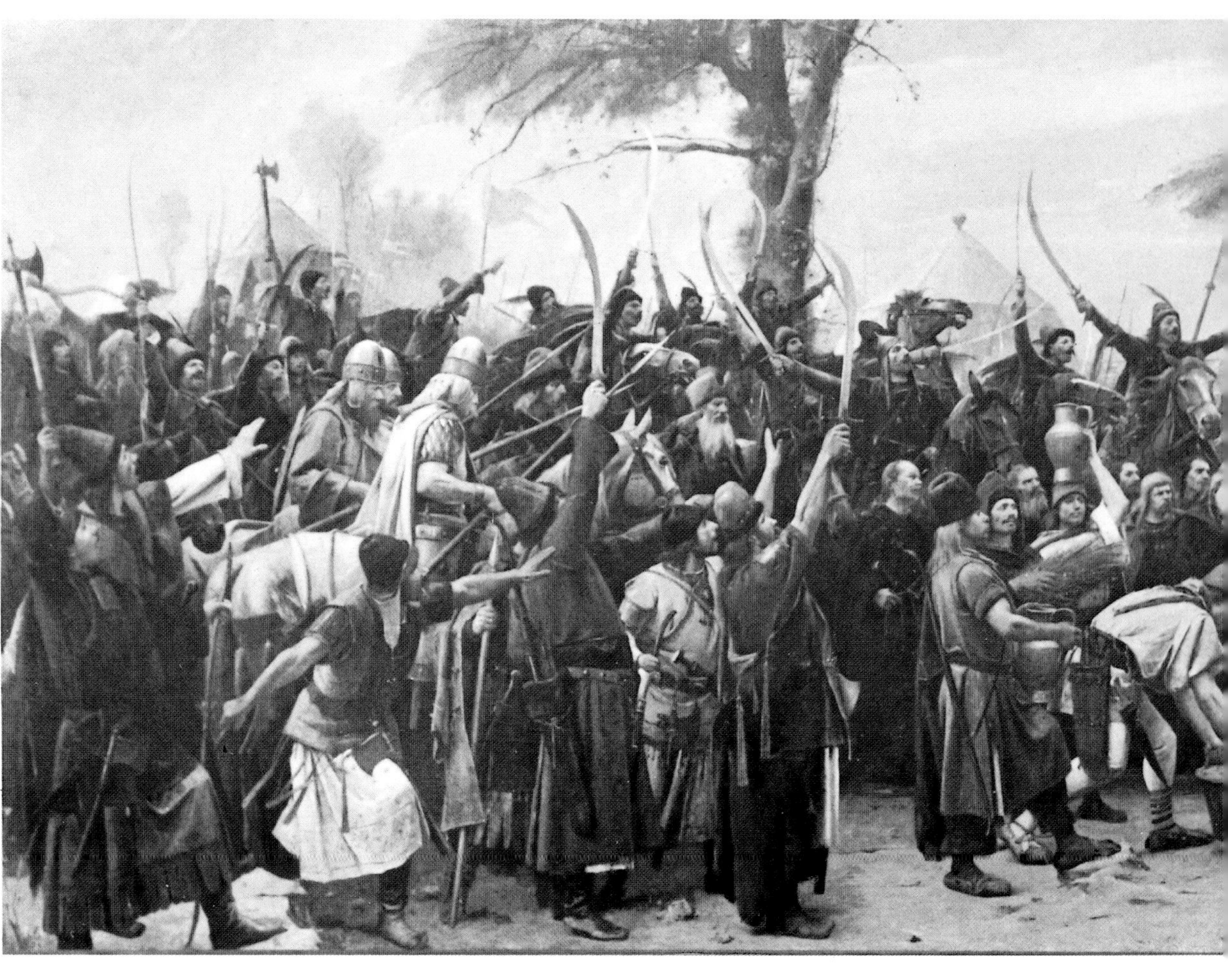

291. MIHÁLY MUNKÁCSY
The Magyar Conquest of Hungary, 1893

Oil on canvas, 459×135.5 cm
Signed bottom right: "Munkácsy M. 1893 December 20"
Budapest, the House of Parliament, (lent by the Hungarian National Gallery)
Inv. No.: 3201

Immediately after accepting the commission to paint the ceiling of the Kunsthistorisches Museum in Vienna, Munkácsy was commissioned to provide a large painting for the building of the Parliament in Budapest. This was eventually executed with the assistance of Munkácsy's pupils who copied his sketches. The painter first named his work *Árpád,* possibly with reference to Mihály Kovács's painting entitled *Árpád Being Lifted on the Shield,* the ceremony whereby the first of the tribal heads was made king, or another similar work by Bálint Kiss. Munkácsy interpreted the theme with all the Romanticism of the 1840s and 1850s. The principal figure, Árpád, is mounted on a white horse surrounded by cheering followers. He receives gifts from the inhabitants of the region he has just conquered and which he intends to annex as part of Hungary. When the painting was completed Munkácsy's health was already failing and he was getting old. He did not understand why his painting received such a cool reception. It was in fact attributable to the political climate at the end of the century, when the problem of minority groups was so critical within the Austro-Hungarian Empire. His intention had been to create a monumental work expressing an ideal situation in which all the nationalities within the borders of Hungary were living together in peace.

292. GYULA BENCZÚR
Buda Regained, 1885–1896

Oil on canvas, 356×705 cm
Signed bottom left: "Benczur Gyula, 1896, Budapest"
Budapest, Hungarian National Gallery
Inv. No.: 2867

In the year of the thousandth anniversary (millennium) of the Magyar Conquest of Hungary, this painting was intended to represent the historical link between Hungary and Austria. In recapturing Buda in 1686–1687 from the Turks, the heroic stand taken by Charles de Lorraine and Eugène de Savoy represented the most notable event in an otherwise bitter relationship between the Austrian Empire and the Hungarian Kingdom.
Ten years passed between Benczúr's first sketch and the completion of this vast painting. Fully aware of the magnitude of his undertaking, he made a series of individual drawings in which he worked out every important detail. His aim was to depict the commanders-in-chief with due dignity and to paint with equal stature the Hungarian and Austrian soldiers triumphantly marching into Buda, the royal residence. His representation of the Turkish dead and wounded, including the Pasha of Buda, serve to indicate the grandeur of the action of recapture.

288

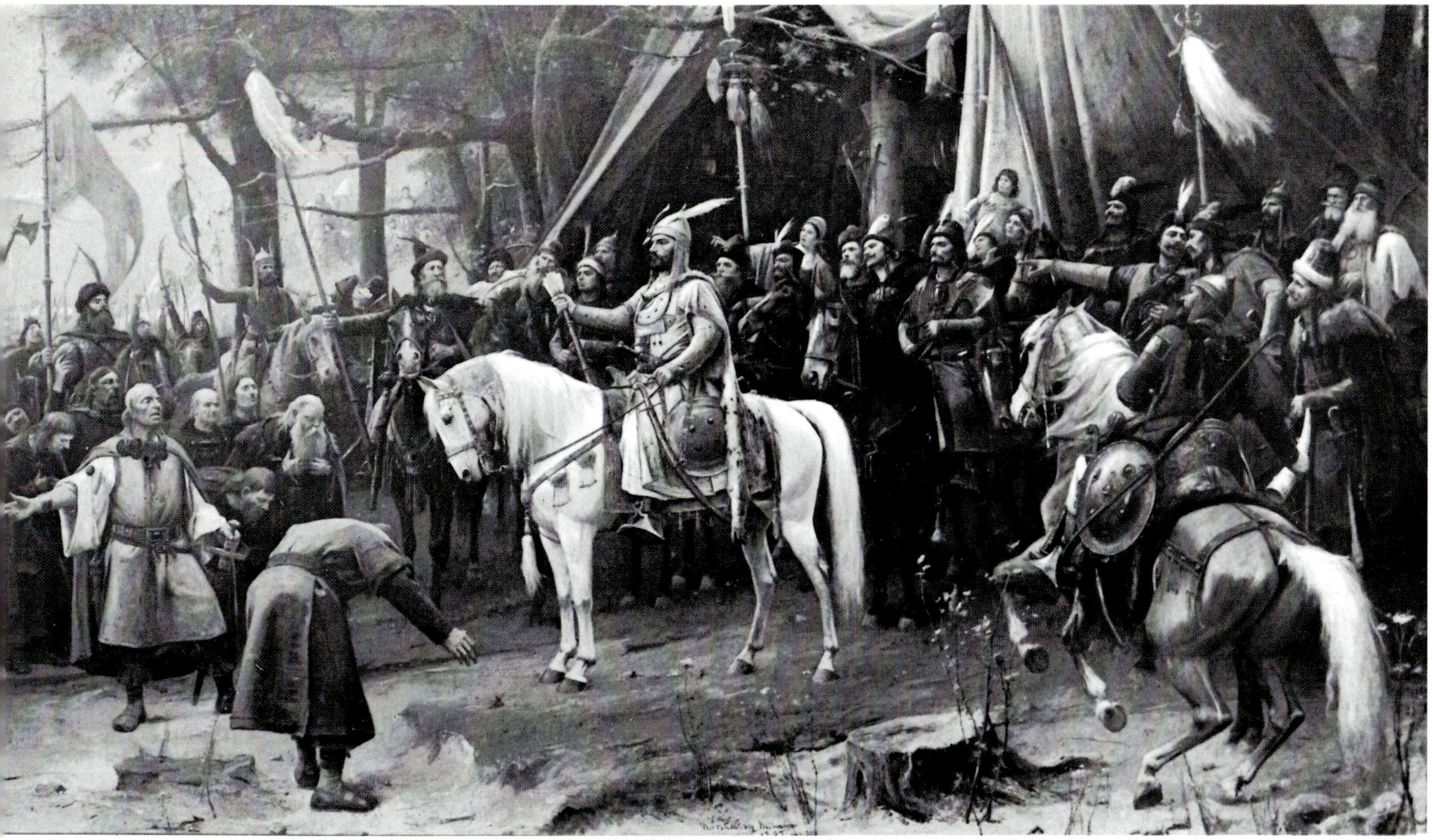

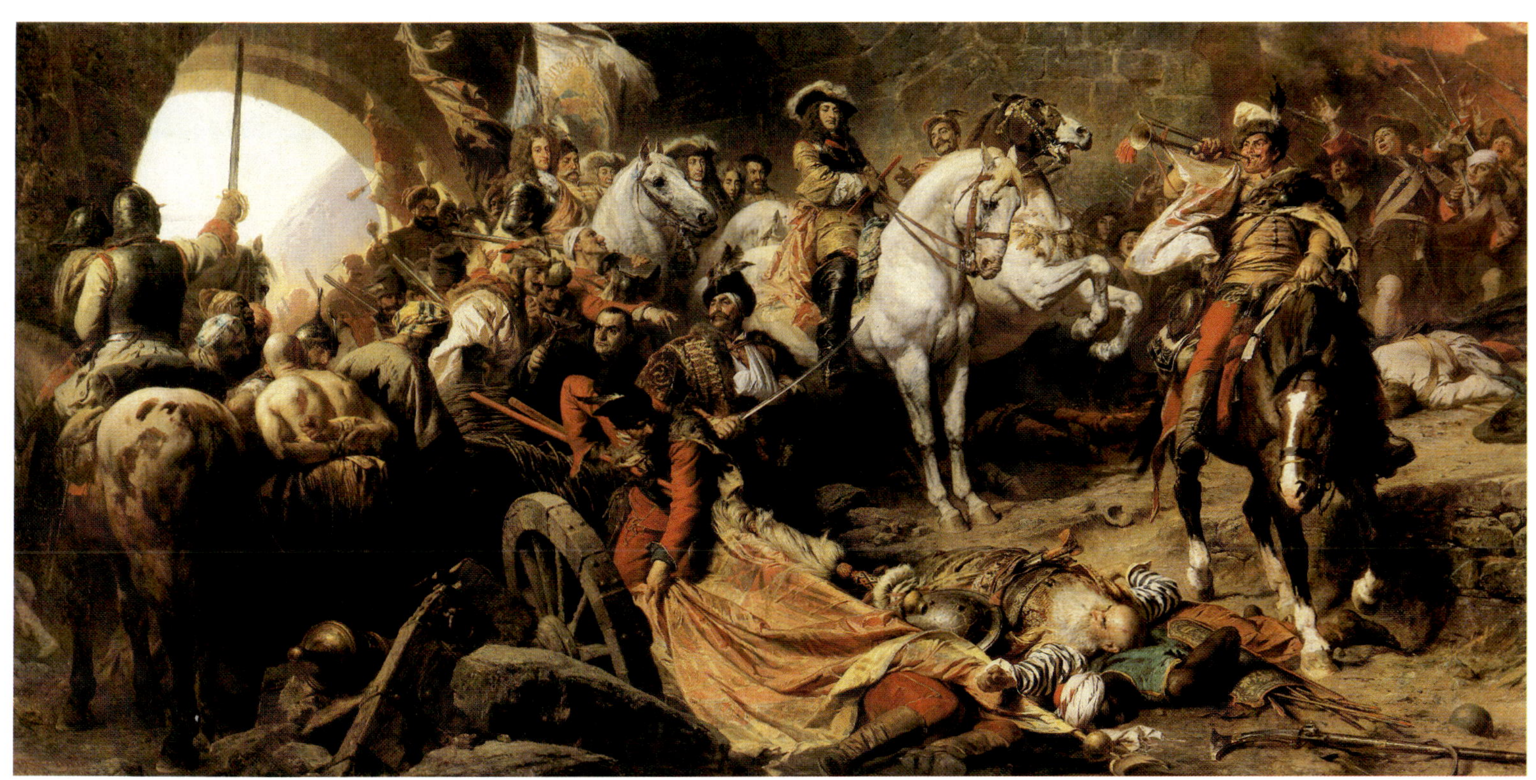

293. AUGUST VON PETTENKOFEN
The Horse Market, II, 1877
Oil on wood, 19.5 × 32 cm
Signed bottom left: "Pettenkofen à son amie de Giczy 877"
Vienna, Österreichische Galerie
Inv. No.: 4705

Pettenkofen visited Szolnok frequently between the years 1851 and 1881 and painted many genre-pieces of the town and its surroundings. He stayed near the market which became one of his favourite subjects. This small sketch of a section of the market was painted on wood and given to a friend.

294. JOHANN GUILBERT RAFFALT
The Market in Szolnok, 1860s
Oil on wood, 31.5 × 50 cm
Signed bottom right: "J. G. Raffalt"
Vienna, Österreichische Galerie
Inv. No.: 1381

Raffalt first went to Szolnok in 1863 to visit his friend Pettenkofen, though he had already spent some time in Hungary. His father, also a painter, used Hungarian motifs for his town scenes and landscapes. Raffalt was possibly following his example in this precise representation of part of the covered market in Szolnok and the 18th century votive column in front of it. The many figures around the house and column are only an anonymous faceless crowd; the painter was mainly interested in the view and the clothes worn by the townfolk.

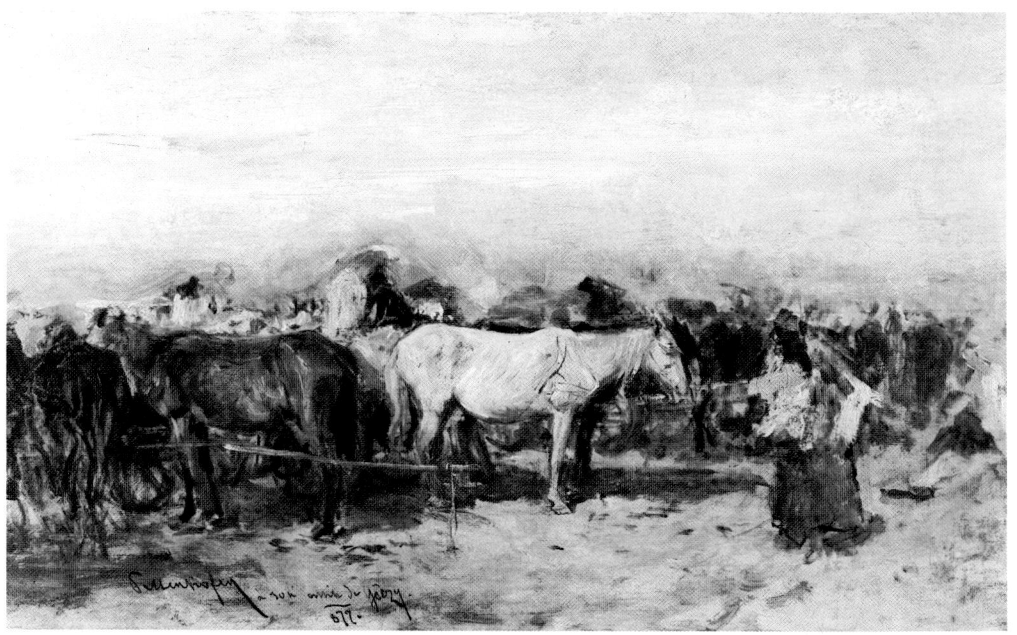

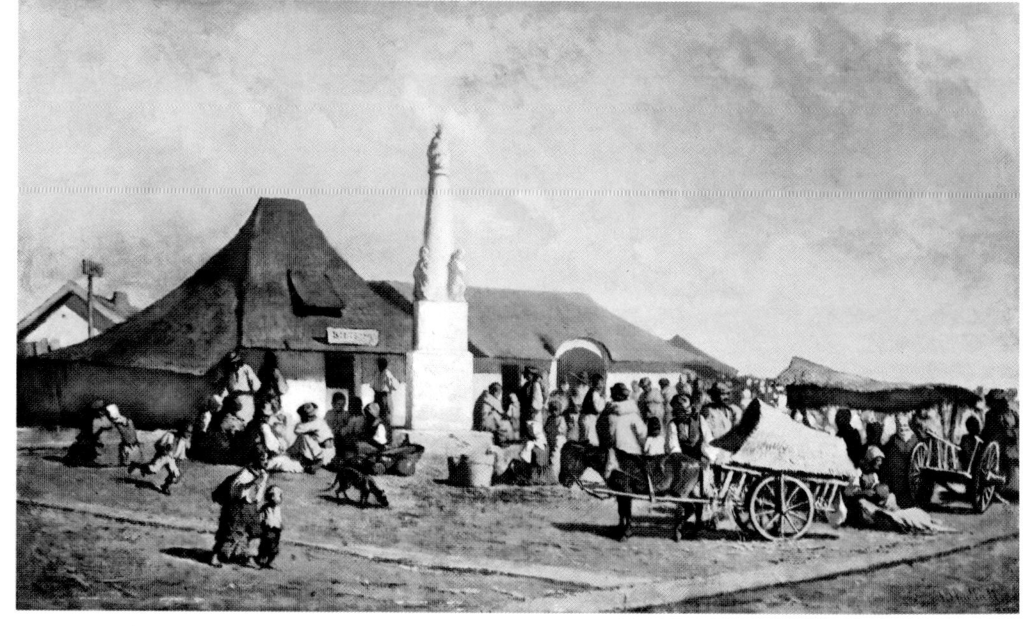

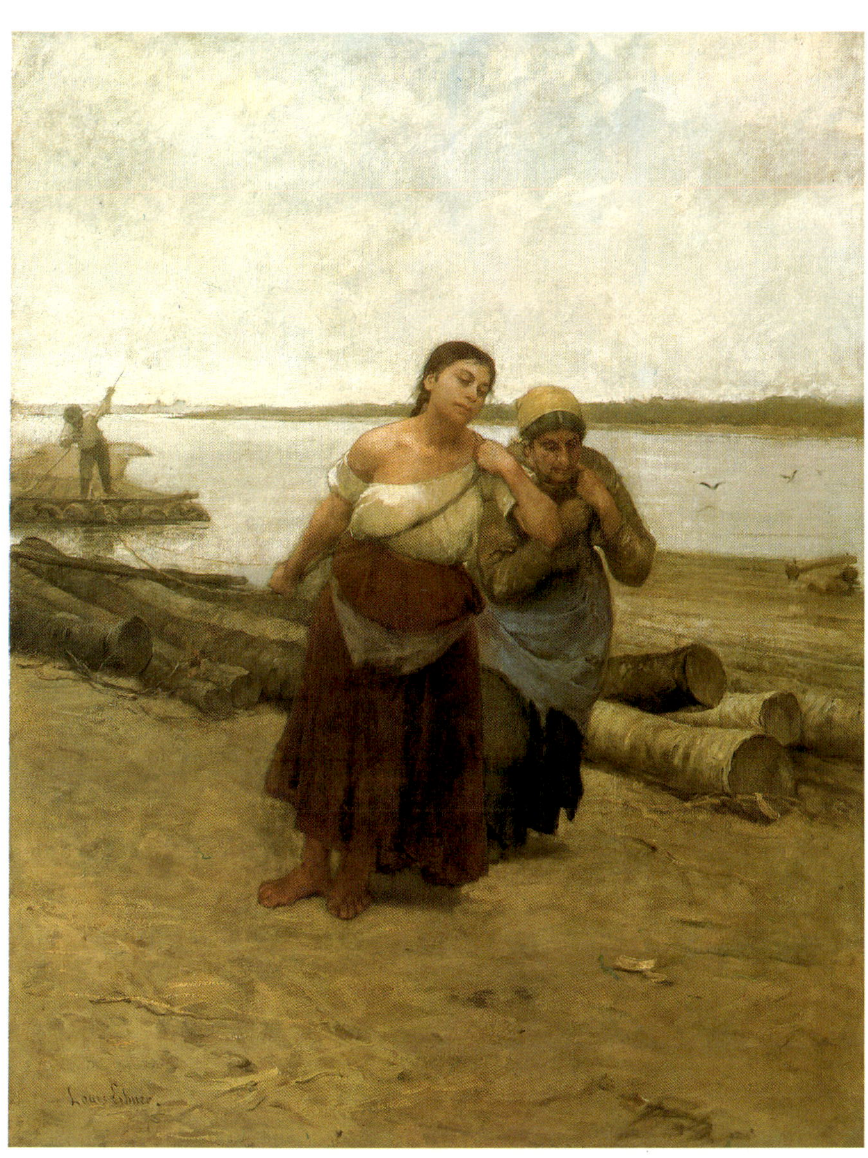

295. LAJOS DEÁK ÉBNER
Hauling Logs, c. 1885
Oil on canvas, 132 × 98 cm
Signed bottom left: "Louis Ebner"
Budapest, Hungarian National Gallery
Inv. No.: 6313

This painting is a fine example of delicate Naturalism, executed in a reserved but most effective style. Using a strong rope, two women are hauling tree trunks, which are tied together, along the shore of the River Tisza. A man standing on a primitive raft pushes a flotilla of tree trunks towards the riverbank, where a heap of logs indicates how much work they have already done.

296. LAJOS DEÁK ÉBNER
At the Market, 1880
Oil on canvas, 54 × 101.5 cm
Signed bottom right: "Ébner 1880"
Budapest, private collection

From 1874 onwards Lajos Deák Ébner visited Szolnok nearly every summer, although between 1873 and 1878 he lived for the most part in Paris. This oil painting may have been made in Paris from sketches done in Szolnok. It differs from Pettenkofen's simple representation of nature, and also from Raffalt's objective topographical interpretations. In fact, Deák Ébner applies Munkácsy's method of genre painting, using a light brush and fluid movements. This canvas depicts the Szolnok fair. Separate groups mingle to form a harmonious composition in which the details nevertheless provide a narrative element.

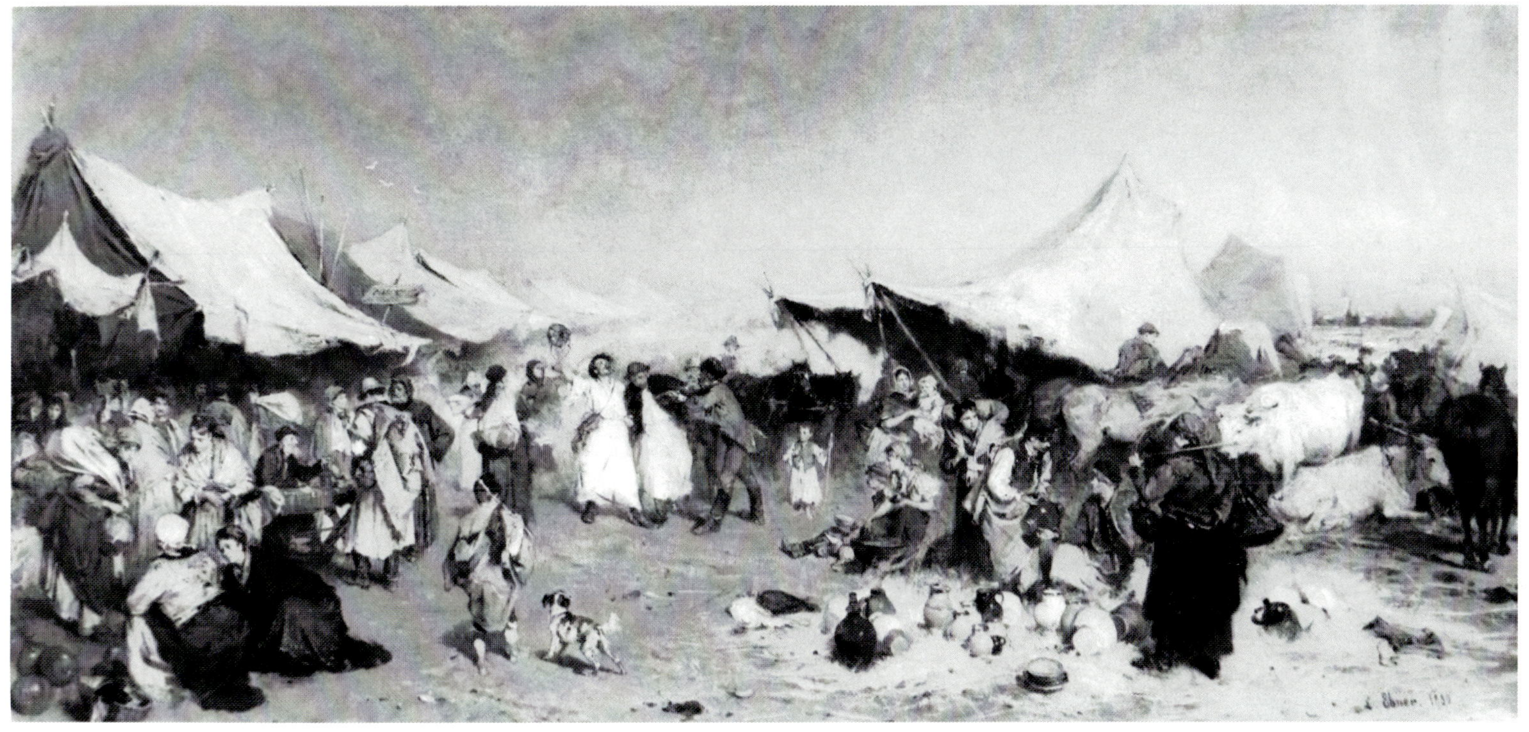

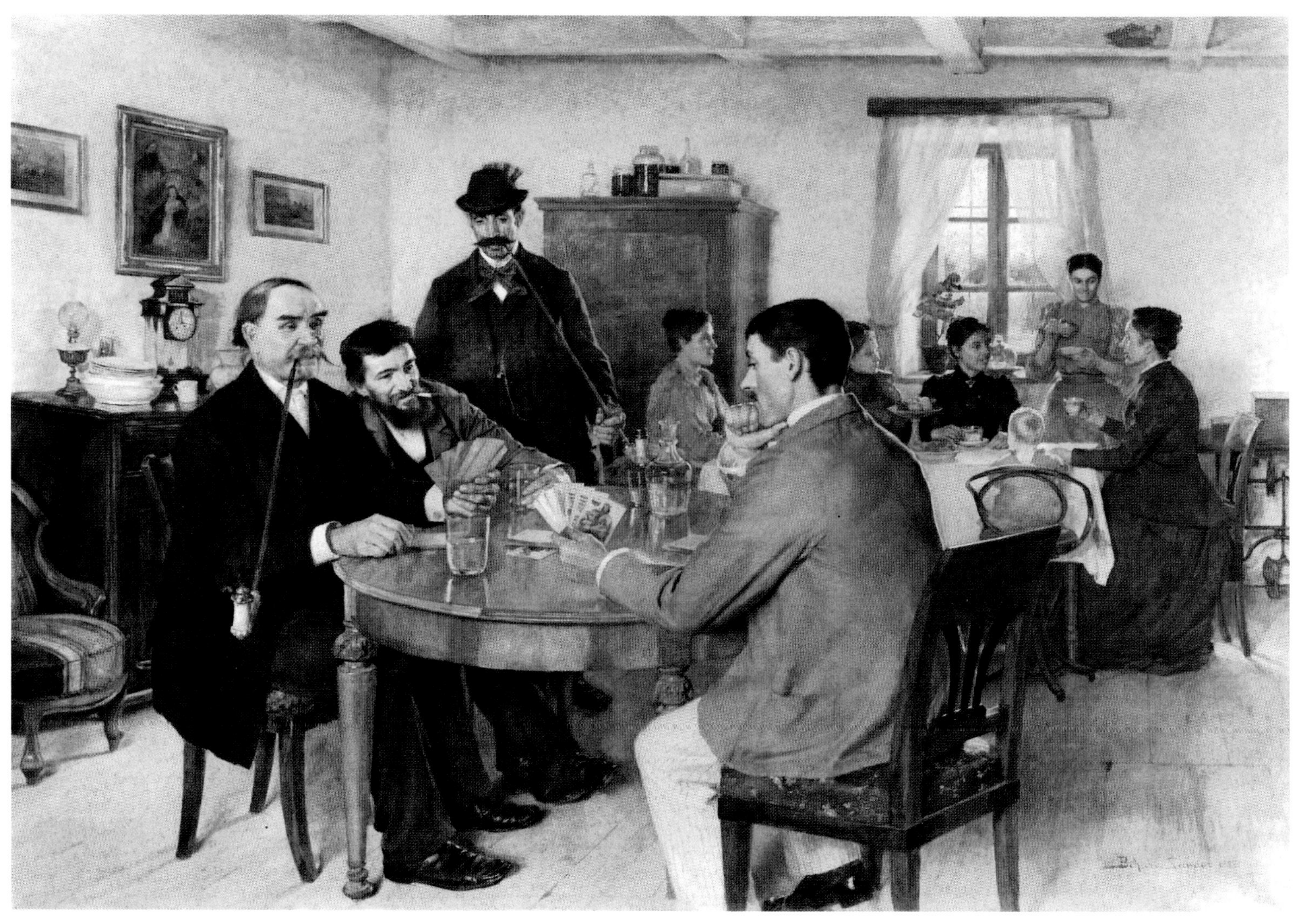

297. SÁNDOR BIHARI
Sunday Afternoon, 1893
Oil on canvas, 113×163 cm
Signed right: "Bihari Sándor 1893"
Budapest, private collection

Sándor Bihari painted this genre-scene in
a friend's house near Budapest. The painter
travelled a good deal in the 1880s and enjoyed visiting both Paris and Szolnok. Here he
projects the homely atmosphere of this scene
in a small provincial town. The figures in the
foreground—three men seated at the round
table, two of them playing cards, the fourth
watching them—are meticulously portrayed, as if recorded through the lens of a camera. By the window, around a smaller table,
five women are chatting and drinking coffee.
Bihari renders every detail of furniture, not
neglecting the preserves on the top of the
cupboard, the clock in a case flanked by pillars and the oil lamp beside it. He even includes details in the pictures hanging on the
wall: two landscapes, one on either side of
a larger religious picture.

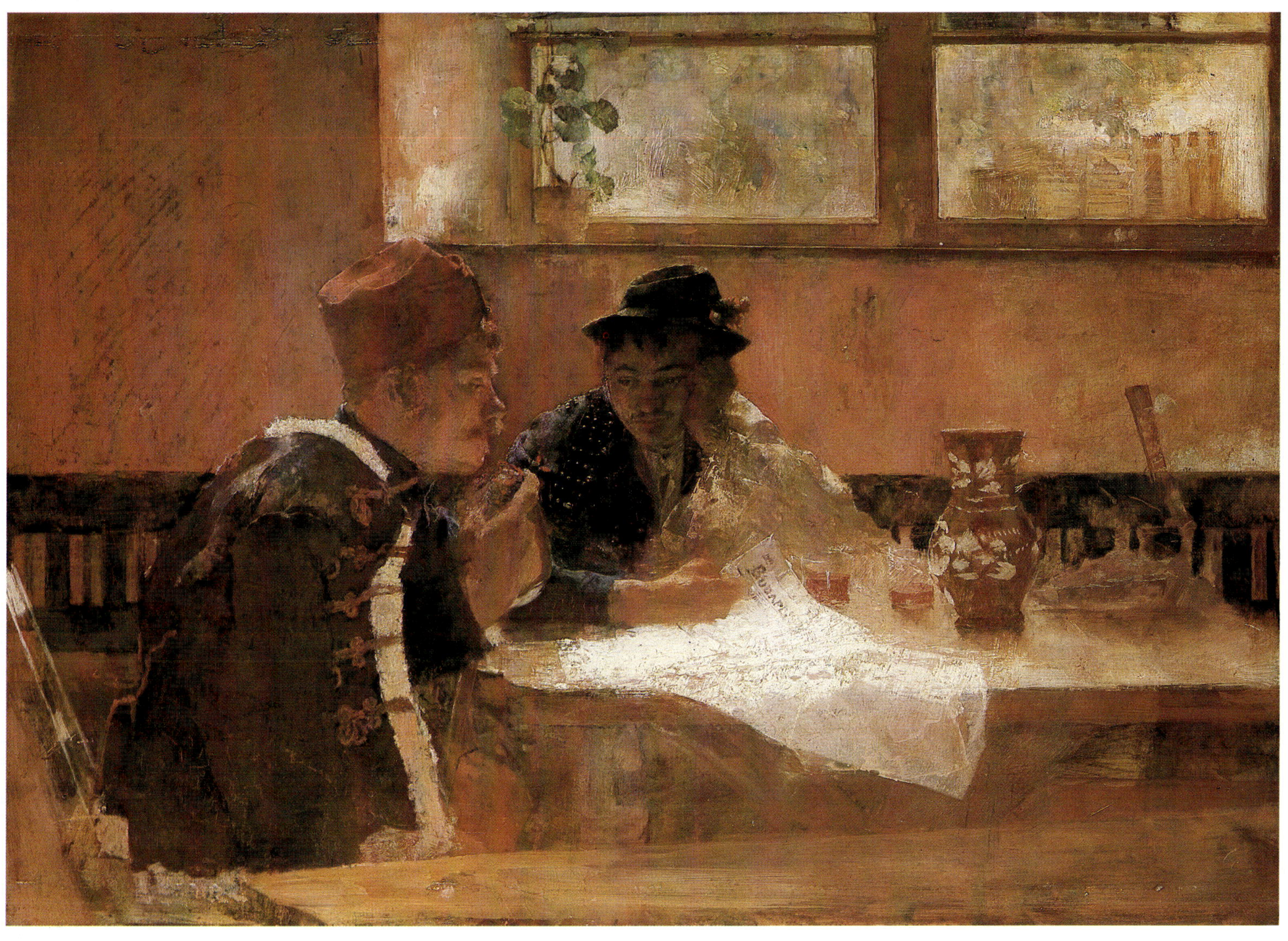

298. SIMON HOLLÓSY
The Problems of the Nation, 1893
Oil on canvas, 52.5 × 83.5 cm
Unsigned
Hungarian National Gallery
Inv. No.: 4954

This painting, executed in two versions by the artist, depicts a Hussar reading his newspaper, and a peasant. They are sitting at a table in an inn with a glass of wine, obviously discussing politics. In 1860 Mihály Szemlér painted the same subject (Plate 249). Hollósy's work includes fewer figures, but the effect of light is more pronounced and the colouring much richer. The bright spring sunshine pouring in through the window, the plant on the window sill and even the sparkling red wine in their glasses do not divert the two men's attention from the problems of Hungary. Their faces express their deep concern about what they read. The peasant's hat is decorated with the posy given to recruits in Hungary. They may be discussing political unrest and the possibility of imminent war.

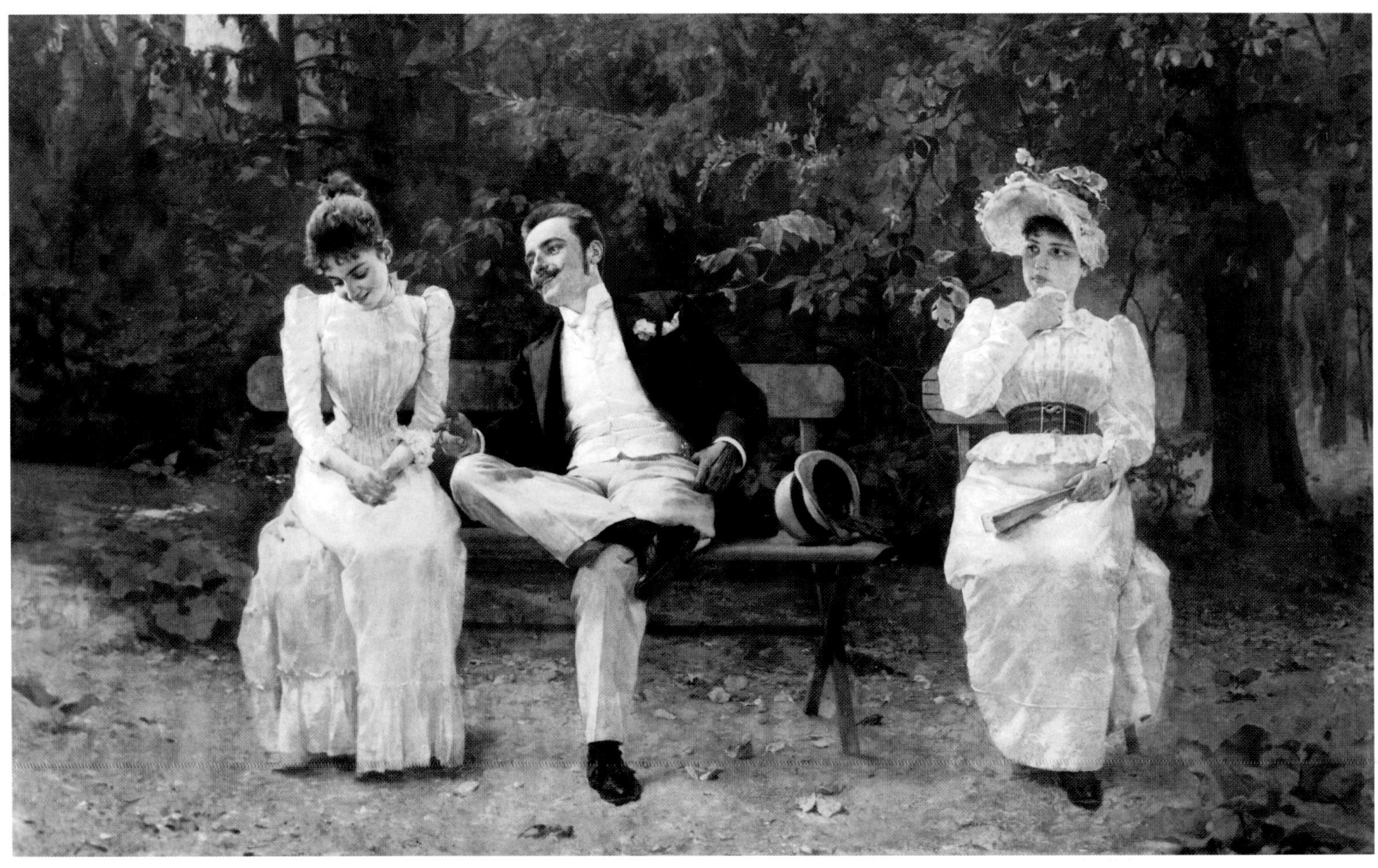

299. TIHAMÉR MARGITAY
Jealousy, 1892
Oil on canvas, 86×137 cm
Signed bottom left: "Margitay 1892"
Budapest, Hungarian National Gallery
Inv. No.: 3646

The art critic Károly Lyka saw the painter Tihamér Margitay as a talented painter with a gift for drawing who wandered from the true path of demanding artistic creation towards fashionable themes and easy genre paintings. He learned to paint under Bertalan Székely at the Academy of Arts in Budapest, and from 1879 onwards repeatedly received grants to continue his studies at the Academy of Munich.

From 1880 onwards, Margitay became a celebrated painter of fashionable society portraits. His themes include the irresistible gallant, the neat, convent-educated young girl receiving her future fiancé for the first time, and the rejected suitor.

His characters are always well educated, elegantly dressed and conventional. Margitay never represented tragic situations. In this painting, the elegant irresistible "Romeo" sits on a bench in the park, indulging in an entertaining conversation with a young lady while his pretty wife or fiancée sulks nearby.

294

300. JÁNOS THORMA
Suffering, 1892–1893

Oil on canvas, 250 × 300 cm
Signed bottom left: "Thorma"
Budapest, Hungarian National Gallery
Inv. No.: 1548

Though Thorma's painting is similar to that of Margitay in terms of graphic detail and narrative character, the two works are in fact totally different. Thorma's painting shows a real tragedy. A couple, dressed in mourning, stand at the gate of the cemetery: the pretty young woman accompanying her older, sickly husband bends forward to kiss a beggar woman's healthy child.

The painting is based on a scene Thorma himself witnessed in Paris. A woman in mourning was walking along a Paris street with her elderly husband when she suddenly kissed a beggar-woman's child. Thorma spent nearly a year working on this rather large painting in a coach-house in Paris specially arranged for the purpose. For the sake of his Hungarian viewers, he changed the setting and depicted instead of a street in Paris, the cemetery at Nagybánya. In the background, poor women with shawls over their heads stand by the simple tombstones. In the foreground, in addition to the mother with her healthy child, there are other weary beggars waiting for alms. Thorma does not attempt to draw a parallel between the lives of the people depicted, nor to contrast them. He simply presents several aspects of human suffering in a gloomy autumnal setting.

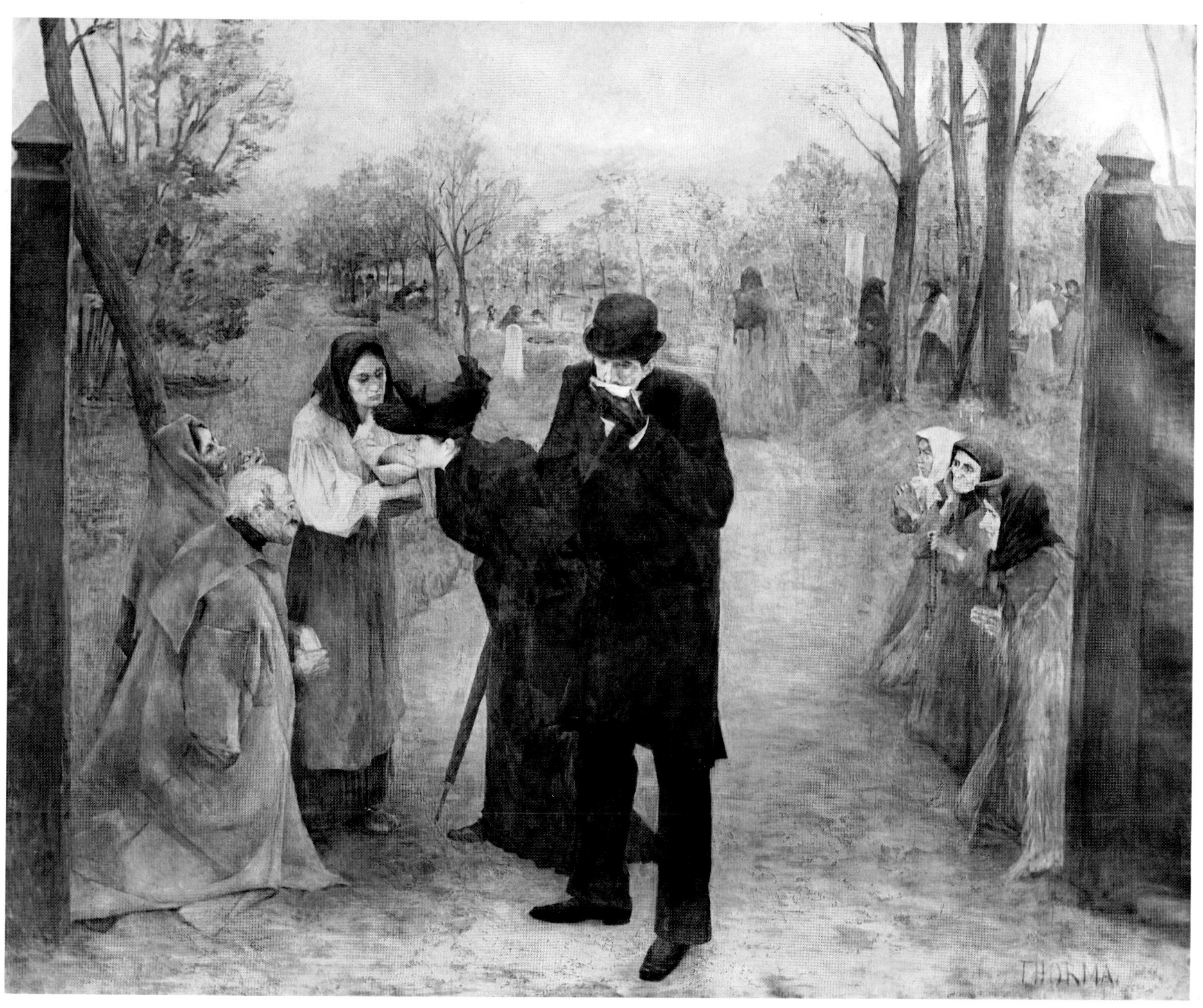

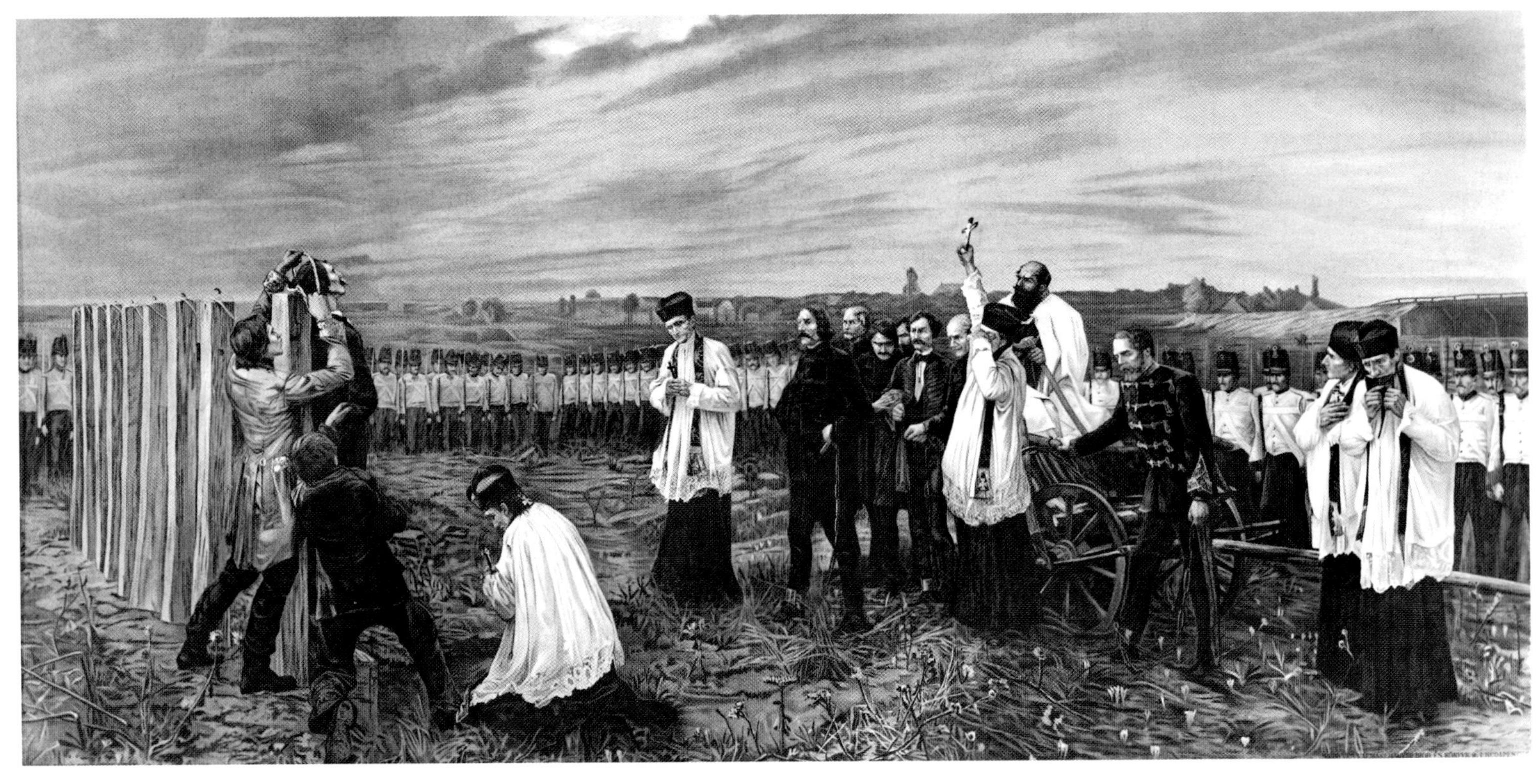

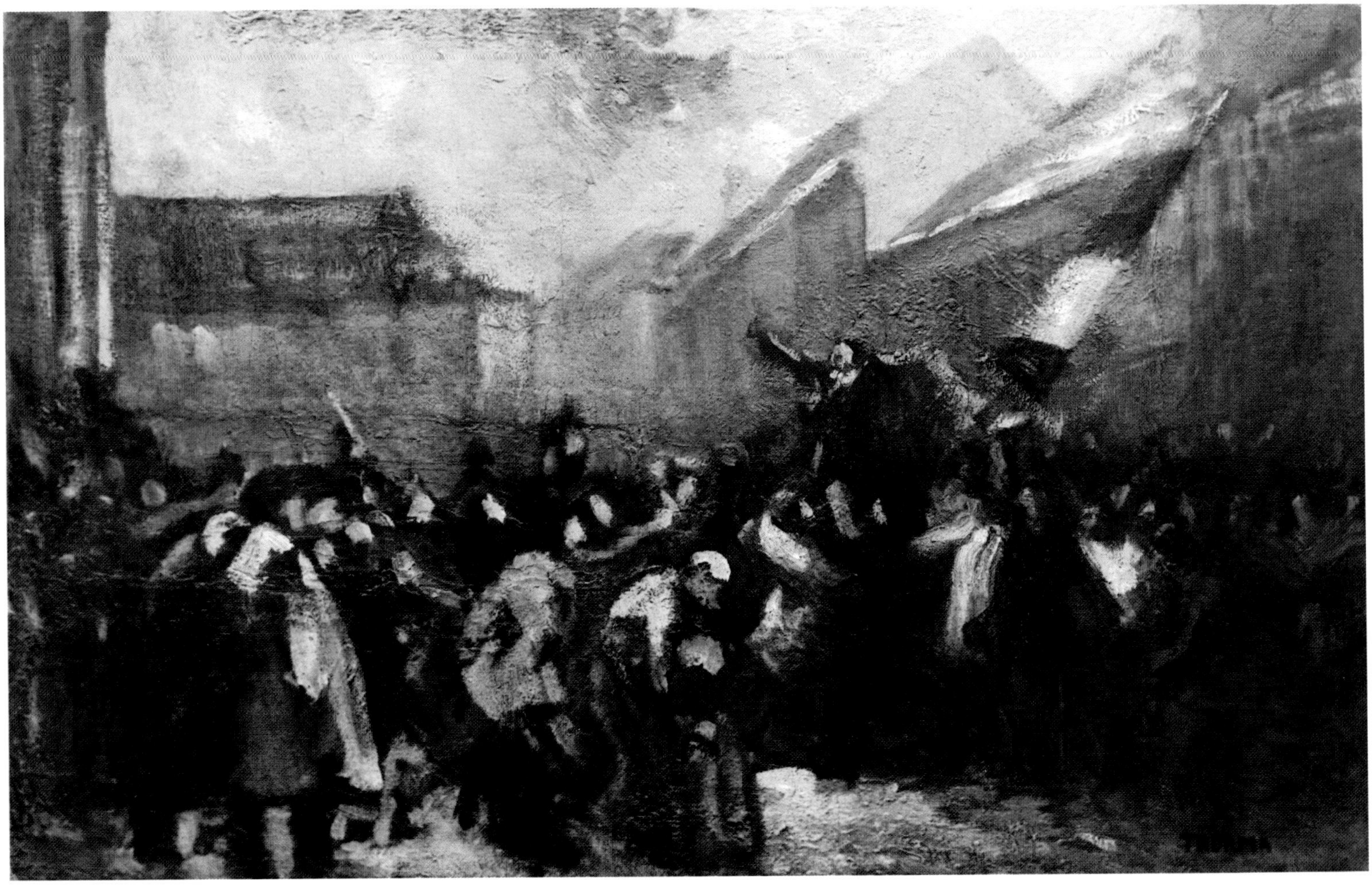

301. JÁNOS THORMA
The Martyrs of Arad, 1893–1896
Oil on canvas, 350 × 633 cm
Budapest, Hungarian National Gallery
Inv. No.: 3308
(Since the painting is being restored, the
reproduction is from an old print)

In the early 1890s, Thorma, who mostly
painted delicate naturalistic genre-pieces, developed an interest in historical themes. In
1893, on the thousandth anniversary of the
Magyar Conquest of Hungary, he began
a monumental work, the *Martyrs of Arad*.
His aim was to depict the execution of the
Hungarian generals of the defeated War of
Independence in a naturalistic way, without
recourse to allegory. As he could not be
given sufficient wall space at the Official Exhibition in honour of the great national
celebrations in the Art Gallery, Thorma
rented a private hall in which to exhibit his
work. It was much approved for its moral
values, but later lost its popularity among
Hungarians who did not care to see such
a tragic scene represented in a matter of fact
style. The rulers of the Austro–Hungarian
Empire, too, thought that the time had
come to relegate the tragic deaths of the
Hungarian generals to oblivion.

302. JÁNOS THORMA
"Rise Hungarians!" (sketch), after 1898
Oil on canvas, 75 × 116 cm
Signed bottom right: "Thorma"
Budapest, Hungarian National Gallery
Inv. No.: 54.1799

In the spring of 1898, Thorma began another
historical painting of a very popular theme.
It depicts the scene on the 15th of March,
1848, when Sándor Petőfi gave frequent re-
citals of his poem, the "National Song", in
the streets and other public places of Pest as
he was carried shoulder-high by his enthusiastic companions. This sketch comprises all the important features of the final
painting on which Thorma worked for
more than thirty years and even suggests
a more dramatic significance in the poet's
gesture which, together with the huge
tricolour placed diagonally beside him,
structures the movement of the composition. In this first sketch for his huge canvas,
the artist gives a restrained indication of the
excited crowd in undulating patches of
colour.

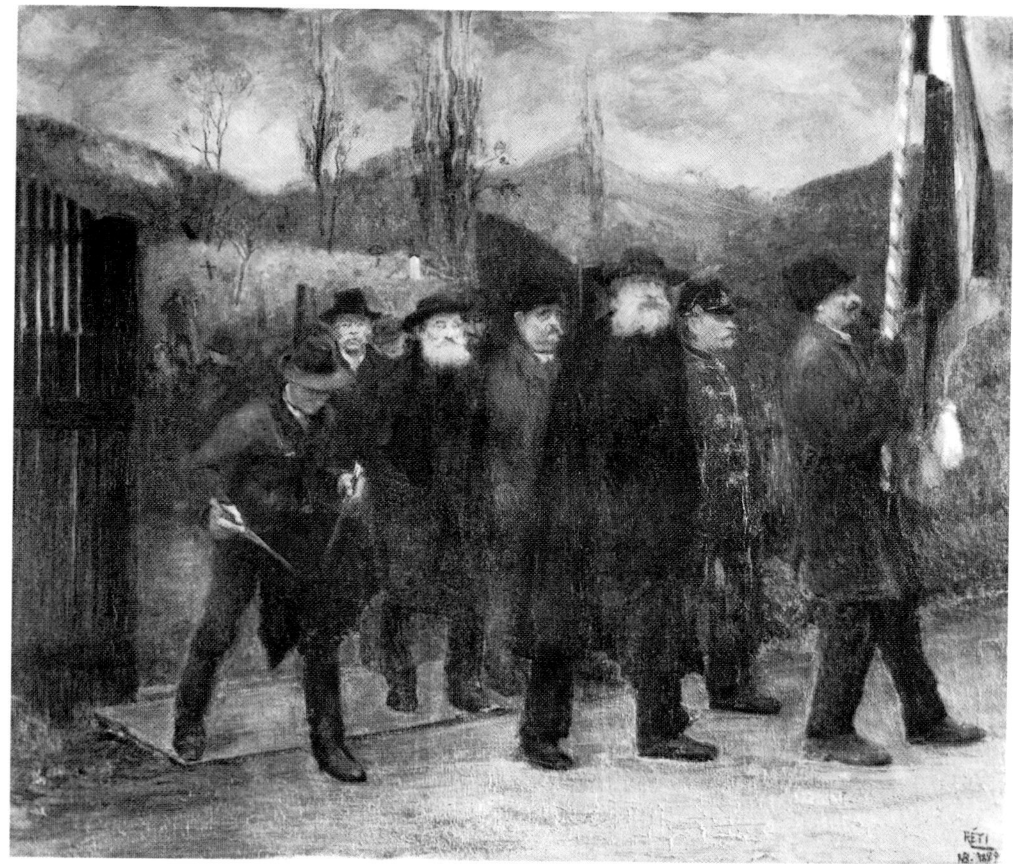

303. ISTVÁN RÉTI
Burial of a Honvéd, 1899
Oil on canvas, 196 × 226 cm
Signed bottom right: "Réti NB 1899"
Budapest, Hungarian National Gallery
Inv. No.: 1745

This painting is one of the best examples of
the historical genre paintings executed in
a naturalistic style in the 1890s. István Réti's
painting was exhibited together with the
work of others of the Nagybánya colony indicating that he, too, took it upon himself to
perpetuate the memory of 1848–1849. From
1892 onwards Réti painted nearly all his important works at Nagybánya. It is not
known where this particular picture was
made, but Réti's own description of the
theme and setting has survived. He tells us
that it depicts veteran *honvéds* (soldiers) from
the War of Independence at the cemetery
gate, on their way home from the burial of
one of their fellows. We also learn that it was
a late November afternoon and that not only
the background, but the figures too, were
drawn from life. The most significant of the
figures is undoubtedly that of the elderly
honvéd bearing the Hungarian tricolour.
In 1900 the painting won the 1000 Crown
Prize of the Lipótváros Casino, the meeting
place of the middle class and the haute
bourgeoisie, and was later bought by the
Museum of Fine Arts.

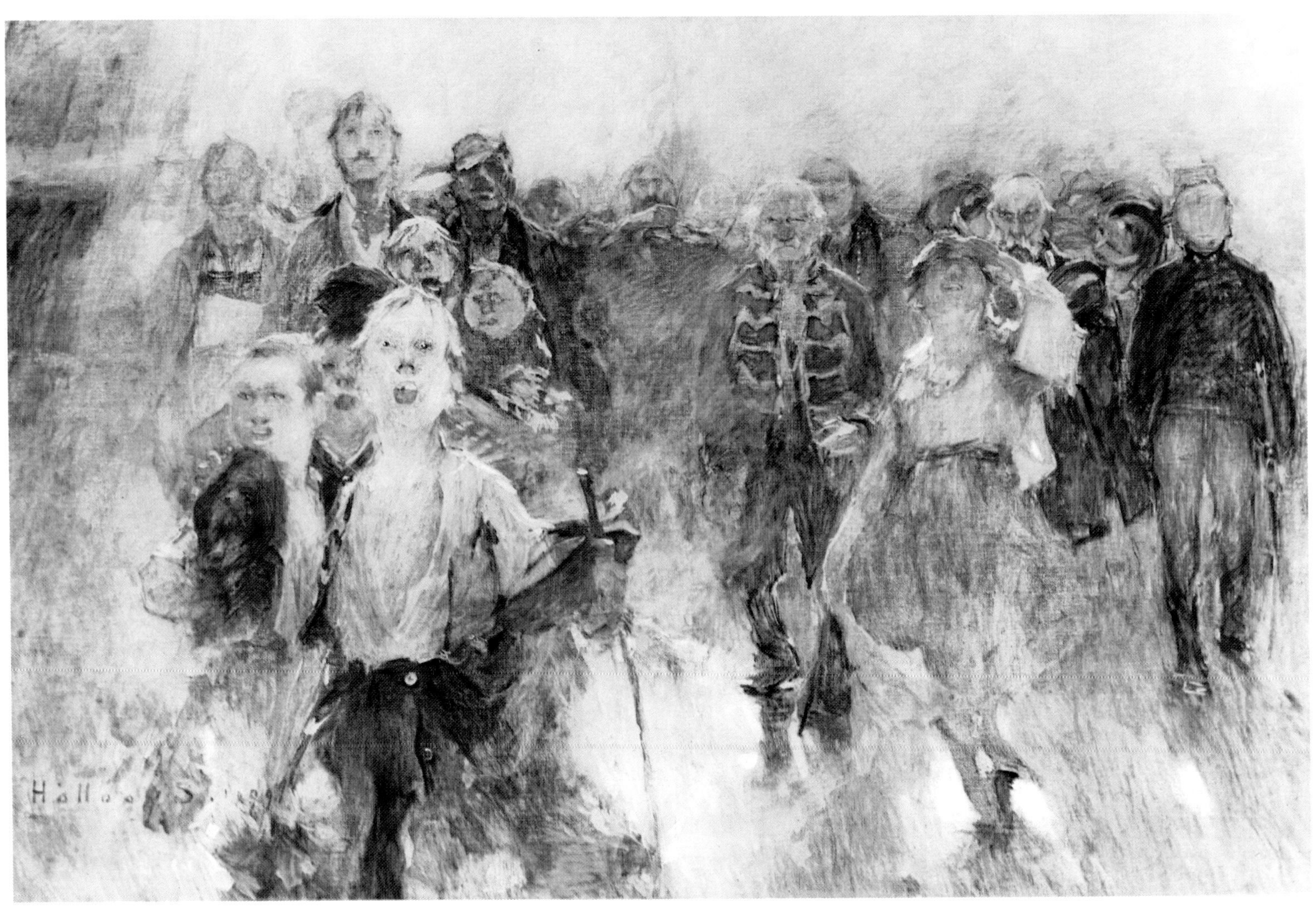

304. SIMON HOLLÓSY
The Rákóczi March, 1899
Oil on canvas, 92×127 cm
Signed bottom left: "Hollósy S. 1899"
Budapest, Hungarian National Gallery
Inv. No.: FK 8032

István Réti tells us that during his period at Nagybánya (1896–1901), Hollósy painted more figure compositions than landscapes. Although before going to Nagybánya he was commissioned to paint the Fortress of Huszt, and although he struggled for a long time over this old-fashioned historical landscape, eventually it was confiscated in place of a debt, and he never finished it.

In the late 1890s he began work with enthusiasm on a very large historical composition (200×200 cm) in which it was his aim to depict *kuruc* soldiers setting out to join the Rákóczi War of Independence against the Habsburgs (1703–1711), singing and marching to the rhythm of the "Rákóczi March". In his first picture Hollósy painted his figure life-size, as did Monet some years earlier in *Déjeuner sur l'herbe,* and János Thorma in *The Martyrs of Arad.* The same fate awaited Hollósy's painting as that of Monet: the artist, dissatisfied with his work, destroyed it. Later, when he was at Nagybánya, Hollósy completed two more sketches on this theme. This painting was exhibited at the 1899 National Salon's show of the Nagybánya School in Budapest.

The problem of rendering the "Rákóczi March" by pictorial means haunted Hollósy throughout his life.

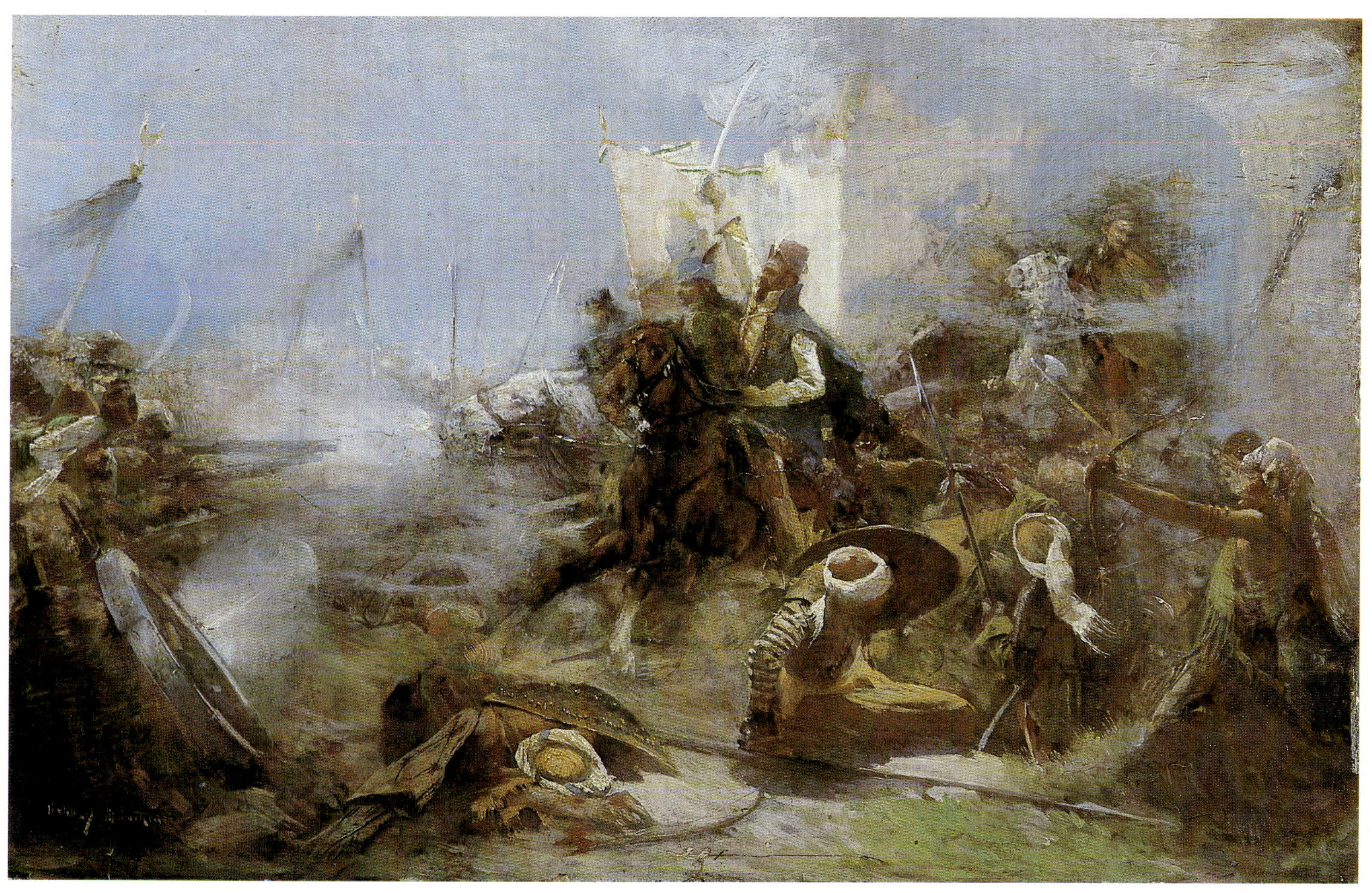

305. SIMON HOLLÓSY
**Zrínyi's Charge on the Turks from
the Fortress of Sziget, 1896**
Oil on wood, 23.5 × 36 cm
Signed bottom left: "Hollósy Münchenben"
(Hollósy in Munich), and on the reverse side:
"1896"
Szeged, Episcopal Collection
Inv. No.: 5.4.4

In this painting of Zrínyi's charge on the
Turks, done before *The Rákóczi March,* Hollósy made no great innovations. This picture
is one of many works painted on the same
theme and it was deliberately conceived in
the tradition of 19th century history
painting.
In this small but powerful sketch Hollósy
does not portray Zrínyi as a great hero who
in a dramatic gesture throws away his life for
the sake of his country; instead, he returns to
the conception of history favoured at the beginning of the century, seeing in Zrínyi's action the reckless bravura of a *huszár.*

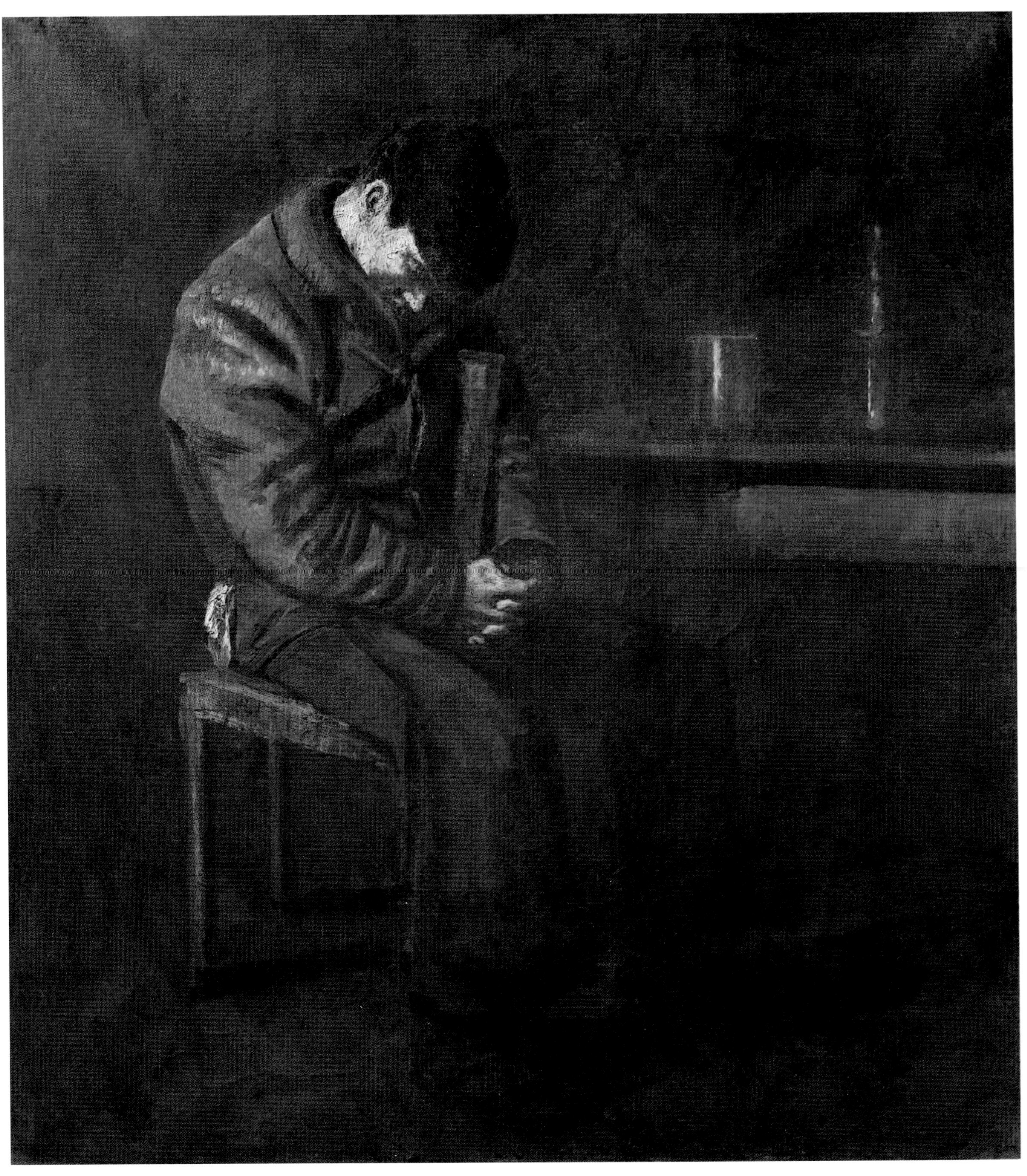

306. LÁSZLÓ MEDNYÁNSZKY
Sleeping Lad in an Inn (Sleeping Worker), c. 1897
Oil on canvas, 95.5 × 85 cm
Signed bottom right: "Mednyánszky"
Budapest, Hungarian National Gallery
Inv. No.: 56.296

Though a rich aristocrat, Baron Mednyánszky did odd jobs such as collecting rugs in Paris or working in the harbour at Marseilles. In Vienna and in Pest, he did not consider it beneath his dignity to visit the outskirts of the town, despite his title as a nobleman.

He recorded his experiences in his sketches from which he later made larger paintings that were both realistic and lively. He first painted his tramps in grey and brown tones against a dark background, with occasional shades of rust to enhance the effect. He probably sketched this young lad, asleep by a table in an inn, in this manner, without adding anything to the actual background. He carefully observed the youth's head, drooping heavily between his shoulders, his peaceful expression and folded hands, his shabby clothes and the handkerchief in his pocket. The bottle of wine and the glass on the table simply serve to indicate the setting; the painter was not interested in their colour or light effects. Mednyánszky's aim was not to idealize the scene, but to depict the everyday reality of a working lad asleep in an inn.

307. LÁSZLÓ MEDNYÁNSZKY
After the Brawl, 1897
Oil on canvas, 85 × 65 cm
Budapest, Hungarian National Gallery
Inv. No.: 56.118

In this portrait Mednyánszky conveys all the anger and resentment felt by a young vagabond as he looks around him like a wild animal at bay. He is a man of the open fields and the forests, a stranger in the town. The self-protective movement with which he turns away, his tense body and blazing eyes indicate his revulsion to his surroundings. Mednyánszky, who was himself brought up in the country and played as a child with the children of peasants and labourers, fully understood the reasons for the tramp's resentment. These young lads came up from the country into the city only to become homeless, wild, uprooted creatures. Mednyánszky had known what it is to wander as a stranger through the great cities of Europe, pacing the streets as if obeying some demonic call.

In this work he reveals the innermost psyche through the means of Realism.

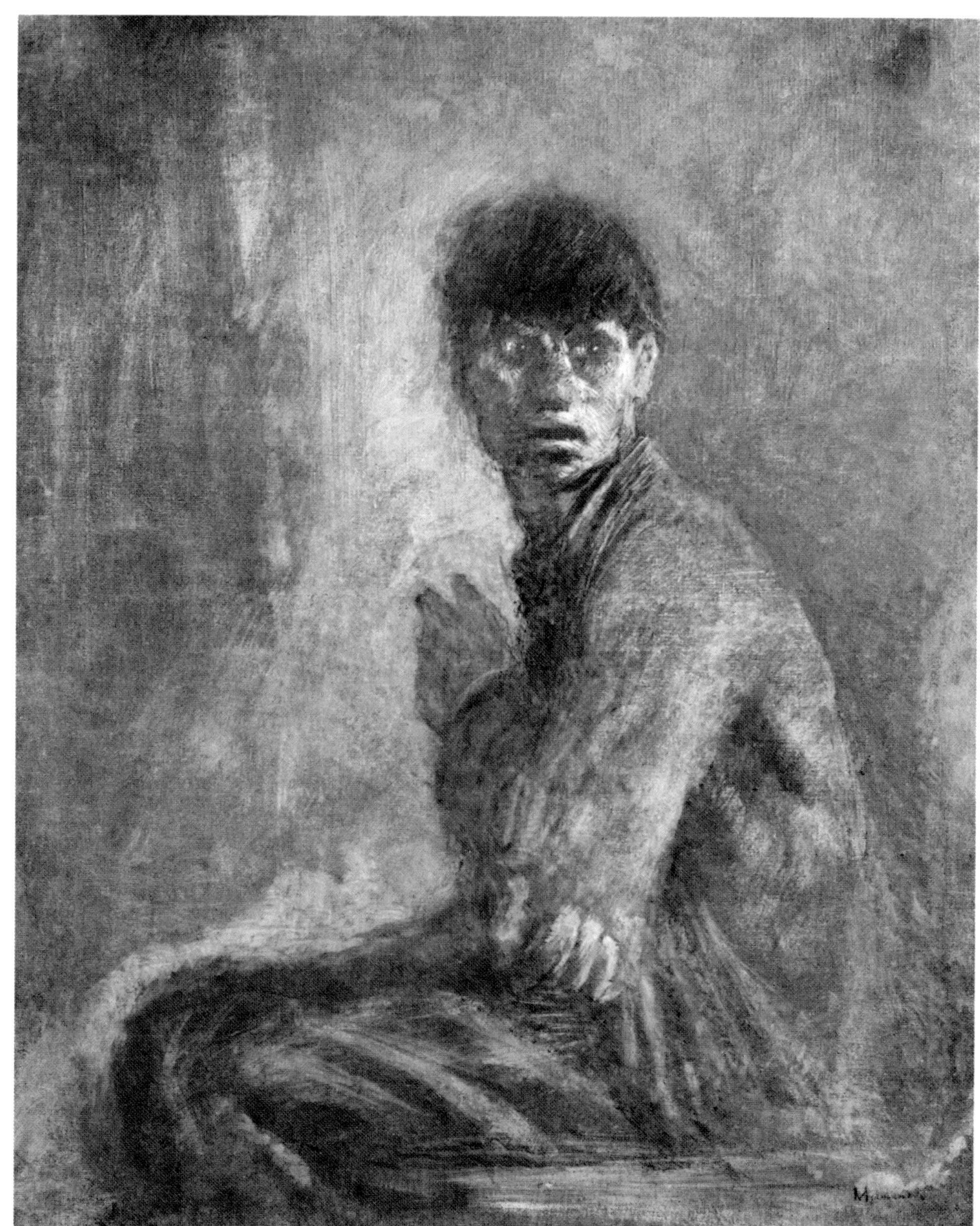

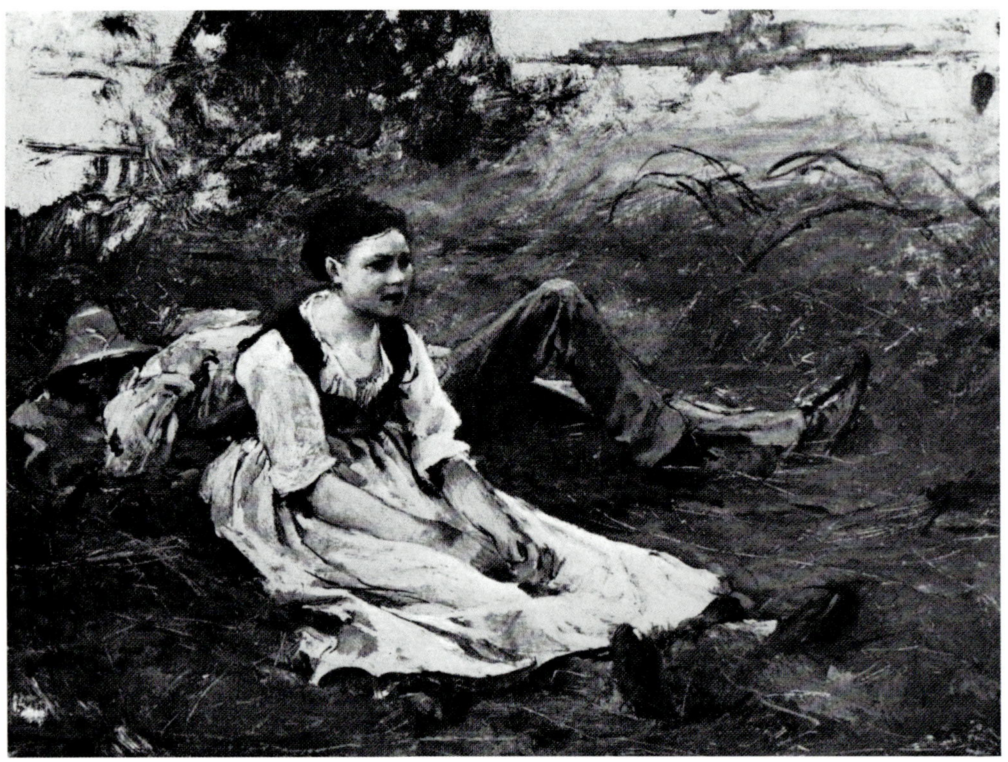

308. JULES BASTIEN LEPAGE
Haymakers, 1877
Oil on canvas
The Hague, Mesdag Museum

This painting was made thirteen years before István Csók chose the same theme (Plate 309), probably under the influence of Bastien-Lepage, though Csók interpreted it anew.

Bastien-Lepage uses identical brushstrokes to depict both figures and landscape, though the girl sitting in the foreground has more plasticity.

A larger size version of this work hangs in the Louvre, but this sketch, too, has been raised to the perfection of a finished work with a few masterly strokes of the brush.

309. ISTVÁN CSÓK
Haymakers, 1890
Oil on canvas, 116×136 cm
Signed bottom left: "Csók 890"
Budapest, Hungarian National Gallery
Inv. No.: 5149

István Csók was born at Pusztaegres in Transdanubia, Hungary. He studied in Budapest, Munich and Paris before he painted this work. Art critics disagree as to where it was executed. Csók possibly conceived the idea in 1877, while he was studying in Paris at the Julian Academy, and was influenced by Jules Bastien-Lepage, whose paintings he might have seen in Munich as well. One of his models is the same pretty black-haired girl of Pusztaegres who also posed for his *This do in Remembrance of Me* (Plate 310), painted the same year. According to some sources, she was also seen with Csók in Munich.

The painting shows a typical Transdanubian countryside, and the models are dressed in the national costume of the region. It conveys a feeling of casual spontaneity and a lack of formal composition: one weary girl lies down on the fresh hay, the other unwraps a picnic whilst sitting beside a young lad wearing a hat. The calculated lack of composition is underlined by the asymmetrical arrangement of the figures.

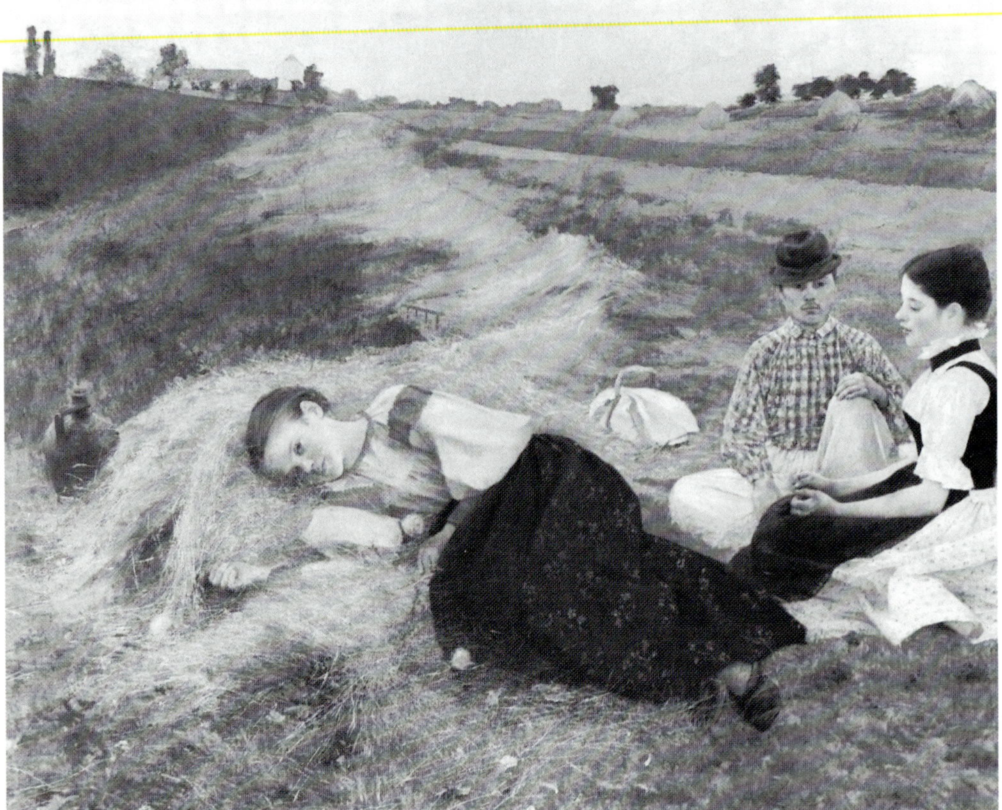

310. ISTVÁN CSÓK
**"This do in Remembrance of Me",
(Holy Communion), 1890**
Oil on canvas, 136.5×111 cm
Signed bottom left: "Csók 1890"
Budapest, Hungarian National Gallery
Inv. No.: 1693
Purchased in 1898

Subject and style are harmoniously united in this simply rendered painting, subdued in feeling and tone.

Any emotive or dramatic details or narrative elements would have been inappropriate for this subject; the Holy Communion represents for Protestants, too, the most sacred moment of the religious service. Even in Wilhelm Leibl's praying peasant women there is more demonstration of their faith and feelings than may be discovered from the expressions of these young peasant girls and women depicted in the Calvinist church of Pusztaegres as they proceed round the Lord's Table which is covered with an embroidered cloth. The minister is seen only from behind, nor are those taking the communion fully visible. The principal figures are the two young girls who have just taken the bread and wine and are moving slowly and solemnly back to their places, each holding in her hands an embroidered white handkerchief. The 16th century traditional costumes, worn at the most important village feasts as well as for the communion service, show the sense of vivid Protestant traditions in Hungary. The young girls' fresh faces and the light coming through the windows suggest the noble simplicity of the ceremony, a feeling shared by the painter himself.

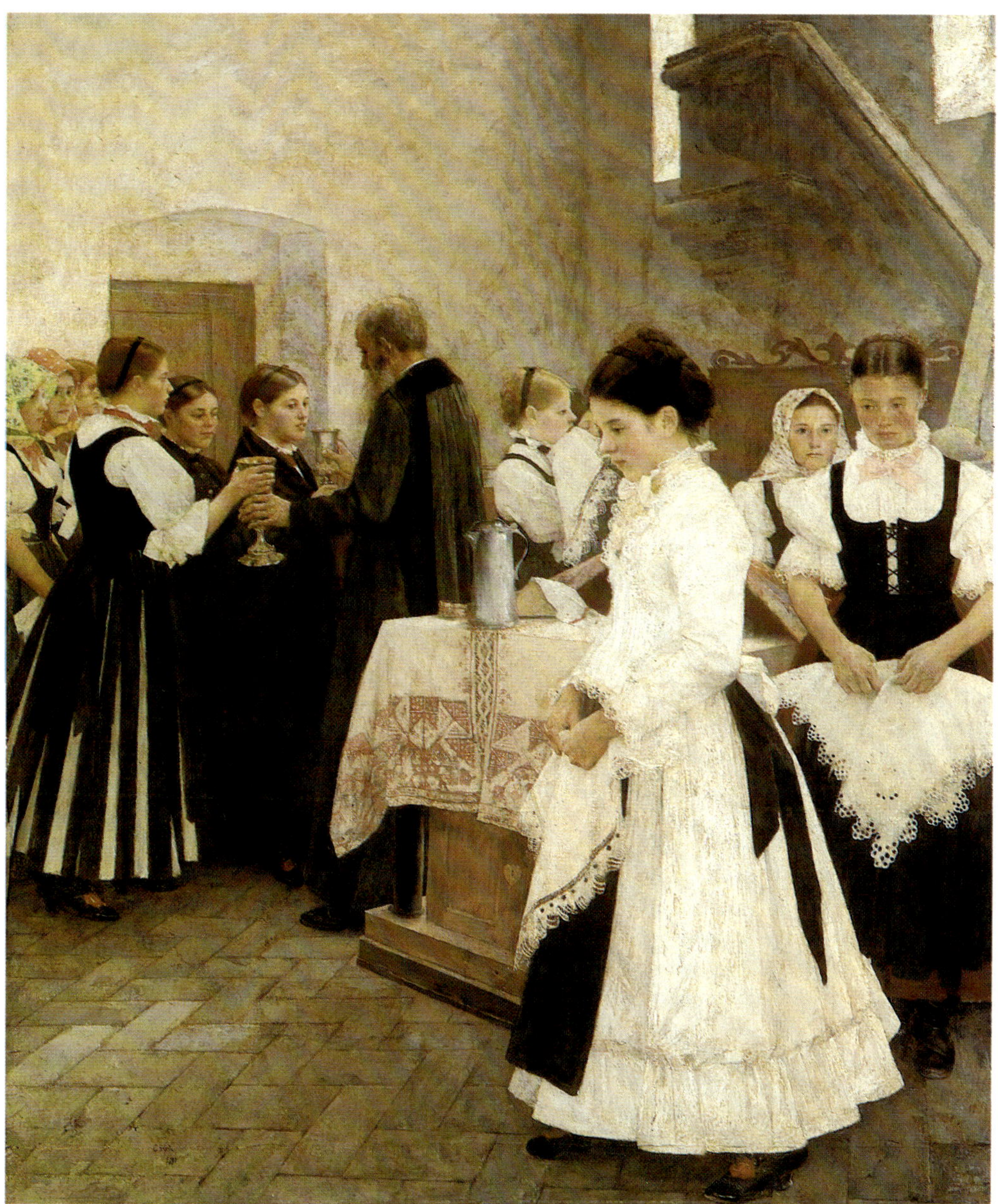

Ferenczy was an unassuming, modest person, but he knew the worth of his own art. "He can take his place with the finest Hungarian artists," writes István Réti, "armed as he is with profound knowledge, inborn talent and strong moral convictions. Sensitivity and will power characterized him as a man; his artistic values were embedded like pearls in a deep instinctive morality."
It was in 1893 in Munich that Ferenczy began to study the pictorial interaction between human figures and nature. The solution of this problem remained one of his chief aims for the rest of his life.

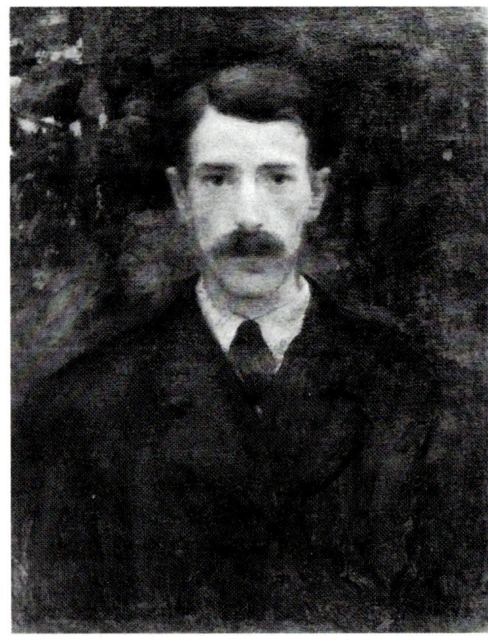

313. KÁROLY FERENCZY
Bird-song, 1893
Oil on canvas, 105 × 77.5 cm
Signed bottom right: "Ferenczy K."
Budapest, Hungarian National Gallery
Inv. No.: 1667
Purchased in 1898

Of all Hungarian painters, Károly Ferenczy was one of the most serious and sensitive. He explored with minute care the possibilities within a new style of genre-painting with a new handling of line and colour. This new type of genre-piece was totally free from anecdotal elements nor did it follow the Academic rules of composition. Later, from about 1893 onwards, Ferenczy began to study the changing effects of light and the variations of juxtaposed pure and compound complementary colours in the open air. Yet Ferenczy never began to paint with a theory; he always based his paintings upon visual experience, even though he painted within a certain stylistic framework. Thus in Munich, and later in Nagybánya, he would set out from the town, walking through the local forests and over the hills together with his models, who were mostly members of his family or friends.
Bird-song suggests at the same time direct experience and thoughtful composition. Thus the artist makes us share the wonder which he experienced when he saw the woman in red amidst the spring colours of the forest, loud with the song of birds.

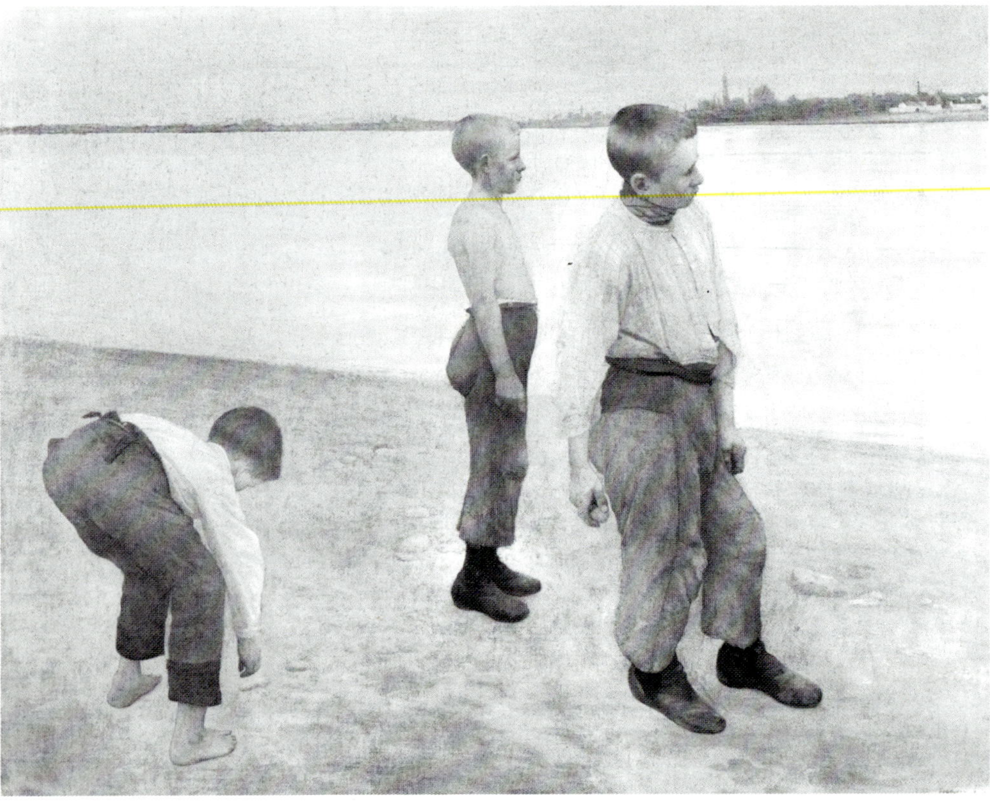

312. KÁROLY FERENCZY
Boys Throwing Pebbles into the River, 1890
Oil on canvas, 119 × 149 cm
Budapest, Hungarian National Gallery

This painting precedes the artist's *Self-portrait* (Plate 311). A *plein-air* composition under an overcast sky, it indicates Ferenczy's way of experiencing nature. Three boys stand on the shore of the grey Danube, their figures outlined against the background, as in István Csók's *Haymakers* (Plate 309). The boys look for contact with the landscape: one has chosen a pebble to play 'ducks and drakes' so that he can stir the water into surface ripples. The boy in the middle stands straight, gazing into the distance; the third is just about to pick up a pebble. This simple scene differs both in its intent and in its form from the usual narrative genre-painting of the 1880s in Hungary.

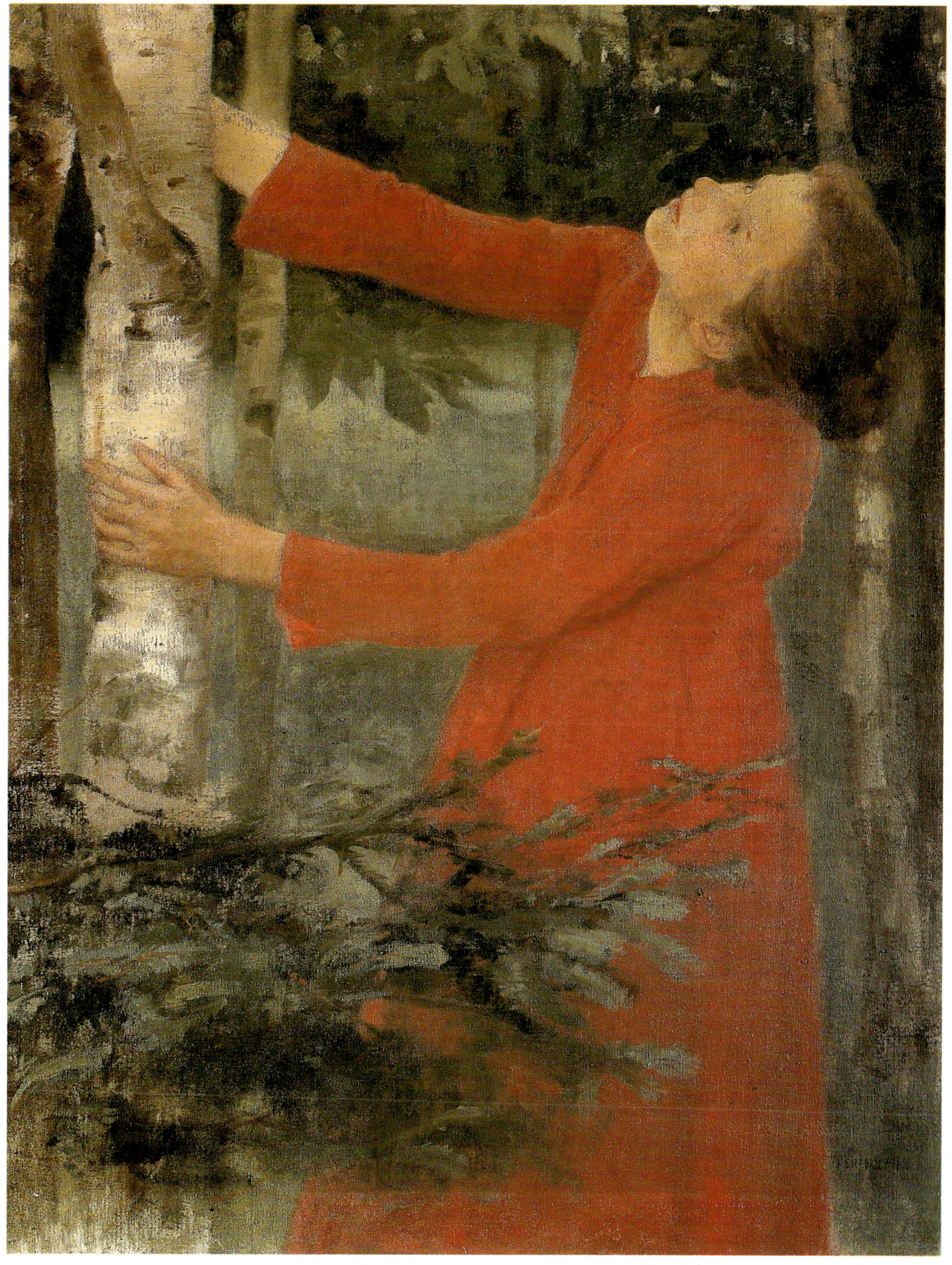

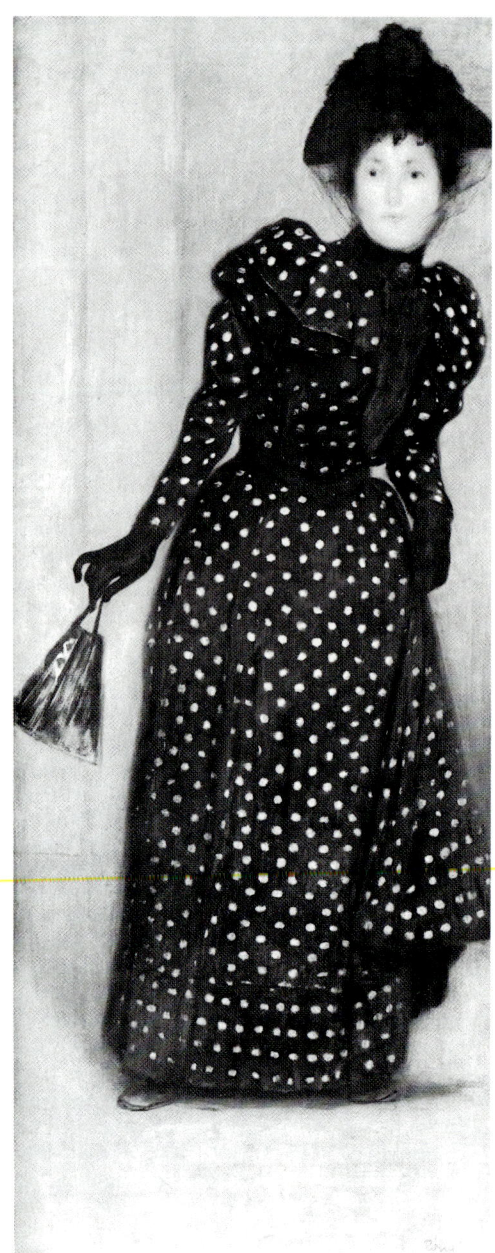

314. JÓZSEF RIPPL-RÓNAI
Woman in a White-dotted Dress, 1889
Oil on canvas, 187 × 75 cm
Signed bottom right: "Rónai"
Budapest, Hungarian National Gallery
Inv. No.: 60.157

In his memoirs published in 1911 in Budapest, József Rippl-Rónai states that this painting was the first work executed in his own personal style. It is indeed a composition which ushered in a new period of Hungarian painting, though several experts have found similar earlier examples in contemporary European painting. Art historian Katalin Keserű goes so far as to compare it, rather ingenuously to Munkácsy's pictures of society ladies. She comes closer to the truth when she points out the direct influence of Whistler's portraits of women of the upper middle classes. In her biography Mária Bernáth praises the bold vertical format of the painting, adding eloquently that "the head is most beautifully drawn, with a hint of Impressionism in the features which are slightly blurred by the lowered veil…" The lines of the left arm, hand and shoulder point towards the stylistic traits of Art Nouveau even before the movement actually existed.

315. JÓZSEF RIPPL-RÓNAI
Uncle Rippl, the Kossuth Enthusiast, 1897
Oil on canvas, 190 × 75 cm
Signed top left: "Rónai"
Budapest, Hungarian National Gallery
Inv. No.: 56.247 T

In 1897, after his second exhibition in Paris, Rippl-Rónai went home to Kaposvár to visit his parents. There he painted this portrait of his elderly relative sitting in a chair with a striped cover. The man is old enough to have known the stirring events of 1848–49 which he keeps in mind and commemorates in his own home where he hung a lithographic print of Louis Kossuth. In this discreet way the painting serves to show the respect and admiration given to Kossuth in Hungary in the late 19th century, which only increased after the great politician's death in 1894. Viewed in this context, the painting is more than a mere portrait. It reflects the attitude of all strata of society to one of the most outstanding figures of 19th-century Hungary.

With simple means, in the unaffected idiom of Post-Impressionism, the painter here pays tribute to the great politician of the 1840s, the leader of the War of Independence, a man who was tireless in the cause of his country's freedom throughout his life.

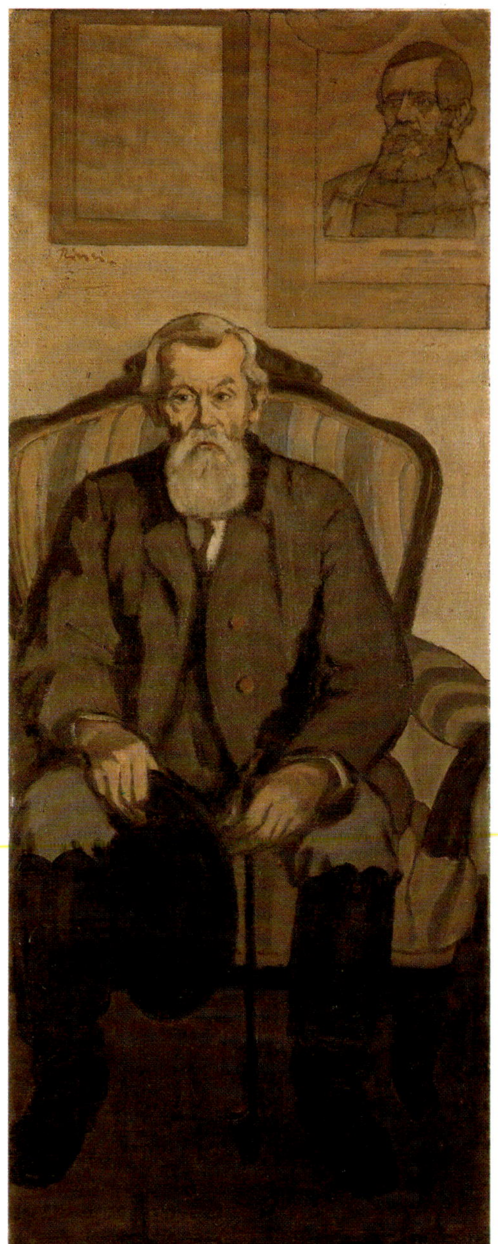

316. JÓZSEF RIPPL-RÓNAI
The Artist's Grandmother, 1894
Oil on canvas, 62.5 × 71.4 cm
Signed bottom left: "Rónai 1894"
Budapest, Hungarian National Gallery
Inv. No.: 1042

Rippl-Rónai's grandmother was nearly 100
years old when he painted this portrait, possibly based on a quick pencil sketch and mostly completed from memory. The old lady
sits in an armchair. The only object in the
bare room is a vase with a flower, withered,
yet delicate, like Rippl-Rónai's grandmother.

The old lady's posture indicates that she
must have often posed for a painter. As a
little girl she was perhaps asked to stand beside her mother, dressed all in white and
with flowers in her hair, either in the garden
or in a simple middle-class interior. Perhaps
she was portrayed to provide a companion-
piece to her husband's likeness; a plain bust
with a single piece of jewellery or a starched
lace collar. Later again, as a mother, she
might have sat with her children for a photographer, facing his camera in a carefully furnished studio where, in those pioneering
days of photography, she would have had to
sit motionless for a long while, as though sitting for a painter.

Here, to please her grandson, she is sitting
for him again, wearing her best brown
dress.

Much has been written in appreciation of
this portrait by both Hungarian and French
art critics. In 1894 Crevalier wrote, "This
powerful picture expresses all the poignance
and poetry of old age. Baudelaire's little old
women are not more heart-breaking or
more sad."

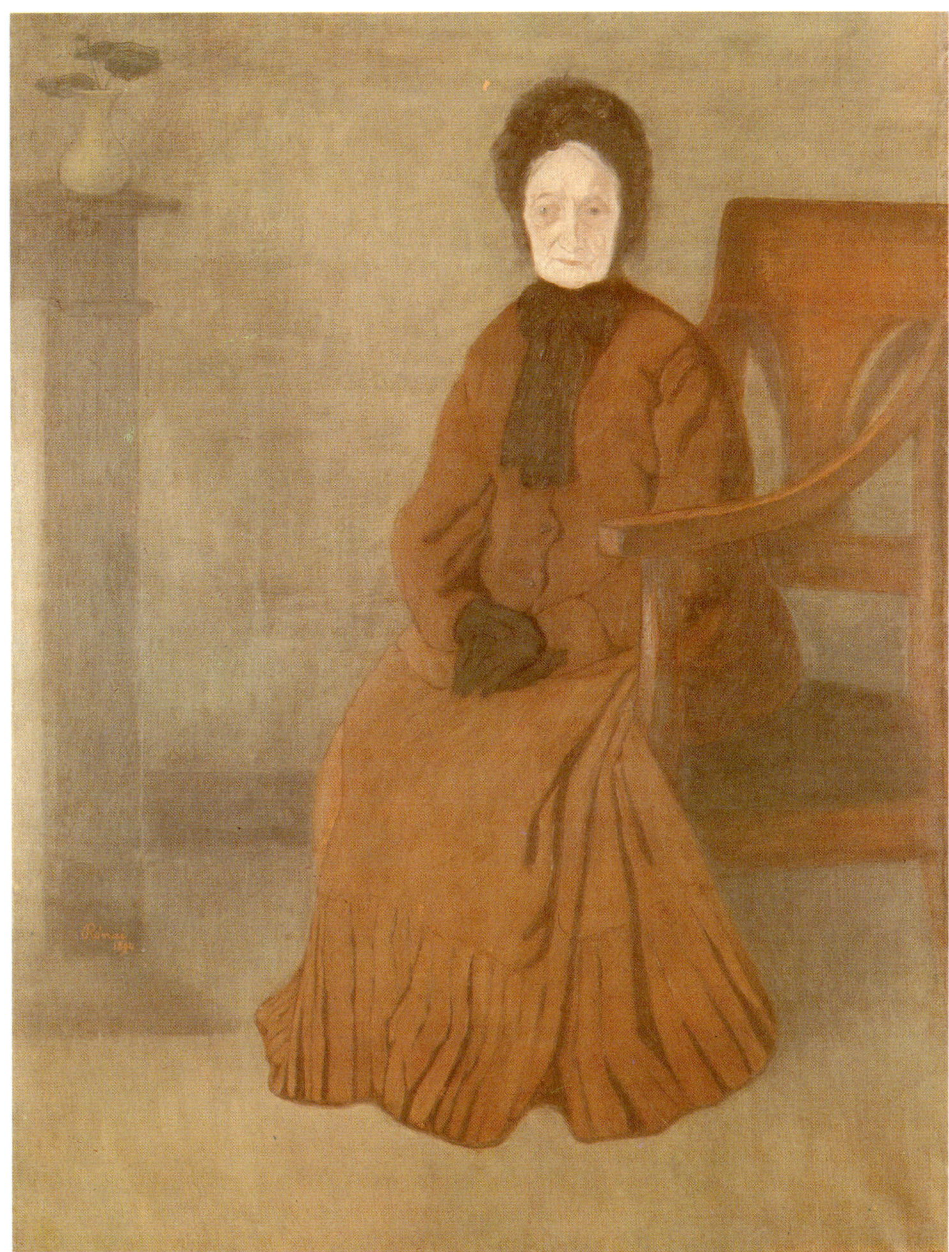

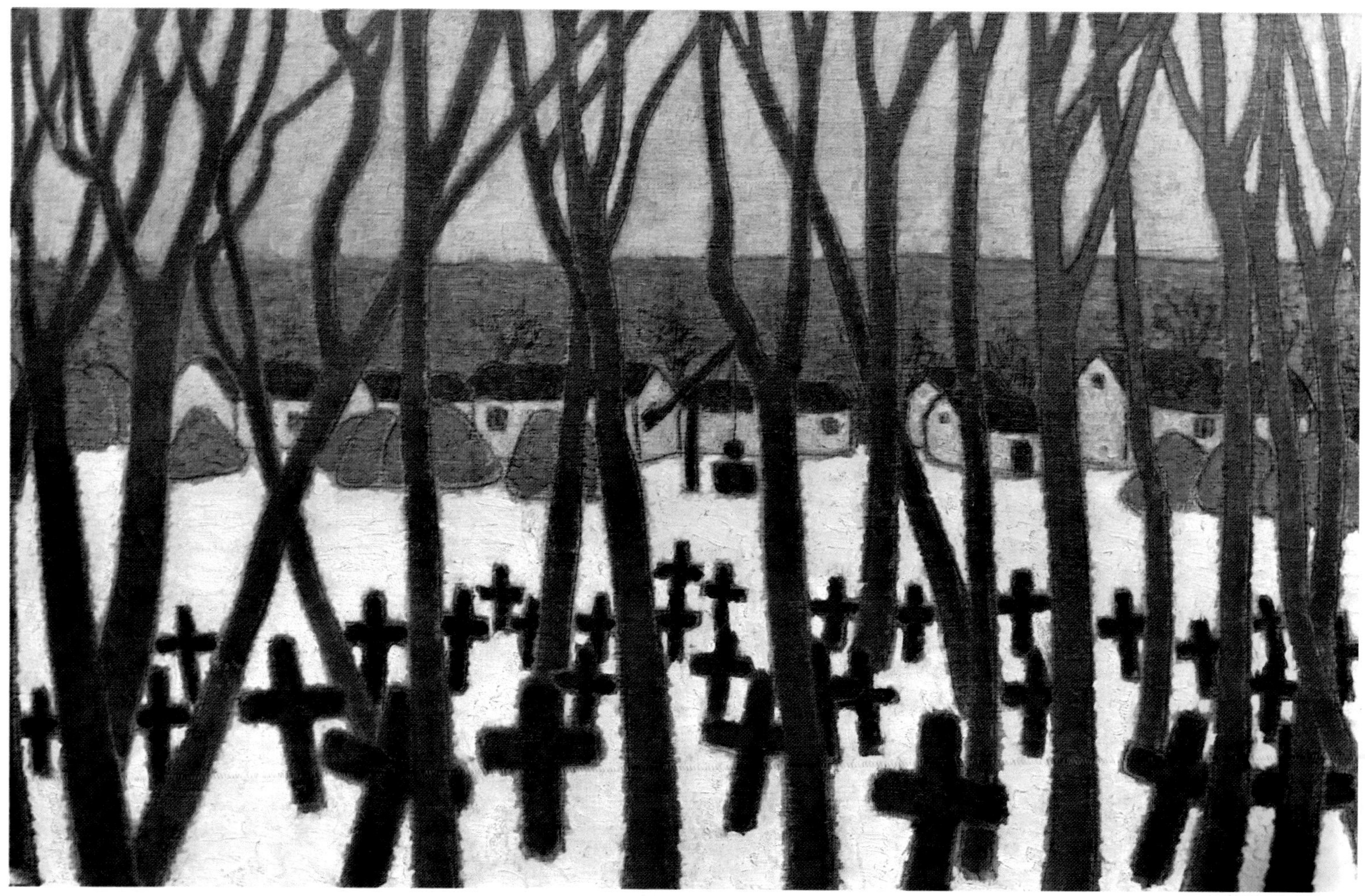

317. JÓZSEF RIPPL-RÓNAI
Graveyard on the Hungarian Great Plain, 1894
Oil on canvas, 58 × 81.5 cm
Unsigned
Budapest, private collection

In the second half of the 19th century the main railway lines were being laid through Hungary. Artists could now travel by rail as well as by coach or on foot. Rushing through the landscape in a train, they could now memorize the visual impressions of a few outstanding details of their home country in a new way.

Rippl-Rónai records that he conceived the idea for this painting during a train journey in winter, when he came home from Paris, probably for Christmas. He first memorized the scenery so that later he could recreate it in a formal composition. He conveys his vision in a horizontal arrangement of the violet-blue sky, the white and deep-violet, snow covered landscape, yellow haystacks in front of a row of peasant houses with their black-green thatched roofs and, most important of all, the little ramshackle wooden crosses in graves blackened by time and weather, under the bare branches of the trees.

In its simplicity, this work is one of the noblest Hungarian landscapes painted in the closing years of the 19th century. Interestingly, Rippl-Rónai made it at a time when he had been living near Paris for many years and had announced that: "there is nothing that could call me back to Hungary; all artistic and literary activities are vain efforts there". He had not realized that there might come a time when he would respond to the call of deeper feelings, of the primary forces: the earth, the countryside, the past, never depicted in this style before, and the very particular atmosphere of those Sundays in autumn in a provincial town. For these he gave up a successful career in Paris, the very centre of European art. He then devoted all his life to a better understanding of the primitive appeal of his own country and an attempt to represent it in paintings worthy of European acknowledgement.

318. JÓZSEF RIPPL-RÓNAI
Portrait of Aristide Maillol, 1899
Oil on canvas, 100 × 76 cm
Signed bottom left: "Rónai"
Paris, Musée National d'art Moderne

In the 1890s József Rippl-Rónai excelled in portraiture. He always portrayed his models using the simplest possible means, and with an admirable gift for characterization, choosing the most appropriate setting for each subject. He achieved his most direct manner in portraits of his artist friends. In these, the facial features, postures, the colour of the clothes and the background hinted at the movements they represented. For example, Rippl-Rónai portrayed his friend Pierre Bonnard in a black coat against a grey background as he was hurrying somewhere. Vuillard is depicted sitting on a chair turning over the pages of a book, while the elegant Pittcairn Knowles is shown wearing a broadbrimmed hat. This portrait of Maillol dates from 1899 and is one of Rónai's most striking works. The background is Banyuls, a small town in Southern France near the Spanish border, where Rippl-Rónai was staying as Maillol's guest. Similar proportions can be observed in the houses and in Maillol's long thin figure and longish face. Bluish-black shadows, blue tones unifying the whole of the painting, and other colour patches unite the artist and his house in a new emotional and intellectual pattern.

It was in this beautiful house in Banyuls, which Maillol so readily shared with his friends, that Rippl-Rónai realized the need for a home, both material and spiritual.

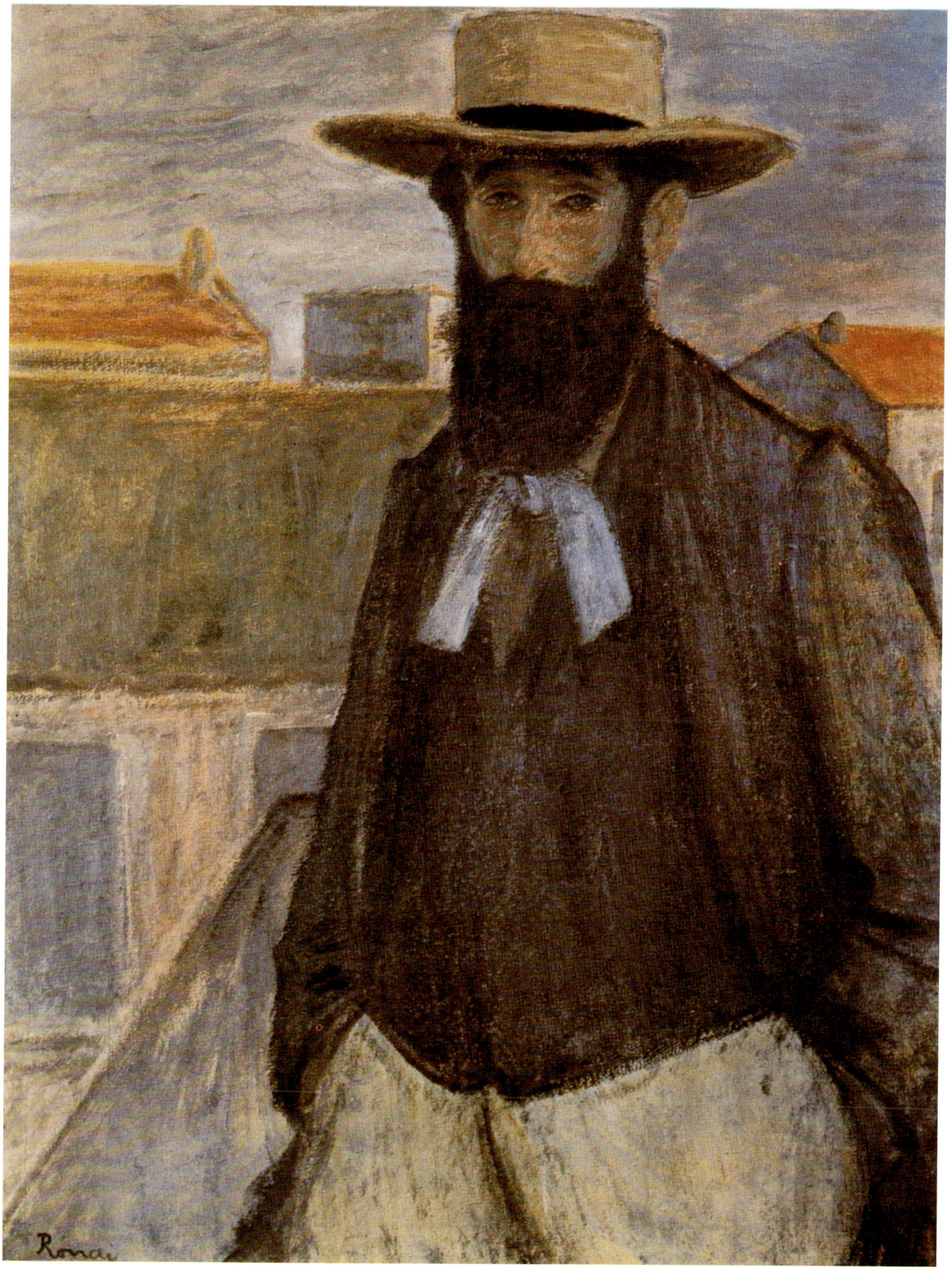
Rónai

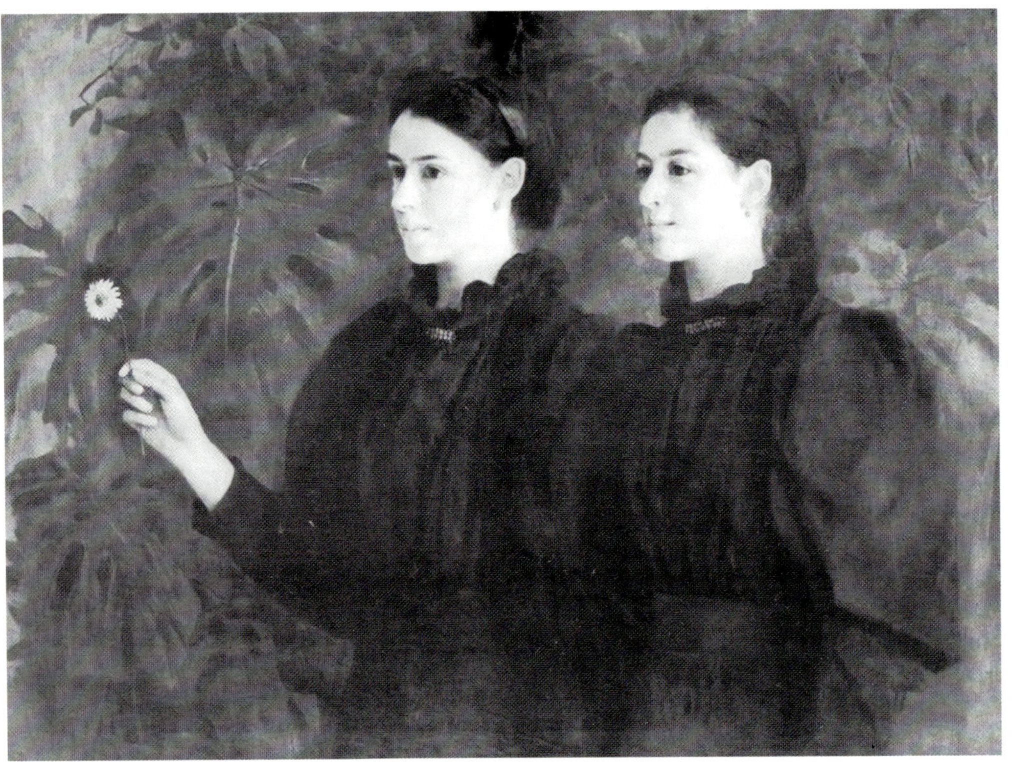

319. ALADÁR KÖRÖSFŐI-KRIESCH
Portrait of Two Sisters, 1894
Oil on canvas, 80×106 cm
Signed upper right: "A. K. 94"
Sabinov, City Museum
Inv. No.: 322

This double portrait is related in its conception to Csontváry's portrait of a girl (Plate 321). It was commissioned by the two sisters, Janka and Gabriella Zeyk in Transylvania. One of the girls was married to Félix Szinyei-Merse, the son of the painter. Like Csontváry's portrait, it bears witness to the painter's close relationship to nature, to the posing of the models as taught at the Academies, and represents a cautious step towards a new decorative style. The painting was exhibited in 1895 in Budapest. Aladár Körösfői-Kriesch went to study painting in Bertalan Székely's class at the School of Decorative Art in 1880. From there he went for a short time to Munich, then to Venice and Rome, where he stayed for two years. Eventually, between 1893 and 1900, he became one of the most industrious pupils in the Master's School for Wall-Painting run by Károly Lotz within the confines of the Budapest Academy of Arts. At the beginning of his career, Kriesch participated in the last phase of such important forms of 19th century painting as portraiture, historical and religious compositions. At the same time he was associated with the initiators through his new understanding of artistic forms, his conceptual innovations and technical experiments. In addition to his own teachers, he revered the Renaissance masters and the English Pre-Raphaelites, whom he perhaps learned about during his time in Rome. The works of this group, which circulated in the form of book illustrations, impressed Kriesch with their literary inspiration, mystical lyricism and message, and their decorative style. Indeed, Kriesch had achieved a harmonious synthesis of these influences by the early 1890s.

This elegant, mysterious double portrait of two sisters was completed the same year as the well-known likeness of the artist's sister. The background to the figures is provided in both cases by a surface of flowers or plants. In this painting the two girls are depicted against luxuriant green vegetation. Both figures stand demurely upright, their dark silk dresses relieved only by the sparkle of a necklace from under high frilled collars. Though one of them holds a daisy up in her hand, they seem to be gazing into the distance, watching as if in a dream the objects of a world far away, of which the plants surrounding them are mere imitations. The dominant dark colours serve to emphasize the pallor of the girls' faces.

By the close of the 19th century portraiture had taken on a new quality. The likenesses created in the 1890s project a symbolic message and a search for a new universal style; they are reserved in character, but rich in true artistic values.

320. UNKNOWN PHOTOGRAPHER
Photograph of Tivadar Csontváry Kosztka's Sister, Anna, 1890s
Budapest, Photograph Collection of the Research Institute for the History of Art, the Hungarian Academy of Sciences

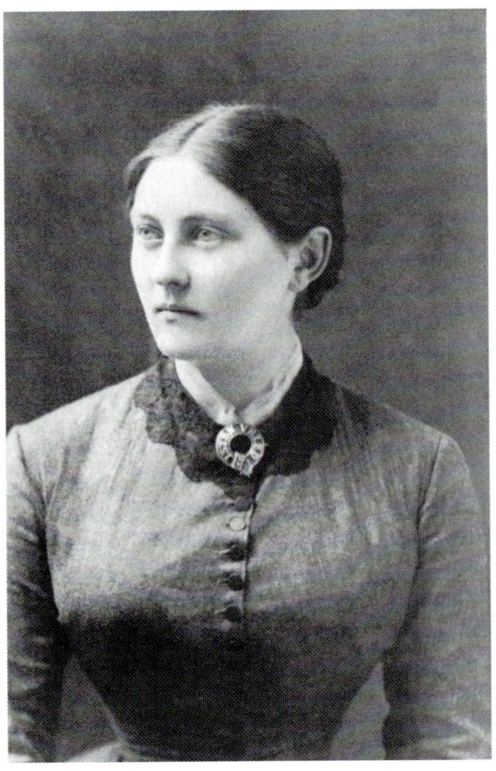

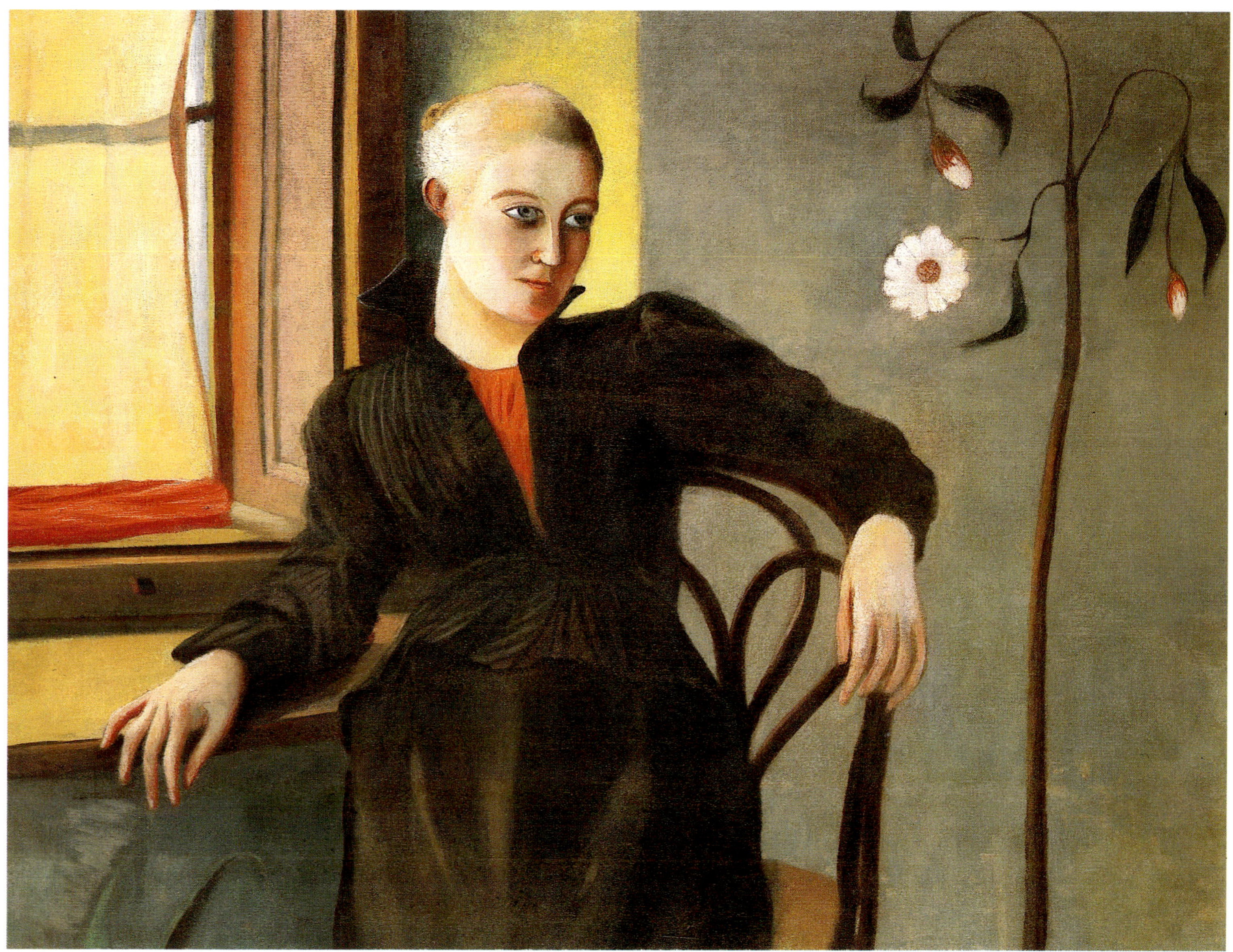

321. TIVADAR CSONTVÁRY-KOSZTKA
Woman Sitting by the Window, 1890s
Oil on canvas, 73 × 95 cm
Unsigned
Budapest, Hungarian National Gallery
Inv. No.: 50.435

Csontváry's work forms a link between the 19th and the 20th centuries. His Romanticism induced him to paint heroic landscapes and throughout his life he repeatedly composed paintings on historical themes. Several of his paintings are deeply symbolic in significance or were based on literary sources; and he also practised portraiture, especially at the beginning of his career.

From 1890 onwards Csontváry attended Academies and schools of painting in Germany and France. Like other artists at that time, he studied for lengthy periods in Munich, Karlsruhe, Düsseldorf and Paris, and like them, he soon sought to develop his own individual style.

His early paintings primarily reflect the influence of what he had learned in Hollósy's School in Munich, though his personal touch was already obvious. In this portrait of a young woman sitting by a window, Csontváry's solution to the problem of light is reminiscent of Hollósy's genre-paintings from Munich in which the latter painted similar interiors where the strong source of light, coming through the curtains, from the outside, lights the faces of his subjects. In Hollósy's works the walls are mostly a warm pink or red. Csontváry selected another colour for this portrait, presumably more suited to the sitter's personality. Here the wall is grey with yellow light cast upon it and, behind the girl's head, there is a translucent, unearthly green tone. The earnest-looking young woman, gazing into the distance, is obviously someone close to the painter. Beside her is a tall Oleander tree with a flower and a half open bud, and there is a clear symbolic relationship between the girl and the flower.

The sitter bears a striking resemblance to the artist's own sister Anna, whom he dearly loved and whose friendship was a source of spiritual strength to him throughout his life. Csontváry painted this portrait in the absence of the sitter, but he accomplished a true likeness within which all the details seem to be real. For this to be so he may possibly have used a photograph. The girl's face with its clear blue eyes, tightly closed lips and simple chignon, strongly resembles a photograph of the painter's sister taken around 1880, which was found among his papers after his death. Although the posture is different the figures are almost identical.

Csontváry's artistic aim was to achieve the most perfect rendering of his own vision. The interval between the act of seeing and the act of painting, allowed the emergence of the lyrical and symbolical traits in his paintings. This special quality gives to this early painting the quality of a genuine masterpiece.

A Short Bibliography

Sources and Contemporary Literature

Kazinczy Ferenc levelezése Vol. I–XXI. (The Letters of Ferencz Kazinczy), ed. János Váczy, Budapest, 1890–1911; vol. XXII, ed. István Harsányi, Budapest, 1927; Vol. XXIII, ed. Jenő Berlász and Klára Cs. Gárdonyi, Budapest, 1979.
Ferencz Kazinczy: *Pályám emlékezete. Fogságom naplója. Magyarországi utak* (My Career. Diary of My Imprisonment. Travels in Hungary). Budapest, 1979.
Imre Henszlmann: *Párhuzam az ó- és újkori művészeti nézetek és nevelések között, különös tekintettel a művészetek fejlődésére Magyarországon* (Parallels between the Old and New Artistic Viewpoints and Teachings, with Special Emphasis on the Development of the Arts in Hungary). Pest, 1841.
János Joó: *Nézetek a magyar nemzet műveltségi és technikai kifejlése tárgyában* (Views on the Cultural and Technical Development of the Hungarian Nation). Buda, 1841.
Károly Kertbeny: *Ungarische Malerrevue. Beitrage zum näheren Verstandnis der bildenden Kunste in Ungarn.* Pest, 1855.
Ungarns Männer der Zeit. Prag, 1862.
Gusztáv Kelety: *A képzőművészeti oktatás külföldön és feladatai hazánkban* (The Teaching of Art Abroad and Its Task at Home). Buda, 1870. *Művészeti dolgozatok* (Essays on Art). Budapest, 1910. Vols. III–IV. Budapest, 1915.
Tamás Szana: *A magyar művészet századunkban* (Hungarian Art in This Century). Budapest, 1890.

Books and Articles

Alexius Lippich de Korong: *La formation de l'esprit artistique en Hongrie.* Budapest, 1901.
Károly Lyka: *A képírás újabb irányai* (Newest Trends in Painting). Budapest, 1906.
Lajos Ernst: *A magyar történeti festészet* (Historical Painting in Hungary). Budapest, 1910.
Simon Meller: "A magyar művészet kialakulása a XIX. század első felében" (The Development of Hungarian Art in the First Half of the 19th Century) in: *Művészet* (1911), 174–186.
Kornél Divald: *A Magyar Tudományos Akadémia Palotája és gyűjteményei* (The Palace and Collections of the Hungarian Academy of Sciences). Budapest, 1917.
Károly Lyka: *A táblabíró világ művészete. Magyar művészet* 1800–1850. (The Art of the World of Hungarian Noblemen, 1800–1850). Budapest, 1922. 2nd ed.: Budapest, 1942. 3rd ed.: Budapest, 1981.
Ernst Kállai: *Neue Malerei in Ungarn.* Leipzig, 1925.
Elek Petrovics: *Jegyzetek művészetünk történetéhez a XIX. század első felében* (Notes on the History of Our Art in the First Half of the 19th Century). Budapest, 1933.
Elek Petrovics: *Magyar mesterművek,* IV (Hungarian Masterpieces). Budapest, 1936.
Gyula Fleischer: *Magyarok a bécsi képzőművészeti akadémián* (Hungarians at the Viennese Academy of Art). Budapest, 1935.
Géza Entz: *A magyar műgyűjtés történetének vázlata 1850-ig* (A Survey of Hungarian Art Collecting till 1850). Budapest, 1937.
Jenő Kopp: *Magyar biedermeier festészet* (Hungarian Biedermeier Painting). Budapest, 1943.
Zoltán Farkas: *La peinture hongroise moderne.* Budapest, 1944.
Gábor Ö. Pogány: *A magyar festészet forradalmárai* (Revolutionists of Hungarian Painting). Budapest, 1946.
Hundert Jahre ungarische bildende Kunst. Wien, 1948.
Károly Lyka: *Nemzeti romantika* (National Romanticism). Budapest, 1942. 2nd ed.: Budapest, 1982.
Magyar művészélet Münchenben (Hungarian Artistic Life in Munich). Budapest, 1952. 2nd ed.: Budapest, 1982.
Lajos Végváry: *Szolnoki művészet 1852–1952* (Art at Szolnok 1852–1952). Budapest, 1952.
György Rózsa, György Spira: *48 a kortársak szemével* ('48 through the Eyes of Contemporaries). Budapest, 1953. 2nd ed.: Budapest, 1973.
István Réti: *A nagybányai művésztelep* (The Artists' Colony of Nagybánya). Budapest, 1954.
A magyarországi művészet története (Hungarian Art History), ed. Lajos Fülep, II, *Magyar művészet* (Hungarian Art), ed. Anna Zádor, by István Genthon, Lajos Németh, Lajos Végvári, Anna Zádor. Budapest, 1958. Last ed.: 1970.
Dénes Pataky: *A magyar rajzművészet* (Hungarian Drawing). Budapest, 1960.
Teréz Gerszi: *A kőrajzolás története Magyarországon a XIX. században* (The Art of Lithography in Hungary in the 19th Century). Budapest, 1960.

GÁBOR Ö. POGÁNY: *Magyar festészet a XIX. században* (Hungarian Painting in the 19th Century). Budapest, 1958. (Also in English, German and Russian.)
Gizella C. Wilhelmb: *Magyarország történetének képeskönyve 896–1849).* (A Pictorial Guide to the History of Hungary 896–1849). Budapest, 1962.
Ernő Marosi: "Das romantische Zeitalter der ungarischen Kunstgeschichtsschreibung." *Annales Universitatis Scientiarum Budapestiensis de Rolando Eotvos Nominatae.* Sec. hist. Tom. VII. Budapest, 1965, 43–78.
Lajos Németh: *Modern magyar művészet* (Modern Hungarian Art). Budapest, 1968. (Also in English, German and Russian.)
Antal Kampis: *A magyar művészet a XIX. és a XX. században* (Hungarian Art in the 19th and 20th century). Budapest, 1968. (Also in English and German.)
Júlia Szabó: *Magyar rajzművészet 1849–1890* (Hungarian drawings 1849–1890). Budapest, 1972.
Lajos Németh: *A XIX. század művészete. A historizmustól a szecesszióig* (Twentieth century art. From Historicism to Secession). Budapest, 1974.
Anna Zádor: *A XIX. század művészete. Klasszicizmus és romantika* (19th century art. Classicism and Romanticism). Budapest, 1976. (Also in English and German.)
György Rózsa: *A Történelmi Képcsarnok legszebb festményei* (The Best Paintings of the Historical Portrait Gallery). Budapest, 1977. (Also in German.)
Művészet és felvilágosodás. Művészettörténeti tanulmányok (Art and Enlightenment. Essays on Art History), ed.: Anna Zádor and Hedvig Szabolcsi). Budapest, 1978.
Éva Bodnár: „Il salone di Parigi a la pittura ungherese nel seccolo XIX" in: *Atti del XXIV. Congresso Internazionale di Storia dell'arte* 7. Bologna, 1979.
Művészet Magyarországon 1780–1830 (Art in Hungary 1780–1830). Catalogue, Hungarian National Gallery, Budapest, 1980 (ed.: Hedvig Szabolcsi and Géza Galavics).
Művészet Magyarországon 1830–1870 (Art in Hungary 1830–1870). Catalogue, Hungarian National Gallery, Budapest, 1981 (ed.: Júlia Szabó and György F. Széphelyi).
Válogatás magyar magángyűjteményekből (Selections from private collections in Hungary). Catalogue, Hungarian National Gallery, Budapest, 1981 (ed.: Katalin K. Sinkó).
Judit Szabadi: *A magyar szecesszió művészete* (The Art of the Hungarian Art Nouveau). Budapest, 1979. (Also in German.)
Magyar művészet 1890–1919 (Hungarian Art 1890–1919), ed.: Lajos Németh, Budapest, 1981.
Endre Csatkai: *Kazinczy Ferenc és a képzőművészet* (Ferencz Kazinczy and the Fine Arts). (With essays by Anna Zádor, György Rózsa, notes by Péter Szabó: Ed.: Géza Galavics). Budapest, 1983.

Works on European Painting which Discuss Parallel Phenomena

Constant von Wurzbach: *Biographisches Lexikon des Kaiserthum Oesterreichs.* Wien, 1857–1892.
E. Waldmann: *Die Kunst des Realismus und des Impressionismus im 19. Jahrhundert.* Berlin, 1927. (Propyläen Kunstgeschichte Bd. 15.).
Gustav Pauli: *Die Kunst des Klassizismus und der Romantik.* (Propyläen Kunstgeschichte Bd. 14). Berlin, 1931.
Bruno Grimschitz: *Maler der Ostmark im 19. Jahrhundert.* Wien, 1940.
John Sloane: *French Painting between the Past and the Present. From 1848–1870.* Princeton, 1951.
Fritz Novotny: *Painting and Sculpture in Europe 1780–1880.* London, 1960 (Pelican History of Art).
Werner Hofmann: *Das irdische Paradies.* Frankfurt, 1961.
Rudolf Zeitler: *Die Kunst des 19. Jahrhunderts.* Berlin, 1966. (Propyläen Kunstgeschichte, Neue Folge. Bd. 11).
Walter Wagner: *Die Geschichte der Akademie der bildenden Kunste in Wien.* Wien, 1967.
Géza Jászai: "München und die Kunst Ungarns 1800–1845". *Ungarn-Jahrbuch,* Mainz, 1970.
Paul Wogt: *Was sie lieben. Salonmalerei im 19. Jahrhundert.* Köln, 1970.
Wolfgang Becker: *Paris und die deutsche Malerei 1750–1840.* München, 1971.
Anna Petrova-Pleškotova: *K počiatkom realismu v slovenskom maliarstva. Josef Czauczik a jeho okruh* (The beginnings of Realism in Slovak painting. Jozsef Czauczik and his circle). Bratislava, 1961.
Albert Boime: *The Academy and French Painting in the Nineteenth Century.* London, 1971.
Alexa Ćelebenović: *Peinture kitsch ou réalisme bourgeois, l'art pompier dans le monde.* Paris, 1974.
Fritz Baumgart: *Idealismus und Realismus 1830–1880. Die Malerei der burgerlichen Gesellschaft.* Köln, 1975.

RAINER SCHOCH: *Das Herrscherbild in der Malerei der bürgerlichen Gesellschaft.* München, 1975.
Rudolf Rosenblum: *Modern Painting and Northern Romantic Tradition.* London, 1975.
Rudolf Bachleitner: *Die Nazarener.* München, 1976.
Jan Białostocki: *Von heroischen Grabmal zum Bauerngebrabnis. Todesmotive in der Kunst des XVIII. und XIX. Jahrhunderts.* Wiesbaden-Mainz, 1977.
(Abhandlungen der Akademie der Wissenschaften und Literatur in Mainz, Gesichtes- und Sozialwissenschaftliche Klasse).
Albert Boime: *Thomas Coutoure and the Eclectic Vision.* Yale University Press, New Haven – London, 1980.
Elisabeth Gilmore-Holt: *The Art of All Nations. 1860–1873.* New York, 1981.
Werner Kitlitschka: *Die Malerei der Wiener Rings Strasse. Mit einem Beitrag Fritz Novotny.* Wiesbaden, 1981.
Éva Gottliebova: Josef Czauczik a jeho okruh. Košice, 1981.

Artist Biographies and Plate References

Artists from abroad who had also worked in Hungary are marked with an *. Artists who worked abroad and made paintings which are referred to for iconographical or stylistic parallels are marked with **. In the Bibliography, certain often-mentioned works are shortened, ex: Wurzbach = Wurzbach. Constant von: *Biographisches Lexikon des Kaiserthum Oesterreich,* Wien 1857–1892. Th. B. = Thieme, U. – Becker, F.: *Allgemeines Lexikon der bildenden Künste,* I–XXXVIII, Leipzig, 1907–1950.

* ABEL, JOSEPH (Aschach, 1765–Wien, 1818). Plate 10 Wurzbach: I, 1.— Th. B.: I, 19. Országh, Sándor: *Budai színházak és játékszín* (Budapest's Theatres and Stages). (Budapest, 1895. 56. "In Memoriam J. A.", *Welser Zeitung,* Jg. 72 (1968), Nr. 41; Jg. 73 (1969), Nr. 35.

ADLER, MÓR (Óbuda, 1826–Budapest, 1902). Plate 194 A. M. Életrajza (M. A.'s Biography). Manuscript, Archives, the Hungarian National Museum, Budapest. 8./1920. Donatello (Dömötör, István) *A. M. M.* 1902, 422–424.—*Művészet Magyarországon 1780–1830* (Art in Hungary 1780–1830). Catalogue, Hungarian National Gallery.

** AIGNER, JOSEPH MATTHÄUS (Wien, 1818–Wien, 1886). Plate 131. N. N.: J. M. A. *Druck im Nachlass Hofrat Ankwicz-Kleehoven.* Wien, Österreichische Galerie.—Th. B. I, 148

ALCONIERE, TIVADAR (Hermann Kohn) (Nagymarton, 1797–Wien, 1865). Plate 68 Czakó, Elemér: *Széchenyi a legnagyobb és leghívebb magyar* (Széchenyi, the Greatest and Most Faithful Hungarian). Budapest, 1941.—Vayer, Lajos: "Széchenyi képe" (Portrait of Széchenyi). *Magyarságtudomány.* Budapest, 1942, I, 115.

* AMERLING, FRIEDRICH VON (Wien, 1803–Wien, 1887). Plates 64, 65, 147. Probszt, Günther: *F. v. A. Der Altmeister der Wiener Porträtmalerei.* Zürich-Leipzig-Wien, 1927.—Schoch, Rainer: *Das Herrscherbild in der Malerei des 19. Jahrhunderts.* München, 1985, 93, Plate 100.

* AXMANN, JOSEPH (Brünn, 1793–Salzburg, 1873). Plate 51 Th. B., II, 287. Balkay, Pál: (Tiszaörs, 1785–Eger, 1846). Plate 9 Naményi, László: "B. P. festő" (B. P. Painter), *Művészet.* II (1903.—Th. B., II, 411.

BARABÁS, MIKLÓS (Márkosfalva, 1810–Budapest, 1898). Plates 62, 75, 80, 81, 82, 83, 84, 85, 91, 92, 98, 100, 101, 109, 111, 121, 125, 189, 193 Th. B., II, 451–452.—Hoffmann, Edith: *B. M.,* Budapest, 1923; 2nd ed. 1950.—Szvoboda, Gabriella: *B. M.,* Budapest, 1984.

** BASTIEN-LEPAGE, JULES (Darmvillers, 1848–Paris, 1884). Plate 308 Boime, Albert: The Academy and French Painting in the Nineteenth Century. London, 1971, Plate 65.

BENCZÚR, GYULA (Nyíregyháza, 1844–Dolány, 1920). Plates 237, 279, 290, 292 Th. B., III, 297–298.—Mihalik, Sándor: *B.,* Kassa, 1944.—Telepy, Katalin: *B.,* Nyíregyháza, 1963.

Bihari, Sándor (Rézbánya, 1856–Budapest, 1906). Plate 297
Szana, Tamás: *Magyar művészek. B. S.* (Hungarian Artists. S. B.), Budapest, 1889, 137–144.—Th. B., IV, 24.

Blaschke, János (Pozsony, 1770–Wien, 1883). Plates 12, 51
Th. B., IV, 102.

Borsos, József (Veszprém, 1821–Budapest, 1833). Plates 97, 99, 105, 106, 132, 133, 145, 146, 148
Th. B., IV, 378.—Pataky-Molnár, Zsuzsa: *B. J. emlékkiállítása katalógusa* (exhibition catalogue), Veszprém, 1971.

** Böcklin, Arnold (Basel, 1827–San Domenico di Fiesola, 1901). Plate 232
Rolf, Andrée: *A. B.,* Basel-München, 1977, 348.—Neue Pinakothek, München. Erläuterungen zu den ausgestellten Werken. München, 1981, No. 9335, 33–34 (Cristoph H. Heilmann).

Brocky, Charles (Károly) (Temesvár, 1807–London, 1855). Plates 94, 95, 96, 138
Wilkinson, Norman: *Sketch of the Life of Charles Brocky.* London, 1870.—Nyáry, S.: *B. K. festőművész élete és művei* (The Life and Works of Ch. B. Painter), Budapest, 1910.—Th. B., V, 40–41.—Lajta, Edit: *B. K.,* Budapest, 1957. New Edition Budapest, 1985

Brodszky, Sándor (Tóalmás, 1819–Budapest, 1901). Plate 215
Th. B., V, 43.—*Magyar Művészet* (Budapest, IV, 1928, 610–612.

* Cajetan–Joseph (biog. data unknown). Plates 116, 130
Th. B., V, 358–359.

** Courbet, Gustave (Ornans, 1819–Tour-de-Peilz, 1877). Plate 244
Lázár, Béla: *Courbet et son influence à l'étranger.* Paris, 1911—*C. C.* (exhibition catalogue). Paris, Grand Palais, 1977–1978.—*Courbet und Deutschland* (exhibition catalogue). Hamburg–Frankfurt am Main, 1978–1979, 27, 259–260 (P. K. Schuster, R. Andrée).

Czauczik (Czausig,) József (Lőcse, 1789–Lőcse, 1857). Plates 7, 18, 36, 39, 42
Szepesházy und Thiele: Merkwürdigkeiten des Königreichs Ungarn. Kaschau, 1825, I, 108.—Kőszeghy, Elemér: *Bildnismalerei in der Zips.* Késmárk, 1922.—Petrova-Pleškotova, Anna: *K počiatkom realismu* (The Beginnings of Realism). Bratislava, 1961.—Gottliebova, Eva: *Josef Czauczik a jeho okruh* (Josef Czauczik and His Circle), Košice, 1981.

Csók, István (Pusztaegres, 1865–Budapest, 1961). Plates 309, 310
Lázár, Béla: *Cs. I.,* Budapest, 1921.—Farkas, Zoltán: *Cs. I.,* Budapest, 1957.

Csontváry Kosztka, Tivadar (Kisszeben, 1853–Budapest, 1919) Plate 321
Németh, Lajos: *Cs.,* Budapest, 1964. rev. ed. 1971 (German, English, French shortened versions, too).

** Daubigny, Charles François (Paris, 1817–Paris, 1878). Plate 265
Hellebrandt, Richard: *Ch. F. D.,* Morges, 1976.

** Daumier, Honoré (Marseille, 1808–Valmondois, 1879). Plates 176, 246
Nochlin, Linda: *Realism, Style and Civilization* (Harmondsworth (Middlesex), 1971.

Deák Ébner, Lajos (Pest, 1850–Budapest, 1934). Plates 295, 296
Th. B., VIII, 494–495.—Möbius, Isabella: *D. É. L.,* Budapest, 1940.

** Delacroix, Eugène (Charenton-Saint-Maurice, 1798–Paris, 1863). Plate 175.
Bertoletto, Luigina Rossi: *D.,* Milano, 1972.

** Delaroche, Paul (Paris, 1797–Paris, 1856). Plate 183
Boime, Albert: *The Academy and French Painting in the Nineteenth Century.* London, 1971, 102–103, Plates 51–52.—Ziff, N.: *D.,* New York, 1977.

Donát, János (Neuzelle an der Oder, 1744–Pest, 1830). Plates 3, 11, 19, 47
Wurzbach, I, 397, XXVII, 267.—Th. B., IX, 420.—*Schloss Wetzdorf. Pargfrieder-Radetzky-Wintzent* (catalogue). Kleinwetzdorf-Haganberg, 1979, 12–22.—Bakó, Zsuzsa: "D. J. magyarországi munkássága" (H. D. 's Work in Hungary, Ph. D. dissertation, ELTE, Budapest), Manuscript, 1981.

Dósa, Géza (Nagyenyed, 1846–Marosvásárhely, 1871). Plate 231
Th. B., IX, 492.—M. Kiss, Pál: "D. G.", *Magyar Művészettörténeti Munkaközösség Évkönyve* (Yearbook of the Circle of Hungarian Art Historians), Budapest, 1952.

Ehrlinger (erlinger), János: (? – Pozsony, 1848). Plate 49
Csatkai, Endre: "Pozsonyi képzőművészek és iparművészek 1750–1850 között" (Artists and Applied Artists in Bratislava between 1750–1850), *Művészettörténeti Értesítő*, XII, 1963, 22.

* Einsle, Anton (Wien, 1801–Wien, 1861). Plate 74
Th. B., X, 423–426.

* Ender, Johann (Wien, 1793–Wien, 1854). Plates 6. 63, 67, 72, 108
Th. B., X., 515–516.—Bártfai Szabó, László: "Ender János levelei gróf Széchényi Ferenc arcképéről" (J. E's letters on Count Ferenc Széchényi's Portrait). *Magyar Könyvszemle,* 1931, 56–59.—Rózsa, Georg: "Die Allegorie der Ungarischen Akademie der Wissenschaften. J. E. und István Széchenyi." *Alte und Moderne Kunst,* 8 Sept, 1966, 28–31.—Koschatzky, W.: *Thomas Ender.* Wien, 1982.

Ferenczy, Károly (Wien, 1862–Budapest, 1917). Plates 311, 312, 313
Th. B., XI, 400.—Petrovics, Elek: *F. K.,* Budapest 1943.—Genthon, István: *F. K.,* Budapest 1963 (2nd ed., 1980).

* Fischer, Joseph (Wien, 1769–Wien, 1822). Plate 22
Th. B., XII, 30–31.—Rózsa, György: "Die ungarische Landschaft im Werk J. F. s", *Mitteilungen der Österreichischen Galerie.* Wien, 1982–83.

Forray, Iván (Soborsin, 1817–Wien, 1872). Plate 87
Horváth, Henrik: *Az árvíz a művészetben* (A pest-budai árvíz 1838-ban) (The Flood in Art. The Pest-Buda Flood of 1838). Budapest, 1938.

* Geiger, Andreas (Wien, 1765–Wien, 1856). Plate 130

Gyárfás, Jenő (Sepsiszentgyörgy, 1857–Sepsiszentgyörgy, 1925). Plates 285, 286, 287, 288
Th. B., XV, 374.—Gazda, József: *Gy. J.,* Bucharest, 1969.—Kisdégi–Kirimi, Irén: *Gy. J.,* Budapest, 1971.

** German Painter (c. 1780). Plate 13
Mojzer, M.: *A Magyar Nemzeti Galéria késő reneszánsz és barokk kiállítása* (Late Renaissance and Baroque Exhibition at the Hungarian National Gallery). Budapest, 1980. Catalogue. N. 548. p. 71.

Györgyi Giergl, Alajos (Pest, 1821–Pest, 1863). Plates 162, 164
Th. B., X, 376.—Bakay, Margit: *Gy. G. A.,* Budapest, 1938.

Haan, Antal (Békéscsaba, 1827–Capri, 1888). Plate 157
Th. B., XV., 386.

** Henner Jean-Jacques (Bernviller, 1829–Paris, 1905). Plate 182.—*Musée JJ.H. Catalogue sommaire.* Paris, 1923, 5.—Boime, Albert: *The Academy and French Painting in the Nineteenth Century.* London, 1971, 111–112, Plate 92.

Hesz, János Mihály (Eger, 1768–Wien, 1833). Plate 20.
Ernst, Lajos: *H. M. tervezete 1820-ban magyar képzőművészeti akadémia felállítása iránt* (H. M.'s Proposal in 1820 about the Establishment of the Hungarian Academy of Art). Budapest, 1898.—Th. B, XVI, 598–599., Jávor, Anna: *H. J. M.* (manuscript). Budapest, 1980.

* Hoffmann, Michael (Wien, 1797–Wien, 1867). Plate 54
Wurzbach, IX.—Th. B., XVII, 277–278.

Hollósy, Simon (Máramarossziget, 1857–Técső, 1918). Plates 298, 304, 305.—Th. B., XVII, 384–385.—Németh Lajos: *H. S.,* Budapest, 1955.

Höfel, Johann Nepomuk (Pest, 1786–Wien, 1864). Plates 46, 90
Th. B., XVII, 189–190.

Jankó, János (Tótkomlós, 1833–Budapest, 1896). Plates 169, 170
Szana, Tamás: *J. J.,* Budapest, 1899.—Takács, Mária: *J. J.,* Budapest, 1936.—Th. B., XVIII, 388–389.

** Jazet, Jean-Pierre Marie (Paris, 1789–Yerres, 1871). Plate 58
Benezit, E.: *Dictionnaire critique et documentaire des peintres, sculpteurs, dessinateurs et graveurs.* V., Paris, 1961, 134.

* JETTEL, EUGEN (Johnsdorf, 1845–Lussingrande, 1901). Plate 269
Wawra, C. J.: *Katalog Künstlerischer Nachlass E. J.,* Wien, 1902.—Th. B., XVIII,
542–543.—Aurenhammer, Hans: "Österreichische Malern in Szolnok". In: *Maler-schule von Szolnok.* Catalogue. Budapest–Wien–Graz, 1975–76.

KAERGLING, HENRIETTA (Pest, 1821–?). Plate 86
Wurzbach X, 351–352.—Th. B., XIX, 422–423.

KELETY, GUSZTÁV (Klette till 1861, Keleti till 1901) (Pozsony, 1834–Budapest, 1902).
Plates 149, 163, 213
Th. B., XX, 88.—Csengery-Nagy, Zsuzsa: Gusztáv Kelety chez les Eötvös. *Annales de la Galerie Nationale Hongroise* No. 1. 1970. 51–62

* KININGER, VINCENZ (Regensburg, 1767–Wien, 1851). Plate 12
Th. B., XX, 331–332.—Nebehay, Ch. M.: *V. K.,* Catalogue. Wien, 1981.

KISFALUDY, KÁROLY (Tét, 1788–Pest, 1830). Plates 51, 54, 57
Th. B., XX, 384.—Vayer–Zibolen, Ágnes: "Károly Kisfaludy. Die Anfänge der Romantik in der Kunst Ungarns". In: *Művészettörténeti Füzetek. Cahiers d'histoire de l'art.* Budapest, 1973.

KISS, BÁLINT (Szentes, 1802–Pest, 1868). Plates 112, 172
Th. B., XX, 386.—Zádor Anna: "K. B. 1802–1868". *Magyar Művészettörténeti Mun-kaközösség Évkönyve* (Yearbook of the Circle of Hungarian Art Historians), 1952, Budapest.

KLIMKOVICS, IGNÁC (Kassa, 1800–Kassa, 1852). Plate 16
Zmetakova, Danica: *Kresba 19. storocia Slovensku* (Slovak Drawings from the 19th Century). Bratislava, 1976. Plate 44, 192.—"Kresbovy odkaz Klimkovivcovcov". (Message of Klimkovics' Drawings). *Sbornik Slovenskei Narodnij Galerie.* 3. Bratis-lava, 1980, 203–219.

** KNAUS, LUDWIG (Wiesbaden, 1829–Berlin, 1905). Plate 254
Th. B., XX, 570–577.—Pietsch, L.: "K. Bielefeld u. Leipzig, 1896–1901". *Katalog der Meister des neunzehnten Jahrhunderts in der Hamburger Kunsthalle.* Hamburg, 1969, 158.

** KOCH, JOSEPH ANTON (Obergibeln, 1768–Rome, 1839). Plate 212
Th. B., XXI, 81–88.—Lutterotti, O. H.: *J. A. K.,* Berlin, 1940.

KOVÁCS, MIHÁLY (Abádszalók, 1818–Budapest, 1892). Plates 120, 139, 143, 161, 177
Th. B., XXI, 362–363.—Noack, F.: *Deutsches Leben* in: Rom, Berlin, 1907, 442.,—Biró, B.: *K. M. élete és művészete* (The Art and Life of M. K.), Budapest, 1930.—Ludányi, G.: *K. M.,* Budapest, 1985.

KOZINA, SÁNDOR (Felsőságh, 1808–Felsőpulya, 1873). Plates 73, 79, 124
Th. B., XXI, 370–371.—Csatkai, Endre: "K. S. elfeledett magyar biedermeier festő" (S. K., A Forgotten Hungarian Biedermeier Painter), *Művészettörténeti Értesítő,* 1970, 31–33.

KŐRÖSFŐI–KRIESCH, ALADÁR (Buda, 1862–Gödöllő, 1920). Plate 319
Lyka, K.: "Drei ungarische Künstler". *Deutsche Kunst und Dekoration.* Darmstadt, 1904, VII, 12.—Dénes, Jenő: *K. K. A.,* Budapest, 1939.—Keserü, Katalin: *K. K. A.,* Budapest, 1977.

KRAFFT, BARBARA (Iglau, 1764–Bamberg, 1825). Plate 17
Th. B., XXI, 384–385.—*Katalog der Galerie des 19. Jhs. im Oberen Belvedere.* Wien, 1924.

** KRAFFT, PETER, sen. (Hanau, 1780–Wien, 1856). Plate 59
Th. B., XXI, 401–402.—Vasić, P.: "Die Kunst P. K. s" In: *Österreichische Zeitschrift für Kunst und Denkmalpflege,* XIV, 1960, 58.—Vancsa, E.: *Aspekte der Historienmalerei des 19. Jhs. in Wien.* Dissertation. Wien, 1973.—Frodl-Schneckmann, M.: *J. P. K.,* Wien, 1983.

* KREUTZINGER, JOSEPH (Wien, 1767–Wien, 1829). Plates 1, 2
Rózsa, György: "Kazinczy Ferenc a művészetben" (F. K. in Art). *Művészettörténeti Értesítő,* VI, 1957, 174 ff.

* KUPELWIESER, LEOPOLD (Piesting, 1766–Wien, 1862). Plate 159
Th. B., XXII, 121–123.—Feuchtmüller, R.: *L. K. und die Kunst der österreichischen Spätromantik,* Wien 1971.

* LACCATARIS, DEMETER (Diamanti Laccatari) (Wien, 1798–Pest, 1864). Plate 53
Th. B., XXII, 174.

LANDAU, ALAJOS (Pest, 1833–Budapest, 1884). Plate 178
Th. B., XXII, 288.—Biography: Archives, Hungarian National Gallery, Budapest.

* LANZEDELLI (LANZEDELLY), JOSEPH, Jun. (Wien, 1806–Wien, 1865). Plate 136
Th. B., XXII, 366.—Rózsa, Gy.–Spira, Gy.: *48 a kortársak szemével* ('48 Through the Eyes of Contemporaries), 2nd ed., Budapest 1973, 122.

** LEIBL, WILHELM (Köln, 1844–Würzburg, 1900). Plate 259
Waldmann, E.: *W. L. – eine Darstellung seiner Kunst. Gesamtverzeichnis seiner Gemälde.* Berlin, 1914, 1930.—Wilhelm Leibl und sein Kreis. Catalogue, München, 1974.

LIBAY, KÁROLY LAJOS (Besztercebánya, 1861–Wien, 1888). Plate 154
Libay, Ludwig: *Ägypten, Reisebilder aus dem Orient… nach der Natur gezeichnet und herausgegeben.* Wien, 1857.—Siorbán, V.: Adatok *L. K. L. életrajzához* (Ammendations to the Biography of K. J. L), Dés, 1917.—Th. B., XXIII, 183.

* LIEDER, FRIEDRICH (Potsdam, 1786–Pest, 1859). Plates 4, 5
Th. B., XXIII, 203–204.—Naményi, László: "L. F.", *Művészet,* II /1903, 344–350.

LIEZEN-MAYER, SÁNDOR (Győr, 1839–München, 1898). Plate 217
Th. B., XXIII, 216–217.—Benkő, Gizella: *L. M. S.,* Budapest, 1932.

LIGETI, ANTAL (Nagykároly, 1823–Budapest, 1890). Plates 155, 156, 167, 168
Th. B., XXIII, 218.—H. Rapaics, J.: *L. A.,* Budapest, 1938.

LOTZ, KÁROLY (Hessen–Homburg, 1833–Budapest, 1904). Plates 153, 166, 220, 225, 226, 227, 228, 281, 283
(Emmerich Henszlmann): "Die Wandbilder des neuen Redoutengebäudes in Pest". *Zeitschrift für bildende Kunst.* Leipzig, 1866, 204–211.—Ybl, Ervin: *L. K. élete és művészete* (The Art and Life of K. L.), Budapest, 1938 (abbreviated, revised ed., Budapest, 1981 with an Afterword by A. Zádor).

* LÜTGENDORFF, FERDINAND VON (Würzburg, 1785–Würzburg, 1858). Plate 33
Lütgendorff, Leo: *Der Maler und Radierer F. v. L.,* Frankfurt am Main, 1906.—*D. v. F. a jeho škola* (D. v. F. and his School). Catalogue. Bratislava, 1969.

MADARÁSZ, VIKTOR (Csetnek, 1830–Budapest, 1917). Plates 179, 180, 181, 184, 187, 190, 200
Th. B., XXIII, 525—Radocsay, D.: M. V., Budapest, 1941.—Székely, Z.: *MV.,* Budapest, 1954.—Rózsa, György: "A magyar történelmi festészet témáinak barokk feldolgozásai" (Baroque Handling of the Subject Matter of Hungarian Historical Painting)", *Művészettörténeti Értesítő.* 1959, 275–280.

** MAKART, HANS (Salzburg, 1840–Wien, 1884). Plates 278, 284
Kelety, G.: "Künstlerbriefe I–VI". *Ungarischer Lloyd,* 1968. 7, 22, Jan. 12, 26., Febr. – 20 March, 21 May.—"Die fünf Sinne." Bilderzyklus von H. M.", *Pester Lloyd.* 1883. 13, Jan.—Frodl, G.: H. M. *Monographie und Werkverzeichnis.* Salzburg, 1974.

** MANET, EDOUARD (Paris, 1832–Paris, 1883). Plate 240
Jedlicka, G.: *E. M.,* Erlenbach-Zürich 1941, 49–70.

* MARASTONI, JAKAB (GIACOMO). (Venice, 1804–Pest, 1860). Plates 102, 122
Th. B., XIV, 51.–Péter, Kornélia: *M. J.,* Budapest, 1936. Szvoboda, G.: *M. J.,* 1981.

MARGITAY, TIHAMÉR (Jenk, 1859–Budapest, 1922). Plate 299
Szana, Tamás: *Magyar művészek M. T.* (Hungarian Artists). Budapest, 1899. 217–225.—Th. B., XXIV, 89.

MARKÓ, KÁROLY the Elder (Lőcse, 1791–Villa Appeggi, 1860). Plates 29, 30, 41, 76, 77, 78, 150, 152
Szana, T.: *M. K. és a tájfestészet* (K. M. and the Art of Landscape Painting), Budapest, 1898.—Th. B., XXIV, 117–118.—Pogány, Ö.: *Id. M. K.* (K. M. the Elder), Budapest, 1954.—Bodnár, E.: *Id. M. K.* (K. M. the Elder), Budapest, 1980.

MEDNYÁNSZKY, LÁSZLÓ (Beczkó, 1852–Wien, 1919). Plates 273, 306, 307
Th. B., XXIV, 330.—Kállai, E.: *M. L.,* Budapest, 1943.—Egri, M.: *M.* Budapest, 1975.—Aradi, N.: *M.,* Budapest, 1983, Sarkantyu, M: *M.* Budapest, 1983

** MEISTER, SIMON (Koblenz, 1796–Köln, 1844). Plate 66
Th. B., XXIV, 348–349.—Schoch, R.: *Das Herrscherbild in der Malerei des 19. Jhs.*, München, 1976, Plate 114.

MELEGH, GÁBOR (Versec, 1801–Vienna, 1832). Plates 21, 60, 61
Th. B., XXIV, 360.—Pataky, D. *"M. G."*, *Művészettörténeti Értesítő*, 1956, 173–175. Jávor, A: "Melegh Gábor Bécsben" [Gábor Melegh in Vienna] (1817–1832), *Művészettörténeti Értesítő*, 1984. 2, 51–57.

MÉSZÖLY, GÉZA (Sárbogárd, 1844–Jobbágyi, 1887). Plates 271, 272
Th. B., XXIV, 437.—Rajnai, M.: *M. G.*, Budapest, 1953.

** MILLET, JEAN-FRANÇOIS (Gruchy, 1814–Barbizon, 1875). Plate 258
Sensier, A.–Malts, P.: *La vie et l'oeuvre de J. F. M.*, Paris, 1881.—Pataky, D.: *Les maîtres de dessin*, Budapest, 1958.

MOLNÁR, JÓZSEF (Zsámbék, 1821–Budapest, 1899). Plates 151, 158, 216
Th. B., XXV, 46–47.—Turchányi, E.: *M. J.*, Budapest, 1938.

** MONET, CLAUDE (Paris, 1840–Giverny, 1926). Plate 241
Isaacson, Joel: *Le Déjeuner sur l'herbe* (Ed. Fleming, J. and Honor, H.), Ann Arbor, 1970.

MUNKÁCSY, MIHÁLY (Munkács, 1844–Endenich, 1900). Plates 250, 251, 252, 255, 256, 257, 260, 261, 262, 263, 264, 275, 291
Th. B., XXV, 271–272.—Végvári, L.: *M. M. élete és művei* (The Life and Works of M. M.), Budapest 1958.—Perneczky, G.: *M.*, Budapest, 1970 (in English, French and German).

MÜLLER, JÁNOS JAKAB (worked at Lőcse between 1780–1828). Plates 23, 24, 25
Petrova–Pleskotova, A.: *Slovenské vytvarné umenie obdobia narodneho obrodenia* (Slovak Fine Arts During the National Rebirth), Bratislava, 1966.

** GERMAN PAINTER (c. 1780). Plate 13
Mojzer, M.: *A Magyar Nemzeti Galéria késő reneszánsz és barokk kiállítása* (Late Renaissance and Baroque Exhibition at the Hungarian National Gallery). Budapest, 1980. Catalogue. N. 548. p. 71.

NEUHAUSER, FERENC, JR. (Wien, 1763–Nagyszeben, 1836). Plate 38
Művészet Magyarországon 1780–1830 (Art in Hungary 1780–1830), Budapest, 1980. Catalogue, Hungarian National Gallery, 152–153, 29, no. 141 (Galavics, Géza).

ORLAI PETRICH, SOMA (Mezőberény, 1822–Budapest, 1880). Plates 142, 144, 165, 171, 191
Th. B., XXVI, 46.—Szij, B.: *"OP. S."* Bulletin de la Galerie Nationale Hongroise, Budapest, 1974 /2, 15–32, 150–159).—Keserű, K.: *OP. S.*, Budapest, 1984.

PAÁL, LÁSZLÓ (Zám, 1846–Charenton, 1879). Plates 267, 268, 270
Lázár, B.: *L. P.*, Paris, 1904—Th. B., XXVI, 111.—Farkas, Zoltán: *P. L.*, Budapest, 1954.—Bényi, L.: *P. L.*, Budapest, 1978.

PETRICH, ANDRÁS (Mitrovica, 1765–Buda, 1845). Plates 27, 28
Th. B., XXVI, 497.—V. Zibolen, A.: "P. A. irodalmi vonatkozású rajzairól" (On A. P.'s Drawings Related to Literature), *Yearbook of the Petőfi Literary Museum*, Budapest, 1964.

* PETTENKOFEN, AUGUST VON (Wien, 1822–Wien 1889). Plates 140, 293
Th. B., XXVI, 506–507.—Kaposváry, Gy.: "P. és Szolnok" (P. and Szolnok), in: *Malerschule von Szolnok*. Catalogue. Budapest–Wien–Graz. 1975–1976.

** PILOTY, CARL THEODOR VON (München, 1826–Ambach, 1886). Plate 198
Neue Pinakothek, München. *Erläuterung zu den ausgestellten Werken*, München, 1981, 253–254. (Schulz-Hoffmann, Carla).

* RAFFALT, JOHANN GUILBERT (Muran, 1836–Rome, 1865). Plate 294
Aurenhammer, H.: see Jettel, Eugen, *op. cit.*

** RAHL, CARL (Wien, 1812–Wien, 1865). Plate 223
Speidel, L.: *R's Athenischer Fries*. Wien, 1867.—George-Mayer, A.: *Erinnerungen an C. R.*, Wien, 1882.—Kitlitschka, W.: *Die Malerei der Wiener Ringstrasse*, Wiesbaden, 1981.

** REBELL, JOSEPH (Wien, 1787–Dresden, 1828). Plate 40
Th. B., XXVIII, 64—Noack, F.: *Das Deutschtum in Rom,* Rom, 1907

RÉTI, ISTVÁN (Nagybánya, 1872–Budapest, 1945). Plate 303
Th. B., XXVIII, 189.—Aradi, N.: R. I., Budapest, 1958.

RIPPL-RÓNAI, JÓZSEF (Kaposvár, 1861–Kaposvár, 1927). Plates 314, 315, 316, 317, 318
Th. B., XXVIII, 376.—Pewny, D.: *R. R. J.,* Budapest, 1940.—Petrovics, E.: *R. R. J.,* Budapest, 1940.—Gachot, F.: *R. R. J.,* Budapest, 1944.—Genthon, I.: *R. R. J.,* Budapest, 1976.—Keserű, K.: *R. R. J.,* Budapest, 1982.—Szabadi, J.: R. R. R., Budapest, 1978.—"J. R. R. et l'art nouveau", *Acta Historiae Artium,* Tom. XXVI (1980), fasc. 3–4–285–316.

** ROMAKO, ANTON (Wien, 1832–Döbling, 1889). Plate 197
Novotny, F.: *Der Maler A. R., 1832–1889,* Wien–München, 1954.

ROMBAUER, JÁNOS (Lőcse, 1782–Eperjes, 1849). Plates 14, 26, 34, 45, 48
Divald, K.: *Adatok R. J. festőről* (Data on Painter J. R.), Budapest, 1904.—Th. B., XXVIII, 555.—A. Tihamiroff: "Rombauer en Russie" (Rombauer in Russia), *Bulletin de la Galerie Nationale Hongroise,* Budapest, 1961, 5–38.—"R. J. ismeretlen műve" (J. R.'s unknown work). *Művészettörténeti Értesítő,* 1965, 268.—Petrova–Pleškotova, A.: J. R. a jeho presovski suchasnici (J. R. and his followers in Prešov"), Catalogue, Bratislava, 1963–1964.

RÓMER, FLÓRIS (Pozsony, 1815–Nagyvárad, 1889). Plate 89
Kumlik, F.: *R. F. élete és működése* (The Life and Work of F. R.), Bratislava, 1907.—Rottler, F.: (ed): *R. F., Ipolyi Arnold, Fraknói Vilmos. Egyház, műveltség, történetírás* (F. R., A. I., V. F., The Church, Culture and the Writing of History), Budapest, 1981.

ROSENTHAL, (DAVID), KONSTANTIN (Pest, 1820–Pest, 1851). Plate 104, 118
Biró, B.: "R. D. önarcképe" (The Self Portrait of D. R.), *Szépművészeti Múzeum Közleményei,* (Bulletin du Musée des Beaux-Arts Hongrois) Budapest, 1949, no. 3, 49–50.

RÓTH, IMRE (EMMANUEL) (Paris, 1812–Kassa, 1870). Plate 103
Th. B., XXIX, 87.

** ROUSSEAU, THÉODORE (Paris, 1812–Barbizon, 1867). Plate 266
Th. B., XXIX, 115–116.

** RUNGE, PHILIPP OTTO (Wolgast, 1777–Dresden, 1810). Plate 15
Traeger, J.: *P. O. R. und sein Werk.* München, 1975, 114.—Hoffman, W. (ed).: *R. in seiner Zeit,* Hamburg, 1977. Ausstellung der Hamburger Kunsthalle, Plate 115.

SCHÄFFER, BÉLA (ADALBERT), (Nagykároly, 1815–Düsseldorf, 1871). Plates 115, 117
Th. B., XXIX, 552.

 * SCHÄRMER, MARTIN (Nassenreith, 1785–Wien, 1868). Plate 51
Wurzbach, XXIX—V. Zibolen A.: see Kisfaludi Károly, *op. cit.*

** SCHLOTTERBECK, WILHELM FRIEDRICH (?, 1777–Wien, 1819).—See Fischer, Joseph, *op. cit.*

SCHMIDT, JÓZSEF (Pest, 1810–Pest, 1842). Plate 93
Wurzbach XXX, 279.—Szvoboda, G.: "A Pesti műegylet megalakulása és első kiállítása 1840-ben" (The Foundation and First Exhibition of the Art Association of Pest in 1840), *Ars Hungarica,* Budapest, 1982, 297, ff.

SCHOEFFT, ÁGOST (Pest, 1809–London, 1888). Plate 71

SCHOEFFT, JÓZSEF, SR. (??) (Pest, 1780–Pest, 1850). Plate 71
Bártfai Szabó, L.: *Adatok gróf Széchenyi István és kora történetéhez* (Additions to the History of Count István Széchenyi and his Age), Budapest, 1943, 224. „Széchenyi István művész kortársai és barátai" (The Contemporaries and Artistic Friends of István Széchenyi), *Magyar Művészet,* VI (1930, 598–599).

SIGRAY, BORBÁLA (dates unknown). Plate 113
Nagy, Iván: *Magyarország családai* (The Families of Hungary), X, Pest, 1863, 180.

SIMÓ, FERENC (Székelyudvarhely, 1801–Kolozsvár, 1869). Plates 69, 70
Th. B., XXXI, 50.—Biró, B.: *Kis-solymosi S. F.* 1801–1869 (F. S. of Kissolymos

1801–1869). Erdélyi Helikon, 1942, no. 8. — „S. F. nyolc képe a Szépművészeti Múzeumban" (Eight Paintings by F. S. in the Museum of Fine Arts), *A Szépművészeti Múzeum közleményei, (Bulletin du Musée Hongrois des Beaux-Arts) Budapest, 1948, 30–33,*

STECH, ALAJOS (Sasvár, 1813–Tata, 1887). Plate 50
P. J.: „S. A. 1852-ben" (A. S. in 1852), *Művészet,* XII (1911), 233.

STEINACKER, KÁROLY (Wien, 1801–Sopron, 1873). Plate 96
Csatkai, E.: „S. K. soproni biedermeier festő" (K. S: A Biedermeier Painter from Sopron), *Művészettörténeti Értesítő* (1953), 149.

STORNO, FERENC, SR. (Kismarton, 1820–Sopron, 1907). Plate 126
Wurzbach, XXXIX, 201.—Th. B., XXXII, 126–127.—Levárdy, R.: „Id. S. F. pannonhalmi működése" (F. S. Sr.'s Work in Pannonhalma), *Soproni Szemle,* 51, (1939), 1–17.

STUNDER, JOHANN JAKOB (Coppenhagen, 1759–Besztercebánya, 1811). Plate 8
Th. B., XXXII, 249.—Petrova–Pleskotova, A.: "K zivotu a dielu maliare Jána Jakuba" Stundera (Life and Work of the Painter Johann Jakob Stunder). *Ars* 2, 1967.

SZÉKELY, BERTALAN (Kolozsvár, 1835–Mátyásföld, 1911). Plates 195, 196, 199, 201, 202, 203, 204, 205, 206, 208, 209, 210, 211, 289
Palágyi, Menyhért: Nemzeti festészetünk, I. Sz. B. (Our National Painting. B. Sz. Sr.) Budapest, 1910.—Th. B., XXXII, 373–374.—Petrovics, E.: „Sz. B.-ről" (On B. Sz.), *Magyar Művészet,* 1925, 309 ff.—*Sz. B. Élet és Művészet,* Budapest, 1937, 30–59.—Dobai, J.: *Sz. B. kiállításának katalógusa* (Catalogue), Műcsarnok, Budapest, 1955.—„Sz. B. művészi arculatának kialakulásáról" (On the Development of B. Sz.'s Artistic Profile), *Művészettörténeti Értesítő,* 1956, no. 2–3.—Bakó, Zs.: *Sz.,* Budapest, 1981.

SZEMLER, MIHÁLY (Pest, 1833–Budapest, 1904). Plate 249
Th. B., XXXIII, 375.—B. Supka, M.: „Sz. M.", *Magyar Művészettörténeti Munkaközösség Évkönyve* (Yearbook of the Circle of Hungarian Art Historians), 1955, Budapest, 1957 (ed. Dávid, K.), 219–252.

SZINYEI MERSE, PÁL (Szinyeújfalu, 1845–Jernye, 1920). Plates 229, 230, 233, 234, 235, 236, 238, 239, 240, 243, 245, 247, 248
Lázár, B.: *P. M. Sz.* Leipzig, 1911, Budapest, 1913.—Th. B., XXXII, 378.—Meller, S.: „Sz. M. P. élete és művészete" (The Life and Work of P. Sz. M.), *Országos Szépművészeti Múzeum Évkönyve* (Annales of the Museum of Fine Arts), VII, Budapest, 1935.—Petrovics, E.: *Sz. M. P.* Budapest, 1941.—Hoffmann, E.: *Sz. M. P.,* Budapest, 1943.—Rajnai, M.: *Sz. M. P.,* Budapest, 1953.—Pataky, D.: *Sz. M. P.,* Budapest, 1964.—Bernáth, M.: *Sz. M. P.,* Budapest, 1982.—Jeszenszky, S.: Le déjeuner sur l'herbe de Szinyei (Szinyei's 'Picnic in May'), *Bulletin de la Galerie Nationale Hongroise,* No. 2. 1960. Budapest, 5–70—Szinyei Merse, A.: „Bildgattungen und Themen im Jugendwerk von Pál Szinyei Merse. Ein ikonographischer Ausblick.". *Acta Historiae Artium.* Tomus XXVII. Fasc. 3–4. Ms. in the archives of the Hungarian National Gallery; SZMP (Corvina, in preparation).

SZOLDATICS, FERENC (Vörösberény, 1820 – Rome, 1916). Plate 207 Th. B., XXXII, 380–381. – Bíró, Béla: Sz. F. 1942–46. Manuscript. Archives of the HNG. 1830–1870, Nr. 230, 343 (György F. Széphelyi).

TELEPY, KÁROLY (Debrecen, 1829–Budapest, 1906). Plate 214
Th. B., XXXII, 511.—Telepy, K.: *T. K.,* Debrecen, 1968.

* TEVELY (TEVELE), FERDINAND (Prague, 1807–Wien, 1893). Plate 188
Th. B., XXXII, 571.—*Művészet Magyarországon 1830–1870* (Art in Hungary 1830–1870), Budapest, 1981. Catalogue, Hungarian National Gallery, no. 199, 343 (F. Gy. Széphelyi).

THAN, MÓR (Óbecse, 1828–Trieste, 1899). Plates 137, 160, 173, 174, 192, 221, 222, 224
Th. B., XXXII, 581.—C. Wilhelmb, G.: *T.,* Budapest, 1982.

THORMA, JÁNOS (Halas, 1870–Nagybánya, 1937). Plates 300, 301, 302
Th. B., XXXIII, 86.—Felvinczy, Takács, Z.: „T. J.", *Magyar Művészet,* 4 (1928), 737–741.—Radocsay, D.: „T. J.-ról" (On J. T.), *Magyar Művészettörténeti Munkaközösség Évkönyve* (Yearbook of the Circle of Hungarian Art Historians), III, Budapest, 1954.

TIBÉLY, KÁROLY (Szepesváralja, 1813–Rimaszombat, 1870?). Plate 88
Th. B., XXXIII, 131.—Kőszeghy, E.: *Bildnismalerei in der Zips.* Késmárk, 1933,
29.—Gottliebova, E.: *Josef Czauczik a jeho okruh* (Joseph Czauczik and His Circle),
Košice, 1981, 77–81.

** TISCHBEIN, JOHANN FRIEDRICH AUGUST (Maestricht, 1750–Heidelberg, 1812). Plate 35
Th. B., XXXIII, 207–209.—August Graf Preysing: „Das Familienbildnis der Grafen
Fries". *Jahrbuch des Vereines für Geschichte der Stadt Wien* (Hrsg. Dr. Rudolf Geyer).
Band: Wien, 1951, 102. 1. Plate 15.—*Katalog der alten Meister der Hamburger Kunsthalle,*
1966, 161, Nr. 604.

UJHÁZY, FERENC (Szolnok, 1827–Budapest, 1921). Plate 141
Th. B., XXXIII, 550.—*Illustrierte Kunst Revue,* vol. 3, nr. 12, Berlin–Leipzig–Wien,
1901.—U. F.: *Gyakorlati oktatás a festészet vagy képírásban Mengs Anton Raffael lovag
olaszul írt munkája után németből magyarítva* (Practical Advice on Painting or Picture-
Writing, Hungarianized from the German after the Italian works of Mengs Anton
Raffael, knight), Pest, 1844. Ms, Hungarian National Gallery Archives.

** VAUTIER, BENJAMIN (Morges, 1829–Düsseldorf, 1898). Plate 253
Pecht, F.: *Deutsche Künstler des 19. Jhs.,* Nördlingen, 1881.—Leipzig. Museum der bildenden Künste. Catalogue.

** VERNET, HORACE (Paris, 1789–Paris, 1863). Plate 58
Kazinczy Ferenc, Levelek (The Correspondence of Ferenc Kazinczy), Budapest, 1979,
225, no. 688–689.—Schoch, R.: *Das Herrscherbild in der Malerei des 19. Jhs.,* München,
1975, 52–54, plates 32–33.

VIDRA, FERDINAND (Veszprém, 1814–Bilka, 1879). Plate 129
Th. B., XXXIV, 334.

** WALDMÜLLER, FERDINAND GEORG (Wien, 1793–Wien, 1865). Plates 31, 107, 110
Th. B., XXXV, 74–77.—Grimschitz, B.: *F. G. M.,* Salzburg, 1957.

WAGNER, SÁNDOR (ALEXANDER) (Pest, 1838–München, 1919). Plates 218, 219
Th. B., XXXV, 28–29.—Laushoffet, M.: A. W., München, n. d.

WALZEL, ÁGOST FRIGYES (Braunau, c. 1790–Pest, after 1860). Plate 92
Th. B., XXXV, 139.—Gerszi, Teréz: *A kőrajzolás története Magyarországon a XIX.
században* (The History of Lithography in Hungary in the 19th Century), Budapest,
1960. Index.

WARSÁGH, JAKAB (dates unknown). Plate 32
Th. B., XXXV, 168.—Horváth, H.: „Zur Aesthetik der altpester Firmtafeln".
A Műgyűjtő, 1931, no. 8–10.

WEBER, HENRIK I (Pest, 1818–Pest, 1866). Plates 119, 123, 127
Th. B., XXXV, 220.—Fleischer, Gy.: *Magyarok a bécsi képzőművészeti akadémián*
(Hungarians at the Academy of Fine Arts in Vienna), Budapest, 1935, 95. — Koday,
E.: *Wh. H.,* Budapest, 1943.

WEBER, HENRIK II (Pest, 1818–?). Plate 128
See Fleischer, Gy. *op. cit.,* 95.

* WERNER, FRITZ FRIEDRICH ALEXANDER (Berlin, 1827–Berlin, 1908). Plate 134
Th. B., XXXV, 407–408.

* WIELAND CARL (dates unknown). Plates 43, 44
Wurzbach, XVI, 18.—Kőszeghy, E.: *Bildnismalerei in der Zips.* Késmárk, 1833, 28.

** WUTKY, MICHAEL (Krems, 1793–Wien, 1823). Plate 56
Th. B., XXXVI, 319–320.—Meller, S.: *Az Esterházy képtár története* (The History of
the Esterházy Picture Gallery), Budapest, 1915, 94 (329); 216, 449.

* ZABRATZKY, JOSEF (active in the mid-19th century). Plate 136
Nagy, Z.: *A magyar litográfia története a XIX. században* (The History of Hungarian
Lithography in the 19th Century), Budapest, 1936, 47.

ZICHY, MIHÁLY (Zala, 1827–Petersburg, 1906). Plates 114, 274, 276, 277, 280
Lándor, T.: *Z. M. élete* (The Life of M. Z.), Budapest, 1903.—„Z. M. önvallomása"
(The Self-confessions of M. Z.), by Ede Iván, *A Ház,* IV (1911), Nr. 1, 1–16.—Th.
B., XXXVI, 476.—Lázár, B.: *Z. M.,* Budapest, 1927.—Bényi, L.—Supka, M.: *Z.
M.,* Budapest, 1953.—Berkovits, I.: *Z. M.,* Budapest, 1964.

Index of Places Outside Present-day Hungary